MANAGERIAL BEHAVIOR, PERFORMANCE, AND EFFECTIVENESS

McGraw-Hill Series in Psychology

Consulting Editors

Norman Garmezy

Richard L. Solomon

Lyle V. Jones

Harold W. Stevenson

Adams   Human Memory
Beach, Hebb, Morgan, and Nissen   The Neuropsychology of Lashley
Von Békésy   Experiments in Hearing
Berkowitz   Aggression: A Social Psychological Analysis
Berlyne   Conflict, Arousal, and Curiosity
Blum   Psychoanalytic Theories of Personality
Brown   The Motivation of Behavior
Brown and Ghiselli   Scientific Method of Psychology
Buckner and McGrath   Vigilance: A Symposium
Butcher   MMPI: Research Developments and Clinical Applications
Campbell, Dunnette, Lawler, and Weick   Managerial Behavior, Performance, and Effectiveness
Cofer   Verbal Learning and Verbal Behavior
Cofer and Musgrave   Verbal Behavior and Learning: Problems and Processes
Crafts, Schneirla, Robinson, and Gilbert   Recent Experiments in Psychology
Crites   Vocational Psychology
D'Amato   Experimental Psychology: Methodology, Psychophysics, and Learning
Davitz   The Communication of Emotional Meaning
Deese and Hulse   The Psychology of Learning
Dollard and Miller   Personality and Psychotherapy
Edgington   Statistical Inference: The Distribution-free Approach
Ellis   Handbook of Mental Deficiency
Epstein   Varieties of Perceptual Learning
Ferguson   Statistical Analysis in Psychology and Education
Forgus   Perception: The Basic Process in Cognitive Development
Franks   Behavior Therapy: Appraisal and Status
Ghiselli   Theory of Psychological Measurement
Ghiselli and Brown   Personnel and Industrial Psychology
Gilmer   Industrial Psychology
Gray   Psychology Applied to Human Affairs
Guilford   Fundamental Statistics in Psychology and Education
Guilford   The Nature of Human Intelligence
Guilford   Personality
Guilford   Psychometric Methods
Guion   Personnel Testing

McGraw-Hill Series in Management

Keith Davis, Consulting Editor

MANAGERIAL BEHAVIOR, PERFORMANCE, AND EFFECTIVENESS

John P. Campbell
Associate Professor of Psychology and Industrial Relations
University of Minnesota

Marvin D. Dunnette
Professor of Psychology and Industrial Relations
University of Minnesota

Edward E. Lawler, III
Associate Professor of Administrative Sciences
Yale University

Karl E. Weick, Jr.
Professor of Psychology
University of Minnesota

McGraw-Hill Book Company
New York, St. Louis, San Francisco, Dusseldorf, London, Mexico, Panama, Sydney, Toronto

**Managerial Behavior,
Performance, and Effectiveness**

Library of Congress Catalog Card Number 74-95796

09675

1234567890   MAMM   79876543210

This book was set in Musica by University Graph-
ics, Inc., and printed on permanent paper and
bound by The Maple Press Company. The design-
er was Merrill Haber; the drawings were done
by B. Handelman Associates, Inc. The editors
were Walter Maytham and Ellen Simon. Sally
R. Ellyson supervised the production.

To the rain, Gull Lake, and the causal arrow.

PREFACE

In late 1965, Dunnette was approached by trustees of the Smith Richardson Foundation to undertake a comprehensive search for available knowledge concerning the identification and enhancement of managerial effectiveness. The request arose because of the foundation's recognition of the crucial roles played in an industrial society by managers and the difficulty of developing and maintaining a sufficiently large reservoir of managerial talent to serve the needs of rapid industrial growth, expansion of investments, and constantly increasing consumer needs. Besides systematizing the available evidence, an explicit aim was to suggest guidelines for future management research that would maximize the payoff of information. The team of Campbell, Dunnette, Lawler, and Weick was formed, and after a series of discussions, a decision was made to interview key personnel in industry, government, and university settings in order to document and describe current practices and research investigations directed toward identifying, developing, and motivating managers. The interviews were conducted in the spring and summer of 1966.

Concomitant with carrying out the interviewing phase of our inquiry, we undertook a survey in depth of the business and behavioral science literature for the purpose of discovering and summarizing the major trends and current status of behavioral scientists' theories, speculations, and research results bearing on the determiners of managerial effectiveness.

In this undertaking we chose deliberately to consider managerial effectiveness in *all* its aspects, including such diverse topics as the identification of personal attributes or competencies shown to be related to effective managing, the development of managerial proficiencies through special programs of education and training, and the particular properties of organizational policies, practices, or environments most likely to elicit effective job performance from managers. This breadth of focus explains, in a way, how the four of us came together in this joint effort—Campbell, psychometrics and organizational psychology; Dunnette, differential industrial psychology; Lawler, applied social industrial psychology; and Weick, experimental social psychology.

We undertook the project primarily, then, for the broad purpose of finding out what practices are currently being used by government and industry in identifying and "growing" managers and the degree to which these practices are or are not attuned to results derived from behavioral scientists' research on the determiners of managerial effectiveness. In particular, we have sought to discover discontinuities between practice and research and to point up areas most in need of increased research attention. In seeking answers to these questions, we found the area of managerial effectiveness to be far more complicated than we had originally realized or imagined. We hope that our readers will not be overwhelmed by its complexity but that they will instead be challenged to do research in this difficult area and to develop further knowledge of how best to identify, develop, or motivate managers so that they can realize full effectiveness in their managerial jobs.

In retrospect, we believe our efforts have produced guidelines and ways of looking at organizational behavior that have broad applicability beyond the management sphere. That is, many of the behavior models and research needs that we suggest are salient for almost any employment role. We believe that this is as it should be since understanding of the whole of organizational behavior would be greatly enhanced by a coordinated research attack. Thus, we think this volume has considerable relevance for anyone who is seriously interested in the study of organizational behavior, whatever work role happens to be the specific target.

We deeply appreciate the initiation and continuous support given to this enterprise by the Smith Richardson Foundation. The many expenses involved in carrying out our surveys and literature searches and the expenses of preparing the many drafts of our manuscript were defrayed by a grant from the foundation. We also deeply appreciate the care given to the typing of the manuscript in its several forms by our hardworking and conscientious secretaries: Charlene Sturm, Connie DeWitte, and Carmen Doren.

JOHN P. CAMPBELL
MARVIN D. DUNNETTE
EDWARD E. LAWLER, III
KARL E. WEICK, JR.

Contents

xiii

Chapter 1 Managerial Talent: A Critical Natural Resource

The key occupational group in an industrial society is management. Effective direction of human efforts—whether in the public or private sectors of an economy—is central to the wise and efficient utilization of human and material resources. In the United States, rapid industrial growth, continuous expansion of investments, and a burgeoning population interact to create a true managerial elite. Yet the flow of high-level manpower into managerial functions is far below current demands. According to a recent survey conducted by the *Wall Street Journal* (Melloan, 1966), more and more managerial jobs are going unfilled because fewer and fewer persons are available to take them. The number of people in the prime managerial age range of thirty-five to forty-five is on the decline because of lowered birthrates during the Depression of the 1930s and losses of young men during World War II and the Korean War. Moreover, lower proportions of current top college graduates are choosing to enter the business world than has been true in previous decades.

The upshot of these serious manpower shortages in the key occupation of management is that business firms and government agencies need desperately to learn more about how to conserve what is perhaps our most important natural resource—our reservoir of potentially effective managers. The problem, quite simply, is one of supplying enough competent managerial talent to meet demands in the years ahead. According to Melloan (1966), frantic activity is already apparent in many of our largest companies. He states:

> Significant changes are being made by most companies in the care and treatment of prospects for top management. They are being tagged earlier in their careers, often through systematic talent scouting. Their progress is being traced by computers that "flag" management when one has gone unrewarded too long. They are given important jobs to handle earlier, and more frequent job changes to test their mettle. To stimulate ambition, they are sometimes given broad hints that they are being closely observed.

That is, many of our best companies are expending money, time, talent, and energy to identify, nurture, and motivate top managerial talent. Thus, the management of managerial talent has itself become big business, an enterprise of prime importance to the continued growth of our economy.

We ask how well the job is being done and whether or not current practices may be improved. What are the strategies used by key firms for identifying, developing, and motivating managers? Are they based on solid evidence derived from behavioral science research on managerial effectiveness, or do they merely reflect fads and fashions and "seat-of-the-pants" thinking and maneuvering? Where are the gaps in our knowledge of what makes a man an effective manager? What avenues of research need to be followed to fill these gaps?

These are the questions that stimulated this book; the reader should find answers to them here—or, at least, ways of coping with them. The above questions led us to survey firms and government agencies to learn about prevailing practices, to evaluate their practices in light of knowledge about managerial effectiveness contained in the behavioral science and business literature, and to suggest the kind of research knowledge required for developing improved practices in the future.

The topic of managerial effectiveness can be made as broad or as narrow as one chooses. We have chosen to treat it broadly in an effort to consider all its aspects, including such diverse topics as selection, training, group and organizational structure, and motivation. Though diverse, these topics have one characteristic in common: each is potentially important as a determiner of, or contributor to, managerial effectiveness. In our effort to consider managerial effectiveness in all its aspects, we have focused in this book on a plethora of independent variables—ranging from individual characteristics and personal experiences to the nature of training and development programs and the kinds of people and organizational characteristics confronting managers in

their jobs. But throughout, we have focused on the same dependent variable—
managerial effectiveness.

We began this work with two major objectives before us. First, we wished
to produce an integrated summary of present literature and to cast it within
an interpretive framework that would constitute a contribution to basic knowledge. Second, we wished to provide a structure for considering managerial
effectiveness that would stimulate and guide future research. Thorough examination of existing evidence and current organizational practices related to
managerial effectiveness has, we hope, accomplished both these objectives.

Our decision to consider managerial effectiveness in all its aspects did
not arise from any compulsive need to "cover the waterfront" or to "leave no
stone unturned." Nor did it come simply from a desire to be eclectic in our
approach. Instead, our decision to consider the several rather than just a few
potential determiners of managerial effectiveness grew out of our firm belief
that the management of managerial talent must be *individualized* according
to the special characteristics of each managerial job, person, and organization. Our belief is stimulated by current commentary by Hinrichs (1966) and
Suojanen (1966) showing that evolution of managerial functions and theories
is necessary for meeting the requirements of the future. Both authors argue
that managerial actions in the future must be increasingly flexible in order to
meet the needs of knowledge-oriented rather than crisis-oriented organizations.
The knowledge-oriented organization rejects the classic functionalism of traditional organizational theory and gives precedence to values of democracy
and to traditions of individual autonomy. Because of rapid changes in managerial jobs suggested by the development of new organizational concepts,
we wish to avoid the classic functional job analysis and selection paradigm
used for so many years by industrial psychologists as they sought to validate
individual characteristics against measures of job "success." Their approach
assumed implicitly that little error was introduced when people who showed
similar success patterns were simply clustered together and then the different
clusters compared for the purpose of discovering differences. Unfortunately, this approach ignores dynamic elements in the man-job system—changes
which may be induced by a particular job incumbent, by external demands
and constraints, by organizational changes, by the obsolescence of human
skills and knowledges (Roney, 1966), or by the press for innovation and change
in a knowledge-oriented society. Applying such a paradigm will nearly always
result in a premature and oversimplified fixing of personnel practices in the
form of across-the-board procedures, leading, in turn, to organizational inflex-
ibility in the use of manpower.

Because of the dynamism demanded by a knowledge-oriented society,
we have been reluctant to pursue any direction dictated by only a limited set
of determiners of managerial effectiveness. We believe that much research

and many company practices imply the stripping away of managerial individuality—that is, "programs" or statistical equations are being used for "managers in general." In contrast, decisions about managers and managers' jobs are *individual* decisions. A specific job with unique responsibilities must be filled; a particular manager shows certain inabilities or weaknesses, and something must be done about *him;* a manager shows occasional flashes of brilliance, but they are few and far between, and he seems to need specialized incentives to keep him going. These are but a few examples of the day-to-day individualized decisions arising constantly in most business firms and government agencies—decisions demanding information bearing on all rather than just a few of the independent determiners of managerial effectiveness, if wisdom is to prevail.

All this points to the need for a truly individualized approach to the task of managing managerial effectiveness—an approach which assumes that no single set of parameters is sufficient and which demands knowledge of the *many* determiners of managerial effectiveness, knowledge to be used in developing individualized programs of managerial recruitment, selection, training, job design, and motivational enrichment. This is our fundamental point of view and structures our approach throughout the remainder of this book. This view of an individualized strategy applied to the management of managerial talent is given further body in Chapter 2, where we present a heuristic model of managerial behavior—an interpretive framework to guide our interpretation of the literature, our evaluation of company practices, and our suggestions for needed further research.

SUMMARY

Management is the key occupational group in an industrial society. Presently, the supply of managerial talent falls far short of meeting demand, and industry and government are expending much time, talent, money, and energy to assure improved methods of managing the critical natural resource of managerial talent.

Unfortunately, though practices related to managerial effectiveness are widespread, most are being undertaken without benefit of research-based evidence defining the nature and effects of determiners of managerial effectiveness. We have written this book for the purpose of considering managerial effectiveness in all its aspects. We seek to consider many independent variables as potential determiners of the single dependent variable—managerial effectiveness. By surveying and evaluating existing practices and by summarizing and integrating the relevant business and behavioral science literature, we hope to develop strategies for individualizing the approaches used in managing managerial effectiveness. We assume that no single set of variables is sufficient for understanding managerial effectiveness and that it is, instead, a result of the multiple determination of many determiners.

In the next chapter, we present a heuristic model of managerial behavior to guide our evaluation of current practices, our interpretation of the literature, and our suggestions for needed research.

Chapter 2   Determiners of Managerial Effectiveness

THE PERSON, THE PROCESS, AND THE PRODUCT

An understanding of effective managerial performance demands answers to several questions: What are the personal demands of the managerial job? What sorts of people are most likely to become effective managers, and what types tend to fail? What do managers do that may lead to success or to failure? What are the products of effective management?

These questions are neither new nor astute. Yet they are important for understanding managerial behavior, and they are difficult to answer. The business literature is full of commentary, speculation, and expressions of opinion about possible answers. These are nearly always based on insufficient evidence —ranging from anecdotes derived from personal experiences to results of opinion surveys and managerial appraisal programs. Nonetheless, it is informative to consider briefly the essence of these conjectures as a prelude to our discussion later of our model or framework for interpreting information bearing on managerial behavior.

Our questions divide conveniently into three groups having to do, respectively, with the *person,* the *process,* and the *product.* What sorts of persons are effective managers? What is the process of effective managing? What are the products of effective management?

Opinions based primarily upon personal observations, hunches, or theories about effective management have been stated by Argyris (1953), Hoffman (1963), Ohmann (1958), Pfiffner (1955), Piotrowski and Rock (1963), Wald and Doty (1954), and Stryker (1958, 1961). Opinion surveys have been the basis for statements by Brooks (1955), Randle (1956), Bailey (1956), Coates and Pellegrin (1957), Eisenberg (1948), Gaudet and Carli (1957), England (1966, 1967), and Jurgensen (1966). Conclusions based on psychological testing of groups of managers include those by Henry (1948); Rosen (1959); Huttner, Levy, Rosen, and Stopol (1959); Piotrowski and Rock (1963); and Miner and Culver (1955).

The person. The various lists of desirable managerial traits gleaned from these many sources seem to include just about every human virtue. Below is a short summary of personal qualities said to be necessary for managerial effectiveness:

Able to sustain defeat	Extraverted
Alert	Fearful of failure
Ambitious—achievement-oriented	Group-oriented
Assertive	Honest
Capable of good judgment	Intelligent
Competitive	Mentally healthy
Concrete	Optimistic and confident (as a cover-up
Creative	for fear of failure)
Decisive	Pragmatic
Dedicated	Predictable
Dynamic	Reality-oriented
Emotionally stable	Self-controlled but defensive
Energetic	Tolerant of frustration

Recently, Jurgensen (1966) asked several groups of personnel men and executives (a total of 210 persons) to sort 120 adjectives to describe "the type of person most likely to succeed as a key executive in top management." The dozen adjectives rated as most descriptive and the dozen regarded as least descriptive of such a person are shown below:

Most descriptive of successful key executive	Least descriptive of successful key executive
Decisive	Amiable
Aggressive	Conforming
Self-starting	Neat
Productive	Reserved
Well informed	Agreeable
Determined	Conservative
Energetic	Kindly
Creative	Mannerly

Most descriptive of successful key executive (cont'd)	Least descriptive of successful key executive (cont'd)
Intelligent	Cheerful
Responsible	Formal
Enterprising	Courteous
Clear-thinking	Modest

Apparently, managerial success demands vigor, intelligence, and originality coupled with stability, good judgment, peak determination, forcefulness, and persistence. Listing qualities is an appealing pastime, but the trait descriptions are loosely defined, and they do not pinpoint with sufficient precision the behavioral elements making up effective management. Perhaps opinions about the management process can be more fruitful.

The process. How do successful managers manage successfully? Here, too, lists are numerous. Successful managers are said to show most of the following job behaviors:

- They manage *work* instead of *people*.
- They plan and organize effectively.
- They set goals realistically.
- They derive decisions by group consensus but accept responsibility for them.
- They delegate frequently and effectively.
- They rely on others for help in solving problems.
- They communicate effectively.
- They are a stimulus to action.
- They coordinate effectively.
- They cooperate with others.
- They show consistent and dependable behavior.
- They win gracefully.
- They express hostility tactfully.

It is not known whether any single manager has been observed who shows all these exemplary behaviors; but at least this list is somewhat more helpful than a list of mere trait names because it does show the range of things perceived as important in managing. Managing is seen to be a complicated, broad-ranging job, requiring a myriad of skills for planning and organizing work, for handling information, and for dealing in a coordinated, consistent, and graceful way with people.

The product. Surprisingly, writers have frequently evaded discussing the outcomes of effective managing. The assumption is common that effective managers (those who are ambitious, dynamic, dedicated, intelligent, stable) and effective managing will lead inevitably to good things. Most authors feel little need to comment upon the fruits of effective management in order to define it. In contrast, respondents to our survey of current practices (described in Chapter 3) placed heavy emphasis on the products of effective management. Stated most directly, our respondents see effective managing as yielding *re-*

sults! But what are results? Depending upon the firm, results include maximizing profits, maintaining organizational efficiency, promoting high employee morale, and producing (selecting, training, developing) effective subordinates who will be capable of taking on added responsibilities and of maintaining the firm in the years ahead.

England (1966, 1967) surveyed 1,072 managers throughout the country, asking them to indicate which of eight organizational goals are most important and which connote greatest success. The percentages of managers who said that a goal was *both* important and highly successful are shown in the table below.

Goal	Percent
Organizational efficiency	60
High productivity	60
Profit maximization	48
Organizational growth	43
Industrial leadership	38
Organizational stability	17
Employee welfare	4
Social welfare	2

Most managers, it appears, are striving toward high productivity, maximum profits, and organizational efficiency. These are the products presumably indicative of effective managing. In the longer term, valued goals are organizational growth commensurate with internal organizational stability with a view probably of attaining industry leadership.

Our respondents emphasized practices established by their firms to assure a results-oriented assessment of their managers. Many firms have developed systematic procedures to ensure that their managers formulate both short- and long-term objectives and lay broad strategies for accomplishing them.

There seems to be a discontinuity between the product and results orientation of our industrial respondents and journal contributors' greater emphasis on managerial processes and manager traits. The discontinuity may reflect differing motives of the two groups—a concern with results or products is a way of specifying ultimate responsibilities (and job functions) for managers already employed by a firm; a concern with personal characteristics and with methods of managing yields prescriptions for psychologists and personnel men for designing manager selection and training programs.

BRIDGING THE GAP

The discontinuity needs to be bridged. Management methods and manager traits need to be studied in terms of the organizational products they yield. But the bridge needs to be built on careful empirical research, showing exactly how personal traits and job behaviors relate to desired organizational outcomes. Conclusions about personal characteristics of managers and how they should do their jobs to achieve effective outcomes cannot continue to rest on such flimsy grounds as hunches, insights by experts, or mere responses to questionnaires. If this is not already painfully apparent from the imprecise trait labels and hazy behavior descriptions already cited, one more example will make it obvious. In an attempt to define the "traits of the successful executive," Piotrowski and Rock (1963) list the following characteristics:

1 Ability to concentrate on achieving a goal
2 Use of the right amount of energy at the right time and in the right place to achieve an intended result
3 Ability to get others to want to share in the achievement
4 Unique insight into the goal and how to reach it in the best way
5 A tremendous sense of timing for bringing the greatest concentration of energy to bear
6 Insight into other people

About all that can be gleaned from such profundity is that successful executives are persons who have the abilities to be successful! The definition is so circular, the wording so imprecise, and the behavioral implications so subjective and so poorly explicated that little is left but a meaningless hodgepodge of words. The definitional problem has been no more clearly illuminated than by Stryker (1958), who surveyed 150 executive readers of *Fortune* magazine for their definitions of various trait labels such as "integrity," "dependability," etc.; "dependability" elicited 147 different definitions.

We can gain little new knowledge about predicting effective executive job behavior from such opinions. Even if definitions were precise and the behavioral components unambiguously specified, they still would be based solely on undifferentiated groups of managers and useful only for crude descriptive purposes rather than for differential prediction.

It may appear that we are laboring the point at too great length, but we firmly believe we cannot overemphasize the essential inadequacy of opinions, hunches, speculations, and expertise as a basis for prescriptions concerning the prediction of effective executive job behavior. Even so, the business journals continue to be filled with such speculations and implicit prescriptions; we have presented here only a limited sampling in order to illustrate the nature of their imprecision and to argue the uselessness of pursuing them further.

A MODEL OF MANAGER BEHAVIOR

What, then, will be an appropriate datum for deriving accurate differential predictions about managerial behavior?

The questions posed earlier are still crucial even though the answers suggested so far are not helpful. The key concepts of person, process, and product can, however, be related to the heuristic model of manager behavior shown in Figure 2.1. It is a schematic portrayal of factors determining the expression of managerial behavior—factors to be considered in predicting managerial effectiveness. The diagram shows that a manager's job behavior is a function of ability, motivation, and opportunity as reflected in various situational or organizational circumstances. A behavior model similar to this was first presented by Maier (1955), who suggested a multiplicative relationship between ability and motivation. He argued that such a relationship is appropriate in that it explains the common subjective observation that if either ability or motivation is low, improvements in the other will still have only negligible effect on job behavior. Unfortunately, evidence in support of a multiplicative relationship is only sketchy at best (e.g., Lawler, 1966a; Locke, 1965; Vroom, 1964), and at least one recent study (Graen, 1967) failed to confirm it. Because of the tentative nature of Maier's proposition, we choose *not* to assume such a multiplicative relationship, indicating by our schema merely the importance of taking into account *both* ability and motivational influences. The exact nature of the relation between the two must await results of further empirical investigations.

Nonetheless, the model makes it apparent that a manager's job behavior is directed by many different factors and by interactions between them. For example, his *abilities* include his intelligence, special skills and aptitudes, technical information and knowledge, and interest and temperamental fac-

Figure 2.1 Schematic portrayal of the determiners of managerial behavior.

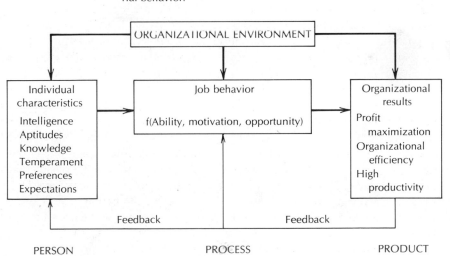

PERSON   PROCESS   PRODUCT

tors equipping him to meet organizational demands made on him. He works in a particular organizational environment which defines desired objectives and broad organizational outcomes and also, more indirectly, the kinds of job behaviors expected of him. Moreover, the organization establishes feedback procedures to inform him of the outcome of his efforts and establishes incentives (such as financial rewards; job challenges; opportunities for status, achievement, recognition, security; etc.) to stimulate and direct his motivated behavior by providing opportunities for satisfying preferences, needs, and expectations. Executive behavior—or, more importantly, *effective* executive behavior—is a function of complex interactions between individual or personal characteristics; the demands and expectations placed upon persons by the physical, administrative, and social environments of their organization; and the nature of the feedback, incentive, and reward systems developed by organizational policies and practices.

Motivational variables are defined broadly to include not only the traditional individual incentives such as money and security but also the temperamental and preference predispositions to stay with the job and to exert effort in performing it. Abilities may be viewed as involving the "capability" of doing some job, and motivation as involving volitional elements such as willingness or desire to do it. This is a usual convention, one adopted by Mace (1935) and Viteles (1953) in distinguishing between "capacity to work" and "will to work."

Finally, the model specifies *opportunity* variables as a third set of determiners of managerial job behavior. These refer to situational and organizational factors that may influence the managerial process. They are distinct from the personal predisposing variables of ability and motivation, but they are, nonetheless, strongly relevant to both the nature of a manager's job behavior and the organizational results flowing from it. They include such things as task characteristics, structural components, and social-psychological concepts such as organizational "climate," group influences, communications patterns, etc.

It should now be abundantly clear that it is incomplete to talk *only* about personal traits leading to managerial success or *only* about the way good managers manage or *only* about the products or results of good managing. All three must be considered concurrently, and the effects and moderating influences of different organizational environments must be included as well. Instead of asking, "Who will be effective?" "How may a person be effective?" or "What does an effective manager produce?" we must ask the broader and more complicated question, "What are the varieties or combinations of organizational circumstances, personal characteristics, and behavior patterns that are likely to be perceived as effective managing?" To predict the occurrence of effective managing demands that all these elements and their interactions be considered.

In sum, our heuristic model in Figure 2.1 portrays factors that need to be taken into account in our attempt to understand more fully managerial behavior and managerial effectiveness. It points up the complexity of managerial behavior in that it also directs us toward considering interactions between factors based on individual characteristics (abilities), motivation, and opportunity variables. In a sense, the model may be taken as simply a checklist or framework to direct our attention during our survey of present industrial practices and our search of the literature on managerial effectiveness. This is the role it has served for us; it should serve the reader in like manner.

We hesitate to complicate the picture further, but we must mention three additional considerations important in thinking about managerial effectiveness. They are only partially implied by our model, and it is therefore important that they be made explicit.

Modifications of the job-man relationship. Psychologists and personnel men have traditionally depended mostly on personnel selection and job placement procedures to assign persons to particular jobs—assuming apparently that both the person and the job are fixed or static entities and that there exists a kind of "best fit" between job requirements and individual characteristics. The assumption is unrealistic for managers and for managerial jobs. A major purpose of widespread managerial training and development programs is to modify managers' knowledge, skills, and other behavioral tendencies in order to equip them to meet more successfully the demands of their jobs; thus, training and development assume modifiability in human traits, and plans for *selecting* managers must be incorporated intimately with plans for *developing* them. At one extreme, if all persons were perfectly modifiable through training, knowledge of individual abilities and motive patterns at the time of selection would be merely surplus information; all managers could be trained to behave effectively in their jobs. At the other extreme, if all persons were unchangeable through training or experience, assessment of individual characteristics would take on great importance; programs of personnel selection and/or job redesign would be the only way of assuring effective managing. Neither extreme is true, but many firms operate as if one or the other were true— some emphasizing individual assessment to the near exclusion of training and development, and others emphasizing only training and tending to ignore individual measurement. In fact, Jennings (1959) claims to have noted distinct differences among industry groupings in their preference for either the "life-process" theory (i.e., managers are born, not made) or the "skill-insight" theory (i.e., managers are made, not born). Our orientation and our discussion in subsequent pages are based on no prior assumptions. To assure optimally effective managers, it is necessary to obtain as much information as possible on what training can accomplish and to design jobs, organizational environments, and selection programs according to the conditions specified by training research results.

Other influences modify the job-man relationship. The *means* for accomplishing managerial job objectives are rarely specified in detail. A particular manager may change the way a job is done in order to capitalize on his own propensities, strengths, weaknesses, and stylized patterns of behaving. We should not expect effective managing to demand any single pattern or "mold" of personal qualities. Instead, we should pursue and hope to discover various kinds of job behaviors resulting in effective managing. Rather than viewing men and jobs as static entities, we regard both as modifiable, and we intend to examine the dynamic qualities of both as they relate to measures of effective and ineffective managing.

Situational, social, and organizational factors. Figure 2.1 clearly shows the potential effects of organizational environment or "climate" on managerial effectiveness. The kind of person a manager works for can affect his own job behavior for good or for ill. The kinds of subordinates a manager has, the industry grouping his firm is in, the relative success and particular job style of his predecessor, and the expectations and managerial style of his own boss are just a few of the situational factors that can affect his own managerial effectiveness. Over twenty years ago, Stogdill emphasized the importance of such situational and social factors in summarizing his classic review of leadership research. He stated (1948, pp. 64-65):

> A person does not become a leader by virtue of the possession of some combination of traits, but the pattern of personal characteristics of the leader must bear some relevant relationship to the characteristics, activities, and goals of the followers. Thus, leadership must be conceived in terms of the interaction of variables which are in constant flux and change. The factor of change is especially characteristic of the situations, which may be altered by the addition or loss of members, changes in interpersonal relationships, changes in goals, competition of extra-group influences, and the like. The personal characteristics of leader and of the followers are, in comparison, highly stable. The persistence of individual patterns of human behavior in the face of constant situational change appears to be a primary obstacle encountered not only in the practice of leadership and in the selection and placement of leaders, but also of situations.

More recently, an equally strong emphasis on the situation was made by participants at a Harvard University symposium on executive selection (Taguiri, 1961). It was agreed that organizational variations had perhaps their most important effects on the definition and measurement of management effectiveness; thus, development of any single measure of effectiveness is precluded because of the differing objectives and demands of different organizations. The many facets of managerial success need to be studied, and dimensions of organizations relevant to manager success need to be defined, described, and measured.

Unfortunately, organizational climate, like the weather, has engendered much talk but little action. Situational and organizational characteristics have not typically been considered along with individual characteristics and job behavior descriptions in studies of manager effectiveness.

Cost considerations and utility. The *costs* of assuring management effectiveness and the relative costs of different kinds of personnel decision errors must also be considered. The term "cost" is most often associated with dollars and cents, but we intend no such narrow construction. We intend a meaning similar to that conveyed by the term "utility" as used by Cronbach and Gleser (1965). We view "cost" and "utility" as convenient terms to signify a particular way of thinking about possible outcomes associated with different personnel actions. Cost does not necessarily imply the desirability of reducing all outcomes to a dollar scale, but it does imply a careful analysis and identification of all possible outcomes associated with personnel actions—accompanied by either objective or judgmental weighting of the values (both dollar and human) associated with each.

Consider the dilemma faced by a physician who suspects, on the basis of evidence obtained with a fallible diagnostic instrument known to be wrong four out of five times, that a patient may have a rare brain tumor. Should the patient be subjected to a lengthy and dangerous surgical procedure to remove a tumor which probably is not there—but which, if present, will cause certain death in a matter of weeks? The relative "costs" of decision errors in this example are evident, but they cannot easily be expressed as dollars, nor would any clarity be added to the alternatives if they were so expressed.

Though less dramatic, similar considerations are involved in estimating relative costs associated with correct or incorrect predictions of effective managerial behavior. The total cost or utility associated with any program—selection, training, organizational realignment, or whatever—designed to assure more effective managing should be estimated and compared against the overall utility of available alternatives. It is uncommon for cost factors to be considered by personnel decision makers; usually they operate with only limited knowledge of the predictive accuracies and associated costs of their personnel programs, and they fail to take account of differential costs due to different types of personnel decision errors. It is our intention to emphasize cost and utility considerations as we explicate more fully the many parameters related to managerial effectiveness depicted in Figure 2.1.

SUMMARY

Much of the business and psychological literature on the topic of managerial effectiveness is based on little more than personal experiences or opinions about traits possessed by "good" managers, what they must do to be effective, or what the products of their effective behavior may be. Much of the literature is one-sided, emphasizing only the persons, only the processes, or only the products related to effective managing.

We have presented a heuristic model of managerial behavior which may be used as a checklist to aid in interpreting current industrial and government practices for identifying, nurturing, and motivating managers and for interpreting research on managerial behavior and managerial effectiveness. The model specifies that managerial job behavior is a function of individual characteristics (abilities), volitions (motivation), and social and organizational characteristics (opportunity). Managerial effectiveness is seen to be a function of complex interactions between ability, motivation, and opportunity variables and the nature of feedback, incentive, and reward systems developed by organizational policies and practices.

Moreover, the model implies the importance of rejecting static concepts of persons, jobs, and their interaction. To be fruitful, practices bearing on managerial effectiveness and research on it must recognize the likelihood of changes occurring in people (through experience, training, growth, etc.), in jobs (through organizational planning, job design, etc.), and in the relationships between the two. Finally, cost and utility considerations should be taken into account at every stage in programs and research related to managerial effectiveness. The utility of any program designed to assure effective managing should be estimated and compared against the estimated utilities of available alternatives.

In the next chapter, we describe current practices followed by key industrial firms and government agencies in identifying, nurturing, and motivating managers, and we evaluate these practices against the specifications of the heuristic model outlined in this chapter.

Chapter 3 **Current Industrial and Government Practices in the Management of Managerial Effectiveness**

AN INTERVIEW SURVEY

As a first step toward unraveling the interactive components of the model of managerial behavior presented in the last chapter, we conducted personal interviews with key officials in a number of industrial firms and government agencies to learn about their strategies for assuring an adequate and even flow of effective managers in their organizations. In our interviews. we focused on organizationally controlled activities believed to have causal impacts on the selection, development, and motivation of effective managers.

The prime goal of most authors who have cataloged current practices has been to give detailed, step-by-step portrayals of organizational strategies. Our goals in surveying current practices were quite different. Our major goal was to learn how well current practices in industry and government fit current research knowledge about managerial effectiveness. We wanted to integrate and evaluate past research in the context of current practices to provide a sound basis for suggesting needed directions for future research. Moreover, the degree of fit between practice and current research knowledge indicates how responsive personnel executives have been to existing research evidence, thereby providing clues about needed changes in current practices as well as leads for needed new research.

Our second goal was to learn about the extent and kind of research being done by organizations in auditing their own practices in the management of managerial effectiveness. Here, our focus was less upon the results of such research than on the mere occurrence of it. In a sense, research is one of the practices presumably designed to enhance managerial effectiveness; and thus we included questions about it in our survey.

Previous Surveys

Many previous surveys have described strategies employed by the big, successful firms in areas related to managerial effectiveness. It is easy to locate detailed accounts of practices followed by such firms as General Electric or International Business Machines. Nearly all such descriptions suffer because evidence about the effectiveness of the procedures is based on testimonials from program developers and participants instead of upon research-based evidence. Still it is difficult for a personnel manager to ignore existing fads and fashions. If he ignores new techniques, he may miss out on something truly useful, and he risks a loss of reputation among his professional peers. On the other hand, if he presents a generous menu of the latest programs, his superiors (who may have no other adequate criteria for judging his performance) will praise his initiative and industry, and other personnel men will regard him as a progressive leader. It is little wonder that so many observers have remarked upon the propensity of personnel practitioners to grasp at every newfangled fad and gimmick. Similarly, the well-established and traditional practices of personnel management tend to persist without any attempt to validate their effectiveness simply because this is what everybody is doing. Dubin (1949, p. 238) has described this situation as follows:

> Most of the issues dealt with by personnel and labor relations men can be handled with little reference to the details of production processes. This has led to an almost universal plagiarism in the field. Industrial relations specialists have an insatiable hunger to know what is being done in other companies. Any policy, technique, or gadget which might be used in the home company is quickly copied. In fact, many of the paid consultants in the field have as their main stock-in-trade a set of gadgets or a "system" which is extolled for universal application.
>
> The logic of the industrial relations specialists can then be best characterized as a preoccupation with the internal consistency of rules, procedures, and operations concerning the processing of groups of people within a company.

Thus, our purpose in this chapter is *not* to add further purely descriptive materials to the already burgeoning literature. The personnel practitioner will not find here any detailed accounts of particular firms' managerial effectiveness practices; presumably, he will not be able to use our survey results to support any claims about "what other firms are doing." Instead, our purpose is to review trends and to evaluate them in the context of our model and of available research knowledge.

A wealth of information has, however, been provided by previous surveys conducted on broad samples of firms of many sizes and representing many industrial groupings. In fact, more than fifty surveys of industrial personnel practices related to managerial effectiveness have been done. Many have been carried out longitudinally and are useful for detecting trends among different practices. This wealth of previous survey information provides useful comparison data for results of our survey.

SURVEY METHOD

Normally, a survey implies developing a random or at least a representative sample of firms from a larger, defined population. Our purpose, however, was to discover research being done on managerial effectiveness as well as to learn something of current practices. Moreover, the existence of information from so many previous surveys based on representative cross sections of firms suggested that random sampling would be less valuable than choosing firms intentionally biased toward learning about any research that may be underway in industry. We sought to identify and contact firms and government agencies widely regarded as being at the forefront in innovating and doing research on the management of managerial effectiveness. Leading firms, we felt, should be the pacemakers in developing patterns for others to follow, and contact with them should provide clues about trends to be expected in other firms in the years ahead. Further, any discontinuities in such forward-thinking firms between present research knowledge and actual managerial effectiveness practices ought to provide an unusually rich source for suggesting additional areas of needed research.

In order to identify such firms, we requested nominations of firms who were doing research in areas related to the identification or enhancement of managerial talent from the 861 members of the Division of Industrial Psychology of the American Psychological Association and from the industrial representatives of the Foundation for Research in Human Behavior, a nonprofit group devoted to promoting applications of behavioral science research in industrial settings.

Nature of the sample. Replies were received from 132 individuals nominating a total of 146 organizations. Table 3.1 lists the six business firms nominated most frequently. Many of the nominations went to academic and research organizations and are not included in this chapter. We visited the non-business organizations or sent letters to them inquiring about their work, and their research is described in later chapters discussing the status of research gleaned from our literature review. With only one exception each firm nominated by two or more people was visited, and a high official was interviewed about current practices related to managerial effectiveness. With the addition of visits to several firms nominated only once, we ended up making a total of 33 industrial interviews. All firms contacted agreed to participate in the study; thus, the response was 100 percent. We also contacted the United States Civil Service Commission, and with its help we collected information about current practices of six government agencies. In this chapter, we describe what we learned about current practices in these firms and agencies. In later chapters, we present information about research projects undertaken by some of them and results obtained.

Table 3.1   THE SIX MOST FREQUENTLY NOMINATED BUSINESS ORGANIZATIONS

Organization	Number of nominations
Standard Oil of New Jersey	22
At&T	17
Sears	11
IBM	9
GE	7
Du Pont	7

As we have said, because only companies known to be doing research were visited, they constitute a distinctly biased grouping of United States industry.[1] Not only are the firms more research-oriented than is typical, but they

[1]We wish to express our deep appreciation to the following persons, who so willingly gave us the benefit of their time and knowledge for interviews about managerial effectiveness practices and relevant research being carried out in their respective organizations and institutions: Mr. Lewis Albright, of American Oil Co.; Mr. Douglas Bray, of American Telephone & Telegraph; Mr. Gene Krause, of Archer-Daniels-Midland Corp.; Mr. Will Maloney, of Armour Corporation; Mr. Jarold R. Niven, of Boeing Corporation; Mr. Willys Monroe, of Booz, Allen & Hamilton; Mr. B. Von Haller Gilmer and Mr. Victor H. Vroom, of Carnegie Institute of Technology; Mr. Edward Kendall, of Case and Company; Mr. Joseph McPherson, of Dow Chemical; Mr. W. R. G. Bender of Du Pont; Mr. Norman Frederiksen and Mr. John K. Hemphill, of Educational Testing Service; Mr. E. A. Woody, of FAA; Mr. Herbert Meyer, of General Electric Company; Mr. Marvin Mandery, of General Mills; Mr. Paul Sparks of Humble Oil Co.; Mr. Richard Dunnington and Mr. Walter MacNamara, of IBM; Mr. Seymour Chad, of the Internal Revenue Service; Mr. Richard Diercks, of International Milling; Mr. Alan Clark, Mr. Frank McCabe, and Mr. Frank Metzger, of International Telephone & Telegraph; Mr. Henry Meyer, of Jewel Tea Company; Mr. Richard Waters, of Kaiser Industries; Dr. Paul Thayer, of LIAMA; Mr. Jack Brenner, Mr. Howard Lockwood, Mr. J. Rusmore, and Mr. Keith Tombrink, of Lockheed Corporation; Mr. Clifford Jurgensen, of Minneapolis Gas Company; Mr. Gerry Morse, of Minneapolis Honeywell; Mr. Harvey Miller, of Minnesota Mining & Manufacturing; Mr. William Howes and Mr. Edward Ossim, of NASA; Mr. Wright Elliot, of National Association of Manufacturers; Mr. Raymond Katzell, Mr. James Kirkpatrick, and Mr. Joseph Weitz, of New York University; Mr. Felix Lopez, of New York Port Authority; Miss Mary Tenopyr and Mr. Stan

are also larger, more profitable, and more growth-oriented and include more highly educated managers than is typical of a random or representative sample of modern-day industry. For example, all but six of the organizations have more than 10,000 employees, a figure often cited as the dividing line between large and small organizations. Thirty of the organizations visited were on *Fortune's* latest list of the 500 leading industrial corporations in the United States. Of the remaining three, one is a large utility, one a large service governmental agency, and one a large insurance company, none of which are eligible for listing in *Fortune's* 500.

The predominance in our sample of large, profitable firms is evidence in itself of where research on management effectiveness is going on. This is corroborated by Goode's (1958) findings showing that only a few large organizations are doing personnel research. Another study (Pierson et al., 1959) found that only growing, profitable organizations hire many college graduates. An easy assumption is that only large, profitable firms can afford either to do personnel research or to hire college graduates. But it is equally likely that the causal arrow goes in the opposite direction. That is, being research-oriented may well lead to profitability, rapid growth, and greater attractiveness for educated men. Regardless of the reason for the relationship between research activities and firm size, the implication for our study is clear. By choosing firms doing research on managerial effectiveness, we obtained a sample of firms biased in the direction of being large, profitable, and growth-oriented.

Interview content. A structured interview was conducted with high officials in each of the organizations. It required about two hours to complete and dealt with the following areas: sources of managerial talent, selection methods used, training and development activities, managerial incentives used, and the nature of performance appraisal systems. The questionnaire used to guide our interviews is shown in the Appendix. It was used solely as a guide

---

Stromberg, of North American Aviation; Mr. Seymour Levy, of Pillsbury; Mr. Irv Pollitt, of Polaroid Corporation; Mr. W. G. Anderson and Mr. Jack Plattner, of Procter & Gamble Co.; Mr. Phil Kriedt and Mr. Robert Selover, of Prudential Insurance Company; Mr. J. R. Schmitt, of Richardson Merrill Corp.; Mrs. Esther Diamond and Mrs. Jean Palormo, of Science Research Associates; Mr. V. Jon Bentz, of Sears, Roebuck & Co.; Mr. Paul Baker and Mr. Harry Laurent, of Standard Oil Company of New Jersey; Mr. Thomas Harrell and Mr. Dale Yoder, of Stanford University; Mr. R. F. Morrison, of Sun Oil Corporation; Mr. George Baker, of Supermarket Institute; Mr. Milt Holmen, of Systems Development Corporation; Mr. Marvin Berkeley, Mr. Earl Gomersall, Mr. Charles Hughes, Mr. M. Scott Myers, and Mr. Earl Weed, of Texas Instruments, Inc.; Mr. Fred Massarik, of UCLA; Mr. Henry J. Duel and Mr. Dennis Seidman, of the United States Air Force; Mr. J. E. Uhlaner, of United States Army Personnel Research Office; Miss Dorothy E. Green, Mr. Albert Maslow, Mr. William McDonald, Mr. Nicholas Oganovic, and Mr. Glen Stahl, of the United States Civil Service Commission; Mr. Albert S. Glickman, of the United States Department of Agriculture; Mr. Frank Friedlander and Mr. Robert Stevenson, of the United States Naval Ordnance Testing Station, China Lake, Calif.; Mr. John MacDonald and Mr. George Murray, of Union Carbide; Mr. Ivo Mersmann, of United Airlines; Mr. Robert Burns, of the University of Chicago; Mr. Edwin Miller, of the University of Michigan; Mr. John B. Miner, of the University of Oregon; Mr. John V. Zuckerman, of the University of Southern California; and Mr. Robert Woodworth, of the University of Washington.

and was modified to fit particular circumstances in different interviews. This was necessary because of wide differences in function and structure from firm to firm.

Even though personal interviews were held with officials presumed to be best qualified to answer our questions, there were difficulties in getting complete information. Typically, the head of personnel or of personnel research was interviewed; however, in many organizations, because of decentralization, some of the questions simply could not be answered. In other organizations more than one individual was interviewed in order to get as complete information as possible. Even so, for many reasons, gaps still existed. For example, in many cases the figures we requested simply did not exist. This problem was particularly evident in areas relating to where managers at different levels in the organization came from and in questions about incentive programs. Still another difficulty was that some officials preferred not to reveal certain information, despite our promises that their responses would be dealt with confidentially. Notable examples of this arose in relation to questions about the cost and evaluation of managerial development and training activities. Because of these gaps in information, we cannot present complete data relevant to all questions asked in the interviews. Rather than focusing on sketchy data and potentially inaccurate responses, we have decided to present information mainly in those areas eliciting the most confident and complete replies. Where possible, respondent information was checked and corrected by gathering supplementary data (such as personnel policy manuals) containing information on the same issues.

In order to identify and eliminate any interviewer distortion of the data, all interviews were tape-recorded. After completing each visit, the interviewer wrote a report describing the practices of the organization he had visited. This report was checked for accuracy by a second person listening to the tapes of the responses. In some instances, the interview reports were returned to the interviewees, who checked them for accuracy. The final descriptions of procedures followed by each firm were then examined for relative frequency of different practices, and these data form the basis for the remainder of this chapter.

SOURCES OF MANAGERIAL TALENT

There are many sources of management talent. Three *internal* sources are promotion from lower level managerial jobs, promotion from nonmanagerial jobs, and lateral transfers. *External* sources include new college graduates and employees from other organizations (which may involve employing executive search firms). The questionnaire asked the percentage of managers at each management level who were drawn from each of these sources. Almost universally (96 percent), the companies we interviewed believed in filling positions from within their own organizations. The most frequent estimate was that at all levels of management, at least 90 to 95 percent of managers had come from internal sources. However, most respondents could not estimate the relative proportions of managers obtaining their positions from promotion or from lateral transfer, although the latter source was acknowledged to be used commonly at all levels in most organizations.

The few organizations that did not universally promote from within seemed to depart from the policy only out of necessity. That is, rapid growth taxed internal managerial resources so greatly that not enough qualified people were available within the organization to fill higher positions. For example, one growth company promoted from within only above the third level of management. At lower levels managers were brought directly into their positions from outside the company. Approximately 75 to 80 percent of this company's lower level supervisory positions were filled with persons having two to four years of managerial experience with other firms. Thus, this organization had a policy of hiring persons who had been tried out in managerial positions by other firms and then using their performance in lower level positions as a proving ground for promotion to middle management. In contrast, most organizations used external sources only for recruiting persons belonging to various technical or professional specialties. Thus, the majority of lawyers, accountants, psychologists, physicians, and certain scientific or technical specialists in relatively esoteric areas had been hired directly from the outside and placed in management positions.

Other studies have found that most organizations adhere to promotion-from-within policies. Megginson (1963) found that 62 percent of 350 firms had a stated policy of selecting managers from within, 4 percent selected from outside, and the remainder obtained managers from both sources. Pamplin (1959, p. 68), in a study of 33 large organizations, concluded that "most companies . . . indicated that their basic policy regarding selection of executives was one in which executives were selected from inside the company." Studies by Newcomer (1955) and the National Industrial Conference Board (1957) also contain relevant data. They both show that over 50 percent of executives obtained their positions through promotion from lower level positions. A study by Scientific American (1965) showed that 80 percent of the executives in a broad sample had previous work experience in other jobs with their present companies. It is difficult to tell from these data whether there has been any increase in the tendency to promote from within in recent years. However, the typical response of the subjects to our interview was that it may be increasing somewhat, particularly in light of the recent emphases on management development programs.

We also asked how important executive search and other recruiting firms were for obtaining managerial manpower. As might be expected, they are used only infrequently and were said to be of only negligible importance as a source of managers. Apparently only about 5 percent of the more technical positions are referred to such recruiting firms. This low estimate is partially supported by the NICB study (1957), which found that only 10 percent of vacancies in a group of companies were filled by executive search organizations. At this point one cannot help but wonder who, then, is making such active use of these firms, for they certainly seem to be thriving (Stryker, 1961; Yoder, 1962). Perhaps the smaller firms are using them to pirate managers from the large, successful firms. This interpretation is partially supported by the fact that several of the firms we interviewed were mentioned by Fortune (Stryker, 1961) as frequently raided organizations.

Obviously it was impossible for either our survey or the previous ones to determine the degree to which promotion-from-within policies are actually practiced. Undoubtedly there is a tendency to overstate their importance since it seems to be socially desirable to have a promotion-from-within policy. Where possible, we asked respondents where all current top executives had been just previous to their present positions. Their answers seemed to support the contention that promotion from within is actually practiced. Thus, it seems safe to assume that promotion from within is a widely accepted and practiced policy in the large, profitable, and growing firms characteristic of our sample.

Evidence from studies by Warner and Abegglen (1955), Newcomer (1955), and Scientific American (1965) clearly shows that fewer and fewer non-college men are moving into top managerial ranks. In 1900, 28.3 percent of business executives had college degrees; by 1950 the figure had risen to 62.1 percent, and by 1964 to 74.3 percent. Bowman (1964) found that 93.4 percent of 2,000 managers reported a college education to be essential for moving into management. We concluded the same thing from our interviews; that is, with the exception of front-line supervisors, a large majority of persons in managerial jobs have college degrees. Our interviewees were careful to stress that it is still possible to move into top management without a college degree; each respondent was able to cite some "hero" who had made it. However, the very fact that those who had made it were regarded as unusual or atypical points up the relative difficulty of making top management without a college degree.

How do the college graduates who eventually obtain management positions enter the organization? With a policy of promotion from within in operation, the answer is that they enter the organization in nonmanagement positions. Indirectly, then, the most important source of managers is ultimately an external one—recent graduates from colleges. After being hired, a college graduate's movement into management comes internally through training, experience in nonmanagement jobs, or combinations of these. A recent survey of 25 firms by the NICB (Habbe, 1963) showed that they all started recent college graduates in nonmanagement jobs. This emphasis on recruiting inexperienced college graduates for positions likely to lead to management jobs rather than recruiting them directly into management is also illustrated by a cursory examination of the help-wanted ads in the New York Times. On July 13, 1966, for example, of 57 ads for management trainees or administrative assistants, only one-third included experience requirements. In contrast, 98 percent of the ads for management positions mentioned experience requirements, and only 12 percent mentioned education requirements.

In summary it appears that most companies subscribe to a policy of promotion from within. One effect of such policies is that college graduates enter organizations in nonmanagement positions, but are perceived to be on the promotion ladder leading to management. Thus college graduates form the prime ultimate source of managerial talent for most organizations. In essence, the major route to management in most present-day firms is through college and through in-company managerial training "programs." External sources are used only rarely by most large firms to hire experienced managers, and this occurs mostly when persons are being sought for very specialized or technical jobs.

SELECTION PRACTICES

The focus in the selection of managers from outside the organization has always been upon the person and upon presumed traits leading to success in management. Implicit in the use of tests, interviews, and other selection instruments is the assumption that certain traits or characteristics relevant to managerial effectiveness can be measured at the time of application for employment. As we saw in the preceding chapter, opinion surveys of traits necessary for management imply that a good manager possesses just about every human virtue. We gained a similar impression from firms we visited; they seemed to be looking for managers scoring high on as many measures as possible. Many were using a great variety of selection instruments in order to identify prospective managers possessing such a "spread of excellence."

Most firms, however, place quite a different emphasis on decisions related to internal selection or promotion from within. There, the emphasis tends to be much less trait-oriented and more results-oriented (or product-oriented). A significant effect of the widespread promotion-from-within policies is that the initial selection decision (to take a person into an organization) becomes even more important. These initial decisions determine the caliber of men who are to make up the future management force in a firm. In contrast, firms hiring experienced managers from outside can, perhaps, afford more "slippage" in the system—if their selection practice also implies less rigidity in promoting from within. That is, greater pressure might be placed on managers to "cut the mustard" in such firms than in those where all higher managers are drawn from the internal ranks.

At any rate, the topic of managerial selection includes decisons of three different types: decisions about hiring college graduates, decisions bearing on promotion and transfer of present employees, and decisions related to hiring experienced managers from outside the organization. We noted quite different emphases and different selection practices for these three decisions among the firms we interviewed. This is perhaps best illustrated by reviewing the selection instruments actually used by the firms in our sample.

Psychological tests. Judging from the widespread attention given recently to the issue of psychological testing, one would guess that tests are being used by all firms for just about every type of selection decision. This is far from the case, however, particularly for decisions involving managers.

Ward (1960) obtained questionnaire replies from 1,610 managers describing test usage in their companies. Fifty-three percent reported that tests were used for salaried employees; forty-two percent reported their use for hourly paid employees. The use of personality tests seems to be on the upswing. Scott, Clothier, and Spriegel (1961) reported an increase in personality test usage from 29 percent of companies in 1947 to 44 percent of companies in 1957. They also noted an increase in the use of mental ability tests (from 38 percent of firms in 1947 to 63 percent of firms in 1957). A more recent survey by the NICB (1964) also indicates that intelligence tests are used by many companies in the country (73 percent of the manufacturing companies surveyed). As an overall figure it is reasonable to estimate that as many as 60 to 70 percent of the firms in the country use ability or aptitude tests, with considerably fewer firms using personality tests.

The more important question for our purpose has to do with the relative frequency of test usage for personnel decisions concerning managers or managers-to-be. Ward (1960) attempted to pinpoint the differential amount of test usage for selecting persons for different jobs, finding somewhat greater use of tests for salaried than for hourly paid employees. Unfortunately, it is still not clear whether managers are receiving more or less testing than others because *salaried* employees include both management and nonmanagement persons. Results from our own interviews show that companies may be more hesitant about giving tests to candidates for management jobs as compared with applicants for other salaried positions. Several firms pointed out that they used tests for selecting many nonmanagement employees but that they did not use them for management positions. In total, the evidence is inconclusive with respect to whether tests are used more or less frequently for management in comparison with nonmanagement jobs.

Tests for internal selection decisions. Policies of promotion from within greatly increase the importance of internal personnel decisions. Of the companies we interviewed, nearly half (40 percent) test managers and prospective managers as part of their assessment for promotion or transfer. This agrees with data given by Pamplin (1959) showing that 33 percent of the firms he studied used tests for internal decision making. Several companies we interviewed reviewed test records obtained at the time of employment for managers being considered for promotion, but most of these firms claimed they placed little weight on these test results as a basis for actual personnel decisions.

The companies that did test used a wide variety of tests. Typically a mental ability test was used, as were some personality and interest tests. A few companies used only ability tests, but most used both ability and personality or interest tests. For example, one company used an eight-hour comprehensive test battery including, among others, the Wonderlic Personnel Test, the Shipley-Hartford Test, the SRA Verbal Test, the DAT Abstract Reasoning Exam, the Watson-Glaser Critical Thinking Test, the Davis Reading Test, the Kuder Preference Record, and the Guilford-Zimmerman Temperament Survey. A number of other testing programs were less comprehensive, typically involving perhaps the Primary Mental Abilities test for the SRA Verbal and the Strong or Kuder interest measures. The federal government has developed its own battery of tests, which is used for most types of internal management selection decisions.

For those companies using tests to help make internal personnel decisions, their use varies directly with the level of the managerial position. The higher the level, the less likely tests are to be used. This finding is not surprising in light of a study by Freeman and Taylor (1950) showing that only 4 percent of a sample of top executives felt that tests were the best selection method for top management jobs. For these managers, their own personal judgment was the overwhelming favorite as the best way to pick good executives.

Perhaps the heaviest use of tests for internal decisions occurs when an individual is being considered for his first move into managerial ranks. For example, the Early Identification of Management Potential (EIMP) test battery used at Standard Oil of New Jersey and the Humble Oil Co. is especially designed to aid this kind of decision. The test scores of each manager become an important part of his record and play a part in his future development. Although these scores are not available to the manager's immediate superior, they are available at higher levels, and they, along with estimates of potential by the manager's superiors, form the basis upon which training and development decisions are made. A number of other companies we interviewed have developed or are beginning to develop tests designed to spot future managers at an early date. Still, of the firms we studied, as pointed out earlier, only about 40 percent use any kind of test information for deciding who is to be promoted into management, and even fewer use them to decide who is to be promoted within management. Ward (1960) in his survey found that 36 percent replied that tests are used for promotion and transfer decisions. Thus, despite the great importance of internal selection decisions in organizations committed to promotion from within, tests are ignored more often than not as decision-making aids.

One issue concerning the use of tests for internal moves involves who does the testing. Only two organizations "bought" testing from outside firms. All others relied on their own personnel departments. The frequency of test administration to a specific individual showed big differences from firm to firm. Some are tested only once after entering the company; others are retested when being considered for promotion. The EIMP approach is a single battery administered a few years after joining the company. Several other organizations test managers again and again as they move up into management— often with different test batteries. In summary, then, it is obvious that all types of tests are used in internal selection decisions, but that they are used mostly at the lower levels of management and even then only in a minority of the companies.

Tests for external selection decisions. Previous studies have shown that tests are more often used in deciding who is hired from outside the organization than they are for internal decisions. Ward (1960) gives the figures of 53 percent use for external and 36 percent for internal. The same trend appears in data gathered in our interviews, as shown in Table 3.2. Ninety percent of the firms test some or all of their external hires, while only about 40 percent test for internal decisions. One reason for this tendency to do more testing externally than internally undoubtedly stems from the belief that testing is really helpful only when little is known about the individual. Managers often expressed the view in the interviews that better judgment about a man's potential is obtained from a careful review of his performance record. In fact, according to some managers, internal testing is often more strenuously objected to than external testing and therefore may create resistance on the part of persons being considered for promotion.

Table 3.2 also shows that companies using tests for internal decisions inevitably use them also for external decisions. These data may reflect the "normal" pattern of growth for testing programs. First, companies test acquiescent

Table 3.2 THE USE OF TESTS BY ORGANIZATIONS INTERVIEWED

		Give tests to some or all for external decisions		
		Yes	No	
Give tests to some or all for	Yes	15	0	15
internal decisions	No	15	3	18
		30	3	

applicants—only later are higher level managers and candidates for promotion considered fair game.

The organizations studied use a wide variety of tests for external hiring decisions. Most frequently used are cognitive, verbal, and arithmetic ability tests. Next come personality and interest tests, which are used by most firms, and finally projective tests, used by only four firms. The government agencies we visited tend to use only ability tests for external hires and, of course, do not use projective tests. No consistent differences appeared between the kind of tests used to hire new college graduates and those used for more experienced managers.

Recent college graduates are more likely to be tested by the firms we interviewed than experienced managers being considered for employment. This is particularly true for those with experience who are being considered for high-level positions. The common practice, when a high-level job *must* be filled from the outside, is to contact an executive search firm, which may provide the names of several qualified persons. These persons are then interviewed by company officials. Typically, the search firms do not test the candidates, although four of our interviewees do request that test information be provided for candidates for lower level (below middle management) slots.

Most firms, then, do test managers hired from external sources. However, they vary considerably in terms of what tests they use and in the proportion of managers tested. Many organizations test only recent college graduates who are applying for management entry positions such as sales and technical jobs. The odds are that most recent college graduates entering such firms will be tested as part of the initial selection program and perhaps later when they are considered for promotion. This somewhat heavy testing of college graduate applicants is probably warranted by the key role that most college men are being asked to play in moving rapidly into managerial jobs.

Company research on testing. Goode (1958), after surveying 131 organizations, concluded that only 5 percent of all personnel research was being done in business organizations. He went on to state that personnel men often have little understanding or knowlege of what research is or how it should be conducted. Such a pessimistic view appears *not* to be warranted concerning the test validation work being done in the companies we visited. Although some companies were making no attempts to validate their tests, 20 firms were doing some type of test validation research. Admittedly we visited firms that were research-oriented and thus secured the "cream of the crop." Business in general is probably better characterized by the 13 firms that were doing no research. Some of the research on test validation that we found taking place in industry was of high quality and is discussed in greater detail in later chapters. The fact that good research is being done indicates that significant research is feasible in industry. However, as we shall see, most of the research being done in industry seems to be focused upon the test validation issue; areas such as training and motivation are receiving almost no attention.

   Interviews. According to Dunnette and Bass (1963, pp. 117-118):

> The personnel interview continues to be the most widely used method for selecting employees, despite the fact that it is a costly, inefficient, and usually invalid procedure. It is often used to the exclusion of far more thoroughly researched and validated procedures. Even when the interview is used in conjunction with other procedures, it is almost always treated as the final hurdle in the selection process. In fact, other selection methods (e.g., psychological tests) are often regarded simply as supplements to the interview.

   Every indication is that the interview continues to be used almost universally as a selection device. Scott, et al. (1961) report that 98.4 percent of a sample of 852 companies used the interview in their selection process. This, of course, does not tell us how important a part of the process the interview is, but the fact that 93.9 percent of the companies in the Scott et al. study said they *never* hired anyone without an interview suggests that it is indeed a critical phase. All the companies we visited placed great importance upon interviews in their hiring procedures. Only in one organization was there a program under way to decrease the importance of the interview in the selection program—and the personnel man responsible remarked upon the stiff resistance he was encountering. We did learn that one company we did not visit had been successful in hiring without the use of interviews. Reportedly they were looking for researchers to staff a laboratory, and they simply wrote to the major universities, asking for the names of their best students. Upon receiving these names, the company mailed very attractive job offers to the 200 top individuals. A startling 199 of these accepted the job offers. In sharp contrast, however, most line managers are absolutely opposed to surrendering their prerogative to judge future employees on the basis of an interview. Obviously the interview must satisfy some very important needs of the interviewer, if not of the interviewee.

   Many different procedures are classified under the broad heading of "interview." They range all the way from a completely unstructured discussion between applicant and employer to a highly structured panel interview during which a group of interviewers asks a predetermined sequence of questions of a single interviewee. This same wide range in types of interview was apparent among the companies we visited, extending from completely unstructured to highly structured situations and from leaderless group discussions among several applicants to face-to-face interviews between one applicant and one company representative. Not surprisingly, each firm we visited seemed to have its own special version of the standard interview, and validity was often claimed for these special variations in the face of general agreement that everyone else's interviews were usually invalid for selection purposes. The variations took many forms—for example, in the order used by different interviewers in talking to the applicant or in special training procedures used for the interviewers. In one firm the applicants are first interviewed by two or three members of upper management, who then exchange quick phone calls in order to decide whether to hire the applicant. If the decision is positive, they send the applicant to a lower level manager whose job it is to "sell" the company. Still, most firms rely on a relatively unstructured format and have applicants interviewed successively by several members of management. This procedure was found to be particularly common in the hiring of new college graduates.

In many companies interviewing of recent college graduates has become a highly ritualized and time-consuming operation. This, of course, is not necessarily bad, since, as we have seen, this hiring decision has a crucial bearing on the subsequent quality of management available to the firm. Typically the college graduate is given a twenty- to thirty-minute campus interview conducted either by a trained personnel man or by a line manager. After this interview, a decision is made about whether or not to invite the graduate to visit the company for further interviewing.

There is some evidence concerning the nature of the on-campus interview. A study by Odiorne and Hann (1961) found that 95 percent of the interviewers hiring at Michigan used open-ended questions and that 71 percent operated without a set pattern. The interviewers tended to shy away from putting stress on the candidate, from focusing on biographical information, and from prying out facts. What do interviewers base their decisions on in these twenty-minute sessions? The three most frequently mentioned factors were grades, good personality, and expressiveness in the interview. Factors leading to unfavorable interviewer impressions were unrealistic goals and lack of sincerity. Apparently, here too the typical firm is looking for someone with all the "right" traits. However, even these data are questionable since Odiorne and Hann found little correspondence between responses to the same questions asked via interview and via questionnaire surveys of company interviewers. This discrepancy was easily explained by one recruiter, who stated, "Well, I guess I can't tick off my standards for acceptance or rejection like some kind of litany. I think I know what I like or don't like however" (Odiorne & Hann, 1961, p. 150).

If the student survives the initial screening interview, he is usually invited to visit the company, where he can expect to face a number of interviews. These are usually unstructured confrontations between one interviewee and one interviewer. The interviewers are typically untrained for interviewing and usually are line managers seeking to decide whether or not to hire the college graduate into a nonmanagement job in their departments. In most companies, after all testing has been done and other selection steps have been taken, the final decision in hiring is based simply on whether or not a particular plant or division manager "likes what he sees" in an applicant sitting across the table from him. Moreover, it is often true that if that one manager does not want a graduate, he will not be hired anywhere in the organization.

The management intern program of the Civil Service Commission uses interviews somewhat differently from the way they are used in the nongovernment settings we visited. Interviews are not used until after the applicant has performed satisfactorily on several tests and after he has provided a considerable amount of personal history data. This often includes obtaining letters of recommendation from a number of people familiar with the applicant. After assembling all these data, if the applicant still appears to be qualified, he is given several interviews. Pairs of interviewers from Washington talk to each candidate, and he is assessed on such factors as his oral expression, adaptability, maturity, and motivation. In addition to individual interviews, group interviews are used. Here, four to seven candidates are observed in a group situation while they discuss two assigned tasks or problems.

A somewhat different situation seems to exist when experienced managers are being hired from outside the organization. Of course there is no campus interview, but there may be some kind of interview with an executive search firm. However, the basic thrust of this interview is likely to be toward gathering background and biographical data to be transmitted to the hiring organization. Only four of the organizations we visited had a search or consulting firm do any in-depth appraisal interviews.

The crucial interviews for the experienced manager are likely to be those which take place once he visits the company. Here, he is likely to encounter the same kind of day-long round of interviews that the new college graduate faces. He may, however, get even more attention. For example, in one firm we visited, experienced applicants for managerial positions are given in-depth interviews with the company psychologist or psychiatrist. Although it is difficult to generalize on the basis of our sample of firms about what kinds of interviews are typically conducted for hiring managers from external sources, our data do suggest that the interview is typically the key input into selection decisions.

Perhaps the one kind of selection decision in which the formal interview does not play a key role is that involving internal promotions and transfers. A study by Pamplin (1959) found that interviews were used in less than 50 percent of the companies he studied when internal moves were made. The same general tendency appeared in the companies we visited. The reasons for this are obvious. In the first place, the people making the decision often already know the individual and therefore regard the interview as superfluous. Also, more complete data are available on an individual being considered for promotion than for one coming in from outside. Interviewing for internal moves is probably restricted primarily to those situations where the future superior is not acquainted with the candidate (as when the opening is in another plant), although we did find some companies that use interviews for almost all internal moves.

At this point a reasonable conclusion would seem to be that the interview remains the key selection instrument for most firms. This is hardly a startling new conclusion since in 1940, 98 percent of a sample of 251 firms used the interview, while in 1957, 98 percent of a sample of 852 firms used it (Scott et al., 1961). Thus, the popularity of the interview is not new, nor has it suffered from the increased use of tests and other selection devices. In later chapters we shall see that management's insistence on selecting people on the basis of interviews can best be explained by reference to the needs of the interviewer, rather than on the grounds of its demonstrated efficacy as a selection device.

Research on interviewing. It was definitely not "in" to do research on the interview in the companies we visited. This is particularly disconcerting in light of the great importance placed on interviewing. In fact, we learned of only one study that had been addressed to the topic of interviewing. At this point one cannot help but wonder what business organizations, if any, are doing research on the interview. The firms we visited certainly would seem to be those most likely to be doing this research. The typical attitude seemed to be that the interview has so much face validity that it is unnecessary and in fact rather useless to consider validating it. Fortunately, however, a great deal of research is going on in nonbusiness settings on the interview, and this is discussed in later chapters.

Application blanks and biographical data forms. Application blanks appear to be used nearly as widely as the interview. Scott et al. (1961) found that in 1957, 99.6 percent of the companies which were surveyed used application blanks—in contrast to 99 percent in 1940. Thus, the application blank has been and continues to be used everywhere. For management personnel, it obviously has its greatest relevance when selection of people from external supplies of manpower is involved. Still, up until the last few years the application blank has typically been the forgotten instrument in the selection package. Recently, more attention has been focused upon the possibility of weighting and systematically scoring application blanks. In some cases long biographical data forms have been developed to supplement the application blanks (for example, this is one of the major approaches used in the EIMP battery); in many cases these resemble personality or interest tests. Whereas the typical application blank may include questions about age, education, and marital status, biographical data forms delve into much more personal areas of the individual's background. Questions about parental relations and childhood sibling experiences are not uncommon.

We could find no previous studies that have attempted to determine how frequently weighted application blanks or biographical data forms are presently being used in the selection of managers, but we did obtain information from our interviews on this topic. Our general impression is that the use of these devices is in its infancy. At the most, only five or six of the firms we visited are making real use of these forms for selecting managers, and these firms have only recently started using them. The forms in use vary considerably, from those weighting just a few items like grades and means of support while at college to long biographical data forms administered in addition to the regular application form. The trend is obviously toward increased use of these instruments, but it is difficult to tell how far their use will go. These matters are discussed in much greater detail in later chapters.

Research on application blanks and biographical data forms. Six of the firms were doing research for the purpose of developing scoring systems for biographical data. Several other firms mentioned that they were moving in this direction. This is not surprising because most firms have files full of completed blanks from both present and past employees, along with records of personnel decisions made about them during their careers. Little more is needed to begin a program of research on the possible "meaning" of biographical data scoring systems for managerial effectiveness.

References. Only one company makes extensive use of references in its hiring procedure. There, references are gathered from an applicant's former superior, his peers, and even his subordinates. Moreover, the firm attempts to judge the relative value of references obtained from different individuals; thus, it sometimes secures references on the references. Other firms we visited tend to be much more casual about checking references, but they still use them extensively. Many said that the best references were those casual comments dropped during a phone call. Thus, they avoid using long forms or having the respondent rank or rate the applicant. In companies we visited references were given most attention when used for hiring experienced managers from outside the organization.

There is little evidence available on the extent of use of references for hiring decisions. Scott et al. (1961) did find that 50.4 percent of a sample of firms required written references. According to their data this figure has remained about the same since 1940. They report 49 percent in 1940, 48 percent in 1947, and 49 percent in 1953, hardly a significant increase in the use of references. It is impossible to tell from these data how much weight is actually given to the results of the reference checking procedure. Our best guess is that little is given. As one respondent observed, "Everybody has three friends."

The current use of references is perhaps best summarized by the following quotation from *Personnel* (1960, p. 19):

> References from former employers, once a major deciding factor in whether the applicant got the job or not, no longer carry as much weight as they used to. In a recent *Industrial Relations News* survey, only 15 of the 25 companies questioned said that they check references. When minor falsehoods are uncovered, they are usually overlooked. Most common fibs: dates of employment, education, salary, age, or reason for leaving previous job.

None of the organizations we visited was doing research on the validity of references. As was true with interviews, they were often classified as having face validity and therefore not meriting particular concern. Perhaps the most difficult thing to assess concerning reference checking is how extensive it is and to what lengths organizations are willing to go to get complete information on a prospective employee. In the case of the one organization mentioned above, the answer is that they were willing to go quite a long way! That is, they were willing to get references for the referencer and to trace the individual's history far back into the past.

Consultants' appraisals. No previous studies could be found on the degree to which organizations use consultants' appraisals in making selection decisions. There does exist a considerable folklore (e.g., W. H. Whyte, 1956) suggesting that they are often called upon to make crucial decisions and to provide extensive psychological information on prospective top managers. Four of the organizations we visited reported that they made use of the consultants' appraisals. In all four cases the organizations seemed to make extensive use of their consulting firm. Two of the four firms said that they referred candidates for internal moves as well as applicants to the consultant for appraisal. Unfortunately, we could not determine from the firms we visited the kind of selection instruments the consultants used to make their recommendations. Apparently they typically were using psychological tests (type unknown), interviewing (type unknown), and reference checking (type unknown).

The way one firm uses consultants gives some idea of how so many of these consultants stay in business even though only a small minority of companies use their services. This particular organization had as many as 20 different consultants working for it at one time. Each division had its own consulting firm working for it, and often the degree of overlap between the work of different consultants did not become apparent until the end of the year, when all the bills were presented to the central personnel office.

It almost goes without saying that no research was being conducted with respect to the validity of consultants' recommendations. They appeared to be taken completely on faith, but as one personnel man enthused, "My consultant is uncanny—he's so good at spotting these guys."

Assessment centers. The assessment center approach has received a great deal of attention lately, much of it laudatory (e.g., Ferguson, 1966). The first industrial firm to undertake this approach was AT & T. Their approach has its roots in the Office of Strategic Services (OSS, 1948) assessment center used for selecting spies during World War II. Briefly, the candidate being considered for a management position goes to the center for 2 1/2 days. While there, he is interviewed and tested, and he takes part in various simulated managerial tasks. At the end, the staff, made up partly of line managers, evaluates the individual's managerial or promotional potential. Since these centers began, about twenty thousand prospective managers have been assessed; the current rate is about five thousand per year. The research staff of AT&T has done a great deal of first-rate research on the assessment center approach for identifying attributes and conditions making for managerial effectiveness. This is discussed in detail in later chapters.

A number of other companies have begun to form their own assessment centers. In fact, one of the most frequent questions we were asked by the companies we visited was, "What can you tell us about assessment centers?" Interest centered on the possible applicability of the assessment center approach to promotion and transfer decisions and may indicate acknowledgment on the part of organizations that promotion from within makes these decisions increasingly important.

Performance evaluation. Every organization makes the point that individual merit is a crucial part of its promotion decisions. Whether it is promotion into or within management, the organizations we visited stressed that they attach great importance to merit or how well an individual is performing his present job. Pamplin (1959) reported that all the 22 organizations he studied which had formal selection programs also used some form of job performance appraisal for promotion decisions. However, 11 of his firms had no formal selection program. We obtained similar results. Although all firms stressed the importance of performance for promotion, a number had neither formal selection systems nor formal appraisal systems. Spriegel (1962) presents some data supporting this observation. He found that only 300 of 567 companies had performance appraisal systems for use in promotion decisions and that many of those having formal systems did not use them at the managerial or executive level. One of the firms we visited, for example, did not keep any performance appraisal records for promotion purposes. All they tried to do was to see that a list of managers with the necessary experience was available for each job opening. Other firms had extensive merit ranking systems covering everyone in the company, and from this it was possible to get a manager's rank, just as it is possible to get a student's rank within his class.

Overall, it is difficult to evaluate the weight given to performance appraisals in promotion decisions. Despite the lip service paid to the importance of merit, one cannot assess its importance when no formal appraisal system exists. In addition, in the case of several firms we got the impression that all managers are put onto the promotion list and that regardless of how they perform in their jobs, they do ultimately receive promotions. Several companies we visited, for example, placed major weight in promotion decisions on the immediate superior's estimate of his subordinate's *potential* rather than on the superior's estimate of his subordinate's *job performance effectiveness*. In some instances the responsibility almost seemed to fall upon the superior of the individual who was slated for top management to see that he did well in his job performance. Poor performance seemed to reflect more upon the individual's superior than upon his own chances for future promotion. Perhaps the most reasonable conclusion is that most organizations do consider merit in promotion, whether it is measured by a formal system or by simple word of mouth among superiors, and/or other influential officials, but that the weight assigned to merit in making promotion decisions varies widely from company to company.

Experience and seniority. As is true of merit, virtually every organization states that experience and seniority are a crucial aspect in determining who is promoted. However, there is considerable variation among organizations in terms of how important it is and how data concerning experience are gathered and used. Recently it has become common for organizations to develop systematic storage and retrieval systems for this kind of data. Under such a system when a position is open, the manager in charge of filling it can ask for and obtain a list of all personnel having the necessary background and experience to handle the job. Typically this information is available from a computer, which can search all available manpower and come up with those employees which best fit the job demands. This information is also often available from replacement charts showing who the likely candidates are for all jobs in the organization.

Ferguson (1966) has recently suggested that computers can be programmed to provide more information than just lists of people who are presumed to be able to fill a certain position. He suggests that computers should supply test data, information on how selecting an individual will affect manpower needs of the organization, and information on the total career development of the individual. Such a system is obviously exciting, but as Ferguson points out, it is still in the future. Limited use of computers and the replacement chart approach, however, is becoming more and more common. Thirteen of the organizations we visited had such systems presently functioning in their organizations. Three other firms were in the process of installing them, and most of the others were in the planning stages. The availability of computers for this purpose has been relatively recent, but as programming capability improves and as more complex decisions and information can be handled, it is probable that the importance of this approach will increase. It is also likely that more will be known about how to evaluate and use previous experience as a criterion of promotability. However, given the typically unsystematic methods for assessing an individual's previous experience, it is virtually impossible to know—now—how previous experience is weighted in organizational promotion and transfer decisions.

Combining predictors. We have already stressed that influences on managerial effectiveness are diverse and complex, involving the interaction of individual characteristics and motivational and organizational environment variables. How should predictors be combined to reflect the complexity of these interactions? Simply adding them by means of equations or statistical rules seems too mechanistic and seems to depart from our aim of individualized prediction. But combination by purely clinical inference also seems precarious. Such predictions may be individualized, but they also seem haphazard and overly conjectural. Granted that certain predictors may be better than others, the questions still remain of how they should be combined to yield accurate predictions about managers' job behavior.

A large number of psychologists believe that the many complicating features of the manager-job interaction can be taken into account only by means of judgmental or clinical processes. They argue that it is unrealistic to assume that crucial behavioral tendencies are adequately tapped by single scales on certain psychological tests and that correlating such scales with estimates of managerial effectiveness results in grossly over-simplified conclusions, representing a serious underutilization of the total information contained in such tests. Thus, it is believed that meaningful prediction can be made only by considering configurations of predictor variables and by taking account of how they may be modified by particular circumstances that a manager may face. It is argued that prediction for each individual managerial candidate cannot depend upon statistical relationships gathered on groups of managers; instead, the psychologist, reviewing predictor information and knowing the job circumstances, can collate and integrate the total amount of information better and can make more accurate judgments about behavior than could be accomplished through use of statistical combination of predictors and criteria.

It should be apparent that the clinical approach is highly subjective; an individual's test scores and other predictor information are interpreted by the clinician on the basis of his own experience with similar cases, his inferences about job requirements, and any theories he may have about the meanings of the various predictor patterns as indicants of specific behavioral tendencies. Clinical prediction requires great skill, in contrast to the simple clerical function of combining predictors statistically. The skilled clinician must know all there is to know about the predictors he is using, the special circumstances for which they are being used, and all the aspects of human behavior for which they may be relevant.

In contrast, predictors are combined statistically according to equations developed specifically for predicting specific types of job behavior in certain circumstances. After the equations have been developed, it is possible to train an ordinary clerk to apply them to the predictor variables and to express the combination in the form of actuarial odds that a particular type of job behavior will occur. Obviously, the prior development of such equations or combining rules demands careful research, validation, and cross-validation of the predictors against the behavior measures to be predicted. But the yield from such research is a publicly communicable and objective procedure that is not dependent on specialized experience or clinical judgment.

The organizations we visited used only clinical combinations of their selection information. Even where carefully developed test and other quantitative measures were obtained, they were combined with data from other sources, such as interviews, by means of a strictly clinical method for the purpose of making the final selection decision. A few firms did have cut-off scores on their tests and other statistical rules, but once someone scored above them, the final decision to hire rested entirely upon clinical judgment. The reason for this seemed to be that the people we talked to simply felt that human judgment was required to combine properly and meaningfully the many predictors of management effectiveness. In no case, however, had any research comparing various methods of combining data been done.

Summary and conclusions: use of selection instruments. The safest thing to do at this point would probably be to conclude with the statement that there are wide individual differences among firms in the use of selection instruments. However, there are certain general trends and tendencies that probably should be noted if we are to reflect an accurate overview of current practices.

First, let us look at the hiring of new college graduates. Our survey shows that the interview is probably the most important factor in selecting recent college graduates. Tests and weighted biographical forms are gaining in popularity. In one sense, organizations seem to rely on the fewest sources of information (basically tests and interviews) in hiring recent college graduates and admittedly probably have less of the kind of information they would like to have in order to make a selection decision. This comes about because such things as performance appraisal and experience are not relevant for the recent college graduate.

An entirely different situation exists where internal movements are involved. Interviews and tests are less important, and such factors as experience and evaluated performance take on greatly increased importance. In addition, several significant new procedures have developed that promise to be widely used as aids for decision making concerning internal moves. Notable here are the assessment center approach and the computerized storage of the experience and performance levels of all managers in the organization. At the present time probably the greatest importance is attached to experience measured often in the form of seniority and to merit measured often in the form of a superior's subjective appraisal. For both internal and external selection decisions, it is clear that the information is combined for decision-making purposes on the basis of "clinical" judgment rather than on the basis of any carefully developed and validated pattern or configuration of predictor information.

MANAGEMENT TRAINING AND DEVELOPMENT PRACTICES

Training and development programs have become big business in their own right in this country. Just how big was amply illustrated by a report from one of the firms we visited stating that 20 percent of its annual investment budget was committed to training and development costs. Another study (Serbein, 1961) found that of a sample of 35 companies employing 10,000 or more employees, 8 spent more than $1 million per year on just in-company-training. One organization spent over $15 million on in-company training and development programs.

These same 35 firms reported spending a smaller but still significant additional amount of money on out-of-company training. A few years ago the aircraft industry estimated that its expenditures for training programs ran about $34 million per year. However, this figure appears to be hopelessly out of date since just one of the aircraft companies we visited said they spent that much in a single year. Another company we visited was increasing the personnel staff substantially, and all the new men were to work in training activities. There are many other figures that could be cited showing the amounts of money and time organizations are spending on training. However, they all point to the same conclusion: Training cost has risen to a point where, along with the costs of salaries and materials, it has come to represent one of the major investments of financial resources made by organizations.

Most of the data available on the amount of money organizations invest in training do not distinguish between money spent for programs that are applicable to management and those applicable to nonmanagement employees. Thus, it is difficult to estimate exactly how much is spent on management training and development relative to other kinds of training. The impression we gained from the organizations we studied was that their major training commitment was to the training and development of management level employees. This showed up first in the type and relative numbers of people in the personnel or training departments working on management and nonmanagement programs. The management training programs often had more people working on them, and the people were usually more highly educated. In addition, the management training and development programs often utilized a number of outside experts, while nonmanagement programs seldom did. The large commitment to management training also appeared in the number of hours organizations said their managers devoted to such activities. Several of these organizations stressed that their average managers spend as much as forty work hours per year in some kind of development program.

The programs vary fantastically in scope and material presented. One company, for example, gives motivation seminars, while another simply provides all managers with a running audit of all the programs available in the country so that they can take advantage of them.

Perhaps the key question at this point is: Why are organizations investing all this money in training and development programs? Some previous research evidence provides a rather clear-cut answer to this question. Both Bailey (1955) and Wickstrom (1964) found that organizations say their most important reason for sponsoring training programs is to improve the performance of managers on their present jobs. Secondarily, they say the programs are designed to prepare managers for possible future promotions. Thus, organizations appear presently to be looking for a rather immediate return on the money they invest in management training. Whether this is a reasonable and indeed a desirable expectation is of course a good question and is considered at length in a later chapter. For the time being we shall focus solely upon what kinds of things organizations are doing in order to fulfill this objective.

Organizations have not always been this committed to the development and training of their employees. Scott et al. (1961) have pointed out that training has been on the increase since 1930 and that the trend continues to be upward. The growth of training for management personnel has been particularly rapid, and much of this growth seems to have taken place since World War II. For example, today there are some forty-three universities offering residential executive development programs, and all but two of these programs started after the war (K. R. Andrews, 1959). Some other currently popular training devices such as T groups (J. P. Campbell & Dunnette, 1968) and Kepner-Tregoe (Kepner & Tregoe, 1965) also date from after the war. A study by Habbe reported that in 1935 only 3 percent of 2,500 companies had executive training programs. Tricket, using a slightly broader definition, reported that by 1954, 50 percent of 500 companies had management development programs. Although their data are not perfectly comparable, these surveys suggest that a dramatic increase in management programs has taken place. Perhaps the best estimate of how many firms currently have management training programs comes from a study by Clark and Sloan. They reported that 77 percent of 350 large companies had management development programs, a figure which is in agreement with findings from our own survey.[2]

Scott et al. (1961) as well as many others have pointed out that most of the training activity is centered in the larger firms. Table 3.3 illustrates this point.

Table 3.3   155 COMPANIES HAVING A COMPREHENSIVE TRAINING PROGRAM, CLASSIFIED BY SIZE GROUP

Employees	Companies	Percent of companies in size group
Less than 1,000	15	7.1
1,000-4,999	57	15.8
Over 5,000	77	32.9
Not given	6	
Total	155	

Source: Scott et al. (1961).

There has been a marked change in the management development programs in the last ten years. The pomp and ceremony of highly formalized and ritualistic training programs has been slowly disappearing (Stolz, 1966). Such programs have been replaced by programs that are organized, but organized to fit the needs of each individual manager, and thus they often appear to be diffuse. Argyris (1961) has described this condition as a situation where there is heavy emphasis placed on self-development but where the trainers control the training program with respect to objective, content, and time. Admittedly this philosophy seems to lack internal consistency, but as Argyris points out, it was subscribed to by the majority of training directors in a sample he studied. In the companies we visited this philosophy was subscribed to extensively. Typically a development committee of the training department decided what kind of development *each* manager needed and then suggested that he enroll in a certain course or program.

Because of this individualization of the training program, it is becoming more and more difficult to generalize about what kind of training managers in any given company have had. It is also equally difficult to make any very comprehensive statements about whether companies are using a certain kind of training device or technique. Indeed at times it appeared during our interviews that every company had at least tried all the training devices or techniques we asked about at one time or in some place in their organization. The individualization of training and development programs has created the need for many specialized programs. No longer do companies assume that a single,

[2] The Habbe, Tricket, and Clark and Sloan studies are cited in Bridgeman (1959).

standardized program is adequate for the developmental needs of all managers. It is currently fashionable to analyze the individual and his work situation and suggest one of a great number of potential programs ranging from simulations to *T* groups. Only a few organizations have the internal capacity to offer all the different kinds of programs. One that can is the federal government, which annually publishes through the Civil Service Commission a listing of the approximately 220 courses or programs that the government offers. More and more managers from organizations are being sent to such places as Bethel, Maine, and Lake Arrowhead, California, for specialized programs run by experts in a given field. These are programs that normally would be exceedingly difficult to provide within any one organization, often because of low demand for the course or unavailability of skilled instructors. Also, since many of these programs focus on behavior, there are difficult professional and ethical issues involved in in-house training programs. The assumption of most companies is that these diverse programs are better fitted to the needs of the individual than a large internal program could be because they focus on the specific area or areas in which each individual needs most help.

Because of the trend toward sending managers outside the organization, it becomes considerably more difficult for the organization to do research on a given program. If, for example, an organization wants to know the value of a program like Kepner-Tregoe, it may find meaningful research impossible because it has sent only a few managers to the program. Even so, many firms do try systematically to gather personal testimonials from every training participant. A second consequence is that firms often lose direct control over the content and objectives of the course. The most they can do is carefully select the programs to which they send their managers. However, this is often difficult because of wide variations among programs which may have the same broad label (for example, *T* groups may differ greatly depending upon who the trainer is). Thus, although organizations may hope a given course will fit the needs of the managers they send, it may not be perfectly designed to accomplish this purpose for everyone.

The current tendency for training programs to multiply outside and to a lesser extent inside organizations, as well as the inclination of organizations to use a multitude of programs, makes it difficult to talk about the validity or frequency of use of individual programs. In a sense, this is the same problem that exists in the testing area, where it is impossible to discuss each individual test. The most that we can hope to do is to focus upon a few broad classifications of training and development programs and consider the frequency of their use. Our approach to this problem is to categorize training programs according to the type of input material used. As will be seen in later chapters, it is also possible to divide programs on the basis of how they are taught; — that is, the method they use — and on the basis of what results they hope to achieve.

The prime distinction here, however, is whether the training program is one based upon largely cognitive or theoretical material, as opposed to those attempting to change participants' behavior by focusing largely on the actual behavior occurring during training.

Cognitive programs include most of the typical training programs consisting of textbook and lecture approaches to training on such subjects as tax law, human relations, economics, etc. One further distinction that is worth making here is whether the cognitive input is of an applied nature or not. Obviously this is a difficult distinction, but it is quite clear that company-sponsored liberal arts programs are not designed to be immediately applicable, while some of the courses offered in human relations or tax laws are. This distinction is important because many organizations will sponsor applied programs readily but will look aghast at liberal arts or other such nonapplied cognitive programs.

Programs that focus upon the behavior and personality of the participants have been rather recent entries into the field of management training and development. But they have come on very strongly. *T* group, Managerial Grid (Blake & Mouton, 1964), and Kepner-Tregoe are perhaps the leading examples of the kinds of training. Some simulations and role-playing sessions would be other examples of training fitting into this classification when they place a major emphasis upon analyzing the behavior of the participants.

Job rotation and direct coaching from one's superior are two frequently used management development techniques that do not fit easily into our classification system. They often combine both cognitive and participant behavior inputs; more often they vary greatly from situation to situation in the inputs they provide. Thus, rather than force them into one classification, we shall consider them separately. In considering the prevalence of different types of training programs, we find that some programs are much more popular at the executive level, while others are typically employed only at the lower levels of management. Thus, we have differentiated between programs designed for the top, middle, and lower levels of management. Top level management includes all company officers bearing titles equivalent to vice-president and above. Lower level management consists of the first and second levels of supervision. Middle level management, of course, is made up of all levels between top and lower management. With this distinction in mind, let us turn to a consideration of the relative use of these different types of programs.

Applied theoretical and cognitive programs. Undeniably the most frequently used types of training programs at all levels of management are those which deal with cognitive material that can be applied directly to the manager's current job. Almost every company is supporting this kind of training to some extent. For example, Wickstrom (1964) found that only 8 percent of a sample of 117 firms said that they did not use outside courses dealing with specific management skills (e.g., production cost, contract, and personnel procedures). Similarly, he found that a high percentage of the companies were running inside courses dealing with similar topics. Some slightly less immediately applicable training also appeared to be getting support; for example, courses on current economics were used by 62 percent of the firms, and conferences on leadership skills were run by 68 percent of the firms. Over 60 percent of the companies in Wickstrom's sample offered courses in problem solving, labor relations, and communication. In short, most organizations appear to offer their managers a great number of courses designed to provide information on particular topics and skills.

In the firms we visited, virtually all foremen had been through a supervisory training program designed to give basic skills necessary for management positions. This was true whether they came up from a nonmanagement position or directly from a management training program for college graduates. Perhaps the best example of this kind of training is a two-year program offered in one of the companies we visited. It covers a number of different topics including work planning, company operations, communication, leadership problem solving, coaching performance appraisals, and salary administration. It is through this program that the company attempts to make its managers knowledgeable with respect to current developments in the behavioral sciences as well as with respect to company practices. Bridgeman (1959) estimates that at least two-thirds of all firms offer some form of training like this. In addition, the lower level managers in firms we visited could typically take outside courses from universities on a tuition refund basis if they established that the courses were work-related. Usually the lower level manager, after his initial supervisory training course, is limited to taking a few skill courses given within the company and perhaps signing up for an outside-the-company course at a local university. He is seldom sent away to a university or other training program for a residence course, nor is he likely to take any course that is not strictly applied.

It is at the middle management level that university residence courses and other off-the-job courses are used heavily. As Bridgeman (1959) points out, companies typically send only middle managers and then often only those with potential for top level positions to these programs. Wickstrom (1964) reports that 64 percent of all firms use general business management courses outside the organization. And as pointed out before, more than forty universities now offer these courses. Most of the firms we visited made some use of such courses for their middle level managers. In addition, several of the companies we visited ran their own residence training programs for middle level managers, and most offered a number of in-company nonresidence training programs for their middle managers. Most of these in-company courses were skills-oriented packaged programs that were given on a regular basis. They varied with respect to whether or not they were residence programs. Often they involved taking a few hours off a week to attend instruction, but in some organizations they involved leaving the job for several weeks of rather intensive training. In addition, the same program for refunding most or all of the tuition for a university course that was applicable at the lower level of management was typically also available for middle level managers.

It is at the top levels of management that training is predominantly an outside-the-organization activity if it is done at all. Few of the firms we visited had extensive internal top management programs. The majority of firms preferred to send top managers away to the better-known university programs such as Arden House, the Sloan program at MIT and Stanford, or the Harvard advanced management program. These programs present a smorgasbord of different material, ranging from occasional *T* groups to classic economics, but they appear to present mostly theoretical and cognitive material. To some extent the executives undoubtedly do participate in some of the packaged courses in such areas as speed reading and public speaking offered within the company. However, in most companies they rely primarily on external rather than internal programs.

Humanities or liberal arts programs. In one sense courses which have as their main input cognitive material drawn from the humanities or liberal arts have never gotten off the ground. K. R. Andrews (1959) says that at least ten programs have been devised but that two of them have been discontinued. Five of these are full-time residential courses for the executives of American Telephone and Telegraph. AT&T is probably the only company making an appreciable use of this kind of program today. Also functioning is the Aspen executive program, which does draw from many different companies. All the programs that have been run so far have been tailored to the top levels of management, and there is no indication that they will be used at the lower and middle levels of management in the near future. In fact, there is some reason to wonder whether they will continue to sustain their present popularity at the executive level.

Behavior input programs. The most rapid recent growth among management training and development programs has taken place in those programs which have as their major input the behavior of the participants. Prior to 1950 such programs were virtually nonexistent. Today they seem to be everywhere. They are typically marketed as separate courses by organizations such as the National Training Laboratories or Kepner-Tregoe, but training of this type is also often included in broader programs such as the Arden House or Sloan fellow programs.

The best-known programs of this type are probably the Managerial Grid (Blake & Mouton, 1964), *T* groups (Schein & Bennis, 1965), and Kepner-Tregoe (Kepner & Tregoe, 1965). These programs have enjoyed a phenomenal growth rate over the last five to ten years, and they all purport to deal largely with the behavior generated by the managers during the training sessions. They differ widely, however, in the means used to generate the behavior and in the way the behavior is analyzed. *T* groups are typically unstructured and depend upon the informal personal interactions within the groups for their data. The analysis of the behavior is facilitated by a trainer. The grid approach and Kep-ner-Tregoe are more automated and structured than the *T*-group approach. They depend on course materials and programs to help generate and analyze the behavior that will be focused upon. The grid and *T*-group approaches both focus on interpersonal relations, while Kepner-Tregoe, like many other simu-lations, focuses more on decision-making behavior.

It is difficult to assess the extent to which these different programs are actually being used in industry. One of the favorite devices of the leading pro-ponents of the various programs seems to be to list all the eminent companies that use their method. As Robert Blake puts it, nine out of the ten largest cor-porations in the world use the Managerial Grid.[3] If we look at the list of firms that have used these methods, as compiled by the proponents, it appears that every company of any consequence is using them. And it is probably quite true that to some extent most of the large companies have tried these programs. However, one thing that our interviews revealed was that some companies had tried and abandoned them, while others used them to only a limited extent. With respect to *T* groups, for example, twenty-five were clearly currently making use of them, while six were not. Three of the six that were not using them stated that they had had a poor experience with them and had dropped them. Appar-ently these poor experiences were due largely to negative feedback received from the participants. Among the twenty five that were currently using *T* groups, only a few were making large-scale use of them, that is, attempting to train a substantial proportion of their managers. Several organizations were highly committed and had hired a number of trainers into the company. They had *T* groups going on virtually constantly within the organization. One com-pany had eighteen managers who they felt were qualified *T* group trainers, although they admitted it was difficult to define a qualified trainer. Two of the other companies that we visited had made extensive use of Blake's material and seemed to prefer it to the *T*-group approach, although they seemed to have no data to support the view that it was more effective.

In the organizations we visited, lower level managers were unlikely to be exposed to the Kepner-Tregoe approach or to *T* groups; however, they were likely to get the Managerial Grid since it is given to all levels within the organ-ization. *T* groups were used quite frequently for middle level managers. Often the *T* group that a middle level manager goes to will be run inside the compa-ny. However, if he goes to a *T* group outside the company, he will probably go to a different session from the one the top executive in his organization attends. The middle level manager might go to Bethel, Maine, for two weeks for his *T* group and pay a total fee of $425. A top level manager, on the other hand, is not likely to go to a *T* group within the company; if he goes, he will probably attend something like the President's Lab, which may be held in a

[3] APA convention, Chicago, 1965.

resort hotel in Florida and costs in the area of $1,000 for a week of training. This lab is limited to the chief executives of large corporations.

The impression we gained from our interviews was that the Kepner-Tregoe program is used most often at the middle levels of management. In summary, then, it is obvious that a number of organizations are using training programs that have as their basic input the behavior of the participants. Perhaps the most popular of these approaches is the *T*-group method, and it enjoys its greatest popularity at the middle and top levels of management.

Coaching and job rotation. Job rotation and coaching are widely accepted methods of management development. Wickstrom (1964) has reported that 72 percent of all companies he studied used job rotation and that 84 percent used coaching from a superior. All the organizations we visited stressed that they believed in both coaching and job rotation as development techniques. However, very few had anything that could be called a program to implement their interest in these approaches. Job rotation, for example, did not appear to be used very systematically. There were, however, a few exceptions to this. One company did have a secret list of potential top level managers who were being rotated through a selective group of jobs. This company also gave the individuals extensive lists of reading material that was designed to prepare them for promotion.

The greatest use of systematic job rotation was with recent college graduates. College graduates were often rotated through a number of jobs as their introduction to the organization. After the rotation program they were often given their first management job. One of the organizations we visited placed heavy emphasis on rotation at all levels of management. Planning sessions were held with top management in order to chart managers' courses through a variety of jobs. However, this type of program was the exception rather than the rule. Typically, rotation at the middle and upper levels of management tended to be rather haphazard and casual.

Megginson (1963) reports that on-the-job training with coaching by a superior is the most frequently used method of training top management. The data we gathered support this conclusion with but one qualification. It is often true that although a program or policy exists calling for coaching by a superior, it is next to impossible to tell how much if any is actually taking place. All the organizations we visited had policies supporting coaching at all levels of management, but in many organizations the personnel man admitted it was difficult to tell how much was actually going on. Some organizations tried to guarantee its occurring by scheduling certain periods for coaching and by setting up appointments specifically for it. Others offered courses to superiors on how to coach their subordinates. Overall it was difficult to determine just how much coaching occurred, although it is clear that potentially this could be the major training device used in any firm.

Research on training. "Evaluation of training in industry is in much the same category Mark Twain placed the weather" (McGehee & Thayer, 1961). In every company we visited, managers stressed their interest in research on training. However, very few were doing any. Only six studies could be found that attempted to evaluate training, and two of these had been done a number of years before. In several cases the personnel man informed us, "I cannot give the studies to you because the results weren't favorable to our programs." In one organization we were informed rather sheepishly by the personnel man that it was organizational policy that the effects of training cannot be measured, and in another we were told rather firmly that the effects of training are unmeasurable. Finally, several organizations said they were systematically evaluating the training programs by getting participant opinions of their worth. As is explained in greater detail in succeeding chapters, the evaluation by anecdote is virtually useless as research evidence.

According to data gathered by Bridgeman (1959), there is no reason to believe that the companies we visited are any different from the others in this country with respect to evaluating training. He reports one study which asked companies to evaluate the training programs they were using. One-third said they made no attempt. The other two-thirds said they had evaluated (?) theirs on the basis of such criteria as a general judgment concerning the subsequent performance of individual participants and the participants' expressed opinions about the courses. Thus, there is little evidence that systematic evaluation of training programs is going on anywhere in industry.

This great lack of an attempt actually to evaluate training is particularly interesting in light of the point made earlier that most organizations train in order to improve present job performance. Admittedly job performance is not easy to measure, but with this limited objective in mind for training it would seem that a substantial amount of research would be under way on the impact of training. The major question at this point concerns how long organizations will follow a policy that is best characterized as spending millions for training but not one penny for training evaluation.

Summary and conclusion: training. The evidence suggests that management training and development is becoming increasingly popular. But perhaps more important is the point that in the last ten years, the characteristics of training have changed in line with a focus on self-development. This has led to a proliferation of programs both inside and outside the organization and to the use by organizations of a number of different programs at each level of management. At the moment, coaching from a superior and job rotation appear to be the main methods practiced at all levels of management. In addition, lower level managers are likely to be exposed to an in-company supervisory training program along with some university night school courses and some "canned" in-company skills courses. Middle level managers are likely to go away to attend residential university courses or other specialized programs, and they may take a few in-company skills courses. Top management almost always leaves the organization for training, and it typically takes place in a university or similar setting and involves a composite of some cognitive material and some behavior material.

MOTIVATIONAL PRACTICES

In our interviews we encountered a number of difficulties in obtaining meaningful data about current practices bearing on manager motivation. One problem is that to some extent, each organization is using all the possible incentives to motivate at least some of its managers. Thus, when we asked a respondent whether pay or the other rewards were an incentive in his organization, he inevitably said "yes" and this made our data essentially meaningless. To deal with this problem, we made the distinction between those organizations with specific policies or programs directed toward managerial motivation and those in which some managers just "happened" to be motivated by an incentive in a way not necessarily planned or intended by the organization. In our survey of current practices we were interested in the former, that is, the extent to which organizations attempted to make systematic and programmed use of the different incentives to motivate their managers. Not surprisingly, with this more restricted definition in mind, it turned out that most organizations are not trying to use all possible incentives to motivate their managers.

A second problem in writing about current practices in motivation is that there exist very little previous data on the topic. With the conspicuous exception of financial incentives, previous writers have not been concerned with whether organizations have tried to make systematic use of incentives. Little data exist on whether organizations have attempted to create more stimulating jobs for their managers or whether they vary group composition in order to improve performance. Despite these problems, it is possible to consider the use of several incentives in addition to pay based upon the data we collected in our interviews.

Financial incentives. Every organization that we visited reported that it attempted to use money as a motivator of effective management performance. There were a few individual personnel men we encountered who were disillusioned with pay as an incentive and felt that it could only be a dissatisfier (to use Herzberg's, 1966, terminology) and, as such, lacked the power to motivate performance. However, even these managers admitted that it was organization policy to use pay as an incentive. In discussing the use of money as an incentive, it is important to distinguish between how it is used at different management levels. In most organizations, entirely different financial incentives are used for lower level managers and for upper level managers.

The great interest in management compensation is evidenced by the large number of reports and analyses of current compensation trends and practices. We rely on findings from the two most widely circulated and comprehensive studies of current practices in management compensation—the annual surveys of executive compensation authored by Arch Patton for the *Harvard Business Review* and the Top Executive Compensation series of the NICB. The NICB (Fox, 1964) series measures total compensation as salary plus bonus (regardless of whether any portion of the bonus is deferred), and Patton (1951) defines total compensation as salary, bonus, and any insurance premiums paid by the company.

Two issues are likely to shed the most light on how organizations are actually using pay as an incentive. The first bears on what factors are actually used to determine a manager's salary; the second bears on the prevalence and possible effects of different kinds of bonus and incentive schemes. In a later chapter we consider questions related to when and why money may be expected to motivate behavior.

Company size is clearly established as a primary factor determining managerial pay; executives of large companies are paid more on the average than executives of small companies, when company size is stated in terms of sales volume (Patton, 1951, 1965). Roberts (1959), analyzing the reports of 410 corporations reporting to the SEC in 1945, 1948, and 1949 and those of 939 reporting in 1950, observes that sales accounted for 53 percent of the intercompany variance in compensation, while Patton (1965) calculated figures of 50.4 and 60.8 percent for the years 1953 and 1964, respectively. Moreover, Patton advises that compensation of the chief executive increases about 20 percent for each 100 percent increase in sales.

Perhaps the most often cited tenet of all organizational compensation schemes is that a man should be paid according to his contribution to the goals of the company. If this principle is converted into practice, its operation should be evident in a correlation between the compensation of top executives and the profitability of the business. Patton (1965) presents a chart of percentage changes in sales, net profits, and chief executive compensation for the ten years from 1955 to 1964. As might be expected, all three variables appear to move together, with profits showing the widest year-to-year variations, and compensation the least. Although Patton believes that the chart "clearly traces the dependence of top executives on profit," he also makes an apparently contradictory observation (p. 114):

> Earlier executive compensation surveys by McKinsey & Company have shown a definite relationship between pay and profitability. . . .
> For reasons that I do not understand at this point, the pay-profit relationships of the past decade are at variance with earlier findings. For example, when we compare the profit gains chalked up during the past

eleven years by the highest paying companies in 1953 in each industry—size for size—with those turned in by their poorest paying competitors, the results are a standoff. In other words, the profit increases between 1953 and 1964 of the companies with the highest paid chief executives (relative to company size) in 1953 were no better than the profit gains turned in by their lowest paid competitors.

Thus, there appears to be a basis for questioning the assertion that high managerial pay leads to high profits. But is the reverse true? This is difficult to answer. Bonuses and incentives tend to increase overall executive pay during high profit years, and this would yield apparent relationships between profitability and executive pay. Unfortunately, however, sales and profits show high correlations, and it is difficult to estimate the separate effects of each on executive compensation. Roberts did, however, locate eleven firms showing low correlations. Thus, it was possible to examine the relationship between compensation and profitability with sales volume partialed out and that between sales volume and compensation with profitability partialed out. Seven of the eleven compensation-sales relationships were statistically significant, for data gathered over the years 1935 to 1950; only one of the eleven compensation-profitability relationships was significant (five showed negative correlations).

These findings, even though based on only eleven firms, cast doubt on the claims made by the NICB and by Patton of positive associations between executive pay and company profits. They may merely be artifacts, resulting from the more pervasive, direct relationship between sales volume and pay levels.

Roberts obtained further corroborating evidence for the lack of relationship between company performance and executive compensation. He used the 1950 Fitch stock ratings to identify 68 low-paying firms and compared them with 272 other companies. His comparison actually shows that the low-paying firms have higher ratings of overall performance than the other firms. Executive turnover rates were also about the same in the two groups during the period from 1948 to 1950.

Turning, then, to the subject of possible effects of pay incentives on the performance of middle and lower level managers, we find surprisingly little information. What there is fails to show any consistent pattern between pay level and performance for managers who are at the same organizational level. For example, Lawler (1966b) found only small relationships between managers' pay levels and their rated performance in seven organizations. Ghiselli (1965) and Haire (1965) have discussed pay and performance in the context of relationships to be expected when pay levels and pay raises are studied longitudinally for a group of managers. If differential job performance is related to differential pay increments (perhaps the latter "causing" the former), we might expect a pattern of positive correlations between salary increments received over a span of years. However, Opsahl and Dunnette (1966) point out that this would be the expected outcome *only* under two assumptions—first, that the acquisition of managerial skills is a predictable and stable process (in the same way that human growth is), and second, that a person's job effectiveness in a given period of time is predictable from past patterns of job performance and predictive of future levels of performance. In fact, Haire's (1965) analysis of the pay histories of groups of executives in two companies showed *no* consistent pattern of correlations between salary levels at the end of each year and raises over five- and ten-year periods. The values of these correlations varied greatly from time to time and between the two companies. Haire argues from these data that pay for managers in these companies shows no relation to performance—that the pay raises might just as well be assigned by lottery. However, such results could also mean that the assumptions mentioned by Opsahl and Dunnette are not true. Then, the patterns of low and haphazard correlations could mean instead that the two companies were using pay in a flexible way to reward managerial job performance on the spot, and that managers in the two companies should neither "rest on their laurels" after receiving good pay rewards nor feel irrevocably cut off from such rewards because of a brief period of ineffective performance.

Several authors (e.g., G. E. Brown & Larson, 1958; H. H. Meyer, Kay, & French, 1965) have, of course, noted that salary actions seem very often to be made independently of performance appraisal information. Where this occurs, it is obvious that managerial salary policies and pay practices can have no incentive qualities. In the view of managers in such firms, pay is determined on bases (often mysterious and unknown) other than how well they do their jobs. Lawler (1966b), in fact, found in a questionnaire survey that managers rarely reported that their own job performance was an important determiner of their pay level.

However, a substantial portion of the companies we visited have developed salary administration policies definitely designed to reward managers differentially according to their job effectiveness. The usual approach in such companies is to give large (12 to 15 percent) and frequent (every eight to ten months) salary increases to highly effective managers and small (5 percent) and infrequent raises (every eighteen months) to ineffective managers. Obviously such policies must be tied closely to some form of systematic performance appraisal. The companies we visited were using all types of appraisals—ranging from management by objectives, used by many, to simple graphic rating forms and estimates of potential. Even though many companies had developed differential salary administration policies, few had established any systematic procedure for learning whether or not they were actually being used by superiors in administering the salaries of managers reporting to them. A common trend is reflected by one personnel manager's comment that "our supervisors just can't seem to bring themselves to pay their people very differently. They just go down the line, giving everybody about the same raise."

Table 3.4 MEDIAN SALARIES OF SECOND, THIRD, AND FOURTH HIGHEST-PAID EXECUTIVES AS A PERCENTAGE OF CHIEF EXECUTIVE'S SALARY

	1953	1954	1955	1956	1957	1958
Second highest paid	72	70	71	70	69	73
Third highest paid	58	58	58	57	57	60
Fourth highest paid	54	51	51	51	52	55
	1959	1960	1961	1962	1963	1964
Second highest paid	72	73	71	NR	NR	72
Third highest paid	60	61	59	NR	NR	58
Fourth highest paid	55	54	54	NR	NR	52

NR: Not reported.
Sources: Patton (1958, 1961, 1962, 1965).

In contrast, two companies did keep track of the incentive use of salary increments by examining the range of raises assigned to subordinates by each manager in the firms, and several other companies were planning to institute similar systems.

Still, it was all too apparent in our visits that few companies had managed to put "new" thinking into their use of money for pay. Most were still shackled by the kind of constraints shown in Table 3.4, which shows that, on the average, salary levels of top executives are probably determined very heavily simply by what the top man makes. Although there is considerable fluctuation between industries for the median rates of the second and third highest-paid men (see Fox, 1964, p. 5), executive salary administration has traditionally operated to maintain certain level differentials in compensation. Individual variance within levels is, of course, present, but much of it is apparently related to differences in function instead of differences in effectiveness. For example, Howe (1956) found that among firms with sales over $15 million, salaries of functional division heads followed a consistent pattern-sales highest, followed by manufacturing, product engineering, control, personnel, industrial engineering, and purchasing. This implies that executive compensation may often be more a matter of following the traditional guidelines of an industrial "caste system" than of providing rational administration of financial incentives to "motivate" maximum managerial effectiveness. Steadfast allegiance to such "traditions" is bound to conflict with incentive objectives of compensation administration.

It is probable that current widespread use of executive bonus[4] plans represents an effort by industry to break some of these traditions. Such plans have

[4]The literature on executive incentive systems is not consistent in its terminology. We cannot be absolutely certain that various sources we are citing have chosen to follow the pattern we shall use, i.e., to include bonuses, profit sharing, commissions, and any other cash incentive plans under the single heading "bonuses." However, it is our impression that most authors tend to use either the term "profit sharing" or the term "bonus" when referring to this genre of compensation plans, but that they rarely use both terms in a conscious attempt to differentiate between the two. Hence, we believe our single category renders the published data most comprehensible.

obvious advantages to profit-minded firms who believe in the motivating efficacy of money. In discussing the history of nonsalary forms of executive compensation, Roberts (1959) states that the executive bonus came into use immediately after World War I. It was widely used up to the Depression of the 1930s, fell off considerably during the 1930s, and returned with business recovery, after World War II. Of 400 firms sampled in 1945, 80 offered executive bonuses; by 1950, out of 914 companies, 491 had bonus plans.

In 1963, the NICB (Fox, 1964) reported that "about half" of the manufacturing and retail firms surveyed had bonus plans, but that only 25 percent of the casualty insurance, 12 percent of the banks, and 6 percent of the life insurance companies provided executive bonuses. In our own sample of 33 firms, 15 had bonus plans for top management, 12 had them for middle management, and 8 had them for lower management. It is probably typical of organizations in general that they are less likely to have bonus plans at the lower levels of management than at the top levels.

Patton (1965), reporting on 1964 pay practices, notes a renewed interest in "executive incentive plans" due to the 1964 revisions of the income tax laws which make possible greater enjoyment of current income (and simultaneously reduce the attractiveness of stock options). Our interviews did indicate that some organizations were considering adding bonus plans in line with the tax law change, and a more recent study by Patton (1966) suggests that many have indeed implemented such plans.

As is true of so many American business practices, the executive bonus has also gained popularity overseas. Patton (1963) reports that from 35 to 55 percent of foreign executives receive bonuses—a figure only slightly lower than that in the United States. At the same time, the foreign executive's bonus tends to amount to a smaller proportion of his total compensation—an average of 15 percent or less—well below the median for the three top-paid men as reported by the NICB (Fox, 1964).

MEDIAN BONUS AS A PERCENTAGE OF SALARY, BY INDUSTRY, FOR THREE TOP-PAID MEN IN COMPANY

Industry	Percent of salary
Retail trade	41
Manufacturing	35
Casualty insurance	16
Banks	11
Life insurance	8

Megginson (1963) reports a 1961 survey of 350 firms, the results of which he believes are generalizable to 95 percent of American firms ("but not the very large or very small ones"). He asked firms what their "main method of payment" was. The results are as follows:

Method of payment	Percent
Straight salary	26
Bonus*	41
Salary plus bonus*	23
Stock options	4
Other	5

*"Bonus" defined as above.

He observed that large firms are more likely to use stock options, while smaller companies favor a bonus arrangement. Roberts (1959) provides some data on the use of bonus systems relative to profitability. There is a slight tendency for firms paying bonuses to fall into the high profit rather than the low profit category. Overall, it appears that bonus plans are most likely to be used for managers at the top levels of large and profitable firms.

Megginson's data also show that stock options are seldom the *primary* element in an executive's compensation. Nevertheless, they are a sufficiently important form of executive compensation to deserve our attention, particularly since they represent an attempt to relate financial outcomes to management effectiveness. In this sense, they represent an attempt to tie pay to performance. Fourteen of the companies we visited provided stock options for top level executives, six for middle level executives, and only one for low level executives. In our sample, then, stock options were only slightly less prevalent than bonus systems. They also displayed the same hierarchical effect that we saw in the use of bonus plans.

Stock options are a relatively recent development compared with executive bonuses. Roberts (1959, p. 29) advises: "An adverse tax ruling in 1946 discouraged the spread of stock option and purchase plans before the trend had become very pronounced. According to Roberts, revisions of the Internal Revenue Code in 1950 gave rise to wide adoption of stock options in industry. Similarly, Patton (1951, p. 61), reporting on compensation practices in 1945, 1948, and 1949, notes, "The use of capital stock as a bonus for executives is comparatively rare." However, by 1955, Patton (1956) found that 47 percent of 606 companies surveyed had some kind of an option plan, and by 1957, 60 percent of 642 companies had stock options (Patton, 1958). In 1963, probably the peak year for stock option plans, the NICB reported the following:

Type of business	Number of companies	Percent with stock option plan
Manufacturing	725	75
Retail trade	77	60
Life insurance (stock companies)	88	33
Fire, marine, and casualty insurance companies	30	33
Gas and electric utilities	107	30
Commercial banking	124	20

Source: Fox (1964, p. 6).

The provisions of the 1964 revision of the Internal Revenue Code have degraded the profitability of stock options, and it is Patton's opinion that companies are now seeking other approaches to executive compensation (Patton, 1965). Our own interviews did not indicate any tendency for large-scale abandonment of option plans; rather, it seemed that some firms were interested in supplementing them with other kinds of incentives.

In 1957 (Scott et al., 1961), a survey of 852 firms revealed that:

Ninety-six percent have some form of group life insurance.
Ninety percent have accident insurance coverage for employees.
Ninety percent have a pension plan other than federal social security.
Eighty-nine percent have some form of health insurance.

Since these benefits are available to all employees, it is virtually certain that practically all managers today receive at least the basic package of fringe benefits available to operating employees, in addition to traditional "perquisites of office." The full range of fringe benefits available in different firms cannot possibly be discussed here. For example, some of the firms we visited provide such things as tax consultants, free vacations, and child guidance services to their managers. Educational opportunities are covered elsewhere in depth — thus we shall direct our attention to the one most significant financial element of the manager's fringe benefit, his pension.

In the area of executive pensions, data are spotty and difficult to compare. However, as early as 1950, the NICB (Fitzgerald, 1950) reported a trend toward liberalization of managerial pension benefits. The following figures were furnished in a 1964 report:

MEDIAN ESTIMATED PENSION FOR THREE TOP-PAID EXECUTIVES

Type of business	Number of executives	Median pension at age 65 as percent of 1963 salary
Commercial banking	338	43
Life insurance	319	42
Fire, marine and casualty insurance	125	41
Gas and electric utilities	282	40
Manufacturing	1,740	34
Retail trade	135	29

Source: Fox (1964, p. 8).

Comparing this table to the table presented earlier showing use of bonus according to type of business, it is clear that industry groups with higher pension benefits are those with lower average bonuses.

As a practical matter, it is sometimes difficult to differentiate clearly between pension plans and so-called deferred compensation arrangements. Deferred compensation plans aim primarily at providing a means for the executive to keep a larger portion of his income by spreading salary payments (or by providing other forms of compensation) into the years after he retires. Both Roberts (1959) and Patton (1958) report increasing use of deferred compensation plans in the period following World War II. As an indication of recent practices, the 1964 NICB (Fox, 1964) provides figures showing that banks are the heaviest users of deferred compensation. Thus, a reasonable conclusion is that fringe benefits are likely to be greatest in those firms tending not to pay big bonuses or to use stock options.

A widely practiced approach in administering salary in industry is to keep pay levels and salary actions secret. We expect that such a practice strips away a considerable amount of money's symbolic motivating value. If others do not know that one has received a healthy pay raise, the raise is less potent as a mark of status, recognition, or achievement. When pay policies are clouded in secrecy, it is also probably much more difficult for managers to see the relationship, if any, between what they do on the job and the salary they receive. Yet only a few of the organizations we visited made any effort to communicate accurate information about salary administration policies and practices. Even most of the firms with strong policies of differential salary treatment based on job performance failed to communicate the policy very broadly. Only two firms had actually included a series of sessions on the motivational aspects of salary and salary administration in their in-company supervisory and managerial training programs. In the remainder of firms, information about these important practices had to be gathered via the grapevine or simply by "being around long enough."

An appreciation for the wide range of salary practices shown in the companies we visited can be obtained by contrasting practices at two extremes related to the use of money for incentive purposes. At the one extreme was a company which admitted their compensation system had badly deteriorated. No incentive bonus or stock option plans were being used. Salary was supposed to be based upon merit, but little provision was made for differential treatment of the best and poorest performers. Salary administration was decentralized, and heads of different divisions made entirely different use of money, creating inequities between divisions as well as within divisions. The central salary administration group provided guidelines, but had been unsuccessful in communicating them to division heads. At the other extreme was a company with both bonus and stock option plans which were tied to achieving a middle level management job. According to the company, these served as a strong incentive for lower managers to reach higher levels. The organization also had a broad system of merit increases. An outstanding performer could receive 12 to 15 percent salary increases as frequently as every eight to ten months, while an average to poor performer could expect only 5 percent increases every eighteen months. According to the organization, this program has been very successful and the managers are responding to it well.

Security and insecurity. The need for security was used as an incentive in two rather different ways in the organizations we visited. In the majority of the organizations managerial security seemed to depend upon a minimal (often mediocre) level of performance—extremely good (rocking the boat) or extremely poor performance was the only grounds for dismissing a manager. Most managers admitted that in such a situation, security probably acts more as a disincentive than as an incentive.

Three of the organizations we visited used security directly as a motivator. Or perhaps it should be said that they used insecurity. Simply put, they made an effort systematically to fire those managers who were not performing well, thus tying security and performance rather closely together and presumably making it a motivator of effective performance. One issue that arises here concerns the type of managers attracted to such organizations. In at least one organization we visited, the inference was that it attracts managers with extremely high ego strength who are looking for the rather large short-term rewards the organization offers. A number of personnel managers in the firms where everyone was secure in his job remarked that their organizations really should fire more people in order to make security more of an incentive, but most admitted that such a policy was not likely to be instituted. In short, it appears that very few organizations are presently using security as a direct motivator of managerial effectiveness or are likely to use it this way in the near future.

Job design. The area of motivation that has probably received most attention in the last five years among social scientists is job design. Argyris (1964a), Herzberg (1966), and others have stressed the motivational advantages to be gained from creating a stimulating job and providing the manager with freedom and autonomy so that he can make his own mark on the job. Apparently, either these pleas have fallen on deaf ears, or organizations cannot figure out how to improve job design. Almost none of our respondents followed a conscious policy of designing jobs so that they would be a rewarding experience *per se*. In fact, some were downright hostile to such ideas as making a manager's job more interesting. As one personnel manager put it, "We're not in business to make people happy." In some instances it was obvious that the managers had not given much thought to the issue of job design. Another manager's response was, "I don't understand! What is an interesting job?"

On the other hand, several of the organizations we visited were concerned with job design—particularly with decentralization. But decentralization was stressed primarily as a means for improving accountability and profits. This philosophy of decentralization tends to stress the need for organizational control and guidance as safeguards against too much managerial freedom and autonomy (for example, see Koontz & O'Donnell, 1959). At the same time, as Pfiffner and Sherwood (1960, p. 190) point out:

> The contemporary trend in large-scale organization is toward decentralization, but we must realize that decentralization is several things to different people. There are those who view it entirely in terms of decision-making; others see it from the standpoint of geographical dispersion of plants and installations; and still others approach it as a philosophy of corporate life, a set of organization values with sociological, psychological, and spiritual facets.

Not surprisingly, given these variations in philosophy, the reaction of the managers we interviewed indicates that decentralization does not always provide the kind of freedom and other positive job design benefits foreseen by social scientists. In fact, several of the organizations we interviewed indicated that they were abandoning decentralization to achieve improved control.

A number of the managers we interviewed did stress that in their organizations, probably the most important motivator was the fact that the managerial jobs were particularly exciting and stimulating. However, they also pointed out that this came about typically not because of any programs or organization policy but rather because of the nature of the business they were in. Finally, there were a few companies that attempted to be sure their managers were confronted with a challenging job by always advancing their men rapidly and throwing them into jobs that were slightly over their heads. Overall, however, our general impression was that in only a small minority of the organizations we visited were any real thinking and experimentation going on in the area of managerial job design.

The typical organization was characterized by having rather narrow jobs and very tightly written job descriptions that almost seemed designed to take the newness, conflict, and challenge out of the job.

In contrast to the approach of the typical organization is that of Texas Instruments, which has been described in detail elsewhere (Scott Meyers, 1966). They do not believe either in having highly structured jobs or in establishing many superior-subordinate situations. Rather, they operate on a team basis. These teams are always changing according to the issue on which they are working. No large departments are established; instead, there are product-customer centers. Managers of these centers operate as bonafide entrepreneurs in developing the plans, goals, and overall activities of their particular organization. They have to create their own team of specialists and thus have a job that Texas Instruments believes is far more challenging than the typical carefully defined industrial job.

Promotion. Every manager we talked to was sure that promotion was an important incentive in his organization. All said that in their organizations, promotion was based largely upon merit, although several firms had neither a formal performance appraisal system nor a formal promotion system. Obviously where there is no performance appraisal system, it is impossible to determine whether promotion is based upon performance. In fact, there are very few data available on the degree to which promotion is actually related to merit under any system.

There was a consistent tendency in the organizations we visited to keep secret information about who was on the promotion list and who was the replacement for a given job. However, one organization did just the opposite; that is, they publicized such information, pointing out that getting on the list could be a potentially powerful incentive for managers. They also argued that such a list can be an incentive only if some people know who is on it and if managers have a goal to work toward.

There is a considerable amount of evidence that promotion is related to things other than merit. For example, it is clear that it helps to have a college degree, preferably an engineering degree and preferably from an Ivy League school (Newcomer, 1955; *Scientific American,* 1965). It also helps to be a white Protestant male and to have a high IQ and strong achievement motivation (Harrell, 1961). Obviously many of the things that are related to promotion are also likely to be indicators of good performance, and this supports the point that merit is the chief determinant of promotion. However, some (e.g., sex and color) are not necessarily related to merit and indicate that the determinants of promotion are multiple and perhaps interactive in nature, so that merit may be only one of a number of factors typically influencing promotion. The question of just how much influence merit has remains to be answered.

Status and status symbols. The use of status as an incentive in industry is quite extensive and often carefully planned. One need only venture into an organization and look around for a few moments to see the rather obvious symbols that abound. However, the important point is that status and status symbols are directly tied by most organizations to organizational level rather than to job performance. That is, typically all managers at the same level appear to possess similar outward signs of status in the organization. One organization we visited was making an attempt to eliminate status that is tied to management level and was trying to tie it to performance. However, in most organizations, status is related to performance only to the extent that promotion is tied to performance. Before we can answer the question of whether status is tied to performance, we must therefore face the unanswered question of whether performance determines promotion.

Research on motivation. Eight of the companies we visited were doing some research on the motivation of their management employees. Several of these companies had a number of projects under way and were heavily committed to this research. General Electric, for example, has been doing research on management compensation and on the motivational effects of the performance appraisal interview. IBM has done and is doing a number of large-scale attitude studies in the motivation area. However, the vast majority of the firms seemed to feel that this kind of research was not worth considering. They pointed out that in contrast to selection research, the payoff is less immediate and often less widely applied. Perhaps the most surprising thing is that only a few organizations, two to be exact, were doing any research on compensation. This is surprising in light of the fact that all organizations had programs designed to use pay as a motivator of effective performance, and of course pay is one of the greatest expenses for all organizations. When asked why no research was going on in the pay area, most firms replied that they did not feel they were ready for it, implying that other kinds of research are more palatable. As was true of the training area, then, the overall conclusion must be that little research is being done in the organizations we visited on the motivational determinants of management effectiveness.

Summary and conclusion: motivation. The managers in the organizations we visited did occasionally stress that they were aware of the possibility that by creating stimulating jobs and providing some freedom, the managers could be motivated by such internally mediated needs as self-actualization. However, in practice it seems that most organizations are relying on the traditional incentives of money, promotion, and status symbols to motivate their managers at all levels of management. The evidence also indicates that despite the claims of organizations that promotion and pay are related to performance and thus are incentives, it is often true that there seems to be little relationship between pay and performance.

Performance Appraisal

McGregor (1957) was perhaps the severest critic of personnel appraisal practices as they were employed in business in the 1950s. Particularly, he attacked the fact that appraisal, having both administrative (salary and promotional) and developmental purposes, tended to place the superior in the incompatible roles of judge and counselor. The act of judging subordinates, McGregor observed (1960, p. 84), tended to elicit defensiveness, so that:

> In attempting to communicate criticisms to a subordinate the superior usually finds that the effectiveness of the communication is inversely related to the subordinate's need to hear it.

As a means of vitiating what they saw as debilitating effects of traditional performance appraisal, McGregor (1957, 1960), Drucker (1954), and other writers have proposed a "management by objectives" approach, which would be an improvement over current practices, particularly with respect to the developmental use of appraisals.

In our interviews, we sought answers to three questions about performance appraisal practices: First, how many firms conduct formal performance appraisals of managers' job performance? Second, to what extent has business followed the advice of McGregor and Drucker in implementing management by objectives approaches? Third, what use do firms make of data gathered from appraisal procedures?

Whisler and Harper (1962) provide the data shown in Table 3.5 on trends since 1930 in the use of performance appraisal techniques. Clearly, performance appraisal, particularly at the management level, has been on the increase since then.

Table 3.5 SURVEY RESULTS: USE OF FORMAL RATING IN BUSINESS FIRMS

Year	Number of companies in survey	Percentage of responding companies answering "yes" on appraisal of rank-and-file employees	Percentage of responding companies answering "yes" on appraisal of managers and executives
1930	195	*	*
1940	231	95.3	45.6
1947	325	80.8	43.7
1953	628	77.5	47.5
1957	852	77.0	58.0

* Available evidence shows that only 41 percent of responding companies used rating scales.
Sources: Adapted from Scott et al. (1948, 1954).

More recently, the NICB has confirmed the trend toward the increasing use of appraisals at the management level—84 percent of 167 companies surveyed said they appraised to some extent (Wickstrom, 1964). It is probable that the figure from the NICB study (84 percent of the firms doing some form of appraisals) is slightly high but is still a reasonable estimate of the use of performance appraisals in this country. The figure is substantially higher than that suggested by the Whisler and Harper data, but it is more recent, and if we assume a continuing upswing in the use of performance appraisals, it is in fairly good agreement with the earlier figure of 58 percent of firms carrying out appraisals in 1957. The data from the firms we visited confirmed the fact that a figure around 80 percent is a reasonable estimate of the number of firms now formally appraising their managers.

The likelihood that appraisal is being done is apparently not uniform at all levels of the organization. Yoder (1962) reports a study of 80 firms conducted by Cresap, McCormick, and Paget in 1961. This study revealed that appraisal of top executives was, in 50 percent of the cases, an informal process. Spriegel's (1962) data for 1960 are more extensive, while revealing a similar trend, as shown in the following table.

PREVALENCE OF APPRAISAL PROGRAMS AT VARIOUS ORGANIZATIONAL LEVELS—1960

Total number of companies surveyed	567
Number engaging in formal appraisal	357
Number rating both supervisors and executives	243
Number rating executives only	14
Number which have discontinued a program of rating executives	256
Number rating supervisors only	100

Source: Spriegel (1962, p. 79).

Apparently, executives are somewhat less enthusiastic about analyzing their own performance than they are about having their subordinates' performance appraised. Still the data indicate that well over half the firms did appraise their executives' job performance in 1960.

A study done by Litterer (1957) provides some evidence on the kind of appraisals being done. In the 47 firms he studied, 10 used an open-ended global approach in which the appraiser was asked simply to write an essay on certain prescribed general characteristics (e. g., performance, ability, and potential). The remainder of the firms asked for ratings on specific traits, and 32 of the 37 provided graduated scales on the rating forms. During this same period, Mahoney et al. (1963) found that 12 of 22 firms were dissatisfied with their appraisal programs—largely because evaluation tended to focus on traits rather than results. Clearly at this time there was little or no use of the management by objectives approach. However, in 1964, Wickstrom reported the following data for the 141 firms that evaluated managerial job performance:

HOW 141 COMPANIES APPRAISE MANAGERS—1964

Type of Appraisal	Present use, percent			Future emphasis, percent		
	None	Little	Much	Less	Same	More
Trait appraisal	26	28	46	24	63	13
Appraisal against specific objectives	39	38	23	2	49	49

Note: Columns do not add to 100 percent because some companies use more than one type of program.
Source: Wickstrom (1964, p. 126).

Obviously, although trait appraisal still predominates, firms are definitely moving toward the management by objectives approach, and if we accept the future emphasis data at face value, it is apparent that the trend will continue.

Whisler and Harper believe that the increased emphasis on appraisal of managers (and the decrease which they found in appraisal at the rank-and-file level) is due to management's mounting interest in using appraisal for developing and improving managers and a growing conviction that operating level employees are undevelopable. G. E. Brown and Larson (1958) surveyed 23 governmental agencies and companies in California, and their conclusions complement those of Whisler and Harper with the exception that they appear to reject the rather dubious conclusion of Whisler and Harper (1962, pp. 51-52) that organizations regard workers as undevelopable:

> The separation of performance appraisal from salary administration was virtually complete. . . . At the present time the major emphasis is on the development of both the employee and the supervisor in the effective performance of their jobs.

Spriegel also presents data to confirm the fact that the purposes of appraisal are currently often conceived to be basically developmental, rather than for use in distributing organizational rewards and punishment. The following table illustrates this assertion.

PURPOSES FOR WHICH APPRAISAL IS USED

Purpose	Number of firms
Counseling	300
Promotion	298
Training and development	265
Considering retention or discharge	240
Salary administration or merit increase	237
Bonus payments	54
Profit-sharing payments	14

Source: Spriegel (1962, p. 82).

However, the data also clearly illustrate that organizations still use appraisals for promotion, discharge, and salary decisions as they traditionally have. Thus the major change in the last ten years may have been an increase in the use of appraisals for developmental purposes with only a slight effect on its use for personnel decision making.

In our survey of 33 organizations, we did not go into appraisal practices deeply and systematically. Nevertheless, some impressions did emerge concerning current procedures in this area; the primary ones are as follows:

1 There appears to be a strong and growing tendency for firms to adopt a results-oriented approach (although many firms also ask for global or trait ratings at the same time). In two instances where the nature of the technology makes managerial performance a highly interdependent process or where personnel change jobs

and assignments rapidly, firms had been forced to discontinue management by objectives approaches because individual performance could not be identified.

2 A few firms have begun to experiment with peer ratings. Many of the management by objectives companies, of course, employ some measure of self-rating.

3 Firms who have developed manager replacement tables, although they may have a systematic and formal appraisal system, tend to use committees to determine lines of succession. These committees may or may not consider performance appraisals in making their decisions, and apparently they never use appraisals as the sole criterion.

4 At higher levels in the organization, appraisal is more likely to be performed by a committee, rather than by the superior alone.

5 A small minority of companies still do not have formal appraisal systems.

6 In large, diversified organizations, widely different systems may be used in various divisions.

7 Many companies have two or more appraisal systems operating concurrently. For example, a manager's budget performance may be appraised to determine whether he gets a bonus, while a global personality evaluation may be made to isolate his developmental needs.

8 A number of companies are beginning to feel that the traditional, relatively narrow ranges of wage and salary administration defeat whatever incentive value might be obtained from tying managerial pay to performance appraisal. On the other hand, those interviewees who stated that their firms did not have a systematic plan of wage and salary administration tended to believe that managers were relatively arbitrary in distributing increases—and that this also destroyed the incentive effects of pay.

A feeling for the range of practices that exist can perhaps best be gained by looking at the performance appraisal systems in three of the companies we visited. In one organization there is essentially a gigantic, organization-wide paired comparison ranking. Rankings are made on the basis of the person's overall contribution to meeting the company's objectives and on the basis of his potential for meeting these objectives in the future. Although these criteria are obviously global, a real attempt is made to tie the company objective aspect very closely to actual job behavior through an extensive system of meetings in which each manager talks about long-range objectives and states what he can do in the short term to help achieve them. Another company uses an approach even more closely tied to specific management behavior. Here the manager himself completes a form describing what his major activities were for the last year, and then the superior evaluates the manager's performance on these activities. A third company has developed a list of types of behavior that it believes to be important to managerial functioning. Each manager is rated every six months by his superior on these eight traits. On the basis of these ratings it is decided whether an individual will get a pay raise or be placed on a secret promotion list.

In summary, then, it would appear that performance appraisal is being used with increasing frequency at the management level and in particular at the lower levels of management. McGregor's writing on management by objectives appears to have had a significant impact, with more and more firms trying this approach. In addition, the use of appraisals for management development and job-related counseling purposes is now very much in style, and in order to handle the conflict between appraisal for counseling and appraisal for personnel decision making, some firms are installing two or more appraisal systems.

OVERVIEW: CURRENT PRACTICES IN THE MANAGEMENT OF MANAGERIAL EFFECTIVENESS

Our model of managerial behavior presented in the last chapter stressed that effective management is a function of many factors and their interactions. In this chapter, we have reviewed separately the practices followed by 33 large organizations in three key personnel areas: selection, training and development, and motivation. Now we ask how practices followed in each of these areas are combined to form total programs designed to enhance managerial effectiveness—programs designed to conserve and utilize wisely the critical manpower reservoir of potentially effective managers. To what extent have organizations been able successfully to develop integrated programs giving proper attention to *all* the factors suggested by our model and balanced, instead of one-sided, attention to the three major areas of selection, training, and motivation?

To answer the above question, we estimated the comprehensiveness of each organization's practices in the areas of internal selection, external selection, training and development, and motivation. We defined a "comprehensive" program as one which deals with all levels of management, is clearly and explicitly formulated, and uses a variety of approaches. This method of "rating" organizational practices, even though subjective, did yield a useful overview of managerial effectiveness practices in the organizations we interviewed. For example, one normal expectation might be that a few organizations do everything—that is, they have comprehensive programs in all areas—and that the rest do little or nothing. Actually, this does *not* appear to be the case. Only eight firms were rated as not having comprehensive programs in any area; these firms placed greatest emphasis on external selection, but even here, their approaches tended to be haphazard and nonsystematic. The best example of this pattern was a billion-dollar corporation with many, almost completely autonomous, product divisions. The central personnel officer and his staff groups literally did not know what practices the various divisions were following. About the only underlying theme was the extensive use of outside consultants for external selection assignments, with no effort at integrating their activities and no mechanism for even becoming informed of them.

Of the remaining 25 organizations, the large majority (20) had comprehensive programs in just one or two areas. We rated only one firm as having comprehensive programs in all four areas. Thus, the pattern seems to be that most of these organizations make substantial managerial effectiveness efforts in one or two areas and come close to ignoring the others. It was therefore a simple matter, after reviewing our field reports and listening to the tapes of our interviews, to classify most firms' practices as essentially selection-oriented, training and development-oriented, or motivation-oriented. The answer to our earlier query is very clear-cut: Most companies *have not* developed finely integrated programs giving the proper balance to all areas demanded for the effective management of managerial effectiveness. Instead, most programs are one-sided, emphasizing one area at the expense of the others.

A better idea of these patterns may be provided by recounting briefly the specific approaches used by some of the organizations we visited.

In one—a selection-oriented firm—a vast array of psychological tests is used for both internal and external selection decisions. A managerial candidate is given several hours of testing before he is employed and an additional eight hours or more after employment, to assess his promotional potential. On the other hand, almost no training is provided by the organization; it is particularly lacking for persons in middle and higher management levels. Moreover, no systematic attempts are made to enrich the motivational milieu for managers. Stock options and bonus plans are not used; little support, even in the form of lip service, is given to the idea of pay level related to merit, and no special programs designed to elicit managerial feelings of achievement, recognition, or job challenge have been developed in the firm.

In a second firm—a training- and motivation-oriented one—quite a different picture emerges. Here, the concept of selection seems to be out of favor; no tests are used, and only limited objective information of any kind is gathered for external selection decisions. Formal performance appraisal information is not used for promotional decisions. However, motivational and social-psychological (in the form of job challenge and coordinated "team" efforts) factors are emphasized heavily. The key function of planning is stressed throughout the organization. Both short-term and long-term company goals are made explicit and communicated widely and accurately. Managers are given heavy responsibility quickly, and they are forced into the "limelight" by participating actively in planning and review sessions with higher company officials. Moreover, the emphasis on accomplishing broad company objectives is reflected in task-force or team approaches to assignments and problem solving, thereby emphasizing and hopefully "developing" coordinative and communicative skills among managers. Although no 'forms" are filled in systematically or formally for performance appraisal purposes, the planning, limelighting, group efforts, and coordinating activities offer many opportunities for observing and "assessing" a manager as he contributes (or fails to contribute) to accomplishing organizational goals.

In a third firm — a training-oriented one — vast opportunities are available for exposure to different learning situations, but little attention is given either to selection or to the development of challenging job situations or other potential motivational influences. The major "program" for developing managerial skills seems to involve a rather massive effort to catalog and maintain a running audit on as many outside-company training programs as possible. The personnel department informs managers throughout the firm of programs that "look good" so that they may plan developmental "packages" for their subordinates, within the context of a management by objectives approach which is practiced for all persons in managerial jobs in the firm. Auditing of the various programs is done by maintaining a file of reports submitted to their superiors by persons who have attended the programs. Thus, this firm maintains a kind of cafeteria of training and development experiences to be utilized as may be deemed appropriate by various managers (in consultation with their superiors) in the company.

A few companies had succeeded in coming very close to implementing fully integrated programs of managerial effectiveness practices. The one company judged by us to have such a program uses a carefully validated battery of tests as a major aid for internal selection decisions; this is complemented by a wide range of training experiences, determined for a particular manager by committee recommendations based on records of his present job performance, his estimated potential for achieving top management, and his previous educational and work experiences. A variety of financial incentives are used and are tied to various measures of a manager's merit, including estimates of his potential as well as of his present job performance. Practices in this company represent one of the few examples we found of a careful blending of validated selection methods and the use of informed and systematic appraisal methods for administering incentives and tailor-making development programs. Thus the testing, compensation, and salary systems as well as the effective use of both company and noncompany training programs are geared toward identifying, developing, and motivating effective people to become effective managers.

No other company we visited had a program as comprehensive as this. Indeed, few approach the same depth of coverage even in single areas that this company's practices show in all the key areas.

SUMMARY

This review of current practices for enhancing managerial effectiveness, followed by a discussion of a select few organizations, confirms the major impression gained from the *Wall Street Journal* survey cited in Chapter 1 (Melloan, 1966). Companies are, by and large, acutely aware of increasing shortages of effective managers. They are meeting the problem in many ways—ranging from testing and purely selection strategies to installing elaborate computerized manpower inventory systems, planning specialized training and development experiences, and providing varieties of incentive systems to elicit motivated managerial behaviors. Thus our respondents, like those in the *Wall Street Journal* survey, describe programs of great variety, reflecting sharply differing views of the determiners and correlates of managerial effectiveness.

Our major disappointment is that so little ongoing research on managerial effectiveness was reported by the firms we interviewed—firms presumably nominated *because* they were doing research. It appears that even these select 33 organizations have based their practices mainly on fad and fashion rather than on research-based evidence. And, even when practices have been implemented quickly because of pressing shortages, their implementation has only rarely been accompanied by research studies designed to determine the nature and extent of their effects.

In subsequent chapters, therefore, we present a comprehensive review of research results and theorizing concerning the measurement, prediction, development, and nurture of effective managerial job behavior.

Chapters 4 and 5 consider problems and possible solutions involved in describing managerial jobs and questions of defining and measuring managerial effectiveness in such jobs. Chapters 6 and 7 review the methodological difficulties involved in assessing or evaluating managerial candidates and predicting their relative levels of job effectiveness. Chapters 8 and 9 present the major research results obtained from several large-scale managerial effectiveness prediction studies. Later chapters consider motivational determinants of managerial effectiveness, the impact of organizational climate factors, knowledge available from experience and research with managerial training and development programs and their effects on managerial effectiveness, and current social-psychological theorizing in relation to managerial effectiveness.

Finally, we present a discussion of areas where knowledge still is lacking and outline programs and methodologies for undertaking needed research. It is our sincere hope that those readers who follow us through all the way to the end will gain a comprehensive and sophisticated grasp of what is and what is not known about managerial effectiveness and, more importantly, that they will be guided and stimulated to undertake and to support the research necessary to fill in the existing knowledge gaps and eliminate the pockets of ignorance now so prevalent.

Chapter 4 **Describing the Managerial Job**

It is difficult to describe *any* job and discover what it calls for in employee behavior, but unusually so for managerial jobs because they change so much
from one setting to another. First, they are subject to time-determined changes;
the things an executive does when preparing an annual budget differ from those
he does when conducting labor contract negotiations. Second, there are per-
son-determined changes; managers are typically given broad administrative
assignments, but they are allowed great latitude in the means they use to accomplish them. Finally, managerial jobs are often subject to situation-determined changes; they may differ according to organizational level and function (for example, sales management versus research management), or they
may differ from company to company, region to region, country to country,
etc.

   Because time-, person-, and situation-determined changes are so prevalent at the managerial level, the sampling of jobs for job analyses must be unusually extensive in order to assure that all important managerial behaviors
have been tabulated in the effort to define the methods used in accomplishing the broad goals required by the jobs. The sampling must be broad enough

both to describe the core responsibilities of the jobs being studied and to map the allowable tolerances of behavior differences related to time, person and situation differences.

DEVELOPING DESCRIPTIVE DIMENSIONS FOR MANAGERIAL JOBS

We are confronted with a problem similar to the one faced by psychologists in their early efforts to discover lawful regularities in human behavior. Because people differ greatly, psychologists had to develop fundamental measures or dimensions for describing the various ways in which they differ. Similarly, because managerial jobs differ greatly and change rapidly, we need to discover the fundamental dimensions along which they differ and to develop ways of measuring them. Ideally, we would like to be able to describe any particular managerial job with a relatively small number of measures, just as any person can be described by referring to such measurements as height, weight, intelligence, age, sex, mechanical ability, clerical aptitude, etc.

How can such dimensions, applicable to a wide range of managerial jobs be developed? In essence, we must learn as much as possible about what managers actually do in accomplishing the requirements of their jobs. That is, how do they go about getting their jobs done? To answer this question and subsequently to develop managerial job dimensions requires the following steps: First, systematic observations, reports, or records of many managers' job behaviors must be accumulated. Second, these records of job behavior must be analyzed either rationally or statistically to discover broader behavioral content categories to define relatively similar groupings of behavioral components. Third, the categories and the behavioral elements defining them should be tried out as a means of observing managerial behavior and describing the major dimensions making up another sample of managerial jobs. Fourth, the categories may need to be modified as indicated by these new observations; only then will the generality and broad usefulness of the categories (dimensions) for defining the major behavioral requirements of different managerial jobs have been shown.

Many investigators have begun various parts of the task of defining the managerial job in this way; they have used a variety of observational or reporting methods and employed many methods for developing and defining behavior dimensions. Unfortunately, most investigators have left the task only half done. Nonetheless, it is instructive to review their efforts, techniques, and results as a way of indicating what we know of managerial jobs and where we need to learn more.

Stewart (1967) lists three methods commonly used to study what managers do on their jobs. First, an observer may record what a manager does. Second, the manager may keep his own record or diary of his activities during a workday. Third, a manager may be asked to estimate (without benefit of systematic record keeping) how he spends his time, or he may use a prepared checklist of job duties or behaviors to indicate what he perceives to be the relatively more and less important behavioral elements and requirements of his job.

Methods of direct observation and behavior recording. Dubin (1962) has called attention to the paucity of actual behavior observations in the study of business organizations. Certainly this is true at the managerial level, where the number of systematic observations of job behavior is limited and, until recently, the number of subjects small. The first and most frequently cited observational study is the one by Carlson (1951). He enlisted the cooperation of many "reporters" to record the job actions of ten executives (nine Swedish and one French) for a period of four weeks. The reporters included the executives themselves as well as persons surrounding them in their work settings—their secretaries, personal assistants, telephone operators, and others who were carefully trained in recording their observations on checklists and questionnaires designed for the purpose. For each executive action, a record was made of (1) the site (inside or outside the firm, in own or someone else's office, at home, etc.), (2) contact with persons and/or institutions, (3) technique of communication (telephone, conversations, written, observational, etc.), (4) nature of question or issue handled, and (5) kind of action taken. Carlson concluded that these executives worked excessive hours, spending one-third of their total working time outside the firm. They had insufficient time for inspecting and overseeing their functions, and since they were subjected to constant interruptions, they had practically no time for reading or for contemplation. Using a similar recording form, Burns (1957) collected diaries of managerial actions kept for three to five weeks by 76 British top managers working in eight middle-sized (500 to 900 employees) companies. Burns's conclusions dealt mostly with differing communications patterns shown by managers in different companies. Top managers in firms with more vigorous programs of expansion spent relatively more time in discussions with one another (up to 80 percent of their total working time). He found little flow of information up and down the hierarchical structure of organizations; apparently, the top management teams tended to form internalized communications "cliques," relatively difficult to penetrate from below and quite retentive of information already possessed.

Dubin and Spray (1964) obtained descriptions of all "job behavior episodes" occurring during two weeks from eight executives scattered among different industries, functions, and organizational levels. The self-recording form used by the executives required that they describe behavioral content and indicate when each episode began and ended, with whom the action took place, who initiated it, and how each interaction was conducted. The authors' major finding was that no two executives had similar patterns. Face-to-face discussion was by far the dominant mode of interaction, although there were great differences among these executives in the amount and nature of such interaction. Higher level executives were more involved with persons outside the company than lower executives, and a large majority of interactions (by all executives) were initiated by them instead of by others.

Horne and Lupton (1965) obtained managers' activity records from 66 managers and their secretaries and assistants for a time span of one week. The managers were from 10 firms varying widely in size (from 170 to 40,000 employees), product, and technology; they were mostly at middle levels of responsibility, but their functional areas ranged widely over both line and staff assignments and over many "specialties" (engineering, comptrolling, personnel, sales, purchasing, etc.). One activity record form was completed for each work activity no matter where it occurred. Respondents indicated by means of these checklists the following nine types of information about each work episode:

Type of information	Example
1 Method and means used	Phone, meeting, letter, etc.
2 Time and duration	Time of day and time encompassed
3 Location	Office, home, other company, etc.
4 Time relationship	For the past, present, or future
5 Level relationship	Organizational unit dealt with
6 Contacts	Person, group, organization, etc.
7 Purpose	Giving, seeking, reviewing, etc., information, plans, advice, decisions, etc.
8 Functional area	Technical, financial, personnel, etc.
9 Managerial "classification"	Formulating, organizing, unifying, or regulating

Tables 4.1 to 4.3 show how these 66 managers, on the average, spent their work time, with whom, and where. Obviously, by far the major portions of their workdays were devoted to giving, seeking, or receiving information in their own offices in face-to-face interaction or informal discussions with just one or a few other persons. This generalization is helpful in describing the broad sweep of managerial jobs, particularly since Horne and Lupton also report that no major differences in behavioral patterns were shown across these companies of widely differing size and technology. According to Horne and Lupton (1965, p. 32):

> Managers talk most of the time, and mostly face-to-face. They seem not to be overwhelmed with paper or formal meetings. They swap information and advice and instructions, mostly through informal face-to-face

contact in their own offices. Middle management does not seem, on this showing, to require the exercise of remarkable powers to analyze, weigh alternatives, and decide. Rather, it calls for the ability to shape and utilize the person-to-person channels of communication, to influence, to persuade, to facilitate.

Although the authors' generalization about the "typical" middle manager's job and their inferences about personal qualities necessary for doing the job are appealing in their simplicity, they run counter to the need we have expressed for discovering fundamental dimensions to use in describing *differences* among various managerial jobs. Indeed, Horne and Lupton gave only passing attention to the rather large differences shown by these 66 managers in the way they spent their work time.

Table 4.1 METHODS OF WORK USED BY THE 66 MANAGERS IN THE HORNE AND LUPTON STUDY (1965)

Method of working	Mean proportion of time spent, percent
Talking with one other person	25
Discussion with two or more others	19
Formal meeting	10
Phone	9
Paper work	14
Reading	10
Reflecting	2
Inspection	2
Visits	9

Table 4.2 PURPOSES OF WORK ACTIVITIES REPORTED BY THE 66 MANAGERS IN THE HORNE AND LUPTON STUDY (1965)

Purpose of work activity	Mean proportion of time spent, percent
Information transmission	42
Advice (giving, seeking, receiving)	6
Decisions (giving, reviewing, etc.)	8
Instructions	9
Plans (reviewing, coordinating, etc.)	11
Explanations	15
Other	9

Table 4.3 LOCI OF WORK ACTIVITIES REPORTED BY THE 66 MANAGERS IN THE HORNE AND LUPTON STUDY (1965)

Location of activity	Mean proportion of time in location, percent
Own office	52
Own department	11
Other office in own company	16
Other department in own company	6
Another company	4
Home	4
Social	3
Anywhere else	4

Behavior sampling. In contrast to recording *all* job behavior episodes, McNaughton (1956) has argued that activity sampling[1] could usefully be employed for learning what managers do in their jobs. Kelly (1964) made 1,800 momentary observations of four manufacturing section managers at randomly selected times over a three-week period. The activities were grouped according to location, function (planning, personnel administration, or technical maintenance matters), and types of interaction (e.g., with peer, superior, or subordinate). Results of the activity sampling showed that these managers spent two-thirds of their time with other persons—one-fifth of this time being spent with their own superiors, one-thirds with peers, and one-half with subordinates. Over half the activities sampled found the manager engaged in planning or programming; about one-quarter involved technical matters and machine maintenance, and only slightly more than 10 percent related to personnel administration. Although based on only four managers, this study is important because it demonstrates the feasibility of using time sampling procedures for studying managers' job behaviors. Kelly also concluded on the basis of the large proportion of planning- or task-oriented activities that his data support the views of Wilfred Brown (1960), who has minimized the importance of personal style in managing in favor of defining effective management as the utilization of resources and techniques for getting the job done.

Exhaustiveness versus purposiveness. Observers in each of the studies discussed so far obtained records of managerial job behavior in natural surroundings and with as little intervention as possible. As is evident from the results, the studies suffer from being strictly descriptive at the expense of developing more general content categories or of differentiating between more and less important aspects of managerial behavior. Apparently the goal of obtaining complete and exhaustive observational accounts has forced too much attention on record-keeping and classifying procedures, with the result that a great deal has been learned about the job behavior of just a few executives; not much has been learned, via these methods, about the general dimensions constituting the job behavior of many executives. A study confirming these inferences was done by O'Neill and Kubany (1959), who gathered 31,886 job behavior observations for 85 foremen over a twenty-week period and correlated the foremen's job behavior "scores" against a variety of objective criteria of supervisory effectiveness. They found no consistent patterns of relationship and concluded that the mechanistic recording of job activities was incapable of revealing crucial differences between more and less effective foremen—that such observations needed to include value judgments about the quality of

---

[1]One innovative approach for sampling job behavior is described by M. W. Martin (1962). He used a random alarm device about the size of a pack of cigarettes to study the reading activities of 701 scientists over a fourteen-day period. The alarm was set to go off an average of about $3\frac{1}{2}$ times per day, and each scientist recorded what he was reading at the time the alarm sounded.

various actions in addition to simply counting them. Weick (1967) has also argued that observer passivity and exhaustiveness need not necessarily be indigenous to observational methodology. He suggests that greater attention be given to purposive observation by more judicious sampling of observational settings and by more imaginative selection of behavioral measures.

Several methods have been used to broaden the sampling of jobs observed and to assure greater efficiency in pinpointing the more important elements of job behavior to be recorded. For example, E. Kay and Meyer (1962), after reviewing sixteen hours of job observations made by Ponder (1958) on 24 foremen, decided that a typical foreman was subjected to a vast array of random inputs from many different sources and that he also initiated a number of outputs or actions. They developed a self-report job activity questionnaire consisting of input items such as "My boss asks my advice on a production problem" or "An employee asks me for a work assignment" and output items such as "I tell an employee how to do a job" or "I ask another foreman to expedite a job for me." The questionnaire was administered to 111 foremen in the same plant as the 24 whom Ponder had observed so extensively. The foremen were asked to estimate the relative frequency of the various inputs and outputs included in the questionnaire. Kay and Meyer concluded that the questionnaire approach, consisting of rationally derived statements, was as useful and valid for comparing work patterns of foremen as the more expensive and time consuming observations made by Ponder.

Critical incidents. One of the best search techniques for sampling many jobs and for focusing on the more important aspects of managerial behavior is the Critical Incidents Method, developed by Flanagan (1954). Flanagan defines the critical requirements of a job as those behaviors which are crucial in making a difference between doing the job effectively and doing it ineffectively. Critical incidents, as the term implies, are simply reports by qualified observers of the things people did that were especially effective or ineffective in accomplishing parts of their jobs. Such incidents are actual behavioral accounts, recorded as stories or anecdotes and obtained from managers, job incumbents, and others close to the jobs being studied. Here are examples of two incidents—one effective and the other ineffective—gathered by Flanagan (1951) in his study of the job behaviors of Air Force officers:

Effective Behavior

A directive was received from higher headquarters requesting certain detailed information that appeared on the surface to be impossible to obtain in the limited time allowed. In the discussion on the matter, various ideas came up such as reporting certain phases of the required information as unknown, requesting higher headquarters to extend the reporting date, etc. This officer spoke up and said, "This is a directive. We should be getting the information instead of discussing alternatives; give me the job and I'll get it." He was given the job as requested and immediately formed a plan of attack and expedited it. Information had to be obtained from over 100 locations all over the United States. He formed a unit to bring the information in and another to compile it in the required phases. The deadline was met due to this officer's initiative and force in handling a seemingly impossible problem. This officer at the time was not assigned to specific duties, having just reported for duty. I forcibly requested this officer and he is working for me now.

Ineffective Behavior

This officer was an adjutant in my squadron. My former adjutant was very energetic and handled most of the administrative functions with little or no supervision. This new officer started out and was given the same authority as my former one. The administration began to slow down, reports were going in late, so I began to check. I found that this officer was very thorough, so thorough that even the most ordinary function was slowed up waiting for his signature. One afternoon I overheard the enlisted men talking. The conversation was to the effect that they were through work at noon and here it was 3 P.M. and the passes were not signed yet. I checked with the adjutant and found that he had been too busy at noon to sign the passes but would get to it as soon as he finished a roster he was making up. I picked up the passes, signed them and got the men started on their way. I checked with some of the men in the unit and found that this delay had become a common occurrence. I then decided that this man was too slow for my unit and got rid of him on the next shipment.

After a large number of such incidents have been collected, they may be abstracted and categorized to form a composite picture of job essentials. These categories, in turn, form a behaviorally based starting point for developing checklists of task behaviors regarded as crucial to the job. Listed below are the categories developed by Flanagan from the nearly three thousand incidents he collected for Air Force officer-executives:

Handling administrative details
1 Understanding instructions
2 Scheduling work
3 Getting information from records
4 Getting ideas from others
5 Checking accuracy of work
6 Writing letters and reports
7 Getting cooperation
8 Presenting finished work

9 Keeping records
10 Keeping others informed
11 Rendering effectiveness reports

Supervising personnel
1 Matching personnel and jobs
2 Delegating authority
3 Giving orders and instructions
4 Ensuring comprehension
5 Giving reasons and explanations
6 Supporting authorized actions
7 Encouraging ideas
8 Developing teamwork
9 Setting a good example
10 Assisting subordinates in their work
11 Evaluating subordinates' work
12 Looking out for subordinates' welfare
13 Maintaining relations with subordinates

Planning and direct action
1 Taking responsibility
2 Solving problems
3 Making use of experience
4 Long-range planning
5 Taking prompt action
6 Suspending judgment
7 Making correct decisions
8 Making forceful efforts
9 Absorbing materials

Acceptance of organizational responsibility
1 Complying with orders and directives
2 Accepting organizational procedure
3 Subordinating personal interests
4 Cooperating with associates
5 Showing loyalty
6 Taking responsibility

Acceptance of personal responsibility
1 Attending to duty
2 Attending to details
3 Reporting for appointments
4 Meeting commitments
5 Being fair and scrupulous
6 Maintaining military appearance
7 Adapting to associates
8 Adapting to the job
9 Conforming to civil standards

Proficiency in military occupational specialty
1 Possessing fundamental training
2 Improving effectiveness
3 Keeping well informed in specialty
4 Applying training and information
5 Showing ingenuity in specialty
6 Handling related assignments

It should be noted that the Critical Incidents Method will typically yield descriptions of both static and dymanic aspects of a job. The behavioral accounts of what actually happened or of what a manager actually did force attention on situationally determined elements and also on modes of behavior that may be unique for the person being described. Thus, by sampling broadly and by gathering many behavioral incidents about managerial jobs, an investigator can be assured of discovering important time-, person-, or situation-determined changes that may be crucial to a full understanding of the job being studied. B. R. Kay (1959) and R. E. Williams (1956) have also described managerial jobs in terms of critical requirements. Kay collected 691 incidents of foremen's behavior from 74 managers and rank-and-file employees in a single firm, and Williams collected over 3,500 incidents of executive behavior from 742 executives who were distributed proportionally by industry, company size, and geographic location.

Table 4.4 CLASSES OF CRITICAL JOB BEHAVIOR INCIDENTS REPORTED BY 742 EXECUTIVES

Content area	Effective incidents		Ineffective incidents	
	N	Percent	N	Percent
Planning, organization, and execution of policy	590	41	379	18
Relationships with associates	380	27	179	9
Technical competence	61	4	151	7
Coordination and integration of activities	117	8	647	31
Work habits	272	19	489	23
Adjustment to the job	19	1	248	12
Total	1,439		2,093	

Table 4.4 shows how the 3,500 incidents collected by Williams were categorized according to six broad content areas. The development of subcategories within each of the six areas named in Table 4.4 led finally to the 80 "critical requirements of an executive's job" shown below:

Planning, organization, and execution of policy
1 Bases plans and actions on a clear, accurate knowledge of the objectives of the company

2 Formulates effective policies to be used in achieving the objectives of the organization for which he is responsible

3 Communicates and interprets policy so that it is understood by the members of his organization

4 Anticipates difficulties to be overcome in achieving objectives of the organization and plans ways of overcoming them

5 Delegates authority and responsibility readily

6 Utilizes his experience and the experience of his associates in achieving objectives of the organization

7 Makes prompt and explicit decisions

8 Applies ingenious methods in reaching the objectives of his organization

9 Perseveres in efforts to reach objectives

10 Reviews plans and actions of his organization and makes adjustments or corrections as necessary to achieve objectives

11 Makes decisions that take into account all available information

12 Initiates necessary plans and actions promptly

Relations with associates

1 Establishes clear channels of communication within his organization and between his organization and other parts of the company

2 Makes his knowledge available to associates when opportunities arise

3 Utilizes the knowledge and services of associates

4 Persuades and influences associates to support policies and to cooperate in reaching objectives

5 Understands the primary requirements of the jobs of his subordinates and superiors

6 Understands the capabilities and limitations of his associates

7 Assigns subordinates to jobs for which they are best suited

8 Assists subordinates with personal difficulties as opportunities arise

9 Demonstrates an interest in working conditions and personal welfare of subordinates

10 Assists associates in performing their jobs by means of friendly advice and help

11 Prevents loss of efficiency due to animosity or differences of opinion among members of his organization

12 Makes clear assignments of authority and responsibility to his subordinates

13 Explains reasons for policies, actions, and conditions

14 Supports policies and actions of superiors under all conditions (though he may privately disagree with them)

15 Supports actions of subordinates conforming to their authority and responsibility

16 Makes sure that subordinates understand policies, decisions, and instructions

17 Stimulates associates by convincing them that their jobs are important in reaching the objectives of the organization

18 Encourages associates to submit ideas and plans

19 Guides subordinates by commendation of good performance and frank discussion of inferior performance

20 Stimulates subordinates by assigning increasing responsibility and authority to them

21 Stimulates associates by means of competitive devices

22 Stimulates pride in the immediate organization and in the company
23 Keeps himself constantly informed of the progress of associates toward achievement of objectives
24 Stimulates associates by setting a good example in work habits
25 Provides opportunities for the professional development of subordinates

Technical competence
1 Displays up-to-date knowledge of management principles (or his specialized field of management)
2 Effectively organizes and applies his knowledge of management to his job
3 Derives cause-and-effect relationships from available information
4 Utilizes all available sources of information in reaching conclusions or decisions
5 Provides information that is technically accurate and reliable
6 Contributes ideas relating to activities outside his immediate responsibility
7 Demonstrates ingenuity in solving management problems
8 Seeks means of improving his proficiency in management
9 Effectively performs managerial assignments outside his immediate responsibility
10 Foresees effects of his judgments and decisions on other activities of the company

Coordination and integration of activities
1 Provides physical facilities required for effective performance of his organization
2 Maintains physical facilities of his organization in good order
3 Assumes responsibility for plans and actions required for the achievement of major objectives
4 Applies his experience and the experience of others in policy making and planning
5 Overcomes difficult obstacles to the achievement of objectives
6 Persists in efforts to reach objectives despite setbacks or opposition
7 Makes vigorous attempts to reach objectives
8 Derives general policies and conclusions from unintegrated facts and estimates
9 Fully supports and carries out company policies
10 Interprets policies to subordinates and promotes policy conformance

Work habits
1 Works diligently on delegated and self-assigned activities
2 Works long hours when necessary to achieve assigned objectives
3 Is punctual in keeping appointments and starting conferences
4 Plans and conducts meetings and conferences so that his time and the time of associates is not wasted by interruptions and diversions
5 Delegates responsibilities and instructs subordinates when he expects to be absent
6 Is honest in all matters pertaining to company property or funds
7 Demonstrates pride and responsibility in his work
8 Makes reasonable and reliable estimates of the time required for the achievement of objectives
9 Schedules his work and the work of his subordinates for efficient performance
10 Regularly reviews progress of his organization and takes necessary corrective actions

Adjustment to the job

1 Demonstrates by actions that the achievement of company objectives is more important than his personal convenience
2 Performs his work without apparent regard for personal advancement or compensation
3 Supports company policies and personnel against unfair criticism or action
4 Participates in community activities as opportunities arise
5 Assumes some of the responsibilities of associates whenever necessary to achieve an objective
6 Fulfills commitments promptly
7 Improves his proficiency by reading, discussion, research, and study
8 Is honest in statements about his work or actions
9 Maintains good attitude toward his job despite strong emotional stress
10 Makes good impression by gentlemanly and temperate social conduct
11 Is neat in appearance
12 Performs effectively despite unusual demands
13 Increases effectiveness of his organization by friendly, cooperative relations with members of his own organization and with other units of the company

Although these "requirements" are helpful for estimating the wide range of activities engaged in by managers, their wording lacks precision and places too much demand on evaluative judgments of different degrees of effectiveness. These categories would need to be used for describing an independent sample of managerial jobs before they could confidently be viewed as representing fundamental dimensions of managerial job activities.

An important question bearing on the usefulness of critical incidents for discovering such dimensions concerns the reliability with which they can be categorized. In order to study this question, Andersson and Nilsson (1964) collected 1,847 critical incidents about the job of grocery store manager from 10 superiors, 122 managers, 100 assistant managers, and 178 customers. After grouping the incidents into 17 categories and 86 subcategories, they chose 100 incidents randomly from each of three broader content areas (relations to customers, relations to personnel, and relations to the store and to sales) and asked psychology students working in pairs to assign them to the previous categories and subcategories. The students agreed with the original categorization for an average of 80 percent of the incidents, thereby demonstrating a reassuringly high degree of interjudge reliability for developing meaningful and nonambiguous category definitions based on critical incidents.

Dimensions based on factor analysis. Roach (1956) obtained 70 essays from sales managers describing the best and the poorest supervisor each had known. From these, he wrote 390 descriptive statements and incorporated them into a job behavior checklist which was administered to 245 office supervisors. He used factor analysis[2] to determine statistically the major clusters or cate-

[2]Factor analysis is a mathematical procedure for identifying the minimum number of dimensions or factors necessary to account for the patterns of correlation or similarity among a much larger

gories for describing supervisory behavior. An examination of his factors suggests that some were descriptive of personal traits such as poise, cheerfulness, and approachability rather than being descriptive of *job* behavior. It is likely that the original essays included many personal references and that Roach failed to delete them when he prepared the 390-item checklist. This means that the original essays were as much descriptive of particular people as they were of the duties and activities of managerial jobs. What is needed is closer attention to behavior and less attention to mere trait descriptions.

Many factor analytic studies of more behaviorally relevant elements have been done in an effort to explicate the basic dimensions of supervisory, managerial, or executive behavior.[3]

It is difficult to summarize all these studies because factor naming depends so importantly on one's interpretations of the statements and behavioral descriptions defining the factor. But many of the factorings end either with two distinct factors or with two groupings of factors roughly analogous to the factors of *consideration* and *initiating structure* first identified and named as part of the Ohio State Leadership Studies. Fleishman (1953b) has described the development of the Leader Behavior Description Scales (LBDS) resulting from this series of research studies. Starting with over eighteen hundred statements descriptive of various aspects of leader behavior, expert judges culled out all but 150 and then classified them into nine categories:

Integration Leader actions helping to increase or decrease cooperation in the group
Communication Leader actions transmitting information to others in the group
Production emphasis Leader actions oriented to the volume of work accomplished
Representation Leader actions designed to represent the group's interests to others outside the group
Fraternization Leader actions involving the leader as an integral member of the group

---

number of measures. In Roach's study, 15 factors were obtained. By examining the descriptive statements highly correlated with each factor, Roach was able to suggest the following names for the factors, and these may be viewed as the major common descriptive dimensions underlying the 390 statements of his checklist questionnaire:

1. Personal compliance
2. Job knowledge
3. Direction of group performance
4. Rewarding of employee performance
5. Company loyalty
6. Decision making
7. Group spirit
8. Personal drive
9. Impartiality
10. Poise and bearing
11. Consideration
12. Open-mindedness
13. Cheerfulness
14. Approachability
15. Overall evaluation

[3] These include studies by Creager and Harding (1958); Fleishman (1953a); Forehand and Guetzkow (1962); Grant (1955); Hemphill (1959, 1960); Peres (1962); Prien (1963); Rambo (1958); Rupe (n.d.); Stogdill, Shartle, and Associates (1956); Stogdill and Coons (1957); and Stogdill, Goode, and Day (1963a, 1963b, 1964).

Organization Leader actions leading to a differentiation of duties and prescribing ways of doing things
Evaluation Leader actions bearing on judgments of how well group products meet established standards
Initiation Leader actions leading to changes in group activities
Domination Leader actions resulting in his will being enforced over that of other members in the group

These 150 items, comprising the LBDS, were administered in many job settings to obtain behavior descriptions of managers and were scored according to the nine dimensions listed above. It was soon evident that the nine dimensions were not independent; thus, their intercorrelations were factor analyzed to yield two relatively more fundamental dimensions of leadership behavior—*consideration* (involving predominantly the behaviors of integration, communication, representation, and fraternization) and *initiating structure* (involving predominantly the behaviors of organization, domination, initiation, evaluation, and production emphasis).

Similar factors have emerged from most other studies, such as Rupe's factors of executive achievement and responsibility for subordinates and society, Prien's job orientation and employee-centeredness, and Grant's two groupings of factors (judgment, planning, and efficiency improvement and interpersonal effectiveness, and effective supervision).

Managerial job dimensions: too many or too few? We seem to have come full circle. The extensive behavioral accounts provided by Carlson, Burns, Dubin and Spray, Horne and Lupton, and Kelly, though impressive in forming a generalized view of what managers do, are of little help in defining dimensions because the authors made only limited and rather unsystematic comparisons between *different* manager's jobs. In contrast, the many studies using questionnaires and checklists for rating and describing managerial job behavior led, through factor analysis, to just two basic dimensions of manager behavior. Certainly, this must be an oversimplification of the characteristics and full range of behaviors demanded by managerial jobs! In fact, we believe it is. Moreover, it seems likely that behavioral dimensions such as consideration and initiating structure are more a part of the person than of the job; they reflect personal behavioral styles that a manager can bring to *any* job, instead of the specific behavioral demands of different managerial jobs. Thus, the two dimensions, even though describing basic human predispositions, are not particularly useful for mapping the characteristics of, and differences between, managerial jobs. We need information about similarities and differences in the requirements imposed by different managerial jobs independent of the personal characteristics or "styles" brought to managerial jobs by different job incumbents. Only two major investigations (Hemphill, 1959, 1960; Stewart, 1967) comparing the behavioral requirements of different managerial jobs have come to our attention. However, they complement each other beautifully because they approach the develoment of managerial job dimensions from different points — Hemphill analyzed responses of 93 managers to a lengthy position description questionnaire, and Stewart analyzed information gleaned from job activity diaries kept for four weeks by 160 managers. Since both investigators took the crucial step of investigating differences and similarities between different jobs, comparisons and contrasts between the two sets of results aid greatly in our effort to describe managers' jobs in terms of a small number of relatively fundamental behavioral dimensions.

Hemphill's dimensional analysis of executive position descriptions. Hemphill (1959, 1960) sought to describe fully the similarities and differences in a number of executive jobs. To do this, he asked 93 executives to complete a 575-item Executive Position Description Questionnaire (EPDQ). Each respondent used an eight-step scale to indicate the extent to which each element (of the 575) was a part of his executive job. Correlations were computed between all possible pairs of respondents, and thus pairs of executive jobs were identified that were either highly similar or very different across the 575 job elements of the EPDQ. Factor analysis of the matrix of correlations identified clusters or groupings of jobs that were similar to one another but different from those in other clusters.

Since Hemphill chose his 93 respondents from five different firms, three different management levels, and five different functions,[4] it is probable that his clusters of executive jobs reflect rather fundamental dimensions for describing any executive position. It is instructive to examine them with regard to the major responsibilities and behaviors common to the jobs in each of the 10 clusters. Below are Hemphill's titles summarizing the duties underlying each cluster along with the three descriptive or behavioral elements most characteristic of jobs making up each cluster and a brief account of the major functional responsibilities of jobs in the cluster:

Cluster A: Providing a staff service in nonoperational areas
Is considered a staff rather than a line position.
Be capable of performing the jobs of all subordinates.
Selection of new employees.
(Services such as gathering information, interviewing, selecting employees, briefing superiors, checking statements, verifying facts, or making recommendations.)

Cluster B: Supervision of work
Troubleshoot special problems as they arise. Plan the best use of available facilities.
Involves firsthand contact with machines and their operation.

[4] The five companies were American Telephone and Telegraph Co., Westinghouse Corporation, American Brake Shoe Co., Diamond Gardner Corporation, and Standard Oil Co. of Ohio. The three levels included *upper management,* positions with the top three levels of management; *middle management,* positions at or above the third level of supervision; and, *beginning management,* positions at the second level of supervision. The five functions were research and development, sales, manufacturing, general administration, and industrial relations.

(Planning, organization, and control of the work of others, direct contact with workers and with the machines they use, and concern with getting work done effectively and efficiently.)

Cluster C: Internal business control
Maintenance of proper inventories.
Reduction of costs.
Review budgets for operations.
(Cost reduction, inventory control, budget preparation, justification of capital expenditures, determination of goals, definition of supervisory responsibilities, payment of salaries, or enforcement of regulations.)

Cluster D: Technical aspects with products and markets
Anticipate new or changed demands for products and services.
Assist salesmen in securing important accounts.
Involves firsthand contact with customers of the company.
(Concern with product-market-customer details and relations, development of new business, checking on activities of competitors, changes in demand, customer contact, data analysis, and assistance in sales.)

Cluster E: Human, community, and social affairs
Be active in community affairs.
Nominate key personnel in the organization for promotion.
Take a leading part in local community projects.
(Working well with others, both in and out of the organization; concern for company goodwill; public speaking; evaluating people and their performance; and participation in community and civic affairs.)

Cluster F: Long-range planning
Keep informed about the latest technical developments in a professional area.
Long-range solvency of the company.
Long-range objectives of the organization.
(Oriented toward the future of the organization; thinking about, and planning for, the future in industrial relations, management development, organizational objectives, corporate solvency, new ventures, new ideas, and new legislation relevant to the organization.)

Cluster G: Exercise of broad power and authority
Provides opportunity for actually managing an important part of the business.
Offers an opportunity to gain experience in management.
Make recommendations on matters at least as important as the construction of a new plant.
(Status, independence, and power are the key characteristics of this dimension.)

Cluster H: Business reputation
Directly affects the quality of the company products or services.
Involves activities that are not closely supervised or controlled.
Avoid any public comment critical of a good customer or supplier.
(Responsibility for reputation of the organization's products or services, for both product design and public relations, requiring little in the way of attention to details but making rather stringent demands on personal behavior.)

Cluster I: Personal demands
Refrain from activities that might imply sympathy for unions.
Involves spending at least ten hours per week in direct association with superiors.
Spend at least fifty hours per week on the job.

(Constraints upon the personal behavior of the incumbent, calling for propriety of behavior, fulfilling the stereotype of the conservative businessman.)

Cluster J: Preservation of assets
Handle taxes (other than personal).
Write or dictate at least 25 letters per week.
Sign documents that obligate the company to the extent of at least $1,000.
(Concern with capital expenditures, operational expenditures of major amounts, taxes, and profits and losses, including authority to obligate the organization.)

Hemphill developed scoring keys comprised of the 50 items most relevant to each dimension and established norms for each of the dimensions based on the responses of the 93 executives participating in the study. It is now possible to use his EPDQ to describe a managerial job and to "profile" the job along the 10 dimensions. This is a distinct step forward in understanding and describing managers' jobs because it provides a set of common denominators for looking at the jobs. Predictions of effective managerial performances should be facilitated by such an instrument because it allows us to know in advance the kinds of performance emphasized in any given executive position. The prediction task then is to discover the personal or organizational qualities contributing to successful performance along each of these dimensions. It is conceivable that lack of a personal quality leading to a prediction of failure in jobs high in certain dimensions would not disqualify an individual for other managerial jobs not emphasizing those dimensions. Thus, Hemphill's study provides guidelines for developing systematic procedures for understanding managerial jobs, job behaviors, and the personal and organizational qualities leading to effective performance on those jobs.

Stewart's dimensional analysis of the way managers spend their time. In the largest study of its type done so far, Stewart (1967) asked 160 managers to record all job behavior incidents of more than five minutes' duration on the recording form shown in Figure 4.1. Since her interest was in studying differences as well as similarities in managerial jobs, managers in many functions (sales, production, accounting, engineering, and research), at different levels (from middle levels up to senior levels), and many different companies (ranging in size from 12 to 30,000 employees) were chosen to take part in the study. Each of the 160 cooperating managers provided records of all job incidents or episodes occurring over a four-week span of time.

The outstanding feature of the results obtained by Stewart is the great diversity in the things different managers do with their time. Her respondents varied enormously in *where* they spent most of their time, with *whom* they spent it, and *what* they did. Table 4.5 shows a few of Stewart's results, highlighting the great diversity of these managers' jobs. Overall, of course, the results agree with those of Horne and Lupton, discussed earlier. The managerial job— on the average—*is* conducted in one's office and involves primarily informa-

Table 4.5 SELECTED RESULTS FROM STEWART'S (1967) TABULATIONS OF THE WAY MANAGERS SPEND THEIR WORKDAYS

	Percent of work time	
	Range	Mean
Where:		
In own company	Under 50 to 90+	75
In own office	Under 30 to 80+	51
Outside own company	0 to 20+	9
With whom:		
Alone	Under 10 to 70+	34
With subordinates	0 to 50+	26
With boss	0 to 20+	8
With customers	0 to 20+	5
How:		
Paper work	Under 20 to 60+	36
Informal discussion	Under 20 to 60+	43
Committee meetings	0 to 30+	7
On telephone	Under 1 to 10+	6
Degree of job "Fragmentation":		
Number of diary entries per day	Under 7 to 19+	13
Number of fleeting contracts (<5 min) per day	Under 3 to 23+	12
Total number of times alone for ½ hr or longer over the 4-week period	Under 10 to 60+	19

tion transmission in face-to-face situations. However, the more important facet by far of Stewart's results involves the large differences between various jobs reflected in the broad ranges in the way various respondents spent their time.

In order to investigate more thoroughly the different types of managerial jobs, Stewart scored each of the 160 jobs on the following 25 variables:

1 Total number of hours worked.
2 Total number of entries.
3 Total number of fleeting contacts.
4 Percentage of total time spent alone.
5 Percentage of total time spent with one other person.
6 Percentage of total time spent with two or more other people.
7 Percentage of total time spent in his own establishment (not including time spent in other units of the company).
8 Percentage of total time spent outside of the company.
9 Percentage of total time spent traveling.
10 Percentage of total time spent with his boss.
11 Percentage of total time spent with his secretary.
12 Percentage of total time spent with his immediate subordinates.
13 Percentage of total time spent with his subordinates' subordinates.

Time of Starting Incident?* _____

Duration: Hrs. _____ Mins. _____(nearest 5 mins.)

DID YOU DO THIS

Alone?[0]. . . . .   With one other person?[1]. . . . .   With 2 or more?[2]. . . . .

	WHERE?		WHO?		HOW?		WHAT?
0	Own Office	+	INTERNAL Boss	+	Committees[d]	0	Finance
1	Other internal	—	Boss's boss	—	Discussion[e]	1	General management[k] 1
2	Other units[a]	0	Secretary	0	Selection interviewing	2	Marketing and Sales
3	External	1	Subordinates	1	Social[f]	3	Personnel
4	Home	2	Subordinates' subordinates	2	Telephoning	4	Production
5	Travelling	3	Colleagues[b]	3	Figure work	5	Public Relations
		4	Fellow[c] Specialists	4	Reading, external	6	Purchasing
		5	Other internal	5	Writing & Co. reading[g]	7	Research and Development
		6	Other units[a]	6	Other work[h]	8	
		7	EXTERNAL Customers	7	Inspection[i]		
		8	Suppliers	8	Lectures and conferences		
		9	Other external	9	Travelling[j]		

FLEETING CONTACTS

	Personal	Telephone	Interruption?
Boss	0	0	0
Secretary	1	1	1
Subordinates	2	2	2
Other internal Other units	3	3	3
External	4	4	4

Figure 4.1 Self-recording diary used by managers in Stewart's study of managerial job behavior

---

FOR EPISODES LASTING 5 MINUTES OR MORE

Please start a fresh sheet whenever there is a change under any one of the headings: 'Did you do this', 'Where?', 'Who?', 'How?', 'What?'. This means that, except for 'Who?', there should never be more than one tick under one of these headings.

* * 'Incident' is what you have taken a fresh sheet to record, that is a change in one of the headings.
* **a.** 'Other units' means other establishments, divisions, or subsidiary companies belonging to the same parent company.
* **b.** 'Colleagues' are those reporting to the same line boss as you.
* **c.** 'Fellow Specialists' are those doing a similar job to you, in another department, or elsewhere in the parent company. They may or may not be at the same level as you.
* **d.** 'Committee' is any pre-arranged group meeting. It may or may not have an agenda.
* **e.** 'Discussion' is talking, which is not classified under one of the other headings.
* **f.** 'Social' is when work is combined with a social activity.
* **g.** 'Writing & Co. reading' includes dealing with correspondence. Company reading is of material produced by the company.
* **h.** 'Other work' means just thinking. But please read more detailed notes.
* **i.** 'Inspection' is a personal tour of work place.
* **j.** 'Travelling' is when you are travelling for your work and *not* doing any other work listed under 'How?'.
* **k.** 'General management' is when you are dealing with two or more management functions, such as sales and production, at the same time, or in the same meeting. But if there is a clear division between the discussions on two functions, please record on separate sheets.

For more detailed information about headings, please see separate instructions.

FOR CONTACTS OF UNDER 5 MINUTES

Please enter in Fleeting Contacts section below.

There may be a number of such fleeting contacts during the main incident that you have recorded above, or before you start a fresh sheet. So you can have a number of ticks in this section.

When recording a fleeting contact no entries should be made in the main section of the diary, but a tick should be put in the adjoining column if this interrupts what you were doing.

---

14 Percentage of total time spent with his colleagues.
15 Percentage of total time spent with his fellow specialists.
16 Percentage of total time spent with other internal contacts.
17 Percentage of total time spent with customers.
18 Percentage of total time spent with suppliers.
19 Percentage of total time spent with other external contacts.
20 Percentage of total time spent in committees.
21 Percentage of total time spent in all other forms of discussion.
22 Percentage of total time spent in all forms of paper work.
23 Percentage of total time spent in inspection.
24 Percentage of total time spent in personnel matters.
25 Percentage of total time spent on the four headings of the "What?" column which took least time, excluding general management. (This was included as a guide to the range of management function with which the manager was concerned.)

Using analytical methods similar to Hemphill's (Hemphill, 1959, 1960), Stewart examined statistically the similarities and differences between every possible pair of jobs and discovered five clusters or groupings of jobs. Jobs in each cluster were relatively similar in the way their managers allotted time but different from jobs in theother clusters. The five groupings, some typical job titles included in each, and résumés of how time is characteristically spent are summarized below.

Managerial job group I
Number of jobs: 45
Characteristics of time expenditure: These managers traveled a great deal and made contacts mostly with customers and officials from other companies or public institutions. They also attended many conferences and exhibitions.
Representative job titles:
  Sales director
  Sales manager
  Marketing manager
  General manager
  Group works manager
  Works and purchasing manager
Managerial job group II
Number of jobs: 33
Characteristics of time expenditure: These managers spent relatively more time by themselves, reading, writing, and dictating reports and memorandums. They made fewer group contacts and tended to work with relatively specialized or technical matters.
Representative job titles:
  Section head, computing
  Head office engineer
  Works manager
  Chief accountant
  Assistant company secretary
  Production manager
  Payroll manager

Managerial job group III
Number of jobs: 35
Characteristics of time expendidture: These managers spent their time in the same way as that shown by the averages for all managers in Stewart's sample. They spent most time with other colleagues at their same organizational level and undertook a diverse sampling of activities and functions.
Representative job titles:
Chief accountant
Office services manager
Financial director
Works engineer
Sales manager
Public relations officer

Managerial job group IV
Number of jobs: 33
Characteristics of time expenditure: These managers made more short, fleeting contacts than managers in other groups. They were called upon to cope more with crises, problems needing immediate solutions and actions. Their work time was highly fragmented, and they spent relatively more time in inspection and within hierarchical relationships.
Representative job titles:
Works manager
Factory manager
Maintenance engineer
General manager, manufacturing
Chief engineer
Brewer in charge

Managerial job group V
Number of jobs: 14
Characteristics of time expenditure: These managers spent most time in group discussions and in committee meetings. Their contacts were nearly all within their own companies and dealt relatively more with questions related to personnel.
Representative job titles:
Production manager
Factory services manager
Principal, training school
Director, production planning
Technical officer

These two sets of results (Hemphill's and Stewart's) lead us to the following observations about managerial jobs: First, as expected, managers' jobs differ greatly from one another in both substance and modes of operation. Hemphill discovered and named 10 relatively fundamental substantive dimensions along which they differ, and Stewart's analysis shows how different managers interact with the requirements of their jobs to develop widely varying patters or "styles" of time expenditure. Clearly, these findings imply the possibility of discovering systematic relationships between managers' personal qualities and their relative effectiveness in pursuing different managerial functions. These empirical findings confirm and extend arguments we made in Chapter 2 about the need for viewing managerial effectiveness in a context of complex interactions between individual characteristics, job and situational demands, and organizational policies and practices.

Second, a job title, standing alone, yields only partial and incomplete knowledge for estimating either the substance of a manager's job or how and with whom he spends his workday. This is shown most clearly in Stewart's study, where jobs with identical titles (such as works manager, sales manager, chief accountant, production manager, etc.) occurred in several different job groups. This finding confirms the necessity for studying exactly what it is that any given manager is responsible for on his job rather than relying simply on his job title to provide a valid portrayal of his responsibilities and activities.

Finally, and most obviously, we may take hope from these two investigations that useful dimensions for describing managers' jobs can be developed. Both investigators successfully identified groupings of jobs based on relative similarities in the patterns of behavior shown by the job incumbents. It is unfortunate that Stewart did not ask her managers to fill in Hemphill's EPDQ. Had she done so, managerial job groups or clusters derived from each of the two approaches could have been compared for similarities and differences, and we would then know much more about possible relationships between the substantive and stylistic attributes of managers' job.

Functional and level differences in managerial job behavior. As it is, Hemphill's research, though well known, has *not* stimulated many others to use his questionnaire or to undertake similar studies to amplify his findings or modify or supplement his 10 dimensions. Additional studies of this type are sorely needed. There is also a paucity of empirical research relating managerial job differences to standard functional classifications or level differences. In their review of literature relevant to level differences in managerial functions, Fiedler and Nealey (1966) located only six studies dealing with manager behavior, and over half of these dealt with only two levels of management. Actually, Hemphill's and Stewart's data are useful for revealing possible level and function differences in managerial jobs. Tables 4.6 to 4.9, drawn from their data, show the relative proportions of managerial jobs from various levels and various functions which are high on the Hemphill dimensions or which belong to the different groups identified by Stewart. Implications concerning differing responsibilities and behaviors important at different levels and in different functions are evident; relatively more planning, broader power, and greater personal demands are characteristic of upper management staff services, concern with products and markets, and supervision of work are relatively more characteristic of second level (beginning) management. And time spent outside one's own company quite obviously is centered among sales and marketing managers and general management officials; production jobs often involve troubleshooting activities, and financial and staff service jobs frequently involve relatively substantial amounts of time spent in analyzing and developing interpretations of specialized information or technical data.

Table 4.6 PROPORTION OF EXECUTIVE JOBS AT DIFFERENT LEVELS MEASURING HIGH ON EACH OF HEMPHILL'S JOB DIMENSIONS

Levels	Dimensions									
	Staff service	Supervision of work	Business control	Products and markets	Human affairs	Planning	Broad power	Business reputation	Personal demands	Preservation of assets
Upper management (24 jobs)	0.46	0.21	0.71	0.29	0.55	0.63	0.55	0.46	0.46	0.42
Middle management (48 jobs)	0.54	0.54	0.60	0.54	0.41	0.47	0.35	0.39	0.23	0.31
Beginning management (21 jobs)	0.90	0.62	0.62	0.71	0.19	0.43	0.14	0.52	0.19	0.19

Source: Hemphill (1959).

Table 4.7 PROPORTION OF EXECUTIVE JOBS IN DIFFERENT FUNCTIONAL AREAS MEASURING HIGH ON EACH OF HEMPHILL'S JOB DIMENSIONS

Functions	Dimensions									
	Staff service	Supervision of work	Business control	Products and markets	Human affairs	Planning	Broad power	Business reputation	Personal demands	Preservation of assets
Research and development (11 jobs)	0.91	0.54	0.55	0.91	0.27	0.82	0.00	0.54	0.27	0.18
Sales (24 jobs)	0.42	0.16	0.79	0.52	0.54	0.29	0.50	0.21	0.17	0.21
General administration (22 jobs)	0.68	0.54	0.67	0.55	0.18	0.49	0.36	0.27	0.27	0.32
Manufacturing (26 jobs)	0.43	0.54	0.81	0.31	0.39	0.46	0.42	0.62	0.27	0.39
Industrial relations (10 jobs)	1.00	0.70	0.00	0.30	0.70	0.70	0.20	0.80	0.60	0.50

Source: Hemphill (1959).

Table 4.8 **PROPORTION OF MANAGER JOBS AT TWO LEVELS FALLING IN EACH OF FIVE JOB GROUPS IDENTIFIED BY STEWART**

	Top level (57 jobs)	Middle level (103 jobs)
Group I (external company contact and negotiation)	0.44	0.19
Group II (specialized analysis and interpretation)	0.16	0.23
Group III (general and diverse managerial contacts)	0.17	0.25
Group IV (troubleshooting)	0.21	0.20
Group V (coordination)	0.02	0.13

Source: Stewart (1967).

Table 4.9 **PROPORTION OF MANAGER JOBS IN DIFFERENT FUNCTIONS FALLING IN EACH OF FIVE JOB GROUPS IDENTIFIED BY STEWART**

	Sales and marketing (36 jobs)	General management (20 jobs)	Staff services (engineering, research, personnel, public relations) (30 jobs)	Production (36 jobs)	Production planning and control (15 jobs)	Accounting and financial (23 jobs)
Group I (external company contact and negotiation)	0.72	0.50	0.14	0.03	0.14	0.08
Group II (specialized analysis and interpretation)	0.14	0.10	0.30	0.19		0.44
Group III (general and diverse managerial contacts)	0.14	0.10	0.20	0.06	0.53	0.48
Group IV (troubleshooting)			0.33	0.53		
Group V (coordination)		0.30	0.03	0.19	0.33	

Source: Stewart (1967).

An unanswered question. Are differences in job demands such as these related to differences in the personal qualities required for effectively performing the jobs? L. W. Porter and Ghiselli (1957) have demonstrated that middle managers and top managers show modest differences in their self-perceptions, the top managers seeing themselves as more action-oriented and the middle managers perceiving themselves as more analytical, careful, and planful. But are these differences stable qualities of persons serving at the two levels, or are they a transitory result of fulfilling the particular and differing job demands at the two levels?

N. H. Martin (1956) observed the decision-making activities of a small, unspecified number of managers operating at four levels (from shift foreman up to works manager) in a manufacturing plant. Higher level decisions involved much less structure, were more poorly defined, and involved much more distant time horizons (i.e., long-term effects) than those at lower levels. These results are neither surprising nor extraordinary, but they do suggest that quite different cognitive qualities may be necessary for effective decision making at higher and lower levels of management—an inference which, to our knowledge, has not yet received empirical research support.

NEEDED NEXT STEPS

How do we stand now in our effort to define the managerial job? The validity of our previous statement—that most investigators have completed only half the task—should now be apparent. Many have observed managerial behaviors, but have been content merely to describe them without developing and testing more fundamental dimensions or categories for generalizing their descriptions. Others have gone to the other extreme of overabstracting their descriptions, so that their categories merely reflect generalized behavior tendencies rather than basic managerial job requirements and persons' interactions or responses to them. A most helpful beginning has been made by critical incidents studies, which have suggested broad, rationally determined taxonomic categories, but these categories have not then been tested for their general applicability to executive jobs existing at different levels and covering a variety of functions. Hemphill also made an excellent beginning in his rigorous sampling of executive positions in several companies and functions and at three different levels. His "discovery" of 10 major dimensions for describing executive positions should have set off a rash of investigations designed to amplify, clarify, and define more fully these dimensions of executive jobs. Surprisingly, neither Hemphill nor anyone else has pressed the advantage gained in his early studies. Why is this so? We do not know. It is true that complexity rarely stimulates interest and eagerness by other investigators; instead, it is usually simplicity—the single elegant answer or simplified theory—that causes other researchers to jump on the bandwagon. Hemphill's research may have lain dormant and relatively unnoticed because of the unwillingness of others to accept the complexities implied by his dimensional analyses. Certainly, it is easier to adopt the illusion (as so many have) that managerial jobs are all essentially the same or that their differences do not "make a difference" than it is to work with more complicated outcomes such as those of Hemphill or Stewart. As we shall see later, a bulk of test validation studies on managers have lumped all managers' jobs together rather than investigating the nature and significance of their differences. Another, and perhaps more important, problem with Hemphill's research is that he left so much of his executives' jobs undefined from a behavioral standpoint. Job dimensions with labels such as "providing staff services," "supervising work," or "Long-range planning" are so behaviorally sterile that they offer few, if any, suggestions about the human qualities necessary for effectively carrying them out, and investigators intent on predicting effective management behavior may have been disenchanted because of this. It may be that Hemphill's investigation was perceived as a failure, not worthy of further effort, rather than as the groundbreaking, pioneering, but far from finished contribution that we believe it to be.

The most pressing research need now is to attach more behavioral relevance to the broad dimensions developed by Hemphill. The Critical Incidents Method should be used to define in more behaviorally relevant ways each of the 10 dimensions of the EPDQ. For example, what behaviors are a part of effective long-range planning? Which are involved in supervising work, and which enter into the exercise of broad power and authority? Hemphill's position elements used to define the dimensions of the EPDQ can serve as starting points, but they need to be supplemented with the behaviorally rich material that can be expected to emerge as a result of collecting and tabulating critical incidents. After the dimensions of the EPDQ have been defined, research should undertake a more thorough mapping of the differential characteristics of management jobs in different settings, and psychometric studies should be carried out to determine the extent of time-, person-, and situation-determined changes on each of the jobs studied. The critical incidents studies must pay special attention to the changing demands of executive jobs. Kelly's rather tenuous conclusion supporting Brown's emphasis on managers' work-oriented responsibilities as opposed to personal style variables ties in with Simon's (1960, p. 48) prediction that advances in computer technology and the possibility of more rational and impersonal bases for executive decision making will assure that the manager of the future

> . . . will find himself dealing . . . with a well-structured system whose problems have to be diagnosed and corrected objectively and analytically [instead of with] unpredictable and sometimes recalcitrant people who have to be persuaded, prodded, rewarded and cajoled.

The manager qualities and managerial processes leading to effective attainment of goals in Simon's system of the future will undoubtedly differ from the "success" qualities and processes generally accepted in current systems. Certainly, the day is not far away when the majority of managerial jobs will be defined by the magnitude of their information processing and coordinating responsibilities instead of by the numbers of persons supervised. Managerial job analyses, critical managerial behaviors, and dimensional studies of managerial jobs must be forward-looking, not only to tap the status quo and the patterns of the past but to describe the patterns of the future as well.

SUMMARY

Describing requirements of managerial jobs is unusually difficult because such jobs are subject to so many changes. Any given job or position at the managerial level changes from time to time, from person to person, and from situation to situation. This means that a managerial job title tells us very little about actual job demands or about how any given manager may meet those demands. Since managerial job titles provide such limited information, other means must be developed for discovering the behavioral requirements of managerial jobs. What is needed is a set of fundamental dimensions to describe or measure the job behaviors desired at a particular time and for a given situation. With such dimensions, a "running record" could be made of any particular job as changes due to time, persons, or situations are induced.

Various approaches have been taken by different investigators in their studies of managers' jobs. Some have actually observed managers as they go about their jobs and have kept records of what the managers do. More frequently, managers have been asked to fill in short reports describing how and with whom they are spending their work time. With the exception of Stewart's study (1967), these investigations have yielded nothing more than descriptive tabulations; no more fundamental dimensions have been developed from them. Other investigators have gone to the other extreme—abstracting their descriptions of managers' behavior to such a degree that the results reflect merely personal styles (such as consideration and initiating structure) rather than specific requirements of different managerial jobs. Hemphill (1959, 1960) is the only investigator who has come close to a middle ground between these two extremes. In his study, 93 executives estimated how important each of 575 job activities was as a part of their own managerial jobs. Hemphill estimated statistically the degree of similarity between every possible pair of job descriptions and, with factor analysis, discovered 10 fairly homogeneous job groupings. Hemphill's results come close to providing the fundamental dimensions necessary for describing managerial jobs, but they need to be studied more thoroughly and modified so that they will contain greater behavioral relevance.

They need, in particular, to be supplemented with the type of behaviorally rich information that could be derived from collecting and tabulating critical incidents portraying unusually effective or unusually ineffective executive job behaviors. The modified dimensions should then be used to map more thoroughly the differential characteristics of managerial jobs in different settings, and longitudinal studies should be undertaken to map the nature and degree of time-, person-, and situation-determined changes in various managerial jobs.

As we pursue the difficult task of defining and measuring managerial effectiveness in Chapter 5, the crucial importance of measuring managerial job requirements will become even more apparent.

Chapter 5 Defining and Measuring Managerial Effectiveness

THE CRITERION PROBLEM

After managerial jobs have been described according to the dimensional analyses and measures detailed in Chapter 4, the differential effectiveness of managers assigned to substantively different jobs should be determined and related empirically to individual, situational, and organizational attributes. In a word, *effective* managerial job behavior must be defined, described, and measured.

Quantifying job effectiveness has been industrial psychology's major bugaboo since its inception. We doubt that many industrial psychologists would be willing, even today, to claim completely satisfactory answers to the issues and questions raised by the so-called criterion problem, although it has been dealt with exhaustively (and exhaustingly) in the psychological and business literature. We make no effort here to repeat or even to summarize these discussions and proposed solutions. Such matter belongs more appropriately in the textbooks of industrial psychology. Instead, we have devoted our energies toward answering the central question posed in Chapter 2: *What are the varieties or combinations of organizational circumstances, personal characteristics,*

101

and behavior patterns that are likely to be perceived as effective managing? We also address ourselves to two subsidiary questions: What do managers do that may lead to their perceived success or to their perceived failure? What are the products and "signs" of effective managing?

ORGANIZATIONAL OPTIMIZATION

A first approximation toward defining what managers must do in order to be regarded as "successful" is offered by Guion (1965a, p. 466):

> The success of an executive lies largely in meeting major organization goals through the coordinated efforts of his organization; in part, at least, these efforts depend upon the kind of influence the executive has upon those whose work his own behavior touches. . . . The executive's own behavior contributes to the achievement of organizational goals only by its influence on the perceptions, attitudes, and motives of other people in the organization and on their subsequent behavior.

As we saw earlier, the "major organizational goals" mentioned by Guion include factors such as industry leadership, long-term organizational growth, internal organizational stability, organizational efficiency, profit maximization, maintenance of high employee morale, and selection and development of effective subordinates. Such broad goals, though eminently worthy, suffer themselves from imprecision of definition and measurement. In fact, Seashore and Yuchtman (1967) argue forcefully that the imputation of purposiveness to organizations (through attributing superficially attractive and plausible goals to their functioning) is misleading because it fails to recognize the gross organizational imbalances likely to occur if such "goals" (e.g., profitability or growth) ever were actually maximized. Their definition of organizational effectiveness, based on a series of factorial analyses of a set of performance indicators applied to 75 insurance sales agencies over a ten-year period, is *"the ability of an organization to exploit its environments in the acquisition of scarce and valued resources to sustain its functioning"* (p. 393). This definition places emphasis on long-term *optimization* of organizational actions in relation to interactions between internal resources and environmental potential. The notion of optimization is justified by their analysis of the relative stabilities over three periods (1952 to 1957, 1957 to 1961, and 1952 to 1961) of the following 10 factorially independent performance dimensions:[1]

- Business volume (highly stable, $r_{mdn} = .95$)
- Production cost (moderately stable, $r_{mdn} = .41$)
- Index of new agent productivity (unstable-cyclic, $r_{mdn} = .20$)

[1] Some of the dimension titles have been changed slightly from those chosen by Seashore and Yuchtman in order to convey their content more clearly.

- Index of relative youthfulness of agents (unstable-cyclic, $r_{mdn} = .21$)
- Business mix (moderately stable, $r_{mdn} = .67$)
- Manpower growth (unstable-cyclic, $r_{mdn} = .15$)
- Manager's commissions (moderately stable, $r_{mdn} = .36$)
- Maintenance cost (moderately stable, $r_{mdn} = .33$)
- Agent productivity (highly stable, $r_{mdn} = .71$)
- Market penetration (highly stable, $r_{mdn} = .89$)

It appears that certain aspects of organizational performance (such as manpower growth, maintenance cost, or production cost) carry a burden of responding to relatively short-term environmental demands and opportunities in order to sustain longer-term acquisition of environmental resources (such as business volume and market penetration). Seashore and Yuchtman argue, therefore, that (1) organizational performance factors must be considered together as a set rather than in terms of any single goal, (2) measurement of organizational performance at just a single point in time fails to highlight the dynamic qualities of organizational processes, and (3) organizational effectiveness should be evaluated according to its systemic qualities instead of just in terms of its ability to accomplish single, more simplistic organizational yardsticks or "goals."

Mahoney (1966, 1967), sampling a much broader array of organizational units, reports results generally compatible with the arguments advanced by Seashore and Yuchtman. He obtained descriptions of 283 organizations[2] on 114 different aspects of organizational functioning from 84 managers in 13 companies. Factor analysis of the 114 descriptive elements and derivation of factorial dimensions showed that seven dimensions accounted for the bulk (55 percent) of descriptive variance in overall organizational effectiveness. The seven are listed and described briefly below:

- **Development (.04)**
  Organizational personnel participate in training and development activities.
- **Reliability (.05)**
  Organization meets objectives without requiring follow-up and checking.
- **Staffing (.01)**
  Organizational personnel show flexibility among assignments; there is emphasis on development for promotion from within the organization.
- **Planning (.14)**
  Operations are planned to avoid lost time; little time is spent on minor crises or "putting out fires."
- **Cooperation (.01)**
  Operations are scheduled and coordinated with those of other organizations.

[2] An organizational unit was taken as any subordinate unit under the purview of a particular manager. The participating managers were in middle or top positions, and each described an average of three to four units. Overall, the 283 organizations making up the sample ranged in size from four employees to over one thousand and covered production, marketing, engineering, research, administrative services, and staff functions.

- **Performance-Support-Utilization (.27)**
  Efficient performance, mutual support and respect of supervisors and subordinates, and effective utilization of personnel skills and abilities.
- **Initiation (.04)**
  Organization initiates improvements in work methods and operations.

Submitting the above dimensions to a multiple regression analysis against global ratings of the organizations' effectiveness, Mahoney showed that the seven dimensions contributed substantially different amounts to managers' overall judgments of organizational effectiveness. The relative proportion of variance contributed by each of the dimensions is shown in the parentheses after each title. As can be seen, the performance-support-utilization dimension carries most weight in managers' judgments of organizational effectiveness. This dimension combines three different organizational characteristics— quality of output and efficiency of performance, mutual support between supervisors and subordinates, and effectiveness of personnel utilization in the organization. Apparently, managers perceive organizational effectiveness both in terms of organizational characteristics *and* in terms of organizational performance. Other components of organizational effectiveness—planning, reliability, development, staffing, cooperation, and initiation—reflect other aspects of organizational behavior seen by these managers as critical in achieving effectiveness.

In summarizing his results, Mahoney suggests that managers probably view organizational effectiveness hierarchically. He states (1966, p. 17):

> Managers view performance as a first-order criterion. . . . Mutual support and utilization of personnel within the organization are viewed as second-order criteria which are so closely related to performance that they are considered equivalently in judging effectiveness. Planning, reliability, initiation, and development are second-order criterion dimensions; these variables are considered indicative of first-order criteria. . . . The remaining seventeen dimensions of effectiveness can be viewed as third-order criteria. They are considered desirable as supplementary goals and as influencing high-order criteria. However, relationships among these variables and between them and higher-order variables are often too complex to warrant assigning them much influence in the judgment of overall organizational effectiveness.

In the context of Seashore's and Yuchtman's conceptualization, Mahoney's "third-order criteria"[3] can be interpreted as relatively short-term and situationally specific adjustments to environmental conditions, and his "first-order criteria" can be interpreted as the more enduring and global estimates of long-

---

[3] Examples of some of these criteria include such dimensions as cohesiveness, decentralization, conflict resolution, low turnover (due to poor performance), and supervisory surveillance.

term interactions and accommodations between internal organizational characteristics and external resources.

THE EFFECTIVE MANAGER AS AN OPTIMIZER

Returning to Guion's statement, quoted earlier, we may now consider how managerial "success" relates to these concepts of organizational effectiveness. Conceptually, it makes good sense to define effective management in terms of organizational outcomes, and we shall do so within the framework provided by Seashore and Yuchtman.

We define effective managerial job behavior as any set of managerial actions believed to be optimal for identifying, assimilating, and utilizing both internal and external resources toward sustaining, over the long term, the functioning of the organizational unit for which a manager has some degree of responsibility.

The effective manager is, in our definition, an optimizer in utilizing all available and potential resources—material, human, and financial—both within and without the organization, toward its sustained, long-term functioning. We recognize that this definition most certainly complicates rather than simplifies any search for measures of effective managing, but it does at least spell out rather well the major benchmarks for evaluating any proposed measures. These benchmarks both explicit and implied, include the following:

- The ultimate product or outcome is the maintenance of organizational functioning.
- The measures must be over the long term, not merely day to day or short term.
- Effective managerial job behavior includes many actions, not just one. In fact, optimization of resource allocation demands a myriad of complex and multifaceted information processing activities.
- No specification is made about the number of potential configurations of effective managerial actions. That is, different managers, utilizing entirely different behavioral patterns, might still accomplish the same or very similar levels of optimization.
- Effective managerial behavior must be measured in terms of *what the manager himself does* on the job to effect optimization.
- Effective managerial behavior—even though measured solely by what the manager himself does—is still subject to any number of causal variables, including not only the manager's qualities but also the nature of human, financial, and material resources available to him and to the rest of the organization.
- The perceived effectiveness of a manager may be altered by the level of effectiveness of other managers as they, in turn, seek to optimize their own allocation of resources toward the maintenance of their own organizational units.
- Finally, any manager's actions can affect all organizational units for which he possesses either full or partial (shared) responsibility. His actions are typically

directed toward optimal resource utilization in many units instead of just one, and measures of his level of managerial effectiveness should take account of the fact of his multiple membership in the many units.

Implications for Measuring Managerial Effectiveness

Since the ultimate product of effective managing is seen to be the maintenance of organizational functioning, we are faced with a dilemma in assessing the effectiveness of any particular manager. Obviously, organizations possess massive inertia, and many may continue on long after, and in spite of, any and all death blows or knockout punches dealt them by incompetent managing. We must not be deluded, therefore, into equating a manager's effectiveness *directly* with the mere fact that his unit stays in existence. No such easy index of managerial effectiveness exists, and we certainly hope the reader has no illusions that we are advocating any such easy or simplistic solution to the measurement problem. Quite to the contrary, the primary emphasis in our definition and the common theme characterizing the benchmarks derived from it are focused on managerial *actions* or *behaviors* believed to be requisites for optimal resource allocation. Thus, in the end, it is crucial to accept the fact that any criterion (measure) of managerial effectiveness must depend on informed judgment to identify those managerial job behaviors constituting successful optimization of resources.

Astin's (1964) distinction between *criterion performance* and the *conceptual criterion* is helpful in this regard. For him, the "conceptual criterion is a verbal statement of important or socially relevant outcomes based on the general purposes or aims of the [organizational] sponsor" (p. 809). As examples of conceptual criteria, Astin cites such desirable outcomes as "effective teaching," "social adjustment," and "flying proficiency." According to our arguments, then, the conceptual criteria for managerial effectiveness may be taken as "maintenance of organizational functioning" or, more proximately, "optimal utilization of resources." Astin proceeds: "A *criterion performance* is any observable event which is judged to be relevant to the conceptual criterion" (p. 810). The relevance of a criterion performance can be judged only on rational grounds, and it is precisely at this point that informed judgment, expert opinion —or whatever—must be brought to bear to specify the full range of managerial behaviors relevant to the conceptual criterion of optimal resource allocation.

SPECIFYING THE CRITERION PERFORMANCES OF EFFECTIVE MANAGING

How shall the effectiveness of an *individual* manager (as contrasted with a total management team) be measured? Perhaps the overriding requirement of a measure of managerial effectiveness—implied by our discussion so far—

is that it be directly relevant to what the *individual manager himself does* in terms of effective or ineffective resource allocation. This is not to say that nothing but measures or observations of individual behavior can properly constitute estimates of managerial effectiveness, but it does point directly to one important continuum along which all measures of managerial effectiveness must be assessed.

A Deficiency-Excessiveness continuum. Statements or measures of a manager's effectiveness should be based on how he handles the optimizing requirements and opportunities offered by his particular job. This requires that the job be described fully (as we noted in the preceding chapter) and that observational and measurement methods be developed to tap the many aspects of his behavior on it. Many measures of job effectiveness—most particularly many at the managerial level—are seriously *deficient* in that they include only a few rather than all or many of the behavioral elements making up a job. For example, a manager might be judged to be highly effective in planning and organizing his activities, but this measure alone would clearly be deficient as a comprehensive estimate of how well he utilizes all available resources. At the other extreme, measures may be *excessive* in that they contain surplus information; that is, they include elements going beyond what a manager can do himself to affect their outcome. In the job of selling, for example, sales volume is usually an excessive measure of an individual salesman's effectiveness; it is affected, often to unknown degrees, by such factors as territory differences in economic resources, differential effectiveness of advertising campaigns, differing competitive advantages from territory to territory, etc. Clearly, the overall conceptual criterion of maintaining organizational functioning is excessive in that many factors in addition to individual managerial job behavior may determine its maintenance status.

We state, then, that a measure of any given manager's effectiveness should be based on a careful definition of the total domain of his job responsibilities along with statements of critical behaviors believed to be necessary for using available and potential resources in the best possible way. The measure itself must encompass a series of observations of the manager's actual job behavior by qualified observers who are able to judge how effectively he accomplishes all the things regarded as important for doing the job properly—no less (deficient) and no more (excessive).

Patton (1960) and McConkey (1962) both argue for essentially this type of objective-oriented approach for measuring managerial effectiveness. McConkey suggests that job objectives be set jointly by a manager and his superior and that they fulfill the following requirements:

1 They should be compatible with overall company plans.
2 They should represent sufficient challenge to the manager.

3 They should be attainable through the manager's own efforts.
4 They should be clearly defined according to actual tasks necessary for accomplishing them.
5 They should include methods for estimating how well they have been accomplished.

Patton calls his approach "planned performance programming"; its essence is that managerial effectiveness is judged in terms of accomplishing certain agreed-upon tasks specified as relevant to maintenance goals of the organization. According to Patton, each manager's objectives are stated as measurable aims whose degree of accomplishment can be judged.

The major requirements of our suggested measures of managerial effectiveness are that they be strongly job-centered, that they be devised rationally in accordance with long-range planning and objective-setting, and that they be based on job behaviors that are observable and measurable. We believe, with S. R. Wallace (1965), that behavior-based measures of this type are the best bets for achieving fuller understanding of the behavioral elements making up the total fabric of effective executive behavior.

Global measures of managerial effectiveness. Most measures commonly used as estimates on managerial effectiveness fail to meet many of the specifications outlined above. There is good reason for this, which we shall discuss shortly, but first we shall mention some of the measures that have had widespread use.

Global estimates of overall management effectiveness are common. One widely used procedure (Dunnette & Kirchner, 1958; Laurent, 1961, 1962; Mahoney, Jerdee, & Nash, 1960) consists simply of rankings from managers' superiors of their total managerial effectiveness. Such rankings have merit in that they constitute a single index encompassing a sort of overall impression or gestalt of a manager's total "success"; evidence is abundant that separate rankers show good agreement in their independent estimates of a given manager's level of effectiveness. Such impressions also possess a number of additional potential advantages: (1) A manager is compared directly with his peers, who presumably are responsible for optimizing similar resource possibilities; (2) the global impression probably encompasses a broad sampling of managerial behaviors, extending over a span of time and—if the ranker has known him in previous settings—over managerial jobs he has held previously; (3) the impression is likely to be affected most by what the manager himself is or has done and to be relatively free of job "successes" due to organizational or societal factors; (4) the impression probably samples reasonably well the effects a manager may have had on the full range of organizational units for which he may be either fully or partially responsible; and (5) the impression is likely to be based on many behaviors rather than only a few. Even so, such judgments may also be contaminated to unknown degrees by factors such as appearance, education, experience, acquaintance, or liking and disliking, which may or may not be correlated with, or relevant to, actual criterion performances. Thus, a major problem with such global ratings is that they "cover up" so much. We cannot discern from a specific manager's standing in a ranked list of several men whether his various rankers formed their gestalts of him from job-relevant or job-irrelevant information. We cannot know with much certainty what portion of any such global impression may be based on actual managerial job behaviors or on contaminants such as physical bearing, friendliness, interpersonal "savvy," etc., which, though constituting aspects of society's conception of desirable characteristics, may be related to none or only a limited number of actions involving resource allocation. In other words, a global judgment does indeed reflect a common way of looking at "success" in our society and in business, but it yields little in terms of better understanding the way in which success in our society and in business is achieved or the job behavioral correlates contributing to it. Moreover, it yields no knowledge about a manager's differing levels of effectiveness in handling various resource allocation problems and thus tacitly ignores the complex and multifaceted information processing requirements of his job.

Other commonly used global measures are salary and organizational level indexes corrected statistically for age or length of time in an organization. These measures also constitute broad conceptions of "success," but they have the added advantage of reflecting pooled estimates of many superiors' judgments (in making salary and promotional recommendations) over an individual manager's total career. In this sense, it may be argued that such indexes constitute a good summation of a manager's ability consistently to optimize organizational systems, to perform crucial managerial job activities, and to do other "successful" things. Still there is no way of knowing in any given instance the degree of contamination by such factors as luck or good fortune ("being in the right place at the right time") or the relative influence of patterns of deficient and behaviorally sparse observations made over time by different superiors in judging a man's job performance and promotional potential. As we shall see shortly, job performance is clearly estimated quite differently according to differing rater and observer characteristics; the kinds of "judges" a man has had over his career can affect his net "score" on such career indexes for good or for ill.

For example, Miner (1966) showed that promotional decisions in one company differed greatly from department to department in their reliance on previous job performance. In the manufacturing department, promotion decisions were positively related to previous performance as follows:

	Job performance	
	Judged above average	Judged below average
Promoted	24	5
Not promoted	11	20

Note: The numbers indicate the number of persons in each cell of the table.

Clearly the odds were heavily in favor of promotion for those persons receiving above-average job performance ratings (odds of promotion: 2 to 1 for above average and only 1 to 5 for below average). In the accounting department of the same company, promotion decisions were negatively related to previous performance as follows:

	Job performance	
	Judged above average	Judged below average
Promoted	8	19
Not promoted	28	29

Note: The numbers indicate the number of persons in each cell of the table.

Clearly the odds in this department were in favor of promotion for below-average performers (odds of promotion: approximately 2 to 10 for above-average and nearly 4 to 10 for below-average). Career patterns and overall success of persons in this company were probably strongly affected by "luck"—whether they were in manufacturing or accounting. Factors such as these are typically hidden by the broad global indexes of career promotional or salary success.

Objective measures. As an alternative to global measures, a number of objective measures have been utilized including job attitude surveys among a manager's subordinates; grievance, turnover, and absence rates; quantity of organizational output; cost-related indexes such as scrappage rates, tool replacement costs, or cost of processing standard work units; etc. Measures such as these usually suffer from both deficiency and contamination—that is, they fail to tap more than a small part of variance due to individual managerial behavior, and their variations are dependent on many job-irrelevant factors not under the direct control of the manager.

Merrihue and Katzell (1955) developed an Employee Relations Index (ERI) by combining into a single index (via factor analysis and multiple regression analysis) eight objective indicators of employee relations effectiveness: absence rate, separation rate, dispensary visits, number of suggestions submitted, disciplinary suspensions, grievance rates, work stoppages, and extent of employee participation in the insurance plan. Working in several plants of the General Electric Company, they found significant relationships between the magnitude of ERI and subjective estimates of group effectiveness such as motivational level. The early high hopes for the index as an indirect indicator of managerial effectiveness failed to materialize, however, and it has since been discontinued in the General Electric Corporation. Turner (1960) used factor analysis to study the relationships between 11 objective measures (e.g., grievances, scrap rates, hospital passes) and general foremen's rankings of foreman performance on eight different variables (quality, quantity, cost control, organization, etc.) in two different General Motors plants. The ranking variables all loaded on a single factor in each plant (evidence of halo effect in the rankings) and showed no important relation to the objective indicators in either plant. Guion (1965) reports other studies using objective criteria by Comrey, High, and Wilson (1955); Robbins and King (1961); Cuomo (1955); and MacKinney and Wolins (1960). None of these has yielded any high hope for using such indicators for measuring managerial effectiveness.

Rating scales and behavior observation. If global estimates of effectiveness and objective measures both fail to fulfill our requirements of a job-centered, behaviorally based measure of managerial effectiveness, what should be used? What is needed is some way of systematically recording observations across the whole domain of desired managerial job behaviors and tabulating how often they accomplish agreed-upon objectives in the most critical areas of managerial behavior. Unfortunately, there is a rather long and sorry history of gallant but essentially failing efforts to develop rating scales for observing and measuring job behavior. In fact, it is probably because rating scales have had such a bad history that they have fallen into disrepute as an alternative to be considered in assessing managerial effectiveness. The global measures (rankings, promotions, and salary indexes) have filled the gap left by the failure of rating scales to carry out successfully the measurement task.

There are many reasons why standard rating procedures have failed. We shall review the major problems in developing and using such devices and then offer suggestions for overcoming these problems and for developing measures which we believe will prove more successful in measuring managerial effectiveness.

It is our contention that psychologists have not paid proper heed to the extreme difficulties involved in accurately observing and reporting behavior. They have given insufficient attention to meaningfulness, behavior definition, and semantic clarity in their development of job behavior rating scales, with the result that most scales either have not been understood or were viewed as irrelevant by observers asked to complete them. Below, we discuss some of the potential errors inherent in behavior observations and research evidence relevant to them.

Sources of Observational Error.

Inadequate sampling of the job behavior domain. As we have indicated, observations of job behavior depend on identifying as fully as possible all the behaviors judged to be relevant to the conceptual criterion. The identification and enumeration of relevant job behaviors is a primary function of job analysis. If job descriptions are incomplete or erroneous, behavior observations based on them are bound to be faulty. Both extremes of the Deficiency-Excessiveness continuum must be avoided, and the only sure means of doing so is to give careful and extensive attention to the job analysis phase. This has rarely been done, primarily, we believe, because of too great an eagerness to administer tests and other inventories in an effort to obtain quick but unfortunately only partial answers to questions about managerial effectiveness. No substitute exists for careful and complete definition of the managerial job behavior domain.

Response sets and chance response tendencies. The most pervasive source of error in job behavior ratings and the one seemingly most diligently ignored by persons designing rating instruments is lack of knowledge, understanding, or rapport by observers asked to record their observations. The specific individual most often asked to serve as an observer and recorder is someone in the immediate job environment of the manager (often his direct superior). The supervisor-observer is therefore the key man. It is he and he alone—not the test developer, not the psychologist, not the president of the firm, and not even the personnel man responsible for managerial candidates—who must view the job behavior observation form as understandable, job-relevant, practical, and acceptable. If he does not, his responses will tend not to be based on careful observations of managerial job behavior but will instead be affected by any or all of several systematic and/or variable response errors. If the observer fails to understand the statements or items on a rating form, if he regards them as irrelevant to job effectiveness or as unimportant, if he does not feel like cooperating with persons asking him to complete the form, or if he has had only limited opportunities to observe the manager's job behavior, he may adopt any one or several of the following tactics:

- *Central tendency.* He may complete all the forms in about the same way for all the people he describes, thereby failing to discriminate either between different persons or within the behavioral repertoire of a single person.
- *Leniency tendency.* This is merely a special type of central tendency error in which the observer tends to give only favorable or highly effective descriptions of everyone.
- *Halo.* The observer, in filling out the form, makes an overall evaluative judgment (e.g., "good" or "bad") about each manager and then proceeds to describe him using all seemingly "good" or "bad" behavioral statements, regardless of the actual behavioral content of the statements making up the form.
- *Other tendencies.* A number of other response tendencies are possible depending upon the special dispositions shown by each observer. One rather common tendency is to make highly variable and inconsistent responses, still without regard to the behavioral content of the statements, which gives the false impression that care has been taken in differentially describing a person's job behavior.

A study by Vielhuber and Gottheil (1965) reveals an instance in which judgments were related to factors entirely irrelevant to the job. They asked four Army officers at West Point to rate the appearance of 117 entering cadets solely on the basis of each cadet's statement of his name and home address (taking about five to ten seconds). The combined ratings of the four officers correlated .31 with Aptitude for Service ratings made by peers and superiors after fourteen weeks at West Point. Thus, ratings based on momentary first impressions are related to estimates of overall potential for service success, suggesting that appearance and manner, though presumably irrelevant to the job, can and do still affect ratings of job performance.

It is easy to state but less easy to implement the requirements for overcoming observer errors due to these job- and content-irrelevant response tendencies. We must be assured that observers understand the content of the job behavior description form, that they regard it as important, and that they make it a point to observe systematically and accurately the job behaviors of managers of whom they will be asked to give descriptions. Assessing the interobserver agreement for statements in a form is one way of estimating whether or not they convey the same meaning to different observers. Better yet, the observers should actually develop the form; then they cannot help but understand it and be committed to using it properly. Securing critical incidents from supervisors is a good first step in this direction, but it must be carried further. Detailed steps for developing such a form (i.e., one actually written, edited, and utilized by the observers themselves) are outlined later.

Observer characteristics. Many studies provide convincing evidence that observers differ in what they see and report in a job setting. A substantial portion of observational variance is apparently due to the differing expectations and perceptions of observers. For example, peers, superiors, and subordinates differ in their ratings of persons. Observers also differ according to their own job effectiveness and according to other individual characteristics.

Evidence of differences in ratings assigned by peers and by superiors is clear-cut. Gordon and Medland (1965) found that peer ratings of overall leadership potential for four companies of army recruits correlated only moderately (r's of .38, .41, .46, and .51) with the squad sergeant's ratings. In addition, peer ratings showed higher stability over time and over different situations[4] than the sergeant's ratings. Dunnette, Perry, and Mahoney (1956) found a correlation of .55 between overall effectiveness rankings by superiors and peers of 29 commanders (lieutenant colonels and colonels) in the Air Materiel Command. Hollander (1954, 1956, 1957, 1965) and Wherry and Fryer (1949) have demonstrated conclusively that peer ratings of leadership potential obtained during training in military settings have higher reliabilities and are more highly related to later ratings of leadership competence than other measures

[4]After four weeks, the membership of two of the companies was "reconstituted," and new peer ratings were obtained at the end of another four weeks. Correlations of peer ratings obtained at the end of the two four-week periods were .80 and .82; correlations between the two sets of sergeants' ratings were only .60 and .45.

or estimates (such as instructor's ratings) obtained during training. Hollander (1956, 1965) and Gordon and Medland (1965) also suggest that extraneous factors (such as appearance and friendship) are less likely to be contaminants of peer ratings than of superior ratings. Hollander, for example, partialed out friendship nominations from his data and found that the long-term validity of the peer ratings was not seriously affected, although Doll and Longo (1962), also working in a military setting, have demonstrated the usefulness of "correcting" low peer rating scores when they can be shown to result from raters' attributing antisocial characteristics (such as self-centeredness, selfishness, contentiousness, boastfulness, etc.) to their peers. After removing low ratings based on such personal characteristics from the total, the power of the remaining low ratings (presumably containing more job-relevant variance) for predicting training failure was enhanced.

Other studies, most notably those by Weitz (1958) and Roadman (1964), have shown the usefulness of peer ratings for predicting later global ratings of success in managerial jobs in industry. Weitz found peer ratings among life insurance salesmen to be moderately related ($r = .40$) to later global ratings of effectiveness for those who had been promoted to manager. Roadman found that peer ratings obtained among 56 managers toward the end of a month-long training course were strongly related to their promotional experiences in the two years subsequent to their participating in the course. Interestingly, the peer judgments of such "traits" as independence of thought, leadership qualities, and ability to think analytically were most strongly related to subsequent promotional actions. Ratings of emotional maturity, cooperation, and tact were unrelated. Barrett (1966) concludes his discussion of the evidence on peer ratings with the comment that peer ratings are potentially the most accurate judgments of employee job behavior.

It appears that peers and superiors perceive different aspects of an individual's behavior. This is not surprising, for it is likely that a person's behavior in the presence of his peers constitutes a more valid portrayal of his "real self" than his behavior in the presence of his superiors. Moreover, peers should be in a better position than superiors to observe more aspects of a manager's behavior (e.g., not only how he utilizes financial and material resources but also his behavior related to allocating human resources available to him through his subordinates and through coordination with colleagues both inside and outside his organizational unit.) It is surprising that industrial firms have so rarely taken account of these differing frames of reference in their measures of managerial effectiveness.

Other rater characteristics have been shown to affect the nature of ratings obtained. One of the most important appears to be the actual job effectiveness of the rater. Studies by Levy (1960) and by Kirchner and Reisberg (1962) are directly relevant. Levy examined the ratings given to accounting supervisors by accounting department heads who themselves had been designated as "highly effective" or "less effective." He found that overall success of subordinate supervisors rated by "highly effective" department heads was best predicted by an intelligence test ($r = .45$) but that overall success of subordinate supervisors rated by "less effective" department heads was best predicted by a clerical aptitude test ($r = .39$). Apparently, the more and the less effective department heads had sharply differing definitions and expectations concerning valued job behavior on the part of their subordinate supervisors.

Kirchner and Reisberg compared the traits named by highly effective and by less effective technical managers as characteristic of their better and less effective subordinates. More effective managers tended more often to value "initiative," "persistence," "broad knowledge," and "planning ability." Less effective managers tended more often to value "cooperation," "company loyalty," "good teamwork" and "tact and consideration." Further evidence is provided by D. E. Schneider and Bayroff (1953) and by Mandell (1956) showing that brighter and more successful managers perceived their subordinates differently from the way less effective managers did and that such differences, when converted to ratings, may have differential validities for predicting other behavioral measures (such as class standing in Schneider and Bayroff's study and overall supervisory effectiveness in Mandell's study).

What does all this mean in the context of errors of observation? Quite simply, it suggests that different observers differ considerably in their ability to do an effective, reliable, and valid job of observing and recording the job behavior of other persons. Not surprisingly, they see different behavioral aspects from different vantage points, and the things they define as effective in others' job behavior depend importantly on their own characteristics and their own job effectiveness. The implications of this, in turn, are that we should be alert to persons' differing perceptions of effective managerial behavior, and we probably will need to be somewhat selective in according greater weight to observations provided by managers who themselves are more effective in the jobs being assessed.

In addition, we shall want observations wherever possible from more than a single vantage point. It appears that peer ratings can add important and potentially more reliable and valid variance to measures of managerial effectiveness. Disagreement between different observers should not necessarily be viewed as a mark of unreliability (as tradition has so often dictated), but should instead be viewed as a possibly valid indication that differing aspects of a manager's behavior are being accurately perceived and reported. In fact, Buckner (1959) showed that ratings of shipboard performance of 50 seamen for whom raters showed high agreement were *less* predictable from aptitude tests than ratings with only moderate or low agreement between raters. In other words, less reliable (defined as interrater agreement) ratings were more predictable than highly reliable ones—a clear indication of the usefulness of adding new observational information from an independent rater if we have reason to believe that he may be in a position to see aspects of managerial behavior not easily apparent from the first rater's vantage point. Lawler (1967a) suggests that job behavior observations of managerial effectiveness should be obtained from persons at many levels and studied according to a multitrait-multimethod (rater) matrix (D. T. Campbell & Fiske, 1959). To illustrate his suggestion, Lawler developed such an analysis from superiors', peers' and managers' own ratings of different aspects of their job effectiveness. His data, portrayed in the multi-trait-multirater matrix shown in Table 5.1, are useful for revealing similarities and differences in the perceptions of managers' effectiveness as viewed from these three vantage points. For example, the degrèe of intercorrelation between the traits being rated, whether due to response set errors (such as halo) or to actual behavioral covariation, is shown by the correlational values included in the three triangles. Values in the diagonal cells (set off by boxes) show degrees of agreement between different raters recording observations for the same traits. Superiors and peers agree somewhat better with each other (median $r = .53$) than the typical level of correlation between different traits (median $r = .44$). However, ratings by managers of their own job quality, ability, and effort agree very poorly with both superior and peer ratings (median $r = .11$). Whether this low degree of agreement arises merely because of low "reliability" or because of valid differences in the behavioral elements observed by raters at the three vantage points cannot be determined from these data, but the analysis does point up the desirability of seeking answers to this question and other, similar ones.

   Changes in the job or job environment. Since different behaviors may be required at different times in any given job and particularly in managerial jobs, an important additional source of observational error is the limited time perspective yielded by many rating systems. The most usual change in job requirements would be related to the changing pattern of job demands while a manager is new to a job. For example, Fleishman and Fruchter (1960) showed that different behaviors are involved during the early stages of learning Morse code from those involved during later stages. In a somewhat similar study, Ghiselli and Haire (1960) showed that the job behaviors related to high overall production (dollar volume of fares collected) during cab drivers' first few weeks of employment were different from the job behaviors leading to high production after 4½ months on the job. Bass (1962a) has also shown how relationships between ratings of effectiveness for salesmen change over time. At the level of managerial jobs, Stewart's study (1967), discussed in the previous chapter, provides ample evidence of large differences from job to job in the relative consistency of patterns of time expenditure from day to day, week to week, etc. Thus, serious observational errors can result if observations

Table 5.1 CORRELATIONS BETWEEN SUPERIORS', PEERS', AND SELF-RATINGS ON THREE ASPECTS OF MANAGERIAL BEHAVIOR FOR 113 MIDDLE AND TOP MANAGERS

	Superior ratings			Peer ratings			Self-ratings		
	Job quality	Job ability	Job effort	Job quality	Job ability	Job effort	Job quality	Job ability	Job effort
Superior ratings									
Job quality									
Job ability	.53								
Job effort	.56	.44							
Peer ratings									
Job quality	.65	.38	.40						
Job ability	.42	.52	.30	.56					
Job effort	.40	.31	.53	.56	.40				
Self-ratings									
Job quality	.01	.01	.09	.01	.17	.10			
Job ability	.03	.13	.03	.04	.09	.02	.43		
Job effort	.06	.01	.30	.02	.01	.30	.40	.14	

Source: Lawler (1967a).

are based on only a short span of time. It is necessary to study possible temporal changes in job demands and in the nature of job behaviors observed and recorded and to determine the possible effects of such changes on relations between predictors and job behavior observations.

Changes in employee behavior. This source of error is closely similar to that induced by changes in the job. Just as job requirements need to be sampled at different times, so must the observations of employee-behaviors. It would be extremely misleading for a supervisor-observer or a peer-observer to base his job behavior descriptions on only a single day's observations. Yet such an occurrence is far from unlikely because most observers remember recent events much more clearly than less recent ones. This has been shown recently in an insightful series of laboratory studies by Whitlock (1963, 1966) showing the marked effects on overall judgments of single behavioral elements of either a favorable or an unfavorable type and the very short time required (a matter of a day or two) for the effects of such information to be entirely dissipated. In order to assure a much better sampling of an employee's behavior, Guion (1965a) suggests keeping a job anecdote file, in which a manager's superior would systematically and periodically (e.g., weekly) record each subordinate's significant job behaviors over a period of time. This file, according to Guion, could then serve as a "memory jogger" when the superior is asked to complete a job behavior description form. It would help him avoid the error of basing his descriptions on only a limited sample focused mainly on the most recent job activities.

Such a file, though probably uncommon in industry, is not unusual in other areas of human performance. For example, note the following words of wisdom concerning job behavior records from a well-known pitching coach, Johnny Sain:

> I keep a notebook on my pitchers and grade them poor, fair, good and excellent. If you don't keep looking at the book over a period to time, you will remember only the excellent performances, and you will be unfair to the staff as a whole. Their positions change all the time as to who is the best starting pitcher at the moment, or who is the best stopper *now* when he is needed. Many times after a pitcher works I will ask him to grade himself or have the pitchers grade each other. Then I will tell them how I graded them. That way each individual is working to be No. 1.

RIDDING THE OBSERVATIONAL SYSTEM OF ERROR

It is apparent that job behavior observation is fraught with potential error, and this is undoubtedly a major reason why behavior-based observational methods are so rare as measures of managerial effectiveness. The most serious source of difficulty is a very fundamental one—stemming primarily from a common tendency for psychologists to impose their own beliefs about job behavior and their own systems for recording it upon the persons whose task it is to observe that behavior. According to P. C. Smith and Kendall (1963b), and we most certainly concur, this has almost always resulted in a lack of understanding and a lack of commitment to the observational task on the part of the observers. As a consequence, they tend to fill in the forms with little conviction; the records contain large, and, for the most part, inestimable errors—errors that can only serve to attenuate seriously any empirical relationships between predictor measures and managerial job behavior observations. It is crucial that these errors be removed from the observational system. Below, we suggest the means for doing so. Our proposed method combines the Critical Incidents Method with Smith and Kendall's retranslation approach (Smith & Kendall, (1963b).

The retranslation method. How can we develop standardized job behavior rating forms possessing necessary psychometric characteristics which will also be completed accurately and enthusiastically by relatively untrained observers of managers' job behavior? In order to answer this question, Smith and Kendall (1963b) assumed that errors could be avoided only by "selling" the observers on the desirability of completing job behavior ratings honestly and carefully. From this, it follows that job behavior forms must have an appearance of obvious usefulness to the observer as well as to the researcher. This requires taking unusual pains to maintain clearly understood and nonambiguous scales for job behavior description. The following comment (Smith & Kendall, 1963b, p. 151) is indicative of principles desirable for guiding development of job behavior forms:

> Better ratings can be obtained in our opinion, not by trying to trick the rater (as in forced choice scales) but by helping him to rate. We should ask questions which he can honestly answer about behaviors which he can observe. We should reassure him that his answers will not be misinterpreted, and we should provide a basis by which he and other can check his answers.

Dunnette, Campbell, and Hellervik (1968) recently used a modification of Smith and Kendall's retranslation method in developing job behavior observation scales for use in describing the job effectiveness of store department managers working for a large, nationwide retailing chain. Summarizing the actual steps taken in developing the scales will illustrate the method:

1 A two-hour workship session was held with 20 store managers to discuss use of personnel evaluation for increasing department managers' level of managerial effectiveness. Through discussion, the major dimensions involved in department managers' effectiveness were defined.

2 During a second two-hour session with the same group of managers, critical incidents of unusually good or unusually poor department manager behavior were written down and discussed briefly.

3 During the ensuing two weeks, the critical incidents were studied by the researchers and categorized according to their relevance to the broader dimensions of department manager behavior developed in the first discussion session. This process forced some changes in definitions of dimensions and the identification of some new dimensions to accommodate certain of the critical incidents.
4 During a third session, the same managers were asked independently to sort the incidents into the appropriate dimensional categories and to "scale" each incident on a nine-step "effectiveness" continuum ranging from grossly ineffective to highly effective.
5 Judgments obtained during the third session were used to eliminate incidents showing low consensus among managers. Dimensions were also eliminated or modified according to the content of incidents assigned to them.
6 The dimensions and their revised definitions and the remaining incidents were used as the basis for a workshop discussion with a different group of about twenty store managers and assistant store managers located in a different city. They also were asked to categorize the incidents into appropriate dimensions and to scale them on the nine-step effectiveness continuum.

This step is the central innovation in the retranslation procedure. It is similar to the language retranslation process undertaken to ensure that translations from one language to another adhere to the connotations as well as the denotations of the original. Material is translated into a foreign language and then retranslated by an independent translator back into the original. Thus the retranslation approach assures that the meaning of both the job dimensions and the behavioral incidents chosen to illustrate them is highly specific and nonambiguous.

7 The same retranslation procedure was undertaken in a workshop session with a group of store managers and their assistants from a third city. Information from these last two store manager groups served as the basis for developing a final set of department manager job behavior scales; these were pretested for actual use by asking store managers in a fourth city to use them in describing the job behaviors of a sample of their department managers.

The final outcome of this painstaking developmental work was a set of job behavior scales for department managers, comprising the following nine behavioral dimensions:

- Supervision of sales associates
- Handling customer complaints and making adjustments
- Meeting day-to-day deadlines
- Merchandise ordering
- Developing and planning special promotions
- Assessing sales trends and acting to maintain merchandising position
- Using company systems and following through on administrative operations
- Communicating relevant information to associates and to higher management
- Diagnosing and alleviating special department problems

Two of the scales—handling customer complaints and making adjustments, and meeting day-to-day deadlines—are illustrated in Figures 5.1 and 5.2. They

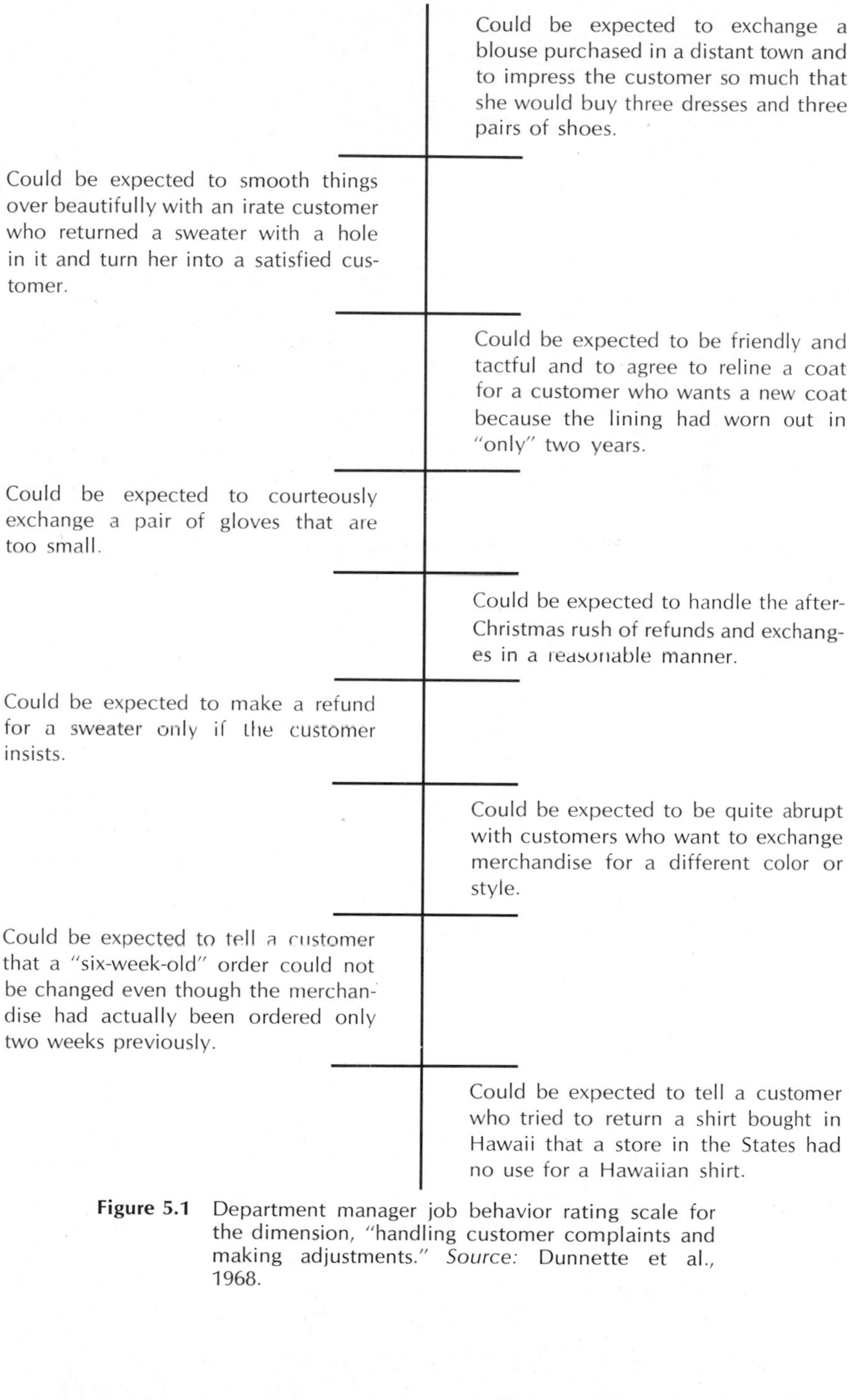

Could be expected to exchange a blouse purchased in a distant town and to impress the customer so much that she would buy three dresses and three pairs of shoes.

Could be expected to smooth things over beautifully with an irate customer who returned a sweater with a hole in it and turn her into a satisfied customer.

Could be expected to be friendly and tactful and to agree to reline a coat for a customer who wants a new coat because the lining had worn out in "only" two years.

Could be expected to courteously exchange a pair of gloves that are too small.

Could be expected to handle the after-Christmas rush of refunds and exchanges in a reasonable manner.

Could be expected to make a refund for a sweater only if the customer insists.

Could be expected to be quite abrupt with customers who want to exchange merchandise for a different color or style.

Could be expected to tell a customer that a "six-week-old" order could not be changed even though the merchandise had actually been ordered only two weeks previously.

Could be expected to tell a customer who tried to return a shirt bought in Hawaii that a store in the States had no use for a Hawaiian shirt.

Figure 5.1 Department manager job behavior rating scale for the dimension, "handling customer complaints and making adjustments." *Source:* Dunnette et al., 1968.

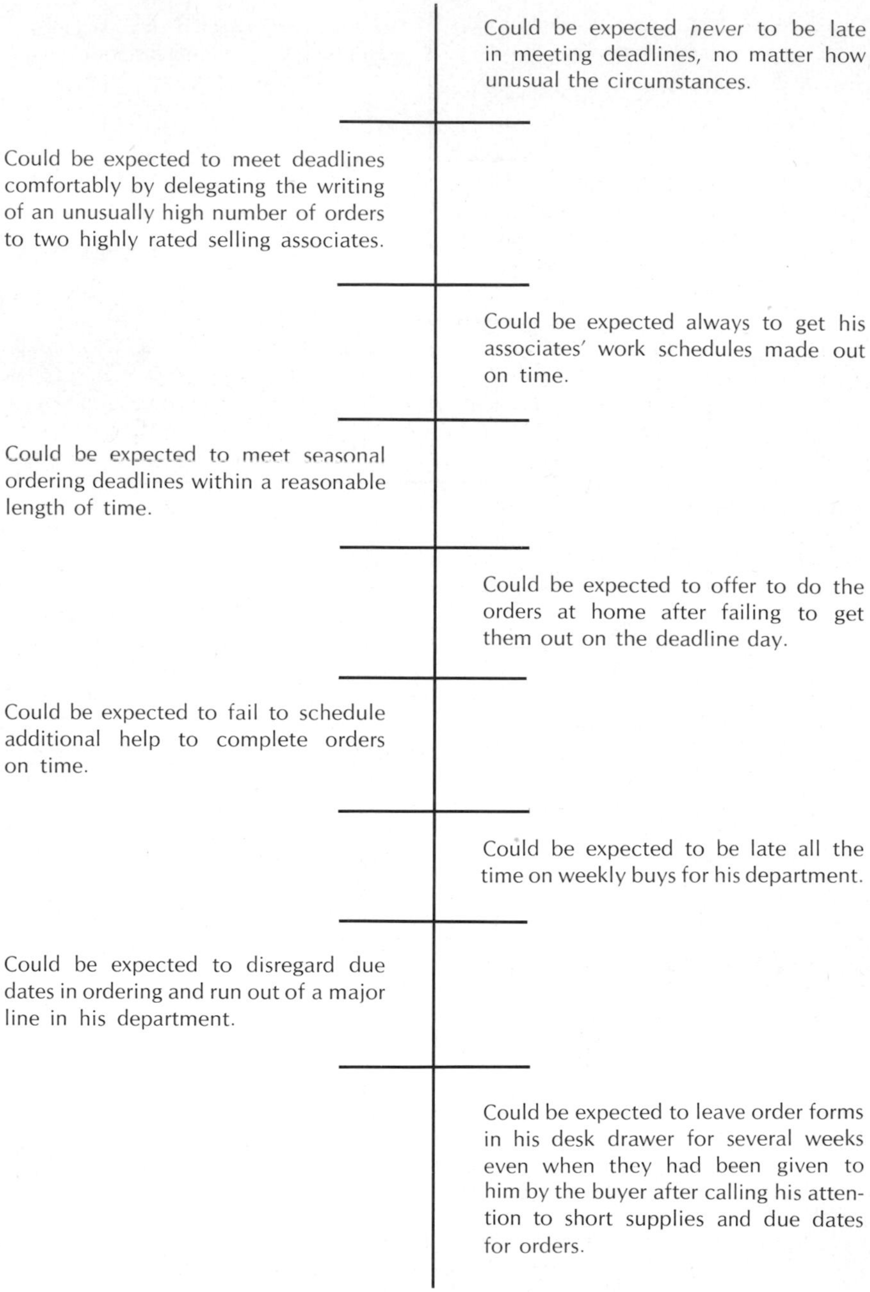

Could be expected *never* to be late in meeting deadlines, no matter how unusual the circumstances.

Could be expected to meet deadlines comfortably by delegating the writing of an unusually high number of orders to two highly rated selling associates.

Could be expected always to get his associates' work schedules made out on time.

Could be expected to meet seasonal ordering deadlines within a reasonable length of time.

Could be expected to offer to do the orders at home after failing to get them out on the deadline day.

Could be expected to fail to schedule additional help to complete orders on time.

Could be expected to be late all the time on weekly buys for his department.

Could be expected to disregard due dates in ordering and run out of a major line in his department.

Could be expected to leave order forms in his desk drawer for several weeks even when they had been given to him by the buyer after calling his attention to short supplies and due dates for orders.

Figure 5.2   Department manager job behavior rating scale for the dimension, "meeting day-to-day deadlines"

show how each of the scales is defined and anchored at various points by the behavioral incidents which had actually been derived from anecdotes about what department managers had done. Thus the scales are derived directly from the various facets involved in the department manager's efforts to allocate and utilize internal and external resources in an optimal way; and, most importantly, they are defined according to the language ("jargon") of the persons (store managers) who will be asked to use them in recording their observations of various department managers' patterns of job behavior.

The modified retranslation method has great promise for overcoming many of the problems and potential errors believed for so long to be inherent in systems of behavior observation and rating. The scales are rooted in, and referable to, actual observable behaviors; behavior observations have been derived from a series of discussions with observers similar to those who are expected to use the scales, and the qualities covered by the scales are rigorously defined and have been shown to be easily and accurately distinguished from one another by raters.

In a sense, the approach allows us to eat our cake and still have it. The job behavior domain is sampled exhaustively in the same way that is typically achieved by any other careful critical incidents analysis; however, the grouping of the incidents is not left up to the psychometrist. Instead, they are developed specifically to illustrate the broad behavior dimensions deemed to be most important for successfully optimizing resource allocation. Happily, the end result is a series of scales based on actual job performance incidents reflecting not a global or unidimensional assumption about job "success" but instead a recognition and use of the several different dimensions and behavior patterns which can lead to success in any given job. We believe this method is ideally suited for developing job observation scales to measure managerial effectiveness.

BEHAVIOR OBSERVATION SCALES IN USE

Job behavior observation scales like those shown in Figures 5.1 and 5.2 should form the basis for learning about both the antecedents and the effects of effective managing. Such scales incorporate all the important benchmarks of an effectiveness measure listed earlier in this chapter. For example, (1) they are derived from experienced observers' reports of actual behavior episodes regarded as illustrative of managerial actions instrumental to continued effective organizational functioning; (2) they sample behavior over the long term, as opposed to short-range judgments or impressions; (3) they specify with precision the myriad information processing activities making up the multiple facets of effective managerial behavior; (4) they imply many possible configurations or patterns of effective managerial resource optimization rather than just one presumed "best" *modus operandi;* (5) they force attention (observation and reporting) on what the manager himself does on the job, thereby guarding against defining his level of success in terms of other causal agents; and, finally, (6) they take account of a manager's membership (full or partial) in several organizational units and of his potential impact on their continued functioning.

It is important to note that these measures of managerial effectiveness serve then to *reveal* rather than to *cover up* the behavioral basis for any particular manager's relative level of success. Thus, they share the many potential advantages of global estimates such as rankings and promotion or salary histories, but they provide, in addition, a behavioral "diagnosis" of a manager's actions. As we note in Chapters 7 and 8, global estimates of managers' effectiveness have indeed proved useful as criteria in many large validation studies, but they provide little new knowledge for pinpointing the varieties of managerial job behaviors contributing to effectiveness. For example, as was noted in Chapter 3, it is common in industry today for personnel decisions about promotions, job transfers, discharges, salary actions, etc., to be influenced greatly by impressions of managers' relative contributions to certain desirable organizational outcomes rather than by carefully documented observations of their actual actions. A manager is bound to be judged by the profitability of his unit, even when it is widely known that many factors other than what he himself does can affect his profit picture. It seems that we are confronted with an interesting and rather surprising paradox: In industry today, job behavior is not typically observed and recorded with any degree of care or precision. Instead, decisions about people are often made on the basis of global impressions formed from job-irrelevant factors reflecting society's stereotypes of success rather than on the basis of factors judged to be directly relevant to realizing broad organizational goals and outcomes. Managerial job behavior is being measured less effectively than we know how in favor, unfortunately, of using measures that suffer from deficiency, excessiveness, or both.

We do not advocate dispensing with global estimates of managerial effectiveness, but their continued use should be supplemented with systematic behavior observation and reporting so that relationships between job behavior and the more common measures of executive success can be examined. Doing this should lead to the following desirable outcomes:

1 As systematic procedures for observing and recording job behavior become more widespread, managers will become more sophisticated in the complex art of making behavior-based rather than purely impressionistic judgments and decisions about others.

2 Managers should become aware of behavior patterns and behavior mechanisms leading to the traditional broad designations of "success" and "failure." Presum-

ably, such knowledge should lead eventually to more fully informed and wiser personnel decisions.

3 Programs related to identifying and developing effective managers will profit considerably from such knowledge. Empirical evidence of how organizational consequences and success patterns are moderated by specific managerial behaviors will contribute to wiser decisions about manager selection and training and organizational structuring because we shall have a more thorough understanding of the nature of linkages between predictors, managerial job behaviors, and organizational consequences.

4 Most important, the validation of predictors against measures of effective managing will be less dependent upon reflections of the status quo than they now are. Simon (1960) contends that the effective manager of the future will be less concerned with managing human relationships and resources and more concerned with making decisions based on rationally developed and objective patterns of information directed toward optimizing *all* available resource utilization. Ohmann (1958), W. Brown (1960), and Kelly (1964) also see these aspects of managing becoming more and more important for managing the firm of the future. Prediction studies based on behaviorally based observations and evaluations should assure greater flexibility in "keeping up" with the changing requirements of management than those global indicators which merely reflect the successful managerial policies and practices of the past.

SUMMARY

In order to predict, develop, or nurture effective managerial behavior, it is necessary that such behavior be defined and measured. We define a manager's effectiveness according to his impact on his organization's continued functioning through optimal acquisition and utilization of internal and external resources (human, financial, and material). Viewing the effective manager in this way—as an optimizer of present and potential resource allocation— yields important implications for measuring a manager's effectiveness. Most important, a measure of a manager's effectiveness should be based on what the manager himself does to affect the *conceptual criterion* of optimal resource allocation. Such a measure can be derived only rationally from experts' designations of the many job behaviors *(performance criteria)* seen as relevant to optimal resource allocation and utilization. In particular, such a measure should avoid both *deficiency* (including fewer than all relevant behaviors) and *excessiveness* (including behaviors or outcomes which either are not relevant to the conceptual criteria or go beyond what the manager himself may do to affect them).

Ideally, then, measures of managerial effectiveness should provide a means for observing accurately and recording systematically the full range of a manager's job behaviors and for evaluating how frequently he accomplishes agreed-upon objectives in the critical information processing and optimizing functions. Rating scales designed to describe aspects of job behavior have fallen into relative disuse in favor of global estimates (such as man-to-man rankings and promotion or salary indexes) of managers' so-called success histories. This is unfortunate because most global estimates, though related indirectly to several aspects of managerial behavior, undoubtedly suffer to unknown degrees from deficiency, excessiveness, or both. Moreover, such estimates tend to reflect society's common stereotypes of what may constitute success rather than affording a "diagnosis" of job-relevant behaviors that could be used to gain better understanding of the diverse parameters making up managerial effectiveness. It is highly desirable, therefore, that a better method for observing and recording managers' job behaviors be developed—one designed to overcome or avoid the plethora of potential sources of observational error (poor sampling of job behaviors, response set tendencies, vantage-point differences in behavior observations, changes in job requirements, etc.) from which nearly all traditional rating techniques suffer.

It is likely that most previous rating scales have been prone to such errors because they were not understood and accepted by the observers asked to complete them. This problem can be overcome, we believe, by involving the potential observers intimately at every stage during the development and definition of job behavior scales. Once such strategy—a modification of Smith and Kendall's (D. C. Smith & Kendall, 1963b) retranslation technique—was used to develop behavior observation scales for the job of department manager in a national chain of retail stores. The final scales comprised a series of nine behavior-based dimensions defined (in the language or jargon of potential observers) by actual managerial job behaviors believed by store managers to sample completely the diverse information processing and optimizing activities required in the job of department manager.

By giving increased attention to developing such systematic procedures for observing and measuring managerial job behavior and by using such measures to learn exactly how managers' job behaviors relate to other estimates such as overall rankings of success, promotion rates, productivity indexes, quality measures, and other gross performance or outcome measures, effective managing will be defined and understood more in terms of the managerial requirements of the firm of the future rather than in terms of current or status quo measures, as is the case now.

Chapter 6   **Possible Predictors of Managerial Effectiveness**

PURPOSE OF THIS CHAPTER

    Throughout, we have argued that effective managerial behavior develops out of complex interactions between managers' personal traits, demands placed upon them by different job situations and the educational feedback and reward systems developed by their organizations' policies and practices. Nonetheless, most research investigations seeking to predict managerial effectiveness have been one-sided, the bulk of them trying merely to correlate trait differences between managers with either their current or their later managerial job effectiveness. In this chapter, we describe the kinds of individual difference (trait) measures used in such studies and review the major trends of results obtained with them. Specific studies are not described in any great detail; instead, review articles summarizing the "records" achieved by various predictors are featured. Our primary intent is to examine briefly the many kinds of predictors available and to suggest which may be most promising for predicting managerial effectiveness.

TYPES OF MEASURES

Maximum performance measures. Cronbach (1960) classifies tests, according to their purpose, as measures of either *maximum performance* or *typical behavior*. The former term designates tests of cognitive and motor abilities, including those tests designed to determine how *much* or how *well* a person can perform. Such tests do have correct and incorrect answers in the sense that the magnitude of the total score implies greater or lesser ability. Examples of tests potentially useful for managers include measures of general intelligence, verbal ability, numerical ability, perceptual speed and accuracy, inductive reasoning, spatial relations ability, mechanical knowledge or comprehension, etc. Factor analysis has been used extensively—most notably by L. L. Thurstone and J. P. Guilford—in order to map taxonomies of human abilities measured by maximum performance tests. However, since factor analyses typically have paid little attention to relationships between test and nontest behaviors, the names or labels assigned to factorially derived measures are based on presumptions about the content of tests comprising a factor rather than on observed relationships with nontest behaviors. This may be a major reason why factored tests of aptitude rarely show any special advantage for predicting specific job behaviors. In fact, as McNemar (1964) has pointed out, general intelligence measures (combining measures of many different abilities) have usually been the more useful predictors of nontest behaviors such as scholastic success. This is particularly true in predicting managerial effectiveness.

Typical behavior measures. In contrast to maximum performance measures, typical behavior inventories have no specified correct or incorrect answers. Instead, an individual's answers are scored or "keyed" to yield descriptions of his major behavioral tendencies or predispositions—his so-called typical behavior—as he pursues his daily activities. Instead of just one scoring key, such inventories often have several—each representing a mode or pattern of observed behavior relevant for describing differences between people. Such a wide variety of typical behavior inventories is in common use that it is difficult to classify them accurately into more meaningful sub-areas. A coarse but useful differentiation is that between *personality* and *vocational interest* measures. Personality reflects the nature of a person's adjustment to the interpersonal and situational demands of his environment; personality measures seek to estimate a person's typical behavior pattern in adjusting to the interpersonal or social aspects of his work environment. In contrast, vocational interest measures are directed primarily toward estimating a person's orientation (likes and dislikes) toward different activities in the work environment. It is presumed that a person will move toward jobs involving desired activities and away from those involving disliked activities. The best-known and most carefully validated vocational interest measure is the Strong Vocational Interest Blank (SVIB).

Two other widely used interest measures are the Kuder Preference Record and the Minnesota Vocational Interest Inventory.

The "record" for maximum performance and typical behavior measures. A number of useful books and articles (Bass, 1967b; Ghiselli, 1966b; Guion & Gottier, 1966; Hedlund, 1965; Kinslinger, 1966; Korman, 1966; Nash, 1965, 1966) have been published recently showing the relative usefulness of maximum performance (cognitive) and typical behavior measures for either reflecting present managerial effectiveness or predicting future effectiveness.

Ghiselli's review (1966a) is the most comprehensive since it covers hundreds of studies (both published and unpublished) of test usefulness appearing between 1919 and 1964. The studies were conducted in a wide variety of settings, using many different tests and many different measures of job effectiveness. In order to summarize so many studies, Ghiselli classified tests into a few broad categories, and jobs into similarly broad groupings based on gross estimates of relative similarity in job demands. Tests were classified according to (1) intelligence, (2) spatial and mechanical aptitudes, (3) perceptual accuracy, (4) motor abilities, and (5) personality and interest. Ghiselli was also forced, because of the large number of studies reviewed, to lump together measures of occupational proficiency differing widely in how carefully they were developed. Finally, he averaged the validities of all these studies simply by converting r's to Fisher's z, averaging the z values, and converting them back to r's.

After all this lumping of tests, jobs, and job criteria of widely differing quality and the averaging of r's without regard to such things as restriction of range, concurrent versus predictive design, differing reliabilities of measures, and size of sampling errors, it is likely that the "summarized" outcome may be a serious underestimate of the actual magnitude of relationships between tested attributes and job proficiency. Even so, such a summary can provide crude guidelines for estimating which measures "look best" for predicting job effectiveness in different occupations. The data for managers (executives and administrators) and for front-line foremen are shown in Table 6.1.

It is apparent that proficiency in executive and managerial jobs has been most effectively indicated by tests of intellectual ability, perceptual accuracy, and personality or interest. Each measure shows average r's ranging around .25 to .30. This level of validity is, of course, low, but it must be judged in light of the severely attenuating influences mentioned above. Probably the *relative* magnitudes of coefficients in Table 6.1 is more important than their absolute values. We conclude from Ghiselli's coarse summary of all studies of executive effectiveness that measures of intelligence and of personality and interest may be "good bets" as potential predictors of managerial effectiveness.

In an additional overview of the antecedents of managerial effectiveness, Ghiselli (1963) reports higher and higher correlations between managers' meas-

Table 6.1 AVERAGE VALIDITY COEFFICIENTS OF VARIOUS TESTS FOR MEASURING JOB EFFECTIVENESS OF EXECUTIVES AND FIRST-LINE FOREMEN

	Executives	Foremen
Intellectual abilities:	.29 [d]	.24 [e]
Intelligence	.30 [d]	.25 [e]
Arithmetic	.26 [b]	.20 [d]
Spatial and mechanical abilities:	.18 [a]	.23 [a]
Spatial relations	.18 [a]	.24 [d]
Mechanical principles		.24 [e]
Perceptual accuracy:	.24 [b]	.14 [b]
Number comparison	.00 [a]	.20 [a]
Name comparison		.08 [a]
Cancellation	.32 [b]	
Motor abilities	*	*
Personality traits: †	.28 [d]	.15 [e]
Personality	.27 [d]	.15 [e]
Interest	.31 [d]	.15 [e]

* No studies of motor ability measures were available for executives or foremen.

† Results are included for only those personality or interest traits which seem pertinent to the job.

[a] Based on less than 100 total subjects.
[b] Based on between 100 and 499 subjects.
[c] Based on between 500 and 999 subjects.
[d] Based on between 1,000 and 4,999 subjects.
[e] Based on between 5,000 and 9,999 subjects.

Source: Ghiselli (1966a).

ured intelligence and global ratings of their effectiveness as the samples for study are chosen from progressively higher managerial levels. However, Korman (1968) disagrees with Ghiselli's conclusion. On the basis of his own review of studies designed to predict managerial performance, Korman (1968, p. 319) concludes the following:

1 Intelligence, as measured typically by verbal ability tests, is a fair predictor of 1st-line supervisory performance but not of higher-level managerial performance. Restriction of range is probably the explanation for this finding.
2 Objective personality inventories and "leadership ability" tests have generally not shown predictive validity, with the exception of the projective measure of managerial motivation developed by Miner.
3 Personal history data as predictors are fair for 1st-line supervisors, but less so for the higher-level individual.
4 "Judgmental" prediction methods, as exemplified particularly by executive assessment procedures and peer ratings, are generally better predictors than psychometric procedures, although allowance must be made for the generally small samples involved.

5   Little has been learned from selection research which can contribute to a theory of leadership behavior.

6   Changes in the orientation of predictive research are needed.

Guion and Gottier (1966), Nash (1965), and Hedlund (1965) have reviewed results obtained with personality and interest measures in measuring managerial effectiveness. Guion and Gottier covered studies appearing during the decade 1952-1962 in the *Journal of Applied Psychology* and *Personnel Psychology*. Although they included studies for all occupations, a review of their summary tables shows that studies on foremen and managers have yielded few validities of any practical magnitude for predicting managerial effectiveness. In over half the studies, the validities failed to reach statistical significance. Guion and Gottier conclude that personality and interest measures have not proved themselves as predictors of managerial effectiveness—a conclusion very different from the more promising expectations suggested by Ghiselli's summary data. Guion and Gottier do, however, find strong evidence that specially made keys validated for specific situations and for specific predictive purposes are of much greater usefulness than standardized scoring keys currently available. They state: "A homemade personality or interest measure, carefully and competently developed for a specific situation, is a better bet for prediction than is a standard personality measure with a standard system of scoring" (p. 159). It is possible that Ghiselli's more favorable conclusion stems from including specially made "homemade" measures along with the standardized keys in the studies he has summarized.

Guion and Gottier (1966, p. 160) conclude their review on the following pessimistic note:

> It is difficult in the face of this summary to advocate . . . the use of personality measures in most situations as a basis for making employment decisions. It seems clear that the only acceptable reason for using personality measures as instruments of decision is found only after doing considerable research with the measure in the specific situation and for the specific purpose for which it is to be used.

Hedlund (1965), after reviewing the use of the Minnesota Multiphasic Personality Inventory (MMPI) in industry, concludes on a similar pessimistic note. He was able to find practically no evidence to support the use of the MMPI in industry; validity studies are rare, and where they have been done, they are disillusioning.

Nash (1965) is less pessimistic about the usefulness of vocational interest measures for predicting managerial effectiveness. He finds a "thread of consistent evidence" supporting the idea that more effective managers have patterns of vocational interest distinguishing them from less effective managers. He notes, however, that correlations between existing interest scales

Table 6.2 **TEST-RETEST CORRELATIONS FOR VARIOUS GROUPS OF SUBJECTS TESTED AND RETESTED OVER 10 DIFFERENT TIME INTERVALS**

Number of subjects	Time interval	Test-Retest correlation
140	2 weeks	.84
102	30 days	.85
253	1 year	.66
160	8 years	.44
175	9 years	.48
137	10 years	.70
165	17 years	.52
178	18 years	.47
202	19 years	.52
191	22 years	.53

Source: Johnson & Dunnette (1968).

and effective management have rarely been high and concludes with Guion and Gottier that tailor-made scales developed for specific measurement situations have usually been better. Nash does, however, suggest that four identifiable interest components seem, on the basis of his review, to be related to managerial effectiveness: (1) social service, humanitarian, and people-oriented likes; (2) persuasive, verbal, and literary interests; (3) a rejection (or dislike) of exclusively scientific, technical, or skilled trades pursuits; and (4) business contact and business detail activities. In his own dissertation research, Nash (1966) successfully developed and cross-validated ($r = .33$) a special scoring key on the SVIB for identifying the more effective managers out of a group of 159 executives in 13 different companies.[1] According to items differentiating between the more and the less effective, the more effective manager prefers activities which involve independent, intense thought and some risk and which do not demand much regimentation. He dislikes technical and agricultural activities and prefers not to spend lengthy periods concentrating on close or detailed tasks. He enjoys being with other people, especially in relationships where he is dominant to them; thus, he is not solely service-oriented. He prefers physical and social recreations, as opposed to aesthetic or cultural forms of entertainment.

Johnson and Dunnette (1968) examined validity and long-term test-retest stability of the Nash scoring key for the 46 items common to both the 1937 and 1966 (D. P. Campbell, 1966) editions of the SVIB. Validity of the key was nearly the same ($r = .30$) as Nash obtained. More important, its stability was high for even lengthy periods of time (up to twenty-two years) separating the two testings. This is shown in Table 6.2. The results led Johnson and Dunnette (1968, p. 292) to conclude:

[1] This research project is described more fully in Chap. 8.

These data provide further support for arguing that potentially effective managers may be identified by a specific pattern of likes and dislikes. This pattern shows a high degree of long term stability suggesting that it appears fairly early in life and that it is invariant under changes in the social, economic, and business milieus of our society.

Long-term stability seems to be the rule for scales on the SVIB. Johansson (1966) studied the relative stability of SVIB scores for all groups in computer storage at the Center for Interest Measurement Research (D. P. Campbell, 1964) who had taken the SVIB two or more times. Table 6.3 shows median test-retest correlations classified according to age of subjects at first testing and length of interval between testings. Clearly, patterns of vocationally related likes and dislikes are stable over long time periods even when subjects' initial testing is done before they have launched their occupational careers (i.e., at age seventeen or eighteen). This relatively high stability is impressive and suggests that empirically developed scoring keys (such as Nash's) based on vocational motivations or preferences should continue to be tried as potential predictors of managerial effectiveness — particularly as they may be used in concert with other typical behavior inventories and/or with maximum performance measures.

Table 6.3 MEDIAN TEST-RETEST CORRELATIONS FOR SCALE SCORES ON THE SVIB ACCORDING TO AGE OF FIRST TESTING AND LENGTH OF INTERVAL BETWEEN TEST AND RETEST

| Age of subjects when first tested | 1 year or less | Time interval between test and retest | | | Over 20 years |
		2 - 5 years	6 - 10 years	11 - 20 years	
17 - 18	.80	.70	.65	.64	
19 - 21	.91	.73	.67	.67	.64
22 - 25		.78	.69	.75	.72
26 and older		.77	.81	.80	

Source: Johansson (1966).

Overall, then, these reviews suggest that standardized personality measures have a rather poor record for measuring or predicting managerial effectiveness. It is best to develop special scoring keys based on measures of effectiveness in particular organizational situations and organizational settings. Interest measures have fared considerably better. As Nash suggests, certain orientations such as persuasion, verbal interest, and interpersonal contact seem more often than not to be common to more effective managers, but the nature of these preference patterns is not well defined, and they need to be explicated more thoroughly.

Projective techniques. According to Gleser (1963, p. 391), projective techniques are

> . . . those techniques which encourage a wide variety of complex responses, presumably determined primarily by the private feelings and attitudes of the subject, and hence revealing something of his underlying psychodynamics. The term is applied to a wide range of techniques, differing as to type of stimulus presented, method of administration, degree of structuring of the task, and nature of response.

The usual rationale for using projective techniques in addition to, or instead of, more structured or objective approaches is that a person's responses to the ambiguous stimuli (such as ink blots) common to them will reveal more fully his underlying personality dynamics, thereby providing an experienced interpreter with much richer content for deriving behavioral inferences.

The most familiar projective techniques probably include the Rorschach test (Rorschach, 1942) and its many offshoots, such as the Structured Objective Rorschach (Stone, 1958) or the Multiple Choice Rorschach (Harrower, 1959); the Thematic Apperception Test (Murray, 1943; Murray, MacKinnon, Miller, Fiske, & Hanfmann, 1948); handwriting analyses of various types (e.g., graphology and graphoanalysis); and many versions of the sentence completion format (Miner, 1968a, 1968b; E. Taylor & Nevis, 1957). Of these, handwriting analysis—though used more frequently in industry than one might expect—is not generally held in good repute, but the others have been used and researched rather widely in industry; most of the studies undertaken since 1940 have been reviewed by Kinslinger (1966). Only 11 studies included managers or supervisors. Of these, 9 yielded results showing that various indicators or "signs" derived from projectives did distinguish between "more successful" and "less successful" managers. However, only 1 of the 11 studies used a cross-validation design; and in that single study, Kurtz (1948) found that Rorschach signs which appeared useful for the validation group of 80 sales managers were completely unrelated to success or failure among the 41 sales managers in a cross-validation group. Kinslinger (1966, p. 134) concludes that the need exists "for thorough job specifications in terms of personality traits and extensive use of cross-validation studies before any practical use can be made of projective techniques in personnel psychology."

Unfortunately, at the time of his review, Kinslinger did not have access to results of a large-scale study undertaken and reported recently by Grant, Katkovsky, and Bray (1967). The American Telephone and Telegraph Company instituted the Bell System Management Progress Study, a longitudinal investigation of the development of young men in a business management environment, in 1957.[2] The raw material for the study consisted of an extensive amount of psychological and behavioral information gathered during a 3½-day assessment of young Bell System employees shortly after beginning their careers with the company. Included among the many assessment procedures (tests of all types, interviews, management simulations, group discussion, etc.) administered to the men were three projective techniques—two sentence completion blanks and six cards from the Thematic Apperception test. Each man's responses to the three projectives were evaluated by a clinical psychologist who wrote a short report giving a general description of his personality with emphasis on characteristics (e.g., feelings about job and career, family, and self) most likely to influence his management career. This projective test report, together with reports written by other staff members based on the various other assessment techniques, was read to the nine assessors making up the staff. They then integrated all impressions and information from the various reports into their ratings of each man's status on the Management Progress Study variables (ability to delay gratification, tolerance of ambiguity, etc.). In order to study the projective protocols statistically, two psychologists, who had not been involved in the assessment, used a manual to code each of the 355 reports on the following nine variables:

Achievement motivation
How ambitious, motivated, and interested in advancement and success is he?

Self-confidence
How confident is he that he will succeed in his work? To what extent does he exhibit self-doubts and anxieties concerning success?

Work or career orientation
How important is work in this man's life compared with other things, such as family and recreation? How much satisfaction does he get from his job compared with other things in life?

Dependence
To what extent is he described as needing or seeking help, advice, direction, and encouragement from others?

Affiliation
How interested is he in being liked and accepted by others, being a part of groups, helping others, and avoiding arguments and friction with others? To what extent does he participate in group situations, and how outgoing is he?

Optimism-pessimism
How optimistic or pessimistic is he about life in general? How positively or negatively does he react to most of his experiences? How satisfied or dissatisfied is he in general?

Willingness to assume a leadership role
How readily will he make decisions and accept leadership or supervisory responsibility? How strong are his dominance or leadership needs?

---

[2] A detailed description of the Management Progress Study and many of the major results obtained from it are presented in Chap. 9. The reader may also wish to refer to reports of the study by Bray (1964) and Bray and Grant (1966).

Willingness to accept a subordinate role

How willing is he to act as a follower or subordinate in his relationships with others? How suggestible and submissive is he?

General adjustment

To what extent does he indicate good adjustment (high self-confidence, ability to adapt to difficult situations and accept frustrations) or poor adjustment (low self-confidence, insecurity, stress or anxiety reactions, emotional conflict, and problems)?

By correlating these ratings with the assessment staff's overall prediction of each man's ultimate potential, it was possible to estimate the relative influence of the projective reports on staff judgments. It was also possible to correlate these ratings with an index reflecting the differential rates of salary progress shown by assessees during the seven to nine years after assessment. Correlations against these two criteria are shown separately for college and non-college men in Table 6.4. Although the magnitudes of the correlations are not overwhelming, it is noteworthy that the projective-based variables correlating highest with staff predictions also correlate best with management progress as reflected in salary advancement. Moreover, it is apparent that "motivational" variables such as achievement and willingness to accept the leadership role are relatively more important to progress than more "adjustment-oriented" variables. Most important, these results suggest that projective techniques can perhaps yield useful predictions when an effort is made to interpret responses to them according to motivations relevant to business management.

Table 6.4 CORRELATIONS BETWEEN RATINGS DERIVED FROM PROJECTIVE REPORTS AND STAFF PREDICTIONS AND SALARY PROGRESS FOR COLLEGE AND NON-COLLEGE MEN

Projective report rating variable	Men with college degrees		Men without college degrees	
	Staff prediction ($N = 207$)	Salary index* ($N = 81$)	Staff prediction ($N = 148$)	Salary index* ($N = 120$)
Achievement motivation	.30	.26	.40	.30
Self-confidence	.24	.11	.29	.21
Work or career orientation	.21	.16	.22	.17
Dependence	−.30	−.35	−.30	−.20
Affiliation	−.07	−.06	−.15	−.07
Optimism-pessimism	.11	−.01	.13	.17
Leadership role	.35	.24	.38	.19
Subordinate role	−.25	−.25	−.29	−.23
General adjustment	.19	.10	.17	.19

*For a variety of reasons, information was not available for many individuals who had gone through assessment years earlier.

Source: Grant, Katkovsky & Bray (1967).

Consideration and initiating structure. Perhaps one reason why most personality measures have shown such poor records is that many of the "typical behaviors" measured by existing scales are not closely relevant to patterns of job behavior necessary in managing. If this is the case, we should expect higher validities with measures more closely relevant to actual managerial requirements. Perhaps the two major managerial tendencies of consideration and initiating structure, if measured, should yield higher validities. Scales designed to measure these managerial tendencies have been developed and used in many investigations, which have been reviewed by Korman (1966). His review includes studies of the Leadership Opinion Questionnaire (LOQ) and the Leader Behavior Description Questionnaire (LBDQ). The former is filled in by a manager and presumably shows, via his own attitudes and opinions, his preference for utilizing consideration, intiating structure, or both in his own "leadership style." The latter questionnaire is similar in content but is designed to be completed by subordinates or by other observers of a manager's behavior to describe his leadership style. Studies of the LOQ are most relevant to our present discussion, but before presenting Korman's review of these studies, we should summarize the definitions given by Fleishman and Peters (1962) of initiating structure and consideration.

Initiating structure involves a manager's acts oriented toward defining or structuring his and his work group's set toward getting work done and toward goal attainment; high scores on initiating structure denote attitudes and opinions indicating highly active direction of group activities, group planning, communicating information, scheduling, trying out new ideas, etc.

Consideration involves managerial acts oriented toward developing mutual trust, which reflect respect for subordinates' ideas and consideration of their feelings; high scores on consideration denote attitudes and opinions indicating good rapport and good two-way communication, whereas low scores indicate a more impersonal approach to interpersonal relations with group members.

The array of evidence reviewed by Korman leaves little room for optimism about the predictive usefulness of the LOQ. The median value of 30 validity coefficients in 7 different studies is $-.02$.[3] The range of coefficients is between $-.19$ and $.51$. Only three studies show r's of any substantial size. Parker

[3]Korman also reviewed studies using the LBDQ. These yielded generally higher coefficients. Thus, descriptions by others of a manager's behavior seem potentially more accurate as predictors of overall effectiveness. Korman points out, however, that all these studies were of concurrent rather than predictive relationships; therefore, it is difficult to know whether the patterns of consideration or structuring are the cause or the effect of managerial effectiveness. A supervisor may well be more "considerate" of a highly effective subordinate than he would be of one who is not effective. No careful experimental studies are available of the mechanism by which consideration or structure may appear as a dominant "style" in a manager's job behavior.

(1963) obtained values of .45 and .51 between consideration and subordinates' ratings of their supervisors; Oaklander and Fleishman (1964) obtained correlations of .37 and .46 between supervisors' consideration scores and their own ratings of the degree of stress present between units in a large hospital; and Bass obtained correlations of .29 and .32 between supervisors' consideration scores and later ratings by their superiors of their overall effectiveness.

USEFULNESS OF TYPICAL BEHAVIOR INVENTORIES

Although typical behavior tests are widely used as aids in making personnel decisions about managers, evidence regarding their accuracy for predicting managerial effectiveness is far from impressive. The poor results obtained so far have a number of causes, but some of the major problems include the following:

1 Only a few of the published typical behavior inventories have been developed empirically. Armchair methods, behavior "theories," and factor analysis have been the bases for most typical behavior measures now in use (the Bernreuter Personality Inventory, the Edwards Personal Preference Schedule, etc.). Since the development of such scales was not behaviorally based, initially, the odds are against their being related to important aspects of managerial job behavior. Even in the case of measures that were developed empirically (such as the SVIB or the MMPI), the behavioral bases for validating them and establishing scoring keys are usually a far cry from the kinds of job behaviors most crucial for defining managerial effectiveness. Thus, scales developed against behaviors such as occupational choice (SVIB) or psychological aberration (MMPI) can hardly be expected to predict managerial behaviors such as effective planning or delegation.

2 Guion and Gottier, as well as Nash, emphasize strongly—and we wholeheartedly concur—that job behavior, particularly at the managerial level, has been inadequately studied in nearly all the investigations cited. Most often, researchers have merely used global ratings or crude objective measures to identify "successful" and "unsuccessful" managers, thereby failing to pinpoint the actual job behaviors contributing to so-called success or failure. Existing scales of typical behavior inventories can be expected to fail to differentiate such global designations because the designations are not behaviorally based and may often not even be behaviorally relevant.

3 Typical behavior tests, as opposed to maximum performance tests, can often be slanted or distorted by an examinee. Thus, a managerial applicant or a manager already on a job would usually have a fairly definite impression (though possibly erroneous) of the typical behavioral characteristics making up the usual stereotype of success in industry. Assuming that such an examinee is eager to paint a good picture of himself, he may try to convince the examiner, through his replies on the test, that his own typical behavior is consonant with what he perceives

to be the desired behavior patterns important on the job. (This is probably the major reason why results with the LBDQ have generally been more promising than those with the LOQ.)

There are no easy or sure answers to this problem. Many studies have shown that typical behavior inventories can be successfully and rather easily slanted when examinees are directed to do so. Probably the best solution, but one which has not been widely employed, would be to base validation studies directly on populations of entering managerial candidates, thereby validating items and scoring systems in the setting most similar to that in which such measures will eventually be used.

What we have said so far should be sufficient to indicate the general nature of possible problems associated with the use of typical behavior measures. Since these measures involve behaviors, however, that are of great potential importance at the managerial level, they should definitely not be discarded permanently from consideration. Instead, the special problems involved in their use should be recognized, and particular pains taken to overcome them. We have already suggested in Chapters 4 and 5 what we believe to be some of the most effective techniques for overcoming such problems through better job definition and more behaviorally based measures of job effectiveness.

SITUATIONAL MEASURES AND TASK SIMULATIONS

However, even the most carefully done study designed to validate typical behavior inventory responses empirically against behavior-based measures of managerial effectiveness may still yield unimpressive results. Paper-and-pencil tests requiring no more than self-descriptions of one's own traits or behavior tendencies may offer far too limited a range of stimuli for sampling adequately the full breadth of managerial job behaviors. Managerial effectiveness is more likely than effectiveness in most other jobs to be strongly affected by situational variables. As a consequence, a test should do better in predicting managerial performance if situational elements can be introduced into it.

Throughout, we have emphasized the importance of situational effects on managerial behavior. Managerial behavior, more than most other behaviors, is likely to be strongly affected by situational, as opposed to strictly individual difference, variables. Thus, test or inventory performance might more usefully forecast managerial effectiveness if it also includes situational elements. Paper-and-pencil measures of typical behavior discussed so far do not take account of, or incorporate into their interpretation, any means of estimating the effects of situational elements on the behavior dispositions being measured. Some might argue that vocational interest measures get at situational elements *indirectly* by asking the examinee to portray his patterns of likes and dislikes (i.e., his reactions to situational elements in previous jobs have produced preference patterns predictive of future preferences for particular types of job situations). Personality and other typical behavior measures can also be viewed as assessing situational variables indirectly through inquiries about an examinee's responses to particular situations, persons, and circumstances. However, these inventories do not actually present the examinee *directly* with stimuli related to specific situational variables during the actual examining procedure.

It has been in response to these needs and in response to the argument that prediction of managerial effectiveness demands more direct measures of situational variables that situational and simulated task measures have been developed. Two of the more widely used measures include the Leaderless Group Discussion and the In-basket technique.

Leaderless group discussion. According to Bass (1954), the Leaderless Group Discussion consists basically in simply asking a group of examinees to carry on a discussion about some topic for a period of time. No one is appointed leader. The examiners do not participate in the discussion, but remain free to observe and to rate the performance of each examinee. It is apparent that the Leaderless Group Discussion method provides a relatively unstructured but directed opportunity for examinees to demonstrate a variety of typical behaviors in interaction with other persons. Observers of such discussions and of such interactions may infer a number of characteristics about the examinees and make predictions concerning expected behavior in future situations involving personal interaction. Bass (1954) reports that the method typically yields high interrater agreement among observers and high test-retest reliabilities, especially when descriptive behavior checklists have been provided for the observers' use in recording their observations. An examinee taking part in a leaderless group discussion is given an opportunity to demonstrate a number of behaviors potentially important to effective management, such as ability to communicate effectively, to overcome group or individual inertia, to solve various interaction problems, to meet deadlines, and to drive for group consensus. It is obvious, then, that the prime advantage of the technique over the usual paper-and-pencil test is the opportunity it affords for observing directly a rich array of leading or structuring behaviors. This advantage is important, and observers will make best use of it by recording and evaluating only the immediate behavior they observe and avoiding the temptation to infer broader personality attributes. Undoubtedly, the Leaderless Group Discussion method has good potential for measuring more explicitly than most paper-and-pencil inventories some of the variables important to effective managerial behavior.

In-basket technique. As its name implies, the In-basket is a simulated managerial exercise structured around the in-basket, the familiar receptacle used in any business setting for collecting incoming mail, memorandums, reports, and other documents. The usual approach is to instruct an examinee that he is to play the role of a manager who has just been told to take over a higher level job after the sudden death of the incumbent. He is told that he has a limited amount of time (about two or three hours) to handle the materials that have accumulated in the in-basket of his predecessor. Hopefully, the examinee will approach the task in the way that he would usually undertake his own managerial responsibilities. Through judicious selection of materials to be incorporated into the in-basket, a rich variety of behavior samples may be elicited. In-baskets have been designed by many different organization and used for a variety of purposes. (The reader should refer to the monograph by Lopez, 1966, for an account of the history and current status of the In-basket procedure.)

In-baskets have played important roles in many managerial training programs. Here, it is used as a simulated exercise, and managers' approaches to dealing with the materials become the basis for discussion of "appropriate" ways of handling such problems. In-basket procedures have also been widely used in assessment programs (e.g., the Bell System Management Progress Study), and it is this use that has greatest relevance for predicting managerial effectiveness. An examinee's responses and actions taken in dealing with his In-basket materials may be scored along many dimensions. Usually the dimensions will be chosen to reflect the kinds of typical behaviors shown to be important in effective management. One such set of dimensions reported by Lopez is given below:

1 Exchanging information
2 Discussing decision with others before deciding
3 Complying with suggestions made by others
4 Analyzing the situation
5 Maintaining organizational relationships
6 Organizing work
7 Responding to outsiders
8 Directing the work of others

Another scoring system derived by investigators studying patterns of behavior in one of the early In-baskets is shown below:

1 Activity level
2 Type of analysis
3 Unwarranted assumptions
4 Decisiveness of judgment
5 Decisiveness of action
6 Planned work distribution
7 Planned work organization
8 Communication with peers and superiors
9 Communication with subordinates
10 Delegation
11 Consideration of others

Frederiksen (1962) administered an In-basket (Bureau of Business In-basket—Frederiksen, Saunders, & Wand, 1957) to 567 subjects ranging from undergraduate students ($N = 25$) to business executives ($N = 75$), Army officers ($N = 45$), and school principals ($N = 232$). Responses were scored on 59 dimensions, and all possible intercorrelations were computed among the 40 showing the highest reliabilities. Factor analysis of the matrix and rotation to an oblique factor solution yielded the following eight factors:

Factor A:	Acting in compliance with suggestions
Factor B:	Preparing for action by becoming informed
Factor C:	Concern with public relations
Factor D:	Procrastinating
Factor E:	Concern with superiors
Factor F:	Informality
Factor G:	Directing subordinates
Factor H:	Discussing

The crucial question concerning simulated procedures of this kind is whether or not behavior during the simulation reflects similar behavioral patterns in actual work situations. Certainly, simulated procedures offer a rich situational background for a manager to demonstrate his reactions and approaches to a variety of problems, situations, and people. They provide more "real" measures of what a manager might run into on the job than paper-and-pencil inventories. Instead of measuring traits or getting at behavior tendencies indirectly, simulated procedures allow *direct* observation of a man's behavior in approaching what appears to be a highly job-relevant but still fairly well-structured and standardized stimulus configuration. Thus the method merits careful study as a predictor of managerial effectiveness. It *has* been widely studied, and results of some of the investigations are given in Chapter 9.

BIOGRAPHICAL INFORMATION AND PERSONAL INTERVIEWS

One of the most promising leads for developing typical behavior inventories is the simple fact that one of the best predictors of future behavior is past behavior. Patterns of typical behavior in the past should be useful for predicting typical job behaviors to be expected in the future. Nearly all programs of personnel selection seek to tap elements of past behavior by using procedures such as personal interviews, reference checking, analyzing application blanks and personal data sheets, reviewing scholastic records, and the like. Unfortunately, it is difficult to know exactly how past behaviors relate to specific future behaviors that may be of interest. The methods just mentioned are poorly standardized, and the type and extent of information obtained may differ greatly from candidate to candidate; predictions must be based on varying knowledge, with the usual result that they can be little more than vague impressions, subjective hunches, and intuitive feelings.

Personal interview. The most commonly used method in selection, the personal interview, is notoriously bad in this regard. It is handled differently by each interviewer, who, in turn, probably uses different methods with each new applicant. At its worst, the personal interview may bog down into merely "passing the time of day," with little time devoted to learning about an applicant's typical behavior patterns from the past. Under the best conditions, a highly skilled interviewer may be able to gather a wide range of fairly accurate information about the past, but even then it is difficult to interpret the meaning of these data as they relate to predicting future behaviors; and, again, reliance must be placed on intuitive hunches and guesses. Some interviewers' hunches turn out to be much better than others'. It is difficult to know ahead of time who the better and more accurate interviewers may be.

In spite of all this, no one would suggest dispensing with the interview as a means of sizing up and predicting the potential effectiveness of managers; it is the only way of seeing what the candidate looks like, of getting an impression of how he might "click" with others, and of becoming acquainted with him as a person. In fact, the personal interview is undoubtedly the most widely used personnel method for predicting managerial effectiveness. Since it is, and since it is usually handled badly, the time is ripe for undertaking careful research on the processes of interpersonal perception, impression formation, and behavior prediction resulting from personal interviews.

Webster (1964) has provided a good start through his direction of a number of doctoral dissertations on the personnel interview. His and his students' research has so far been focused on how the interviewers form impressions of their interviewees. Their findings suggest that each interviewer brings his own special frame of reference or "personal construct" to the interview setting and that this colors the way he perceives others.[4] Each interviewer also possesses a stereotype of what he expects in the ideal job candidate, depending upon his own characteristics and on what he perceives to be the demands of the managerial job to be filled. Once the interview is underway, the interviewer forms a quick first impression (within the first four or five minutes) of the interviewee. If the interview is very unstructured, many interviewers will then tend to gather subsequent information selectively in order to confirm the first impression. Even if the interview is standardized (i.e., even if information about the interviewee is gathered according to a prearranged structure or plan), an interviewer's handling of information depends on his own characteristics; he

[4] Incidentally, such personal constructs are also major factors leading to some of the errors in job behavior observation discussed previously. Very carefully developed standardized procedures for observing interpersonal behavior are necessary in both interviewing and job settings in order to reduce the frequency and magnitude of such errors.

may assimilate all of it and come to an integrated decision, or, finding discordant information hard to handle, he may depend most heavily on just the most recently received knowledge (such as Whitlock, 1963, showed in his research on job performance evaluation). It is likely that unfavorable information will carry more weight than favorable information. Webster's research along with the reviews of personnel interviewing by R. Wagner (1949), Mayfield (1964), and Ulrich and Trumbo (1965) shows that different interviewers tend more often than not to disagree in their impressions and that interviewer predictions of interviewees' later job behavior patterns usually have negligible validity.

On the other hand, impressive evidence that the personal interview *can* occasionally have good predictive validity is shown in Ghiselli's (1966b) results based on a follow-up of stockbrokers (account executives) whom he had interviewed as applicants before they were employed by a large investment firm. Over a span of seventeen years (from 1945 to 1962), Ghiselli interviewed 507 men. His interviews were disarmingly simple, dealing briefly with *what* the applicant had done (educationally and occupationally), *why* he had done it, *how well* he had done it, and why he wanted to be a stockbroker (what he knew about the job and what he thought he would get out of it). At the end of the interview, a single rating of potential for success was made on a five-point scale. Only 275 (54 percent) of the 507 were actually hired, but for them, the interview rating correlated .35 with success defined as "surviving" in the job for three years or more. Had all the men interviewed been hired, thereby retaining a broader range of potential effectiveness, the correlation against the success measure would have been .51.[5] Ghiselli's demonstration of moderate validity for a personal interview is an excellent illustration of using knowledge about previous behavior to predict future behavior. It should be noted, however, that he carefully avoided inferences about personality dynamics or complicated behavioral predispositions. He merely used the interview as a medium for gathering evidence about each man's previous achievement history; the only inferential "luxury" he allowed himself was based on his estimate of what each man knew of the job he was trying to get, namely, that a man who knew accurately "what he was getting into" had a higher likelihood of success than a man who did not.

Until more solid evidence becomes available defining the optimal strategies for forming accurate impressions and making behavior predictions on the basis of personal interviews, we will be well-advised to follow Ghiselli's strategy of keeping things simple, staying close to the data, and avoiding convoluted behavioral inferences. Research on this most often used personnel

[5] The value .51 was obtained by correcting the coefficient of .35 for restriction in range; the standard deviation of ratings for all 507 applicants interviewed was 1.25; it was only .77 for the 275 actually employed.

procedure must, of course, be continued in order to discover interviewing principles and approaches most likely to yield reliable judgments and increasingly valid job behavior predictions. Large-scale research programs and data analyses are now under way at the Life Insurance Agency Management Association (Mayfield & Carlson, 1966), at Minnesota and Ohio State Universities (Dunnette & Hakel, 1965), and as part of the Bell System Management Progress Study (Rychlak & Bray, 1967).

Biographical information. In the meantime, until more research on interviewing is forthcoming, another way to capitalize on past behavior for predicting future behavior is to use empirical procedures to develop scoring weights for the items of a standardized biographical inventory. In effect, elements of persons' past behaviors—marital histories, jobs held, activities in high school and college, educational levels, hobbies, past successes and failures, etc.—are treated as separate items to be compared against defined job behavior categories. In this way, items of a biographical inventory may be scored to yield predictions of typical behavior in the future. The resulting typical behavior inventory does not suffer from many of the usual difficulties encountered in personality and interest tests. For example, (1) the inventory is empirically developed; (2) it is linked directly to job behavior, thereby forcing a more careful study of job behavior than has been done for most typical behavior inventories; and (3) it is less likely to be "faked" because it includes information of actual past behavior which can, if necessary, be checked by independent means. In fact, Mosel and Cozan (1952) and Keating, Paterson, and Stone (1950) showed that biographical information supplied by applicants correlated very highly (all r's in the .90s) with information obtained from other records (such as those of previous employers).

In their recent evaluation of the usefulness of biographical information for predicting job behavior, Owens and Henry (1966) cite a number of other advantages for its use, including:

1 The method is merely an extension of the typical application blank and is likely to be more acceptable than many tests.
2 Results showing which items significantly predict job behavior can aid greatly in understanding the important antecedents of managerial effectiveness (this will be seen more clearly in our discussion of research results in Chapter 8).
3 Empirical validation of biographical items against actual managerial behavior assures that only job-relevant questions will be asked of a job candidate, thereby guarding against charges of willful discrimination against minority groups or "invasion of privacy" by tests designed to "explore the psyche."

Since biographical inventories first came into wide use about thirty years ago, they have been used in a large variety of studies and in many selection programs. Very often, a carefully developed typical behavior inventory based on biographical information has proved to be the single best predictor of future job behavior. Thus biographical information constitutes one of the most fruitful sources of information to be considered along with measures of cognitive abilities, personality and interest measures, and situational procedures for predicting managerial effectiveness. As we shall see in Chapter 8, biographical information has proved particularly useful for assessing managerial effectiveness and for discovering some of its important correlates.

SUMMARY

A manager's job effectiveness is determined not only by his personal attributes but also by the special characteristics of his job and his situation and by his organization's motivational policies and practices. Convincing evidence of the limited and partial role played by the manager's personal attributes has been presented in this chapter. Rarely have correlations between individual difference measures and managerial effectiveness exceeded .40. By and large, existing scales on typical behavior inventories yield little when they have been evaluated by calculating correlations between scale scores and effectiveness estimates. Special scoring keys, tailor-made from existing inventories or from biographical information to fit a particular company or job situation, have shown better results. Other techniques (situational procedures) designed to bring elements of the managerial job more realistically into the assessment procedure have been developed, but they have been used so far in only a limited number of companies and subjected to systematic study in still fewer companies. One extremely important finding does emerge from the results reviewed here. Best results have been obtained either with those instruments and procedures which have relieved the investigator completely of the task of drawing behavioral inferences (as with tailor-made scoring keys) or where the investigator has himself steered clear of making inferences about complicated personality dynamics in favor of seeking to observe or describe only those behaviors judged to be directly relevant to the job of managing. This common thread of evidence connects the better results obtained with such diverse instruments as the Leaderless Group Discussion, projectives, and the personnel interview.

The poor results obtained in many of the studies reviewed in this chapter could also be due in part to methodological inadequacies in the way predictor measures have been combined to form predictions of managerial behavior. Since our purpose in this chapter has been primarily to present a kind of catalog or "montage" of possible predictors, we have given no attention to such methodological questions, nor have we described the major programs of research already completed or under way in some of the major research locations.

In Chapter 7, we consider the relative merits of mechanical and clinical approaches for combining predictors. And, in Chapters 8 and 9, we discuss more fully some of the major research programs now under way and the results being obtained.

Chapter 7 Collecting and Combining Predictors of Managerial Effectiveness

THE NATURE OF BEHAVIOR PREDICTION FOR MANAGERS

Predicting behavior categories. Description and measurement in the physical sciences, where the degree of measurement error is typically low, allow precise estimation of outcomes along continuous scales such as length, mass, or kinetic energy. In contrast, most personnel decisions involve category judgments. To be sure, *some* behavior outcomes are estimated on continuous scales (such as grade point average in college or number of cigarettes smoked per day), but the more usual prediction is in the form of nominal designations of different modes or categories of expected behavior (such as smoker versus nonsmoker, sociable versus nonsociable, or success versus failure). Predicting outcomes of such important behavioral events as graduating from college, entering a particular occupation, or succeeding in one's occupation or marriage is commonly done by psychologists. In predicting managerial effectiveness it is useful, of course, to consider the various dimensions of managerial behavior that may be involved in getting the job done properly and to attempt to assess dispostions toward such behavior patterns. Thus, it is more impor-

148

tant to predict differing modes of managerial job behavior than merely to at-tempt an overall, global success or failure designation. In other words, we seek ways of identifying managers according to broad similarities in their expect-ed job behaviors—some effective and some ineffective.

Individualized prediction. Moreover, the prediction for each manager should be *individualized* according to his special characteristics, his job and organizational circumstances, and the many interactive components illustrat-ed in Figure 2.1. It is likely that managers and managerial jobs differ in their predictability. Extensive research is necessary to learn the job situations, job behaviors, and organizational circumstances for which predictions of man-agerial effectiveness may be more or less accurate. Such knowledge may be used to specify individualized prediction strategies using the particular pre-dictors and other measures shown by research to be most accurate for a par-ticular person, job, and job situation. By individualizing manager job behav-ior predictions, the likelihood is greater that the *right* persons will move into the *right* managerial jobs under the *right* organizational circumstances to assure the desired outcome—effective managing. To be sure, this is an idealized end result, but it is one toward which we are striving when we set out to predict effective managerial behavior. We need to know about the managerial job, effective behaviors on that job, individual and organizational predictors of such behaviors, and the best ways of collecting information and combining it to accomplish accurate individualized predictions.

CLINICAL AND MECHANICAL METHODS

In Chapter 6, we concluded that the measures with the greatest potential for predicting managerial effectiveness are general intelligence tests, specially developed personality and interest scales (as opposed to standard scales already available), and biographical inventories. Situational and simulated measures have considerable promise and are discussed in detail in Chapter 9. The personal interview, though widely used, has not been thoroughly researched, and evi-dence of its validity is meager.

Perhaps interviewing has shown up poorly because facets of information obtained in interviewing have been inefficiently or improperly combined to form behavioral predictions about managerial candidates. The correlation-al studies of typical behavior inventories reviewed by Guion and Gottier (1965), Nash (1966), and Korman (1966) probably also represent oversimplified expec-tations of how different personality and interest facets combine to find expres-sion in different job behaviors. We have seen that influences on managerial job behavior are diverse and complex, involving the interaction of individu-al characteristics and motivational and organizational environment variables.

How should predictors be combined to reflect the complexity of these interactions? Simply adding them by equations or by statistical rules may be too mechanistic and seems to depart widely from our aim of individualized prediction. But personnel interviewers have done poorly because they have *no* rules to go by. Their predictions may be individualized, but they also seem haphazard and overly conjectural. Granted that certain predictors may be better than others, how should they be combined to yield accurate predictions about managers' job behavior?

Clinical combination. A large number of psychologists believe that the many complicating features of the manager-job interaction can be taken into account only by means of judgmental or clinical processes. They argue that it is unrealistic to assume that crucial behavioral tendencies are adequately tapped by single scales on typical behavior inventories and that correlating such scales with estimates of managerial effectiveness results in grossly oversimplified conclusions, representing a serious under utilization of the total information contained in such inventories. Thus, it is believed that meaningful prediction can be made only by considering configurations of predictor variables and by taking account of how they may be modified by particular circumstances that a manager may face. It is argued that prediction for each individual managerial candidate cannot depend upon statistical relationships gathered on groups of managers; instead, the psychologist, reviewing predictor information and knowing the job circumstances, can collate and integrate the total amount of information better and can make more accurate judgments about behavior than could be accomplished through use of a statistical combination of predictors and criteria.

It should be apparent that the clinical approach is highly subjective; an individual's test scores and other predictor information are interpreted by the clinician on the basis of his own experience with similar cases, his inferences about job requirements, and any theories he may have about the meanings of the various predictor patterns as indicants of specific behavioral tendencies. Clinical prediction requires great skill, in contrast to the simple clerical function of combining predictors statistically. The skilled clinician must know as much as possible about the predictors he is using, the special circumstances for which they are being used, and the many aspects of human behavior for which they may be relevant.

Mechanical combination. Predictors are combined mechanically according to rules (e.g., statistical equations or scoring systems) developed specifically for predicting specific types of job behavior in certain circumstances. After the rules have been developed, it is possible to train an ordinary clerk to apply them to the predictor variables and to express the combination in the form of actuarial odds that a particular type of job behavior will occur. Obviously, the prior development of such equations or combining rules demands careful research, validation, and cross-validation of the predictors against the behavior measures to be predicted. But the yield from such research is a publicly communicable and objective procedure that is not dependent on specialized experience or clinical judgment.

It is important to distinguish between the use of mechanical or statistical methods for combining predictor information, which we have just discussed, and the use of statistics for estimating the accuracy of personnel decisions. Some form of statistical comparison *must* be used to calculate the relative "hit rate" of the predictions made, whether based on clinically or mechanically combined predictors. The use of statistics for checking the validity of predictions is not the point at issue. The only question relevant to the so-called mechanical versus clinical controversy is the mode used in collecting and combining the predictors.

It is important also to distinguish the mode used in *combining* predictors from the mode used for *collecting* predictor information. Sawyer (1966) argues that it is important to maintain this additional distinction in order to assure more informed or complete comparisons between clinical and mechanical modes of measurement and prediction. Sawyer (1966, p. 181) draws the distinction between clinical and mechanical modes of data collection as follows:

> Data collection is mechanical if rules can be prespecified so that no clinical judgment need be involved in the procedure. Thus, on the one hand are all the self report and clerically obtained data: psychometric tests, biographical data, personnel records, etc.; on the other hand are the usual clinical interview and observation.

With this distinction, prediction strategies can be classified according to the cells shown in Table 7.1. The names entered in the cells are chosen to suggest typical illustrations of each.

Table 7.1 CLASSIFICATION OF PREDICTION STRATEGIES ACCORDING TO MODE OF DATA COLLECTION AND MODE OF DATA COMBINATION

Mode of data collection	Mode of data combination	
	Clinical	Mechanical
Clinical	One Pure clinical	Two Behavior or trait rating
Mechanical	Three Profile interpretation	Four Pure statistical
Both	Five Clinical overview or composite	Six Mechanical composite (e.g., regression equation)

Each of the methods is described briefly below:

1 *Pure clinical;* clinically collected data combined clinically. Here a clinician bases his predictions on an interview or other behavior observations without using any objective information. The typical "write-up" of a job candidate after he has been interviewed is an example of this strategy.
2 *Behavior rating;* clinically collected data combined mechanically. Here a clinician, after observing a candidate's behavior or after interviewing him, summarizes his impressions in the form of ratings on one or more prespecified scales. Ghiselli's (1966b) use of a five-point scale to summarize his interview impressions (described in Chapter 6) is an example of this strategy.
3 *Profile interpretation;* mechanically collected data combined clinically. Here, a clinician, without interviewing or observing a candidate, interprets his pattern or "profile" of scores obtained on a set of tests. The profile interpretation of scores obtained on a personality inventory such as the Minnesota Multiphasic Personality Inventory or the California Psychological Inventory is an example of this strategy.
4 *Pure statistical;* mechanically collected data combined mechanically. A standard example of this strategy is the use of biographical information and test scores in a multiple regression equation to predict managerial job performance. This is the strategy employed by the Standard Oil Company of New Jersey's Early Identification of Management Potential investigation, which is presented in detail in Chapter 8.
5 *Clinical composite;* both modes used for collecting data to be combined clinically. This is perhaps the most frequently encountered clinical situation, where all information—interview, observation, and test scores—is integrated by either one clinician or a team of clinicians to develop an overview and behavior predictions about a candidate.
6 *Mechanical composite;* both modes used for collecting data to be combined mechanically. This method differs from the clinical composite only in its use of pre-assigned rules (such as a multiple regression equation) for deriving final behavior predictions from all the data (both clinically and mechanically collected) available. A good illustration of this strategy is the use of factor scores to summarize all the clinical and objective test information gathered on assessees in the Bell System Management Progress Study (described fully in Chapter 9).

Sawyer's method for classifying prediction strategies is used throughout our subsequent discussions of the relative merits of different strategies in the remainder of this chapter and the two that follow.

Clinical assessments and personnel appraisals. The relative merits of mechanical and clinical strategies have special relevance to managerial behavior prediction because of the widespread use in industry of so-called manager or executive appraisal techniques.

Guion (1965a) has described the major elements making up such techniques:

1 The most obvious element is the interview, usually carried out somewhat extensively. The interview is most often used to obtain information about a candidate's
family, educational, and work backgrounds but may also delve into the nature
of prior adjustment patterns and the candidate's personality dynamics.

2 An extensive battery of tests is also usually administered. The choice of tests is
dictated by the constructs the psychologist in charge considers important for the
job in question and his understanding of the construct validities of appropriate
tests. Assumptions about construct validity are often quite subjective. Some paper-
and-pencil tests will almost always be included, with the possible addition of situational tests and simulated tasks, according to the orientation and preferences
of the psychologist doing the appraisal.

3 There must be some data concerning the nature of the job. A routine job description is minimal; it is better to have indications also of the character of the organization, some of the psychological characteristics of the people with whom the
man must eventually work, and so on.

4 The usual outcome of all this is a final, integrating judgment. This takes several
forms. In some cases, a recommendation to hire or to reject is made. In others,
there will be ratings along various pertinent dimensions to represent the conclusions of the appraiser, or the report may end with a series of questions suggested by the conclusions reached. This preference is based upon the idea that questions force the person ultimately responsible for a hiring or promotion decision
to attempt an independent check on those conclusions instead of abdicating his
own responsibility for the final decision. Thus, the outcome of the typical "executive appraisal" fits into the clinical composite strategy (cell 5) of Sawyer's classification.

RELATIVE MERITS OF CLINICAL AND MECHANICAL STRATEGIES

Two major arguments, already touched on in our prior discussion of the
clinical method, have been advanced in support of using clinical strategies
to gather and combine personnel information. They are:

1 Often, regardless of the mode of data collection, there is only a clinical basis for
combining the information to form predictions about a candidate. Hundreds of
firms throughout the country employ only small numbers of managers, far too
few to conduct careful selection research or test validation studies. In such instances, the usual recourse is to combine the predictor information clinically,
taking account of the accumulated validity information available for the predictors and inferring their meaning for the specific situation. Of course, it would still
be possible to develop combining rules rationally and use them in the same way
on all managerial candidates. But such an approach would run counter to what
is said by its advocates to be one of the major advantages of clinical data combination—the ability of the clinician to take account of special circumstances,
situational variables, and varying organizational requirements which presumably
cannot be incorporated properly into any across-the-board set of rules for com-

bining the information available on a candidate.[1] Granting the reasonableness of this argument, we should like to emphasize that the psychologist or personnel specialist who bases predictions on such clinical combinations should be constantly on the alert for opportunities to find out how his predictions turn out over the long run. In time, he should accumulate evidence showing how accurate his recommendations have been. Examples of studies assessing the accuracy of clinical predictions for managers are those by Dicken and Black (1965); Albrecht, Glaser, and Marks (1964); and Bray and Grant (1966).

2 Cronbach and Gleser (1965) suggest that clinical methods of data collection are capable of providing many elements of information about an applicant, whereas data collected mechanically and validated statistically can make only narrow behavioral predictions restricted to those specific behaviors chosen originally as performance criteria. The clinician (in industry, the employment interviewer or "managerial" psychologist) is said to elicit a wide range of responses from a candidate and thereby obtain information otherwise inaccessible because no mechanical method could be designed to "anticipate" the full range of relevant information available from all possible candidates. For example, a personal interview yields a plethora of information. Much of it, of course, may be of limited dependability and only remotely relevant to selection decisions, but its breadth still represents a rich source of hypotheses to be confirmed or refuted by other procedures. However, an important note of caution must be sounded: it is all too easy when using clinical procedures to develop hypotheses which become self-fulfilling by affecting the very nature of job observations and interpretations made subsequently. That is, later observations may be unconsciously distorted to conform with and confirm earlier inferences. That this occurs in personnel interviewing is strongly suggested in Webster's research (1964) on the personnel interview, described in Chapter 6.

What evidence do we have of the relative merits of clinical and mechanical strategies in collecting and combining predictor information? The first complete documentation of studies comparing clinical and mechanical methods was provided by Meehl (1954). Since publishing this book, Meehl has continued to collect accounts of such studies. His last tally shows only one instance (Lindzey, 1965) in fifty studies where clinical analysis of information has yielded more accurate predictions than combining rules based on a statistically derived scoring scheme.

Sawyer's more recent review (1966) of 45 studies is especially valuable because he took account of the distinction between mode of collection and mode of combination depicted in Table 7.1. The studies included a total of 49 direct comparisons between various of the cell pairs shown in Table 7.1. For example, there were 4 comparisons of the predictive accuracy of the pure clinical strategy (cell 1) versus the behavior rating strategy (cell 2), 14 comparisons of the accuracy of the pure statistical strategy (cell 4) versus the clinical composite strategy (cell 5), and so on. Sawyer examined the statistical significance of the difference between the predictive accuracies (expressed either

Table 7.2 NUMBER OF COMPARISONS MADE AND PERCENTAGE OF COMPARISONS
IN WHICH EACH STRATEGY WAS SUPERIOR, EQUAL, OR INFERIOR IN
PREDICTIVE ACCURACY TO THE COMPARISON STRATEGY

	Number of comparisons	Percentage of comparisons		
		Significantly superior	Equal	Significantly inferior
Pure clinical	8	0	50	50
Behavior rating	12	8	76	16
Profile interpretation	12	0	75	25
Pure statistical	32	31	69	0
Clinical composite	24	0	63	37
Mechanical composite	10	60	40	0

as percentage of correct designations or as a correlation coefficient) yielded
by the two strategies involved in each comparison. The two strategies were
called equal when they failed to show an accuracy difference significant at
the .05 level or better.[2] Table 7.2 summarizes the outcomes of these comparisons, and Tables 7.3 and 7.4 rank the six strategies according to the relative
proportion of times they yielded significantly superior accuracies and according to the relative proportion of times they yielded significantly inferior accuracies. Clearly, the mechanical mode of combining predictors is superior to
the clinical mode *regardless* of the method used for collecting predictor information. In spite of the compelling logic arguing the advantages of and the
occasional necessity for, clinical combinations of information, the evidence
is overwhelmingly in favor of the rigorous and systematic procedures involved
in mechanical or statistical combinations. However, the evidence is in favor
of Cronbach and Gleser's argument. The best strategy of all, it appears, is one
which supplements data collected mechanically with the presumed broader
range of data collected clinically but which "protects" the data from the clinician's potentially faulty inferences by combining them into a predictive composite by a set of common rules or equations developed mechanically.

In addition to the comparisons summarized in Tables 7.2 to 7.4, Sawyer
reviewed studies showing that predictions based on a clinical composite strategy are improved if the clinician is given the prediction derived from a mechanical combination but that they still fall below what is achieved by the mechanical composite strategy alone. As might be expected, then, a prediction based

al specialty, age, sex, race, and so on. Rationally derived and explicit sets of rules based on the best
available information concerning the job relevance of various predictors would seem preferable
to practices based on such implicit "equations."
[2] In comparisons involving percentages, the smallest difference significantly favoring one strategy
over the other was 12 percent based on 1,000 subjects; the largest difference called equal was one
of 13 percent based on only 30 subjects. In comparing correlations, the largest difference called
equal was one of .13 based on 232 subjects; in addition, five other differences, all smaller than .13,
were called equal even though statistically significant because of the large number of subjects used
(Ns averaging 2,000).

on a mechanical composite strategy is *not* improved by adding the clinically based prediction to it.

Though the results described above are clearly damaging to clinical modes of combining predictors, we should call attention to Holt's (1958) argument that comparisons between the two modes have been between what he terms "sophisticated" statistical procedures and "naïve" clinical procedures. He claims that combining rules have always been developed on one group of subjects and cross-validated on another group, thereby making a wealth of previous experience available to subsequent applications of the equations. He argues that an analogous level of sophistication, applied to clinical methods, would give the clinician a like opportunity to validate his inferences on a previous

Table 7.3 RANKING OF STRATEGIES FROM "BEST" TO "POOREST" ACCORDING TO PROPORTIONS OF COMPARISONS YIELDING SIGNIFICANTLY SUPERIOR PREDICTIVE ACCURACIES

↑ B E S T P O O R E S T ↓	Strategy	Mode of data collection	Mode of data combination	Percentage of "superior" outcomes
	Mechanical composite	Clinical and mechanical	Mechanical	60
	Pure statistical	Mechanical	Mechanical	31
	Behavior rating	Clinical	Mechanical	8
	Profile interpretation	Mechanical	Clinical	0
	Clinical composite	Clinical and mechanical	Clinical	0
	Pure clinical	Clinical	Clinical	0

Table 7.4 RANKING OF STRATEGIES FROM "BEST" TO "POOREST" ACCORDING TO PROPORTIONS OF COMPARISONS YIELDING SIGNIFICANTLY INFERIOR PREDICTIVE ACCURACIES

↑ B E S T P O O R E S T ↓	Strategy	Mode of data collection	Mode of data combination	Percentage of "inferior" outcomes
	Mechanical composite	Clinical and mechanical	Mechanical	0
	Pure statistical	Mechanical	Mechanical	0
	Behavior rating	Clinical	Mechanical	16
	Profile interpretation	Mechanical	Clinical	25
	Clinical composite	Clinical and mechanical	Clinical	37
	Pure clinical	Clinical	Clinical	50

group and to apply them in a "cross-validation" situation to an independent group. According to Holt, such procedures would need to employ careful job analyses and work from extensive job specifications. Moreover, the clinician might even employ a manual outlining the kinds of inferences shown to be accurate in previous situations. Holt's argument is a good one, but it should be noted that the kinds of procedures he describes (that is, an extensive validation of the individual clinician and cross-validation to subsequent samples) demand the same kind of group information and group statistics that typically are required for combining data statistically. If clinical prediction, to be effective, demands the same number of subjects and same amount of data analysis demanded by the statistical study, much of its presumed advantage over the mechanical method is lost. The burden of proof for demonstrating the accuracy of predictions based on clinical combinations of data seems to us to rest rather heavily on the shoulders of anyone advocating the usefulness of such procedures for assessing managerial effectiveness.

Whence clinical prediction? Overall, the best conclusion about clinical methods is that they can be used for collecting data but that extreme caution should be exercised when using them for combining data. The best bet for predicting specifically defined job behaviors is very likely a statistical combination of predictors developed mechanically from prior research. Clinical methods and judgments do, however, represent a broader kind of information gathering which may yield many behavioral hypotheses and can often be the first step toward developing more objectively based applied prediction strategies. The clinical approach is, of course, the most individualized prediction strategy possible; as such, it might represent an ultimate aim for predicting managerial effectiveness. But it is also necessary to be certain that personnel decisions possess a degree of accuracy. Careful validation studies and selection research should always be done to produce evidence bearing on the potential accuracy of such decisions.

Synthetic validity. It should be clear that both mechanical and clinical methods have certain advantages and disadvantages for making predictions about managerial effectiveness. The major advantages of the statistical method are its precision in stating the actual odds that a particular level of job behavior will occur and the knowledge to be gained from learning empirically the exact predictors associated with different job behaviors. Its disadvantages include the difficulty of conducting rigorous validation and cross-validation studies, the inability of the method to take easily into account dynamic changes in job and organizational circumstances, and the difficulty of using it for deriving truly individualized decisions. The clinical method has advantages in dealing somewhat more appropriately with each individual and in utilizing the special skills and experiences of the psychologist to take account of special circumstances idiosyncratic to specific prediction situations, but it suffers from imprecision, in that we have little prior knowledge of the potential accuracy of personnel decisions, and from the myriad problems arising out of difficulties detailed earlier related to unstandardized procedures, subjective judgments, problems of impression formation, and the optimal rules for combining information to form predictions. Can we combine the special advantages of statistical methods with the special advantages of clinical procedures? Can we ask personnel decision makers to operate as statistical clinicians?

We believe that methods now are available pointing the way to a possible happy wedding of the two methods and that they have particular relevance for predicting managerial effectiveness. Holt's suggestions for developing greater sophistication in utilizing clinical procedures help to point the way; greater capacity and clarity for the path to be followed are offered by the relatively new analytic procedures suggested by the concept of *synthetic validity.*

Balma (1959, p. 395) defines synthetic validity as "the inferring of validity in a specific situation from a logical analysis of jobs into their elements, a determination of test validities for these elements, and a combination of elemental validities into a whole." As we have seen, differences in the demands and activities performed in different managerial jobs will ordinarily result in predictors showing substantially different relationships with global ratings of proficiency from job to job. This is one of the major difficulties acting to attenuate the size of validities in research done so far. Greater consistency should be observed if validities are computed between predictors and ratings or observations of effectiveness on specific tasks or behavioral dimensions in different managerial jobs. This is the essential assumption involved in the concept of synthetic validity. The approach involves assembling a set of tests to predict proficiency in a job on the basis of the tests' predetermined relationship with the specific behavioral elements or dimensions of the job. We recommended in Chapters 4 and 5 that managerial jobs be studied according to specific behavioral requirements and that effectiveness measures be developed separately for each of the major dimensions discovered. The method of synthetic validation can then be employed to develop "families" of validities for various predictors against each of several managerial job components, and this knowledge may serve as the basis for "synthesizing" estimated validities for any given managerial job of known dimensional configuration.

The methodology of synthetic validation may not be entirely clear from this brief discussion. Guion (1965b) recently carried out a demonstration of synthetic validation which should make the methodology easier to see. For his study he used the 46 employees of a small electrical goods company in which no more than three persons were doing any one kind of job. After careful job study, it was decided that the various jobs could be described in terms of the amounts demanded of seven elements: salesmanship, creative business judgment, customer relations, routine judgment, leadership, handling detail work, and organizing duties. The president and vice-president of the firm, after deciding which jobs contained each of the elements, spent many hours independently ranking employees according to their relative proficiency in performing each of the job elements. Finally, the two men also ranked all employees according to their "overall worth to the organization." The two men agreed closely in their rankings of employees' proficiency (r's ranged from .82 to .95). The scores obtained by employees on a variety of tests (including both ability measures and typical behavior inventories) were compared with their rated levels of proficiency on each job element. Several of the tests showed large relationships with different aspects of proficiency. For example, proficiency in creative business judgment was highly related to scores on a design judgment test; leadership ratings were strongly associated with verbal ability scores; proficiency in salesmanship was most closely related to sociability test scores; etc. Guion then developed two-variable expectancy charts for each of the job elements by examining proficiency rankings for employees with different patterns on selected pairs of tests and calculating their mean values. For example, 80 percent of employees scoring in the highest categories on the design judgment and adaptability tests were given "superior" ratings on creative business judgment, but only 25 percent of employees scoring in the lowest categories on both tests were rated as superior. Guion used these expectancy charts to develop scoring patterns to reflect expected proficiency ratings for configurations of predictor scores.

To sum up, seven job elements were found to be sufficient for describing 46 jobs in a small firm and for evaluating the proficiency of employees doing these jobs. Test scores were found to be differentially indicative of proficiency in performing each of the various job elements; and these data were used to form expectancy charts so that each test score could be interpreted directly as an estimate of expected proficiency level in one or more of the job elements.

Cross-validation was carried out on an additional group of 13 employees who had been hired since the study had been undertaken. First, their jobs were studied to decide which job elements each encompassed. Second, the expectancy charts and scoring systems developed from the previous data were used to estimate the relative job proficiency of each one of the 13. Third, the president and vice-president ranked the 13 according to their proficiency in performing various job elements and in terms of overall worth. Finally, the estimates based on test scores were compared with the top executives' rankings. The results obtained are shown in Table 7.5. Clearly, the test patterns developed in this demonstration of synthetic validation "hold up" effectively in the cross-validation group; of 13 classifications, 10 (77 percent) are correct.

In a second phase of this study, Guion ignored possible job differences

Table 7.5 DEGREE OF AGREEMENT BETWEEN JOB PROFICIENCY ESTIMATE BASED ON TEST SCORES AND ACTUAL JOB PROFICIENCY RATINGS FOR 13 EMPLOYEES IN THE CROSS-VALIDATION SAMPLE

		Job proficiency observed and rated by top executives	
		Among lower half	Among top half
Job proficiency estimated from test scores }	Among top half	2	5
	Among lower half	5	1

and developed an expectancy chart describing the relationship between the two best tests and the ratings of overall worth for all 46 employees. However, when these results were applied to the cross-validation sample, only a chance number (six, or 46 percent) of correct classifications was made. Apparently, overall worth was too global a concept for describing and assessing proficiency in these many different jobs. The contrasting results in the two phases of Guion's study are testimony to the usefulness of defining job proficiency explicitly in terms of job elements rather than relying on a global, overall rating.

This study illustrates how systematic procedures can be applied to small numbers of persons doing very different kinds of jobs under different circumstances to develop rather precise predictions about their expected job behavior. Moreover, the study shows that (1) rather small Ns can yield both statistically and practically useful results, (2) a global estimate of job effectiveness such as the "overall worth" rating in this study may often be insufficiently rich behaviorally to yield stable results on cross-validation, and (3) statistical precision can be combined with clinical judgments about important aspects of job behavior to yield a kind of statistical-clinical "weighting" of the predictor scores. Finally, Guion's careful methods of job analysis and the ratings of proficiency on different job dimensions illustrate the approach that we believe will be most feasible and fruitful for learning more about the factors and behaviors indigenous to effective managing. In broad outline, Guion's procedure is similar to the methods of job analysis and effectiveness measurement we have advocated for managerial jobs. The executives who did the rankings were involved at each stage; they helped develop the definitions of the various job elements, focusing as closely as possible on specific examples of observable behavior to be used in making the ratings. Moreover, the rankings were obtained independently from two equally well-qualified observers, and the independent rankings were correlated, thereby yielding a "check" on the semantic clarity of the job element definitions as well as on the relative precision with which the behavior had been observed and recorded for different employees. Guion's study constitutes a solid example of successful test validation carried out in a situationally complex setting involving many different jobs with only a limited number of subjects available for study.

It should be clear that synthetic validation leads directly to development of the individualized prediction strategies that we desire for predicting managerial effectiveness. Any given managerial job can be described according to the critical behaviors necessary for getting it done properly. Maximum performance and typical behavior measures shown to be predictive of these job behaviors can then be obtained on job candidates and the odds of their showing the critical behaviors estimated. In effect, individual candidates are assessed only with those predictors shown to be best for predicting relevant job behaviors. Prediction strategies are *individualized,* therefore, in the sense that they may differ from candidate to candidate according to the specific behavioral demands of different managerial jobs and according to the differential accuracy of different predictors for predicting them. Other methods, closely similar to synthetic validation, for individualizing prediction strategies have been summarized by Dunnette (1966). We shall not describe these methods here; it is sufficient simply to note that effective methods *do exist* for developing individualized prediction strategies at the managerial level, that these tend to combine the advantages of clinical and mechanical methods, and, most important, that they incorporate the distinctive features of methods we have proposed for studying managerial jobs and for measuring managerial effectiveness. Dimensional analyses of managerial jobs and behavioral observations of managers based on these dimensions are the basic raw materials for developing and implementing the individualized managerial prediction strategies suggested by the schematic model of managerial performance outlined in Chapter 2.

SUMMARY

Personnel decisions about managers and their careers are individual decisions. A specific job with unique responsibilities has to be filled, or a particular manager needs to overcome certain specific weaknesses in order to improve performance in aspects of his job. In order to assure greater likelihood that the *right* man will be placed in the *right* managerial job under the *right* organizational circumstances, we need to develop *individualized* strategies for predicting managerial effectiveness.

Two broad strategies—mechanical and clinical—have been used in collecting information from managers and in combining the information to develop predictions of effectiveness. Data collection is mechanical if it is done according to preestablished guidelines, rules, or procedures; it is clinical if it is carried out in a flexible manner, which may differ from candidate to candidate at the discretion of the person (clinician, personnel specialist, managerial psychologist) collecting it. Standardized tests and biographical data blanks are examples of mechanical methods of collecting information. Personal interviews and observations of behavior in a leaderless group discussion are examples of clinical methods of collecting information.

Mechanical combination of information is done according to rules or statistical equations developed by prior research, and these rules can be applied to the data, after training, by an ordinary clerical person. Clinical combination of information is done by experts (clinicians, personnel specialists, or managerial psychologists) who believe they can take better account of a candidate's overall pattern or configuration of attributes in the context of relevant, special job requirements and situational circumstances than can be done by any across-the-board rule or equation.

Thus, the rationale for using clinical procedures for predicting managerial effectiveness rests on two major arguments: (1) Often, no sound basis exists for writing any single set of rules to use in combining all the information about a candidate, the job, and the organization to form job behavior predictions (e.g., data are unavailable or too limited for carrying out a statistical study), and therefore clinical judgment is the best basis for developing predictions, and (2) clinical methods of data collection provide richer samples of behavioral information because no mechanical method available can fully anticipate all the information potentially relevant for predicting managerial effectiveness.

When it has been possible to compare the efficacy of mechanical and clinical methods for predicting behavioral outcomes on the same sample of persons, the latter argument has often been upheld, but the former has never been. This conclusion is based on comparisons showing that predictions derived via clinical combinations of information (no matter how gathered) have *never* yielded more accurate predictions than those based on mechanical combinations of the same information. But the best possible prediction strategy (in that it has always proved either equal to, or better than, competing strategies) combines information mechanically that has been collected by *both* mechanical and clinical methods.

These findings suggest that clinical methods should be used to complement mechanical methods in gathering information about managers but that mechanical procedures should be used for formulating optimal individualized prediction rules. New and more sophisticated methods of mechanical combination are available, but they have not yet been widely used for predicting job behavior. One such promising method is synthetic validation. Applied to managerial jobs, the method takes as raw material the dimensional descriptions of managerial jobs and behavior-based measures of managerial effectiveness discussed in Chapters 4 and 5. Predictors (both mechanical and clinical) can then be validated mechanically against the effectiveness dimensions and individualized rules or strategies written. The strategies would be individualized in the sense that they would differ from candidate to candidate according to the behavioral demands of different managerial jobs and the differential patterns of accuracy shown by the various predictors for predicting how well a candidate can meet them.

Chapter 8   Research Results: Actuarial Studies of Managerial Effectiveness

We turn now to descriptions of major research studies directed toward defining more fully the personal characteristics related to effective management. Our emphasis in this chapter and in the following one is mostly on studies involving individual difference measures. In emphasizing these, we caution the reader not to infer any lessening in the importance we attach to process and situational characteristics or to the modification through training or development of persons destined to undertake management responsibilities. These latter aspects of predicting and/or developing managerial effectiveness are treated at length in Chapters 10 to 16. In a sense, we seek in these two chapters to summarize relevant research enabling us to round out or define a sort of *construct* of effective executiveship. The construct, although focusing mostly on person characteristics, will be based on empirical research results instead of on opinions, hunches, and conjectures such as those mentioned in Chapter 2.

Our review of research on managerial effectiveness is limited to larger studies dealing with middle and higher level managers. We have chosen *not* to describe or to discuss many of the research studies directed toward predicting effectiveness at the entering or first level of supervision. Decisions about the magnitude or so-called largeness of studies have, of course, been somewhat arbitrary, determined mostly by a desire to avoid studies carried out on limited samples or under conditions that seem to limit the generality of results. A prime criterion for inclusion is the extent of knowledge contributed by a study either to defining the construct of effective management or to developing significant methodology for subsequent studies of managerial effectiveness. The interested reader will find other useful reviews of research in the literature (Guion, 1965a; Harrel, 1961; Ramfalk, 1957; Stogdill, 1948; Tiffin & McCormick, 1965).

A second goal is to cast studies against the substantive and methodological issues posed in previous chapters. Thus, we review relevant research against the backdrop formed by our discussions of managerial job descriptions, problems of measuring managerial effectiveness, and modes used for collecting and combining predictor measures to predict managerial effectiveness.

PURE STATISTICAL OR ACTUARIAL STUDIES

Most studies of managerial effectiveness have used mechanical methods for both collecting and combining information about managerial candidates. These studies fall into the pure statistical strategy according to the scheme shown in Table 7.1. Although clinical methods are widely used for actually making personnel decisions about managers, only rarely have they been evaluated for their relative accuracy. In the remainder of this chapter we describe methods used and major results obtained in the larger statistical investigations. Chapter 9 presents studies that have used clinical procedures to supplement mechanical methods in collecting data and either clinical or mechanical means for combining data.

Standard Oil Company of New Jersey. Perhaps the best-known and most extensive validation of tests and biographical inventories against measures of management effectiveness is the pioneering Early Identification of Management Potential (EIMP) study carried out by the Standard Oil Company of New Jersey (SONJ).[1] Since the initial validation, the statistical equations have been applied to a number of other subsidiary companies in the Standard Oil organization, including Interesso, Imperial, ESSO Metropolitan Services Corporation, International Petroleum Company (Laurent, 1966), ESSO Europe, Inc.,

---

[1] This is a prime example of a long-term staff study, and many people contributed to it, including C. P. Sparks, A. M. Munger, Carl H. Rush, Paul F. Ross, Douglas Fryer, McE. Trawick, Paul C. Baker, Treadway Parker, Henry Laurent, and E. R. Henry. It is described in detail in *EIMP (Early Identification of Management Potential)*, published by the Standard Oil Company of New Jersey, Social Science Research Division, Employee Relations Department, and available from them.

and the Humble Oil and Refining Co. (Sparks, 1966). Management of SONJ undertook support of this research in order to shed light on two questions: (1) How can success in the job of managing be measured? and (2) How can employees who possess the potential to be successful in management be identified early in their careers?

A total of 443 managers working for SONJ and five of its affiliate companies were the subjects. Because a major purpose of the study was to investigate the broad core of what constitutes managerial success and potential, the sample included managers in many different functions including marketing, research, production, accounting, and staff specialties such as medicine and law. Management of SONJ was more hopeful of identifying young men with potential for general management positions and less concerned with pinpointing potential narrowly oriented toward specific functional areas. This reflects a management philosophy which values diversity in different functions, as opposed to narrow specialization. Thus, wide variation in actual responsibilities exists within as well as across functional designations in the SONJ organization. For example, managers in marketing departments include not only those concerned directly with product marketing but also accountants, analysts, engineers, bulk plant managers, etc.

After studying many possible measures of managerial effectiveness, three measures were chosen:

> *Position level.* The relative level in the organizational hierarchy to which a manager had advanced.
> *Salary history.* Each manager's salary history during his entire career was studied. Various adjustments for the effects of inflation, age, and rate of salary progress were made so that the final index could be regarded as reflecting actual differences in the "worth" of various managers to the organization.
> *Effectiveness ranking.* Managers at similar levels in the organizational hierarchy were grouped together and ranked on the basis of "overall managerial effectiveness" by higher company officials who had observed the job behavior of the managers being ranked.

These measures were combined to form an overall success index, and, very importantly, precautions were taken (by factor analytic methods) to assure its independence from both age and length of experience in the firm. Although this measure of relative managerial effectiveness did not explicitly identify or quantify directly actual managerial behavior dimensions, it undoubtedly *did* identify managers differing substantially in how well they had utilized organizational resources over their careers. Moreover, because of SONJ's emphasis on general management, it is likely that those with high standing on the overall success index included men who had been able to adapt effectively to changing conditions in the past and who—in some degree—had brought about desirable changes. To the extent that such patterns of past flexibility and innovation are similar to the patterns necessary for meeting the organizational demands

of the future, results using such an index *will* identify personal qualities leading to future organizational "success" as well as those which have led to past
organizational success.

Each of the managers took a lengthy battery of tests and completed a background survey covering home and family background, education, vocational planning, finances, hobbies and leisure time activities, health history, and
social relations. The tests included measures of verbal ability, inductive reasoning, and management judgment (the ability to size up and choose an
effective action in different human relations situations); an inventory of managerial attitudes; and personality measures (the Guilford-Zimmerman Temperament Survey). The scores on the tests were correlated with the standings
of the managers on the overall success index. In addition, each of the *items*
in the background survey and in the management judgment and Guilford-
Zimmerman inventories was examined statistically to learn its degree of relationship with the overall success index. Since many items and even more responses
were examined, double cross-validation was used to assure the stability of relationships discovered. The total of 443 managers was divided randomly into two
subsamples of 222 and 221. Scoring keys were developed on each subsample and
cross-validated on the other sample.

Finally, the tests and responses showing the highest and most stable correlations with the overall success index were combined to yield a single score on
the test and questionnaire materials. The correlation between the composite
test score and the overall success index was .70. Figure 8.1 is a theoretical expectancy chart showing the accuracy of the composite test score for reflecting a
manager's status on the overall success index.

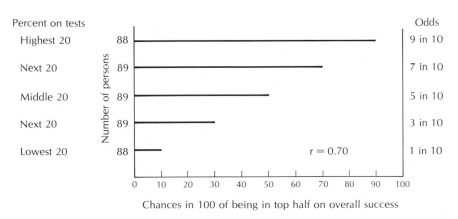

Figure 8.1   Expectancy chart showing chances of being in the
top half on the overall success index for Standard
Oil managers with different composite test scores.

It is useful in attempting to define our construct of effective managerial characteristics to examine the content of the more significant predictors in SONJ's EIMP study. Table 8.1 shows the correlations obtained between scores on standard tests and inventories and status on the overall success and ranking measures for each of the two groups of managers. It is clear that the standardized scales of the Guilford-Zimmerman survey show no useful relationships with either of the effectiveness measures. The two measures of intelligence show moderate, though far from substantial, relationships. Table 8.2 shows the correlations between scores on the special scoring keys and status on the overall success and ranking measures for each of the two groups of managers. The special scoring keys yield substantially higher r's than the standardized scales. Overall, the four best measures are the special biographical survey scales, the special keys on the Guilford-Zimmerman survey, the Management Judgment Test, and the two measures of intelligence. It should be noted that the Management Judgment Test and the biographical keys show rather large differences in their correlations with the two effectiveness measures. This could be a reflection of the degree to which each measure is affected by managers' perceptions of their own career success, a possible contaminant of the study, discussed in more detail later.

Unfortunately, since the major correlates of the success and ranking measures are the two special scoring keys and since the item content of these keys is understandably secret, we cannot say much about the specific nature of per-

Table 8.1 CORRELATIONS BETWEEN STANDARD TESTS AND INVENTORIES AND STANINE SCORES ON THE SUCCESS AND RANKING MEASURES FOR TWO GROUPS OF SONJ MANAGERS

| | Sample A ($N = 222$) | | Sample B ($N = 221$) | |
	Overall success	Ranking	Overall success	Ranking
Miller Analogies Test	.18	.18	.17	.20
Nonverbal reasoning test	.20	.29	.08	.26
Guilford-Zimmerman Temperament Survey				
General activity	.05	.07	.08	−.02
Restraint	.03	.04	.05	.08
Ascendance	−.08	.06	−.07	−.01
Sociability	−.07	.02	−.01	−.08
Emotional stability	.14	.14	.13	.04
Objectivity	.08	.17	.17	.07
Friendliness	.04	.10	.11	−.01
Thoughtfulness	−.01	−.01	−.10	−.06
Personal relations	.05	.14	.20	.11
Masculinity	.06	.23	.04	.16

Table 8.2 CORRELATIONS BETWEEN SPECIAL SCORING KEYS AND STANINE SCORES ON THE SUCCESS AND RANKING MEASURES FOR TWO GROUPS OF SONJ MANAGERS

	Sample A ($N = 222$) Overall success	Ranking	Sample B ($N = 221$) Overall success	Ranking
Special keys based on item analyses of Guilford-Zimmerman survey	.31	.24	.32	.22
Self Performance Report	.24	.07	.23	.04
Survey of management attitudes	.25	.08	.14	.09
Interview (career information)	.21	.21	.19	.06
Interview (human relations rating)	.19	.32	.19	.20
Management Judgment Test	.51	.16	.47	.17
Biographical survey keys	.63	.44	.50	.33

sonal qualities contributing to managerial effectiveness in SONJ. In private correspondence with Dr. Laurent, however, it appears that successful executives in the SONJ organization have shown a total life pattern of successful endeavors. They were good in college, are active in taking advantage of leadership opportunities, and see themselves as forceful, dominant, assertive, and confident.

Table 8.3 shows that the equations developed from the overall groups were approximately equally valid for different companies contributing man-

Table 8.3 CORRELATIONS BETWEEN MULTIPLE REGRESSION SCORES AND SUCCESS INDEX AND RANKING SCORES FOR MANAGERS IN DIFFERENT COMPANIES AND DIFFERENT FUNCTIONS

	N	Success index	Ranking
Company:			
Parent company	134	.75	.55
Marketing and manufacturing	160	.68	.56
N.Y. office of overseas affiliate	21	.46	.47
Foreign sales	28	.70	.28
Shipping	33	.65	.71
Research and engineering	67	.69	.57
Function:			
Exploration, producing	12	.74	.37
Transportation, traffic, purchasing	50	.75	.66
Refining	45	.72	.55
Marketing	107	.67	.42
Economics, engineering, research	99	.75	.56
Financial	86	.74	.55
Employee relations	28	.82	.62
Law	9	.78	.35
Medical	7	.59	.52

Table 8.4 CORRELATIONS BETWEEN SELECTED TEST SCORES AND MULTIPLE RE-GRESSION WEIGHTS (SONJ) AND SUCCESS INDEX AND RANKING SCORES FOR 29 MANAGERS WORKING WITH ESSO METROPOLITAN SERVICES CORPORATION

	Success index	Ranking
Biographical survey (early years)	.39	.34
Biographical survey (adult years)	.42	NS
Management Judgment Test	.57	.64
Miller Analogies Test	.50	.34
Nonverbal reasoning test	.34	.33
Regression equation (SONJ)	.36	.34

NS: r too small to be statistically significant

agement subjects to the study and for managers working in different functions. This is impressive evidence that the qualities identified in the study are indeed those related to general potential for management, regardless of functional, company, or job differences within the SONJ organization.

The multiple regression equations have also been tested against similar success measures for managers in other subsidiaries of SONJ. Table 8.4 shows results obtained for 29 managers employed with ESSO Metropolitan Services Corporation who had been with the firm sufficiently long to obtain stable success index and ranking information. It is apparent that the levels of validity are less (accounting for only one-half to two-thirds as much variance) than those obtained in the initial validation.

Very recently, Laurent has reported, in private correspondence, the results of applying the EIMP materials and regression equations to ESSO Europe, Inc., managers in Denmark, Norway, and the Netherlands. The results are shown below:

	N	r
Denmark	315	.79
Norway	277	.70
Netherlands	70	.75

The managerial effectiveness measure used in each of these studies was salary level adjusted for age. According to Laurent,[2] the higher correlation for Denmark was probably due to the fact that new keys for the biographical survey were developed against the criterion measure, but results for Norway and the Netherlands are based on the same regression equations developed in the EIMP study.

The equations have also been applied to the tests administered during 1962, 1963, and 1964 to nearly one thousand young men shortly after coming to work for the Humble Oil and Refining Co. Each man's immediate superior also estimated the organizational level to which he might be expected to ad-

[2] Private communication, June, 1968.

Table 8.5 SCATTER TABLE SHOWING DEGREE OF AGREEMENT BETWEEN PREDIC-
TIONS OF CAREER POTENTIAL (PDS) AND SUPERVISORS' ESTIMATES OF
POTENTIAL FOR YOUNG PROFESSIONAL EMPLOYEES IN FIRST-LINE
SUPERVISORY JOBS IN THE HUMBLE OIL CO.

Estimated ultimate career potential	Predicted potential* based on SONJ regression equation		
	E and F	C and D	A and B
A and B (top management)	25 (19%)	157 (36%)	185 (57%)
C and D (middle management)	55 (41%)	193 (43%)	99(30%)
E and F (lower management)	54 (40%)	96 (21%)	43 (13%)

*The frequencies of A, B, C, D, E, and F designations on the test predictions were established with
norms based on the original sample of 443 SONJ managers. Cutting scores were set to yield the
following percentages of letter designations: A, 8; B, 17; C, 25; D, 25; E, 17; F, 8. Note that considerably more high scores (A & B) were obtained among Humble managers than among those in
the original norm group.

vance. This estimate of ultimate career potential was compared with potential success estimates derived from Series I [3] of the EIMP inventories (called
the Personnel Development Series [PDS] in the Humble organization). The
results, reported by Sparks (1966), are shown in Table 8.5. The correlation based
on these data is .28. This relatively low value (in comparison with other EIMP
correlations) should not be interpreted as being due entirely to validity "shrink-
age" because only part (Series I) of the EIMP battery was used and, more importantly, because of the markedly different criterion used by Sparks. In fact,
ratings of career potential are difficult to make and show only limited agreement from year to year during the early years of a man's career. This is shown
clearly in the data below, collected by Sparks:

Years of service completed in 1964	N	Correlation between ratings of career potential obtained during the years 1963 and 1964
Less than 2	60	.22
2 or 3	56	.41
4 or 5	55	.37
6 or 7	79	.72
8 or 9	31	.74
10 or more	26	.67

[3] In its present form, the EIMP (or PDS) battery consists of two series. Series I is appropriate for administration any time after a young man joins the company and consists of the two intelligence measures, the Guilford-Zimmerman survey, and biographical items applicable to the man's life through
college. Series II consists of the Management Judgment Test, the Self Performance Report, and biographical items applicable to the early adult years. Responses to questions in Series II can be influenced by maturity and job experience and are more appropriate for administration after a man has
been with a company for five to seven years.

The sharp "jump" in correlation from four or five years of service to six or seven years of service may be due to the relatively greater proportion of persons who have, by then, moved into lower management positions, thereby affording opportunities for observing job behaviors relevant to long-term career potential.

The increasing reliability of the estimate of potential criterion and the effect of including Series II in the predictor battery are shown by the following data, also provided by Sparks:

Tests used	Years of service with Humble (range and mean)	N	Correlation between PDS prediction and supervisory potential estimate
Series I of PDS	1-3 (mean = 2.4)	73	.11
Series I of PDS	4-6 (mean = 4.8)	91	.20
Series I of PDS	7-10 (mean = 8.0)	35	.53
Series I and II of PDS	1-44 (mean = 22.9)	443	.70

In a second study, Sparks compared PDS results for 69 young managers who had risen to high managerial positions with results obtained by 95 older managers who had not advanced beyond lower managerial levels. Table 8.6 shows results of this comparison. The point biserial correlation for the data in Table 8.6 is .78. This coefficient is impressively high, but it is probably an overestimate of the true overall correlation because it is based on results obtained with managers selected from the extremes of the "success" distribution. It is apparent, then, that the special keys and weighting methods developed in the SONJ study do reflect characteristics of managers rising rapidly in the Standard Oil organization. The equations can apparently be applied across different companies and even different countries with some, but not severe, loss of predictive effectiveness. In terms of the numbers of subjects tested,

Table 8.6 SCORES ON SONJ REGRESSION EQUATION FOR HIGHER LEVEL AND LOWER LEVEL MANAGERS IN HUMBLE OIL AND REFINING COMPANY

		Younger* high level managers (N = 69)	Older* low level managers (N = 95)
	A	16	0
Predicted potential	B	30	3
based on SONJ	C	18	12
regression equa-	D	5	21
tion	E	0	19
	F	0	40

*"Older" managers had been with Humble ten years or more and had not risen beyond the middle managerial pay grades; "younger" managers had been with Humble less than ten years but were already in the top five pay grades.

the sizes of validities obtained, and the successful generalization of the validities to other than the original settings, the SONJ studies must be regarded as examples of successful studies designed to discover the personal or trait correlates of managerial effectiveness.

It is particularly noteworthy that these studies yielded high validity coefficients (r's = .70) and high predictive accuracies even though no special attempts were made to study possible differences in managerial jobs, nor were behavioral observations used as measures of managerial effectiveness. Why is this so? At least two important factors stand out as elements contributing to these outcomes.

First, SONJ has for years followed a policy of "rotating" managers from job to job, location to location, and function to function. Over a career with SONJ, a manager will have served in many different jobs and functions, so that assessment against particular kinds of activities or job responsibilities is less important than it would be in a firm with less active rotational job transfers at the management level. Thus, the managers in the SONJ study have been more fully developed as "generalists" than most, and for them, a global measure of managerial effectiveness is probably more meaningful than it would be in more functionally rigidified firms. A second effect of many job changes is that managers, over a period of time, probably become much more widely known than they would in many other firms. This means that their "getting ahead" through promotion and salary increases is less apt to be subject to the biasing influences of being in particular departments or serving under certain managers than could be the case in many other firms. In other words, the influences noted by Miner and discussed in Chapter 6 are probably much less serious contaminants of SONJ's global measures of success than they would be in many firms. In discussing the advantages of the overall success index, Laurent (1966, p. 9) states:

> A measure of a man's success should take into account his entire career—the many judgments, the many decisions that many managers and supervisors have made about him. The success index attempts to do this, and in so doing, tends to minimize the effects of favorable or unfavorable biases held by one or a few supervisors.

We believe that the policy of widespread rotational job transfers for managers and the rigidly followed policy of promoting managers from within the organization[4] assure that biasing components are much less prevalent in the SONJ measure than they would be in similar measures in many other firms.

[4]Our interviews with officials of SONJ and Humble Oil and Refining Co. revealed that virtually no one is hired directly into management jobs from outside the two firms.

A second difficulty in interpreting the high correlations obtained in the series of EIMP studies is that most of them are based on concurrent investigations rather than predictive investigations. It is possible, then, that some responses showing significant relationships with the success index may be descriptive of people who have gotten ahead; that is, they may *result from* "success" rather than be predictive of it. To the extent that this is true in the SONJ studies, the validities obtained could be viewed as being overestimates of the *predictive* accuracy that might be expected from applying the same tests and inventories to groups of entering managerial candidates. Laurent and his colleagues attempted, in a number of ways, to counteract the effects of age and/or experience on the results obtained. First, as already mentioned, the overall success index was "corrected" statistically so that it was independent of both age and company experience. Second, no item from the biographical survey was included in the final scoring key if it showed a significant association with either age or experience. Third, the EIMP battery was separated to form Series I and Series II. Items and tests more likely to be affected by early career experiences and training were placed in Series II for administration five to seven years after coming with the company.

Although each of these strategies does help to guard against effects due to age and experience, they still do not handle fully all possible differential response effects due to different degrees of career success.

The measures showing highest r's with the Overall Success Index were the biographical keys (r's of .63 and .50), the Management Judgment Test (r's of .51 and .47), and the special keys of the Guilford-Zimmerman survey (r's of .31 and .32). Although we do not know the actual items receiving greatest weight in these three measures, it is reasonable to assume that some include content that may be affected by management experience and by different degrees of success.

For example, consider the data shown in Table 8.7, based on hypothetical responses to a biographical item made by long- and short-service managers of varying levels on a global overall success index. These hypothetical responses are strongly related to the overall success index (a substantially larger number [55 percent] of successful managers report getting good or very good grades in college than less successful managers [only 25 percent]) and yet are not related at all to length of service. A crucial question—not handled fully merely by finding a lack of relationship with length of service—is whether or not the differential responses about grades in college might not, in part at least, be due to perceptions of present levels of life success. In other words, some (not all) successful managers, perceiving their own relatively high level of success (as indicated by promotions and good salary standing), might "remember" having done better in college than was really the case. Likewise, some

Table 8.7 HYPOTHETICAL DATA SHOWING RESPONSES MADE BY LONG- AND SHORT-SERVICE MANAGERS OF HIGH AND LOW OVERALL SUCCESS TO THE ITEM:

How good were your grades in college?
_____Very good (VG)
_____Good (G)
_____Average (A)
_____Rather poor (RP)
_____Poor (P)

		Long-service managers (20 years or more)	Short-service managers (10 years or less)	Percent responding in each item category				
				VG	G	A	RP	P
High overall success index (among top third)		Total = 50 VG 10 G 15 A 20 RP 5 P 0	Total = 50 VG 15 G 15 A 10 RP 5 P 0	25	30	30	10	0
Low overall success index (among bottom third)		Total = 50 VG 5 G 10 A 20 RP 10 P 5	Total = 50 VG 5 G 5 A 30 RP 15 P 0	10	15	50	25	5
Percent responding in each item category	VG G A RP P	15 25 40 15 5	20 20 40 20 0					

(not all) less successful managers, perceiving their own relatively low level of success (as indicated by few promotions and poor salary standing) might "remember" having done more poorly in college than they really did. We realize full well that any number of equally likely hypotheses could be advanced; [5] we wish simply to argue that some part of the valid response variance in biographical and self-descriptive items (such as those of the Guilford-Zimmerman survey) and therefore scales derived from them may be only concomitantly related to, rather than *predictive of*, different levels of overall

_____
[5] The most parsimonious one, of course, would probably hypothesize no differential patterns of memory distortion between more and less successful managers.

career success. A major need, already suggested forcefully by Laurent and others, is to study such response patterns longitudinally over the years of managers' occupational careers.

We do not, of course, have any evidence that any substantial portion of the variance represented by the EIMP r of .70 is subject to the "spurious" effects mentioned here, but it is clearly necessary to call attention to the possibility of these influences in *any* concurrent study of managerial effectiveness. It points strongly to the need for studying managers early and throughout their careers in addition to using the retrospective or concurrent approaches employed in the SONJ series. More importantly, this discussion affords us yet another opportunity to argue for the desirability of learning more about the *process* of effective managing by seeking to predict actual job behavior rather than being content with predicting only such gross career outcome measures as promotion or salary advancement.

Industrial Relations Center, University of Minnesota. A second large-scale study of the personal correlates of managerial effectiveness was done by the Industrial Relations Center of the University of Minnesota and is reported by Mahoney, Jerdee, and Carroll (1963); Mahoney, Jerdee, and Nash (1960); and Mahoney, Sorenson, Jerdee, and Nash (1963). Their sample included 452 managers from 13 firms operating in Minnesota, representing manufacturing, finance and insurance, public utilities, agricultural products, and wholesale trade. The managers were drawn primarily from middle management levels (only 3 were at the highest organizational level, and only 34 were at the lowest supervisory level) and from all functional areas. Each was administered a battery of tests, including the following measures:

> *Wonderlic Personnel Test.* A short, twelve-minute test of general intelligence
> *Empathy Test.* An Inventory designed to measure how accurately an examinee discerns musical, reading, and social preferences of groups of people
> *Strong Vocational Interest Blank (SVIB).* Measures the degree of similarity between examinee's likes and dislikes (for school subjects, lines of work, hobbies, activities, etc.) and those of men in different occupations
> *California Psychological Inventory (CPI).* Measures tendencies toward such "typical" behaviors as dominance, sociability, social poise, responsibility, etc.
> *Biographical questionnaire.* A questionnaire asking for descriptions of educational and job experiences, activities, and personal and family circumstances prior to age twenty-five.

Managerial effectiveness was measured for subjects from each of the 13 firms by asking a panel of top company officials to rank them on the basis of overall management competence—essentially the same ranking approach used in the SONJ studies. The ranking scores were shown to be independent of managers' age but related to organizational level in some (not all) of the companies. The total sample of subjects was split in half randomly, and scores on the various tests and inventories were studied in terms of their ability to differentiate between the top- and bottom-ranked 75 managers in one of the two groups; a scoring system based on the measures showing statistically significant differences was developed and tested (cross-validated) on the managers in the other sample. Table 8.8 shows results obtained in the cross-validation group from applying the patterns of predictors and cutting scores shown to be optimal in the validation group.

Table 8.8 RELATIONSHIP BETWEEN PREDICTOR COMBINATION SCORES AND EFFEC-TIVENESS JUDGMENTS FOR MANAGERS IN THE CROSS-VALIDATION GROUP OF THE MINNESOTA IRC STUDY*

	Judged "less effective" (lowest third)	Judged "more effective" (top third)	Total
Above cutting score on predictor combination	23 (29%)	45 (62%)	68
Below cutting score on predictor combination	55 (71%)	28 (38%)	83
Total	78	73	151

*$r_o = .32$.

Of the 98 predictors tried by the Minnesota investigators, 18 showed statistically significant (at the 10 percent level) relationships with the rankings of effectiveness. These were:

- Wonderlic Personnel Test.
- Dominance measured by the CPI.
- SVIB. Higher-ranked managers scored lower on occupational scales of dentist, veterinarian, farmer, carpenter, printer, and vocational agriculture teacher and higher on purchasing agent, sales manager, president of a manufacturing firm, and occupational level.
- Biographical questionnaire. Higher-ranked managers had more education; had better-educated wives; participated in more sports, hobbies, and organizations at age twenty-five; and had wives who worked for a shorter time after marriage than lower-ranked managers.

On the basis of these findings, Mahoney, Sorenson, Jerdee, and Nash (1963, p. 21) characterize the more effective manager as follows:

A more effective manager tends to have interests that are similar to other men in the business field and tends *not* to have interests similar to men in agriculture and skilled trades. On the average, he tends to be somewhat more intelligent and more dominant than less effective managers. His biographical background shows that he has had more educational training and was more active in sports and hobbies as a young man. Also, his wife has had more educational training and worked less after marriage.

The personal elements contributing to effective management suggested by these results can be supplemented by the more detailed study carried out by Nash (1966) of more effective managers' responses to items of the SVIB. Nash's results have already been discussed in Chapter 6.

His SVIB scoring key showed a cross-validation correlation of .33 with the global rankings of managers' effectiveness.

In contrast with the high initial validities (accounting for about 50 percent of the variance) obtained in the SONJ study, the validities obtained in the Minnesota studies are substantially lower (accounting for slightly over 10 percent of the variance). We believe that the Minnesota study may reflect the true level of validity to be expected when company differences are not taken into account and when a global measure is used to estimate effectiveness instead of behavior observations such as we have proposed. The biographical form used by the Minnesota investigators was much less broad in eliciting a range of descriptive information than the background survey used in the SONJ studies. It was much more like the typical application blank and was restricted to strictly biographical items (such as education, activities at age twenty-five, marital status, etc.) rather than incorporating perceptual and self-descriptive material of the type employed in the SONJ biographical forms.

American Chamber of Commerce. A large-scale study of the biographical correlates of job effectiveness for Chamber of Commerce executives has been under way for nearly a decade. Some of the major results have been described by J. J. Kirkpatrick (1960, 1961, 1966). He developed an 11-page biographical questionnaire after conducting depth interviews with 18 Chamber of Commerce executives. The questionnaire included all background information thought to be important on the basis of these interviews, covering early history, family background, education, employment history, military service, social information, and physical condition. The form was mailed to 1,300 Chamber executives, and completed copies were returned by over 600.

Kirkpatrick then used Flanagan's (1951) listing of the critical requirements of Air Force officers' jobs to form a checklist of effective executive behaviors. This was presented to the national board of directors and to several regional managers of the Chamber of Commerce and was used by them as a guideline in designating each of the 600 responding Chamber executives as either above average, average, or below average in meeting the critical requirements outlined by Flanagan; a "forced" distribution was employed so that 50 percent of the subjects were designated "average" and 25 percent each as "above average" and "below average." Kirkpatrick then chose 50 above-average men and 50 below-average men who were matched on age and length of job experience and for whom raters had shown high agreement on the effectiveness designations. Comparisons between questionnaire responses of the two groups yielded 35 items which were combined into a scoring system to "predict" above-average executive performance. The scoring system was cross-validated on two additional groups of 30 below-average and 39 above-average Chamber executives. The results are shown in Table 8.9. The point biserial correlation for these data is .56.

J. J. Kirkpatrick (1966) has also reported results of a five-year follow-up study on the use of the scored biographical questionnaire. Since 1960, 1,129 candidates for executive positions with the Chamber had completed the form. It was decided to use current salary as an estimate of the effectiveness of the managers who had filled out the questionnaire. Salary information and biographical forms were finally recovered for 336 of the 1,129 original candidates, and 80 "high salary" managers were matched on age and size of chamber represented with 81 "low salary" managers and compared on the biographical score. The mean biographical score of the high salary group was about two standard deviations above the mean biographical score of the low salary group. Moreover, an analysis of the differentiating items showed that nearly all the items (31 of 35) that had been significantly related to the rating measure in the earlier study were also related to the salary measure in this study. Although the actual content of these items is secret, Kirkpatrick[6] stated that it is similar to the content of the items found most useful in the SONJ study. Accord-

Table 8.9 **RELATIONSHIP BETWEEN BIOGRAPHICAL QUESTIONNAIRE SCORE AND RATED EFFECTIVENESS OF AMERICAN CHAMBER OF COMMERCE EXECUTIVES***

	Executives judged below average (N = 30)	Executives judged above average (N = 39)
56-60		2
51-55		7
46-50	2	11
41-45	4	9
36-40	6	5
31-35	10	4
26-30	5	1
21-25	2	
16-20	1	

*rpb = .56.
[6]Personal communication, 1967.

ing to Kirkpatrick (1961), the successful Chamber executive has a middle-class socioeconomic background, spent his childhood in a happy and stable family, was well educated, engaged in many extracurricular activities in high school and college and held offices in many of them, emphasized communications skills (debating, oratory, dramatics, editorial responsibilities), and entered the Chamber of Commerce field relatively early (before age thirty-five). Some of the biographical items found in the Chamber study seem descriptive of success rather than necessarily predictive of it. Thus, the successful Chamber executive sees his present family situation as highly satisfying, places heavy emphasis on his career, participates actively in community affairs, enjoys excellent health, and emphasizes policy making and planning in his job instead of selling.

These studies by Kirkpatrick are impressive because they did utilize initially a behaviorally based definition of management effectiveness to define the bases for the global ratings obtained from senior Chamber executives, because men differing in degree of success were matched for age and job experience (i.e., opportunity to accomplish success), and because the *predictive* usefulness of the biographical questionnaire was established by following up persons who had filled out the questionnaire as job candidates or applicants.

Other studies.   A number of other investigators (Bray, 1962; Harrell, 1967; Holland & Richards, 1965; Husband, 1957; Selover, 1962; F. J. Williams & Harrell, 1964) have studied relationships between career success and college success (defined both scholastically and in terms of extracurricular participation). The largest-scale study of this type is the AT&T follow-up investigation reported by Bray (1962). The subjects in the study were all presently employed Bell System college men hired prior to 1950 and who were hired within five years of graduating from college. College records were available for about 10,000 of the sample of 17,000. The measure of career success was each man's salary standing in comparison with that of others having the same length of service in the company. Corrections were made to adjust for differences between salary levels in different parts of the country and between different departments. The distributions of adjusted salary levels were divided into thirds and compared with three predictor measures: rank in college graduating class, college "quality,"[7] and amount of participation in extracurricular activities. Table 8.10 shows the degree of relationship between these three measures of college achievement and the salary measure of career success in AT&T. These data point clearly to the joint action of scholastic and nonscholastic factors in predicting career success as defined by salary progress in the AT&T organi-

---

[7]The classification of college "quality" was admittedly a subjective one based on published materials showing the levels of scholastic aptitude characteristic of different college populations and on off-the-record discussions with college deans and placement directors. Unfortunately, the AT&T report includes no explanation of how the amount of extracurricular participation was derived.

zation. High-achieving students from high-rated colleges who participated actively in campus activities were much more likely ($P = 67$ percent) to earn high salaries at AT&T than low-achieving students who were inactive in college activities and who attended lower-ranked colleges ($P = 20$ percent). Among college men who had graduated in the top tenth of their classes, 51 percent were in the high third on the salary classification, and only 17 percent were in the low third. Unfortunately, the AT&T report gives no Ns; therefore, correlation statistics or overlap information cannot be calculated, and it is somewhat difficult to discern from Table 8.10 the exact magnitude of the relationship between the three predictor variables and salary status for these AT&T employees.

Selover (1962) related information available at the time of hiring managerial candidates to their later promotional patterns in the Prudential Insurance Co. First, he studied 118 college men hired during 1956 and 1957 who were still employed at the end of 1961 and who showed substantial differences in their rate of advancement. Of the many types of information available at the time of hiring,[8] the following five measures showed good relationships with advancement and were combined into a single advancement potential score:

1. Scores on the arithmetic reasoning and vocabulary tests.
2. Level of scholastic achievement in college.
3. Extent of extracurricular participation in college, including part-time work.
4. Previous leadership patterns—offices held in college and/or rank attained in military service.
5. Number of jobs held between college graduation and employment by Prudential. (This factor was related negatively; that is, men who had had a number of jobs but still started with Prudential at the normal starting salary showed slower promotional progress.)

The advancement potential score was then tried on four additional groups in order to estimate the degree of its general applicability for predicting promotional advancement in Prudential. It was applied to 85 men hired from 1952 to 1955, 30 men hired from 1948 to 1951, 36 men hired from 1958 to 1959—all of whom were still with the company in 1961 and had shown different rates of advancement. Finally, advancement potential scores for 48 men who had been asked to resign within one year after being hired were compared with those of 25 men who had stayed with the firm and been promoted to high level jobs. The scoring system was moderately related to the advancement measures in all four groups, yielding phi coefficients of .36, .40, .35, and .65.[9]

---

[8] The kinds of information considered in the study included the schools attended, course of study followed, college activities, previous work and military experience, transcripts of college grades, and tests of verbal and arithmetic reasoning ability.

[9] Since the last coefficient is based on groups chosen from the extremes of the success distribution, it must be interpreted with caution.

Table 8.10 PERCENT OF AT&T EMPLOYEES IN THE TOP THIRD ON THE SALARY DISTRIBUTION ACCORDING TO RANK IN COLLEGE CLASS, QUALITY OF COLLEGE ATTENDED, AND AMOUNT OF EXTRACURRICULAR PARTICIPATION

	Top third in class College quality			Middle third in class College quality			Bottom third in class College quality		
	Above average, percent	Average, percent	Below average, percent	Above average, percent	Average, percent	Below average, percent	Above average, percent	Average, percent	Below average, percent
Substantial extracurricular participation	67	47	50	52	38	34	37	25	26
Some extracurricular participation	61	44	37	42	33	24	32	24	18
No extracurricular participation	47	37	37	35	28	25	31	24	20

These results agree well with the AT&T results in showing the joint action of scholastic and nonscholastic college factors in predicting career success for managers.

In summing up his study, Selover (1962, p. 14) gives the following general description of the typical candidate with high potential for advancements:

> The college graduate who has been promoted rapidly received high scores on our tests of general ability; he achieved a high academic record in college and took an active part in college life or contributed substantially to his support by working; he demonstrated capacity for leadership in college or the armed services by holding a class office, a commission, or other positions demanding responsibility; and he came with the Company shortly after graduation without false starts with other concerns.

Williams and Harrell (1964) and Husband (1957) have followed up graduates from particular institutions—Stanford University Graduate School of Business and Dartmouth College—in the effort to discover the relation between college success and career success. Williams and Harrell found that the current salary (adjusted for length of time out of school) of 196 men who had received their MBA degrees from Stanford between 1927 and 1943 was slightly related to grades received in school (r's of .13, .14, and .22), to professors' ratings of overall school accomplishment ($r = .18$), and to leadership in campus activities (offices held) as an undergraduate ($r = .24$).

Harrell (1967, pp. 31-32) concludes his most recent report of his continuing study of the business careers of Stanford MBA graduates with the following observations:

> The most predictable and feasible criteria of business job success were Hemphill's Position Concern questions, Present Compensation, Present Job Success as perceived by the MBA and number of hours in Work Week. There was little consistency in the relations between predictors and criteria from year to year and from large companies to small companies. Predictors with some positive results justifying consideration to be used for admission to Graduate Schools of Business were:
>   Public Opinion Questionnaire
>   Initiating Structure
>   Decision Making on the Ghiselli Self-Description Inventory
>   Undergraduate Grade Point Average
>   Individual Background Survey
>   Ascendance on the G-Z Temperament Survey
>   Initiative on the Ghiselli Self-Description Inventory
>   Manic Scale on the MMPI
> The personality profile of the MBA who was successful in business included self-confidence in decision making, social boldness, initiative, a history of leadership, energy, plus scholastic ability. Second Year G.S.B. Grades

correlated significantly in Small Companies positively with Present Compensation, Increase in Compensation, Work Week, Present Job Success, Peers View of Job Success; and negatively with Work Week.

Husband (1957) sent questionnaires to 368 graduates of Dartmouth's 1926 class and received replies from 275. He reports no correlational information or overlap data, but he did find rather large median differences in current income between men at the two extremes of scholastic and nonscholastic success during college. Table 8.11 shows some of the results obtained.

Taken together, these four studies indicate a consistent thread of evidence showing that scholastic success in college, extracurricular participation, and particularly the assumption of college leadership postions are predictive of later career success when measured by such global indexes as salary and organizational advancement.

In reviewing some of the above and other, similar studies, Holland and Richards (1965), impressed with the relatively low magnitude of the relationships, argue that scholastic success in college has probably been overrated as a predictor of nonacademic accomplishment and suggest that other kinds of predictors need to be discovered and given more attention.

Sears, Roebuck studies. Over a number of years, the Psychological Research and Services Section of Sears, Roebuck has conducted a series of investigations related to the prediction of executive effectiveness in the Sears organization. The bulk of these studies have been summarized recently by Bentz (1963, 1967).

Over two decades ago (1944), the Sears organization, with the help of Professor L. L. Thurstone, established a psychological testing program. The executive battery of tests included the following:

American Council on Education Test (ACE)
Problem-solving score
Linguistic score
Total score

Guilford-Martin Inventories
Sociability   (S)
Reflectiveness   (T)
Optimism   (D)
Emotional control   (C)
Seriousness   (R)
General activity   (G)
Social leadership   (A)
Masculinity   (M)
Self-confidence   (I)

Table 8.11 MEDIAN INCOMES REPORTED BY VARIOUS GROUPS OF DARTMOUTH GRADUATES FROM THE YEAR 1926 WHO HAD ACCOMPLISHED VARIOUS LEVELS OF "SUCCESS" IN COLLEGE

College experience	N	Income
B + grade average	25	$18,350
C — grade average	66	$13,320
Outstanding success in extracurricular activities	16	$20,000
No extracurricular activities	78	$13,840
Earned one or more athletic letters	33	$18,300
No athletic participation	194	$14,280
Leaders in two or more campus "leadership" organizations	38	$20,000
No leadership experience at Dartmouth	185	$14,250

Composure	(N)
Objectivity	(O)
Agreeableness	(Ag)
Tolerance	(Co)

Allport-Vernon Survey of Values
Scientific
Economic
Aesthetic
Social
Political
Religious

Kuder Preference Record
Mechanical interest
Computational interest
Scientific interest
Persuasive interest
Artistic interest
Literary interest
Musical interest
Social service interest
Clerical interest

Over the years, Bentz has conducted many validity studies of the executive battery. Executive effectiveness has usually been estimated by such factors as promotional rates or by nominations of high success potential managers made by higher organizational officials. Since attitude scales are widely used by Sears, employeee morale has also been used as one measure of store managers' effectiveness, and the the tests have been correlated against it. Discriminant function and multiple regression analyses have been the usual mode

Table 8.12 MEDIAN BISERIAL CORRELATIONS OBTAINED FOR 12 TEST VARIABLES SHOWN TO BE CONSISTENTLY STATISTICALLY SIGNIFICANT FOR SEVEN HIGH SUCCESS OR HIGH POTENTIAL MANAGERIAL GROUPS IN SEARS, ROEBUCK & CO.

	Median biserial correlation
ACE:	
Problem solving score	.14
Linguistic score	.21
Total score	.21
Guilford-Martin:	
General activity	.19
Masculinity	.21
Self-confidence	.25
Objectivity	.17
Tolerance	.20
Allport-Vernon:	
Economic	.15
Political	.28
Kuder:	
Persuasive	.21
Musical	.16

of statistical analyses. Multiple correlations reported in these various studies are often high, occasionally approaching .75 and rarely falling below .40.

Perhaps the best way of summarizing results obtained with the Sears battery is to review results with seven different success groups. The groups, made up of men singled out as being highly successful or potentially the most successful managers at various times over the last decade, are listed below:

1 Senior reserve groups (1957); $N = 350$
2 Special senior reserve group (1955); $N = 117$
3 Highly upwardly mobile executives (1961); $N = 99$
4 Store managers (1960); $N = 556$
5 Parent company supervisors (1956); $N = 42$
6 Parent company special reserve groups (1955); $N = 55$
7 Attendees at staff school (1959 to 1961); $N = 156$

Persons in each of these groups cover a wide range of job responsibilities; the groups are composed of either high status managers (store managers and parent company supervisors) or of men who by dint of exceptional work performance have been singled out (staff school groups, reserve groups, etc.) as potentially the most ready for promotion to high level positions. Biserial correlations were computed between the means of these seven groups and company-wide averages for all persons tested with the executive battery; percentile comparisons were also made separately for each group against the company averages. Of the 31 test variables, 12 showed fairly consistent, statistically significant correlations across the seven groups. These 12 are shown in Table 8.12 along with median biserial correlations obtained for the seven comparisons.

On the basis of these relationships, Bentz (1967, pp. 117-118) has described successful Sears executives as follows:

> It would seem that powerful competitive drive for a position of eminence and authority provides a strong impetus for these men; the need to be recognized as men of influence and status, and ambition to govern, and the desire to excel appears to be of primary importance in enabling these men to utilize their talents fully and appropriately. Accomplishment of these goals appears . . . possible because [they] are superior . . . in intellectual endowment, social competence, and emotional stamina. They are fully confident of their abilities to cope with and control unfamiliar situations, have the facility to deal with problems impersonally, and possess the physical vitality to maintain a steadily productive work pace. . . . Their intensified business orientation is reflected by heightened emphasis on economic values as well as increased liking for persuasive and managerial activites. . . . They are exceptionally open-minded, tolerant and unbiased in their attitudes; while they prefer a dominant position within a group, they are also cooperative teamworkers who willingly listen to the ideas and suggestions of others. . . . Their strong power motive is tempered somewhat by consideration for other people, so that they are not likely to run roughshod over others in their efforts to gain success and renown.

Bentz argues from the above studies and from ones on specialized functional groups (e.g., labor relations executives, retail credit managers, auditors, and the like) that "a cluster of psychological characteristics contributes to general executive competence that transcends the boundaries of specialized or non-specialized assignments." There undoubtedly is a good degree of truth in this assertion, but it is not strongly supported by the concurrent correlations based on extreme group comparisons summarized in Table 8.12.

Other industrial investigations. Several other companies have studied predictors of management effectiveness, but their studies have been somewhat less well publicized, carried out on a smaller scale, and less systematic than those described in previous pages. We refer to investigations carried out by researchers in the Jewel Tea Co., the American Oil Co., the Lockheed Aircraft Corp., North American Aviation, and the Minneapolis Gas Co.

We shall attempt brief descriptions of the more important outcomes of these investigations, but the reader must be cautioned against overinterpreting the results and against attributing too much importance to them. We say this because of the following considerations.

First, the studies suffer from one or more weaknesses such as lack of cross-validation, potentially contaminated criterion measures (e.g., several of the studies using promotion as a criterion have employed subjects whose promotions may have been influenced by knowledge of their status on the predictor variables), and inadequate reporting of statistical information.

Second, their interpretation is difficult because they have used different predictors, different criteria, and widely differing methods for estimating the magnitudes of relationship between predictors and criteria.

Third, some of the investigations have been done on first level supervisors instead of on higher management officials, and this, of course, means that we depart from our previous plan to exclude such studies from discussion. We choose now to include them simply because they *do* capture the flavor of research being done in industry, and, thus, they do add to our description of "what companies are doing" in identifying effective managers.

The upshot of these considerations is that these studies should best be viewed simply as additional bits of evidence—undoubtedly rather subjective, impressionistic, and lacking rigorous statistical justification—to be added to our developing construct of management effectiveness.

Jurgensen's[10] correlational studies of supervisory and management effectiveness in the Minneapolis Gas Co. are useful for identifying the more important concurrent correlates of supervisory and executive salaries, adjusted for length of service and age. Correlations were computed between test and biographical variables and the salary criterion separately for 115 supervisors and administrators (at various organizational levels) and 41 top executives.

The variables yielding correlations above .20 are listed below:

Supervisors and administrators (N = 115)

Biographical
Education	.46
Age	— .79
Length of service	— .60

Cognitive measures
Wonderlic Personnel Test	.53
Shipley-Hartford:	
Abstraction	.49
Total score	.44
SRA Test:	
Linguistic	.43
Quantitative	.52
Total score	.49
Differential aptitude tests:	
Abstract reasoning	.56
Spelling	.26
Sentence usage	.40

[10] Personal communication, 1966.

Watson-Glaser Critical Thinking	.48
Davis Reading Exam	.50
Number comparison	.45
Number completion	.45

Personality
Guilford-Zimmerman Temperament Survey:

General activity	.22
Masculinity	.28

Interest
Kuder Preference Record:

Computational	.37
Scientific	.26
Artistic	— .24

Top executives ($N = 41$)

Biographical

Education	.43
Age	— .06
Length of service	— .05

Cognitive measures

Wonderlic Personnel Test	.38
Watson-Glaser Critical Thinking	.47
Teman Concept Mastery	.31
Differential Aptitude Abstract Reasoning	.38
Michigan Vocabulary test	.55
Moss Social Intelligence Test	.41

Personality and values
Adams-Lepley:

Firmness	— .25
Tranquility	— .20
Stability	— .23
Tolerance	— .29

Thurstone Temperament:

Reflectiveness	.36

Allport-Vernon-Lindzey:

Theoretical	.36
Social	— .30

Interest
Kuder Preference Record:

Scientific	.20
Literary	.49
Social service	— .38

It is apparent that rapid salary advancement for supervisors and executives in the Minneapolis Gas Co. is moderately related to ability factors as reflected in educational attainment and by various measures of intellectual capacity and achievement. It is much more weakly related to personality and interest measures. If only a single measure of management effectiveness (defined by speed of salary advancement) were to be used, educational level would be about as good as any of the others, but it would still account for only about 15 to 20 percent of the criterion variance.

Very similar findings were made by H. D. Meyer (1963, 1965a, 1965b) in a series of studies in the Jewel Tea Co., but he proceeded to study the usefulness of test measures when other factors related to promotion (such as education) were held relatively constant. Meyer's findings are somewhat difficult to interpret because he reports only mean scores, failing to give standard deviations, overlap statistics, or correlational data. However, he asks pertinent questions of his data, and because of this his results provide suggestive leads for looking at management effectiveness somewhat differently from the way it is approached in the studies we have been reviewing.

In 1959, the Jewel Tea Co. initiated a psychological assessment program for managers as part of a broader management development and manpower inventory program. A major purpose was to identify promotable managerial talent; thus, each manager was assigned a promotability rating on a six-point scale. In 1965, a follow-up was made of 178 managers assessed during 1959 and 1960 in order to relate the assessment ratings, biographical factors, and test scores to actual promotion experiences during the intervening five to six years. The assessment ratings showed a strong relationship to later promotions; of 85 persons rated as promotable during assessment, 67 (79 percent) actually received promotions in the ensuing five to six years, and of 93 persons rated as nonpromotable, only 12 (13 percent) received promotions. Of course, the assessment ratings of promotability probably played an important role in actual personnel decisions; thus, Meyer also investigated other factors related to personnel decisions. He found that age, education, initial management level, and functional area were all moderately related (phi coefficients [computed by us] of .45, .54, .31, and .48) to promotional experience. Each of these factors and the assessment rating were then weighted equally to yield a "promotability probability index," which was shown to be strongly related to promotion experience. This is illustrated in the table below.

NUMBER OF MANAGERS WITH DIFFERENT PROMOTION EXPERIENCES DURING THE PERIOD 1959 TO 1965

| | | Promotions | | |
		Two	One	None
	5	10	11	0
Promotion	4	8	16	2
probability	3	5	10	12
index	2	3	11	17
	1	0	5	30
	0	0	0	38

In summary, Meyer's follow-up showed that promotion policies in the Jewel Tea Co. from 1958 to 1965 gave precedence to those managers who were relatively young, were well educated, had begun at lower initial levels, and were working in three key functions (buying, merchandising, and administrative) with the company. The next step was to determine the degree of relationship between various cognitive and personality tests used in the assessment program and promotion experience when the above factors were held relatively constant. To this end, he examined test information for promoted and nonpromoted persons with the same or similar scores on the promotability probability index. The results must be viewed with caution because the numbers of persons in the various subcells (equated according to the promotability probability index) are small, and the results have not been cross-validated. However, the promoted managers clearly scored somewhat higher on a general intelligence test than the nonpromoted managers. The personality test also showed modest differences, which Meyer (1965b, pp. 6-7) has described as follows:

> The pattern for the high probability but not subsequently promoted group is one of outwardly feigned social competence of an emotionally cold and anti-socially manipulative and independent variety, given away by a high social desirability bias score not accompanied by socially desirable scores in personal adjustment and warm and considerate inter-personal relationships.[11] . . . Contrasted with this . . . the low promotion probability but subsequently promoted group . . . reflects no social desirability bias. [Their score average] shows low detail interest, higher emotionality and frankness, and low recognition anxiety. . . . Those promoted are better delegators, are more flexible with details, are less manipulative of people, have less anxiety about approval from superiors and are less inclined to present themselves in an artificially favorable light. They are also probably more warmly emotional.

This series of studies by Meyer is useful in suggesting that the more straightforward, open, and confident men are, the more likely they are to be promoted when "other things (education, job function, etc.) are equal."

Albright (1966) has recently reported a study relating test information to various effectiveness measures for 183 field sales managers working with the American Oil Company. The study dealt with both predictive and concurrent relationships; concurrent relationships are based on tests administered to the managers shortly before effectiveness ratings were obtained. Predictive relationships are based on tests administered to nearly one-third of the men in 1955 when they were working as salesmen for the firm. Measures of effectiveness included global performance and promotability ratings made by their supervisors and salary growth rate corrected for the effect of across-the-board increases. Correlations were computed between all test scores and each of

[11]Measured by scores on the Bass Orientation Inventory.

the criteria; computations were done for the total group and for subgroups separated according to age (above and below forty) and according to different functional areas (retail, consumer, or field sales managers). Results can be summarized as follows:

1 Low to moderate concurrent relationships (ranging between .15 and .40) were obtained against the global performance rating for vocabulary knowledge, measures of dominance, self-sufficiency, and decisiveness and for SVIB scales such as president of a manufacturing company, personnel manager, and certified public accountant.

2 Moderate predictive relationships (ranging between .25 and .45) were shown against the global performance rating for SVIB scales involving positive interest in sales, advertising, verbal, and business occupations and negative or a rejecting pattern of interests in skilled trades and outdoor occupations (such as farmer, industrial arts teacher, carpenter, policeman, etc.). These relationships were particularly marked for retail managers (ranging from -.55 for the policeman scale to +.60 for the sales manager scale).

3 Low to moderate concurrent and predictive relationships (.15 to .35) were obtained against the global promotability ratings for intelligence and vocabulary measures, political and business-oriented values, personality measures of flexibility and agreeableness, and SVIB interests involving business, verbal, and administrative jobs (such as certified public accountant, lawyer, and school superintendent).

4 By and large, concurrent relationships were greater for men over forty than for those under forty. Albright suggests that this was due to the greater range of ability, education, and job experience present in the over-forty group.

Results of this study are in general agreement with those of other studies in pointing up the significant role of dominance, self-confidence, intelligence, and interest in verbal, persuasive, and directive activities for predicting management effectiveness. They also agree with previous studies in showing the same modest degrees of relationship between these measures and global estimates of managerial job effectiveness.

Even more modest relationships were obtained in a series of supervisory effectiveness studies carried out at North American Aviation (Tenopyr, 1960, 1961a, 1961b, 1961c, 1962, 1963, 1965; Tenopyr & Ruch, 1965). The early studies in 1960 and 1961 were undertaken to assess the validity of various tests (such as the Otis Mental Ability Test, supervisory knowledge tests, the Thurstone Test of Mental Alertness, etc.) for predicting different estimates of success (such as salary advancement, promotability, and job performance rating, etc.) of production supervisors and engineering managers. None of the tests showed useful relationships with criteria of supervisory effectiveness. Correlations were uniformly close to zero, and mean differences on tests for supervisors and managers showing varying degrees of job effectiveness were inconsequential.

In later studies, however, somewhat more positive results were obtained. For example, test and biographical comparisons between 23 "successful" and

23 "unsuccessful" computer systems managers [12] showed the former to be bright-er ($r = .66$ with Otis IQ) and more proficient in mathematics (score distribu-tions were nonoverlapping between the successful and unsuccessful men). In the most recent study (Tenopyr, 1965; Tenopyr & Ruch, 1965), a series of tests (supervisory style measures, intelligence tests, etc.) were concurrently validated against salary corrected for age and seniority for 113 production man-agers. A measure of verbal comprehension and a test designed to assess a su-pervisor's ability to handle human relations problems (Leadership Evaluation and Development scale) yielded useful but not overwhelming correlations of .29 and .36, respectively. The possibility of curvilinear relationships were also checked by computing correlation ratios (etas) between the tests and the salary criterion. The relationship with verbal comprehension showed no important change ($r = .29$; eta $= .30$), but the relationship between salary and the human relations measure did depart somewhat from linearity ($r = .36$; eta $= .46$), thus confirming the usefulness of examining the possibility of curvilinear relation-ships between predictors and criterion measures.

Three studies (Brenner, 1963a, 1963b; Flanagan & Krug, 1964) done of man-agers working for the Lockheed Aircraft Corporation are illustrative of a num-ber of important points. The first shows clearly how certain valid biographical items may be merely descriptive of managerial success rather than predictive of it. It also illustrates the necessity of cross-validation. Brenner (1963b) ad-ministered a 120-item personal history form to 293 production supervisors in 1956 and found that 14 items differentiated between high-rated and low-rat-ed men consistently in validation and cross-validation groups. In 1963, these items, along with about thirty additional ones, were administered to 50 depart-ment managers, 91 staff supervisors, and 193 production supervisors. The pro-duction supervisors were divided into validation and cross-validation groups, and item responses were compared against the most recent supervisory per-formance ratings. Similar comparisons were made separately for department managers and staff supervisors, and finally a "status" comparison was made between responses of the production supervisors and the combined groups of staff supervisors and department managers. Five group comparisons were made for each of the 45 items in the questionnaire; of these 225 comparisons, only 26 involving 20 different items were "significant" at the 5 percent level. Of the 20 items differentiating in one or more comparisons, 15 showed only one significant differentiation. Four items differentiated twice; only one item differentiated in three of the five comparisons. Moreover, *no* item showed sig-nificant differentiating power for both groups (validation and cross-validation) of production supervisors. Thus, no items "held up" as indicators of manage-rial success, and Brenner concluded that "it would presently be inadvisable

---

[12]Designated by global ratings obtained from higher management officials.

to use personal history data for the selection of supervisory personnel." Even though these results are entirely negative, it is instructive to examine some of the items showing differences between more and less successful supervisors. A sampling of these items is given below:

Item content	Success response
1 Time at present address	Five to eight years
2 Eventual expected weekly salary	Over $250
3 Present amount of life insurance	$10,000 to $15,000
4 Preferred type of work	Administrative
5 Kind of people respondent wants most frequent contacts with	Managerial
6 Least preferred leisure time activity	Active sports
7 Preference for next vacation	At a resort

None of these items showed consistent differences between successful and less successful managers. Even if such differences had been shown, it is obvious that these items tend simply to reflect present success, financial and geographic stability, and an interest in continuing in administrative jobs. We cannot say whether or not the same responses would have been made earlier, before administrative assignments had been made or before success had been experienced.

A second study (Brenner, 1963a) constitutes one of the few instances where intelligence measures have not shown positive relationships with a measure of management effectiveness. The criterion of success used in this study was essentially a nomination criterion. In 1963, the Lockheed organization instituted a program called the Management Replacement Strength Analysis, which involves asking a manager to rate his subordinates in terms of their readiness to replace him. The ratings involve simply a "yes" (ready now) or a "no" (not yet ready) designation. Brenner chose 42 men who had been nominated as immediately capable of fulfilling the responsibilities of the next higher job and matched them on age, education, and company experience with 42 men designated as not yet ready to move up. Point biserial correlations were computed between test scores and the dichotomous criterion. Only four tests yielded coefficients larger than .20. They were:

Total mental ability score	—.22
Language ability	—.27
Persuasive interest (Kuder Preference Record)	+.23
Literary interest (Kuder Preference Record)	—.22

These relationships are, of course, rather inconsequential, but they are of interest in showing the negative relationship between mental ability and this nomination criterion; perhaps there is a slight tendency for managers to feel threatened by their brighter subordinates.

The third study (Flanagan & Krug, 1964) is a nice illustration of how tests can usefully designate specific patterns of job effectiveness in different job functions. Flanagan and Krug administered the lengthy SCORES battery[13] to 60 Lockheed engineers who had been carefully chosen to fit four homogeneous subgroups. The subgroups were as equally matched as possible on age, education, and company experience and differed on two criterion dimensions (supervisory versus nonsupervisory position and rapid versus slow advancement). High and low promotion rate managers obtained nearly identical scores on the creativity (C) and engineering (E) dimensions, but high promotion rate managers were substantially higher (up to a full standard deviation) on the other four dimensions: supervision (S), organization (O), research (R), and salesmanship (S). The engineers who had been assigned to management jobs also differed sharply from those who had been left in strictly technical activities. In fact, Flanagan and Krug were able to make fairly accurate ($r = .65$) assignments of the men into each of the four subgroups, solely on the basis of a "blind" analysis of each man's SCORES profile. These favorable results suggest that a battery of tests specifically designed to pinpoint functional area aptitudes and traits such as the SCORES battery may be promising both for identifying "general" effectiveness in management and for making personnel placement decisions between management and nonmanagement jobs or in different functional areas in management. Unfortunately, this study is based on limited sample sizes; to our knowledge, it has not been repeated on an independently selected sample of engineer-managers—either in Lockheed or in any other organization. Thus, even though the results appear favorable, they must be interpreted with caution.

IMPLICATIONS OF ACTUARIAL STUDIES FOR PREDICTING MANAGERIAL EFFECTIVENESS

Taken together, these studies provide good evidence that a fairly sizable portion (30 to 50 percent) of the variance in general managerial effectiveness can be expressed in terms of personal qualities measured by self-response tests and inventories and combined by predetermined rules or statistical equations. The *construct* of effective executiveship that we set out to define in this chapter includes such factors as high intelligence, good verbal skills, effective judgment in handling managerial situations (as measured by SONJ's Managerial Judgment Test), and organizing skill; dispositions toward interpersonal relationships, hard work, being active, and taking risks; and temperamental qual-

[13]The SCORES battery is a series of tests requiring twelve hours for administration and measuring 38 variables in 6 broad areas: supervision (S), creativity (C), organization (O), research (R), engineering (E), and salesmanship (S).

ities such as dominance, confidence, straightforwardness, low anxiety, and autonomy. Moreover, men rating high in overall success report backgrounds suggesting a kind of "life-style" of success—excellent health, scholastic and extracurricular leadership in high school and college, assumption of important responsibilities rather early in life, high ambition, and active participation in religious, charitable, or civic groups. The nature of this *construct* is not surprising. What is impressive is that indicators of past successes and accomplishments can be utilized in an objective way to identify persons with differing odds of being successful over the long term in their management career. People who are already intelligent, mature, ambitious, energetic and responsible and who have a record of prior achievement when they enter an organization are in excellent positions to profit from training opportunities and from challenging organizational environments.

In addition to the substantive findings summarized above, these studies yield certain implications for methodological refinements to be considered in future research investigations.

First, all these studies used global measures of managerial effectiveness such as corrected salary or promotion indexes or man-to-man ranking systems. This is both good and bad—good because we have learned that certain core personal and individual background factors *do* relate to overall, career-long estimates of managers' optimizing effectiveness, and bad because the findings tell us little about how such qualities are related to the way in which a person may *behave* in his managerial job. Future studies should supplement global effectiveness measures with observations of what managers actually are doing in their jobs that leads to greater or less overall success.

Second, only occasional lip service has been paid to the desirability of studying and taking account of differences in managerial jobs. As was amply illustrated in SONJ's EIMP study, such potential differences in managerial job requirements are probably unimportant in an organization placing major emphasis on potential for *general* management. In contrast, the considerably lower validities (accounting for only 10 percent of the variance, as compared with the 45 to 50 percent accounted for in the SONJ series) obtained across managers employed in 13 widely different firms in the Minnesota study suggest that jobs and job differences should be studied comprehensively. Existing job titles or functional distinctions should not, of course, be the only basis for comparisons. Instead, job "families" shown empirically to be homogeneous with respect to required reponsibilities, duties, and behaviors should be compared. We believe that careful study of such job differences among samples with diverse organizational requirements, policies, and practices (such as were used in the Minnesota study) is imperative if likely validity differences for predicting managerial effectiveness in jobs varying widely in their behavioral requirements are to be discovered.

Finally, the most serious "gap" in studies reviewed here is the absence of longitudinal investigations of managing and managerial effectiveness. The typical concurrent investigation is limited not only because of the difficulty of interpreting some of the relationships obtained between self-reports and success criteria but also because it yields only a cross-sectional slice in time of managerial effectiveness. We need studies of managerial behavior as a developmental process. Bray (1964) has noted that psychologists have spent their major resources in the study of developmental processes during infancy, childhood, adolescence, and old age but relatively little in an effort to learn about developmental processes during the productive career years between ages twenty-one and sixty-five. Results from concurrent investigations will, of course, be valuable in planning such long-term studies. In time, results from both types of study will be additive, and we shall know much more about the normal developmental patterns, the rewards and traumas, the advances and declines, and the facilitators and inhibitors of managerial effectiveness experienced by managers during the critical periods of their careers.

SUMMARY

A number of carefully planned and comprehensive actuarial studies designed to discover personal qualities related to managerial effectiveness have been conducted. The most notable investigations include the SONJ study, the Minnesota Industrial Relations Center study, the series of Sears studies, the American Chamber of Commerce study, and the AT&T study of college quality and scholastic and extracurricular activities in college. In these (as well as the other studies reviewed), measures of managerial effectiveness have been either career indexes of promotional and/or salary status or global nominations or rankings of overall success. In each, the effort has been to discover correlates of *general* managerial effectiveness rather than correlates of effectiveness specific to certain groupings of managerial jobs or organizational circumstances. Most studies, with the notable exception of the Chamber of Commerce and the AT&T studies, were concurrent or "cross-sectional" validations of psychological test and background information against the success criteria.

Although results vary considerably from study to study, it does appear that from 30 to 50 percent of the variance in estimates of overall general managerial effectiveness can be expressed in terms of personal qualities claimed by managers taking part in the investigations. In spite of this impressive pattern of results, certain gaps are evident in the information derived from these studies, and additional research needs to be done to fill them in.

Managerial effectiveness should be studied developmentally. Careers should be examined sequentially as the stream of men's careers unfold over time. The impact of special experience, of training and development procedures, and of differing organizational circumstances should all be studied as they interact with individual difference factors to eventuate in effective or ineffective managerial behavior. Global estimates of effectiveness need to be supplemented with observations of managers' actual job behaviors. These observations should help to discover the various "roads to effectiveness" followed by different managers. In turn, this information should prove useful for mapping developmental patterns of managerial effectiveness as it occurs in interaction with differing job requirements and differing qualities brought to the job by different managers. We should then be better able to plan effective conservation and utilization of managerial resources as new requirements emerge in the managerial jobs of the future. This will become possible as we grow more aware of the accommodating processes between people and jobs, so that combinations of organizational practices, individual qualities, and desired managerial behaviors can be *synthesized* rather than merely *analyzed.*

Chapter 9 Research Results: Clinical Studies of Managerial Effectiveness

In our survey (reviewed in Chapter 3) of current practices followed by key industrial firms and government agencies for identifying and nurturing managerial potential, we pointed out that personnel decisions nearly always involve some degree of clinical combination of the information available for any given managerial candidate. This happens even when elaborate procedures have been taken to develop valid statistical combinations of predictor variables. In such instances, the prediction based on the statistical regression equation is often taken as additional information to take into account along with other data (e.g., appraisal information, career history, availability, and age) and a prediction made based essentially on a clinical composite strategy. Only rarely have these clinical procedures been subjected to careful study of their relative accuracy for predicting managerial effectiveness. Since the clinical approach *is* used so widely, it is important to summarize what evidence there is about its relative accuracy.

Western Reserve studies. For a number of years, the psychological Research Services (PRS) of Western Reserve University assessed persons being considered for responsible jobs in business settings. Recently, it has been possible to follow up a number of these persons to determine their relative job effectiveness. The nature of the Western Reserve program and the results of the follow-up studies have been described exhaustively and somewhat redundantly in a lengthy series of articles (J. T. Campbell, 1962; J. T. Campbell, Otis, Liske, & Prien, 1962; Hogue, Otis, & Prien, 1962; Huse, 1962; Otis, Campbell, & Prien, 1962; Prien, 1962; Prien & Liske, 1962).

Unfortunately, the authors do not report results separately for managerial and nonmanagerial candidates; in fact, many of their subjects were applicants for sales or engineering jobs; therefore, we shall describe their studies only briefly, primarily in order to provide the reader with an illustration of clinical assessment procedures, how they are used in industry, and how research can be done to determine how good they are for predicting job effectiveness.

The program established by the Western Reserve group took the following form: Shortly after a company requested help in "sizing up" candidates, a PRS staff member made a personal visit to the company in order to obtain information about the job to be filled, the so-called company climate, and the social environment in which the successful candidate would be working. No objective measures of the job, the climate, or the social environment were used, but the impressions formed were the basis for selecting tests for the candidates and for giving the interviewers and report writers background information which presumably would be helpful during the assessment procedure.

Each candidate was then tested. Tests such as the following were used: the American Council on Education Intelligence Examination, the Cooperative Reading Test, the Guilford-Zimmerman Temperament Survey, the Edwards Personal Preference Schedule, the Kuder Preference Record, and projective instruments such as the Thematic Apperception Test and the Worthington Incomplete Sentence Test. Two psychologists having no knowledge of the candidate's test results interviewed him and completed sets of rating scales. A clinical psychologist examined the candidate's responses to the projective instruments and completed a set of ratings without seeing the candidate. A report writer then collated all information available on the candidate and prepared a report for the client firm. Additional ratings were made based (1) solely on the objective test results, (2) solely on the written report, and (3) on full and complete information. The following eight dimensions, used for all the above ratings, were person- or trait-oriented rather than job-oriented: social skills, persuasiveness, leadership, intellectual capacity, creativeness, planning, motivation and energy, and overall effectiveness.

Thus the strategies used for developing the various ratings used both clinically and mechanically collected data to form trait ratings. In making trait ratings based partly on personality test profiles, profile interpretation was necessary, and in making an overall effectiveness prediction, the information had to be combined clinically. Thus the various modes of data collection and combination yield predictions based on four strategies (see Table 7.1): pure clinical, behavior (trait) rating, profile interpretation, and clinical composite.

At least six months later, global ratings of job effectiveness were obtained from supervisors of the candidates who had been hired. These ratings were a kind of "action" rating, ranging from "A"—outstanding in every way, will be promoted as soon as an opening occurs, would go to some effort to keep him as an employee—to "E"—a failure in this position, transfer or discharge is imminent, his resignation should be encouraged.

Ratings based on the various assessment procedures were correlated with the supervisory ratings. The results are shown in Table 9.1.

The correlations in Table 9.1 are not bad, considering the many extrapolations made between the applicants' responses and the behavior ratings and predictions. Moreover, the subjects were employed in several different jobs with many different firms. It is particularly noteworthy that ratings based solely on objective tests (mechanically collected) were generally more valid than those based either on the interview or the projective responses singly or on the combined information of tests, interview, and projective responses.

Table 9.1 CORRELATIONS BETWEEN BEHAVIOR RATINGS BASED ON VARIOUS TYPES OF ASSESSMENT EVIDENCE AND SUPERVISORY RATINGS OF OVERALL JOB EFFECTIVENESS FOR 107 JOB INCUMBENTS ASSESSED AT LEAST SIX MONTHS PREVIOUSLY

Rating dimension		Projective measures	Objective tests	All information	Based only on report
Social skills	.12	.18	.24	.13	.13
Persuasiveness	.11	.33	.22	.22	.24
Leadership	.38	.26	.15	.44	.28
Intellectual capacity	.26	.13	.35	.32	.32
Creativeness	.27	.17	.34	.41	.23
Planning	.12	.18	.35	.21	.29
Motivation and energy	.08	.03	.29	.17	.07
Overall effectiveness	.16	.21	.28	.28	.11
Median correlation	.14	.18	.29	.25	.24

Source: Huse (1962).

GENERAL COMMENTS ABOUT CLINICAL INVESTIGATIONS

The Western Reserve studies illustrate a number of points about the clinical mode of data handling that should be kept in mind as we describe other clinical investigations.

First, the studies are true predictive studies in that the assessment information was obtained at a time prior to gathering the job effectiveness ratings;

therefore, the results can more safely be generalized to similar predictive situations than studies using only concurrent validation designs. Clinical studies tend more often to be predictive; statistical studies (as we saw in the immediately preceding section) are more likely to be concurrent, although this is in no sense necessarily true.

Second, the clinical judgments of the Western Reserve staff members were put into the form of written reports and delivered to company officials charged with making personnel decisions about the candidates. This is a uniform practice whenever assessments are being done in order to aid actual personnel decision making. Such reports usually discuss the candidates' personal characteristics and expected job behaviors, areas which will also usually be the basis for later supervisory ratings. Such reports can seriously color or "contaminate" results of later job behavior observations. In many follow-up studies of clinical judgments, it is difficult to know how seriously contaminated the job behavior observations may be by knowledge gained from the earlier clinical reports. The Western Reserve researchers tried to guard against such contamination by not informing the supervisors ahead of time that they would be asked to make ratings; the staff members made no appointments and merely appeared (by surprise) at each supervisor's office to obtain the global job effectiveness ratings. This tactic certainly should have been effective in keeping the supervisors from reviewing the written reports or even thinking back to them at the time they made their ratings, but it is still impossible to estimate the extent to which their memory of the reports or simply the original "set" created by either a favorable or an unfavorable report might have affected their overall effectiveness ratings; thus clinical follow-ups must be interpreted with caution unless special steps have been taken to guard against the possibility of criterion contamination.[1]

Third, as with most predictive studies, results of clinical follow-ups may actually yield underestimates of the true validities of the clinical judgments. This is so because the subjects available for follow-up study include only those who were hired; persons showing up poorly in the clinical assessment will usually not be hired and will be unavailable for study. The potential magnitude of this effect on test validity has been demonstrated by Peterson and Wallace (1966). Shortly after showing that a scored biographical information blank (the Aptitude Index) had no useful relationship with measures of success for insurance salesmen, Peterson and Wallace persuaded company officials to continue to administer the Aptitude Index to all applicants, but not to score it.

---

[1] In spite of the possibility of such contamination, it should be noted that psychologists' predictions of overall effectiveness based solely on the reports correlated only .11 with the supervisors' ratings. If psychologists did so poorly in discerning potential from the reports when they had direct access to them, it is doubtful that the reports could have had much effect on the supervisors' ratings. This finding may reflect the common tendency for such reports to be phrased in glowing generalities and to tend toward "fence straddling" as far as any solid recommendations are concerned.

Table 9.2 RELATIONSHIP BETWEEN APTITUDE INDEX SCORES AND SIX-MONTH SURVIVAL RATES FOR INSURANCE AGENTS*

Aptitude index score range	Number of agents hired	Number surviving 6 months or longer	Percent survivors
32-39	24	13	54
29-31	38	13	34
27-28	39	7	18
25-26	40	6	15
20-24	18	1	6

*r_{pb} = .30.

After a period of time, the Aptitude Index scores for 159 agents were compared with their survival[2] as insurance salesmen. The results are shown in Table 9.2. It is apparent that the Aptitude Index actually does have good predictive validity for success in insurance selling but that its use as a selection device had probably curtailed the range to such a degree that its apparent validity was negligible. Thus it is very important in interpreting follow-up studies to estimate what the results *might* have shown if the assessment evaluations had not played a part in the initial hiring and placement of the subjects.

One final property of most clinical studies (also illustrated by the Western Reserve series) deserves special comment. Results from such studies do not typically specify exactly the rules or procedures for obtaining valid clinical judgments. In this sense, a clinical study possesses less potential for generality of results than a carefully conducted statistical validation. Clinical studies do not usually yield expectancy tables or precise statements about the odds of certain job behaviors' being associated with particular patterns or configurations of test scores. For example, even though the Western Reserve studies did yield modest correlations, there is nothing in their research reports showing the mechanisms used by the psychologists for deriving their clinical judgments. Other investigators and other psychologists gain less, probably, from such a report than they might be able to gain from a similar report of a validation of a statistical combination of predictor measures. What is needed is more careful attention to the mechanisms used by the clinicians in coming to their ratings and their overall judgments. The usefulness of the clinical approach will be greatly enhanced if the bases for judgments can be explicated and communicated to other psychologists so that they, too, can utilize similar procedures for making predictions of job behavior.

OTHER CLINICAL STUDIES OF MANAGERIAL EFFECTIVENESS

As we proceed now to discuss additional clinical investigations, we shall be alert to the features and problems discussed above—the dangers of con-

[2]Survival was defined as staying with the company six months or longer and earning at least $700 in insurance sales commissions.

taminated criteria, the effects of restriction of range due to use of the clinical reports for personnel decisions, and the need to learn more explicitly what the clinician is doing and how he does it when he derives judgments from the information available for any given candidate.

Dunnette and Kirchner (1958) validated three clinical hypotheses concerning managerial effectiveness. A battery of tests including the Miller Analogies Test (MAT), the Wechsler Adult Intelligence Scale (WAIS), the Strong Vocational Interest Blank (SVIB), the California Psychological Inventory (CPI), and the Edwards Personal Preference Schedule (EPPS) was administered to 26 sales managers working with the 3M Co. At about the same time, the general manager and vice-president of their product division compared each manager with every one of the remaining managers and designated the more effective of each pair of managers. This yielded a global effectiveness score for each man—simply the proportion of times that each was selected as the more effective member of the various pairs. The authors reasoned that more effective managers should (1) be more intelligent, (2) have broader interests, and (3) have "stronger" personalities than less effective managers. To test the hypothesis concerning intelligence, the effectiveness scores of managers above and below the median on the MAT and those above and below an IQ of 125 on the WAIS were compared. To test the hypothesis concerning broad interests, the effectiveness scores of managers with moderate to strong interest patterns in at least two occupational groupings on the SVIB were compared with those of managers showing interest in either none or only one occupational grouping. To test the hypothesis about strong personality, the managers' profiles on the CPI and the EPPS were examined and divided into those with strong personalities (highly confident, outgoing and sociable, dominant, and self-accepting) and those with weak personalities (lacking in confidence, showing dependency needs, nondominant, and introverted), and their effectiveness scores were compared. Finally, managers having "favorable" designations on two or three of the three hypothesized variables (intelligence, interests, and personality) were compared with those having "unfavorable" designations on at least two of the three variables. These clinical interpretations involved mechanical data collection and a combination of mechanical information (for the intelligence tests) and clinical information (profile interpretation) for the personality and interest inventories.

The results of these comparisons are shown in Table 9.3. Even though based on only a small sample of managers, this is an important study because it shows how the clinical combination of tests can be specified according to definite hypotheses based on characteristics believed to be important for effective management. The clinical methods used by the authors for identifying broad interests and strong personalities are clearly stated and can be used by other investigators interested in replicating the clinical processes used by Dunnette

Table 9.3 MEANS AND STANDARD DEVIATIONS OF EFFECTIVENESS SCORES FOR
SALES MANAGERS DIVIDED ACCORDING TO INTELLIGENCE, BREADTH
OF INTERESTS, AND PERSONALITY CHARACTERISTICS

Tests and test score patterns	Effectiveness score			
	N	M	SD	r*
MAT:				
Top half	12	.71	.28	.50
Lower half	12	.44	.34	
WAIS:				
IQ 125 and above	15	.69	.27	.47
IQ 124 and below	11	.35	.32	
SVIB:				
Broad interests	18	.64	.31	.55
Narrow interests	8	.34	.31	
CPI and EPPS:				
"Strong" personality	17	.62	.34	.44
"Weak" personality	9	.40	.30	
Overall:				
Two out of three "favorable"	15	.70	.28	.61
Two out of three "unfavorable"	11	.34	.30	

* The correlations given in the above table are product moment coefficients for MAT and WAIS scores; the remaining are phi coefficients.

Source: Dunnette & Kirchner (1958).

and Kirchner. Moreover, the results show that the combination of inferences derived from the separate designations yields a more powerful relationship with rated effectiveness than any of the three variables considered singly.

Albrecht, Glaser, and Marks (1964) and Dicken and Black (1965) carried out follow-up studies of the later job effectiveness of managers who had gone through clinical appraisal programs earlier. Subjects in the Albrecht et al. study were 31 district marketing managers who were each assessed by clinical procedures (filling out personal history form and taking a sentence completion test and a human relations test, participating in a two-hour interview, and taking brief intelligence and critical thinking tests) shortly after being promoted to managerial jobs. The assessment procedures were carried out for the purpose of validating recommendations based on them; thus they were not used in any way in the selection process, and no reports about the assessment results were given to the company during the period of the study. It is quite certain, therefore, that the later ratings of job effectiveness were not contaminated by knowledge of the assessment results, nor did any restriction in range occur as a result of the use of the assessment data for selection purposes. The three psychologists conducting the assessments ranked the subjects according to predicted job effectiveness in four broad areas: (1) forecasting and budgeting

Table 9.4 CORRELATION COEFFICIENTS BETWEEN CLINICAL PREDICTIONS, TEST
SCORES, AND COMPOSITE RANKINGS OF EFFECTIVENESS IN FOUR JOB
AREAS FOR 31 MARKETING MANAGERS

Job area	Clinical prediction	Intelligence test	Critical thinking test
Forecasting and budgeting	.49	.41	.30
Sales performance	.58	−.07	.12
Interpersonal relationships	.43	.18	.18
Overall effectiveness	.46	.23	.24

Source: Albrecht et al. (1964).

effectiveness, (2) sales performance, (3) interpersonal relationships, and (4) overall performance. Selection of the first three dimensions was based on the informed opinion that they were the most critical for doing the job properly. After a year on the job, the managers were ranked on each of the above skills by two managers above them and by their peers; the three sets of rankings were combined to form a composite index for each subject in each job area. The psychologists' clinical predictions were correlated with the composite index scores, and scores on the two tests were also correlated with the composite rankings. The correlations obtained are shown in Table 9.4.

It is obvious that the clinical combination of information yielded better predictions of later effectiveness for these managers than either of the tests. The difference is least marked for predicting forecasting and budgeting effectiveness (a job behavior which one would expect to be most effectively predicted by intelligence measures) and most marked for predicting sales performance (a part of the job that one would least expect to be predicted by intelligence measures). Moreover, the psychologists making the clinical predictions revealed a fair degree of diagnostic accuracy; that is, their rankings of the subjects on a particular job dimension (such as sales performance) were more highly related to the effectiveness rankings on that dimension than to rankings on other dimensions. This is shown in Table 9.5. This study is an effective demon-

Table 9.5 CORRELATIONS BETWEEN CLINICAL PREDICTIONS IN FOUR JOB AREAS
AND COMPOSITE RANKINGS OF EFFECTIVENESS IN THE SAME JOB AREAS
FOR 31 MARKETING MANAGERS

Clinical predictions	Composite effectiveness rankings			
	Forecasting and budgeting	Sales performance	Interpersonal relationships	Overall effectiveness
Forecasting and budgeting	.49	.15	.33	.34
Sales performance	.02	.58	.39	.39
Interpersonal relationships	.03	.24	.43	.27
Overall effectiveness	.35	.33	.40	.46

stration of the feasibility of seeking to predict different important aspects of managerial behavior and of the ability to do so with an appropriate clinical combination of information.

Two studies reported by Dicken and Black (1965) yielded results generally similar to those obtained by Albrecht et al., but their test battery was much more extensive, including the Strong Vocational Interest Blank (SVIB), the Minnesota Multiphasic Personality Inventory (MMPI), the Otis Quick-scoring Mental Ability Test, and many other tests of clerical aptitude, spatial relations ability, supervisory knowledge, etc. Candidates for promotion to supervisory positions were tested for two firms (one a manufacturing company and the other an insurance firm). A narrative report of about five hundred words was written for each candidate which emphasized his relative strengths and limitations in terms of future jobs and promotional possibilities in his company.

At the time of the study, follow-up information (criterion personality ratings and management personnel decisions) was obtained for 31 of the assessees in the manufacturing firm and 26 assessees from the insurance firm. The information was obtained on the manufacturing firm employees an average of 3½ years after assessment, and on the insurance employees an average of seven years after assessment. Clinical ratings based on the assessment results and scores on the various tests were correlated with the criterion information. Concerning the question of criterion contamination in this study, Dicken and Black (1965, p. 38) state:

> Such contamination is probably minimal in this study, though it cannot be ruled out entirely. White two raters in each company had had direct access to the test reports, none had read them in recent years. . . . Although the reports may have initially confirmed or cast doubt upon opinions held about the subjects, the long time span since testing and the intimate day-to-day contact of the raters and subjects argue against criteria reflecting much from the test reports not well confirmed by direct observation.

The narrative reports were read by four psychologists who used seven-step scales to rate each subject on eight variables:

1 *Effective intelligence.* Able to understand and solve problems efficiently. Grasps problems clearly—perceives the issues. Learns readily. Emphasis is on intellectual ability which can be applied in action. Versus: Slow to learn new materials, routines. Cannot perceive the issue clearly.
2 *Personal soundness.* Mature in personal relationships both on the job and in family and personal life. Personal life is satisfying; is comfortable with himself. Free from emotional instability. Tolerates pressure without difficulties. Versus: Worry or stress causes symptoms like trouble on the job, physical illness, frequent absence, wife trouble, drinking, and accidents.
3 *Drive and ambition.* Active and energetic in pursuing a course of action. Ready to assume initiative. Persistent in seeking goals; willing to extend extra effort to reach them. Is personally ambitious; demonstrates a desire to get ahead. Versus: Not energetic. Not persistent. Has little initiative or ambition.

4 *Leadership and dominance.* Is poised and self-confident in dealing with others. Confident without arrogance. Maintains authority easily and comfortably. Has a matter-of-fact way of expecting his orders to be obeyed or his suggestions to be accepted. Is positive and decisive in making decisions and directing others. Versus: Lacks confidence; is ill at ease in position of authority. Cannot be decisive; is easily confused or uncertain about decisions.

5 *Likableness.* Gets along well with other people. Is popular with associates. Is tactful and adept in social contacts. Versus: Unlikable, unpopular. Tactless, blunt. Has annoying habits. Irritable; makes others uncomfortable.

6 *Responsibility and conscientiousness.* Can give him a job and count on him to see it through properly. Thorough and prompt in carrying out assigments. Takes his duties seriously. His work is accurate. Versus: Needs to be checked or jogged frequently to get job done. Careless, sloppy work.

7 *Ability to cooperate.* Works effectively with other individuals and departments. Can discuss differences freely and effectively. Can compromise and admit own errors or those of own department without undue need to defend himself or his program. Is a good team worker. Tries to "get the job done" in the way which is best for the entire organization without regard for personal feeling. Versus: Defensive about own program if criticized or compromise is needed. Not a good team worker.

8 *Estimate of potential functioning level.* The level of responsibility at which the man might ultimately be capable of functioning in the organization.

Raters in each of the two companies used the same eight variables to rate each subject on the basis of their knowledge of him in the work setting. The ratings were obtained from higher company officials in an interview situation so that the eight dimensions could be carefully defined and so that each rater would give diligent and perceptive attention to the rating task. The clinical

Table 9.6 CORRELATIONS BETWEEN COMPOSITE CLINICAL RATINGS AND SUPER-VISORY RATINGS FOR 31 MANUFACTURING COMPANY MANAGERS AND 26 INSURANCE COMPANY MANAGERS

| | Manufacturing sample | | Insurance sample | | |
| | Relevant report rating | Mean of nonrelevant report ratings | Relevant report rating | Relevant test rating* | Mean of nonrelevant report ratings |
Supervisory rating					
1 Intelligence	.40	.31	.65	.63	.06
2 Soundness	.37	.27	.29	.16	.17
3 Drive	.30	.16	.17	.43	−.10
4 Leadership	.41	.22	.19	.29	.07
5 Likableness	.30	.14	.40	.36	.16
6 Responsibility	.38	.09	.03	.19	−.04
7 Cooperativeness	.20	.24	.21	.40	.20
8 Potential	.51	.38	.31	.18	.19
Median	.38	.23	.25	.33	.12

* For the insurance sample, psychologists made ratings based on the test results in addition to making ratings based on their readings of the reports.

Source: Dicken & Black (1965).

ratings by the psychologists were correlated with the supervisory ratings. Results are shown in Table 9.6. The most impressive fact shown by these results is the diagnostic capability of the clinicians. In nearly every instance, the correlation between the clinical rating (whether based on the report or on the test information) and the corresponding supervisory rating is clearly higher than the mean of its correlations with noncorresponding scales. In other words, the psychologists showed in this study that they could discern behavioral tendencies from assessment information that agree fairly well with the things supervisors will discern about the same people after working with them for a period of months or years. Dicken and Black also correlated all the various test scores against the criterion ratings. Only the intellective and ability measures came close to the clinical ratings in their ability to predict the criterion ratings. A sample of results with the test predictors is shown in Table 9.7.

Although we shall discuss large-scale assessment programs in detail later, it is instructive at this point to present results of three follow-up studies of assessees employed by AT&T. In 1957, the personnel research staff of AT&T instituted its Management Progress Study. In broad outline, the purpose of the study was to obtain extensive psychological information on a large sample of graduating college seniors recently hired by various of the Bell System companies as the first step of a career-long study of managerial progress at AT&T. To this end, a number of recent college hires went through a thorough three-day assessment program during the summer of 1957. The assessees took a large number of tests, participated in situational and leaderless group discussion exercises, were extensively interviewed, and were observed informally. An outstanding feature of the Management Progress Study is that all this information was gathered strictly for research. No one in AT&T except members of the personnel research staff has had access to any of the assessment results; thus there

Table 9.7 **REPRESENTATIVE CORRELATIONS BETWEEN VARIOUS TESTS AND SUPERVISORY RATINGS FOR 31 MANUFACTURING COMPANY MANAGERS AND 26 INSURANCE COMPANY MANAGERS**

		Manufacturing sample				Insurance sample		
		Otis	General clerical	How supervise?	SVIB prod. mgr.	Otis	Minn. clerical	SVIB banker
1	Intelligence	.55	.44	.23	.02	.65	.47	−.24
2	Soundness	.07	.09	.18	.12	.22	.09	.16
3	Drive	.42	.09	.13	−.02	.23	.21	−.23
4	Leadership	.37	.40	.29	−.10	.21	.31	.12
5	Likableness	−.09	−.02	.07	.29	.18	.31	.42
6	Responsibility	.07	−.02	.11	.00	.19	.22	.12
7	Cooperativeness	−.04	−.03	.28	.27	.07	.21	.48
8	Potential	.43	.42	.37	.13	.29	.31	−.14

Table 9.8 RELATIONSHIP BETWEEN ASSESSMENT ESTIMATES OF CAREER POTEN-
TIAL FOR 59 AT&T ASSESSEES AND THEIR MANAGERS' RATINGS OF THEIR
JOB PERFORMANCE FIVE YEARS LATER*

| | | Rated job performance (1962) | | |
		Below average	Average	Above average
Estimate of career potential (1957)	High potential	2	10	8
	Lower potential	11	24	4

*r_{pb} = .35.

Table 9.9 RELATIONSHIP BETWEEN ASSESSMENT ESTIMATES OF CAREER POTEN-
TIAL FOR 23 AT&T ASSESSEES AND THE DECISION TO SEND SOME TO
A SPECIAL EXECUTIVE DEVELOPMENT INSTITUTE AT NORTHWESTERN
UNIVERSITY*

		Not selected for NWU	Selected for NWU
Estimate of career potential (1957)	High potential	3	7
	Lower potential	11	2

*r_{ϕ} = .55.

Table 9.10 RELATIONSHIP BETWEEN ASSESSMENT RATINGS OF 24 AT&T SUPER-
VISORS ASSESSED "FOR PRACTICE" IN 1959 AND THEIR PROMOTIONAL
EXPERIENCE IN THE ENSUING FOUR YEARS*

| | | Status in 1963 | |
		Not promoted	Promoted
Assessment rating	Good supervisory potential	0	8
	Questionable supervisory potential	6	6
	Poor supervisory potential	4	0

*r_{pb} = .70.

has been no problem of criterion contamination and no restriction in the range of effectiveness due to using assessment results for making personnel decisions. In addition to a myriad other clinical ratings (described later) of each assessee, the members of the assessment staff made an overall, global estimate of each man's career potential.

In 1962, Campbell[3] and his colleagues interviewed the managers of 59 of the assessees in order to compare their present job performance with the estimates of career potential made during assessment five years previously. Results of the comparison are shown in Table 9.8. In a second study, Campbell followed up 23 assessees who had been placed initially on management trainee jobs where their performance was closely observed. As a result of outstanding performance, some were chosen to attend an intensive summer executive development institute at Northwestern University. The career potential estimates of the men chosen for Northwestern are compared with the estimates of those not chosen in Table 9.9. In a third study, Campbell followed up 24 men who had been assessed in 1959 "for practice" during the training of new assessment staff members. He compared global ratings of the assessees with their promotional experience during the ensuing four years. Results are given in Table 9.10.

These studies, even though based on fairly small samples, provide rather impressive evidence of the validity of clinical assessment procedures for predicting such personnel actions as promotion, managerial performance evaluation, and success nominations (i.e., being singled out for specialized executive training) in the AT&T organization.

CONCLUSIONS CONCERNING CLINICAL STUDIES

We can now compare the methods and results of these clinical investigations with those of the statistical studies summarized previously. Perhaps the most general impression is that the clinical studies have involved more analytical thinking about managers, managerial jobs, and managerial job effectiveness than the statistical studies. Admittedly, this impression is vague and rather imprecise. Still, the feeling persists; clinical investigations have usually focused more completely on the key personal traits to be measured, the significant job behaviors to be predicted, and the *diagnostic* use of psychological measures and assessment techniques.

Although there may be much less certainty about the stability of valid inferences based on clinical modes of collecting and combining information, it is a distinct advantage to be able to refer to evidence showing that such inferences have yielded *predictive* validities in relation to managerial effective-

[3] Personal communication, 1966.

ness. Moreover, it is reassuring to note that clinicians can apparently designate with fair accuracy some of the major trait and behavioral tendencies that will be observed later, after a man has been on the job for a period of time. Thus, we are impressed that the clinical studies summarized here have been analytic, rational, and thoughtfully conducted.

NEEDED RESEARCH STEPS

The greatest need now is to combine the analytic approaches characteristic of clinical studies with the evidence-oriented and quantitative attitudes characteristic of statistical investigations. We have already outlined in Chapter 8 how we believe this can be done by using synthetic validity concepts in studies of managerial effectiveness. It is possible now to state some further recommendations based on our foregoing review of clinical investigations.

First, studies need to be done which do not use the results of clinical assessments to help make operational personnel decisions. The Albrecht et al. study is one such example; many more need to be undertaken so that the relative validities of clinical procedures for predicting uncontaminated behavioral criteria for managers showing the total (rather than a restricted) range of assessment attributes can be estimated.

Second, more objective methods or measures of situational attributes need to be developed and applied in future investigations. One of the presumed advantages of clinical procedures is that organizational and situational circumstances can be taken into account in making behavioral predictions. Undoubtedly, clinical judgments do seek to take account of such variables, but we have been unable to locate any published studies specifying the nature of factors considered or how clinical judgments may be affected by them. Future studies should either measure these situational variables or at least explicate the inferential processes used by clinicians as they seek to take such differences into account. Similarly, job differences and their effects both on clinical judgments and on the validities of behavioral predictions need to be specified. Several of the studies reviewed above dealt with relatively homogeneous groups of jobs (e.g., Albrecht et al., 1964; Dunnette & Kirchner, 1958); others dealt with many different managerial assignments for which the clinicians presumably "corrected for" the differences, but the nature of such corrections was not spelled out.

Third, as already suggested, the bases for clinical judgments need to be spelled out so that other persons can learn the techniques of successfully making clinical assessments. It may be that clinicians do not always know or may find impossible to communicate the exact basis for their judgments. This need be no permanent deterrent to learning what the bases for their inferences are and how they may go about making them. Computer technology now provides methods for capturing the policies used by personnel decision makers. Such methods have been successfully applied to clinicians' diagnoses of emotional maladjustment and to the interpretation of personality test information (Kleinmuntz, 1963a, 1963b, 1963c, 1964). Thus, once it is shown that a clinical combination of information can yield valid behavioral predictions for managers, the processes and the combining rules should be discovered and explicated. Steps for doing this should enter into the planning stages of future clinical investigations.

Finally, greater emphasis in future studies should be given to the possibility of placing persons in taxonomic categories on the basis of assessment information and then determining their later behavioral patterns in their managerial jobs. This approach was essentially the one used by Dunnette and Kirchner (1958) when they formed test-based categories of "persons with broad interests" and "persons with strong personalities." The rationale for this type of approach has been well stated by Sines (1964, 1966). Briefly, it is based on the assumption that in many instances, the same or similar criterion behaviors may be exhibited by persons with widely differing psychological characteristics. When this is the case, identifying persons showing a particular behavioral pattern may add little or nothing to efforts designed to discover underlying correlates of the behavior; in fact, such efforts might simply yield confusing and seemingly inconsistent results and lead to a series of culs-de-sac. In contrast, persons belonging to the same subgroup defined by measurable psychological characteristics may be observed, and the relative frequency of particular criterion behaviors discovered. This is essentially the approach of actuarial pattern analysis suggested by Lykken (1956) and later demonstrated to be a feasible approach by Lykken and Rose (1963).

Many of the features outlined above have been or can be incorporated into the Bell System's Management Progress Study. By describing it at some length, we hope to convey an understanding of the procedures involved and to outline the latest results reported by the staff of the Management Progress Study.

THE AT&T MANAGEMENT PROGRESS STUDY

A most ambitious and carefully conceived investigation of career development during the years of maturity, AT&T's Management Progress Study was begun in 1956. A number of significant reports of results (Berlew, 1965; Berlew & Hall, 1964, 1967; Bray, 1962, 1964, 1966; Bray & Grant, 1966; Bray, Grant, Berlew, Rychlak, & Katkovsky, 1965) have been made, and it seems apparent that the last decade of painstaking data collection and analysis promises a rich harvest of knowledge bearing on the identification and enhancement of managerial effectiveness.

Design of the study. Defining management development as "those changes in individuals resulting in increased capability to manage," Bray (1962, 1964) designed and undertook the Management Progress Study in order to study longitudinally the unfolding business careers of managers from the time they take their first jobs in the Bell System onward, tracing the total range of their experiences, their successes, and their failures and noting changes in their cognitive, motivational, and attitudinal characteristics as they affect and are affected by their job experiences. The intention, therefore, was to obtain as complete a psychological assessment as possible of a number of young men newly employed in various companies of the Bell System and to follow them periodically throughout their careers. The design for initial data collection and subsequent follow-ups is shown below:

Time	Data from men in the study	Data from the men's companies
First year	Psychological assessment	
Second to fourth year	Intensive interview; questionnaires of attitudes and expectations	Intensive interview with departmental personnel supervisor
Fifth year	Intensive interview; questionnaires of attitudes and expectations	Intensive interview with departmental personnel supervisor; interviews with two former bosses
Sixth year	Intensive interview; questionnaires of attitudes and expectations	Intensive interview with present boss
Seventh year	Intensive interview; questionnaires of attitudes and expectations	
Eighth year	Reassessment	Collection of present appraisal, level, and salary information

Intensive data-gathering methods were employed. The complete range of techniques available was used in conducting $3\frac{1}{2}$-day psychological assessments; methods included paper-and-pencil tests, work samples (e.g., an In-basket test), projective tests, clinical interviews, and participation in group problems and leaderless group discussions. Equally thorough studies were planned of each subject's life and work environments, descriptions of his various jobs, his training experiences, his salary treatment, the traditions and goals of his organization, the morale of his work group, etc. Plans were also made to follow up men who terminated their employment with AT&T as well as those staying with the Bell System.

In accordance with these plans, 422 men employed in six companies were assessed over several summers as shown in the table below:

	Year	Original sample	Still employed (1965)
Company A:			
College hires	1956	67	44
Company B:			
College hires	1957	79	55
Company C:			
Non-college managers	1958	84	83
Company D:			
College hires	1959	56	29
Non-college managers	1959	40	39
Company E:			
College hires	1960	36	20
Non-college managers	1960	24	23
Company F:			
College hires	1960	36	26
Total college hires		274	174
Total non-college managers		148	145

The subjects spent 3½ days at the assessment center in groups of 12. Immediately following, the assessment staff discussed each participant extensively and rated him on each of 25 characteristics (described later), and shortly thereafter a narrative summary of each man's performance was written.

It should be emphasized that no information about any man's performance during assessment has ever been given to company officials. All information collected from the 422 subjects during assessment and subsequently has been held in strict confidence. There has been no contamination of subsequent criterion data by the assessment results; judgments of the assessment staff have had no influence on the careers of the men being studied.

Description of assessment procedures. The first use of multiple assessment procedures on a large scale is credited to German military psychologists (OSS, 1948). The British adapted the procedures for screening officer candidates, and the U.S. Office of Strategic Services took over the approach from the British during World War II (OSS, 1948). Since that time, several studies of various applications of these procedures have been reported in the literature (Cronbach, 1960; Taft, 1959).

In general, the procedures employed have involved the use of multiple methods for obtaining information on individuals, standardization of these methods for making inferences from them, and the use of several assessors whose judgments are pooled to develop trait or behavior ratings of the persons assessed. As might be expected, many variations in methodology have been reported. Information is obtained by both clinical and mechanical means and is combined mechanically to derive trait ratings and clinically to yield global predictions and narrative accounts. A major contribution of the multiple assessment approach has been the use of situational tests or exercises. As we have seen, situational methods offer good potential for adding to the scope of personal behavioral tendencies that can be observed and evaluated.

At the time of assessment, the 422 men were employees of six Bell System companies. Approximately two-thirds of the sample were college graduates who were assessed soon after employment. The remaining third had been employed initially for nonmanagement positions and had advanced into management relatively early in their careers. These men were not college graduates when employed; a few have since earned degrees by part-time and evening study.

The first step in designing the assessment procedures was to select and define the characteristics to be assessed. In doing this, a thorough review of the literature was supplemented by the securing of opinions from experienced Bell System personnel men about the qualities they believed to be important to success in the business. The many characteristics which this process produced were finally reduced to a list of 25 qualities. Techniques were then selected or developed to reveal these variables. A listing of the techniques with brief descriptions of them follows:

> *Interview.* A two-hour interview with each man directed toward obtaining insights into his personal development up to that time, work objectives, attitudes toward the Bell System, social values, scope of interests, interpersonal relationships, idiosyncrasies, etc.
>
> *In-basket.* A set of materials which a telephone company manager might expect to find in his in-basket. The items, 25 altogether, range from telephone messages to detailed reports. In addition, the subject was furnished with such necessary materials as a copy of the union contract, organization chart, and stationery. He was given three hours in which to review the materials and take appropriate action on each item (by writing letters, memos, and notes to himself). Following completion of the "basket," he was interviewed concerning his approach to the task, his reasons for taking the actions indicated, and his views of his superiors, peers, and subordinates (as inferred from the materials).
>
> *Manufacturing problem* (devised by John Hemphill). A small business game wherein the participants assumed the roles of partners in an enterprise manufacturing toys for the Christmas trade. They were required to buy parts and sell finished products under varying market conditions, to maintain inventories, and to manufacture the toys.
>
> *Group discussion.* Also a leaderless group situation, focused around a management personnel function. Participants were instructed to assume the roles of managers, each having a foreman reporting to him considered qualified for promotion. Participants were required to discuss the merits and liabili-

ties of their hypothetical foremen and to reach a group decision regarding their relative promotabilities.

Projective tests. (1) Rotter Incomplete Sentences Blank. (2) Bell Incomplete Sentences Tests (developed by Dr. Walter Katkovsky and the late Dr. Vaughn Crandall with the advice and assistance of Dr. Julian Rotter). (3) Thematic Apperception Test (six of the cards from this test were administered).

Paper-and-pencil tests and questionnaires. (1) School and College Ability Test, Form 1. (2) A Test of Critical Thinking in Social Studies. Now out of print, this test was designed to measure several aspects of critical thinking, including the ability to define problems, select pertinent information, recognize unstated assumptions, evaluate hypotheses, and make valid inferences. (3) Contemporary Affairs Test. Annually, since 1956, the Personnel Research Section of AT&T has developed up-to-date versions of this test. (4) Edwards Personal Preference Schedule. (5) The Guilford-Martin Inventory of Factors (GAMIN). (6) Opinion Questionnaire, Form B. Unpublished, this questionnaire was adapted from Bass (1955) and yields three scores: authoritarianism (A), acquiescence (a), and negativism (n). (7) Survey of Attitudes Toward Life. Unpublished, this questionnaire, made available to the Bell System by Dr. Irving Sarnoff of New York University, is designated to reflect a person's attitudes toward making money and advancing himself.

Miscellaneous. (1) Personal history questionnaire. (2) Short autobiographical essay. (3) Q sort (70 items, self-descriptive).

All the assessment techniques were administered according to standard instructions by the staff member or members responsible for each method. Naturally, the ways in which this was accomplished varied according to the nature of the technique. Thus all interviews were conducted by individual staff members with individual assessees. All tests, questionnaires, and situational exercises were administered to groups of participants. The two group problems involved six participants at a time. Two staff members observed each group problem, recorded their impressions of each participant, and independently evaluated the performance of each.

For each method, one or more of the staff members prepared written reports. The interviewers dictated reports of their interviews. One staff member reviewed each completed in-basket, along with the accompanying interviewer's report on the handling of the basket, and prepared reports describing how each man dealt with the materials in the exercise and evaluating his effectiveness in so doing. Similarly, one of the observers for each group problem prepared reports describing and evaluating individual performance in these exercises, including ratings and rankings by both peers and observers. A clinically trained psychologist reviewed the projective protocols and prepared individual reports. The paper-and-pencil tests were scored and summarized.

The personal characteristics selected for evaluation reflect the many and varied behavioral tendencies and descriptive characteristics believed to be important to managerial effectiveness. Some are directly related to things a manager is required to do in his job (e.g., organizing, planning, decision making, problem solving). Others refer to interpersonal behavior and influence (e.g., communications skills, personal impression, sensitivity, dependence on others). Motives, attitudes, and values are also included (e.g., importance of work, desire for advancement, desire for security). All, of course, are behavioral tendencies that should be related to the manager's ability to identify, allocate, and utilize optimally the financial, human, and material resources available to him. The 25 evaluation variables are listed below:

1	Organization and planning	14	Perception of social cues
2	Decision making	15	Self-objectivity
3	Creativity	16	Energy
4	Human relations skills	17	Realism of expectations
5	Behavior flexibility	18	Bell system value orientation
6	Personal impact	19	Social objectivity
7	Tolerance of uncertainty	20	Need for advancement
8	Resistance to stress	21	Ability to delay gratification
9	Scholastic aptitude	22	Need for superior approval
10	Range of interests	23	Need for peer approval
11	Inner work standards	24	Goal flexibility
12	Primacy of work	25	Need for security
13	Oral communications skills		

Immediately following the 3½ days of collecting information on the subjects, the assessment staff, consisting usually of nine persons, assembled, reviewed, and discussed the results. Each man assessed was evaluated separately, 1 to 1½ hours being required per man.

A typical evaluation consisted of first reading the man's short autobiographical essay. An interviewer then read a summary of his interview with the man. Reports on the In-basket, group exercises, paper-and-pencil test scores, and projectives followed, concluding with a reading of the Q-sort items the man selected as "most" and "least" like him.

Following presentation of the reports, each staff member independently rated the man on a five-point scale on each of the 25 characteristics. Each of the variables was then reviewed. Where differences of opinion occurred, the evidence was discussed and staff members were permitted, though not required, to adjust their ratings.

After the variables had been rated, the staff evaluated the man's potential as a management person in the Bell System. Separate judgments were recorded, independently, regarding the man's likelihood of remaining in the system and, assuming that he would, of achieving middle management in ten years or less. In addition, the staff noted their judgments as to whether the man "should" advance to middle management. Again, the ratings of potential were discussed and adjusted where staff members wished to do so.

Research investigations. A number of studies related to the nature of judgments made during assessment and of the relationship between these judgments and later job performance for the assessees have been completed. Results of these studies give evidence in four areas:

1 Factors underlying the ratings on the 25 assessment variables
2 The relative contributions of the various assessment methods and tests to staff ratings on different assessment factors and their overall prediction
3 Relationships between the staff's overall predictions and later promotional and salary status of the assessees
4 Relationships between early job challenges and job performance and career success shown by the assessees

Factor analysis of rating variables. The rating variables used during the first summer's assessment differed somewhat from those used in all subsequent assessments; therefore, the ratings for the 67 men assessed in 1956 were excluded from factor analyses. Ratings for the remaining men were divided into those with college degrees at the time of employment ($N = 207$) and those without degrees ($N = 148$). Correlation matrices were computed for each of the two groups and factored according to Wherry's (1959) hierarchical method. Though not completely identical, the factors obtained were similar for the two samples. Each analysis yielded a higher-order general factor and several first-order factors. Factors common to both groups are listed below, along with the rating dimensions loading most highly on each:

1 **General effectiveness**
Overall staff prediction
Decision making
Organization and planning
Creativity
Need for advancement
Resistance to stress
Human relations skills

2 **Administrative skills**
Organization and planning
Decision making

3 **Interpersonal skills**
Human relations skills
Behavior flexibility
Personal impact

4 Control of feelings
Tolerance of uncertainty
Resistance to stress

5 Intellectual ability
Scholastic aptitude
Range of interests

6 Work-oriented motivation
Primacy of work
Inner work standards

7 Passivity
Ability to delay gratification
Need for security
Need for advancement (negatively loaded)

8 Dependency
Need for superior approval
Need for peer approval
Goal flexibility

These factors portray the underlying taxonomy used by the assessment staff members in evaluating the young potential managers who were assessed during the summers from 1957 to 1960.

Contributions of assessment methods to taxonomic variables. Earlier in this chapter we said that clinical judgments (such as those used by the assessment staff) often suffer from a lack of specification as to how they are made. Recognizing this, Bray and his associates calculated the correlations between the various tests and assessment methods[4] and scores on each of the variables identified in the factor analytic studies. The results, shown in Table 9.11, help to identify exactly which methods are most important to assessment staff members in making their judgments about the assessees. It is apparent that the group exercises and the performances on the In-basket Test were most important in determining the staff members' assessments on most variables; paper-and-pencil measures were accorded relatively less weight in the ratings. It is also clear, however, that some of the methods and measures had rather precise diagnostic meaning in the view of the assessment staff. For example, behavior on the In-basket carried great weight in judging administrative skills; scores on mental ability measures were most important in estimating intellectual ability; and personality measures affected few judgments other than those of passivity and dependency. This analysis makes very clear the heavy influence that

---

[4] The results of the projective tests were summarized briefly in Chap. 6. Interview results have not yet been reported, although a preliminary report (Rychlak & Bray, 1967) describing a method of content analysis for life themes has been made.

Table 9.11 ASSESSMENT METHODS SHOWING HIGHEST RELATIONSHIPS WITH EACH
OF THE EIGHT FACTORS UNDERLYING THE STAFF ASSESSMENT RATINGS
FOR COLLEGE AND NON-COLLEGE SUBJECTS

	College men	Non-college men
1 General effectiveness:		
Performance in mfg. problem		.60
Performance in group discussion	.67	
Performance on In-basket	.60	.59
2 Administrative skills:		
Performance on In-basket	.76	.68
Score on mental ability test		.72
3 Interpersonal skills:		
Performance in mfg. problem		.52
Performance in group discussion	.62	
Performance on In-basket	.45	.49
4 Control of feelings:		
Performance in group discussion	.47	.36
5 Intellectual ability:		
Score on mental ability test	.79	.64
6 Work-oriented motivation:		
Performance in mfg. problem		.39
Performance in group discussion	.45	.36
Performance on In-basket	.44	
7 Passivity:		
Performance in mfg. problem		−.43
Performance in group discussion	−.39	−.41
Personality measure of activity level	−.43	
8 Dependency:		
Personality measure of achievement	−.29	
Personality measure of authoritarianism		−.34

the three situational exercises had on staff judgments. According to Bray and Grant (1966), the three combined account for 50 percent of the variance in the overall staff predictions for the college sample and for 30 percent of the variance in the non-college sample. In contrast, the mental ability measure accounted for only 6 percent and 12 percent, respectively, in the two samples.

Predictive relationships between staff predictions and later status. In July, 1965, five of the telephone companies submitted information on the progress made up to that date by the men in the study. The data included management level achieved and current salary. Comparisons between staff predictions at the time of assessment and the level achieved by mid-1965 are shown in Tables 9.12 and 9.13. The predictive validities of the assessment staffs' global predictions are moderately high: 31 (82 percent) of the 38 college men who have made middle management were correctly identified by the assessment staffs; 15 (75 percent) of the 20 non-college men who have made middle management were correctly identified. Similarly, of the 72 men (both college and non-college) who

Table 9.12 RELATIONSHIP BETWEEN ASSESSMENT STAFF PREDICTION AND LEVEL ACTUALLY ACHIEVED BY JULY, 1965, FOR 125 COLLEGE ASSESSEES*

		First level management	Second level management	Middle management or above
Staff assessment prediction	Will make middle management in 10 years	1	30	31
	Will not make middle management in 10 years	7	49	7

*$r_{pb} = .44$.

Table 9.13 RELATIONSHIP BETWEEN ASSESSMENT STAFF PREDICTION AND LEVEL ACTUALLY ACHIEVED BY JULY, 1965, FOR 144 NON-COLLEGE ASSESSEES*

		First level management	Second level management	Middle management or above
Staff assessment prediction	Will make middle management in 10 years	3	23	15
	Will not make middle management in 10 years	61	37	5

*$r_{pb} = .71$.

have not advanced beyond the first level of management, the assessment staffs correctly identified 68 (94 percent).

Since the original predictions were for ten-year periods, insufficient time has elapsed for evaluating completely the predictive accuracy of the assessment staffs; follow-up studies will continue to be made in subsequent years. Hopefully, additional studies will also be made using other than global criteria of success. For example, it will be very useful to know how accurately the assessment staffs' estimates of specific proficiencies on the various rating variables (e.g., administrative skills, interpersonal skills, work-oriented motivation, passivity) prove to be. For the time being, since it is apparent that their global predictions are reasonably valid, it is instructive to examine the relationships between each of the methods and these predictions. These are shown below:

	College sample ($N = 207$)	Non-college sample ($N = 148$)
Performance in manufacturing problem	.41	.42
Performance in group discussion	.60	.38
Performance on In-basket test	.55	.51
Mental ability test (SCAT)	.27	.41
Contemporary affairs test	.29	.09
Critical thinking in social science	.31	.22
Personality measure of dominance (EPPS)	.29	.24
Personality measure of abasement (EPPS)	—.15	—.20

Again, the situational procedures are seen to carry the greatest weight in affecting the global judgments (in this instance, the overall predictions) of the staff members; the cognitive measures carry less; and the personality measures are used to only a limited degree.

Operational use of personnel assessment program. Since the Management Progress Study was undertaken, two-thirds of the operating companies in AT&T have set up modified assessment centers (making no use of personality tests or projectives) for aiding in selecting persons for promotion into management. By 1965, 12,000 craftsmen and 4,000 women had been assessed, and by 1968, 3,000 men and 2,000 women were being assessed for promotion per year.

A follow-up study (AT&T, 1965) was done in 1965 to determine the effectiveness of the program. Since the results had been used for making personnel decisions, special precautions had to be taken to obtain special ratings of job performance and potential and to overcome problems of restriction in range and possible criterion contamination.

Five groups were identified for follow-up. The two most crucial groups included men rated as "acceptable" in assessment who were actually promoted and a group of men promoted just prior to the start of the assessment program. If the acceptable group were found to be superior in performance and potential, it would be solid evidence that the assessment program had improved the accuracy of promotion decisions. The other three groups were made up of (1) men rated as "questionable" in assessment who were subsequently promoted anyway, (2) men rated as "not acceptable" in assessment who were promoted anyway, and (3) men who were promoted after the assessment program was underway but who were never assessed. The numbers of men from four cooperating companies included in the study are shown below:

| | Company | | | | Total |
	A	B	C	D	number
Assessed men:					
Acceptable	40	39	29	28	136
Questionable	19	19	14	9	61
Not acceptable	16	6	4	0	26
Men not assessed:					
Promoted since					
program	37	25	40	30	132
Promoted before					
program	40	39	39	33	151
					506

Ratings and rankings of performance and estimates of potential were obtained in personal interviews with managers two levels (district level) above the men in the study. A combined rating and ranking was used to designate whether each man was an "above-average" or "below-average" performer in his job. In a similar way, immediate supervisors' ratings of potential were combined with the district managers' rankings of potential to designate each man as having either "high potential" or "low potential."

Results of the two comparisons are shown in Tables 9.14 and 9.15. Clearly, the institution of the personnel assessment program on an operational basis has brought an increasing proportion of persons who perform well and have high potential into first-line management positions.

Early job challenge and career success. In our survey of industry practices for identifying and developing managers, we found that many companies—notably such companies as Texas Instruments, Honeywell, Inc., and the 3M Co.—give a good deal of attention to providing challenging job circumstances as a means of stimulating effective managerial performance. Current popular-

Table 9.14 PERCENTAGE OF MEN IN EACH OF THE FIVE GROUPS WHO WERE DESIGNATED AS ABOVE-AVERAGE PERFORMERS IN THEIR MANAGERIAL JOBS FOR ALL COMPANIES COMBINED

| | | Number and percent "above average" | |
	Total	N	Percent
Assessed men:			
Acceptable	136	93	68
Questionable	61	40	65
Not acceptable	26	12	46
Men not assessed:			
Promoted since program	132	83	63
Promoted before program	151	83	55

Source: AT&T (1965).

Table 9.15 PERCENTAGE OF MEN IN EACH OF THE FIVE GROUPS WHO WERE DES-IGNATED AS HIGH POTENTIAL FOR ADVANCEMENT FOR ALL COMPANIES COMBINED

	Number and percent with high potential		
	Total	N	Percent
Assessed men:			
Acceptable	136	68	50
Questionable	61	24	40
Not acceptable	26	8	31
Men not assessed:			
Promoted since program	132	25	19
Promoted before program	151	42	20

Source: AT&T (1965).

ity of the management by objectives approach (a form of job challenge) was also apparent.

One of the most intriguing studies done of the Management Progress Study data has attempted to assess the effects of early job challenge on later managerial effectiveness. Results of this study have been reported by Berlew and Hall (Berlew, 1965; Berlew and Hall, 1967).

The subjects of the study included the 44 college men assessed during 1956 who were still with the company in 1962 and an additional 18 college men assessed in 1957 and still with the company in 1962.

The degree of job challenge during each man's first year with the company was estimated from interviews conducted with company officials[5] who were able to describe the job held by each man, the personalities and management styles of his superiors, and the organizational and physical context in which he worked. From the interview protocols, Berlew and Hall estimated the level of expectations the company had for each man in the 18 different behavioral areas listed below:

1 *Technical competence:* the ability to perform non social, job-related tasks requiring some degree of technical knowledge and skill.
2 *Learning capacity:* the ability to learn the various aspects of a position while on the job.
3 *Imagination:* the ability to discover new methods of performing tasks; the ability to solve novel problems.
4 *Persuasiveness:* the ability to present effectively and convincingly a point of view (may be the employer's point of view or that of the company, a department, or a supervisor). Persuasiveness should be differentiated from leadership and popularity.

[5] Actually, interviews were held with company officials annually, but we shall describe only the results of comparisons between *first-year* job challenge and later job performance and success.

5 *Group membership skills:* the ability to work productively with groups of people. A group may consist of individuals at different levels in the company or of individuals from outside the company.
6 *Communication skills:* the ability to make well-organized, clear presentations orally and in writing.
7 *Supervisory skills:* the ability to supervise and direct effectively the work of others.
8 *Decision making:* the ability to make responsible decisions well without assistance from others.
9 *Organizing ability:* the ability to plan and organize own work efforts or those of others.
10 *Time-energy commitment:* the expenditure of time and energy for the benefit of the company.
11 *Sacrifice of autonomy:* the degree to which the employee accepts company demands that conflict with personal prerogatives.
12 *Sociability:* the establishment and maintenance of pleasant social relationships with other members of the company off the job.
13 *Acceptance of company norms:* conformity to the folkways of the organization or work group on the job in area not directly related to the job performance.
14 *Self-development:* formal or informal education pursued on employee's own time for purposes of increasing his value to the company.
15 *Maintenance of public image:* the maintenance of favorable impression outside the company by acting as a representative of it.
16 *Loyalty:* the taking on of company values and goals as the employee's own; identification with the company.
17 *Productivity:* results, job output; the extent to which the employee gets the job done.
18 *Initiative:* drive; self-motivation; the ability to see what should or must be done and to initiate appropriate activity.

The degree of expectation for each area for each man was rated from 1 (low) to 3 (high), and *job challenge* was defined simply as the sum of the rated expectations held by the company for each man. In other words, the entirely reasonable assumption was made that men would be most challenged in jobs for which expectations were high, and relatively less challenged in jobs with lower expectations.

In 1962, a global appraisal of each man's overall performance and potential was made. This was combined with an index based on present salary (corrected for starting salary) to form a success index. In addition, a number of measures of job performance (such as annual appraisals and interviewers' estimates of how well each man accomplished the above expectations) were summed to form a so-called performance index. Table 9.16 shows the correlations between first-year job challenge and these two indexes, separately for men in Company B and Company D. Clearly, men judged to have more challenging first jobs are judged to be performing better and accomplishing more after four or five years in the company than men judged to have less challenging first jobs.

Table 9.16 CORRELATIONS BETWEEN DEGREE OF FIRST-YEAR JOB CHALLENGE AND STANDING IN 1962 ON A SUCCESS INDEX AND A PERFORMANCE INDEX FOR 44 MEN HIRED IN 1956 BY COMPANY B AND 18 MEN HIRED IN 1957 BY COMPANY D

	Company B (N = 44)	Company D (N = 18)
Success index	.32	.37
Performance index	.54	.29

Source: Berlew & Hall (1966).

One reason for this could be that the best men were originally assigned to the more challenging jobs. This is unlikely, however, because the assessment results were unknown to anyone in the operating companies, but Berlew and Hall investigated the possibility anyway. They correlated test scores and assessment staff ratings with the job challenge ratings for all 62 men in the two companies. Most of the correlations were nearly zero; however, three of the rating variables and two of the cognitive measures showed moderate relationships with the job challenge scores:

Cognitive measures	
Verbal ability (SCAT)	.22
Critical thinking tests (CTSS)	.32
Rating variables	
Inner work standards	.27
Range of interests	.26
Tolerance of uncertainty	.25

Since Berlew's study, Bray (1966) has reported data yielding a correlation of .33 between assessment staffs' overall predictions and degree of job challenge for a larger number of assessees (N = 98).

Thus it is apparent that something occurs very early in a man's career with AT&T to single him out for more or less taxing job assignments. Surprisingly, the evidence seems to suggest that the men judged more capable during assessment may tend to receive the more challenging job assignments. We remain unconvinced that this actually occurs. It seems more likely that the interviewer's estimates of job challenge at the end of a man's first year are affected by what he knows of the man and his relative effectiveness. Moreover, it is likely that the more effective men may be able to demonstrate their effectiveness early in their jobs (within a matter of months) and that they will then actually receive more challenging job assignments as a result. To the extent that this occurs, it is testimony to a desirable degree of organizational and supervisory flexibility within the Bell System. It is possible to make crude corrections in the correlations in Table 9.16 for the effects discussed above. In an earlier

Table 9.17 PARTIAL CORRELATIONS BETWEEN DEGREE OF FIRST-YEAR JOB CHAL-
LENGE AND THE SUCCESS INDEX AND PERFORMANCE INDEX WITH
ASSESSMENT STAFF PREDICTION HELD CONSTANT STATISTICALLY (FOR
44 MEN HIRED IN 1956 BY COMPANY B AND 18 MEN HIRED IN 1957 BY
COMPANY D)

	Company B $(N = 44)$	Company D $(N = 18)$
Success index	.24	.30
Performance index	.48	.21

report of this study, Berlew and Hall (1964) present correlations between the
assessment variables and their salary success criterion. From these results, we
estimate that the correlation between the global assessment prediction and
success four to five years later for these subjects would be about .30. Using
Bray's value of .33 for the correlation between the assessment prediction and
first-year job challenge, we have computed partial-order correlations between
first-year job challenge and the success and performance indexes with assessment predictions held constant. The values are shown in Table 9.17. It must
be emphasized strongly that these estimated corrections are of the crudest
sort—based on small samples and estimated values as they are. Still the evidence is suggestive that first-year job challenge is moderately associated with
later judgments of success and job performance, quite aside from the modest
tendency noted previously for the judgments of degree of job challenge to
be affected somehow by the overall effectiveness of the men assigned to these
jobs.

This finding is provocative because it is a clear illustration of the kind of
interaction between individual difference and social variables that we have
been emphasizing in the context of the "model" of managerial effectiveness
presented in Chapter 2. We have evidence from these studies that men who
do better during assessment also do better in their management jobs; we also
have evidence that men who receive especially challenging job assignments
early in their careers do better in later managerial jobs. Most important, the
evidence points to the possibility of multiplicative effects of providing challenging early job assignments for men identified as most capable during assessment. Future research should tackle the difficult problem of tracing further the complex linkages between ability variables (broadly defined as those
dimensions capable of assessment), social and job variables (such as those
studied by Berlew and Hall), and the emergence of effective managerial job
behavior. Fortunately, the materials gathered by the staff of the Management

Progress Study constitute a rich source for undertaking studies of this kind in the years ahead.

Summary and Conclusions from the Management Progress Study

It is apparent that the Management Progress Study incorporates many features we have recommended in our discussions thus far. First, it is a predictive study, having obtained extensive psychological measures and assessment information from young men at the time they first entered upon their business careers. Later measures of effectiveness and descriptions of their job behavior remain uncontaminated by company officials' knowing about the assessment results, and the range of abilities among the subjects remains unconstrained by any selectivity based on the assessment results. Second, the study incorporates extensive information about managerial careers *in progress* through numerous follow-up contacts with the assessees and with company officials about the assessees' job experiences, their relative effectiveness, their behavioral tendencies, and the organizational circumstances under which they are working. Third, the staff of the Management Progress Study has taken pains to identify the types of information used by members of the assessment staffs in making their assessment ratings; thus their analyses provide a first picture of the sorts of variables—test scores, biographical information, behavior during situational exercises, etc.—most likely to affect the process of clinically combining information to yield behavioral descriptions and predictions. Fourth, a most obvious contribution of the Management Progress Study has been the development and careful analysis of new kinds of predictor variables, incorporating richer and broader behavior samples into the predictor matrix than have been provided by the heavy reliance on paper-and-pencil tests and responses to questionnaires. The scores obtained from behavioral observations during the group exercises, the "work samples" from the In-basket exercise, and the rating of expectations and job challenge variables constitute innovative and, as we have seen, potentially very useful approaches for identifying the factors—both individual and situational—contributing to effective managerial behavior. Finally, the diagnostic nosology developed for use in the Management Progress Study has been impressive and should form a basis for defining categories used by other investigators in future studies of managerial effectiveness.

Unfortunately, the Management Progress Study has been undertaken in just one large corporation—AT&T. Personnel policies and practices in this firm provide for rather extensive job rotation for managers among different functions and different locations. Strict adherence to a promotion-from-within policy and extensive job rotation probably combine as in the SONJ organization to develop or at least to reward managers who are "generalists" rather than

Table 9.18 CORRELATIONS BETWEEN STAFF JUDGMENTS BASED ON ASSESSMENT
AND SALARY PROGRESS OVER AT LEAST SIX YEARS FOR FOUR GROUPS
OF ASSESSEES IN THREE COMPANIES

Staff assessment rating	College men, Company A (N = 54)	College men, Company B (N = 83)	College men, Company C (N = 27)	Non-college men, Company C (N = 39)
General effectiveness	.41	.45	.51	.52
Administrative skills	.33	.57	.24	.45
Interpersonal skills	.26	.34	.36	.33
Control of feelings	.34	.17	.50	.32
Intellectual ability	.48	.31	.30	.07
Work-oriented motivation	.16	.29	.20	.41
Passivity	—.30	—.41	—.33	—.41
Dependency	—.25	—.01	—.25	.01

"functionalists." Thus the staff of the Management Progress Study, like Laurent and his colleagues in the SONJ studies, has had less need to consider managerial job differences or to seek to predict direct managerial behaviors in addition to making global estimates of career success and job performance. We still maintain that the broad study of managerial effectiveness across many administrative settings (e.g., many different industrial firms and including as well such "nonindustrial" organizations as service organizations or educational institutions) will profit from greater attention to managerial job differences and the prediction of short-run behavior episodes in addition to the longer-run global career measures that have been used almost exclusively in the studies so far.

In summarizing the clinical investigations, we also called for systematic study of the job behavior patterns of persons who have been "clustered" on the basis of assessment information into relatively homogeneous subgroups. To our knowledge, this approach has not yet been tried by the research staff of the Management Progress Study. We should also note that neither the clinical studies summarized previously nor the Management Progress Study has given attention to utility considerations in addition to reporting validity coefficients for the assessment staff's inferences. The large costs of using assessment procedures to aid in personnel decisions have not to our knowledge been evaluated against the possible costs of not using them. This step is particularly important for assessment programs because the procedures shown to contribute most to staff judgments and presumably to the validity of job behavioral predictions are by far the most costly parts of the assessment package.

Bray and Grant (1966) gave some attention to this problem—not directly in the context of utility but indirectly by considering whether or not judgments based on the group exercises added any significant variance to the staff predictions of career success. [6]

As a criterion of progress, Bray and Grant used the differences between each man's salary on June 30, 1965, and his salary at the time he was assessed. These data were gathered for men in all six companies, but it was decided to interpret the data only for men (employed in three companies) who had been assessed at least six years previously (1956 to 1958); presumably, the salary criterion was more stable for the assessees who had been with their companies longer. The correlations between staff ratings on the factored dimensions and the salary measure for the assessees are shown in Table 9.18. The judgments of administrative and interpersonal skills, intellectual ability, control of feelings, and lack of passivity are more highly correlated with management progress than work-oriented motivation or dependency. In order to investigate whether or not the staff judgments were "better" than the results obtained with paper-and-pencil tests and whether they added significantly to the predictive efficiency of the tests, Bray and Grant chose the judgment variable and the ability test correlating highest with salary progress in each of the four groups. Partial correlations were then computed between the judgment variable and salary progress with ability held constant. The values obtained were .32, .39, .29, and .42, respectively, for the four groups. This still does not get at the overall utility of using these procedures as against other possible personnel actions (such as hiring large numbers of persons for trial periods and letting each one simply "sink or swim"), but it does show at least that the staff judgments, which in turn are heavily influenced by the situational procedures, *do* add reliable predictive variance beyond what any of the tests provide.

SUMMARY

A number of investigations of managerial effectiveness using the clinical mode of collecting and combining predictor information have been de-

---

[6] This is a very important facet of the data presented by Bray and his colleagues because it copes directly with a problem brought to light in a widely cited study by Glaser, Schwarz, and Flanagan (1958), which showed that situational and clinical procedures added little to what could be accomplished by two paper-and-pencil tests for predicting supervisory effectiveness. In their study, they chose 40 subjects who were from each of the two extremes on ratings of supervisory effectiveness but who were equated for age, job experience, and scores on ability and supervisory knowledge tests. Panel and individual interviews, a leaderless group discussion session, a role-playing situation, and a simulated management work situation were then applied to the subjects in order to pinpoint differences between the effective groups which were not related to the test scores. The biserial correlation coefficients between the assessment procedures and status on the dichotomous supervisory effectiveness designation were depressingly low—ranging from .08 for the management work simulation to .17 for the leaderless group discussion.

scribed and discussed in this chapter. Taken together, they illustrate a number of features usually characteristic of clinical studies: They tend to be predictive rather than concurrent investigations; many are open to charges of possible criterion contamination because clinical reports may have been available to persons responsible for completing later descriptions of managers' patterns of job behavior; and even though validities have often been moderately high, the research reports only rarely specific the actual steps taken by psychologists as they develop their clinical judgments and predictions.

Nonetheless, it is clear from these investigations that clinicians can apparently designate with fair accuracy the kinds of behavioral tendencies a man may be expected to show after he has been in a managerial job for a period of time. Moreover, clinical investigations have, for the most part, been more diagnostic and analytic than most of the statistical studies reviewed previously.

Future clinical studies should more uniformly seek to ensure that measures of job behavior remain unaffected by prior knowledge of the outcomes of the clinical evaluations, and additional attention should be given to more fully describing the types of information and major strategies used by clinicians in developing their predictions. Situational parameters also need more complete specification, and actuarial pattern analysis should be tried as a likely means of increasing overall predictive accuracies.

The Management Progress Study, undertaken in 1956 by AT&T and continued since then, is the largest and most comprehensive study of managerial career development ever undertaken. As it continues, information from it will constitute an ever more important and fruitful source of research data for answering many questions related to the development and maintenance of managerial job effectiveness.

Chapter 10 Training and Development: Methods and Techniques

The terms "training" and "development" are often given somewhat different meanings. They may be distinguished on the basis of either the subject matter involved or the level in the organization from which the participants are drawn. In the former instance training usually refers to rather specific, factual, and narrow-range content, while development implies a focus on general decision making and human relations skills. Relative to the latter distinction, development usually refers to activities provided for middle and upper management.

However, the two terms are used synonymously in the following four chapters and are meant to entail the following general properties and characteristics:

1 Management training and development is, first of all, a learning experience.
2 It is planned by the organization.
3 It occurs after the individual has joined the organization.
4 It is intended to further the organization's goals.

The first item implies that a relatively permanent change in the individual must be intended, whether it be an increased body of knowledge, new methods for solving problems, or more effective interactions with other people. Programs that are meant only to stimulate momentary feelings of goodwill, company zeal, or other marked but temporary behavior changes are not training programs. It is obvious that a considerable amount of learning relative to the managerial job is not consciously planned by the organization and that an individual learns a great deal, both good and bad, about managing before he joins the organization. However, these kinds of learning are excluded from our definition of management development for the following reason: Some of the areas most in need of research involve the *interaction* of the organization's training efforts both with the skills, knowledge, and attitudes that the individual brings to the job and with the unplanned kind of training that goes on between superior and subordinate and among coworkers. To include all these learning experiences under the rubric "management development" might obscure some of these very important joint influences.

Management development is thus a teaching activity planned and initiated by the organization. The word "planned" is not meant to imply negativistic things about manipulation or efforts toward eliciting conformity behavior, nor does it necessarily mean the planning must be done by the management hierarchy—in fact, it is usually delegated. Its aim is to further the goals of the organization by enhancing the managerial inputs which are in the form of abilities, skills, motives, and attitudes of individuals. However, participants in programs that fall within our definition of management development need not be managers. In fact, such training programs tend to break down into two general classes: those which are directed toward *preparing* nonmanagement people for future management responsibilities and those which are intended to improve the performance of individuals who are already functioning as managers (Miner, 1966). Although the development effort must have something to do with the organizational goals, the particular goals under consideration need not be restricted to narrow economic aims. Personal development for personal development's sake may indeed be a conscious objective of the organization.

Given the obvious and overwhelming importance of the managerial inputs to an organization and the tremendous amount of time and money that is spent on trying to enhance these inputs through training, it is little wonder that a considerable body of written literature has accumulated on the topic of management training and development. It is the purpose of the next four chapters to examine and summarize, in some coherent fashion, this body of knowledge. Special attention will be paid to reports of research that try to e-valuate whether or not the managerial inputs to the organization are indeed being enhanced by means of the various training and development efforts. On the basis of this look at "what is known" in the training area, some suggestions will be made as to what kinds of research and investigation must be carried out in the future to make management development as meaningful and fruitful as possible.

The professional literature seems to organize itself under four general headings:

1 Descriptions of the various training programs and techniques
2 Discussions of the application of principles of learning and motivation to problems of training
3 Methodological articles on how the effects of training should be evaluated, including discussion of the necessity of various aspects of evaluation
4 Empirical or quasi-empirical studies of the effects of training on the attitudes, opinions, and job performance of managers

The literature will be summarized and discussed under each of these headings in turn. The present chapter deals with methods and techniques. We hope that an organized look at each of these topics will prove fruitful in terms of the strengths and weaknesses that are uncovered.

Papers and articles describing, or proselyting for, particular training techniques constitute by far the largest category of literature on management development. They number in the hundreds and are characterized by a great deal of repetition and a definite ebb and flow with regard to the popularity of specific development techniques. When a new technique is developed, articles describing its use and arguing for its virtues appear at an increasing rate, until a peak seems to be reached and the number of papers begins to decline. This decline is usually helped along by the appearance of a new training method which takes over the limelight, and the cycle is then repeated. We shall make no attempt to summarize this mountain of material but rather shall try to give a concise description of each of the different training methods that have appeared in the literature and organize them into some sort of meaningful classification scheme.

TRAINING TECHNIQUES, OR "HOW TO TEACH"

Management development and training methods seem to fall roughly into three different categories, which we shall label *information presentation techniques, simulation methods,* and *on-the-job practice.* Specific training methods will be discussed under each of these categories.

Information Presentation Techniques

These are devices which have as their aim the teaching of facts, concepts, attitudes, or skills without requiring simulated or actual practice on the job itself.

The lecture. This most traditional of teaching methods has taken its share of lumps from educators and industrial training personnel. McGehee and Thayer (1961) conclude that as usually employed, the lecture is of little value in industrial training. Its principal difficulties seem to be that no provision is made for individual differences on the part of the learners, the lecturer must be an outstanding teacher, it is very difficult for the learners to obtain feedback regarding how they are doing, and there is little opportunity for the learner to participate in the process. The lecture method is not without its friends, however. D. S. Brown (1960) argues that this technique is valuable because of its sheer information-giving ability, its wide acceptance, the fact that it is economical, and the opportunity it affords a master teacher to provide an inspirational model of scholarship for his students. Bennett (1956) makes the point that managers are an intelligent lot and lectures by recognized authorities are in keeping with the status and complexity of the managerial job. Both these writers agree, however, that the lecture must be used sparingly and with due regard for its shortcomings. Tiffen and McCormick (1965) also point out that the lecture might profitably be considered for the presentation of new material or when summarizing material developed by another instruction method.

The conference method. This technique is really the management development analog to the graduate school seminar. The emphasis is on small group discussion, and the leader provides guidance and feedback rather than instruction. Its usual objectives are to develop problem-solving and decision-making capabilities, present new and complex material, and modify attitudes. The keystone is active participation of the learner, primarily by means of verbal discussion with the other group members. The conference is almost always oriented toward discussion of specific problems or new areas of knowledge. The topics for discussion may be chosen by the leader or by the participants themselves (Buchanan & Ferguson, 1953). Each of the participants may also be given practice in leading conference sessions (Zelko, 1952). Along with the participative aspect, feedback to the participant regarding his performance and attitude is an extremely important part of the conference method. It may be provided by the leader, the other participants, or a trained observer. The conference technique was really one of the first products of the reaction against the lecture method and has served as the backbone of the "human relations" type of training. It is most often used to teach such things as effective communication, supervisory techniques, and general approaches to problem solving and decision making. The conference method is perhaps the most widely used managerial training technique (Yoder, 1962).

A serious constraint on this method is its restriction to small groups. However, a large group may be broken down into smaller groups called "buzz" groups (H. A. Boyd, 1952), which then operate as problem-solving or discussion groups and report back to the main body. This technique may be used to illustrate approaches to the same problem, or each group may be assigned a portion of the main topic.

Criticisms of the conference method as a training technique center around its inability to cover much substantive content in a reasonable length of time, the frequent lack of organization, and an emphasis on demonstrating verbosity rather than learning (Jennings, 1956).

Yet another embellishment of the buzz-group technique is the method of forced leadership training described by Jennings (1953a). In most buzz groups a natural leader usually emerges to guide the discussion and keep the conversation going. This individual is identified, and in the second training session the leaders from the first buzz groups are all placed together and new buzz groups are formed, using individuals who did not act as leaders during the first session. Thus in the second buzz-group session an individual who has not previously acted as leader is almost forced to assume this role. The cycle of regrouping nonleaders into new buzz groups is repeated until as many as possible have been given practice in leading the group.

T **(training) groups, or sensitivity training.** This is a difficult technique to describe in a few words or paragraphs, chiefly because there are now so many different variations with different characteristics and different goals. In general, the method is a direct descendant of the conference technique, with its emphasis on small groups and individual participation. However, in the *T* group as it originally evolved, the subject matter for discussion is the actual behavior of the individuals in the group, or the "here and now." That is, the group members discuss why they said particular things, why they reacted in certain ways to what others said, and what they thought was actually going on in the group. They examine one another's ability to communicate, the defenses an individual throws up to protect his self-image, why some people seem to attack or reinforce others, why cliques or subgroups seem to form within the main group, and so on. This is accomplished by having the group members honestly and openly communicate as best they can what they are thinking and feeling relative to what they or someone else is saying or doing. For example, one individual may inform another that even though he is verbally expressing approval, his facial expression says the opposite. The other individual may then try to communicate what he was actually thinking and feeling as he was talking.

Perhaps the most succinct characterization of a *T* group is given by Shepard (1964, p. 379), who defines a *T* group in terms of a norm that must be shared by the members. It consists of a "joint commitment among interdependent persons to process 'analysis,' that is, to shared examination of their relationships in all aspects relevant to their independence."

Descriptive accounts of some specific *T* groups have been given by Schein and Bennis (1965); Klaw (1962); Kuriloff and Atkins (1967); Bradford, Gibb, and Benn (1964); and Tannenbaum, Weschler, and Massarik (1961). A basic ingredient of this technique seems to be a certain amount of frustration and conflict (Argyris, 1963), which occurs when an individual attempts to use his previous modes of operation in the *T* group and is brought up short by the other group members, who wonder aloud why he tries to project his particular self-image, why he gets defensive when questioned about certain things, or why he tries verbally to punish other participants.

Many of the variations in the *T* group method revolve around the role of the trainer. In most *T* groups the trainer acts as a resource person and as a behavior model for the other group members; that is, he expresses his own feelings openly and honestly, does not become defensive and withdrawn when criticized, and exhibits an acceptance of the behavior of others. Beyond this, however, some trainers may try to be as nondirective as possible and let the group move along as it sees fit. Others may exhibit considerably more guidance and periodically attempt to point out to the group what is happening and offer an interpretation of what people are really saying to one another. Another kind of *T* group, referred to as the "instrumented group" (Blake & Mouton, 1962), operates without any trainer at all. The participants are provided with a set of rating scales with which they can rate themselves, the other group members, and the group itself on such things as openness, willingness to express feelings, ability to listen to other people, defensive behavior, and the formation of cliques. The positive ends of the scales implicitly define desirable behavior on the part of the group members, and over a series of ratings made during the life of the group the members tell themselves how they are progressing.

Although sensitivity training originally dealt only with behavior expressed in the group, more recent variants of the technique have introduced a specific problem-solving element, and the group members may examine their interpersonal skills as they affect efforts to work out a solution to a problem. This is frequently the technique used when all the people in the group are from one organization (Morton & Bass, 1964).

The type of group composition is another dimension along which groups can vary. They may be "stranger" groups made up of people from different organizations or "family" groups comprised of people from the same organization. In the latter case participants might be from the same level within a firm, or they might represent a vertical slice that includes a number of levels of responsibility.

Other variations of this basic technique include systematically introducing additional conflict in the group (Reed, 1966), to give the group members more practice in handling severe interpersonal stress, or running the group continuously for twenty-four or forty-eight hours instead of a few hours each day. Supposedly a process which normally stretches over a period of one to three weeks can be compressed into one or two days in this fashion and have even greater impact.

Very distinct from the weekend *T* groups, but still aimed at a compression of time, are the so-called micro *T* groups. With this method sessions are compressed into ten- or fifteen-minute intervals with brief lectures and problem-solving sessions interspersed.

Lastly, a procedure described by Tannenbaum and Bugental (1963) involves breaking the parent *T* group into smaller groups of four to six people or even into pairs. The pairs and smaller groups are intended to allow more interaction per person and provide additional feelings and impressions that the entire group can discuss when it meets together.

The objectives of this kind of training have been stated by many (Argyris, 1964b; Bradford et al., 1964; Schein & Bennis, 1965; Shepard, 1964; Tannen-baum et al., 1961) and in summary they seem to amount to the following:

1 To give the trainee an understanding of how and why he acts toward other people as he does and of the way in which he affects them
2 To provide some insights into why other people act the way they do
3 To teach the participants how to "listen," that is, actually hear what other people are saying rather than concentrating on a reply
4 To provide insights concerning how groups operate and what sorts of processes groups go through under certain conditions
5 To foster an increased tolerance and understanding of the behavior of others
6 To provide a setting in which an individual can try out new ways of interacting with people and receive feedback as to how these new ways affect them.

Which of these relative specific objectives is adopted by a particular training effort depends upon whether the general objective is to teach individual self-awareness and personal development or to enhance understanding of group processes for the sake of organizational effectiveness.

In addition, *T* groups that are made up of individuals from one organization usually have as their aim the release and subsequent understanding and acceptance of the repressed feelings on the part of superior and subordinate that often inhibit communication. They also usually strive for increased tolerance and understanding among the various levels of management and for the building of a cohesive "team" feeling. The implicit assumption in all this seems to be that if these objectives are met, the result will be improved managerial performance.

Laboratory education. Laboratory education is the label applied to a more complete program of training experiences in which some form of *T* group is the prime ingredient. The other ingredients may consist of short lectures, group exercises designed to illustrate problems in interpersonal or intergroup behavior, role-playing sessions, and the like. Specification of the content of the various elements, their duration, their participants, and their sequencing constitutes the training or laboratory "design." Designs may vary depending on the training needs and situational elements the planners feel to be crucial. The laboratory education practitioner responsible for guiding the program is often referred to in the literature as a "change agent."

The variations in the laboratory designs are numerous, and we shall attempt no summary.

Discussions may be found in Bradford et al. (1964), Schein and Bennis (1965), and almost any issue of the *Journal of Applied Behavioral Science*.

Systematic observation. A little-used technique, but one advocated by Crow (1953), involves having the individuals in the development program observe an experienced manager or management group in action by sitting in on management committee meetings or observing a manager's meeting with his staff. The learner is cast in a very passive role, but the material being presented is the "real thing" and is presumably relevant for the trainee. A potential drawback is that the relative importance of what is observed is left to the judgment of the trainee.

Closed-circuit television. Although this technique has found wide application in educational institutions, it has had very limited use in management training. A rather unique utilization of television in a large aircraft company was reported by Niven (1966). After a certain hour in the evening, the educational television station in the region scheduled no regular programs, and the company used this open time to present courses in supervision, industrial relations, etc., to its managers and supervisors. Achievement tests were given to all those who participated, which turned out to be several hundred people.

Programmed instruction. The programmed technique involves defining what is to be learned, breaking it down into its component elements, and deciding on the optimal sequence for the presentation and learning of these elements. The presentation may be by "teaching machine," programmed textbook, or some other device, but the essential ingredient in the procedure is that the learner must make an active response to each element (or "frame") such that his response reveals whether or not he has learned what he is supposed to have learned at that point. There is immediate feedback concerning whether the learner was right or wrong, and the entire procedure is automated, which allows each individual to proceed at his own rate. The sequencing of the elements and the proper feedback are provided by the machine or the programmed book.

There are two principal variants of the above procedure—the so-called linear technique, developed by Skinner (1954), and the branching technique, developed by Crowder (1960). With the linear method the objective is to lead the learner from the simple to the complex in such a way that he almost never makes an incorrect response. The branching technique adopts the notion that incorrect responses may be indicative of certain misconceptions, and subprograms are provided to explore and correct the reasons for an incorrect response. After completing a subprogram, the learner continues on with the main program.

The programmed technique has not been widely utilized in management training, although the situation may be changing. It has been used in one instance to teach motivational principles to managers in a photochemical firm (Lysaught, 1961). At the National Institute of Health a program (teaching machine) was used in an attempt to increase supervisory skill in scheduling appointments, conducting meetings, handling reports, and delegating responsibility (Prather, 1964). It would also seem to have possible merit for teaching factual material in such areas as accounting, finance, contract management, and the like.

The advantages that have been claimed for programmed instruction are that it recognizes individual differences by allowing each individual to set his own pace, requires that the learner be active, provides immediate knowledge of results, and forces the people doing the teaching to break down the topic into meaningful elements and then present these elements in a sequence conducive to optimal learning (Hilgard, 1961). Also, once a program is ready, it obviously has a great deal of operating flexibility.

Some disadvantages often pointed out are its high initial cost, the considerable amount of time required to develop and perfect a program, and the seductive nature of the hardware itself (teaching machines, computers, etc.). Pressey (1963) has forcefully warned that the glamour value of the technique may detract from the fundamental and very difficult task of defining what is to be learned, breaking the subject into its component elements, and sequencing their presentation in an optimal fashion.

Training by correspondence. This method was used in one company to teach principles of business administration and personnel management to supervisors located in over two thousand scattered offices around the country (Krist & Prange, 1957). An achievement test was given at the end of each section, and small study groups were encouraged at each office to discuss the individual lessons.

Motion pictures. A survey reported by Bobele, Maher, and Ferl (1964) showed that some firms do use films in management training, but primarily at the lower levels and usually for introducing new subject matter and stimulating discussion relative to human relations problems. One drawback of films, according to the survey, seems to be the entertainment stigma. A variant of the film presentation is the so-called interruption technique, in which a problem is presented or a situation partially portrayed and the participants are asked to respond to the problem or complete the situation.

Reading lists. Besides providing straight information, executive reading programs can be organized around regular discussion sessions (Hook, 1963), in which managers can exchange opinions and ideas about what they have been reading.

Simulation Methods

In this category are included the techniques in which the trainee is presented with a simulated or artificial representation of some aspect of an organization or industry and is required to react to it as if it were the real thing. In other words, these techniques require actual practice of the managerial role with varying degrees of realism, but the actions of the trainees have no effect on the operation of the organization.

The case method. With this technique certain aspects of the firm are simulated by describing the organizational conditions on paper. The trainees are then usually required to identify problems, offer solutions, and otherwise react to the paper organization which is presented. Cases vary a great deal in length and complexity, but the objective is to be as representative of the problems of the real organization as possible. Cases are usually presented to groups of trainees, and active participation in suggesting a solution is encouraged. This allows an individual to obtain feedback regarding his own suggestions and to learn from watching others approach the same problem. Critics of the case method point to its inability to teach general principles and the general lack of guided instruction concerning the inferences the trainees draw from discussion of the case. Advocates point out that self-discovery is more meaningful and that general principles generated by the trainees themselves are learned better and remembered longer. Of course, cases can also be used in conjunction with other training techniques for the purpose of illustrating and reinforcing general principles that have been previously presented in some more direct fashion.

A variant of the case method is the "demand" technique described by Potter and Strachan (1965). With this procedure the trainees are divided into small groups of three or four individuals, and each team is given an organizational problem to research and present to the entire group. The various solutions are then discussed and critiqued within the entire group.

The incident method. Closely related to the case method is the incident technique (Pigors & Pigors, 1955). With this procedure the trainees are given a sketchy outline of a particular incident which requires action on the part of the manager, and they have to ask questions of the trainer to get more information. When the trainees think they have enough information, they try to come up with a solution. At the conclusion of the session, the trainer reveals all the information that he has, and a solution based on complete information is compared with the solution based on the information the trainees obtained.

Role playing. Here the realism of the simulation is heightened by having trainees "act out" the roles of individuals who are described in the case. With this technique the focus is almost exclusively on the human relations aspect of management and supervision, and the trainee has the opportunity to work through the problem exactly as he would if he were on the job. The success of the method rests on the ability of the players actually to adopt the roles as specified in the case problem and to react to the actions of the other players just as they would if they were in the work situation. If they are successful, the trainee can try out various solutions and judge their success. He can also receive feedback regarding his supervisory techniques, communication skills, and attitudes toward superiors and subordinates.

The method is time-consuming and expensive in that only a few people can play at a time. Some variants of the role-playing method designed to overcome this problem are described by Maier, Solem, and Maier (1957). One of these is the multiple role-playing procedure, in which a large group breaks down into smaller groups and the same problem is role-played within each group without a trainer. All the players then reassemble and discuss, with the trainer, what happened in their groups, what sort of solutions were suggested, what kinds of human relations problems emerged, and how they were handled. A less satisfactory solution is to have some members of the group role play the situation while the rest of the trainees act as observers and take part in the critique session later.

Another type of role-playing method is described by Speroff (1959). He calls it the "substitution method," and it consists of role playing a meeting between a superior and a subordinate or between a union and a management representative in such a way that one of the pair is kept constant but a number of different people take turns playing the other role. The relative successes and failures of each of the substitutes are then analyzed in a critique session.

Speroff (1954) has also described a technique that combines the notions of job rotation and role playing and allows every manager to continue in his job while attempting to learn about the operations and problems of other parts of the organization. For example, a production manager might be given a sales problem along with all the relevant information the sales organization possesses. He may then adopt the role of the sales manager and sit in on sales conferences, ask questions, and talk to various sales personnel. After a week or two, the production manager (still role playing the sales manager) meets with the appropriate sales people and role plays a problem-solving meeting, centered around the sales problem originally given him. (At the end of each session all the participants join in a critique session.) The production manager may continue to role play the sales manager for a period of several months, and over the course of one to five years each manager role plays the jobs of managers from many different parts of the business.

Business games. The nature of the simulation in this method is considerably different from that in role playing or the case method. The business game attempts to represent the economic functioning of an industry, company, or organizational subunit. The game actually consists of a set of specified relationships or rules which are derived from economic theory and/or from detailed studies of the operations of relevant businesses and industries. These relationships describe how variation in the inputs to a firm (raw materials, capital, equipment, and people) coupled with variation in certain mediating factors (wage rates, price of finished product, advertising budget, amount spent on research and development, etc.) influences the firm's outputs (amount sold, profit, net worth, etc.). The trainees play the game by making decisions about what price to charge for products, how much to spend on advertising, how many people to hire, and so on. The quality of their decisions is reflected by the variation in the output variables. The objective may be to teach general decision-making skills or to convey information as to how a specific business or industry actually operates. In either case the trainee is also supposed to come away with a realization of the complex interrelationships between various parts of an organization and an appreciation for how the effects of a decision made in one department may be felt in another.

There are literally hundreds of business games in use today of varying shades of complexity and realism (Croft, Kibbee, & Nanus, 1961). Some require as many as several hundred operating decisions every period (K. J. Cohen, 1960) and incorporate a number of firms in competition with one another. Several players may make up a firm. With the larger games there must be a division of labor among the players, and this allows some of the supervisory and human relations aspects of management to come into play. One of the characteristics of the business game is that it may become extremely realistic for the players. The frequent use of a computer to calculate the effects of operating decisions on outputs adds to the status and glamour of this training method.

The business games in use tend to fall into two general categories: top management games and functional games. Top management games are those which attempt to simulate the major decision-making functions of the chief officers in an organization. Functional games are much narrower in scope and are intended to simulate the operations of specific functional areas in an organization such as production control, marketing, or finance.

Some of the criticisms that have been voiced are that games do not allow for the novel approach and may teach an overreliance on particular kinds of decisions unless they are a balanced representation of the real world. A great deal of reliance is placed on the validity of the simulations. For example, if the model used in the game incorporates an oversimplified relationship between research and development investment and profits, the participants may carry away the notion that a surefire way to increase profits is to divert more funds into developmental research. On the other hand, the game may be too realistic, and the trainees may play with such fervor that the training objectives fall by the wayside. The participants may also spend too much time trying to discover "gimmicks" in the model which can be exploited. Most of the users of business games recommend lengthy critique meetings at the end of each session to help avoid some of these pitfalls.

The task model. Keltner (1965) describes a technique which he claims combines the advantages of role playing and business games. Some complex but easily built physical object is constructed, and a group of trainees is assigned the task of duplicating the model, given the proper materials. Various communication arrangements are used, and only certain trainees are allowed to view the object. Difficulties in communication are discussed as they arise, and solutions are obtained through group discussion. The method may also be used to incorporate competition between teams of trainees, or a portion of the training group can be used as observers to train them to recognize emerging leadership patterns and the like.

The in-basket technique. As described by Frederiksen, Saunders, and Wand (1957) and Lopez (1965), this development method consists of presenting the trainee with a description of a managerial role he is to assume and an In-basket containing such things as customer complaints, correspondence, operating statements, requests for advice from subordinates, and the like. The In-basket materials are intended to resemble a realistic operating situation with a variety of problems of varying complexity. The trainee must work through the In-basket, making decisions and giving advice where called for. The heart of the training is in the follow-up discussions, which allow the trainer and trainees to evaluate and interpret what each man did.

As is the case with business games, the objective seems to be primarily the teaching of decision-making skills, with little or no attention paid to learning new facts, human relations attitudes, or interpersonal skills.

A variant of the In-basket technique which does tend to incorporate some of these other considerations is the Kepner-Tregoe approach (Kepner & Tregoe, 1960). Instead of one trainee working in isolation, four individuals operate together as members of one company. The training begins with each man seated at his desk faced with an In-basket of work. The four In-baskets are meant to simulate an interrelated set of organizational problems typical of those faced by any management group. The participants may call each other on the phone to obtain additional information relevant to their own problems, or they may meet together in a conference room. All these things take time, however, and in the evaluation of the session a premium is placed on obtaining the most relevant information as quickly as possible. Again, the heart of the training is in the critique session, and although a certain number of interactive elements are introduced, the main objective is still to teach problem-solving and decision-making skills.

To incorporate still more realism into the In-basket format, Gibson (1961) suggests using a movie along with the In-basket. The film shows a vice-president who periodically interrupts the trainee's work on the In-basket to suggest additional problems that must be handled immediately. Supposedly this builds a realistic amount of tension into the situation.

On-the-job Training

The methods within this category all incorporate the notion of practice—practice on the actual task to be performed, i.e., the managerial job itself.

Job rotation. This technique is by far the most long-term and expensive way to train management personnel, but many people argue that it is both a necessary and an effective development method (Koontz & O'Donnell, 1955). The main objective is to give the trainee factual knowledge about the operations of different parts of the organization and practice in the different management skills that are required. Learning is largely by trial and error, unless combined with some other technique, and this lack of guidance or structure is the focus of most of the criticism of the method. Wall (1963) suggests that for job rotation to be effective, managers must be given instruction in how to coach and give feedback to the trainer and that definite training goals should be set for each job assignment. The success of job rotation also depends on the job assignments' being actually different so that the trainee learns more than he would by spending all his time on the job for which he was actually selected.

As noted by Koontz and O'Donnell (1955), the general term "job rotation" obscures a number of variations in the method which may or may not be important for a particular organization. First of all, the trainee may be rotated through a series of *nonsupervisory* work situations so as to acquaint him with the range of activities actually undertaken by the firm. Although such a scheme allows the trainee to learn the "production" end of things, many of the training positions may not offer enough of a challenge to the management trainee and indeed may bear little relationship to the skills that will be eventually needed in the management position. It is not inconceivable that such a rotation plan would make the trainee a less effective manager than he would be otherwise. However, for certain types of managerial jobs this kind of training could be very valuable. Rotation among actual managerial positions is perhaps the most common variant and obviously entails something quite different from rotation among nonsupervisory jobs. This difference is illustrative of the argument over whether a potential manager should concentrate on learning administrative and supervisory skills or become proficient in the actual work he is going to manage. Koontz and O'Donnell also discuss rotation among "assistant to" or "acting" managerial positions. Such rotation plans obviously attempt to use actual job experience for training in administrative and supervisory skills, but with some of the risk removed. However, there is also a risk that some of the commitment and involvement of the trainee will be diminished and that much of the substance of the job to be learned will be withheld from him.

Committee assignments or junior executive boards. A more short-term and less comprehensive method involves having the trainees form committees, which then are given real organizational problems to tackle and solve (McCormack, 1938). Problems may be selected from a number of different functional areas, and the trainees may be required to do a considerable amount of information gathering before suggesting a solution. This method differs from the role-playing committee assignment in that the solutions given are the ones actually utilized by the organization.

On-the-job coaching. With this method the superior-subordinate relationship is also a teacher-learner relationship, and the superior acts very much like a tutor in an academic setting. Coaching may vary from being very systematic to being very unsystematic and informal. Regardless of the particular form it takes, most people would argue (e.g., Haire, 1965) that it is one of the prime responsibilities of a superior. However, others (e.g., Argyris, 1961) have pointed to the difficulty of the teacher-learner roles and to the fact that they require the learner to continually try new methods and the teacher to be tolerant of mistakes. These are activities which may not be rewarded by the organization, and the roles of the superior as a good manager and as a good coach may be in conflict.

Performance appraisal. One of the stated goals of performance appraisal usually found in most textbooks is to provide feedback to the subordinate concerning good and bad features of his performance. Presumably this will motivate the individual to improve his performance. As a development technique, appraisal provides an opportunity for the superior and subordinate to discuss means of improving the subordinate's performance. In this sense it is systematic coaching and is distinct from the use of appraisal to identify training needs which may then be approached using other training and development techniques.

Other specialized practice techniques. In addition to exposing trainees to operational and managerial problems in various parts of the organization, other on-the-job techniques seem aimed at more specific goals. For example, some firms (Wilson, 1965) provide opportunities for managers to serve as recruitment and selection interviewers of college graduates. The manager may operate by himself or with other managers on a selection committee. Another firm (P. B. Smith, 1964) has used its management trainees as interviewers to follow up on company-wide attitude surveys. The trainees are first given instruction and practice in nondirective interviewing techniques. Then after the survey results are complete, they conduct interviews with personnel in the departments which showed dissatisfaction in certain areas. The objectives are to find out whether the sources of the dissatisfaction are such that they can be remedied by the company and at the same time to train the prospective managers in this type of face-to-face interaction. The problems of establishing rapport and assuring the employees of his anonymity are obvious. Lastly, in order to train managers in public speaking and simultaneously serve the cause of company public relations, some organizations often set up speaking engagements for their managers and encourage them to give talks at professional meetings.

TRAINING CONTENT, OR "WHAT TO TEACH"

Up to this point we have been talking about techniques and methods in management training and development. When an organization decides to institute or alter a development program, the decision regarding which technique(s) to use is not the only decision that must be made. The decision about *what* to teach also looms large on the horizon and obviously should be made even before techniques are considered.

On their face at least, management training programs have been used to teach a bewildering variety of topics; however, for the sake of a meaningful organization, we have attempted to group them into five categories:

1 *Factual content.* Such a category would include everything from company rules and policies to courses in the humanities. Perhaps the most popular topics in this category are personnel management and business administration concepts. A somewhat novel body of knowledge is utilized by Miner (1965) in a carefully worked-out program to teach managers the causes of ineffective managerial performance and some means for overcoming them.
2 *Approaches and techniques for problem solving and decision making.* Examples of this sort of content are skill in adequately defining the problem or elements in the decision, an appreciation for the interrelatedness of decisions, the importance of planning or optimal sequencing of the steps in the decision-making process, and the realization that many problems do not have one best solution or any permanent solution. Attempts to teach creativity such as those by Parnes and his associates (Meadow & Parnes, 1959) and the means for effective group problem solving as discussed by Maier (1963) would also have to be included here. The creativity work tends to focus on the individual's approach to obtaining solutions and stresses nonroutine, or "divergent," thinking. Maier's efforts, on the other hand, are aimed at teaching leaders and groups how to utilize more effec-

tively the knowledge and contributions of the individual members to achieve a more effective combined solution.

3 *Attitudes.* Although extremely difficult to define, this sort of training content refers to such things as a positive regard for democratic leadership, consideration for the contributions of others, tolerance for other people's mistakes, and the like. It seems vital to many people that such attitudes go hand in glove with the teaching of human relations skills in order to avoid teaching a role that is only manipulative and not effective (Jennings, 1953b). Somewhat unique in this category is the training program developed and described by McClelland (1965), which attempts to instill in the trainees a high need for achievment. This program attempts to go somewhat beyond attitude change and actually tries to modify the individual's motivational structure.

4 *Interpersonal skills.* In this category fall such things as effective communication, how to listen to other individuals, and how to be an effective group member.

5 *Self-knowledge.* Knowledge concerning how one's behavior affects others and what other people think of one and a realistic perception of one's abilities and limitations should be included here. The state of one's physical health, as it may influence job effectiveness, is also relevant.

MODIFIERS

When one looks at the myriad training efforts described in the literature, the two dimensions of "*what* is taught" and "*how* it is taught" still do not satisfactorily describe all the variations in programs. There is an additional set of characteristics, which we shall label "modifiers," that various writers and investigators in the field sometimes view as important for training outcomes. Included here are such things as whether the training is on company time or individual time, the total time involved in the training (can the same learning be accomplished in less time?), and the locale of the training session, that is, whether the training is conducted inside or outside the plant. With regard to this latter modifier, the virtues of university versus company programs have often been argued (Anshen, 1954; Boudreaux & Megginson, 1964; Huneryager, 1961), and the prestige, teaching facilities, and isolation of the university setting are pointed to as either desirable or distracting elements. T-group advocates often speak of the "cultural island" as a necessary or unnecessary part of such training. Here the choice is between conducting the training sessions at a very isolated setting where little contact with the outside world is allowed and holding the program in-house. A great deal of discussion has also centered around who does the training—the line, the staff, or some outside consultant. Here there are the obvious considerations of relative costs, trainer competence, and flexibility. However, the motivational considerations relative to both trainer and trainee are also often pointed out as having a direct bearing on deciding who trains. Many people argue that trainees respond much more favorably when the training is carried out by their own management and management has obviously assumed the responsibility (e.g., Blake & Mouton, 1966b).

In brief, these things we have called "modifiers" can be summed up in a few questions: Where should training take place? Who should train? How much time should be spent for training? Whose time?

Obviously, not all training and development programs utilize just one technique or are intended to teach one particular topic. The objectives and scope of a two-year job rotation program are not all comparable to those of a two-hour seminar on human relations employing role playing and the conference method. By arranging all these methods in an organized "list," we do not mean to imply that they are comparable in terms of the "domain of behavior" they seek to influence.

However, it is also true that many more than one combination of training method and modifier can be used for a particular training or development objective. For example, a programmed booklet may attempt to teach the same thing as a business game, or role playing may be used to reach the same objectives as a *T* group. It is a truism to say that given a particular objective, different costs and different payoffs are associated with different combinations of techniques and modifying circumstances.

Perhaps it would be well for people interested in training and development to examine a number of possible combinations with a view toward systematically justifying, on the basis of theory and empirical findings, the pros and cons of each one. As we shall discuss later, Briggs (1966) suggests that there is an optimal combination of training method and "what is to be learned" and that it behooves educators, organizational training specialists, and learning theorists alike to get on with the job of finding out what these optimal combinations are.

TEAM TRAINING

Up to now we have been talking about training and development efforts in the context of the individual trainee. Somewhat distinct from this orientation is the notion of team training (Blake, Mouton, & Blansfield, 1962; Boguslaw & Porter, 1962; Porter, 1964). Instead of developing individual managers, the emphasis is on training teams of managers. Blake et al. (1962) use the analogy of a baseball team to illustrate that individual training cannot do the whole job. The team must be trained as an interacting unit. Porter (1964) has pointed out that the skills, information, and attitudes obtained from team training revolve largely around problems of coordination and thus are not the same as what is learned in individual training. Viewed in this fashion, it would seem that for team training to be effective, a great deal of individual training must have gone before. That is, there must be individual skills and attitudes available for coordination in the team setting. On the other hand, it also seems reasonable that an individual must learn something about the various aspects of team performance before the crucial requirements for individual training become apparent. The two interact.

The literature regarding the use of team training for executive development is rather sparse. Not much has been said about possible training techniques, what is to be taught, or what the modifiers of such training are. However, some of the simulation methods seem especially appropriate for this kind of training. Porter (1964) describes the use of a simulated situation to train the entire work force in an air defense installation, including people with managerial responsibilities. The larger, more complex business games which allow a number of trainees to make up a firm and which require effective coordination among the trainees could be used for team training if the players making up a firm were a functioning management group in real life.

A very specialized method which, according to Blake, Mouton, Barnes, and Greiner (1964), does attempt to develop both individual and team or organizational skills is the Management Grid approach. The content is also quite specialized, and the initial objective is to teach a particular management style, referred to as the "9,9 style." Managerial style is conceived as having two dimensions—a concern for people and a concern for production—and Blake and Mouton (1964) have developed questionnaire-type measures to locate individual managers on these two dimensions (or grids). A 9,9 style describes a manager who has both a maximal concern for people and a maximal concern for production. The first steps in the training focus on the individual, and a modified T-group method is used to teach each participant how the other group members see his managerial style. Trainees are first familiarized with the grid language and theory. The group then proceeds to work through a series of exercises and case problems which allow each individual to exhibit his management style, and this behavior then becomes the object of T-group type of feedback. Participants supposedly develop skills which enable them accurately and candidly to reflect the management behavior of each individual. This process is intended to instill an appreciation for the human problems of production and move the trainees toward the 9,9 region of the grid.

After this initial phase, the trainees are supposed to go back to their functional groups and use what they have learned to move the entire team to 9,9 methods of operating. It is intended that the "openness" and "candor" learned in the first group carry over to the functional group, starting with the boss and his chief subordinates, and that they become a part of the daily work routine. Finally, attempts are made to extend the utility of the 9,9 approach beyond a particular work team by identifying actual sources of intergroup or interdepartment conflict and incorporating the 9,9 approach in intergroup problem-solving exercises. New attempts are also made to redefine problems and set goals for the organization as a whole. In order for these objectives to be realized, all the managers in an organization must take part in the training. Blake et al. (1964) thus conceive of their program as organizational development rather than management development. The same is true for certain advocates of laboratory education (Schein & Bennis, 1965).

It should be emphasized again that team training is meant to be something distinct, but not entirely independent, from individual training and that the success of the former depends to a degree on the success of the latter. The two obviously interact. As with the other training techniques, team training can potentially at least be directed at a number of content areas. For example, the "family" type of *T* group can be used to familiarize members of a management team with one another's methods of communication, self-images, etc. It is hoped that this will reduce some of the interpersonal barriers that dampen effective coordination. Notice that in such an instance the contribution of team training would be knowledge about the behavior of specific people, i.e., the people who work together in the job situation. The functional team must thus be trained intact. As another example, perhaps a business game could be used to teach team procedures for planning an organization's short-term and long-term goals. The team members could learn which individual functions best as a "critical evaluator," who is an "idea" man, etc., and then devise means for coordinating these specialized skills in future goal-setting tasks.

The interactions between the objectives of individual and team training are obviously complex, and not all aspects of these interactions are always relevant. However, the notion of team training as applied to the management development sphere deserves more attention than it has received.

SUMMARY

In this chapter we have made no pretense of being evaluative. Instead we have tried to give a picture of the types of methods and techniques that are available for changing management behavior through training and development. In fact, the bulk of the training and development literature is devoted to descriptions of these methods. If nothing else is gained from this material, the reader should at least come to the conclusion that training and development is a fertile field for research and theory. The relevance of learning theory, attitude change, task analysis, criterion analysis, and measurement is obvious.

Chapter 11 **Applications of Basic Research and Theory**

It is obvious from even the cursory discussion of management development activities presented in the previous chapter that organizations are trying actively to influence learning in a multitude of areas. For very practical and utilitarian reasons, attempts are made by the firm to teach concepts, create skills, change attitudes, and alter group processes. However, the activities of the organization trainer have remained relatively untouched by the theorist, even though many people in universities and military organizations have been concerned for a long time with the theoretical foundations of the learning process, attitude change, and group dynamics.

PRINCIPLES OF LEARNING

Of all the relevant areas of basic research, the one which has had the most influence on training and development is the field of learning. Even here, however, the cross-fertilization has not been great, and when more contact of theory and practice is suggested (Fryer, Feinberg, & Zalkind, et al., 1956; McGehee & Thayer, 1961), what is most often advocated is that the trainer make more use of certain "principles of effective learning" that have been developed by the basic researcher. A number of sets of such principles, differing only slightly, have been presented in the literature in the context of training and development, and a synthesis of them is given below. Again, these principles are usually offered as things which the organizational trainer can use to improve the effectiveness of his training efforts.

Distributed or spaced learning periods. If one has thirty hours to devote to a management development program, should it be given all at once (along with lots of black coffee), an hour a day five days a week for six weeks, five hours a day for six days, or what? In general, the implication is that distributed practice is better than massed practice. Note the word "PRACTICE." Almost all of the research on which this principle is based has utilized such things as the memorization of word lists and the mastery of motor skills as the experimental task. Such activities are a far cry from learning to deal with intergroup conflict or exploring the influence of R & D spending on corporate profits. As it stands, this principle cannot specify any optimal procedure for any particular kind of management development, but can only point toward an important variable to be considered. The fact that it can very well be important is suggested in a study by Mahler and Monroe (1952) which showed that a group of 300 supervisors trained over a two-week period made fewer mistakes in training their subordinates than a similar group which was trained in three successive days.

Whole versus part learning. In effect what this principle says is that there is an optimal size "chunk" of the training program that should be presented to the learners at any one time. However, this principle suffers from an inability to define what is a part and what is a whole, and we found no references which tried to relate it empirically to the training of individuals in organizations.

Reinforcement. In general, this principle states that the responses made by the trainee in the learning situation which are rewarded will tend to be repeated, remembered, and utilized in other situations. It also says that punishment will not have a similar effect in the opposite direction and, in fact, is relatively ineffective as an influence on learning. One of the difficulties in transporting this principle to the management development area is defining before the training starts what will function as a reward. Will praise from the trainer be enough (perhaps it may even be viewed as punishment), or will some external sort of reward have to be offered, a promotion or salary increase, for example? And when would a salary increase function as a reward? Another difficulty in trying to incorporate reinforcement in training programs is that there are a number of sources in the organization from which rewards can originate (Schien, 1963). Haire (1948, 1964) and Mosel (1957) have pointed out that although certain kinds of responses may be reinforced by the trainers or by the other trainees during the training period, such behavior has little chance of being translated back to the job situation if the trainee's boss does not reward the learning or allow it to be utilized. Haire applies the term "encapsulation" to the kind of learning that never gets beyond the training sessions. He also points out that it is the superior and not the trainer who controls *most* of the rewards and determines the value system in the everyday work situation. The superior by necessity must act as a reinforcer. In sum, the value of reinforcement can hardly be denied, and if the learning theorists have provided a valuable principle at all, it is this one. Its application, however, presents difficulties.

Knowledge of results (feedback). Feedback can enhance learning in two general ways: by allowing the learner to correct mistakes and by making the task more intrinsically interesting or rewarding. This principle has been widely recognized by many people involved in training and development. It is the backbone of programmed instruction, and in this context feedback is important both for the elimination of errors and for its reinforcement properties. With the Skinner method of programmed learning, however, the reinforcement aspect of feedback seems to be the more important because incorrect responses are to be avoided in the first place. The *T*-group methods and many of the simulation techniques (e.g., business games) also make specific provisions for feedback to the participants. It does not seem to be quite so integral a part of the other techniques.

In general this principle says that knowledge of results is a good thing and that the sooner it comes after the learner's response, the better. However, Mosel (1958) has warned that it is not enough just to say that feedback enhances learning. Merely informing a trainee that he was wrong is not as effective as telling him why he was wrong and how he can avoid making similar mistakes in the future. In fact, merely informing an individual of an incorrect response may prove overwhelmingly frustrating for people who want to know "why."

The only study uncovered which focused specifically on the effects of knowledge of results on management training was one by Ayers (1964). In this study a questionnaire—the Ohio Leadership Opinion Questionnaire (LOQ)—was given to the training participants at the beginning and at various stages in the training. The questionnaire is intended to measure certain leadership qualities and was discussed in some detail in an earlier section. The experimental group was allowed to score their own questionnaires and to refer to the scoring key to see what their "leadership profile" looked like. The number of changes over the course of the training was considerably greater for the experimental group than for the control group, which participated in the same training program but did not receive any information concerning changes in their leadership profile.

Motivation. This principle says that to learn one must *want* to learn. However, being too motivated may lead to a decrement in performance. There is some evidence to suggest a curvilinear relationship. As distinguished from reinforcement, motivation usually refers to the forces which cause the individual to approach the training actively and with interest. Many trainers seem to be well aware of this principle and have gone to great lengths to make training interesting. It is perhaps useful to contrast learning which is inherently interesting, or motivating for its own sake, and learning for which external motivation must be supplied. A frequently advocated ingredient of the former is the notion of "participation," which has been consciously incorporated in a number of the training methods described in the previous chapter. Besides participating in the actual training sessions, a number of writers (Argyris, 1961; Schein, 1963; Timbers, 1965) have suggested that the trainee participate in the *planning* of his development program. The rationale for this type of participation is that self-development is the most motivating training activity of all. Argyris (1961), however, has pointed out what he considers to be a paradox concerning self-development as a motivator. Almost everyone undoubtedly agrees that a manager who feels responsible for his own development is more motivated and ultimately learns more than a manager who does not. On the other hand, it is the trainer who usually defines the content of the course, the time and the place, etc. Also, the responsibility for determining training needs often rests exclusively with the training staff. An example of an external source of motivation is suggested by Ingenohl (1962), who advocates that management development be made a competitive opportunity to appeal to the managerial spirit of competition. Perhaps a less useful means of external motivation would be a "suggestion" by a superior that a manager go through a training program.

All motivated trainees may not be motivated to learn, however. Chowdhry (1964) interviewed 29 executives at a university management training program and concluded that participants who select themselves for the program often use the training to escape from the stresses of the job and to plan the next phase of their career strategy, rather than for the purpose for which the training was intended.

Transfer of training. This principle attempts to state under what conditions the behaviors learned in the training session will be utilized in other situations. For management development it points to the very crucial consideration of whether or not skills learned in training will transfer to on-the-job behavior. The empirical evidence relating to the transfer of training will be discussed at some length in a later chapter.

Much of the theoretical discussion of transfer (McGehee & Thayer, 1961; Tiffeen & McCormick, 1965) centers around the question of why transfer takes place. One answer often given is that transfer occurs to the extent that the elements of the behavior learned in training are identical to the elements of behavior required for good job performance. In other words, the training situation must be just like the job situation, at least in part. The training methods which obviously seek to take advantage of this mechanism of transfer are the on-the-job techniques and the simulation methods. For example, one of the objectives of role playing is to provide an opportunity for the trainee to learn to deal with human relations problems just as he would in an actual job situation. Also, some business games are intended to give the trainee actual experience in reacting to such things as changes in the price of labor and the like. However, this sort of transfer may run into difficulty if the organization intends the training situation to be identical with the job situation when actually it is not. In such a case the trainee may learn an inappropriate response, and *negative* transfer may occur; that is, the training may actually make job performance worse.

Another explanation of why transfer occurs has to do with the application of *principles* learned in training to problems faced on the job. This is the intent of most of the information presentation techniques and to some extent the simulation techniques. For example, a business game can be used to teach an appreciation for the interrelatedness of the decisions which must be made in a complex organization. It is then hoped that this concept will carry over to the job and be brought into play whenever an individual is faced with an important decision situation. The crucial aspects of this kind of transfer revolve around the conditions under which a principle is seen as relevant to the job situation and is fruitfully applied.

In sum, the question of transfer is perhaps the most important learning consideration that must be faced by the organization that wishes to develop managers. If the goal of development and training is to further the goals of the organization, then training that does not transfer is of no use and may even have considerable negative utility. More will be said about this problem later.

Practice. This principle implies that in order for the training effort to reap its full benefit, the behavior learned must be practiced; that is, it must be overlearned to ensure smooth performance and a minimum of forgetting at a later date. Many would argue (e.g., Allen, 1957) that this cannot be done away from the job and that practice must be provided for in the actual work setting. On the other hand, it might be difficult to practice the type of skills involved in T-group training without the presence of a supportive trainer and group. Also, the meaning of practice itself is unclear for such things as courses in the humanities and the case method. In sum, the means for applying this learning principle to management training problems remain a bit fuzzy, although its value for certain kinds of skill learning seems readily apparent.

The principles outlined above encompass what is most often discussed by those who try to apply the knowledge of the learning theorists to the training situation. These topics are not theory as such, but are *principles* that might profitably be applied by the organization (This & Lippitt, 1966). Not everyone agrees as to how much use has been made of these principles, but most writers seem to concur that a lot more could be done with them.

As we have already mentioned, the above principles make up the bulk of the "training theory" literature. Although their importance for management learning seems obvious, demonstrations of their effects have been carried out almost exclusively in terms of animal behavior and human psychomotor skills. Consideration of the complex learning involved in management training and development introduces some additional notions that might be important for the organizational practitioner.

Bass and Vaughan (1966) point out that there are different "ways" to learn that these have important implications for the particular training methods which are selected to achieve specific objectives. For example, one obvious way to learn is through *trial and error*. In its purest form, trial and error would constitute random sampling (without replacement) from a population of available responses until the correct or most useful one is identified. Although self-discovery through trial and error may facilitate motivation and retention, it may also be very inefficient.

Another way, perhaps more important for complex learning, is *modeling*, or the imitation of the behavior of others who are observed being reinforced for particular responses. In this type of learning the attraction of the model and the numerous factors which affect his relationship to the learner become quite important.

Perhaps most important of all for the acquisition of responses in complex learning are the various *intermediary processes* that can be provided for the learner. Written instructions, graphic displays, and actual demonstrations are some examples; that is, the responses to be learned are presented in an organized fashion via some kind of coded or symbolic means.

These three ways to learn—trial and error, modeling, and intermediary processes—are really descriptions of the process by which the desired responses are acquired. Their relevance for various training objectives is crucial, and they should be carefully considered in the planning of any management development effort. For example, the people involved with *T*-group and laboratory training have chosen to focus on trial and error and modeling as the principle means by which their training objectives can be achieved. Although intermediary processes are provided through lectures and observation of group exercises, such processes are anathema to the *T* group itself. In the *T* group the trainer provides a model of desirable behavior, and the participant discovers new responses (both attitudinal and behavioral) through trying out new modes of responding in an atmosphere of psychological safety.

In sum, once a learning process (or a combination of processes) has been chosen, the implications of the learning principles should then be considered. Trial and error, modeling, and symbolic processes actually describe *how* a response might be acquired, while the principles are potential influences on the relative speed with which the response is acquired and the rate at which it is forgotten.

Recently, the general utility of the principles of learning has been called into question by Gagne (1962), who says that concepts such as distributed practice, reinforcement, and the like are not what is really important in the learning situation. Their focus is entirely too one-sided in that they overemphasize the *process* of learning rather than *what* is learned (Gagne & Brown, 1961). In other words, the trainer's first allegiance should be to his subject matter rather than to his methods.

Gagne proposes a series of questions to be used in analyzing a training problem:

1 What are the task components of the job?
2 What "mediates" or influences performance on these job tasks; that is, what must be learned in order to enhance job performance?
3 How should these mediators (the training content) be broken down into elements for purposes of training?
4 How should the learning of these elements be sequenced in order to ensure optimal progression from one learning stage to another and to provide for maximum mediation effects, or transfer to the job?

In this schema the notion of "what is to be learned" is elevated to the peak of importance, and while the traditional learning principles are not unimportant, they are definitely relegated to a secondary position. For example, if the virtues of programmed learning are argued from this point of view, one could point to the fact that programmed learning forces the trainer to consider exactly what he wants to teach and why, then to break the topic down into its proper elements, and finally to sequence the learning of these elements in an optimal fashion. The benefits of reinforcement and feedback are appreciated, but they are not the main reason programmed instruction is valuable.

If we adopt the Gagne approach to training, and his arguments for doing so are compelling, we run into the same stumbling block that has been haunting us throughout this volume. To say that we can analyze a manager's job into its task components is akin to saying that we are able to describe what a manager does. The difficulties involved in this objective have already been discussed at length in an earlier chapter. Gagne derived most of his thoughts from investigations of skill training in the military, where perhaps it is a bit easier to make a thorough analysis of the tasks which make up the job and to specify the mediating training elements than in the case of managerial jobs. Nevertheless, these operations are just as necessary for planning managerial development as for planning the job of the tank driver if managerial development is to consist of anything more than trial-and-error attempts to change behavior.

In the management literature the analysis of task components goes by the name of "establishing training needs." Almost no substantive studies have been published in this area, and most of the discussions of needs analysis center around the methods used to uncover them. A number of writers (Bellows et al., 1962; Ghiselli & Brown, 1955; Gilmer, 1966; Sterner, 1965; Tiffen & McCormick, 1965) describe checklist or questionnaire procedures in which lists of possible training needs are given to potential trainees or their superiors with instructions to indicate which aspects of the job are most in need of training. The items on the questionnaire usually reflect someone's "best guesses" as to possible training needs, however, and in no case has such a list been based on actual systematic observation of managerial job behavior. Perhaps a more prevalent method, especially for middle and upper management, is to include a discussion of the subordinate's training needs as a regular part of the performance appraisal procedure. In actual practice, however, as was true in a number of the firms included in our survey, many participants in management development programs select themselves and thus perform their own needs analysis. We were able to find no example of a task analysis even approaching the scope demanded by Gagne's schema.

One procedure that does hold considerable promise is the "critical incident" technique used by Glickman and Vallance (1958) to assess the training needs of line naval officers and feed back the results to the people responsible for the OCS curriculum. A critical incident is defined by Flanagan (1954) as a concrete piece of job behavior that is considered critical for either good performance or poor performance. Critical incidents are recorded on the job as they happen, usually by the immediate superior; they were discussed in much greater detail in an earlier chapter. In the Glickman and Vallance study, over a thousand critical incidents of ensign behavior were recorded by superior officers. Similar incidents were grouped into categories, and the categories that reflected poor performance were fed back to the training command. Changes were then made in the training program to try to remove the causes of negative critical incidents and enhance the causes of positive ones.

Leaving one unsolved problem behind and pursuing Gagne a bit further, the next consideration that must be faced is specifying the mediators of good job performance; that is, what skills and attitudes that can be brought under the control of the training program will facilitate effective job performance?

The organization must be able to verbalize publicly what it is going to teach for the purpose of enhancing managerial effectiveness. In other words, what is to be learned? One of the difficulties in this task with respect to management development has been pointed out by Lundberg (1962). He observes that many of the crucial mediating factors of management performance are postulated to be attitudes. However, demonstrating the link between a change in an attitude and a change in job performance is difficult indeed. The management trainer could certainly benefit from an improved conceptualization of the attitudes he is attempting to alter or reinforce. The term "attitude" has been used rather loosely by training specialists. We shall discuss the empirical evidence regarding this link in a later section. Furthermore, few management training efforts have yet tried to incorporate any theoretical analysis of attitude change in their programs. Specifying the mediators of management performance for training purposes indeed has its problems.

OTHER THEORETICAL APPLICATIONS

Discussions of learning principles exhaust most of the theoretical literature devoted to training efforts. However, the body of psychological theory potentially applicable to problems of management training and development is certainly much broader. Theories of attitude formation and attitude change are directly relevant. Basic research efforts in the areas of group structure and process, person perception, personality, and cognitive structure also have considerable potential. In fact, consideration of these topics is vitally necessary. For example, one potential objective of the T group (Tannenbaum, Weschler, & Massarik, 1961) is to help an individual come to terms with previously unacceptable aspects of his self-image by means of obtaining feedback on his defense mechanisms from a nonthreatening audience. Such a process seems to imply an actual alteration in the self-image, i.e., a kind of personality change. If trainers hold these kinds of objectives, then they might properly search the literature of personality theory for fruitful insights to apply systematically to their training activities.

Besides considering the implications of personality theory for trainee behavior, it might also be useful to consider its application relative to the influence of superiors and peers on training outcomes. For example, Schein (1963) uses personality concepts to explain the failure of superiors and peers to reinforce what the trainee has learned. The "trained" manager might be a threat to the boss's security and self-image, and the boss might therefore try to squelch any changes in the trainee's job performance. Again, it might be fruitful to hypothesize what kinds of training outcomes would be most likely to be positively or negatively reinforced by particular kinds of superiors. To date, however, there has been almost no direct application of basic research in personality theory to problems of management development.

In addition to the learning principles, the area of basic research and theory which has had perhaps the most direct application to training has been that of small group theory, or "group dynamics." The work of Lewin (1947, 1948) on the effects of individual participation and democratic versus autocratic leadership formed much of the foundation for the group methods of training. The conference technique, *T* groups, and the simulation methods all owe a great deal to this area of theoretical work. In the management development context much of small group theory fits into the learning principles as a means for increasing learner motivation, providing opportunities for practice, and mediating learning through the self-discovery of insights.

Another aspect of small group research with potential relevance for certain kinds of management training might be labeled theories of "group process" or "group development." For example, Tuckman (1965) postulates that task-oriented groups, such as training groups, go through four stages. In the first stage the members try to test one another to find out where they "fit" in the status ladder and also attempt to make themselves dependent on the trainer so that he carries the full responsibility for what the group does. Since most of the participative methods of training attempt to thwart such behavior, the group then enters a period of conflict in which the participants thrash out all the difficulties involved in shedding their previous status symbols and accepting their fair share of the responsibility for training. Once this is accomplished, the group becomes very cohesive, and the members practice being "close" to one another by means of a great deal of very open communication. Once the newness of this team feeling wears off, the group enters its fourth and final phase, in which it can attack the training problems in a democratic, open, and efficient manner. Similar "stage" hypotheses have been proposed by other writers (Bales, 1951; Bennis & Shepard, 1956; Harvey, Hunt, & Shroder, 1961; Schutz, 1958). This aspect of small group theory might possibly have relevance when considering how to break down the training program into meaningful parts and wholes (e.g., perhaps it would be desirable to structure the training program so that the individual sessions correspond to particular phases of group development) and otherwise take advantage of the processes that go on in groups.

ATTITUDE CHANGE

Implicitly, at least, a major part of management training and development is concerned with attitude change. The attitudes in question may be focused on the firm itself, subordinates, methods of supervision, management techniques, or a number of other objects. A further assumption is that such attitudes have relevant implications for the behavior of the individuals involved. Given the potential relevance of attitudes and attitude change for management development, it is surprising to note that almost no basic attitude research or theory has been incorporated into the management development literature. The attitude literature that has potential relevance is voluminous, and it is beyond the scope of the present volume to integrate it with the objectives and practices of management and development. However, we would like to sketch briefly some of its implications in hopes that it might stimulate a closer examination by potential researchers of the training and development process.

What is an attitude? How the variable is conceptualized obviously has implications for the means used to change it. Previous writers have provided definitions which tend to converge along certain dimensions. First of all, attitudes are viewed as internal states which occur within the individual but which are focused on certain objects in the environment (e.g., organization A, theory Y, or unions). The relative specificity of the focal "object" is a point still at issue. Postulating very specific objects (e.g., all the various things a union might do or stand for) necessitates having to deal with a large number of attitudes and has very different training implications from postulating a general sort of attitude structure, such as liberalism versus conservatism (e.g., Eysenck, 1953). The specific view seems to reflect the majority opinion.

Beyond the environment and within the individual it becomes necessary to postulate what elements make up an attitude. At least three have been mentioned, but not all of them by every theorist (Krech, Crutchfield, & Ballachey, 1962; Secord & Bachman, 1964). First, the *cognitive* component of an attitude refers to the intellectual beliefs or knowledge that an individual might have about an object. For example, one might have a certain belief about the goals that unions are trying to achieve, if the union is the attitude object under consideration. The most important cognitions are those which make a positive or negative judgment about the object according to some set of criteria (Krech et al., 1962). The *feeling,* or *affective,* component of an attitude refers to the emotions connected with the object and whether the object is felt to be pleasing or displeasing. It is this affective quality that tends to give the concept of attitude its motivational quality. However, whether strong attitudes actually motivate is an empirical research question that is by no means answered. The third element is the *behavioral* component, or action tendency. Allport's early definition of an attitude was that it is a "predisposition to respond." That is, if an individual holds a negative attitude toward an object, he will be more likely to hinder, degrade, punish, or harm that object, and the reverse will be true in the case of positive attitudes.

Given these three possible elements, different implications for research and practice flow from a consideration of which elements are most important and how they interact. For example, Shaw and Wright (1967) hypothesize that the affective component is the central variable and that an individual's feelings about an object result from his cognitive associations. Further, the affective components form the antecedents of the behavior. Thus the direction of the relationship has been specified (cognitions → feelings → behavior), and this identifies which are the independent variables and which are the dependent variables. Conversely, one could also postulate that it is the behavior toward an object that results in certain feelings, which in turn lead to a selective building up of cognitive beliefs justifying the action. Or perhaps both of these processes operate at different stages of an individual's relationship with the object. Which of these is true obviously has implications for efforts to change attitudes through training. It also has implications for how attitudes should be measured. For example, Shaw and Wright (1967) conclude that since they believe the affective component to be most salient, the proper way to measure attitude is by assessing an individual's feelings toward the object.

Methods of attitude change. A number of methods have been used in experimental and field settings to attempt to change attitudes (see, for example, A. R. Cohen, 1964). Most of these can be summarized under four headings:

1 *Communication of additional information.* That is, additional inputs are focused on the cognitive elements making up the attitude in hopes that the individual's beliefs will change. This immediately raises research questions concerning the relative effects of variability in the credibility of the communicator, the amount of change advocated, the effects of one- versus two-sided communication, and the order of presentation. Such questions have been researched in varying degrees, and practitioners attempting to change attitudes via management development should become well aware of the results.

2 *Approval and disapproval.* That is, making rewards or incentives contingent on a particular type, magnitude, and direction of attitude change. One would expect that for this method to be effective, the nature of the change must be made clear to the individual, the contingency of reward on change must be perceived, and the value of the reward must clearly override the value to the person of keeping the original attitude.

3 *Group influences.* In general, what are the effects of interacting with group members whose attitudes are considerably different.

4 *Being induced to engage in discrepant behavior.* For example, in a number of studies, subjects have been asked to role play a situation in which they took the opposite side of an issue or otherwise played the role of a person whose attitude was discrepant from their own. In the field setting this may not be simply role playing. The individual may be *required* to engage in behavior which is contrary to his attitude (e.g., socialize with union officials even though he thinks they are bad).

In some way or other, all the above methods involve introducing discrepancies among the elements making up the individual's attitude in hopes that the elements will be rebalanced through changing the *affective* component of the attitude. Thus in practice, the central variable in attitude change research is the feelings component associated with the attitude object.

Given these external means for changing attitudes, previous research and theory suggest that there are a number of additional characteristics of the attitude itself that must be taken into account. Krech et al. (1962) summarize these under seven headings:

1 *The extremeness of the attitude.* In general one would expect the difficulty of attitude change to vary with extremeness, but the practitioner should be aware of the possible asymmetry between changing positive and changing negative attitudes.
2 *Multiplexity.* This refers to the breadth of the attitude or the number of specific subelements making up the focal object. For example, an attitude toward "unions" is much broader than an attitude toward "union wage demands."
3 *Consistency.* That is, consistency among the cognitive elements, affective elements, and behavioral tendencies making up the attitude. An attitude which already contains some inconsistent elements should be easier to change.
4 *Interconnectedness.* To what degree is the attitude in question interrelated or closely connected with other attitudes? Attitudes which are strongly supported by other attitudes should be more resistant to change.
5 *Consonance of the attitude "cluster" of which the focal attitude is a part.* While the interconnectedness dimension emphasizes the number of supporting attitudes in the cluster, consonance refers to their intercorrelation or the degree to which they reinforce one another. Again, the greater the consonance, the more difficult it should be to change the attitude under consideration.
6 *The number and strength of the needs which are served by the attitude.* This is essentially a motivational aspect and implies that the stronger the individual needs to which the attitude is attached, the more difficult it will be to change. For example, an attitude related to an individual's need for security should be more resistant to change than an attitude related to his need for entertainment.
7 *Centrality of related values.* In essence, this refers to the centrality of the attitude in the individual's personality makeup. Attitudes which reflect the core or principal component of an individual's personality would most likely be very resistant to change.

The above concepts are not theory in the formal sense, but they do represent parameters that should be taken into account before any attempt is made to change managerial attitudes by means of training and development programs. In this sense, they are similar to the learning principles discussed in a previous section.

Whether attitude change implies behavioral change is still a moot point, even when the total spectrum of the attitude literature is considered. Both Festinger (1964a) and Rokeach (1968) lament the fact that there is virtually no empirical research linking attitudes and behavior, no matter what the content area.

Rokeach (1968) has suggested a reformulation of the attitude-behavior change problem which may help to explain why it occurs and how it may be made to occur. He postulates that behavior is a function of at least two kinds of attitudes in any particular situation. In general, these are attitudes toward objects and attitudes toward situations. For example, a restaurant owner may have a particular attitude toward members of a minority group (object) and a particular attitude toward serving customers in his restaurant (situation). These two attitudes interact in a kind of figure-ground relationship, and the behavior of the owner toward minority-group members in his restaurant is a resultant of the two. This can explain why a very prejudiced individual might still deal with minority-group members in his place of business. Rokeach suggests that in any situation where behavior change is desired, these two classes of component attitudes must be dealt with. Certainly in the organizational situation there are many striking examples of this figure-ground relationship. As just one instance, consider attitudes toward employees (object) and attitudes toward "getting the work out" (situation). A training program that succeeds in creating more employee-centered attitudes among supervisors may or may not result in behavior change. The critical factor is the nature of interaction of the "trained" attitude with the situational attitude. Both types of attitudes could be assessed before training begins, and the resultant considered. Perhaps the situational attitude carries such a great weight that giving training attention exclusively to the object attitude is futile.

Other conceptualizations of the attitude-behavior change problem have been given by Fishbein (1967) and Doob (1947). Fishbein explains the negative results of previous research with two principal points. First, complex behavior is multidetermined, and we should not expect a terribly high relationship of attitude change with behavior change. Second, most previous research has focused on the relationship between rather *general* attitudes and behavior in a fairly *specific* domain, for example, attitudes toward a general class of people (women) and behavior relative to specific people (Suzy Smith). Thus, Fishbein argues that the attitude objects studied have often been inappropriate. They have been much too general. There are obvious similarities between this notion and the specificity achieved by Rokeach through the interaction of an object attitude and a situational attitude.

For our purposes, the most salient feature of Doob's (1947) formulation is that while an individual may learn a new attitude, he must also learn a new set of *responses* in order for there to be any relationship between attitudes and behavior. Thus a learning experience that stresses only attitude change might be doomed to failure from the start.

In sum, careful consideration of the elements making up an attitude, the methods available for changing attitudes, and the possible parameters affecting behavior change should provide a great deal of guidance for training and development efforts. To date, very little of this body of knowledge has been exploited.

THE SYSTEMS APPROACH

Since we are using the term "applications of theory" rather loosely, it might also be appropriate to include in this section a brief look at some past and current thinking regarding how the management training function shoud be conceptualized; that is, how does the training function fit into the rest of the organization? The traditional description of the training process, whether it be for managers or other types of personnel, usually sets down a number of steps, such as the following:

1 Determine training needs.
2 Choose a theoretical approach (or approaches) appropriate to the types of things that must be taught.
3 Define the objectives of the training effort.
4 Develop a training program to meet the objectives.
5 Identify the individuals to be trained.
6 Conduct the training.
7 Determine whether the training has met its objectives.

Recently, however, this view of the training function has come under critical scrutiny from those wanting to conceptualize training from the point of view of systems or communications theory (Brown, 1966; Crawford, 1962; Odiorne, 1965). According to these writers, several things are wrong with the above formulation.

First, starting with a determination of training needs is not enough. The goals of the entire organization must first be examined to see whether training needs identified among individual managers are relevant to these goals. A manager may be very deficient in human relations skills, but if such skills are irrelevant to the organization's goals, they are not an appropriate subject for training. By the same reasoning it may be far more important to institute training for an aspect of management performance that is judged less deficient than some other aspect if the former is many times more important for the organization than the latter. The importance of training needs must be judged relative to the organization's overall goals.

Second, the steps in the training process listed above really imply that the training program has a definite beginning and end and that once it has been satisfactorily demonstrated that the training has met its objectives, the program is complete. Not so, say the critics. For example, Odiorne (1965) argues that we should borrow the cybernetics model from the communications theorist and view training as a continuous process. Ideally the evaluation procedure should make a systematic provision for feeding back information as to how the determination of training needs and the training process itself could be improved. In jargon terms he is proposing a "feedback loop," which really serves two purposes. It makes it possible for the training program to be constantly improved and to be reused more effectively with new training groups, and it enables the training program to change if the goals of the organization or the training needs change. Training is thus viewed as a continuous and self-correcting process.

Third, the degree to which a training program meets its objectives cannot really be assessed or measured at any one particular point in time, as seems to be implied by the traditional view. Feedback to the process should continue to occur for a considerable time after the trainee has left the formal training environment. The organization is not necessarily worried about the manager's change in performance during the twenty-four hour period immediately after the conclusion of the program, or even a week or a month later. It is the sum of his behavior changes over a substantial period of time which is at issue.

Finally, the traditional conceptualization tends to ignore the fact that the output of organization training programs (in the form of new knowledge, skills, or attitudes) interacts with the output of the other programs conducted by the organization. For example, Schein (1964) illustrates how a recruiting and selection program that obtains topnotch college graduates and promises great opportunities in the firm can interact in a very negative fashion with a job rotation program that provides no challenges or opportunities to learn. On a somewhat more subtle but no less important level, the values instilled by a training program may conflict with the values held by top management, and a great deal of dissatisfaction and conflict may result (Sykes, 1964). Also, the systems analyst himself may so change the manager's job that previous training programs teach entirely the wrong things.

The college trainee example mentioned above is a specific case of a general class of interactions between the objectives of the training program and individual differences in trainees. Fiedler (1965) points out that it might be tremendously expensive to try to teach a particular leadership style to an individual who by the very nature of his personality is almost incapable of practicing it. It might be much better for the organization to change the job rather than the man. From a somewhat different examination of the same problem, Cronbach and Gleser (1965) convincingly argue that the benefits of training may be greatly enhanced if the methods used can be varied to suit the abilities and characteristics of the trainees. Teaching human relations to engineers, for example, might require a very different sort of procedure from that used to teach the same skills to line supervisors who have come up through the ranks. The initial value orientations and expectations of these two groups are probably considerably different.

In sum, the above points are meant to characterize the "systems approach" to conceptualizing the training function. Such an approach goes beyond merely recognizing that it is the line's ultimate responsibility to train, with the training staff acting in a consultive capacity. It implies that the training function is a subsystem within a larger system and that while it has its own inputs and outputs, these overlap and interact with the inputs and outputs of the entire organization. Pushed to its logical extreme, this means that the time a manager spends in a training session must be demonstrated to be worth more in terms of the organization's goals than a similar period of time spent on some other activity (e.g., working). While it may be impossible to demonstrate such things in dollars and cents terms, the admonition of the systems approach to consider as carefully as possible all the points in the organization where training activity interacts with other programs must be heeded.

One implication of the systems approach often pointed to is the choice between improving performance through training and through the selection of better personnel. Certainly these two activities are directed toward many of the same goals, and for certain goals and in a particular organizational situation one may be more useful than the other. However, while it is an improvement to think in terms of alternatives, an either/or approach to the choice between selection and training still falls short of the systems view. Instead of taking an either/or approach, we should really consider things in terms of interactions; that is, for the particular kinds of people brought into the management ranks by the selection program there is an optimal kind of training experience, and we must be able to change this training experience to take advantage of changes in selection policy. It may indeed be somewhat better to change the selection policy rather than continue with a particular training program. However, once the selection rules have been changed, management performance can be even further enhanced if the training experience can also be changed to interact optimally with the trainee inputs. This same sort of argument should be applied to the interaction of selection and training activities with the motivational and situational variables discussed in other sections of this book.

SUMMARY

In this chapter we attempted to face the frustrating task of specifying the theoretical developments in behavioral research that have implications for training and development. There have been almost no explicit attempts to connect such theory with the objectives and problems of developing managers through training. We briefly reviewed some of the implications of the so-called principles of learning and cited the opposing views of Gagne, which concentrate on the specification of *what* is to be learned. Also briefly mentioned were the theory of small group processes, theories of attitude change, and the systems approach to conceptualizing the training and development function. It was argued that each of these areas has much to contribute to management development, but so far few efforts have been made to bridge the gap.

Chapter 12   The Methodology of Training Evaluation

In this chapter we shall take a brief look at the methodological tools and procedures people have used to gather information for determining the effects of training. Decisions about the utility of training cannot be made in a vacuum. The person or persons in the organization responsible for such decisions must have in front of them information about training effects that is meaningful and unambiguous. The twin questions of (1) what kind of information on training effects we can get and (2) how we should go about getting it are the crucial considerations that will be the topic of the present discussion.

CRITERIA

The literature relevant to the first question consists almost entirely of discussions of possible criteria that can be used to evaluate training effects, plus a great deal of argument about their relative merits. For example, Odiorne (1964) is of the opinion that training must prove its worth in strict economic terms. He argues that if management development connot be demonstrated to contribute to the economic goals of the organization, then it should not be carried out. Mahler (1953) has taken a somewhat different view and argues that if training programs are not initiated because of a fear that the benefits cannot be measured in terms of economics, then evaluation is being overemphasized. He believes that attaching cost accounting concepts to training is just not possible, especially in the context of the managerial job, and that people who are responsible for judging the worth of a training program must be satisfied with something less.

It is our view that it probably is not possible to demonstrate the worth of training in cost accounting terms, for reasons which will be developed later. However, neither should the organization's money be spent on programs whose effects are entirely unknown. The question then, as always, is: "Where lies the fruitful middle ground?"

A number of classification schemes of training criteria have been offered as aids to viewing the problem (Goodacre, 1955; D. L. Kirkpatrick, 1959a, 1959b, 1960a, 1960b; Korb, 1956; Lindbom & Osterberg, 1954). In sum, it seems useful to view such criteria along three dimensions:

1 What types of information are gathered?
2 From which individuals or organizational units is the criterion information obtained?
3 At what point in time, relative to the actual training session, are the data gathered?

Types of criterion information. Some representative types of criterion measures that have been used are the *opinions* of various interested parties, questionnaire measures of certain kinds of *attitude changes, objective examinations* designed to determine whether the trainee learned what the program tried to teach, and various measures of actual post training *job performance.* Relative to job performance measures, Odiorne (1965) suggests that the criterion should vary depending on the level of manager being trained. Training effects should be evaluated for general managers by looking at changes in profits, for production managers by looking at changes in costs, for the production supervisor by looking at units produced, for sales managers by looking at sales revenue minus costs, and for staff managers by comparing programs completed with budget considerations. Other measures that have been suggested are managerial turnover, rate of effective horizontal and vertical communication, fluctuation in frequency of critical incidents, and, of course, ratings of job performance.

An interesting example of an achievement test designed to measure training effects is described by Blansfield (1955) and also by Suttell (1955). In these two studies standardized role-playing situations were developed to test for learning in supervisory and human relations skills. A team of judges rated the performance of each trainee and gave him a score on a number of dimensions.

Along much the same line, Lawshe, Bolda, and Brune (1959) have developed a scoring system for human relations case problems presented via filmstrips. Their procedure for arriving at the scoring system was as follows: After the case problem was shown to a group of subjects, they were asked (1) what the supervisor should have done and (2) why the employee acted as he or she did. The first question was intended to measure "employee orientation" (i.e., to what extent the respondent considered the employee in arriving at a solution), and the second question was supposed to tap "sensitivity" to others. This sample of responses was then given to a group of judges who assigned them to steps along one of two nine-step scales according to how employee-centered or sensitive a particular answer seemed to be. If the judges agreed as to where on the scale a particular answer belonged, that answer was included in a master scale. This master scale could then be used to score future responses to the case problem by comparing and matching a new answer with the answers on the master scale. Another example of a training achievement measure is the one developed by Frederickson, Saunders, and Ward (1957), who have standardized an In-basket problem which can be objectively scored to test a trainee on a number of different aspects of decision making. Of course, many other kinds of achievement tests have also been used to test an individual's knowledge of specific subject matter, such as business law, data processing, and the like.

In the area of attitude change, a number of different measures have been used to assess training effects, and these center largely around attitudes toward the "human problems" of supervision, attitudes toward supervisors and subordinates, attitudes toward various leadership methods, and attitudes toward the organization itself. In the empirical studies that will be summarized in the next section, two specific questionnaire-type measures of these kinds of attitudes appear quite frequently. They are the Leadership Opinion Questionnaire (LOQ) (Fleishman, Harris, & Burtt, 1955), developed by the Ohio State University group, and the How Supervise? developed by File and Remmers (1948).

The LOQ was described in some detail in a previous chapter. Briefly, it is a paper-and-pencil measure of leadership attitudes which yields scores on two dimensions labeled "consideration" and "initiating structure." These dimensions correspond roughly to a concern with the human relationships in the work situation and a concern for the productive task itself. The LOQ is used by the subject himself for purposes of self-description, while a companion instrument, the Leadership Behavior Description Questionnaire (LBDQ), can be used by subordinates, peers, or superiors to describe the leadership behavior of the individual in question. The LBDQ yields the same two scores of consideration and initiating structure. The How Supervise? is also a paper-and-pencil instrument which the individual uses to describe his attitudes toward a number of different aspects of the work environment and the supervisory or leadership role. The individual is asked whether he agrees or disagrees with certain supervisory practices, policies, or beliefs and whether or not he would follow certain courses of action. A high score tends to reflect a participative, human relations type of orientation somewhat along the same lines as the consideration dimension on the LOQ.

Just as it is unfortunate that so little use has been made of basic research in attitude change, it is also unfortunate that so little has been done with other types of attitude measures. Some of the consequences of an overreliance on this type of questionnaire measure will be discussed later.

After considering many of the possible criteria for evaluating training, H. O. Martin (1957) has suggested that they be grouped into two classes, internal and external. *Internal criteria* are those directly linked to the activities of the training program, such as attitude scales and achievement tests designed to measure what the program is intended to teach. *External criteria* are measures designed to assess actual changes in job behavior, such as ratings, economic indicators, grievance rates, or turnover with a manager's unit. For example, a questionnaire asking trainees whether the participants have become more "sensitive to the needs of others" is an internal criterion, if such was the intended context of the training program, while a rating of a manager's job performance made by a subordinate is an external criterion. Or suppose a group of executives are trained in speed reading. If the training is evaluated by means of a standardized test of reading speed and comprehension, an internal criterion has been used. However, if the criterion is some measure of how quickly the executive can read reports in his daily work situation, it is still external. Both types of criteria are necessary, and certainly the relationships between them must be explored if meaningful conclusions are to be drawn from training evaluations.

Who provides the criterion information? Most of the criterion information used to evaluate training effects is obtained from the trainees themselves. However, data may also be gathered from the individuals planning and conducting the training, or from the trainee's superiors, immediate associates, or subordinates. For example, the opinions of any one of these groups could be sought concerning how they thought the training affected the trainee. A frequently used device to evaluate *T*-group training (Bunker, 1965) requires subordinates or associates to report any "changes" they think they have observed in the trainee over a certain time period.

An example of attitude change data that might be gathered from individuals other than the trainees would be that derived from a job attitude survey among subordinates to see whether a "trained boss" results in more positive attitudes toward various aspects of the work situation (Buchanan, 1957). Relative to job performance criteria, it might be appropriate to assess the performance of subordinates as well as the performance of the trainee, by means of either ratings or some sort of objective measure (Lindbom & Osterberg, 1954).

In addition to considering individuals as sources of training criterion information, it might also be possible to get some index of work unit effectiveness such as various cost or profit measures, the grievance rate, morale, turnover, or the frequency of production or scheduling problems. Of course, the behavior of the manager must have an influence on these latter kinds of indexes.

When is the information obtained? The information provided by a particular criterion may be gathered before the training starts, during the training, immediately at the conclusion of the training, or after a certain post training time interval. Collecting criterion data at particular points may make a great deal of difference in the kind of information made available to the organization for the evaluation of the program. The goals of the training , in relation to the goals of the organization, may specify long-term objectives or relatively short-term objectives, but in either instance the behavior of the trainees at some point in time *after* the conclusion of the training is certainly crucial. Furthermore, it is not the absolute level of behavior that is crucial but the change in criterion behavior between the time the training started and some time after it was concluded. That is, did the training really result in a change in performance that transferred back to the job? Conclusions drawn from an assessment of the change in the trainees over just the course of the training period may be far different from those based on an examination of the degree of change that occurred between the start of training and twelve months after its conclusion. On the other hand, comparing the changes made over the course of the training session with the changes exhibited over a longer time interval may offer valuable information concerning the extent to which the things learned in training are retained or the ways in which other forces in the organization interact with the training effects to change the overall picture.

EXPERIMENTAL DESIGN

Besides considering criteria that can be used, a good deal of the literature is devoted to the second of our two initial questions: What plan or procedure should be used for collecting the information so as to make the results as meaningful as possible? In the jargon of researchers everywhere, the name given to such a plan or procedure is *experimental design*. The fundamental objective of any such plan, or experimental design, is to make the results less ambiguous and more amenable to a causal interpretation. In other words, can we or can we not say the training is really responsible for the change in criterion behavior?

MacKinney (1957) has given perhaps the most concise description of various types of experimental designs that may reduce the ambiguity in eval-

uation results by varying amounts. The lowest level, or most ambiguous, procedure would be to secure an *after* criterion measure only. With such a plan it is
not possible, strictly speaking, to attribute anything in the criterion behavior
to the effects of the training. There may indeed have been no change as a result
of training. One step above this approach would be to measure the trainees
both before *and* after the training experience. This would at least demonstrate
whether some change had taken place. However, any changes observed could
still not be attributed solely to the training program because there may have
been other things going on in the organization at the same time that could have
caused the changes in the trainees. What is needed, of course, is a second group
of people, or a control group, who are also given a before and after measure but
who do not receive any training. This group can be influenced by all the forces
within the organization that impinge on the training, or experimental, group
except for the training experience itself. Such a design reduces the ambiguity in the results a great deal and greatly increases the confidence with which
one can point to the training program as the cause of any changes in the experimental group not observed in the control group. MacKinney argues that
this last procedure, which entails an experimental group and a control group,
both of which are measured before and after, is the only one worth the effort.

Even at this point, however, there are still sources of ambiguity in the results. The organization is really interested in finding out whether change resulting from the training program is due to the learning that supposedly went
on or is actually due only to a general increase in work motivation. The so-called
Hawthorne effect is the possible heightening of motivation which results from
being singled out by the organization for special attention and consideration.
If the change in the experimental group can be attributed to the Hawthorne
effect, then almost any training will do, and neither the technique not the content makes much difference. To account for this type of phenomenon, another
feature may be added to the experimental design in the form of a second control group which receives, instead of the training, a placebo. The placebo must
be just as capable of stimulating the Hawthorne effect as the actual training,
but it must not produce any of the learning entailed in the actual development
program.

At this point three groups have been included in the design, with each
measured before and after. Solomon (1949) has described yet one more com-
plication in an attempt to point to the training program as the cause of changes
in the criterion measure. Suppose the mere operation of measuring the individuals in the training, placebo, and control groups changed them in some
fashion. For example, the mere fact that a manager knows he is being rated
may stimulate him to greater output, or just the act of administering an attitude scale to an individual may indeed change his attitude. In other words,
the pre test may teach. The solution proposed by Solomon is to include yet

another control group which is not given the pre measure. Then if all the groups are random samples from the same population, any effects of the pre measure should be reflected in the difference between the after scores for the control group with both a before and an after measure and the control group with only an after measure. This form of group design is illustrated below.

Time 1		Time 2
E measure	Train $\longrightarrow$	Measure
C_1 measure	Placebo $\longrightarrow$	Measure
C_2 measure	No activity $\longrightarrow$	Measure
C_3	No activity $\longrightarrow$	Measure

Solomon also suggests that the control group which received no pre measure could then be trained and an after measure given at time 3. Still another group could be selected to act as a control for this new experimental group, and in effect the entire evaluation study would be replicated. However, it indeed may not be merely a replication to run the training program again with new experimental and control groups. The first training program may have changed the organization in some fashion such that the managers who enter the second training session have already been influenced. We must then consider the interaction of the second training program with the first. For example, in an initially naïve organization a group of managers could be put through a development program which includes a large dose of the T-group experience. The trainees may return to the organization and act much differently toward their superiors, subordinates, and fellow managers. In addition, they might talk a great deal about their experiences, in either a positive or a negative fashion. As a result of all this, the second group of managers may have somewhat different expectations, attitudes, and even human relations skills from those of the first group, and the effect of the training on them may be considerably different. It is interaction effects such as these which the systems view of the training process tries so hard to point out in advance.

The above design accounts for most of the sources of bias that it is possible to control in one experimental design. D. T. Campbell and Stanley (1963) have succinctly summarized these potential sources of ambiguity, and they mention 12. Some of these we have already discussed in the course of introducing the above design. Some we have not.

1 *History,* or the specific events occurring between the before and after measurement in addition to the experimental variable (in our case, the training program).
2 *Maturation,* or ongoing processes within the individual, such as growing older or gaining more job experience, which are a function of the passage of time and which may "change" the individual in some fashion.
3 *Testing,* or the effect of the pre test or post test performance.
4 *Instrumentation,* or the degree to which the criterion instruments may measure

different attributes of the individual at two points in time. An example would be using different raters to rate trainee behavior before and after.

5 *Statistical regression,* or changes in criterion scores resulting from selecting extreme groups on the pre test.

6 *Differential selection,* or using different methods to select individuals for the experimental and control groups.

7 *Experimental mortality,* or the differential loss of respondents from the various groups.

8 *Interaction of differential selection and maturation,* or the compounding of the disparity between groups as a result of differential selection, with the interval changes occurring within the individuals over the course of the training period. That is, the experimental and control group may have been different to start with, and these differences become even greater because of interval changes occurring during the experimental period.

9 *Interaction of pre test with the experimental variable,* which refers to the possibility that something in the training experience reacts with the pre test in such a way that the pre test has a greater effect on the trained group than on an untrained group.

10 *Interaction of differential selection with the experimental variable,* or a different effect for the training experience if it is applied to one group versus another. Because of differential selection the groups are not comparable at the beginning on the criterion variables, and they may also react differently to the training.

11 *Reactive effects of the research situation,* or the phenomenon that exists when the efforts required by the research design so change the participants' expectations and reactions to the training that results cannot be generalized to future applications of the training.

12 *Multiple treatment interference,* or the differential residual effects of previous training experiences. For example, if one group had previous exposure to courses in social psychology and another did not, they may not react in comparable ways to a *T* group.

Quasi experimental designs. The four-group design described above is an ideal that can probably seldom be reached in a field setting. It may simply be impossible, or the cost may be more than either the researcher or the organization is willing to pay. There is also the possibility that the effort required to set up the experimental and control groups may so change the expectation of both the trained and untrained subjects that a new source of bias is introduced and the results are made less meaningful than for a less "well-controlled" study.

Researchers and organizations low in the need for achievement may be inclined to give up at this point, but for those of us who are not D. T. Campbell and Stanley (1963) suggest a number of "quasi" experimental designs that can still provide useful data even though a true experiment is not possible. Their justification for these "patched-up" designs is as follows: The real purpose of an experiment is to eliminate rival hypotheses that compete with the hypothesis proposed by the experimenter as an explanation for the results that are obtained. To the extent that a patched-up design might eliminate nontrivial alternative explanations, it may be worth the effort. Both researcher and organization should keep in mind that training "effectiveness" is neither a dichotomous nor a unidimensional variable and that one experiment, no matter how ideal, will not "prove" that the program is either effective or ineffective. Since training research is actually a process of eliminating competing explanations for the ability of the training to produce certain results, makeshift designs can be used if they contribute to this objective. The central question is still whether the reduction in ambiguity achieved by the study is worth its cost. Such a question must be answered in light of the specific situation faced by the researcher.

One quasi design relevant for the study of managerial training and development is labeled the "time series experiment" by D. T. Campbell and Stanley (1963). In essence the procedure is to collect criterion information on one group of individuals at several points in time, including several time periods before and several time periods after the introduction of the training experience. The relevant experimental comparison involves the criterion measures obtained before the introduction of the training program versus those obtained after. For an effect to be demonstrated, the training program must produce a discontinuity in the curve describing criterion performance over the trial periods of a type that does not occur at any other point. The change may be in the form of an abrupt change in either the slope or the intercept of the curve.

The one-group time series design is similar to the simple before and after study except that it provides considerably more information as to whether the change observed after the training program represents typical or atypical fluctuation in criterion behavior. Of course, there is still the possibility that the training may have been concurrent with some other organizational change that could have produced the same result.

A second patched-up design that may be useful in many instances, especially for recurring types of training programs, is the so-called institutional cycle design. This procedure is really the combination of two or more before and after studies which occur at different points in time. That is, one group is given a pre test at time 1, they experience the training program, and they are administered the post test at time 2. Also at time 2, a second group is given a pre test. The second group is then trained and given a post test at time 3. Thus at time 2 an experimental and a control group have, in effect, been created. The information yield could be enhanced even more if the first group could be measured at time 3 and the second group could be be measured at time 1. A schematic representation of this situation is shown below.

	Time 1		Time 2		Time 3
Group I	Measure	(Training)	Measure	(No training)	Measure
Group II	Measure	(No training)	Measure	(Training)	Measure

This design would seem to have great applicability in situations where a number of people were to be trained but not all at the same time. It might even be possible to randomly assign individuals to time periods if the implicit understanding was that everyone would be trained in due course. The data obtained at time 3 and the post measures for all subsequently trained groups also provide information as to how the training program is interacting with other organizational changes to produce changes in the criterion measure.

One additional variant of the above design would be applicable if the training program itself were made up of discrete segments which could be presented in different orders to different groups. Thus the differential effects of various training elements and the effects of certain combinations could be tested by applying the criterion measures at various points to all groups simultaneously. However, we should point out that this design as well as the previous one precludes follow-up studies with external criteria. By the time the training program is finished, all participants have received the same experience, and there is no longer any control group on which to obtain external criterion data. The fruitfulness of the "cycle" design is limited to internal criterion measures. In contrast, the time series procedure is most relevant for external criteria that are normally available in the organization on a recurring basis.

Campbell and Stanley discuss other quasi experimental procedures that might have applicability in specialized situations, but those discussed above, together with various combinations of them, seem to cover the major options available to the researcher.

SOME RECOMMENDATIONS

Up to now we have been discussing the possible forms that an evaluation study of a training program might take. The nagging question still remains regarding what form it *should* take. In other words, what kinds of criteria should we use, what individuals should we measure, when should we measure them, and what sort of data-gathering plan or experimental design should we use? As has already been pointed out, Odiorne (1965) recommends that if training effects cannot be demonstrated in economic terms, then training should be forgotten. MacKinney (1957) says essentially that if it is impossible to set up an experimental and control group with before and after measures, then the whole thing is not worth bothering about because nobody will know what the training is doing.

K. R. Andrews (1957, 1966) argues strongly that the best measures of a training program's worth are the opinions of the trainees, with the opinions of the trainers, superiors, subordinates, and peers bunched closely in second place. Although Andrews recognizes all the flaws inherent in this sort of criterion, the opinions of the trainees win by default since in his view there are really no accurate tools available for distinguishing before and after states.

Although other measures may appear to be more objective and relevant, their own particular biases make them less useful than systematically gathered opinion, which can reflect a great deal more information in spite of its flaws.

Andrews makes little mention of the need to link explicitly the training criteria to the goals of the organization or to account for all the sources of ambiguity in determining causation that were discussed in previous paragraphs. It is a truism to say that these questions must be dealt with by anyone trying to decide the worth of training and development. Therefore, it is almost implicit in Andrew's argument that if a development program is evaluated by asking the trainees, "In what ways did it help?" then the linkage of the training activity to the organization's goals, the comparison of before and after states, the comparison with a placebo, and the examination of interaction between training effects and other organizational forces all must go on within the individual before he renders his opinion. In other words, the individual trainee himself must act as his own before and after measure, control group, and systems analyst. These operations must be performed by the individual trainee, or his opinion cannot be considered in any sense a valid means of evaluation. Comparing a procedure such as this with an *explicit* use of before and after measures, control groups, and interaction assessments is closely analogous to the statistical versus the clinical argument regarding the prediction process. Whether an individual is capable of making such judgments is a matter for argument. Indeed there may be vast differences among individuals regarding their ability to make these kinds of judgments.

Korb (1956), in an excellent statement of the practical problems involved in trying to evaluate training, accepts the opinions of trainees and superiors as minimum criteria. In general, according to Korb, evaluation is the process of determining whether progress is being made toward stated training objectives at "reasonable speed and expense." The essential flavor of his argument is that in a real-life situation, there is no one best criterion measure and that it is probably impossible to arrange an optimal experimental design. As a result, the organization must (1) define its training goals as well as it can, (2) bring as much expert judgment to bear as possible on an analysis of whether the content and process of the training can be expected to do what they are supposed to do, (3) systematically solicit opinion from participants and their associates, and (4) obtain data on as many criteria as possible with as many controls as possible. After as much as is reasonably possible has been done along these lines, the organization must decide whether the criteria of reasonable speed and expense have been met. If they have, then the training is judged useful. If they are not satisfied or if there are not enough data to enable a judgment to be made, the training is judged unsuccessful and should be discontinued. Such a decision is not black or white, and there are no well-defined steps in the process of information gathering that signal "sufficient data." Making such decisions is frustrating and always ambiguous to a degree, but Korb implies that such is the real world.

If the four writers discussed above are viewed together, they seem to fall along a continuum from Odiorne at one end to Andrews at the other, with Mac-Kinney and Korb in between and in that order. These four positions represent the bulk of the opinion concerning what should be demanded for training evaluation. Randall (1960) uses a trichotomy to classify feelings about training evaluation and talks about positivists, negativists, and frustrates. Positivists are people like MacKinney who insist on unambiguous evaluation, while negativists imply that it really is not necessary or possible. The hapless frustrate recognizes the need for evaluation, but as yet has no means for accomplishing it. It is our feeling that MacKinney's view probably represents the position of most academic types, while Andrews's thoughts are what is most often put into practice.

Which position along this continuum is best? We should like to argue that while all of them have their strong and weak points, they all suffer in varying degrees from too narrow a view of the problem. For example, the use of economic indexes obtained from the performance of operating units is subject to a great deal of bias. Measures such as unit costs are not always under the exclusive control of the manager, and the biasing influences that may be present are not always obvious enough to be compensated for. Even if there were no biases in such measures, few people would claim they represent the sum and substance of the organization's goals. Managers are usually responsible, implicitly or explicitly, for many things besides certain narrow-range economic indicators. Contributing to the growth of the organization, relative to both its human and economic resources, is just one example.

Similar arguments to the above could be made for any other *single* criterion used to evaluate training effects. We hope that the notion of *the* criterion has already been laid to rest in the discussion of the prediction of management effectiveness. The arguments against a single measure of job performance are just as relevant in the context of training evaluation as in that of executive selection. The effects of training must be evaluated against a number of criteria which reflect more than one aspect of the organization's goals. All the criteria mentioned in previous paragraphs do not measure the same thing by any means, and reliance on any one of them may hide many important training effects from view.

In addition, we should know something about the interrelationships between the various criteria themselves. For example, if two criteria are very simialr to each other, then the training program should affect each one in a similar manner, or we should be able to explain satisfactorily why it does not. Also, we should know something about the relationships of the criteria to other properties of the organization. For example, how are ratings of management effectiveness related to the production cycle, to the general company profit picture, or to the activities of the wage and salary department? Examining a number of relationships such as these gives a great deal more meaning to the training criteria and provides considerably more information about possible interactive effects with other organizational programs than the exclusive use of one criterion. In other words, as much relevant information as possible should be obtained concerning the criteria in use, and this should go beyond the mere inclusion of a criterion as a before and after measure in an experimental design.

Some attempt should also be made to study the relationship between the internal criteria and external criteria. If the development program affects the internal criteria but not the external criteria, then even though learning may be taking place, it apparently does not have any relevance for the organization's goals. If the converse is true, then the training program apparently has an effect on job performance, but not for the reasons intended by the trainers.

There is also a certain narrowness implicit in the discussions which focus on the experimental design elements of evaluation. Before and after measures, with or without one or more control groups, imply that the organization is looking for significant changes that can be attributed to the training. Often this translates to *any* change being used to signal the success of the training, even if it is relatively small. Thus the misleading notion of "statistical significance" rears its ugly head here as well as in the selection area. Demonstrating that a difference between the before and after measures is statistically significant is only a minimal step. The crucial consideration is whether or not the training changes managerial behavior enough to make a difference to the organization. "Trained" managers may decrease their production costs ½ of 1 percent, but if that is of no consequence to the goals of the organization, then the training has not demonstrated its utility. Likewise, showing that the trained group changed significantly, in a statistical sense, on certain attitude measures is of little value unless it can also be shown that this amount of change has important implications for the organization's goals. In other words, what does it mean to say that the trainees became significantly less "authoritarian" or significantly more "employee-centered"?

There are really two considerations implicit in any attempt to explore the importance of a significant training effect. One is the notion of *practical* significance, or utility for the organization, which has just been discussed. The other consideration might be labeled *theoretical* or *scientific* significance. This is a concept with which a particular organization may not be directly concerned. However, it is the concern of investigators who want to be able to say something in general terms about the effects of certain kinds of training. For example, if it can be established that a program in creativity training does alter an individual's approach to many different kinds of problems, it has important implications for management and adult education in general, even though such a change may have no importance for the goals of a particular organization. Once the effects of such a program are mapped out for different kinds of trainees and for different types of criterion problems under various organizational situations, the *general* body of knowledge concerning management training has been enriched. Other organizations and investigators may then use this new knowledge to advantage in the planning of their own programs. Stated in another way, practical significance is concerned with what the training is worth to the organization, and theoretical significance is directed at the contributions of the development program to a general theory of management learning. In neither case, however, is the concept of statistical significance of much help.

Besides relying a bit too heavily on the notions of single criterion and statistical significance, most of the literature on training evaluation also neglects the importance of a systematic look at the process and content of the training. Korb (1956) bears down heavily on this point and says that a panel of all available experts should always be asked such questions as: Were the goals of the training clear to both the organization and the trainees? Were the methods and content of the training *really* relevant to the goals? Were the proposed methods actually used and the proposed content actually taught? Did it appear that learning really was taking place? Is the training program in conflict with any other program in the organization? What kinds of criteria should really be expected to show change as a result of the training?

If such questions were systematically asked in the course of planning and evaluating a development program, our understanding of the results would be greatly enhanced. For example, it seems unreasonable to expect that the effects of a twenty-hour management development program would be manifested in many of the criteria we have previously discussed. Training effects should not be expected where none are really possible. On the other hand, such a logical analysis of the training effort should greatly facilitate the search for an explanation of any unexpected results that are found.

The above arguments are in no sense meant to imply that objective criteria and experimental designs are inherently bad. They are not. However, we do feel that a ceaseless quest for the one true criterion or an exclusive reliance on the notion of statistical significance is misleading. Any attempt to evaluate training should include:

1 Utilization of multiple criteria, not just for the sake of numbers but for the purpose of more adequately reflecting the multiple contributions of managers to the organization's goals.
2 Some attempt to study the criteria themselves, that is, their interrelationships and their relationships with other relevant organizational variables. The relationship between internal and external criteria is especially important.

3 Enough experimental control to enable the causal arrow to be pointed at the training program. How much is enough will depend on the possibility of an interactive
   effect with the criterion measure and the susceptibility of the training program
   to the Hawthorne effect.
4 Provisions for saying something about the practical and theoretical significance
   of the results.
5 A thorough, logical analysis of the process and content of the training itself along
   the lines suggested in Chapter II, Applications of Basic Research and Theory.
6 Some effort to deal with the "systems" aspects of training impact, that is, how
   training effects are altered by interaction with other organizational subsystems.
   For example: How are the reinforcement contingencies in the training situation
   strengthened or weakened by the reward practices (formal or informal) in the organization setting? Is the nature of the job situation such that the skills learned
   in the development program can be put to use, or are other organizational changes
   required? Will the new skills learned by the participants hinder or facilitate the
   functioning of other organizational subunits? These and other questions must
   be faced before any truly meaningful evaluation of training impact can be made.

Unfortunately, the enterprise suffers from a lack of specification concerning
what subsystems are important and how their characteristics should be measured. Certainly, as House (1968) points out, previous research has established
that the organizational reward structure and the social influence of the work
group have pervasive effects. However, even these subsystems have not been
tied down to the particular types of skills and behaviors for which they are important.

   If the information implied by the above points is not obtained, then little
that is unambiguous can be said about the training program. However, if such
data are gathered, then the relationship of the training effort to the overall
system can be substantially mapped out. The "utility" of the information-gath-
ering efforts must also be kept in mind; that is, if the cost of trying to decide
whether the program is beneficial outweighs any possible benefit, then it is
obviously not worth the effort. Given the high payoff of management performance, however, the probability of this being true would seem rather small.

   The dynamics of the interactions between the training function and the
entire organization take on paramount importance if we accept the argument
of Schein (1965) that one of the prime objectives of training and development
is more adequately to prepare managers for an "uncertain future." That is, management education must somehow enable an individual to cope with job demands which have not yet been created. Gilmer (1963) makes much the same
point and calls attention to the rapid rate at which even managerial jobs are
changing. Development and utilization of optimal management training experiences based on the most useful information we know how to gather cannot be overemphasized.

SUMMARY

The question of how training and development programs should be evaluated is not answerable in any absolute sense. In this chapter we have tried to elaborate on the types of questions that must be considered before a decision can be made as to the utility of a training experience. We focused first on the criterion problem and distinguished between external and internal criteria. These two kinds of criteria are aimed at two different questions, what is learned versus what is transferred. Next we discussed possible experimental designs for evaluating training and attempted to catalog prevailing expert opinion as to how much experimental control is necessary, without success. Finally, we argued strongly for a systems approach to training evaluation.

The final decision concerning the worth of a training or development program must always reduce to a subjective judgment on someone's part. To make this judgment as intelligently as possible, information of the type discussed in this chapter must be gathered.

Chapter 13   Empirical Studies
of Training Effects

So far we have examined the literature revolving around (1) the types of training and development programs that have been used, (2) the theory that has been brought to bear on these activities, and (3) the various methodologies proposed for evaluating the impact of training. All such discussions inevitably lead to the fundamental question which many try to avoid but which must be faced in some form by all: If an organization chooses to enhance its managerial inputs by means of planned teaching efforts, do these efforts indeed make a "difference"? In other words, are there desired changes that are attributable to the training program?

In this chapter we shall attempt to review the empirical evidence relevant to this question, that is, the kinds of effects that *have* been demonstrated for management development programs. Obviously the term "effects" has a wide range of meanings, as illustrated in the previous discussion of criteria. For the sake of bringing some order to the situation, H. O. Martin's (1957) notion of internal and external criteria will be used to initially divide the studies into two groups, those which attempt to demonstrate some change in behavior relevant to the training itself and those which are directly concerned with changes in job behavior. In the former category are criteria such as attitude measures, tests of decision-making ability, and general opinions concerning whether or not the training was "successful." External criteria include objective measures of unit and manager performance in the job situation, turnover or grievances in a manager's unit, and ratings of job performance by superiors, peers, or subordinates. In the latter case an attempt has been made to estimate directly the effects of the training on job behavior. With the former judgment it remains to be demonstrated whether the behavior changes observed have anything to do with management effectiveness.

Within each of these two initial categories the most attention will be devoted to the studies with the least ambiguity, that is, those which make the greatest efforts toward experimental control. A distinction will be made between studies with "some" control, defined as the use of experimental and control groups, with either a before and after measure or just an after measure, and those with "few" controls, defined as studies with before and after measures but no control groups. Scant attention will be given to investigations employing no control group or no before measure unless other means were used to reduce the ambiguity in the link between the training activity and the criteria.

To further organize the discussion, the studies will be categorized, in rather rough fashion, along content lines. The following five categories will be used:

1 *General management or general supervision programs.* This is the broadest type of development effort and typically includes material on human relations, labor relations, labor economics, company policies and practices, supervision, leadership, decision making, and the like.
2 *General human relations programs.* The content of these programs is narrower than that of the above in that the focus is on the human relations problems of supervision, attitudes toward employees, and communication problems.
3 *Problem-solving and decision-making programs.* Here the emphasis is on teaching generalized problem-solving and decision-making skills that would be applicable to a wide range of work problems that managers must face.
4 *Laboratory education programs.* As was apparent from our previous discussion of methods and techniques, the laboratory method represents a distinct training content as well as a unique method. Also, the relatively large number of studies devoted to determining its effects dictate its treatment as a separate category.
5 *Specialized programs.* A number of studies have been devoted to evaluating programs designed to achieve very specialized objectives, such as reducing the "halo" error in personnel appraisals. Although their content is rather diverse, they are all lumped in one category for the sake of convenience and ease of identification.

The above five categories, considered together with external versus internal criteria, yield a tenfold classification of studies as shown on the following page.

	General mgt. & supervision	General human relations	Problem solving & decision making	Laboratory education	Specialized programs
External criteria					
Internal criteria					

Such an approach may seem like an overcategorization of the literature; however, some sort of organization is necessary for the sake of the reader's sanity, and this appeared to be the only feasible one. It was impossible to categorize studies by either the training method used or the specific type of criterion, since the great majority employed a combination of techniques and a combination of criteria.

Special attention will also be given to studies which attempted to compare the relative effects of two or more training methods or which tried to assess the interaction of individual differences with training impact. As a final point, it should be remembered that we have no direct concern with attempts to change the attitudes, opinions, or performance of nurses, teachers, salesmen, or college students, although research has been conducted in these areas. Our focus is on the managerial, supervisory, and administrative roles.

EXTERNAL CRITERIA

General management programs. Goodacre (1955) reports an evaluation study done at B. F. Goodrich on 800 individuals from a number of different managerial and supervisory jobs. Training was by the conference method, and total training time was about thirty hours. Both external and internal criteria were used, and these included measures of job satisfaction, attitudes toward the company, and self-confidence, along with achievement tests geared toward the course content and actual job performance ratings made by the participant's immediate superior. The 800 people were randomly divided into an experimental and a control group, and the criterion data were obtained both before and after. In general, the control group did not change on any of the variables, but the experimental group did show improvement in the achievement tests and in rated self-confidence. The experimental group was also given somewhat higher post training performance ratings; however, the differences were not as great for this external measure as for the internal criteria. The after measures were obtained within a relatively short time after the training, and no further follow-up was made.

Although this particular study is a good one, it illustrates a number of difficulties in such research. When ratings of job performance are used as a criterion, a serious source of contamination results, if the person doing the rating knows who was in the experimental and control groups. Goodacre frankly states that this was the case, but many other investigators give no indication one way or the other. Also, as is true for a number of studies, no attempt was made to examine the interrelationships of the various criteria, although the data for doing so were certainly available. Lastly, the decision rule for change versus no change was a statistical test of significance (t test), which with a sample size this large conveys relatively little information.

In another relatively well-designed study, Schwarz, Stilwell, and Scanlon (1968a, 1968b) examined the effects of a general university program on managers and executives from an insurance company. The "cycle" or time-lag design was used, and the participants were randomly divided into two groups which were trained six months apart. The Leader Behavior Description Questionnaire (LBDQ) was administered to the subordinates of each group before and after the training program. Also, between the two training sessions each former participant and prospective participant was interviewed and asked to describe critical incidents in his job and how he handled them. The interviews were divorced from any connection with the university program. Changes on the LBDQ were not the same for the two groups. The managers in the first group were described as becoming less active, less definitive, less production-centered, less oriented toward superiors, and more oriented toward subordinates. However, the second group was described as moving toward more structure and becoming more active. The researchers argue strongly that this finding represents a definite interaction of the first training program with other parts of the organizational system. However, the specific nature of the interaction and the ultimate result is unknown. The content analysis of the incidents also showed significant results. The trained group reported more personnel incidents and talked in terms of "employee development" and changing attitudes, while the untrained group reported more incidents dealing with staffing and conflict problems. The trained group also seemed to be using sounder strategies in attempting to resolve their work problems.

A study by T. F. Hull and Powell (1959) is an example of a much larger number of evaluation efforts which utilize few controls and achieve a minimal reduction in ambiguity. A questionnaire was sent to 98 alumni of a university program asking them to evaluate the effects of the program along a number of dimensions. The means for the 58 returned questionnaires showed a slightly positive opinion on almost all the dimensions.

General human relations programs. Three studies fall in this category. Buchanan (1957) attempted to evaluate a program for the first-line supervisors by asking a superior and a subordinate of each trainee to report any changes in the trainee's job performance which they believe to be a result of the training. This change was estimated by the observer directly rather than by comparing a before and an after measure. A relatively unstructured conference format was used as the method of instruction, and of the 154 supervisors attending the training, 108 were evaluated by either a superior or a subordinate, and 25 by both. One year after the training another questionnaire was sent to the participants asking them to examine a list of 15 possible types of learning and then indicate which of the 15 they had actually learned in the training program and which had been helpful back on the job. The questionnaire was returned by 35 of those originally judged to have benefited from the program and by 13 judged not to have benefited. On all but one of the 15 items a significantly higher proportion of the benefited group said the learning helped in the performance of their jobs.

A large-scale study to evaluate the effects of the Grid approach to individual and team training is reported by Blake, Mouton, Barnes, and Greiner (1964). It involved all 800 managers in a 4,000-member division of a large petroleum corporation. A large number of evaluation criteria were used, some administered or collected before and after and some used as after measures only. For example, the development program lasted for approximately one year, and during that time the firm experienced a considerable rise in profits and decrease in costs, which the investigators claim cannot be explained on the basis of changes in the prices of raw and finished products, reductions in the labor force, and the like. A substantial increase in productivity per employee without increased investment in plant and equipment is also pointed to as an objective measure of the Grid program's effectiveness. Other improvements cited as criterion changes are a catalogue of organizational problems that were solved during the experimental year, increased frequency of meetings, a change in criteria for management appraisals, and a definite shift toward the 9,9 variety of attitudes and values. These later changes were inferred from the results of a post test only.

The worth of these results is difficult to judge. For example, the rise in the productivity per employee index appeared to be the result of an almost constant level of output but a drastic decrease in the size of the work force during the twelve-month period. The question of whether productivity would have fallen along with the size of the work force if the Grid program had not been functioning or would have remained about the same cannot really be answered. A development program that relies so heavily on group participation and team spirit must also live in the shadow of the Hawthorne effect. The *specific* content of the Grid program may have made little difference, but it is impossible to tell.

Beer and Kleisath (1967) also sought to determine the effects of the Grid program on managerial and administrative behavior. However, they were concerned with the effects of only the first phase of the program, and the participants consisted of the bulk of the managerial staff of a subunit of a manufacturing organization. The before and after criterion measures consisted of a large number of questionnaire scales which a subordinate could use to describe his superior's behavior. Included were the LBDQ and scales measuring perceptions of within-group processes, intergroup processes, communication, and job attitudes. A total of 41 scales yielded 37 changes in the predicted direction, but only 14 of the 37 were statistically significant, and some of these differences were quite small. Also, as in the Blake (1964) study, it was not possible to obtain a control or comparison group. However, the consistency of the results over such a large number of scales provides some support for the ability of the Grid to change management and supervisory behavior in the "employee-centered" direction.

Problem-solving and decision-making programs. We were able to locate only one study in this category that used any sort of external criterion. Hillman (1962) studied a program using participative conferences, case discussions, role playing, and movies. The trainees were branch managers in a large "multiple" organization, and significant before and after changes were shown on the How Supervise? turnover in the organization dropped 30 percent, and accidents decreased 50 percent. No control group was used, and similar criticisms apply as with the Blake et al. and Beer and Kleisath studies.

Laboratory education programs. Besides being the most controversial area of management development (Argyris, 1963, 1967; Bass, 1967a; Odiorne, 1963), laboratory and T-group training has also generated a fairly large research literature. Since this literature has been reviewed in detail elsewhere (J. P. Campbell & Dunnette, 1968; House, 1968), we shall try to summarize only the major findings.

The bulk of the studies in this category employed an open-ended "perceived change measure." That is, one or more subordinates or associates of the experimental and control subjects were asked some variant of the following question: "Over a period of time people may change in the way they work with other people. Do you believe the person you are describing has changed his or her behavior in working with people over the last year as compared with the previous year in any specific ways? If your answer is "yes", please describe the change."

Estimates of change were usually obtained from several (three to seven) observers for each subject several months after the laboratory program. This method was used in studies by Miles (1965), Bunker (1965), J. B. Boyd and Elliss (1962), Valiquet (1968), and Underwood (1965). In the Boyd and Elliss study the observers were interviewed by the researchers, while in the other four studies data were obtained by including the above question in a mailed questionnaire. Observers were not asked to judge the positive or negative aspects of the behavior changes, but merely to describe those which had occurred. All studies used at least one control group, and in the Bunker, Miles, and Valiquet studies they were chosen in a similar, but unusual, fashion. Controls were matched with experimental subjects by asking each person in the experimental group to nominate a "control" individual who was in a similar organizational position and who had never participated in a *T* group. It is not clear from the report how the control subjects were chosen in the Boyd and Elliss study.

Subjects in the Miles and Bunker studies were participants in National Training Laboratory programs. Miles used 34 high school principals as an experimental group and two groups of principals as controls. One "matched" group of 29 was chosen via the nomination procedure, and a second group of 148 was randomly selected from a national listing.

Besides the open-ended measure, two other external criterion measures were also used: the LBDQ (Stogdill & Coons, 1957), which was completed by observers, and the Group Participation scale, a peer nomination form originally developed by Pepinsky, Siegel, and Van Alta (1952) as a counseling criterion measure. Data from both these instruments were collected before and after the training for one-half of the experimental group and the matched pair control group. To check any treatment-measurement interaction effects, data for the second half of the experimental group were collected post training only. There were no interactions.

A large number of other measures were also included in the study. Five measures of the individual's organizational situation were obtained: (1) security, as measured by length of tenure in present job; (2) power, as measured by the number of teachers in the participant's school; (3) autonomy, as measured by length of time between required reports to the immediate superior; (4) perceived power, as measured by a Likert type scale; and (5) perceived adequacy of organizational functioning, also as measured by a Likert type scale In addition, a number of personality measures were administered, including items intended to assess ego strength, flexibility, and self-insight.

No significant results were found with the LBDQ or the Group Participation scale, and the personality measures were not predictive of anything. However, results obtained with the perceived change measure were statistically significant. The observers reported perceived behavioral changes for 30 percent of the experimentals, 10 percent of the matched controls, and 12 percent of the randomly selected controls. The corresponding percentages for self-reported changes were 82, 33, and 21 for the three groups. The participants tended to report considerably more changes than the observers. An informal content analysis was carried out, and Miles concluded that the nature of the changes reported included increased sensitivity to others, heightened egalitarian attitudes, greater communication and leadership skills, and patterns of increased consideration and relaxed attitudes in their jobs. No details are given as to how the content analysis was performed.

With certain exceptions, most of the other relationships were not significant. One of the exceptions was a correlation of .55 between the perceived change measure and trainer ratings of amount of change during the *T* group.

Also, two of the situational variables, security and power, correlated .30 and .32 with the perceived change measure. That is, more changes in job behavior tended to be observed for the high school principals with longer tenure and more subordinates.

Bunker's experimental group included 229 people from six different laboratories conducted at NTL during 1960 and 1961. The participants were presumably rather heterogeneous, but a substantial proportion had leadership or managerial responsibilities. The matching by nomination procedure yielded 112 control subjects. Eighty-four percent of the observers returned questionnaires.

Bunker presents a list of 15 inductively derived categories that were used for content analyzing the perceived change data. The 15 categories are grouped within the three major classes labeled (1) overt operational changes, i.e., communication, relational facility, risk taking, increased interdependence, functional flexibility, and self-control; (2) inferred changes in insight and attitudes, i.e., awareness of human behavior, sensitivity to group behavior, sensitivity to others' feelings, acceptance of other people, tolerance of new information, self-confidence, comfort, and insight into self and role; and (3) global judgments, which is really a catchall for changes with no specific referent. An agreement rate of 90 percent is reported when trained, independent judges use the categories to classify the responses. Eleven of the fifteen subcategories yielded statistically significant differences between experimental and control groups, with the trained group showing greater change in each category. The greatest differences (ranging up to 20 to 25 percent were in areas related to increased openness, receptivity, and tolerance of differences; increased operational skill in interpersonal relationships; and improved understanding of self and others. Again, about one-third (ranging up to 40 percent) of the members of the experimental group were reported to have changed, in comparison with 15 to 20 percent in the control group. Categories showing no differences between the groups reflect such things as effective initiation of action, assertiveness, and self-confidence. However, Bunker (1965) emphasizes that changes among the trainees differed greatly from person to person and that actually there was "no standard learning outcome and no stereotyped ideal toward which conformity is induced" (p. 42).

Both the Boyd and Elliss study and Valiquet's investigation used managerial personnel from a single organization. Boyd and Elliss employed an experimental group of 42 managers selected from three different *T* groups conducted at a large Canadian public utility. Their two control groups consisted of 12 control individuals who received no training and 10 managers who received a conventional human relations training program employing lectures and conference techniques. Perceived changes were collected by interviewing each manager's superior, two of his peers, and two of his subordinates. The percentages of observers reporting changes for the laboratory-trained group, the conventionally trained group, and the no-training group were 65, 51, and 34, respectively. The percentages of subjects showing changes "substantially" agreed upon by two or more observers were 64 for the experimental group and 23 for the two control groups taken together. All the above differences are statistically significant. Of 22 reported changes judged to be unfavorable (e.g., an increase in irritability or loss of tolerance) by the researchers, 20 were attributed to members of the laboratory-trained group. The observers were also asked to Q sort a deck of 80 statements describing different kinds of job behavior changes. No significant differences were found with this instrument.

Valiquet randomly selected 60 participants from an ongoing laboratory-type training program in a large multiproduct corporation. Final results were available for 34 trained subjects and only 15 matched control group subjects. The change categories developed by Bunker were used to content-analyze the descriptions obtained from each observer. Statistically significant differences were obtained between experimentals and controls on total number of changes observed, total changes agreed upon by two or more observers, and total number of changes reported by the subjects themselves. Results by category were much the same as in the Bunker study except that differences were greater in this study for the categories of "risk taking" and "functional flexibility," defined as the ability to accept change and to be an effective group member. Valiquet believes these differences occurred because the program involved in-plant training conducted with coworkers and because the trainers were from within the firm, thereby facilitating the transfer of actual behavior to the work situation.

The above investigations seem to form the backbone of the evidence used to support the utility of the T group method for the development of individuals in organizations. Certain summary statements can be made. In all the studies, between two and three times as many "changes" were reported for the experimental groups as for the control groups. In absolute terms about 30 or 40 percent of the trained individuals were reported as exhibiting some sort of perceptible change. The percentage was somewhat higher in the Boyd and Elliss study, where the observer opinions were gathered by means of an interview rather than by questionnaire. Within the limits of the method, the types of perceived changes which seemed to discriminate best between experimentals and controls have to do with increased sensitivity, more open communication, and increased flexibility in role behavior.

Obviously, the studies incorporate a number of methodological limitations. The observers responding to the criterion measures apparently knew whether or not the individual they were describing had been through T-group training. Several of the authors suggest that the effects of such contamination were probably not serious, arguing that the variance in the types of changes was always greater for the experimental groups than for the control groups and that the proportion of changes verified by more than one observer was always higher for the trained group. Such arguments may or may not satisfy those who worry about this type of bias. There is a second potential source of error in that the multiple describers for each subject were nominated by the subject and probably had varying degrees of interaction with one another. It is not known to what extent the observers might have discussed the fact that they had been asked to describe a particular individual and thus contaminated one anothers' observations. Also, no before measures were used, and the estimation of change depended solely on the observers' recollection.

Moreover, it is important to remember at this point that the kinds of changes reported in these four studies have no direct or established connection with job effectiveness. Even if an individual does actually exhibit more "sensitivity" or "functional flexibility" on the job, we still know nothing about how these constructs may be related to performance effectiveness. The relationship between such measures and job effectiveness constitutes an additional research question which has yet to be examined.

Underwood (1965) did ask observers to rate behavior changes according to their effects on job performance, but his study used fewer subjects and describers than those discussed above—15 experimentals and 15 controls. Each subject was asked to recruit one observer, who was then given a sealed envelope containing instructions for observing and reporting on any behavioral changes in the subject's "characteristic behavior pattern."

Nine individuals in the experimental group were reported to have changed in some fashion versus seven in the control group; however, there were nearly 2½ times as many changes reported for the experimental group as for the control group. Although the frequencies are small, it is interesting to note that in the control group the ratio of changes judged to increase effectiveness to those judged to decrease effectiveness was 4 to 1, while in the experimental group the ratio was only 2 to 1. In other words, the suggestion is that while the T group produced more observable changes in job behavior, it also produced a higher precentage of unfavorable changes with respect to their rated effects on job effectiveness. This is the only study of its kind, and it is unfortunate that the Ns are so small.

Finally, a study by Morton and Bass (1964) dealt with self-perceived changes in job behavior. Conducted in an aerospace corporation, the study focused on a T-group type of program (referred to as an "organizational training laboratory") for managers from different levels within the same department. Feedback was speeded by requiring written descriptions from the trainees as to what they were thinking and feeling. Three months after the training, the 107 managers who attended the laboratory were asked to report any critical job incidents which had occurred since the training and which they considered a consequence of the laboratory. Replies listing 359 incidents were received from 97 of the original trainees, and almost all of the incidents were "judged" by the researchers to have a favorable influence on job behavior. Almost two-thirds of the incidents dealt with personal improvement and improved working relationships. Unfortunately, there were no attempts at experimental control.

A second group of studies in this category used questionnaire measures of perceived changes in job behavior as indexes of training effects. Thus the behavior under consideration is much the same as for the studies using the open-ended measure; however, in this case the content dimensions are given an a priori specification. Studies by Zand, Steele, and Zalkind (1967); F. C. Taylor (1967); and Buchanan and Brunstetter (1959) fall in this group. All three studies used managers from a single organization, but only the last employed a comparison group.

Zand, et al. used two criterion measures. One consisted of a 42-item questionnaire designed to assess a manager's perceptions of his own behavior, his relations with his superior, the situation in his work group, the organizational climate, and the behavior norms in the company. The second was an eight-item questionnaire originally developed by Haire, Ghiselli, and Porter (1966) to measure an individual's attitudes toward theory X versus theory Y (McGregor, 1960), a dichotomy roughly akin to authoritarian and directive management versus democratic and participative management.

Perceptions of trust of others, openness in communication, seeking help, and superior receptivity to others' ideas declined significantly immediately after training and then returned to pre training levels on the one-year follow-up. No changes were found on the theory X - theory Y measure. These results were interpreted as supportive of the laboratory program. The less favorable perceptions immediately after training were seen as reflecting the adoption of "more realistic" standards, and the return to former levels after one year represents perceptions of real behavior change, given the lower standards. Obviously, there are strong competing explanations which cannot be ruled out because of the lack of control. The lack of change toward theory Y was explained on the basis of the already strong orientation toward theory Y for the managers in the sample. Almost all the initial item means were between 3.0 and 4.0 on a five-point scale.

Some of the difficulties involved in using perceptual data as criteria are illustrated in the study by Taylor. The primary criterion measures were 20 bipolar adjective rating scales used to describe the trainee, 25 pairs of statements defining scales for describing the trainee's work group, and the eight-item Likert scale for measuring the trainee's orientation toward theory Y or theory X. All the measures were completed before and six months after a one-week T-group laboratory conducted for 32 managers in a single organization. Some of the measures were also administered one month after the T group. An average of four associates of each subject also responded to the criterion measures with the aim of describing the participants' observed behavior. While the results tended to show a number of significant changes in the participants' own responses, corresponding changes were not observed by the trainee's associates. This general result was also true regarding the theory Y- theory X measure.

Finally, Buchanan and Brunstetter (1959) used trainees' perceptions of how their work units changed as a measure of the effects of an intraorganizational laboratory program directed at organization development. All the managers in one large department ($N = 224$) were used as an experimental group, and all the managers in a second department ($N = 133$) constituted a control group. Three to seven months after the completion of the training, the participants were asked via a questionnaire to rate changes in the effectiveness of various functions occurring in their own subunits during the previous year. No before measure was used. On those functions judged by the researchers to be under the control of the manager, the experimental group reported a greater number of effective changes. Unfortunately, it is difficult to draw conclusions from the results of such a study. There is no way to estimate how comparable the two departments were before the training began. Also, the trainees were actually being asked to judge what kind of an effect they themselves had had on the department, since it was only through them that the training could have an impact.

Specialized programs. At least five attempts have been made to determine the success of certain specialized training efforts by means of external criterion measures. McClelland (1965) reports some evaluation data relative to his own development program aimed at teaching need achievement. Matched experimental and control groups of 16 executives were evaluated with certain measures of performance and rate of promotion (unspecified in the article). Over a two-year follow-up it was claimed that the executives with need achievement training had done better on the average than the controls. In the same article, data were reported on two other studies that used only post measures and were without a control group. In these two studies, samples of executives from two different cities in India ($Ns = 52$ and 32) were given the training and then followed up. The investigators report that about two-thirds of the trainees became "unusually" active in business after the training, as compared with their performance before the training.

The lack of detail concerning the criterion measures makes it very difficult to draw conclusions from this study. Unfortunately, this is a charateristic which plagues much of the training literature, and it severely complicates the task of trying to build generalities.

Moon and Hariton (1958) evaluated a training program consisting of thirty hours of lectures, discussion, and role playing directed at teaching managers to provide more effective feedback to subordinates. The trainees were 50 managers in an engineering section within a division of General Electric. Two years after the start of the program the subordinates of the original trainees were surveyed to obtain their opinions concerning changes in their superiors' job behavior. Data were obtained on the different dimensions of effective supervision from 66 subordinates in the engineering section and from 67 "analogous" subordinates in a manufacturing section of the company who served as controls. The subordinates evaluating the experimental group perceived their superiors as higher on 8 of the 10 dimensions when compared with the controls. The dimensions showing the greatest differences between experimentals and controls were those such as giving recognition for good work, providing opportunities for subordinates to express their viewpoints, and expressing concern for an employee's future. No before measures were taken. The length of the time interval between the training program and the criteria measure argues well for the retention of any training effects and reduces the danger of the subordinates' reacting on the basis of their knowing the boss has been trained.

McGehee and Gardner (1955) explored an attempt to teached foremen to handle supervisory problems arising from time study procedures. Training was primarily by discussion and laboratory practice and was directed at foremen's attitudes toward time study, the principles and procedures in time study, and the organization's reasons for using time study. The criteria consisted of a multiple-choice achievement test, a Thurstone type of attitude scale designed to evaluate attitudes toward time study, and ratings of supervisor performance in the handling of on-the-job time study problems. A group of 10 experimental and 11 control individuals were matched on the basis of age, company experience, education, and initial scores on the three criteria (before and after measures were used). The attitude measure reflected no changes for either group. The experimental group did show significant changes on the achievement and performance rating measures, but the control group did not. After the completion of the first phase of the study, the control group was trained, with similar results. In contrast to most studies criterion reliabilities were evaluated, and they proved quite satisfactory for the achievement and performance rating measures but disappointingly low for the attitude scale.

Levine and Butler (1952) divided 29 first-line supervisors into three roughly equal groups and compared the lecture method and a group discussion technique with regard to teaching supervisors to reduce the "halo" error in ratings of subordinates. The third group was used as a control. Both training sessions lasted just 1½ hours. The degree of halo in their actual on-the-job ratings of subordinates was examined before and after, and only the discussion group showed any reduction in this type of rating error.

The final study included in this category utilized military personnel as participants. Mayo and DuBois (1963) studied the improvement in rated leadership behavior of chief petty officers who attended a leadership training school.

The course lasted for five weeks and stressed the military aspect of leadership. Leadership ability was rated before and after by superior officers who also rated the leadership of personnel not in the training program. There were 211 individuals in the experimental group and like number in the control group. Other criterion measures used were a 100-item achievement test given before and after and peer ratings of relative improvement which were obtained after training only. Using certain statistical correction procedures, the investigators determined that the dichotomy of trained versus not trained correlated .34 with gains in rated leadership ability. The gain in leadership also correlated significantly with final course grades but essentially zero with the other criteria. A large source of ambiguity in this study, however, is the fact that the same group of superior officers rated both the experimental and control individuals and were well aware of which was which.

INTERNAL CRITERIA

We found considerably more studies that employed internal criteria of training effects than studies that utilized external criteria. Such criteria are of course easier to use, but at the same time they are much more difficult to interpret in the context of the organization's goals. The discussion will be organized under the same headings used in the discussion of external criteria. Again we shall devote the most attention to the studies which made the greatest efforts to reduce ambiguity in the results.

General management programs. Within this category there exist a number of programmatic research efforts relative to training effects. That is, instead of being content with a one-time, one-place evaluation, the researchers have carried out a series of related studies in an attempt to handle some of the complexities of the situation and obtain more generality concerning results. Although such programs have been all too few and may only serve to reveal even more important interactions that must be considered in the future, they are perhaps the only hope for illuminating significant portions of the system.

Perhaps the most frequently cited research program is the one carried out at the International Harvester Company and reported by Fleishman (1953b); Fleishman, Harris, and Burtt (1955); Harris and Fleishman (1955); and Harris (1958). Some of these studies utilized control groups, and some did not. However, we shall discuss them all at this point for the sake of maintaining continuity.

There were four studies in all, and the training effort under consideration was an intensive course for supervisors conducted at the company's Central School in conjunction with the University of Chicago. Techniques employed were lectures, small group discussions, role playing, and reading lists, and the content included labor relations, economics, public speaking, problem-solving techniques, organizational planning, personnel management, and principles of motivation. One of the studies in the series also considered the effects of a week-long refresher course which covered many of the same topics but which was conducted in the plant. The criteria used for evaluating training effects were the Leadership Opinion Questionnaire (LOQ) and a supervisor form of the LBDQ which is filled out by his subordinates.

The first study did not utilize a control group but focused on an experimental group of 46 supervisors who were trained at the Central School. There was a significant decrease in the average initiating structure score and a significant increase in the average consideration score. The second study utilized three experimental groups (Ns =30, 31, and 29) and a control group of 32 foremen. Both the LOQ and the LBDQ were used as criteria, but as post measures only. The three experimental groups were differentiated on the basis of the length of time between their completion of the course at the Central School and the post test. These time intervals were 2 to 10 months, 11 to 19 months, and 20 to 39 months, respectively, for experimental groups I, II, and III. All groups were matched on the basis of age, education, and experience. The results of this phase of the research program were somewhat surprising for the researchers and for human relations advocates in general. No differences were found on the LOQ between the control and experimental groups, and the only significant difference in the subordinate descriptions of the supervisor's behavior was in the "wrong" direction. The first experimental group was described as being significantly lower on consideration after training than the control group.

A third study (Harris & Fleishman, 1955) was conducted to determine whether the findings of the above study may have been an artifact of experimental and control groups that were not equal to begin with. Thirty-nine supervisors who had attended the Central School served as the experimental group, and 59 who had not attended the school were used as controls. The LBDQ given to subordinates before and after training was the criterion measure. Almost a year separated the pre and post tests. There were no changes in mean scores on initiating structure or consideration for either group, but the correlation between pre and post test scores was lower for the experimental group than for the control group (.46 versus .22 and .58 versus .27 for initiating structure and consideration, respectively). Evidently the training did "something," but it is impossible to say what it was. It certainly did not improve the general level of the group on these measures.

A fourth study dealt with the effects of the refresher course. Experimental and control groups were made up of supervisors who had all attended the Central School and were matched on age, education, experience, and the two criterion variables—the LOQ and the LBDQ. Post measures were obtained several months after completion of the refresher course, and the only statistically significant change was in the right direction but in the wrong group. The controls were rated significantly lower on initiating structure on the behavior description post test as compared with the pre measure.

As in the previous study the correlations between the pre and post measures were significantly lower for the experimental group than for the control group. In other words, the leadership patterns, as measured by these questionnaires, were less stable for the experimental group than for the control group. It is conceivable that different subgroups of foremen (doing different kinds of work perhaps) might have reacted differently to the training, but lumping them all together in the same group had the effect of canceling out any significant differences.

Also included in International Harvester studies was an attempt to relate the criterion variables to external measures of foreman performance such as absenteeism, accidents, grievances, turnover, and ratings by superiors. A number of the correlations were statistically significant, but tended to show a different pattern for foremen in production departments and foremen in service departments. In the production departments, consideration was negatively related to superior ratings but also negatively related to absenteeism. Conversely, production foremen who were high on initiating structure "tended" to be rated as more proficient by their superiors but to have higher absenteeism and grievance rates. There were fewer significant correlations in the service department, and none involved superiors' ratings of foreman performance. There was a significantly negative relationship between consideration and accident rate and a significantly positive correlation between initiating structure and turnover. These results offer some evidence for a link between the internal evaluation criteria and external measures of job performance, although it is not always in the expected direction. One can speculate that if the training had been effective (and it appeared to have had very little effect), it would possibly have reduced things like absenteeism and turnover but would have lowered supervisors' opinions of foreman performance. This last point illustrates what is probably the main object lesson of these studies. The behavior change rewarded by the management climate back on the job may not be the same as that rewarded in the training setting. However, such conflicts must be reconciled before any training program can hope to contribute to advancing the organization's goals.

The work by Miner (1960, 1961, 1965) is another example of a programmatic approach to the study of management training. It centers around the integrated course he has developed to teach an appreciation for the management role and the reasons for ineffective performance. The criterion used to evaluate the effects of his training program is the Miner Sentence Completion Scale, described earlier, which uses the sentence completion format to measure an individual's attitudes toward various aspects of the management role, e.g., relationships to authority figures, willingness to exercise power, willingness to take care of administrative problems, and the like.

Positive results have been demonstrated in an R & D department by utilizing before and after measures and an experimental group ($N = 55$) and a control group ($N = 30$) and with MBA students at the University of Oregon. The change in attitudes in the R & D sample was quite striking and was made even more so because the control group actually decreased on the criterion measure, presumably because of some organizational changes that were going on.

Miner also conducted a follow-up of the R & D managers using an external criterion rather than the sentence completion scale. The period of the follow-up was approximately five years. Fifty-two managers were identified who had taken the course, and 49 other managers were used as controls. At the time of the training the experimental and control groups did not differ in salary or grade level, and performance appraisal data indicated that the two groups were fairly well matched. The follow-up criteria were the degree of advancement achieved by those who stayed with the company and the rehiring recommendations made for those who left the company. Both of these indexes were significantly higher for the experimental group, although the total number terminated was quite small.

An Air Force study (Mosel, 1959; Mosel & Tsacnaris, 1954) which incorporated a control group used the How Supervise? to assess the effects of a program in general supervision given to commissioned and noncommissioned officers. The gain in favor of the experimental group was small but statistically significant.

A number of studies of the no-control, before and after type have also used the How Supervise? test as a criterion measure. Barthol and Zeigler (1956) gave Forms A and B of the How Supervise? pre and post to 210 foremen, general foremen, and department supervisors who participated in a thirty-hour training program. The methods used were lectures and group discussions. The training group was divided into those who had some college education and those who had none and then was further broken down according to the amount of previous supervisory training. All groups were significantly higher on the post test, although the subgroup with some college education improved their scores significantly more than the other groups. The college group's lowest score of 43 was only four points below the mean of the noncollege group. No follow-up was made.

Katzell (1948) used the How Supervise? to evaluate a specific method of training that he calls the "determinate discussion method." It is essentially a structured conference technique which requires flow charts of the training activity to be prepared in advance and passed out to the participants as reference material. Participants were 60 second level foremen and middle managers at a railroad. Alternative forms of the How Supervise? were administered before and after the thirty-two-hour program, and scores significantly increased.

Lindbom (1953) also used the How Supervise? to evaluate a training program in supervision given to all the managers in the home office of a small insurance company. Both males and females were trained. A total of 50 people took the course, which ran over a sixteen-week period and used the conference method, role playing, and filmstrips. In addition to the How Supervise? a measure of job satisfaction was used as a before and after measure. There were statistically significant increases on both the How Supervise? and the job satisfaction measure.

Although we have made no attempt in this chapter to review reports of participant opinion, one such study stands far above the rest and deserves mention. K. R. Andrews (1966) and his associates surveyed 6,000 former participants in various general management programs conducted on campus by Harvard University. The programs were of the "live-in" variety and had to be at least two weeks long for the participants to be in the study. Preliminary interviews with over one hundred managers led to the construction of a questionnaire, which was then put through several careful pre tests. The final product consisted of 48 items, and 19 required essay-type answers. The areas covered were the participant's background, his reasons for attending the program, his expectations, his reactions and evaluations of various elements in the program, his career progress since the program, and his opinions concerning whether or not his career progress was in any way connected with the training experience. Careful procedures were also worked out for coding and classifying the essay responses.

As might be expected, the reaction was overwhelmingly favorable, and almost everyone said he would like to repeat the experience. Some specific benefits frequently mentioned were (1) an increased confidence in their own ability, (2) a wider knowledge of segments of business other than their own, (3) a deeper appreciation of the nature of the human and social problems of business, (4) a realization that many different approaches to a problem are available, and (5) a wider tolerance of differences of opinion. Perhaps one of the most significant findings was that reported changes in attitudes and problem-solving approaches were very highly associated with the degree to which the learning experience had been structured by the faculty. Related to this was the finding that participants placed a higher value on classroom experiences than small study groups or informal discussions.

General human relations programs. There is also one series of programmatic studies in this category.

Articles by Lawshe, Bolda, and Brune (1958, 1959) report five investigations of a program designed to teach (1) an employee orientation to supervisory problems and (2) sensitivity to the reasons why people behave as they do. The principal method was a role-playing situation in which the trainees were re-quired to spontaneously act out the completion of a case problem. The five groups were construction foremen (two groups, $N = 40$), school custodians ($N = 26$), staff supervisors participating in a sixteen-week management program ($N = 27$), line and staff supervisors from one firm ($N = 16$), and supervisors in a five-week human relations program ($N = 14$). The groups were given vary-ing kinds of feedback experience and varying amounts of experience with the training method. Only the fifth study included a control group ($N = 15$). The criterion measure was a case problem presented via a filmstrip. After the trainees viewed the filmstrip, they were asked two questions: (1) "What would you have done if you had been the foreman?" (employee orientation) and (2) "Why did the employee behave the way he or she did?" (sensitivity). Answers to the two questions were scored on the two dimensions according to the scoring system described previously in the discussion of training criteria (Chapter 12). All groups were measured before and after except the staff supervisors in the third study. No significant differences were found with the first group. In the second study the school custodians who took the foreman part in the role playing increased on both employee orientation and sensitivity, while those who played the em-ployee part increased on only the sensitivity dimension. In the third study (no pre measure) the foremen role players also did better on the sensitivity scale. In the fourth and fifth studies the experimental groups changed significantly on sensitivity but not on employee orientation. Thus almost all changes were ob-served on the sensitivity dimension. Only one-half of one group (the second study) showed any change on employee orientation.

In discussing the results the investigators talk about something called "im-pact" as an important factor. Impact is defined as a characteristic of a training experience which allows a trainee to criticize his own performance, provides adequate feedback, and serves to emphasize human relations factors in a strong emotional manner. This factor was supposedly present in the last four studies, and this explained the pattern of results. The investigators conclude that skit completion role playing is an effective method for increasing sensitivity *and* employee orientation, as long as impact is present. The data do not seem to support quite so strong a conclusion, especially for employee orientation. Fur-thermore, this particular technique was embedded in much broader overall training programs which differed for the five groups. This is one of the "system" factors that makes drawing inferences very difficult.

The next series of articles cited represent what might be described as the typical kind of evaluation study found in the literature. In general, they are one-time, one-place efforts and take something of a shotgun approach to cri-terion measure.

Carron (1964) describes an evaluation of a training program directed at R & D supervisors which continued over a six-month period in a chemical firm.

There were 23 supervisors in the experimental group and 12 in the control group, and they were matched on such things as age, job level, and time with the company. The criteria administered before and immediately after training were the LOQ and an attitude measure of authoritarianism (Adorno et al., 1950). There was a statistically significant reduction in initiating structure and authoritarianism, but no significant change in consideration scores. Seventeen months after the training the experimental and control groups were measured again, and only the decrease in initiating structure scores was still significant. The actual mean difference was much less than it had been for the pre and post comparisons.

In one of the earlier studies Carter (1951) developed a twenty-hour course for supervisors in three large insurance companies utilizing lectures and small group discussion techniques. The program was given to 18 supervisors in an experimental group and 18 controls matched on age, sex, and years of education. Criterion measures used were a 25-item achievement test, the How Supervise? a logical reasoning test (Watson-Glaser), a social judgment test for supervisors developed by H. H. Meyer, and a questionnaire which asked supervisors to estimate what percentage of their subordinates held certain opinions.

There were significant changes in favor of the experimental group on the achievement test and the How Supervise? with superiors' ratings of supervisory performance also increasing from pre test to post test. However, the superiors helped plan the program and made their ratings after the program had been under way for a time. Thus the ratings could have been contaminated with knowledge of training performance or perhaps even with knowledge of pre test scores. In spite of this, and even though there was no follow-up, the results of this study must be classed as generally positive.

Stroud (1959) studied the effects of a human relations program at Bell Telephone. A questionnaire was administered five months after the program to the superiors of the 103 supervisors in the experimental group and 91 supervisors in the control group. It consisted of the consideration scale from the Ohio State LBDQ and four additional items requesting successful and unsuccessful critical incidents relative to trainee interactions with other individuals and interactions with a group. The questionnaire was also completed by the trainees themselves.

Comparisons of the post training scores revealed no significant difference between experimental and controls for *self*-perceived consideration, but there was a significant difference between the two groups when superiors described the consideration of their subordinates. The critical incidents provided by superiors did not reveal any significant differences, but the incidents recorded by the subjects themselves showed a tendency for the trained supervisors to indicate awareness for the feelings of others and to be somewhat more conscious of the nature of their role.

Maier (1953) tried out a participative type of human relations program with 176 first-line and middle managers. The experimental group was given an eight-hour program featuring practice in role playing and group problem solving, but the 144 control managers were given only a half-hour lecture on attitudes. There was no pre test, and the post test consisted of a multiple role-playing problem. Fifty percent of the control group and fifty-nine percent of the experimental group "accepted change" in the test problem, and the percentages of subordinate roles viewed as a "problem" were 11 for the experimentals and 25 for the controls. The experimentals were thus concluded to be far superior to the controls on the criterion measure.

Using pre and post measures and a control group, Alves and Hardy (1963) studied training effects on managers from three departments in Los Angeles County. Sociometric data were obtained from the subordinates of the trainees, and questionnaires were administered to the participant's superiors asking whether there had been any "changes" in trainee behavior. In general the results were in favor of the experimental group, but again, both subordinates and superiors probably knew who had been trained and who had not.

In an English study Handyside (1956) evaluated the effects of a human relations program on 40 supervisors in a manufacturing plant. The experimental group consisted of all members of one department, and the remaining supervisors in the plant made up the control group. An attitude survey was conducted among subordinates before and after the training, and the attitudes of the supervisors toward the program were also measured. Attitudes of the participants toward the program were largely neutral, and only 4 out of the 40 said the course produced any changes in their job behavior. The pre and post surveys of subordinate attitudes were separated by a twelve-month time interval, and no changes were found for either group. However, there was a significant increase in the external criterion for the experimental group. The productivity of that department rose about 12 percent over a six-month period. No additional follow-ups were made. There was no increase in productivity for the other departments in the plant.

In one of the better studies on employee-centered versus production-centered attitude change, Blake and Mouton (1966) used a measure derived from the goals of the Management Grid to assess changes in union and management attitudes toward supervisory practices. The researchers' attention was concentrated on changes in attitudes toward five "distinct" managerial styles: maximum concern for both production and people (9,9), minimum concern for both production and people (1,1), maximum concern for production and minimum concern for people (9,1), maximum concern for people and minimum concern for production (1,9), and a moderate but balanced concern for both production and people (5,5). The criterion measure consisted of 40 attitude items in a forced-choice format. The inventory was given before and after identical grid programs conducted for 33 management personnel and 23 union representatives, all of whom had management or staff responsibilities within the local. Significant differences in the predicted directions were obtained between the two groups on the pre test. Managers scored higher than union members on the styles with a high production orientation and lower on those with a low production orientation. No initial differences were found on the 5,5 style. Relative to the before and after comparisons, the managers tended to exhibit more shifts than the union personnel, although both groups tended to move in the same direction. The management group increased on 9,9 (the largest difference), decreased on 5,5, on and decreased 1,9. The differences for the other two styles were not significant. Union members increased on employee centeredness and decreased on production centeredness.

While these results are encouraging, several problems remain. There were no comparison groups, and the strong possibility that any one of a number of other human relations training methods would produce similar results cannot be entirely discounted. Also, the items appeared to be geared to the goals and content of the training program. Thus, the "correct" answer may have been apparent to the respondent, and a positive response bias may have been elicited.

In a study described by House and Tosi (1963), 252 managers were originally trained in a forty-hour course by means of lectures and discussions. The before and after measures were a lengthy series of questionnaires dealing with delegation, authority, responsibility, and job satisfaction. Complete data were collected on only 24 experimentals and 33 controls. Most of the changes over the course of the training were not significant.

Another study which attempted to assess training effects by means of a before and an after measurement of general employee attitudes was carried out by Hazeltine and Berra (1953). The survey was given before the program to all 200 supervisory personnel in a division of a large chemical firm. The survey was repeated a year later, and significant improvements in attitudes toward subordinates, superiors, and the organization were shown.

The last two studies to be included in this category (Hayes, 1956; Soik, 1958) were both before and after designs without control groups, and both used criterion measures similar in content to the How Supervise? Both studies showed a small but significant increase in scores which persisted several months after the completion of the development program.

Laboratory education programs. *T*-group and laboratory studies using internal measures to assess change have yielded more negative than positive results. This may be due to the fact that such experiences produce no effects or the fact that relevant internal criteria have not been used. In any event, the studies in this category can be grouped around five different types of criterion measures: (1) self-awareness, (2) interpersonal sensitivity, (3) attitude change, (4) personality change, and (5) performance on simulated problems.

Four studies focused on attitude change, and three of these used the Fundamental Interpersonal Relations Orientation—Behavior (Schutz, 1958) questionnaire (FIRO—B) as the before and after criterion instrument. FIRO—B includes a series of attitude items designed to measure six relatively homogeneous dimensions related to three major types of an individual's behavior in groups: control (i.e., attempting to influence the proceedings), inclusion (i.e., initiating contacts with others in a group), and affection (i.e., moving toward others in a close and personal way). The questionnaire contains a pair of scales for each behavior category, one to assess the respondent's own tendency or desire to show the behavior and the other to assess how much he wants others in the group to show it.

In the best and most relevant study, P. B. Smith (1964) used only the four scales measuring attitudes toward affection and control to obtain responses from 108 English managers and students before and after they had been trained in *T* groups (11 groups in all) and compared them with responses obtained from a control group of 44 students (6 groups in all) who merely took part in a series of discussions. The overall disparity between the individual's own behavioral tendencies and that desired in others decreased for the *T*-group trainees, but showed no change for those in the control group. The largest changes occurred for those who initially showed strong control and weak affection tendencies and who desired low control and high affection from others in the groups. Such changes are consonant with the aims of the *T*-group method.

Schutz and Allen (1966) and Baumgartel and Goldstein (1967) also used FIRO—B to assess laboratory impact on heterogeneous student and adult groups. However, the results of these two studies are difficult to interpret and not very clear-cut.

Finally, Kernan (1964) used the LOQ (Fleishman et al., 1955) to study possible attitude changes resulting from *T*-group training. The LOQ yields scores labeled "consideration" and "initiating structure," corresponding roughly to a concern for employee human relations and a concern for getting the work out. It was administered before and after a three-day laboratory training program conducted within a single organization. Experimental and control groups consisted of 40 and 20 engineering supervisors, respectively. No significant before or after differences were obtained for either group on either of the scales of the LOQ.

No evidence has been found indicating that laboratory or *T*-group programs can bring about personality change. The *F* scale (authoritarian personality) was used in the study by Kernan (1964) and the California Personality Inventory (CPI) in a study by Massarik and Carlson (cited in Dunnette, 1962).

No changes were found. However, as the authors of these articles point out, changes in basic personality variables are perhaps too much to expect from such a relatively short training experience.

Three studies attempted to assess changes in self-awareness by asking subjects to describe their "actual self" and their "ideal self" before and after the T group. The general method was to have individuals select adjectives or personality items which they thought were descriptive of them.

Burke and Bennis (1961) and Gassner, Gold, and Snadowsky (1964) observed a reduction in the discrepancy between actual and ideal self-descriptions, but the latter study also showed a similar effect for the control group. In contrast, a study by Bennis, Burke, Cutter, Harrington, and Hoffman (1957) yielded no significant effects at all.

In a fourth study, Bass (1962a) asked 30 trainees participating in a ten-day T-group laboratory to describe their mood at five different times during the training period. They did this by indicating on a four-point scale how well each of 27 adjectives (previously selected to reflect nine different moods such as pleasantness, anxiety, etc.) fit their feelings. Four of nine mood factors showed statistically significant trends. Skepticism decreased throughout the period; concentration increased initially and then declined; depression increased initially and then declined; and activation decreased, went up, and then came down again. Contrary to Bass's expectations, very little anxiety was expressed at any time, and it showed no significant trend either up or down over the period of the training.

In summary, we can say that the way in which an individual sees himself may indeed change during the course of a T group. However, there is no firm evidence indicating that such changes are produced by T-group training as compared with other types of training, or merely by the passage of time.

Relative to a somewhat different type of criterion measure, a major aim of the T-group method is to increase skill and accuracy in interpersonal perception, in addition to increasing the clarity of self-perceptions. In spite of the complex measurement problems involved, several studies have attempted to assess how a T group affects the accuracy of interpersonal perception.

In the Bennis et al. (1957) study cited above, a measure of "social sensitivity" was derived by first computing the discrepancy between an individual's prediction of another subject's response and the subject's actual response to items from a personality inventory. For each individual the discrepancies were then summed over all the items and all the other group members. While there was a slight tendency for the accurate predictors to be predicted more accurately themselves, no changes occurred in this measure over the course of the T group.

Gage and Exline (1953) also attempted to assess how well T-group participants could predict the questionnaire responses of the other group members.
Two National Training Laboratory groups of 15 and 18 persons, respectively,
responded to a 50-item questionnaire before and after a three-week laboratory.
The items were opinion statements concerning group processes, leadership
styles, the scientific study of human relations, and so on. To control for the
effects of taking the same items twice, two 50-item forms judged to be "equivalent" by the researchers were administered before and after. An accuracy score
for each person was obtained by correlating his predictions on each of the 50
items with the group's composite response on each of the items. In addition
to the accuracy measure, a "similarity" index was obtained by correlating the
actual responses of each subject with the group response. The actual responses
of the subjects were also correlated with their predictions of the group response
to yield a measure of "assumed similarity." None of these three indexes changed
significantly over the course of the training.

Lohman, Zenger, and Weschler (1959) gave the Gordon Personal Profile
to 65 students at UCLA before and after their participation in semester-long
courses utilizing T groups. The students filled out the inventory and indicated
how they thought the trainer did. There was a slight but not significant increase
in the degree of agreement between students' predictions and the trainer's responses. In sum, the studies incorporating a measure of how well an individual can predict the attitudes and values of others before and after T-group training have yielded largely negative results.

An alternative strategy for assessing changes in interpersonal sensitivity
is illustrated in the following series of four studies. In his report of a laboratory
program conducted by Argyris, Harrison (1962) found that T-group participants
(19 middle and top managers) used a larger number of interpersonal terms in
describing others than 12 control group managers selected from the same organizational levels did. However, the trained managers did this only when they
were describing individuals who had been in the T group.

In a later study employing a larger sample ($N = 115$) but no control group,
Harrison (1966) used a modified version of Kelly's Role Construct Repertory
Test to secure self-descriptions and descriptions of 10 associates before, three
weeks after, and three months after participation in NTL training. The modified
form of the Kelly test required the describer to respond to triads of individuals
by selecting a word or phrase that discriminated one member of the triad from
the other two and then to give its opposite. In sharp contrast to the usual finding
of an effect shortly after training with a subsequent drop-off over time, Harrison
found significant increases in the frequency of subjects' use of interpersonal
concepts to describe associates three months after training, but no short-term
(three-week) differences.

Oshry and Harrison (1966) asked 46 middle managers to evaluate some possible causes of unresolved interpersonal work problems, and the resources available for dealing with them, before and after they participated in a two-week NTL program. The problems were actual ones faced by the subjects in their back-home work situations. The subjects were given a standard set of 45 items which listed a number of antecedent causes and possible ways of dealing with such problems. According to Oshry and Harrison, the managers, after training, viewed their work as more "human" and less impersonal, and they saw more distinct connections between getting work done and the satisfaction of interpersonal needs than before training.

In a similar study, Bass (1962b) showed the film *Twelve Angry Men* to 34 executives before and after two weeks of T-group training, asking them to finish a series of incomplete sentences to describe the behavior of the characters portrayed in the film. Bass concluded that the training resulted in participants' becoming more sensitive to the interpersonal relationships exhibited in the film. Although no control group was used, two other groups of trainees were shown the film only after training in order to assess possible effects of seeing the film twice. All groups responded similarly on the post training questionnaire, suggesting that the increased sensitivity to interpersonal relations was due to the training and not merely to seeing the film twice.

In contrast to the negative findings regarding perceptual accuracy scores, the four studies cited above establish fairly well that people who have been through a T group describe other people and situations in more interpersonal terms. However, there is still the more important question of whether this finding actually represents increased sensitization to interpersonal events or merely the acquisition of a new vocabulary.

The last class of criteria to be considered consists of situational tests or artificial tasks that are intended to simulate job activities or job behavior. Performance in a business game or on a case problem is an example of this kind of dependent variable. Only two studies fall in this subcategory.

Deep, Bass, and Vaughan (1967) used the Carnegie Institute of Technology Management Game (K. J. Cohen et al., 1960) to study the effects of T-group training on the simulated managerial behavior of a number of University of Pittsburgh graduate students in business administration. Nine T groups (without trainers) met for fifteen weeks. At the end of the fifteen weeks, three of the groups were divided into thirds and reformed into three new groups, three of the groups were split in half and reassembled, and three of the nine groups remained intact. The nine teams then competed with one another in the game. The splintered groups broke even or made a profit, but the intact groups lost an average of $5.37 million over the fifteen-week trial period, even though they gave the most positive descriptions of their openness, communication, and cooperation. On the basis of their own subjective observations, the researchers attributed the lower performance of the intact groups to their neglect of the management control function. These results are somewhat difficult to assimilate into an evaluation of the *T*-group experience per se since both the splinter and intact groups had identical training. However, the study does point up the danger of assuming relatively straightforward transfer from the *T* group to another setting.

Argyris (1965) used a case discussion as a situational task and then attempted to measure, via observational techniques, the changes in interpersonal competence over the course of a laboratory program conducted for executives in a university setting. On the basis of previous work, an extremely complex method for content analyzing sound tape recordings of group sessions was developed such that scores on various dimensions of interpersonal competence could be assigned to each individual. The dimensions were originally derived by rationally grouping discrete individual verbalizations and were given such labels as "owning up versus not owning up," "experimenting versus rejecting experimentation," "helping others to be open versus not helping others be open," etc. Behaviors are also categorized according to their expression of cognitive ideas versus feelings, and the feelings component is given much greater weight. Case discussions were scored before and after the *T*-group experience, which was part of a six-week "living-in" executive development program. There were 57 managers in the experimental group and 56 in the control group. In general, the results were mixed and fell short of what the author considered to be success.

Problem-solving and decision-making programs. In view of the importance of this activity in the management function, it is surprising that so few studies have attempted to assess these kinds of training effects. We found only three.

Mahoney, Jerdee, and Korman (1960) conducted a very carefully designed study to evaluate a management training program utilizing case analyses, group discussions, reading assignments, and supplemental lectures. Five groups of 12 second level managers were used, with one of the groups trained at a later date and thus originally serving as a control group for the other four. The evaluation instruments used were a test to measure course content, a test to measure problem-solving approaches to case analysis, and an attitude scale designed to measure responsibility for self-development. No differences were found with the knowledge test, but there were significant differences on the attitude measure and on one subscale of the case analysis test. One disheartening finding was that the instructors scored no higher on the criterion measures than the trainees. The investigators were frankly pessimistic about the linkage between their criteria and job performance.

A twenty-hour course given to three levels of management at a paper mill was studied by Moffie, Calhoon, and O'Brien (1964). Fifty individuals were trained, and a control group of similar size from another mill was matched with the experimentals on the basis of biographical and psychological test data. Criteria were the Watson-Glaser Critical Thinking Appraisal and the systematic observation of participant behavior with the aim of measuring any increase in interpersonal skills. No significant differences were found with any of the measures.

Although it is an extremely popular training technique, no research efforts were uncovered that attempted to measure the impact of the business game on management behavior. However, Raia (1966) has recently reported such a study using 139 business administration seniors as participants. The students, who were taking a course in business policy, were divided into three groups, two experimentals and a control. The first experimental group played a "simple" kind of management game, and the second experimental group played a much more complex one. The control group played no management game, but all three groups used a series of analytic case problems, which made up the normal course content. The criterion measures were a standardized test based on a case problem, the final examination in the course, and a questionnaire designed to measure attitudes toward the course. The standardized case problem was the only measure given before and after. There were no differences between groups on the attitude measure, but the groups using a business game did improve their scores on the standardized case problem test. Both experimental groups were superior to the controls on both the case problem and the final examination. However, there were no differences between the two types of games.

Thus with the exception of the Raia study, no evidence has been uncovered indicating the ability of management development programs to change problem-solving behavior.

Specialized programs. Two rather interesting studies have been concerned with the effects of university programs in the humanities. Obviously, such development efforts are more lengthy and are less directly aimed at job behavior than the development programs considered so far.

One of two controlled evaluation studies dealing with instruction in the humanities for executives was done by Viteles (1959). A total of 57 executives from Bell Telephone took a nine-month humanistic studies program at the University of Pennsylvania. About thirty executives constituted a control group. Some of the before and after measures employed were the Graduate Record Examination (GRE), the Cooperative General Culture Test, the Kuder Preference Record, the Allport-Vernon-Lindzey Scale of Values, the Conservatism-Radicalism Opinionaire, and the Significant Issues Questionnaire. The control group changed significantly on only the social science subtest of the GRE. The experimental group changed on the humanities subtest of the GRE and on many of the other measures, with the exception of the interest test (Kuder). In general, the values and attitude measures moved in the direction of more liberal opinions, increased theoretical and aesthetic values, and decreased economic values.

It is unfortunate that no follow-up data are presented since the chances for conflict between the values reinforced in the training situation and the prevailing organizational climate are not the least bit remote.

In an investigation intended to replicate the Viteles study, Gruenfeld (1966a) used the Allport-Vernon Study of Values to evaluate the effects of a program in humanistic studies conducted at Wabash College. The Wabash program was similar in content to the University of Pennsylvania program except that it was conducted during the summer and the participants attended for several summers (five), rather than staying for a full academic year. There were 69 managers in the experimental group and 28 in the control group.

The two significant differences on the Allport-Vernon found by Viteles were a significant decrease in economic values and a significant increase in aesthetic values. Gruenfeld was able to replicate the first of these findings but not the second. When the experimental group was broken down according to the number of summers of attendance, there was a uniform decline in economic values associated with longer participation in the course.

Finally, Goodacre (1963) attempted to evaluate several variations in a training program designed to teach managers how to use a performance appraisal system. A total of 700 managers participated, and they were divided into four groups. Three of the groups were taught the principles and procedures entailed in the goal-setting approach to performance appraisal. They varied in the type of feedback provided. The first group was given the new system, allowed to try it out, given feedback in terms of anonymous comments from employees, and then given more training. The second group was not given additional training after feedback, and the third group was not given any feedback at all. They were merely instructed in how to use the new system. The fourth group, which acted as a control, used the traditional "trait" approach to appraisal. A 17-item questionnaire designed to measure practices stated as occurring among good "developers" was given to subordinates before and after. The greatest number of changes were, as expected, in the first group, but the *control* group was a close second. Thus the training effort yielded a relatively small increment in "utility."

COMPARATIVE STUDIES OF TWO OR MORE METHODS

A very valuable type of research effort, from both the scientific and the organizational point of view, is one which compares the relative effects of two or more training methods against the same criteria. For the organization such a study directly attacks the question of cost versus utility for alternative approaches to the same goal. Unfortunately, very little training and development research has been of this form. We can mention only one study using external criteria and only three employing internal measures.

In the single external criterion study, Jennings (1954) contrasted the forced leadership method described earlier with the usual sort of conference technique for teaching human relations principles and skills. A group of 40 first-line supervisors were divided into two groups of 20 in such a way that they were comparable on initial performance as rated by superiors. An equal amount of time was devoted to each training method (16 sessions). The 40 supervisors were again rated in terms of overall performance six months after the completion of the training program. Whereas initially 50 percent of the group using the forced leadership method was rated in the top half of the total group, 70 percent were rated above the median of the total group at the time of the post measure. This offers some evidence in favor of the forced leadership method, but again we do not know whether the raters were aware of who was trained with what method.

The next three studies compared the relative effects of alternative training methods on some kind of internal index. Di Vesta (1954) used personnel being trained as medical administrative supervisors in the Air Force to compare a student-centered and an instructor-centered approach to human relations training. A total of 94 participants received both human relations and technical training, and 24 received only technical training. Of the 94, 27 were trained via a group discussion (conference) technique and 67 with a lecture format. The experimental group of 27 gained significantly more than the 24 controls on the Personal Relations Test, on the consideration scale of the LOQ, on the judgment in social situations scale of a social intelligence test, on the How Supervise? and on certain subscales of some comprehensive attitude and leadership skill measures. In sum, there was considerable change as compared with the control group. However, the only significant difference between the discussion and the lecture methods was a slight superiority for the discussion method in improving scores on the leadership test.

Also in the human relations context, Kight and Smith (1959) compared two varieties of a highly participative five-day development program. One utilized a *T* group, and one did not. Thirty-three supervisors constituted the experimental group, and sixty-nine supervisors made up the controls (no *T* group). Criteria were an adaptation of the old Twenty Questions game and a self-insight index obtained by comparing an individual's own impression of his skill in taking leadership roles with the estimates of the course instructors. There was no pre measure. The trainees who had the benefit of a *T* group scored higher on Twenty Questions, but there were no differences on the self-insight index. Interestingly enough, anonymous opinions revealed that the trainees seemed to favor the non-*T*-group method.

Even though it used only trainee opinion, a study by Wilson, Mullen, and Morton (1968) did attempt to compare the effects of an individual-centered and an organizationally centered laboratory education program. In terms of trainee opinion the organizationally centered laboratory was seen as being much more relevant for the individual's work role.

THE ROLE OF INDIVIDUAL DIFFERENCES

It does not seem reasonable to expect the impact of a training program to be the same for all individuals. Individual managers differ in their attitudes, abilities, values, skills, and expectations. The question of how these differences in individuals interact with the technique and content of a training program is of paramount importance. In fact a knowledge of any such interactive effects is crucial to the planning and conduct of any program. However, the empirical literature devoted to examining the interaction between individual differences and the training program is quite meager.

Blocker (1955) attempted to determine the effect of a training program on participants who had previously been judged to be either authoritarian or democratic managers on the basis of two years of observation by supervisory and staff personnel. The training program consisted of twenty hours of discussions, role playing, and films. The content was devoted to principles of leadership, motivation, employee counseling, and employee attitudes. There was no control group, and 15 managers in an insurance company made up the experimental group. Seven were judged to have authoritarian supervisory styles, and eight were labeled democratic. The criterion measure consisted of a series of reports submitted by each manager describing interviews he had with his subordinates. These reports were a normal part of the yearly appraisal routine, and the supervisors did not know they were being used for research purposes. On the basis of the supervisory techniques the subjects reported they used, it was concluded that the democratic managers remained democratic and the authoritarian managers remained authoritarian. There were thus no main effects and no interactive effects. The unfavorable results were explained by the author as being due to an unfavorable management climate (the training goals were not reinforced) and a training program which was really too short.

Papaloizos (1962) studied the effects of a twenty-hour course in human relations and supervisory practices on 150 foremen drawn from several different industries in Switzerland. The primary technique employed was the case method. There was no control group. The criteria were two different measures of attitudes toward subordinates. Before the training started, the participants were given the Maudsley Personality Inventory, which allows individuals to be divided into four classes: normal introverted, normal extraverted, neurotic introverted, and neurotic extraverted. As measured by pre and post comparisons on the criterion variables, the only participants to be significantly affected by the training were the normal extraverts.

In an excellent investigation of leadership training for prospective non-commissioned Army officers, Showrl, Taylor, and Hood (1966) studied both the comparative effects of an "automated" versus a conventional method of training and the interactive effects of high ability versus average ability learners. The automated method consisted of a programmed tape recording of lectures and questions which was integrated with programmed text material. Subjects were randomly assigned to treatments and compared to a matched control group that received no training at all. The criterion measure was a 30-item achievement test. The two trained groups were superior to the control group at both ability levels, but the automated method was significantly superior to the conventional method only for the average ability group. The design of this study is one that deserves to be evaluated.

Gruenfeld (1966b) investigated the interaction of personality characteristics with trainee expectations and judgments concerning the effects of the university humanities program described earlier. The personality measure was the Edwards Personal Preference Schedule (A. Edwards, 1959). Correlations of .33 and .41 between the abasement scale of the EPPS and expected benefit (pre) and perceived benefit (post), respectively, lend support to the notion that feelings of inadequacy lead to more positive expectations and greater feelings of benefit. Small but significant correlations suggested a number of other potentially important interactions.

In another study involving evening university classes, Gruenfeld (1966a) found that managers and supervisors who had to pay their own tuition reported more benefits from the program than those who had their tuition paid by the company. In the same study Gruenfeld also found a correlation of $-.41$ between intelligence and perceived benefit. He concluded that those who find it harder perceive more benefits.

Also with regard to trainee perceived benefits, Buchanan (1965) has demonstrated that participants whose bosses have a positive expectation about the program tend to see more benefits in the program. This finding, together with those mentioned above, suggests a number of troublesome interactive effects if trainee perceptions are used as indexes of training impact.

Essentially negative results were found by Steele (1968), who used the Sensation-Intuition scale from the Myers-Briggs Type Indicator (Myers, 1962) to predict changes for 72 participants in an NTL laboratory education program. The S-N scale is conceptualized as measuring a preference for basic modes of perceiving or becoming aware of the world, with the sensation end of the scale corresponding to preferences for facts, realism, practicality, and thoroughness and the intuition end representing preferences for multiple causation, abstractness, experimentation with stimuli, and a chance to generate individualistic ideas.

The criteria were trainer ratings and a questionnaire consisting of seven open-ended items designed to measure interpersonal values. In general, the S-N scale was related to the value orientation of the participants and to their general style of group behavior, as rated by the trainer. However, it was not related to changes on any of these variables, and thus there were no interactive effects.

Finally, Harrison and Lubin (1965) divided 69 people in a 1962 Western Training Laboratories program into two categories on the basis of their orientations toward people versus tasks as expressed via a questionnaire. Judgments of learning during training were made by the trainers. The investigators concluded that while the person-oriented members were more expressive, warm, and comfortable, the task- or work-oriented members learned the most over the course of the laboratory program. However, the authors do not report whether the work-oriented participants were still judged to be less effective than the person-oriented individuals, in spite of what they had learned, or were equal or superior to the person-oriented group after training. They were only "observed" to exhibit more "change." The data are quite subjective.

THE INFLUENCE OF SITUATIONAL VARIABLES

Time and time again in this volume we have sermonized about the importance of situational variables in the determination of management effectiveness. Nowhere is this more important than in the transfer of training-produced changes to the work situation. That is, when the influence of the training subsystem is considered, the interactive influence of other subsystems must be considered simultaneously. Obviously, there are major problems in defining and measuring relevant situational variables and in assessing their influence. Some of these have already been mentioned, and they will be taken up again in a later chapter.

Very few empirical studies have attempted to deal with situational effects. The International Harvester studies again pointed to the type of job or task involved and suggested a significant interactive effective effect for production versus staff supervisory jobs. Two other studies illuminate the possibility of negative interactive effects.

Form and Form (1953) studied a program in supervision conducted in a medium-sized auto parts manufacturing firm. A total of 115 individuals who hoped to be promoted to a foreman's position participated in the twenty-two-hour program. The teaching method consisted of a series of informal discussions of various topics relevant to the foreman's job. The criterion measure was an opinion questionnaire administered before and after. Over the course of the training the participants developed much more negative opinions regarding the job of foreman and also more frequently rated their own foreman as being poor. Attitudes toward the company itself did not change. The investigators attribute the negative findings to the trainees' unfavorable comparison of their actual foreman's behavior with the picture of the ideal foreman presented in the course. In the absence of a control group the shift in opinions cannot be explicitly attributed to the training program; however, the study does suggest a danger that might be present in many such programs.

In a widely quoted study by Sykes (1962), a general conference technique was used to teach general human relations and supervisory skills to a wide range of incumbent supervisors, approximately 95 in all. As in the Form and Form study the trainees apparently compared the actual behavior of management with the idealized picture presented in the course and perceived considerable room for improvement. According to Sykes, when the supervisors submitted a list of grievances to management, management's responses were too slow in coming and did not reveal any real change in attitude. During the year following the training program, 19 supervisors quit and 25 more were planning to do so. This was in contrast to a normal turnover of one or two individuals. Again because there was no control group, the conclusions can be only tentative; however, the warning is clear.

SUMMARY

Much of the evidence concerning the effects of management training and development programs has also been examined by Miner (1965). His general conclusions seem to be the following: (1) In terms of volume, a great deal of research has been done on the impact of management development; (2) almost all these research studies offer positive evidence for change, although there is relatively little evidence for the long-term retention of such changes; and (3) there is enough consistency among the results to offer substantial proof of the ability of development programs to bring about certain types of changes, namely, the acquisition of human relations attitudes and problem-solving skills. While others may view the management training field with considerable negativism, Miner is optimistic and, by his own admission, enthusiastic concerning the achievements and potential of management education.

We do not share all Miner's generally positive feeling about the state of the art (as reflected in the empirical studies), but neither do we wish to adopt the gloomy, negativistic view held by others (e.g., Odiorne, 1964). That is to say, we want to be middle-of-the-roaders.

Before trying to summarize this chapter, one major qualification is in order. We have been discussing the *published* results of research on training effects.

We have no way of knowing whether there is a substantial body of unpublicized findings for which the relative proportion of positive versus negative findings is significantly different. Although 90 percent of the research in a particular category may yield positive results, it is conceivable that the ratio might be just the opposite for the unpublished findings. We can only hope that if someone carries out a well-designed study, he will publish the results, regardless of the outcome.

A frequency count of the studies in each category is shown in Table 13.1. A separate count is shown for those exhibiting "some control" and those having "few controls" as defined at the beginning of this chapter. In addition, four studies compared the effects of two or more alternative methods, and seven dealt with the interaction of the training method with individual differences.

Table 13.1

		General management programs	General human relations programs	Problem solving and decision making	T-group and laboratory education programs	Specialty programs	
External criteria	Some controls	2	-	-	6	5	
	Few controls	1	3	1	3		
		3	3	1	9	5	21
Internal criteria	Some controls	8	10	3	8	3	
	Few controls	5	6	-	9	-	
		13	16	3	17	3	52
		16	19	4	26	8	73

As can be seen from the table, the preponderance of studies employed internal criterion measures, and a very slight majority were of the controlled type. Surprisingly enough, the highest frequency count is for T-group and laboratory education research. This is even more surprising in view of the fact that the laboratory method is a more recent development than any of the others.

What can be said concerning the substantive results of these research efforts? We can talk in general terms about the results in each category, although it is not possible to be specific about particular techniques or particular criterion measures.

1 Approximately 80 percent of the studies in the general management and general human relations categories yielded significant results on most of the criteria which were used. These kinds of programs do produce results in a wide variety of settings. However, 29 of the 35 studies in these two categories used internal criterion measures, and over half of these were focused on a particular kind of attitudinal content. Such content has been labeled "con-

sideration" by Fleishman et al. (1955), "employee centeredness" by Blake and Mouton (1964), and the "human relations" approach by many others. In general, it implies a positive regard for employees and a desire to be supportive, to communicate effectively, to involve subordinates in decision making, to show concern for their welfare, and so forth. There is certainly enough positive evidence to suggest that such attitudes can indeed be taught to managers. However, the carryover of these attitudes to the work situation can run into difficulties, as the International Harvester studies demonstrated. In addition, there is very little direct evidence showing that individuals who are high on consideration or employee centeredness are more effective managers. For example, the previously cited review by Korman (1968) turned up very little evidence for a positive relationship between scores on the consideration scale of the LOQ and measures of performance.

The evidence is not all negative, however. A series of studies carried out by University of Michigan researchers (Likert, 1961) tended to show that supervisors of high producing groups were described as being less production-centered, being more considerate of their men, and allowing more participation in decision making than supervisors of low producing groups. However, the differences between supervisors in employee centeredness were not the results of a training program but were merely observed to exist. Consequently, one could just as easily say that high producing groups lead to employee-centered leadership as that employee-centered leadership leads to high production. Effective work groups probably do not need much supervision, and the supervisor does not have to be production-centered and crack the whip. On the other hand, in an experimental study by Morse and Reimer (1956), supervisors who were *trained* to be democratic and participative tended to have less productive work groups than supervisors who were trained to be authoritarian and production-centered. This study stands without replication, however, and can be only suggestive. For example, it is not known whether the superiority of the authoritarian supervisors was only a short-term phenomenon and really operated at the expense of long-term effectiveness or whether it actually constituted a long-term change.

All this merely serves to point up again the folly of expecting any simple relationship between an attitude change and a change in performance. Unfortunately, a significant proportion of the studies reviewed here seem to have incorporated such an expectation.

One criterion measure which implies a considerably different aim from that discussed above is the Miner Sentence Completion Scale (Miner, 1965). With this instrument a high score is intended to reflect a positive attitude toward certain aspects of the management role. These are such things as feeling comfortable with authority figures, adopting the masculine role, liking competitive situations, feeling comfortable imposing one's wishes on others, and wanting to stand out from the group. If not actually antagonistic, such an orientation is at least considerably different from the human relations approach reflected in such measures as the LOQ and the How Supervise? Training designed to increase scores on one would almost by necessity have to be different from the training implied by the other. More work is needed to determine the relationship between these two kinds of attitudes and how they are both related to job behavior.

In general, however, the thrust of these studies reflects an overreliance on one particular class of criterion variables, namely, measures of "human relations mindedness." Although it may be very valuable, this kind of variable cannot be expected to reflect all that is important concerning the objectives of a training program.

2 The evidence, though still limited, is reasonably convincing that T-group training and the laboratory method do induce behavioral changes in the "back-home" setting. This statement is based primarily on results from the studies using the open-ended perceived change measure as a criterion. However, our subjective probability estimate of the truth of this generalization is not 1.00 because of the confounding elements already discussed, namely, the manner of choosing control groups and the fact that most observers probably knew who had or had not received the T-group experience.

Given the fact of actual behavioral changes attributable to the T-group method, there remains the vexing problem of specifying the nature of these changes. Here the data are not very clear. Several researchers (e.g., J. B. Boyd & Elliss, 1962; Bunker, 1965) strongly resist discussing the nature of any "typical" training effect; they imply that each trainee's pattern of change on various behavioral dimensions is unique. If this is true, the present lack of knowledge about how individual difference variables interact with training program variables makes it nearly impossible for anyone to spell out ahead of time the outcomes to be expected from any given development program. That is, if training outcomes are truly unique and unpredictable, no basis exists for judging the potential worth of T-group training from an institutional or organizational point of view. Instead, its success or failure must be judged by each individual trainee in terms of his own personal goals.

However, in spite of this strong focus on uniqueness, it is true that group differences have been obtained which seem to be compatible with some of the major objectives of laboratory training.

Still another problem in evaluating the back-home changes is that the perceived change measures have not usually related observed changes to actual job effectiveness. Observers have been asked to report changes in behavior, not changes in performance. The only study to attack this problem directly was Underwood's (1965). His results lead to the suggestion that while laboratory training seems to produce more actual changes than the simple passage of time, the relative proportion of changes detrimental to performance is also higher for the laboratory method.

Results with internal criteria are more numerous but less conclusive. For example, evidence concerning changes in self-perceptions remains equivocal. We still cannot say with any certainty whether *T* groups lead to greater or lesser changes in self-perceptions than other types of group experience, the simple passage of time, or the mere act of filling out a self-description questionnaire.

The special problems of measuring changes in sensitivity and accuracy of interpersonal perception have already been touched upon. People who have been in a *T* group do apparently use more interpersonally oriented words to describe certain situations, but this says nothing about their general level of "sensitivity" or the relative accuracy of their interpersonal perceptions.

We lament the small number of studies using well-researched attitude measures and/or situational measures as criteria. If such criteria were more widely used, we might have a clearer idea of exactly what kinds of attitudes and skills are fostered by laboratory education. As it is, no conclusions can be drawn. The P. B. Smith (1964) study using FIRO—B is suggestive of positive effects, but the studies by Kernan (1964) and Beer and Kleisath (1967) using the LOQ yielded mixed results. Deep et al.'s use of a simulated exercise has rather negative implications.

3 The small number of research studies dealing with attempts to teach problem-solving and decision-making skills is disappointing. So is the generally negative tone of the results. Either such programs do not produce changes in behavior or we have not yet learned to detect them. Both alternatives are undesirable.

4 Studies comparing the effects of two or more methods are too few to warrant any attempt at generalization. Similarly, these include just enough studies examining interactions with individual differences to suggest that some are important and some are not and that the overall pattern is a complex one. Both of these research areas deserve a great deal more attention.

It is also possible, and necessary, to make a few summary comments about the methodological characteristics of training and development research. We have already lamented the lack of comparative studies and research incorporating measures of individual differences.

In addition, there is reflected in these studies an almost exclusive reliance on the notion of statistical significance as an indicator of training success or failure. Few investigators attempted to say very much about the practical or theoretical significance of the magnitude of the changes they observed. The intensity of their comments, pro or con, concerning a result did not seem to depend on the relative magnitude of the difference but on whether or not statistical significance was achieved. While this is one way of judging the outcome of an evaluation study and must be demonstrated as a first step, it is certainly not the whole story. It also seems to be a quirk of researchers (not only in this area) to go through all sorts of explanatory gymnastics when the results of a study do not reach statistical significance. Few people seem to be able to say, "No effects were demonstrated."

Another conclusion that seems to stand out from this review concerns the relatively small range of content and techniques examined by the majority of the studies. A wide range of methods and content was discussed in Chapter 10, but the bulk of the research seems to focus on just a few. For example, human relations courses are overrepresented. This is not to say that such content is not important, but only that other kinds of programs are just as deserving of research. By far the most frequently used methods were combinations of lectures, conferences, role playing, and *T* groups. Relatively little *research* attention has been given to business games, the In-basket, or any of the on-the-job techniques.

The multimethod nature of most of the programs points to another research problem. It would be advantageous to know which element or elements of these programs were actually responsible for the training effect, if any. However, no studies attempted to assess the relative effects of the various parts, except by trainee opinion. The whole question of which technique is best for which type of content remains meagerly explored.

We have already noted that the vast majority of studies utilized internal criteria. Only eight investigations were found that used external criteria and employed a control group. Three of these (Levine & Butler, 1952; McGehee & Gardner, 1955; Moon & Hariton, 1958) were directed at very specialized goals, and another (Jennings, 1954) did not really use a control group but compared two teaching methods. Thus with regard to the *bulk* of the literature on training effects, it remains to be demonstrated whether the changes in the criteria used to measure training effects have any importance for the organization's goals. It unfortunately follows that the present empirical literature on the relationship of training content to management performance tells us very little about what kind of knowledge and skills contribute to managerial effectiveness. In order for this to happen, it *must* be demonstrated that "what is learned" in a training program contributes to making an individual a better manager. For example, to be able to say that a positive attitude toward the human relations aspects of work contributes to managerial effectiveness, a change in such an attitude must be reflected in a change in performance.

All this points up something which should be obvious anyway. It is too much to expect that any simple relationship should exist between measures of attitudes and measures of performance. The multitude of studies on the relationship of job satisfaction to productivity points this out only too clearly (Brayfield & Crockett, 1955; Herzberg, Mausner, Peterson, & Capwell, 1957). Similar complex relationships undoubtedly exist between other internal and external criteria, and they will not be reasonably understood until a substantial portion of the interrelationships within the entire system are understood. A few studies have pointed to the importance of the managerial climate for the post training behavior of trainees, but the surface has barely been scratched. In the light of such considerations, the almost exclusive reliance of management development research on internal criteria and the lack of attention given to their linkage with the organization's goals loom as the most negative conclusion to come from our review.

All the above is not meant to imply a sense of pessimism or an overly negativistic attitude. Research on the effects of management development *has* demonstrated significant effects, and it *has* made a contribution to knowledge. It will undoubtedly continue to do so. However, what we have tried to make clear is that the problem is much more complex than the efforts to attack it to date would seem to imply. Trying to assess the effects of management training on an organization by administering a narrow range of criteria before and after a relatively short-term teaching effort made up of a number of techniques which are not differentially understood can convey only so much information. It is not that management development research has been of no value; rather, there simply has not been enough of the varying kinds of efforts it will take to map out a significant number of the relationships in the system.

Chapter 14 A Balanced Methodology for Management Research

Before pressing forward with discussions of managerial motivation, situational factors, and proscriptive management methods, we shall pause to discuss alternative methodological approaches to the study of managerial effectiveness in hopes of further delineating what we mean by the interactionist's point of view. Although there will be no substantive content, we believe the methodological bias a researcher adopts greatly influences the types of problems he investigates and the kinds of data he gathers. This latter state of affairs is unfortunate since a rational scientist attempting to maximize payoff should choose meaningful problems first and appropriate methodologies second. We hope that an internalization of the present chapter will help facilitate such an aim.

Cronbach (1957) has beautifully characterized two distinct approaches to the study of behavior, the correlational (or differential) and the experimental. In general, the differential approach focuses on the dimensions of behavior which already exist in nature and along which individuals differ. The objectives are to define these dimensions as meaningfully as possible (e.g., general intelligence, mechanical aptitude, job satisfaction, scholastic achievement) and then develop operational measures of these variables which possess useful reliability and validity. Once this is accomplished, the crucial correlates of the measures can be determined. In fact, the ultimate goal of the differential approach is to determine the patterns of covariation among the relevant dimensions that account for the complexity of individual differences.

The experimentalist, on the other hand, seeks to impose some sort of experimental treatment on individuals and then note the differences in behavior introduced by his manipulation. As pointed out in the chapter on training evaluation, this latter inference requires that alternative sources of variation be controlled. While the correlationist tries to determine how relevant aspects of behavior tend to "go together," the experimentalist is after causal explanations. However, what he gains in the ability to make causal inferences he is in danger of losing to the lack of realism and meaningfulness in the experimental situation.

From a statistical perspective, experimenters are concerned chiefly with variance between treatments. Measures of central tendency constitute their prototypic statistic. Individual differences have tended to annoy rather than challenge experimenters because within-treatment variance suggests that the experimenter has not been entirely successful in controlling behavior. Experimenters tend to derive their hypotheses from theoretical premises and to embed their results in theories. Their investigations typically contain multiple dependent measures, but these outcomes tend to be analyzed and interpreted separately. This is perhaps another fault of the experimental approach, since "no response measure . . . is an adequate measure of a psychological construct. Every score mixes construct-relevant variance with variance specific to the particular measuring operation" (Cronbach, 1957, p. 676). Also, the assumptions concerning people that are associated with the experimental method have a somewhat distinctive flavor. A basic purpose of this approach, especially when it is directed to applied problems, is to discover those conditions which produce the highest average level of performance when all persons are treated similarly. It is presumed that persons are self-directing and creative and that they shape rather than conform to their environments. "The organism which will adapt well under one condition would not survive under another. If for each environment there is a best organism, for every organism there is a best environment" (Cronbach, 1957, p. 679).

The correlational method involves a different set of properties. Statistically, correlational studies are concerned with variation within treatments, and the standard deviation exemplifies the prototypic statistic. Since the designs used by the correlational psychologist demand uniform treatment for every case contributing to a correlation, variance among treatments is a source of error. Investigators who work within this tradition are less sophisticated than experimentalists concerning theory and more sophisticated concerning multivariate analysis. The assumptions about people that underlie this tradition differ considerably from those associated with the experimental method. Correlational psychology is directed toward raising the average level of performance by treating persons differently (e.g., hire versus not hire). The correlational psychologist "takes the system for granted and tries to identify who will fit into it. His devices have a conservative influence because they identify persons who will succeed in the existing institution. By reducing failures, they remove a challenge which might otherwise force the institution to change" (Cronbach, 1957, p. 679).

Cronbach also points out that these two types of inquiry have become associated with different substantive areas, to the detriment of behavioral science research. However, each approach has its unique advantages, and we echo his plea for a strong emphasis on studying the interactions of experimental treatments with individual differences. As we have implied several times already in this volume, the ultimate question concerns what type of organizational treatments are best for what kinds of individuals, given certain situational conditions or constraints.

THE CURRENT BALANCE

With regard to the methodologies employed, how does research on managerial effectiveness look when held up to Cronbach's dichotomy and his plea for an integration of the two approaches? In sum, the dichotomy tends to appear quite clearly, while the necessary integration is only beginning to emerge. A number of points are relevant.

Instrument-centered research. As is obvious from the literature reviewed in previous chapters, the bulk of the research dealing with managerial effectiveness revolves around the correlational-differential point of view. There has been a heavy concentration on attempts to develop and refine measures of managerial attributes, and herein lies a danger. It is probably best illustrated in Kaplan's (1964, p. 28) charming description of the "law of the instrument": "Give a small boy a hammer and he will find that everything he encounters needs pounding." The impression one gets is that investigators have chosen to formulate their problems in such a way that they can be solved only if the refined testing instruments in hand are applied. This may have the unfortunate effect of generating problems that preclude the use of other methodological approaches and leaving the field vulnerable to the shortcomings of the correlational method.

This vulnerability is illustrated by what happens, or fails to happen, in the context of the classic validity model (Dunnette, 1963) when a puzzling result is found. Aside from considerable ad hoc speculation, it is difficult for the researcher to carry out further work in any meaningful way to discover the reason for the strange outcome. Despite occasional pleas for more integrated research (e.g., Haire, 1959), there have been few attempts to take advantage of the power of convergent strategies, if our review of the literature is any indication.

The neglect of the stimulus. Either because of, or concomitant with, the emphasis on the correlational approach, there has been a severe neglect of research concerning the stimulus conditions in organizations that influence managerial effectiveness. The differential approach focuses on *R-R* relationships and uses this paradigm to account for behavior. It seems obvious that the *S-R* paradigm is also a potent model for investigating differences in managerial performance; however, the only research area where the stimulus has been investigated with any frequency is in training and development. Only sporadic attempts have been made to study other stimulus variables such as organizational climates, structural properties, etc.

One reason for the neglect of the stimulus may be the impression of overwhelming stimulus complexity that the organization presents. One reaction to this seems to be a focusing on highly visible and easily measured properties of the organizational environment such as size, span of control, and tallness or flatness of the organization. Unfortunately, such variables are probably quite confounded, resulting in considerable decrement in explanatory power. Much more attention must be given to developing a taxonomy of relevant organizational stimuli. One possible aid here is the tendency of individuals to simplify their environment through such mechanisms as selective perception and remembering, expectancies, and generalization. For example, an explanation for the potency of hierarchical level in a number of studies (L. W. Porter & Lawler, 1965), even though such a variable is highly confounded, might reside in these simplifying mechanisms. Level is a much more easily perceived and immediate property around which to organize perceptions and expectancies than organizational size or "shape."

The isolation of the experiment. As noted above, the one research area employing the experimental approach is management training and development. That is, rather than hunt for individuals who had received varying amounts and kinds of training in the past and correlating these differences with differences in later performance, investigators have at least attempted to obtain comparable experimental and control groups and impose the development experience on the experimental group. However, the studies reviewed in Chapter 13 have been interpreted almost exclusively in terms of main effects. Differences in outcomes within treatments have been regarded largely as experimental error, and interactions between treatments, individual differences, and situations have not been studied. Also, relationships between dependent variables are infrequently examined, and the benefits of multivariate analysis have not been used to advantage by the training researchers.

In sum, while the experimental approach has been used to a certain extent in a specific research area, it has not been subjected to very much cross-fertilization from the differential point of view.

AN ARGUMENT FOR MORE EXPERIMENTATION

We have seen that the predominant methodology used for research on managerial effectiveness is the correlational approach. Experimentation has been restricted largely to the evaluation of training effects. At this point we would like to argue briefly for more experimental studies to help redress the balance.

One of the more useful descriptions of experimentation has been proposed by Kaplan (1964). He states that "experimentation is a process of observation, to be carried out in a situation especially brought about for that purpose" (p. 144). This definition is useful because it preserves the essential feature of experimentation—namely, control of the conditions for observation—and yet it also is sufficiently general to include studies conducted in a variety of settings utilizing a variety of techniques. It seems especially crucial at the outset to discard the notion that experimentation is a relatively specific, homogeneous approach which occurs in a given setting. Experiments involving managers may not be common because investigators have maintained narrow ideas about the properties of an experiment. For example, experiments are typically regarded as the means to test theories, and in the absence of theories of managerial effectiveness, there is less apparent need for experiments. However, experiments are actually useful methods for both deduction and induction. When we argue that experiments are a valuable approach to study managerial effectiveness, it is presumed that they will be useful in *both* ways. Some notion of the variety that is possible within an experiment is suggested by the sample continuum or organization-relevant experimental tasks described by Weick (1966b). It is possible to arrange experimental tasks along a continuum according to the degree to which they contain properties of an organization in abstract or concrete form. When this is done, it becomes apparent that technologies ranging from highly abstract models of organization (e.g., the group reaction timer developed by Zajonc, 1965) to very concrete models (e.g., the simulated aircraft maintenance organization developed by Enke, 1958) involve organizational issues. In short, considerable discretion exists within the experimental approach concerning the content of the exercise.

Some standard objections. Undoubtedly the main objection to experimentation concerns its relevance to organizational problems. Experimental settings, after all, are not organizations, nor are they intended to be. Confusion about the issue of relevance is often collapsed into the simple assertion that "experiments are artificial." Before such an assertion is used to discount much of this chapter, some points should be considered. Zigler has described a prominent reason why experimental and natural settings differ and why this should not deter the use of experimentation. He observed (1963, p. 353) that persons often regard experiments as irrelevant because they do not realize that one of the properties of an explanatory system

> . . . is that the processes suggested or the principles specified somehow transcend the world for which they were constructed and are applicable to other worlds as well. . . . What the experimenter is saying is that if such and such holds in the real world because of the principles expounded in the particular theory under investigation, then such and such should hold in the world which the experimenter has created. This translatability is what gives theoretical importance to experiments that involve phenomena which, taken in isolation, not only appear picayune but seem to have little relationship with what one observes in nature.

Notice that Zigler's description does not justify all experiments, but it does shift attention away from value-laden labels such as "artificial" to more specific issues such as the accuracy with which the experimenter has extrapolated from one set of observations to another. If anything, Zigler's argument places an even greater burden on the experimenter to be explicit about the properties of his experimental setting, but the argument also makes it less essential for the experimenter to defend the value of experiment on the grounds of superficial similarities. Relationships between natural events and laboratory events are mediated by theoretical properties, not by a visual resemblance.

Experimental settings are quite varied, and at times they actually resemble natural organizations quite closely. This does not mean that the investigator is necessarily hypersensitive to appearances. Realism may be added to an experimental setting to accomplish several aims. For example, it is common to find that extremely unrealistic settings are adopted when the investigator wants to conceptualize a phenomenon at a higher level of abstraction, transpose a natural event, test hypotheses, or enhance the visibility of processes (Weick, 1965b, pp. 200-204). However, if he has other aims such as developing a theory, preserving the interaction of variables, increasing subject involvement, or testing comprehensive theories, then his experimental settings are apt to be more realistic. Notice that all eight of these aims are appropriate at some stages in the development of concepts about managerial effectiveness; consequently, it is incorrect to argue that only realistic settings should be used to study managerial effectiveness. Legislating the content of experiments on the basis of superficial similarities would hinder chances of learning significant information about managers.

One should also be hesitant to conclude that knowledge about unfamiliar topics is best gained if there is a steady progression from unrealistic to realistic studies or from realistic to unrealistic. *Both* the strategy of realism and the strategy of unrealism can provide information about *both* familiar and unfamiliar phenomena. For example, if an investigator wants to learn about an unfamiliar phenomenon, he can choose an unrealistic setting (he conceptualizes the elusive phenomena at a higher level of abstraction, or he strips away most of the natural properties to get a close look at some portion of the process), *or* he can choose a realistic setting which duplicates the puzzling phenomenon and then systematically simplify it to see which properties are most crucial. Once a great deal is known about a phenomenon, there still is no apparent advantage to either the realistic or unrealistic setting. Realism may assist the study of familiar topics because the investigator wants to preserve interaction of variables or test comprehensive theories, but familiarity may also be the occasion for unrealistic settings because the investigator wishes to explore specific theoretical propositions or because he wants to transpose a natural event.

If experimentation is construed in this manner, there are several implications. First, the realism of an experiment is sometimes a spurious basis on which to judge its worth. Second, realism and unrealism serve different purposes, so the appropriateness of a methodology should be judged against the experimenter's aims, not his referent reality. Third, artificiality is an exceedingly poor criterion to use in the evaluation of any experiment. It tends to becloud issues. "Artificiality" is a dangerous label to attach to experiments because it focuses attention on pseudoissues and suggests self-defeating solutions. If a situation seems artificial, the only thing to do is to make it more real or natural. And this usually means that more "props" are added so that the setting *looks* more natural. But as more props are added, controls flounder, and it becomes more difficult to observe what happens. The behavior that is evoked is made no more real by these additions, and in fact the experimenter has probably made his propositions less accessible (Weick, 1966b).

Another commonly expressed roadblock to more experimentation centers around a reluctance to learn about managerial effectiveness from anyone except managers. Researchers seem to have adopted the "myth of necessary bias," which Tumin (1964) suggests is a prominent assumption made by members of organizations. Necessary bias is the belief that only those who have vested interests in organizational success have the ability and right to make relevant criticisms and observations about the organization. Perhaps the myth is preserved most pungently in the question: "Have you ever met a payroll?" Many studies of managerial effectiveness seem to imply that unless the sample has met a payroll, it can be ignored. It is the contention here that such a view is unduly narrow.

Suppose an investigator were faced with the following choice in designing a study of managerial effectiveness. He could study either actual managers performing simple laboratory tasks (e.g., learning nonsense syllables) or college sophomores performing quasi organizational tasks (e.g., supervising the activities of seven peers who are constructing objects for distribution). Which would furnish the more useful information? If the investigator assumed that managers are unique, that their perspective is significantly different, that they are more "mature," and that individual differences are crucial in the determination of actions, then he would probably opt for the design in which managers perform simple tasks. However, if the investigator assumed that the significant factors about a manager are the task that he performs, the demands that are made on him, and the position that he holds, then he might conclude that a study which preserves these demands is more relevant than one in which the environment is highly abstract. Probably most persons would argue in favor of a study in which managers perform quasi organizational tasks. However, this design has flaws.

Studies in which actual managers perform realistic organizational exercises may produce outcomes that are difficult to interpret. What could possibly happen in these sutdies is that managers might compare the simulated organization with the organization in which they work and then "redefine" the simulated organization. These redefinitions are in the direction of making the simulated organization either more like the one with which they are familiar or more *unlike* (i.e., artificial) the one with which they are familiar. In either case, treatments may not be comparable across subjects, and it would be more difficult to explain the outcomes. These alterations have been documented in several simulations involving actual managers (e.g., Bass, 1963). If such redefinition occurs with tasks that resemble those found in organizations, then it seems probable that redefinition would become even more of a problem with simple tasks.

Suppose that the investigator decides to study managerial effectiveness by using college sophomores who perform tasks that resemble managerial tasks. What problems might occur? Initially, there would be strong reservations concerning whether sophomores have very much in common with managers. As Dill (1964, p.52) has remarked, "What college sophomores do, alas, may not be much more relevant than the behavior of monkeys for predicting how executives, nurses, or research scientists will perform." College sophomores, however, do resemble managers on some dimensions, and managers, after all, are increasingly being recruited *from college populations.* The problem is that we do not know which dimensions discriminate most clearly between these two populations. It would seem useful to clarify this question because of the greater "accessibility" of college populations and because extensive research with managers is time-consuming and companies are often unwilling to release valuable managerial time for research purposes. It should also be noted that differences between sophomores and managers, even if they exist, are not crucial unless the dimensions on which these two populations differ are correlated with the effects being investigated.

An additional problem with samples concerns the fiction of the typical manager. It seems clear that experimenters probably will never find a subject population that is equivalent to a typical manager simply because there is no such thing as a typical manager. There may be just as much variation among managers as there is between managers and college students.

If investigators argue that managerial effectiveness can be studied only by observing actual managers, they bypass other important issues. It seems likely that managers are distinguished as much by their assignments as by their individual qualities. This suggests that a profitable methodological departure would be to explicate the properties of the prototypical managerial task and then incorporate these properties into experimental settings. We are arguing that quasi managerial tasks can furnish a substitute for actually studying managers. Once these tasks are designed, nonmanagerial populations can be studied because their assignments resemble closely those of the manager.

The above should not be taken as an argument *against* the use of managerial samples. We are merely trying to point out why viewing managers as a "sacred sample" for experimentation may be unduly restrictive and hurt more than it helps.

Finally, a criticism sometimes leveled at experimentation in the organizational setting pertains to its relatively short duration and compressed nature. Investigators seem to value the longitudinal approach above all others.

No one will deny that if events are observed over longer periods of time, they look different from the way they do viewed for only a short time. A longitudinal study tends to produce a more complete picture of events (complete in the sense that more is known about them), but the completeness or preciseness of explanation is often sacrificed. When relationships are viewed over long periods of time, intervening events frequently provide several alternative explanations for observed outcomes. If an investigator selects a population of persons who should become managers and a population who should not and then waits to see whether his predictions were correct, intervening events provide more and more competing explanations for the eventual outcome. While a longitudinal study may provide a comprehensive view of natural events, it may also hinder attempts to explain these events in a parsimonious way.

Our argument is that while it is important to see what happens to events which extend over time, there are other ways to determine this than by simply waiting passively while events unfold. It seems possible that events can be shortened and intensified without losing time-relevant variables. It is not necessarily true that if an event is hurried or if its history unfolds in a burst, it differs significantly from an event that unfolds at a more leisurely pace. If time-relevant properties can be retained in settings which actually are fairly short-lived, then investigators can have the dual benefits of a longitudinal view and fewer intervening events which must be taken into account when the outcome is explained.

Most attempts to preserve time-relevant properties in studies of short duration consist of simple definitional reinterpretations. Thus in many laboratory simulations of organizations (e.g., Guetzkow & Bowes, 1957), each participant is told that one hour of actual time is equivalent to one year in the history of the organization. This technique of time compression requires the subject to role play, and it is not at all clear how this affects his behavior. The alternative solutions that we have in mind are detailed in Weick's (1965b, pp. 214-218) discussion of ways in which short-term groups can be made equivalent in their formal properties to long-term groups. This approach builds upon the finding that as persons interact over long periods of time, certain things happen, members learn more about the strengths and weaknesses of their associates, there is more differential allocation of responsibilities for task accomplishment, and norms develop. It is argued that if each of these properties can be implanted into a "young" experimental group, the members will come to interact as if they had been together for some time. An example may clarify this distinction. In the early stage of a group, interaction is relatively undifferentiated. Differences in ability, leadership, attractiveness, responsibility, etc., do not become apparent immediately, and they are not formalized until considerable interaction has occurred. When a young group is given a task which requires immediate differentiation (e.g., members have to assemble a story in a wheel communication network), in order to accomplish it they will confront problems which normally would occur much later in their history, and in solving these problems they age quickly. Assuming that groups follow orderly sequences of development, it seems plausible that it is the occurrence of crises during this development, and not just the lapse of time, which is the crucial component in longitudinal studies. And it is possible to hasten the incidence of such crises. Thus it is possible for the investigator to have a controlled longitudinal study which preserves properties that emerge over long periods of time but in which intervening events are less of a problem. Under these conditions, it should be possible to construct more concise explanations of managerial effectiveness.

While there is little precedent for this approach, it seems worthy of attention. If an investigator is dubious about the comparability between groups with contrived and natural histories, then he can examine the outcomes that occur in both settings to determine the "goodness of fit." If the argument presented above is valid, there should not be significant differences between the outcome observed under these two widely different conditions. If differences do occur and they cannot be explained on the basis of ineffectual manipulations within the contrived group, then the value of this approach is less clear. At this point we can plead only for a more venturesome approach to methodological alternatives.

It should not be concluded from the above that generalizing between the laboratory and the field is easy. It is not. But what is needed is greater specificity concerning the blocks to generalization, not a general indictment in terms of diffuse artificiality.

Other issues. There are at least four troublesome and specific issues concerning experiments which render generalization from the laboratory to the referent event precarious, especially in organizational research. These problems are discussed at length by Weick (1966b), but a short summary of them here may suggest their nature:

1 *Task prominence.* When subjects work on a laboratory task, their attention is focused on a single task, and there are seldom competing demands which they must also handle. This contrasts sharply with the managerial setting, in which diffuseness of attention is probably the rule.
2 *Limited alternatives.* Most subjects have minimal commitments to experimental groups and have attractive alternatives when these fleeting relationships prove unappealing. Commitments within organizations are considerably less transitory. Recent research by Kiesler and Corbin (1966) clearly indicates that as commitment varies, so does the person's tendency to conform to an unattractive group. Highly committed subjects conform more to an unattractive group than noncommitted subjects. The troublesome implications of this finding should be apparent.
3 *Recruitment.* In many experiments it is difficult to recruit participants, and as these difficulties increase, there is a lessening of the populations to which results can be generalized. D.T. Campbell (1957, p.308) has stated this issue clearly: "The greater the cooperation required, the more the respondent has to deviate from the normal course of daily events, the greater will be the possibility of nonrepresentative populations. . . . The longer the experiment is extended in time, the more respondents are lost and the less representative are the groups of the original universe."
4 *The first day at work.* A person who participates in an experiment is more like a person on his first day at work than a person on his first decade at work: "A person who is in an experiment, like the newcomer on the job, often has low confidence in his judgments, is easily influenced, misunderstands instructions, is uninformed, finds the job novel and interesting, is cautious, and tolerates many demands that would anger him in more familiar settings. Many of these behaviors dissipate as he becomes more accustomed to the assignment" (Weick, 1966b).

The preceding points imply that caution must be exercised in generalization, but they also suggest specific points at which problems occur. Furthermore, each of these problems can be solved by appropriate modification of experimental settings. Recent writing about laboratory methodology is characterized by an increasingly critical look at the shortcomings of experiments. Rosenthal (1964) has compiled impressive evidence that experimenters can unintentionally bias the responses which their subjects give. These findings have alerted experimenters to a crucial problem, and efforts are now being made to diminish the effects of bias (e.g., Aronson & Carlsmith, 1968). Webb et al. (1966) have detailed numerous unobtrusive measures which can be used to assess phenomena, and Weick (1967) has suggested ways in which naturalistic observation can be a more potent methodology. Persons interested in managerial research should pay close attention to these developments in experimental methodology since they are directed toward some of the very issues which have caused this approach to be viewed with lack of interest.

It is probably safe to predict that a body of comparative literature will have to be built up around the experiment itself; that is, the manipulations and structuring used to facilitate generalization from the experimental setting will themselves have to be varied and their effects noted. Certainly there are enough heuristic models already available to guide such investigation meaningfully. For example, Strother (1963) has defined an organization as a *cooperative relationship* and has described a number of elements of the cooperative process that might prove fruitful to incorporate in an experiment. Zelditch and Hopkins (1961) outline the *bureaucratic* properties of an organization, and Rapoport (1959) details the nature of organized *activity*. All such models provide means for increasing the utility of the experimental method for the study of organization.

Again we should point out that the above discussion is not meant to degrade the correlational-differential approach to the world or argue for a shift in emphasis to the experimental method. After all, behavior must be measured and predictions made. It is as fallacious to regard within-treatment differences as merely experimental error as it is to measure individual differences and pretend that treatment differences do not exist. The understanding of human behavior in organizations simply cannot go forward until the relevant interactions are mapped out.

SUMMARY

The correlational and experimental approaches to studying behavior were summarized and contrasted. We then argued that the study of managerial effectiveness has suffered from a one-sided emphasis on the correlational method, but even where experimentation has been used, it has not been cross-fertilized by the differential psychologist. In an effort to redress the balance, the applicability of the experimental method and its application to the study of interactive effects were discussed at length. We examined the common objectives to experimentation in organizations: (1) lack of realism, (2) lack of managerial subjects, and (3) short time duration. We also discussed the more specific issues of (1) task prominence, (2) limited alternatives, (3) recruitment of subjects, and (4) the first day at work.

Chapter 15 Managerial Motivation

The topic of managerial motivation has been receiving increasing attention in the past few years (Vroom, 1965), and it is one of the central topics in the relatively new field of inquiry labeled "organizational psychology" (Leavitt & Bass, 1964). Given the importance of the concept, it remains exceedingly difficult to define and research.

Very generally, we can begin by saying that an individual's motivation has to do with (1) the *direction* of his behavior, or what he chooses to do when presented with a number of possible alternatives; (2) the *amplitude,* or strength, of the response (i.e., effort) once the choice is made; and (3) the *persistence* of the behavior, or how long he sticks with it. The term "motivation" conveniently subsumes a number of other variables such as drive, need, incentive, reward, expectancy, etc. It is these variables which are important for the study of motivated behavior and to which our attention will be directed.

This chapter is divided into two main sections, one on theory and the other on data. We first attempt to summarize the major "themes" in motivational theory, as they relate to managerial behavior, and see what they suggest regarding research questions that should be investigated. Then we try to organize the available empirical research and assess the fit of the research questions that *have been* asked with those which *should be* asked.

MOTIVATIONAL THEORIES AND ORGANIZATIONAL BEHAVIOR.

As will become obvious, there is an abundance of theory, but it is extraordinarily difficult to identify the similarities and differences across theories. Different theories stem from different traditions and do not always focus on the same elements of behavior. There is also a tendency to assign different labels to the same behavioral element or process. The reader has our sympathy. We would welcome his.

Theories of motivation have tended to divide themselves into two groups, which we have labeled (1) *mechanical or process* theories and (2) *substantive or content* theories. The former try to explain and describe the process of how behavior is energized, how it is directed, how it is sustained, and how it is stopped. They first try to define the *major* classes of variables that are important for explaining motivated behavior. For example, a theory might talk about rewards, needs, and incentives as three general classes of variables that are important for understanding motivation. Such theories then attempt to specify how the variables interact and influence one another to produce certain kinds of behavior. A simple example of such a process statement might be the assertion that "individuals exert more effort to obtain rewards that satisfy important needs than to obtain rewards that do not." Vroom's (1964) instrumentality-valence theory is very much a process theory.

By contrast, content theories are more concerned with the specific identity of *what* it is within an individual or his environment that energizes and sustains behavior. That is, what *specific* things motivate people? For example, we might theorize that individuals have three fundamental needs: food, sex, and security. Thus the content theories attempt to identify and define the specific entities within a general class of important variables (e.g., promotion, salary, job security, fringe benefits, recognition, and friendly coworkers might make up the general class of valuables labeled "rewards"). The content theories are not centrally concerned with specifying the precise form of the interactions between variables.

We acknowledge that our process-content distinction does not yield two completely mutually exclusive categories. Process theorists sometimes attempt to specify the specific variables making up a class, and content theorists may try to embed their variables in a process framework. Nevertheless, the emphasis does seem to be on one or the other. Also, we do not mean to argue that the dichotomy is a desirable one. A motivational theory is useful for making predictions only to the extent that it specifies both content and process, that is, to the extent that it specifies the identity of the important variables and the processes by which they influence behavior.

MECHANICAL, OR PROCESS THEORIES

Currently, there are three major theoretical positions one could adopt concerning the motivational process as it relates to organizational behavior: (1) stimulus response, drive x habit theory; (2) expectancy theory; and (3) equity, or social comparison theory.

Stimulus-Response, or Drive x Habit Theory

Certainly the most influential statement of this type of theory is that of C. L. Hull (1943). Behavior is pictured as resulting from a combination of drive and habit strength. Thus the motivational process deals with these two classes of variables, and the theory specifies that they combine in a multiplicative fashion to produce effort.

Habit strength is defined as the strength of a stimulus-response connection resulting from previous reinforcement experiences. An explanation for how S-R connections are built up by past experience was proposed in Thorndike's law of effect (Thorndike, 1911, p. 16). Much of Thorndike's work was carried out on animals, and his statement of the law of effect is as follows:

> Of several responses made to the same situation, those which are accompanied or closely followed by satisfaction to the animal will, other things being equal, be more firmly connected with the situation, so that, when it recurs, they will be more likely to recur; those which are accompanied by discomfort to the animal will, other things being equal, have their connections with that situation weakened, so that, when it recurs, they will be less likely to recur. The greater the satisfaction or discomfort, the greater the strengthening or weakening of the bond.

Drive level was originally viewed simply as representing the level of temporal deprivation relative to assumed needs such as food, water, or sex. However, it was soon demonstrated that an organism would respond to stimulus conditions which were totally unrelated to physiological need states. The concept of drive was broadened to incorporate the need to reduce any strong internal stimulus, not just genuine hunger pangs. This conceptualization also proved unsatisfactory when it was further demonstrated that both animals and men will often strive to *increase* the amount of stimulation they receive (see, for example, Cofer & Appley, 1964). The current theoretical position seems to view the organism as striving toward an *optimal* level of stimulation or arousal (Cofer,

1967). Obviously, this optimal level may change over time, and Helson (1959) has suggested the notion of adaptation level to explain why the value of incentives may change with repeated reinforcement. For example, an initially novel stimulus may become less novel after repeated appearances.

Expectancy Theory

Expectancy theory, because of its greater potential relevance to managerial behavior, will be discussed more fully.

Early cognitive theories. Concomitant with the development of drive x habit theory, Lewin (1938) and Tolman (1932) developed and investigated cognitive, or expectancy, theories of motivation. Even though Lewin was concerned with human subjects and Tolman worked largely with animals, much of their respective theorizing contained common elements. Basic to the cognitive view of motivation is the notion that individuals have cognitive *expectancies* concerning the outcomes that are likely to occur as the result of what they do and that individuals have preferences among outcomes. That is, an individual has an "idea" about possible consequences of his acts, and he makes conscious choices among consequences according to their probability of occurrence and their value to him.

Thus for the cognitive theorist it is the anticipation of reward that energizes behavior and the perceived value of various outcomes that gives behavior its direction. Tolman spoke of a *belief-value* matrix that specifies for each individual the value he places on particular outcomes and his belief that they can be attained.

Atkinson (1964) has compared drive theory and expectancy theory. Although he points out some differences, he emphasizes that both theories are actually quite similar and contain many of the same concepts. Both include the notion of a reward or favorable outcome that is desired, and both postulate a learned connection contained within the organism. For expectancy theory this learned connection is a behavior-outcome expectancy, and for drive theory it is an *S-R* habit strength.

However, the theories differ in two ways which are important for research on motivation in an organizational setting. For example, they differ in what they state is activated by the anticipation of reward. Expectancy theory sees the anticipation of a reward as functioning selectively on actions expected to lead to it. Drive theory views the magnitude of the anticipated goals as a source of general excitement—a nonselective influence on performance.

Expectancy theory is also much looser in specifying how expectancy-outcome connections are built up. Drive theory postulates that *S-R* habit strengths are built up through repeated associations of stimulus and response; that is, the reward or outcome must actually have followed the response to a partic-

344	Managerial Behavior, Performance, and Effectiveness

ular stimulus in order for the *S-R* connection to operate in future choice behavior. Such a process is sufficient but not necessary for forming expectancy-outcome relationships. An individual may form expectancies vicariously (someone may tell him that complimenting the boss's wife leads to a promotion, for example) or by other symbolic means. This last point is crucial since the symbolic (cognitive) manipulation of various *S-R* situations seems quite descriptive of a great deal of human behavior.

These two differences make the cognitive or expectancy point of view much more useful for studying human motivation in an organizational setting. In fact, it is the one which has been given the most attention by theorists concerned with behavior in organizations.

Instrumentality-valence theory. Building on expectancy theory and its later amplifications by Atkinson (1958), W. Edwards (1954), Peak (1955), and Rotter (1955), Vroom (1964) has presented a process theory of work motivation that he calls *instrumentality theory*. His basic classes of variables are expectancies, valences, choices, outcomes, and instrumentalities.

Expectancy is defined as a belief concerning the likelihood that a particular act will be followed by a particular outcome. Presumably, the degree of belief can vary between 0 (complete lack of belief that it will follow) and 1 (complete certainty that it will). Note that it is the perception of the individual that is important, not the objective reality. This same concept has been referred to as *subjective probability* by others (e.g., W. Edwards, 1954).

Valence refers to the strength of an individual's preference for a particular outcome. An individual may have either a positive or a negative preference for an outcome; presumably, outcomes gain their valence as a function of the degree to which they are seen to be related to the needs of the individual. However, this last point is not dealt with concretely in Vroom's formulation. As an example of these two concepts, one might consider an increase in pay to be a possible outcome of a particular act. The theory would then deal with the valence of a wage increase for an individual and his expectancy that particular behaviors will be followed by a wage increase outcome. Again, valence refers to the perceived or expected value of an outcome, not its real or eventual value.

According to Vroom, outcomes take on a valence value because of their *instrumentality* for achieving other outcomes. Thus he is really postulating two classes of outcomes. In the organizational setting, the first class of outcomes might include such things as money, promotion, recognition, etc. Supposedly, these outcomes are directly linked to behavior. However, as Vroom implicitly suggests, wage increases or promotion may have no value by themselves. They are valuable in terms of their instrumental role in securing second level outcomes such as food, clothing, shelter, entertainment, and status, which are not obtained as the direct result of a particular action.

According to Vroom, instrumentality, like correlation, varies between $+1.0$ and -1.0. Thus a first level outcome may be seen as always leading to some desired second level outcome $(+1.0)$ or as never leading to the second level outcome (-1.0). In Vroom's theory the formal definition of valence for a first level outcome is the sum of the products between its instrumentalities for all possible second level outcomes and their respective valences.

To sum up, Vroom's formulation postulates that the motivational force, or effort, an individual exerts is a function of (1) his expectancy that certain outcomes will result from his behavior (e.g., a raise in pay for increased effort) and (2) the valence, for him, of those outcomes. The valence of an outcome is in turn a function of its instrumentality for obtaining other outcomes and the valence of these other outcomes.

A hybrid expectancy model. Since his formulation first appeared, a number of investigators have attempted to extend Vroom's model to make it more explicit and more inclusive in terms of relevant variables (Graen, 1967; L.W. Porter & Lawler, 1968). Although we shall not discuss the contributions of these writers in detail, we would like to incorporate a number of their ideas in our own composite picture of an expanded expectancy model. However, any imperfections in what follows should be ascribed to us and not to them.

One major addition to Vroom's model is the necessity for a more concrete specification of the task or performance goals toward which work behavior is directed. Graen (1967) refers to this class of variables as *work roles*, but we prefer to retain the notion of *task goals*. Task goals may be specified externally by the organization or the work group, or internally by the individual's own value system. Examples of task goals include such things as production quotas, time limits for projects, quality standards, showing a certain amount of loyalty to the organization, exhibiting the right set of attitudes, etc.

We would also like to make more explicit a distinction between first and second level outcomes. First level outcomes are outcomes contingent on achieving the task goal or set of task goals. A potential first level outcome is synonymous with the term "incentive," and an outcome which is actually realized is synonymous with the term "reward." The distinction is temporal. Like task goals, first level outcomes may be external or internal. Some examples of external first level outcomes granted by the organization are job security, pay, promotions, recognition, and increased autonomy. An individual may also set up his own internal incentives or reward himself with internally mediated outcomes such as ego satisfaction.

As pointed out in the discussion of Vroom's model first level outcomes may or may not be associated with a plethora of second level outcomes; that is, the externally or internally mediated rewards are instrumental in varying degrees for obtaining second level outcomes such as food, housing, material goods, community status, and freedom from anxiety.

The concepts of valence for first and second level outcomes and the instrumentality of first for second level outcomes are defined as before, but the notion of expectancy decomposes into two different variables. First, individuals may have expectancies concerning whether or not they will actually accomplish the task goal if they expend effort (expectancy I); that is, an individual makes a subjective probability estimate concerning his chances for reaching a particular goal, given a particular situation. For example, a manufacturing manager may think the odds of his getting a new product into production by the first of the year are about 3 to 1 (i.e., expectancy I = 0.75). Perhaps the primary determiner of expectancy I is how the individual perceives his own job skills in the context of what is specified as his task goals and the various difficulties and external constraints standing in the way of accomplishing them. Certainly, then, an employee's perceptions of his own talents determine to a large degree the direction and intensity of his job behavior. This first kind of expectancy should be more salient for more complex and higher level tasks such as those involved in managing.

Second, individuals possess expectancies concerning whether or not achievement of specified task goals will actually be followed by the first level outcome (expectancy II). In other words, they form subjective probability estimates of the degree to which rewards are *contingent* on achieving task goals. The individual must ask himself what the probability is that his achievement of the goal will be rewarded by the organization. For example, the manufacturing manager may be virtually certain (expectancy II = 1.0) that if he does get the new product into production by the first of the year, he will receive a promotion and a substantial salary increase. Or, and this may be the more usual case, he may see no relationship at all between meeting the objective and getting a promotion and salary increase.

None of the authors cited so far have explicitly labeled these two kinds of expectancies. Indeed, in a laboratory or other experimental setting the distinction may not be necessary since the task may be so easy that accomplishing the goal is always a certainty (i.e., expectancy I is 1.0 for everybody) or the contingency of reward on behavior may be certain and easily verified by the subject (i.e., expectancy II is 1.0 for everybody). Vroom (1964) defines expectancy as an action-outcome relationship which is represented by an individual's subjective probability estimate that a particular set of behaviors will be followed by a particular outcome. Since Vroom presents no concrete definitions for the terms "action" and "outcome," his notion of expectancy could include both expectancy I and expectancy II as defined above. Thus effort expenditure could be regarded as an action, and goal performance as an outcome; or performance could be considered behavior, and money an outcome. Vroom uses both kinds of examples to illustrate the expectancy variable and makes no conceptual distinction between them. However, in the organizational set-

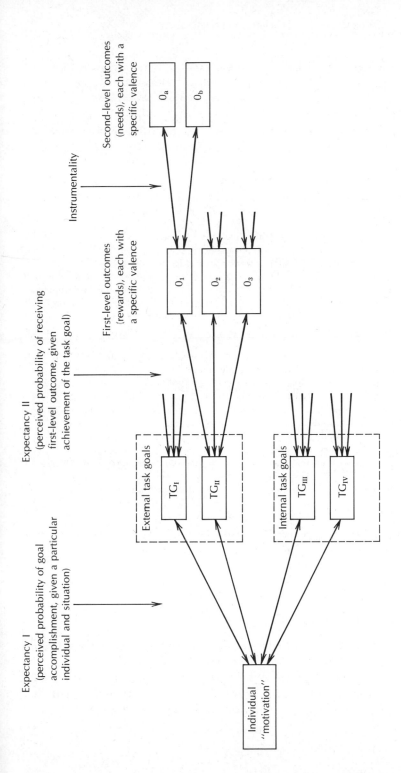

Figure 15.1 A schematic representation of a hybrid expectancy model of work motivation outlining the determinants of the direction, amplitude, and persistence of individual effort.

ting, the distinction seems quite necessary. Rewards may or may not be contingent on goal accomplishment, and the individual may or may not believe he has the wherewithal to reach the goal. A schematic representation of this hybrid model is shown in Figure 15.1.

We have purposely been rather vague concerning the exact form of the relationships between these different classes of variables. This schematic model is in no way meant to be a formal theory. To propose explicit multiplicative combinations or other configural or higher order functions is going a bit too far beyond our present measurement capability. Rather, we shall sum up the relationships contained in our expanded model as follows:

1 The valence of a first level outcome (incentive or reward) is a function of the instrumentality of that outcome for obtaining second level outcomes (need satisfactions) and the valences of the relevant second level outcomes.

2 The decision by an individual to work on a particular task and expend a certain amount of effort in that direction is a function of (a) his personal probability estimate that he can accomplish the task (expectancy I), (b) his personal probability estimate that his accomplishment of the task goal will be followed by certain first level outcomes or rewards (expectancy II), and (c) the valence of the first level outcomes.

3 The distinction between external and internal goals and rewards leads to a number of potential conflict situations for the individual. For example, an individual might estimate his chances for accomplishing a particular task as virtually certain (i.e., expectancy I $= 1.0$). However, the internal rewards which are virtually certain to follow (i.e., expectancy II $= 1.0$) may have a very low or even negative valence (e.g., feelings of extreme boredom or distaste). If external rewards, such as a lot of money, have a very high valence, a serious stress situation could result from outcomes which have conflicting valences. It would be to an organization's advantage to ensure positive valences for both internal and external rewards. Other conflict situations could be produced by high positive valences for outcomes and low estimates of type I expectancies (i.e., the individual does not think he can actually do the job).

Even though this kind of hybrid expectancy model seems to be a useful way of looking at organizational behavior and even though we have devoted more space to it, the reader should keep in mind that it is not the only process theory that one could use. Equity theory is its major competitor, and it is to a discussion of this formulation that we now turn.

Equity, or Social Comparison Theory

There is a constellation of theory dealing with social comparison processes that Cofer and Appley (1964) have lumped under the rubric "dissonance theory" or "discrepancy theory." It makes up the third major theme underlying our discussion of motivational process theories. The central idea is that if a *discrepancy* exists within the individual, he is motivated to reduce it, and the greater the discrepancy, the greater the motivation. The discrepancy under consideration is that which exists between two elements or two sets of elements, for example, two attitudes which do not follow from each other, such as being prejudiced against a particular race and developing a fondness for a next-door neighbor who is a member of that race, or a subjective perception and an objective reality that do not fit, such as believing one is a top-notch manager and then not receiving a promotion for a long time. A number of methods obviously exist for reducing discrepancies (e.g., becoming less prejudiced, starting to dislike one's neighbor, changing perceptions about one's ability, devaluing a promotion, etc.). A broad discussion of discrepancy theory is beyond the scope of this book. Perhaps the most general statement is given by Festinger (1957) under the label "cognitive dissonance."

However, one variant of discrepancy or cognitive dissonance that has special relevance for managerial motivation is so called equity theory as described by Adams and Weick (Adams, 1963, 1965a; Weick, 1965a). The theory has dealt primarily with compensation practices, but can be broadened to encompass a variety of "inputs" and "outputs" that might be present in the organizational setting. That is, the relevant comparison, or discrepancy, is between the ratio of a person's job inputs to job outcomes and the same ratio for a comparison person. If the two ratios are unequal, the person is motivated to reduce the discrepancy. The ratios are shown below.

Inputs include anything the individual perceives as an investment in the job and as worthy of some return. They might include effort, education, or time. Outcomes are anything that is perceived as a return from the situation. Money, recognition, and working conditions might be examples. The elements in the total input-outcome package are weighted by their importance. Adams (1963) postulates that unequal ratios produce "tension" in the individual which he strives to reduce by a variety of means. He may cognitively distort his inputs or outcomes, leave the situation, attempt to change the inputs or outcomes of the comparison person, change his own inputs or outcomes, or change his comparison person. The method most likely to be used for reducing inequity is a function of its "cost" to the individual. For example, an individual will be more prone to changing his perception of the comparison person's input-outcome ratio than his own.

As summarized by Pritchard (1969), equity theory incorporates three classes of variables that require specification:

1 *The nature of inputs and outcomes.* Besides identifying salient inputs and outcome elements and weighting properly, the theory also has to deal with the level of correlation among the elements. That is, if an individual perceives his outcome elements to be highly correlated (i.e., they all represent more or less the same thing such as salary, vacation time, and office furniture), then they do not represent as much of a total outcome package as they would if they were uncorrelated (i.e., represented different things).

2 *The comparison person and the comparison process.* Here the theory must consider the number of Others an individual will use, the relative importance of various Others, and the change in Others over time. In addition, Weick and Nesset (1968) have postulated six ways the comparison process can yield an inequitable comparison.

Person		Other	
Inputs	**Outcomes**	**Inputs**	**Outcomes**
Low	Low	High	Low
Low	Low	Low	High
Low	High	Low	Low
High	Low	Low	Low
High	High	High	Low
High	High	Low	High

In all these situations the ratios are unequal, and yet the nature of the inequity is different and may have different motivational effects.

3 *Modes of inequity resolution.* This seems to be the weakest part of equity theory as a theory. Methods for resolving inequity are numerous, and individual differences undoubtedly exist regarding preferences among methods. For example, one intriguing method might be the manipulation of the perceived correlations among inputs and outcomes.

Comparisons of equity theory with the other process theories and some of the research findings which equity theory has generated will be discussed in later sections of this chapter.

SUBSTANTIVE, OR CONTENT THEORIES

Now that we have briefly touched on some of the major theoretical formulations that might be used to describe the *process* of motivation in the organizational setting, we would like to mention even more briefly some *substantive* suggestions concerning what specific variables should be studied. That is, the theorizing described below has attempted to suggest the specific identity of variables discussed in general terms above.

Murray's Needs

H.A. Murray influenced a great deal of later motivational and personality theory when he hypothesized the existence of a relatively large number of specific needs which human beings attempt to satisfy. The exact number in the list varies according to the particular stage in Murray's career, but about twenty basic needs were usually included. For example:

- Need for achievement
- Need for aggression
- Need for autonomy
- Need for affiliation
- Need for sex
- Need for nurturance

We should point out that Murray's list and his accompanying definitions were not based on empirical research. Rather, they represent his conceptualization of what internal states govern human behavior and were generated from his clinical experience and observation.

The Work of McClelland and Atkinson

Building on Murray's theory, McClelland and Atkinson and their associates (Atkinson, 1958: Atkinson & Feather, 1966; McClelland, 1951; McClelland, Atkinson, Clark, & Lowell, 1953) have sought to refine and intensively investigate a subset of motives from Murray's list. The three which have received the most attention are (1) the need for achievement (n Ach), (2) the need for affiliation (n Aff), and (3) the need for power (n Pow). Within this subset, the achievement need has been given the most emphasis, and the result has been a formalized theory of achievement motivation (Atkinson & Feather, 1966). The achievement motive is viewed as a relatively stable disposition, or potential behavior tendency, to strive for achievement or success. The motive is presumed not to operate until it is aroused by certain situational cues or incentives, which signal the individual that certain behaviors will lead to feelings of achievement (Atkinson, 1957). According to Atkinson, a particular motive— achievement, affiliation, or power— is actually a label for a class of incentives, all of which produce essentially the same result. This end result is an internal experience of satisfaction such as pride in accomplishment (n Ach), a sense of belonging and being warmly received by others (n Aff), or the feeling of being influential and in control (n Pow). These motives may be conditioned to a wide range of incentives, are learned, and have their fundamental origins in relatively early childhood experience (McClelland, 1951).

The fundamental method for assessing the strength of these motives has utilized the Thematic Apperception Test (TAT), which asks respondents to relate what they see in a series of very simple pictures. That is, achievement, affiliation, or power needs are inferred from an individual's associative responses to ambiguous stimuli. The subjects are asked the following questions about the pictures: What is happening? Who are the persons? What has led up to this situation? What has happened in the past? What is being thought? What is wanted? What will happen? What will be done? Scoring methods have been developed by comparing the responses of people under benign conditions with those obtained under conditions where the motive was assumed to be operating. For example, college males in a testing situation were made to feel very relaxed, neutral, or very ego-involved relative to their performance. After the subjects had finished the test, the TAT was administered under the guise of a test of creative imagination. The scoring system thus derived has proved to be reliable across scorers and meaningfully associated with other criterion groups that could be reasonably expected to represent differences in achievement motivation. Similar procedures have been used to derive scoring procedures for the other two motives.

Because of the early research results stemming from the theory, Atkinson (1957) postulated the existence of another class of motives whose end result is the minimization of pain. The specific motive which has received the most attention is the so-called fear of failure.

The above specification of motives is embedded in what is essentially an expectancy-valence model of the motivational process. That is, behavior is seen as resulting from (1) the strength of the motive, (2) the valence of the cue or incentive which arouses the motive, and (3) the individual's expectancy that behavior will lead to the incentive or reward. Expectancy and valence are hypothesized to be inversely related, and the implication is that low expectancies or a low subjective probability of success leads to a higher value for the incentive, and vice versa.

Formally stated, the tendency to approach a task with the intention of performing successfully (T_s) is a multiplicative function of the strength of the achievement motive (M_s), the subjective probability of success (P_s), and the valence or incentive value of success (I_s). That is, $T_s = M_s \times P_s \times I_s$. Conversely, the behavioral tendency to avoid failure by avoiding the task (T_f) is a multiplicative function of the strength of the need to avoid failure (M_{AF}), the subjective probability of failure (P_f), and the incentive value of failure (I_f). That is, $T_f = M_{AF} \times P_f \times I_f$. For any given task the observed behavioral tendency is the resultant of T_s and T_f.

It is beyond our present means to discuss in any detail the specific hypotheses that flow from this theory. However, for illustrative purposes we would like to mention two implications. These are taken from Atkinson and Feather (1966):

1 The tendency to achieve success should be strongest when a task is one of intermediate difficulty, but the difference in strength of the tendency to achieve success that is attributable to task difficulty will be substantial only when n Ach is
relatively strong.

2 When the difficulty of a task is held constant, the intention to achieve success
is stronger when n Ach is strong than when it is weak, but the difference in the
strength of the intention to achieve success that is attributable to a difference
in the strength of n Ach will be substantial only when the task is one of intermediate difficulty.

Consideration of points such as the above leads to additional implications
about what might happen to behavior over time. For example, the law of effect
states that behavior which is rewarded tends to recur at a higher frequency.
In need achievement terms this would be true only if the value of the incentive remained constant. But this may not happen if the behavior under consideration is salient for the achievement motive. Under these conditions the
incentive value of the reward is negatively related to the perceived probability of success. Thus if the individual experiences repeated successes on the
task, the perceived probability of success will increase, the value of the incentive will decrease, and the individual may go off and do something else.

Maslow's Hierarchy

Owing more to the views of existentialism and psychoanalysis than to
those of Murray and the instinct theorists, Maslow (1954) has postulated a *hierarchy* of human needs incorporating several levels. Basic to Maslow's theory is
the notion that needs at a particular level of the hierarchy must be "largely"
satiated before the needs at the next higher level become operative. This is
not to say that two levels cannot be operative at the same time, but the needs
at the lower level take precedence. It follows that if lower level needs are substantially satisfied in our society, they may never actually be very important
for energizing and directing behavior.

The basic outline of Maslow's hierarchy from the lowest level to the highest level is as follows:

1 *Physiological needs.* As one might expect, these include such things as hunger
and thirst. Maslow also goes on to talk about a number of specific hungers.
2 *Safety needs.* These refer primarily to freedom from bodily threat and in our culture are probably most active for young children.
3 *Belongingness or social needs.* These include the need for friendship, affection,
love, and perhaps something akin to affiliation as that term is used by Murray and
McClelland.
4 *Esteem needs.* These represent an individual's need for self-respect, for the respect
of others, and for a stable, positive evaluation of himself.
5 *Self-actualization..* At the top of the hierarchy is the need level most existential

in nature and most difficult to define. A succinct definition is simply that the individual's need to self-actualize is his need to be what he wants to be, to achieve fulfillment of his life's goals, and to realize the potential of his personality.

Self-actualization is similar to the construct of need achievement except that *n* Ach is a more normative concept and is intended to have a similar meaning across a wide range of people, situations, and cultures. Self-actualization must be defined individually.

As was true of Murray's theory, Maslow's characterization of human needs is not based on any empirical foundation, but was derived primarily from Maslow's clinical experience.

Herzberg's Two-factor Theory

On the basis of an extensive review of the earlier literature on job attitudes (Herzberg, Mausner, Peterson, & Capwell, 1957) and his well-known study involving a series of interviews with engineers and accountants (Herzberg, Mausner, & Snyderman, 1959), Herzberg has postulated the existence of two classes of work motivators—extrinsic and intrinsic factors. They are listed below:

Extrinsic factors	Intrinsic factors
1. *Pay*, or salary increase	1. *Achievement*, or completing an important task successfully
2. *Technical supervision*, or having a competent superior	2. *Recognition*, or being singled out for praise
3. The *human relations* quality of supervision	3. *Responsibility* for one's own or other's work
4. *Company policy and administration*	4. *Advancement*, or changing status through promotion
5. *Working conditions*, or physical surrounding	
6. *Job security*	

The intrinsic factors are viewed as being derived from the individual's relation to the job itself. An alternative label is "job content factors." Extrinsic factors are sources of motivation or need satisfaction that stem from the organizational *context* and are thus somewhat divorced from the direct influence of the individual.

Herzberg has more recently (1966) referred to intrinsic and extrinsic factors as "motivators" and "hygiene factors," respectively, and to his theory as the "motivation-hygiene" theory. Interestingly enough, the behavioral implications of the theory are not stated in terms of energizing, sustaining, or directing effort, but are concerned with changes in job satisfaction. Extrinsic factors, or hygiene factors, are seen as being able only to prevent the onset of job dissatisfaction or to remove it once it has become manifest. In contrast, motivators, or intrinsic factors, have no influence on job dissatisfaction but operate only to increase job satisfaction. Thus satisfaction and dissatisfaction are hypothesized to be two distinct entities stemming from different antecedents and should have no particular relationship to each other.

A summary of the research surrounding the two-factor hypothesis is presented later in this chapter.

Summary Comments concerning Motivational Theory

Obviously, there has been a lot of theorizing that is of some relevance for the study of managerial behavior. With some realization of the psychic risks involved, we would like to make a few summary comments about the previous discussion.

The concepts of need, motive, and drive all seem to reflect the same class of variables, even though the mechanisms by which they operate on behavior have been given different interpretations by different theorists. In essence, they are fundamental states within the individual that are altered in some fashion by goal-directed behavior. As mentioned previously, these variables are represented as clusters of highly correlated second level outcomes in our hybrid model. Outcomes representing hunger (food, cooking utensils, etc.) or security (paid-up mortgage, retirement annuity, etc.) are examples.

The first level outcomes in the expanded model correspond to the usual meanings of the terms "incentive" and "reward" in the motivation literature. Incentives, or behavior consequences, are the chief controllers of goal-directed behavior, and they derive their power from their association with motives or drives. Once the goal is achieved, the incentive may then also act as a reinforcer and serve to strengthen the behavioral tendency under consideration. These behavioral tendencies are called *habit strengths* or *S-R* bonds by the *S-R* theorist and are represented as type II expectancies in the expanded instrumentality model. However, the notion of expectancy represents a much more cognitive or conscious awareness of what outcomes might follow behavior than the more mechanistic notion of habit strength.

Relative to the substantive or content theories, most of the theories are "need" theories in the sense that they postulate certain pressures on the organism to act. In the *S-R* framework, the term "need" is most closely allied with "drive." That is, Murray, McClelland, and Maslow have attempted to specify the nature of the drives which energize individuals and which are aroused by certain cues. In terms of our expanded model of expectancy theory (Figure 15.1), central needs such as security, esteem, and achievement could be conceptualized as constructs underlying clusters of interrelated second level outcomes. That is, a cluster of second level outcomes could be highly intercorrelated because they all operate to satisfy the same need. For example, large amounts of insurance, retirement annuities, paid-up mortgages, and a new furnace all might operate on the need for security. Vroom (1965) also speaks of motives as constellations or clusters of interrelated outcomes.

Herzberg does not quite fit the above pattern. As we mentioned previously, his factors stem from a different line of inquiry, and as he defines them (Herzberg et al., 1959), they are closer to what S-R theorists have called "incentives" or "rewards" and what we have called "first level outcomes" in the context of instrumentality theory. That is, they are the cues which call into operation certain needs, drives, or motives.

It is not easy to establish the common elements of equity theory and the cognitive or S-R theories.On the surface the concept of outcome in the equity context appears similar to that of reward, or first level outcome. However, its role in motivation is not really analogous to that of an incentive or reinforcer. The whole notion of the *relative* comparison between inputs and outcomes has no explicit parallel in S-R or expectancy theory.

However, the tension created by unequal ratios between the individual and the comparison person is an internal state which energizes the individual and thus falls under the heading of "drive" or "need." In the instrumentality sense, reducing such tension would be the major component of a broad range of second level outcomes. Although S-R and expectancy theory deal explicitly only with the behavior of a single individual, it is not unreasonable to postulate that outcomes or incentives may take on value through social comparison processes.

Perhaps the fundamental difference between equity theory and the other theoretical formulations is that the only motives under consideration are those established via social comparison. Thus outcomes take on valence or value only to the extent that their attainment would affect the comparison of the two ratios.

Research Questions Suggested by Previous Theory

We would now like to list some of the more salient research questions strongly suggested by our overview of motivational theory. In hopes of making the reader's task easier, we shall group the questions into interrelated clusters. They are not necessarily arranged in order of importance.

1 A number of questions, such as the following, that are important for understanding the motivation of people in organizations have to do not with perceptual data but with the objective reality of the situation.
   a What are the first level outcomes, or rewards, that are *available* to individuals in various job situations? Such a question really has to do with the establishment of a meaningful taxonomy of outcomes.
   b What are the *actual* reward contingencies that seem to characterize organiza-

tional life? That is, what are the objective probabilities that the accomplishment of certain goals will be followed by certain rewards?

c What kind of task taxonomy should be used to study managerial motivation? That is, what task goals are the most salient for research investigations?

2 The theory also suggests that we should have a great deal of information concerning individual preferences for first level outcomes and their behavioral effects.

a What preferences do people have among specific first level outcomes, and what individual differences are associated with preferences for certain outcomes?

b How does the valence or incentive value of first level outcomes change over time as the result of obtaining the outcome? For example, does obtaining additional income raise or lower its valence (incentive value)?

c Which have the greater influence on behavior, internally or externally mediated reward outcomes? For whom?

3 Central to almost all theoretical discussions of motivation is the concept of behavior-reward contingency, or type II expectancy. To exert an influence on behavior, an outcome must be dependent in some fashion on the desired behavior.

a What reward or behavior outcome expectancies do individuals have in various situations?

b How do these change over time as the individual gains experience in the organization?

c How do perceived contingencies differ from actual contingencies, and how can the discrepancy be influenced?

d For a given outcome, what values for expectancy II (stated in probability terms) have the greatest influence on behavior?

4 A fourth group of questions concerns type I expectancies and the influence of perceived task requirements.

a What kind of type I expectancies do individuals prefer? That is, are individuals more "motivated" to achieve goals they perceive as easy, difficult, or something in between? What individual differences are associated with different preferences among type I expectancies?

b How do variations in type I expectancies influence effort expenditure or choice behavior?

c How are type I expectancies influenced by the valence of the incentive—positively, negatively, or not at all?

d Which are more important for behavior change, internally or externally set goals? Under what conditions?

5 A fifth major set of questions revolves around the instrumentality variable.

a For what second level outcomes (needs) are the first level outcomes (rewards) instrumental? What individual differences are associated with differences in instrumentalities?

b How does the instrumentality of rewards change over time, in terms of both the strength of the instrumentality for specific second level outcomes and additions or deletions of second level outcomes for which a reward is instrumental? For example, the instrumentality of a wage increase must surely change drastically as the absolute value of an individual's pay level increases. Cofer (1967) speaks of the consummatory versus sign value of money. That is, at lower pay levels a wage increase represents more of life's necessities, but at higher levels it is *symbolic* of greater achievement, more status, etc. The utility curve for money might thus be discontinuous at a number of points.

c Questions about instrumentalities also force a consideration of what taxonomy of needs is most meaningful for understanding managerial motivation. That is, what needs do managers have? Does a hierarchical formulation such as Maslow's make the most sense? Is achievement dominant? Is the reduction of inequity dominant?

6 Finally, a rather large number of research questions are associated with how the various theoretical constructs are interrelated. We shall mention only a few. The reader can generate others.

    a How is type I expectancy related to type II expectancy? For example, are higher perceived probabilities of reward associated with higher perceived probabilities of difficult task accomplishment?

    b How is the valence of the outcome related to both expectancy I and expectancy II? That is, is the value of the reward related to the individual's perceptions that he can accomplish the task goal and that his accomplishment will indeed be followed by the reward? It hardly seems likely that valences are independent of expectancy levels although a number of current models of individual choice (decision-making) behavior assume them to be (Becker & McClintock, 1967).

    c What are the directions of these relationships? For example, does high valence lead to high type I expectancies, or vice versa?

EMPIRICAL RESULTS RELEVANT FOR MANAGERIAL MOTIVATION

The title of this section reflects the fact that very few data exist that were gathered directly on management samples or with managerial behavior in mind. However, a number of other studies are "relevant," and these will be included.

Historically, almost all research on motivation has been carried out with animals. The bulk of this research initially concentrated on trying to determine the existence of various drive or need states and/or their influence on behavior; however, in recent years the emphasis has shifted to the role of incentives (Harber, 1967). A parallel development really does not exist in the study of organizational behavior. In practice, the bulk of the organization's attention has always been devoted to the influence of incentives, and research has tended to follow this lead. Needs, or second level outcomes, have been examined only recently.

It would be wise at this point to reemphasize the distinctions among several concepts that find their way into motivational research as *dependent* variables. The literature has been concerned with four: (1) effort expenditure, (2) choice behavior among stated alternatives, (3) performance level, and (4) job satisfaction. Although the published literature relevant for organizational behavior tends to ignore the problem of how behavior is sustained, we could further subdivide the concern for these four classes of variables into a consideration for behavior at *one time and in one place* and a consideration of the *persistence* of effort, performance, choices, or job satisfaction through time. This two-way classification is illustrated below.

	Short-term behavior change	Persistence over time
Effort		
Choice		
Performance		
Job satisfaction		

There are important qualitative distinctions among these dependent variables. Theories of motivation have the most direct implications for the variables of effort and choice behavior. Faced with a task, an individual makes choices concerning how to proceed and then expends effort in that direction. Choices and effort (or direction of response and magnitude of response) are the behaviors which came under the direct influence of expectancies, incentive valences, instrumentalities, need strengths, and the like. By contrast, task *performance* is a resultant of effort and choice behavior as they are moderated by situational factors and the ability of the individual (see, for example, L. W. Porter & Lawler, 1968). For example, no matter what choices are made or how much effort is expended, "motivated" behavior may not lead to a change in performance if the work situation does not permit it or the individual does not have the abilities necessary for turning effort into results. Of course, the individual's past performance history may influence his expectancies and preferences, which in turn influence future effort and choice behavior. However, in this instance, performance is not a dependent but an independent variable.

Although job satisfaction has frequently been used as a dependent variable in "motivational" studies, it is actually several steps removed from a direct concern with behavior. That is, job satisfaction results from achieving certain first level outcomes or rewards, but the reward may not depend (be contingent) upon the individual's behavior. For example, the organization may grant an across-the-board salary increase which in no way reflects individual accomplishment. However, if job satisfaction is valued and if certain rewards are instrumental for high job satisfaction, and if rewards indeed are contingent on behavior, then the individual may expend effort in that direction. Thus job satisfaction is a function of rewards, but rewards may or may not be a direct function of behavior.

A discussion of the empirical evidence follows. We shall try to identify the major themes in the empirical research and compare these research findings with the research needs suggested by our theoretical discussion.

The Needs and Motives (Second Level Outcomes) of Managerial Personnel

There exists a substantial body of research on the issue of what needs managers possess. These studies have measured the importance of a number of motives by such methods as asking managers to rate them on importance via a questionnaire (L. W. Porter, 1961, 1963), asking managers to respond to projective test instruments and then content analyzing their responses (McClelland, 1965), and conducting semistructured interviews (Pellegrin & Coates, 1957). In effect, these studies have attempted to determine the differential importance of various needs (i.e., preferences among clusters of second level outcomes). The studies seem to organize themselves around the types of group comparisons that have been made, such as comparisons of the needs of managers with the needs of nonmanagers, those of top management with those of middle management, etc. The motives or needs that have been considered have been drawn primarily from the work of McClelland and Maslow. Our discussion rests heavily on the previously cited review by Vroom (1965).

Managers versus nonmanagers. The available data indicate that there are consistent differences between managers and nonmanagers in terms of their motives. Managers are more concerned with such factors as achievement, power, and status and with income and advancement. In comparison with nonmanagers, managers score higher on projective measures (TAT) of achievement motivation than persons in other kinds of jobs (Veroff, Atkinson, Feld, & Gurin, 1960). McClelland (1961) has measured the achievement imagery of male college graduates and compared it with that of middle level managers; he found that the managers had higher achievement imagery. Other studies (e.g., McClelland, 1961, 1962; Meyer, Walker, & Litwin, 1961) have reported essentially the same finding. Morse and Weiss (1955) found that managers tend to rate achievement and accomplishment in their jobs as more important than members of most other occupational groups do. They also rated "having an interesting job" as more important. Ghiselli (1956) reports that managers achieve higher scores on initiative than the general population. Overall, then, the evidence indicates that managers have strong motives for achievement and like to exercise initiative.

An indication of the strength of the power and influence motive in managers can be seen in the data from interest test measures. Managers obtain exceedingly high scores on the persuasiveness key of the Kuder test (Wald & Doty, 1954) and on the Strong Vocational Interest Blank (SVIB), and they score high on directing people and on the initiation of other persons' and group activities (Strong, 1943). There is also some evidence that managers score higher on TAT measures of power. Veroff, et al. (1960) reported that managers are above average on the need for power.

Cross-cultural comparisons. Comparisons among managers in different countries have yielded somewhat conflicting results. Haire, Ghiselli, and Porter (1966) found basic similarities in patterns among the self-perceived motives of managers in a 14-country study. However, McClelland (1961) has reported that a substantial difference exists among countries in need achievement (n Ach), with the United States having the highest scores.

Functional areas. A considerable number of studies have focused upon differences between managers in various fields of specialization. Perhaps the most definitive of these was the study by Strong (1943). He found that personnel managers tend to have interests more like those of people-oriented professionals such as YMCA secretaries and social science teachers; they showed high humanitarian interests. Sales managers were found to be more similar to other salesmen than to other managers, showing high interest in social factors. Finally, the presidents of companies were a unique group, not resembling members of other occupations. As Vroom (1965) notes, the picture presented by Strong is in essential agreement with that of Kuder (1946). However, L. W. Porter and Lawler (1965) have reviewed the studies comparing line and staff managers, and they point out that there are essentially no important differences. Overall, the differences found between managers in different types of jobs do not seem to be as substantial as those found when managers are compared with nonmanagers and where the different levels of management are compared. It also appears that the same motive differences that distinguish managers from nonmanagers distinguish higher from lower level managers.

Effective versus less effective managers. A third type of comparison and the one most relevant for our purposes is that between more and less effective managers. Better managers tend to show a lifetime pattern of high achievement, power, and economic motivation. In addition, they are more dominant (Mahoney, Jerdee, & Nash, 1960) and tend to score higher on the political and economic scale of the Allport-Vernon-Lindzey test. They are more interested in directing others (E. E. Wagner, 1960), and they have strong desires for status and prestige (Ghiselli, 1963; Goodstein & Schrader, 1963). In terms of their preferences, a good summary is given by Nash (1963), who made comparisons on responses to the SVIB. More effective managers tend more often to prefer independent activities with some risk. They reject regimentation and enjoy interpersonal contact—especially when they are in a dominant position.

The most striking point about the differences between effective and less effective managers is the similarity with the results of the comparison between managers and nonmanagers and the comparison between the different levels of management. The achievement, power and status, and economic and advancement motives tend consistently to appear as the major sources of differences. The key question at this point concerns what accounts for these differences. The finding that managers differ from nonmanagers in terms of motives might be due to the kind of expectancies managers have about the outcomes associated with holding a managerial job. This argument is based upon the evidence (reviewed by Vroom, 1965) which shows that students high in achievement motivation had a much greater preference for the position of manager than students low in achievement motivation. This would suggest that more high than low achievement-oriented students actually choose managerial jobs. This is an indication that people do not acquire high achievement motivation as a result of holding a management job, but rather seek out a management job because they have high achievement motivation. The same sort of "selection" argument could be applied to motive differences between good and poor managers.

Differences among management levels. A number of studies have focused on differences in expressed needs or motives across two or more levels in the management hierarchy. The most comprehensive study was that of L. W. Porter (1964), who devised a 13-item questionnaire based on Maslow's hierarchy and administered it to a sample of 2,000 managers drawn at random from the membership lists of the American Management Association. On a scale from one to seven, each item asked the respondent to answer three questions regarding the manifestation of the need reflected in the item: (1) How much is there now in your job? (2) How much should there be? (3) How important is it to you? Respondents were grouped into five levels ranging from presidents and vice-presidents to supervisors and general foremen. The items attempted to tap the relative strengths of security needs, social needs, esteem needs, autonomy needs, and self-actualization needs.

In general, higher level managers placed greater emphasis on self-actualization and autonomy needs, but there were no differences across levels for the other three need categories. In terms of specific item content, the higher level managers rated as more important the opportunity for personal growth and development, the opportunity for independent thought and action, the opportunity for participation in the setting of goals, and the authority connected with their management position. Using the same questionnaire, similar small but significant hierarchical differences have been found in a military organization (L. W. Porter & Mitchell, 1967). It is interesting to note that within Porter's AMA sample, neither the size of the company nor the distinction between line and staff had any appreciable effect on the importance ratings for various needs.

Pellegrin and Coates (1957) drew the same kind of conclusions from their interview study of 50 executives and 50 first-line supervisors. The executives were described by the researchers as defining success in terms of pride in personal accomplishment and securing the esteem of others. They placed a high value on the opportunity to use and develop their skills. In contrast, the supervisors tended to define success in security and job satisfaction terms and placed a much higher value on being respected as a citizen and a good family provider.

Somewhat different from the above findings are those of an earlier study by L. W. Porter (1961) and one by Rosen and Weaver (1960). Both these studies tended to look at supervisors and managers only at the lower levels and within a single firm. The similarities in need preferences are much more pervasive than the differences across levels.

Data obtained from a small sample of managers using the TAT fantasy method of assessing need achievement (McClelland, 1961, 1962, 1963) tended to suggest that in small companies, expressed need achievement increases monotonically with management level, but that in larger firms the relationship is curvilinear. The highest level managers seemed to express less of an achievement need. Unfortunately, very little other data exist as to how n Ach, n Aff, and n Pow vary across management levels. The previously described AT&T Management Progress Study will be an excellent longitudinal source of such data, but it is not yet available.

As with all cross-sectional research, the above studies do not answer the question of whether higher level jobs *produce* differences in motive strengths or whether individuals with different motive hierarchies find their way into such jobs. A few studies are relevant for this question.

A longitudinal study by Festinger (1964b) points up the complexity of the relationships that are encountered with such a global variable as management level. Festinger and his associates interviewed 175 "promotable" managers and then followed them for approximately four years, at which time about half had been promoted and the entire sample was reinterviewed. In general, the motive and value orientations seemed to be unchanged by promotion. However, the varying nature of the promotions suggested an interactive effect. If it was not perceived by the individual as a dead end and in fact raised his level of aspiration, then work achievement tended to take on more importance. However, if the promotion attenuated the individual's level of aspiration, then family and other outside considerations took on greater importance.

Further support for the self-selection hypothesis is provided in a study by Vroom (1966), which tended to show that MBA students tend to select jobs that will complement their expressed need preferences. In sum, the major thrust of what little data there are is that expressed motives do not, generally speaking, seem to change a great deal as an individual rises in the organization.

Preferences Among Rewards, or First Level Outcomes

In addition to asking what motives or needs are most salient for managers, we might also ask what managers tend to prefer in terms of rewards or incentives. That is, which rewards are linked to which motives, and which rewards are most instrumental for satisfying specific needs?

Considerable evidence exists concerning the reward preferences of nonmanagement personnel (Davis, 1948; Jaques, Rice, & Hill, 1951; L. V. Jones & Jeffrey, 1964; Larke, 1953; Nealy, 1963; Watson, 1939; Worthy, 1950). The general conclusion to be drawn from all these studies is that nonmanagement, nonprofessional personnel in the United States tend to value job security, opportunities for advancement, interesting work, and interesting coworkers most highly. Financial rewards are usually fifth to eighth in the list. However, this may not be true of other countries (Ganuli, 1954; Wilkins, 1949, 1950).

Very few similar studies exist with regard to management samples. A 1947 study conducted by *Fortune* magazine presented managers with a choice among hypothetical jobs which varied along certain reward dimensions. Managers tended to prefer hypothetical jobs consisting of low security and high pay. In a questionnaire survey of 228 managers in five firms, I. R. Andrews and Henry (1964) found that subjects expressed much the same preference for high pay and low security. Working entirely within the context of compensation preferences, Mahoney (1964) sampled 459 managers in three firms and asked them how they would prefer to allocate their total compensation package among nine different alternatives. The results indicate a strong preference for straight salary and little interest in pensions, insurance, or vacations. There were few differences in preferences among the three firms, across hierarchical levels, or for managers of different ages.

In a very interesting study of individual reward orientations, Ghiselli (1968) built an indirect measure of outcome preferences via an item analysis procedure. Several hundred undergraduates were asked to describe themselves with an adjective checklist and at the same time to rate the importance of several different kinds of possible job outcomes. Adjectives were selected that differentiated between four sets of criterion groups which rated four different outcomes—job security, high financial reward, power over others, and self-actualization—as being of either high or low importance. The resulting four scales served as indirect preference measures for the four outcomes and were administered to a sample of 300 "men in general" and 400 middle managers. Compared with the general population, middle managers are low on preferences for job security and financial reward and high on self-actualization. The power-over-others scores were about the same for the two samples.

In sum, it seems fairly well established that on a self-report questionnaire, managers will say they prefer a high salary to guarantees of job tenure and fringe benefits. The indirect measures used by Ghiselli agree with this generalization on job security; however, they seem to contradict the notion that managers value high salaries.

There are no data available concerning what kind of trade-offs managers might make among other first level outcomes such as advancement, more interesting work, interesting coworkers, good working conditions, and the like.

The Effect of Incentives (Money) on Behavior

Beyond the questions of what motives are the most salient for managers and what preferences they have among outcomes or rewards, we must ask the more fundamental question of how various incentives and rewards affect actual behavior. Since the bulk of what data are available deals with the effects of pay, we shall devote the present discussion to money and treat other incentives in a later section.

Possible roles for money. Opsahl and Dunnette (1966) have summarized the possible roles that money might play, in a theoretical sense, in influencing the behavior of people in organizations. First, money could exist as a *generalized conditioned reinforcer* because of its repeated pairings with a number of primary reinforcers (food, housing, entertainment, etc.). In the terminology of our hybrid model, a conditioned reinforcer is analogous to a first level outcome, and a primary reinforcer is analogous to a second level outcome. Since the individual is probably in some sort of deprivation state at any given time, the application of money following a specific behavior should strengthen that type of behavior in the future. Second, money may act as a *conditioned incentive* which is perceived as being capable of satisfying certain needs. Again, the distinction between a reinforcer and an incentive is a temporal one. Money acts as an incentive before the response is made and as a reward after the response is made. The question is whether the incentive value or the reinforcement value has the greater effect on behavior. Third, in line with modifications of Hullian theory, J. S. Brown (1953, 1961) has postulated that money acts as an *anxiety reducer*. That is, a generalized drive or need to reduce anxiety underlies much of human behavior, and the acquisition of money becomes associated with anxiety reduction (also a second level outcome) at a number of points. Others have criticized this point of view (e.g., Harlow, 1953). In contrast to the above, Herzberg, et al. (1959) have proposed a fourth role for money. In effect, they say that money has no direct influence on behavior and can operate only to prevent or erase feelings of dissatisfaction. Lastly, the role given to money by Vroom's (1964) expectancy theory is in terms of its *instrumentality* for obtaining other outcomes. The expectancy view is distinguished not so much by its incompatibility with the above views as by its emphasis on expectancy as well as incentive value or valence. That is, the force money exerts on behavior is a multiplicative function of both the valence of money and the individual's estimate that the behavior will indeed be followed by the reward. Of course, making money contingent on behavior is implicit in the reinforcement, incentive, and anxiety-reduction views, but its explicit statement in terms of conscious awareness gives the expectancy point of view special appeal, we think, for dealing with motivation in organizations.

Early research on incentive payment. Since the incentive value of pay and its contingency on behavior are deemed so important on theoretical grounds, research on incentive payment plans in organizations should take on a high priority. In fact, there is a fair amount of field research comparing incentive and nonincentive payment plans among nonsalaried personnel. These findings have been thoroughly reviewed by Marriott (1957) and Viteles (1953). The general conclusion has been that incentive plans do tend to increase performance when they are instituted. However, the results of previous field studies are difficult to interpret since changes in work methods, supervisory behavior, and organizational structures frequently accompany the switch from nonincentive to incentive pay.

In contrast to the above findings, another body of evidence, again obtained on nonsalaried personnel, suggests that incentive plans may not realize their full potential in increasing performance because of the "rate restriction" phenomenon (Hickson, 1961; W. F. Whyte, 1952, 1955). Consideration of the conflict between these two lines of evidence, in light of our previous theoretical discussion, points up the horrendous complexity of trying to do field research on incentives. Obviously, the outcomes of money, job security, and co-worker approval may all have high valence. However, the expectancies concerning these outcomes are not independent and, in fact, may be negatively correlated. That is, people who place a high value on job security may tend to assign a low valence to money. We have no evidence concerning how individuals attempt to trade off these various incentives and maximize their overall benefit.

The above discussion must be restricted to nonsalaried groups. No data have been obtained from managerial samples. This is unfortunate in view of the fact that managers apparently place a high value on financial incentives and less value on job security.

Managerial pay curves. It is no secret that almost all organizations believe they are using money as an incentive and as a reward for managers. However, only about one-fifth of the 33 firms in our sample made any effort to tie incentive payment directly to the achievement of performance goals. It seems proper to ask whether there is any research evidence that attempts to determine whether organizations *do in fact* make pay increases contingent on performance. This is completely aside from the question of whether managers *perceive* improved performance or greater effort as leading to more money or whether the organization *intends* this to be the case. Data relating to this point will be discussed later.

Most of the available evidence is contained in one study by Brenner and Lockwood (1965) and a series of studies reported by Haire, Ghiselli, and Gordon (1967). The general procedure in these studies has been to obtain longitudinal data on managers' salary increases over a number of years. One can then search the data for clues as to how the organization has been using its financial reward package. For example, the slope of an individual's pay curve over time can be examined to determine what general salary level and size increase the organization has felt to be necessary to elicit whatever behavior it had in mind. The variability in pay from year to year gives some indication of the extent to which an organization chooses to differentiate among individuals at various stages of their careers. Also, the correlation of pay with pay across years (which reflects the way raises are administered) might give some indication of what the organization is trying to reward.

Haire et al. obtained data from three firms over approximately a twenty-five-year period, and Brenner and Lockwood dealt with one sample over a twenty-seven-year period. The only financial rewards considered were straight salary and salary increases. No bonuses, stock options, etc., were included. In general, the results indicate that managerial compensation follows a decidedly positively accelerated curve over time and becomes much more variable from year to year. That is, pay increases become larger and larger on the average but also much more variable. One could make the reasonable inference that organizations believe that a man's contribution to the company becomes progressively greater with time and that in the process he becomes much more easily distinguished from his associates. Given the same total amount of money, however, the firm could also choose to put people on a negatively accelerated curve. The motivational implications of the two curves are quite different. In the latter case, for example, larger raises early in a man's career might ensure that he will exert maximum effort toward his self-development and also that he will not leave the firm for a better-paying job elsewhere. A number of other such speculations could be generated.

More to the point of the current discussion are the data on the correlation of pay with pay. One can look at either the correlations between adjacent years or the correlations of some arbitrary base period salary with pay over successive years. The latter type of correlation is more relevant for our purpose. The pattern of these correlations is a function of the correlation of the size of raises with the original base period salary. If raises are assigned at random (the correlations equal zero), then a theoretical curve can be plotted which describes what the decrease in correlations should look like across successive years. Data for two of the three firms reported by Haire et al. tend to follow the random curve very closely. They conclude that, in these two firms at least, the size of the pay increase does not appear to depend on performance. If increases were dependent on performance, one would expect a smaller decrease in correlations from year to year. Conversely, since performance is certainly not perfectly consistent within individuals, one would not expect a perfect correlation from year to year. Something in between would lend the strongest support to the notion that organizations do indeed reward improvements in performance.

It should be remembered that the above data are limited to differential increases. They do not address the question of whether a salary increase versus no increase is related to performance. Nevertheless, these rather startling results suggest that firms and motivational theorists alike should reassess how pay is actually being used in organizations. If there is no contingency between behavior and money, the individual manager cannot be expected to respond as if there were.

Equitable versus nonequitable payment. It is unfortunate but true that there has been no *experimental* research using managerial samples that has examined the effects of incentives on job behavior. However, a number of studies have used students as subjects and have tried to "simulate" a job situation in some fashion. A series of such studies has been carried out within the context of equity theory for the purpose of determining the effects of underpayment and overpayment on behavior. Our discussion leans heavily on two recent reviews of equity research provided by Lawler (1969) and Pritchard (1969).

The original experimental work was carried out by Adams and his associates (Adams, 1963; Adams & Jacobsen, 1964; Adams & Rosenbaum, 1962; Arrowood, 1961). In this series there were a total of five experiments. In four of them the simulated job consisted of collecting marketing information via a brief interview with people on the street. That is, the students were hired as professional interviewers. In the fifth study subjects were hired to proofread manuscript copy. In each of these studies an experimental group was led to believe that they were very unqualified for the job but that since they were the only people available, they had to be hired anyway. This was labeled "overpayment." Both hourly payment and piece-rate wages were studied, and both quantity (number of interviews or number of pages) and quality (amount of information gathered in each interview or number of errors corrected per page) of performance were used as dependent variables.

The results from these five studies tend to support the following conclusions: Subjects who are made to feel overpaid under the hourly payment condition will increase the *quantity* of their production. Subjects who are made to feel overpaid under the piece-rate condition will decrease the *quantity* of their production and increase the *quality*. Both of these conclusions are in line with equity theory predictions. In the first instance, balance is restored by increasing the quantity of an individual's inputs. Under the piece-rate condition, increased production would lead only to more inequity because the higher financial return would produce even more overpayment. However, inputs can be brought into line by increasing the quality of work.

Notice, however, that in all the above studies overpayment was created by manipulating inputs—the individual's evaluation of his own qualifications. The wages paid actually seemed to be reasonable for that kind of work. Other types of inequity were not considered.

Two more recent studies (I. R. Andrews, 1967; Lawler & O'Gara, 1967) did investigate the effects of both overpayment and underpayment by manipulating the level of the financial reward (an output), not the perceived inputs. In the Andrews study subjects were paid on a piece-rate basis for one of two tasks, interviewing students or checking pages of data, and they were underpaid, overpaid, or equitably paid. Independent checks confirmed that the subjects perceived payment conditions as they were intended to. Lawler and O'Gara also used an interviewing task and a piece-rate wage system. Only the effects of underpayment versus equitable payment were studied, and inequity was again created by manipulating the outcome (piece rate) rather than the input (perceived self-image).

These two studies, which manipulated outputs instead of inputs, tend to support the findings of the early work but at a significantly weaker level. The Andrews data also suggest a greater behavioral effect for underpayment than overpayment. The Lawler and O'Gara data do not say anything about the effects of overpayment.

Further research by Lawler, Koplin, Young, and Fadem (1968) investigated the effects of overpayment over a lengthened time period. The task was again interviewing, and equity was manipulated by inducing the subjects to feel either qualified or underqualified. That is, inputs were manipulated, while the piece rate remained the same for all the subjects over three two-hour work periods. The usual effect of decreased quantity and increased quality for the overpaid group was found for the first work period, but this mode of inequity reduction was not continued over time. Rather, the subjects tended to change their perceptions of their qualifications to bring them in line with their outputs. Thus a subject who was originally induced to feel underqualified can earn more money (via the piece rate) and still reduce inequity if he reevaluates his qualifications (inputs) and sees them as being higher than he was originally led to believe.

Friedman and Goodman (1967) have considered another complicating factor when inequity is produced by manipulating subjects' perceptions of his qualifications (inputs). They point out that each subject has some perception of his own qualifications prior to being "hired" and that the interaction of these prior perceptions with the perceptions produced by the experimental manipulation must be considered. For example, a subject who feels well qualified to perform the job but who is told by his employer (i.e., the experimenter) that he is not should experience cognitive dissonance. One way to reduce the dissonance would be to do a "good job" and change the employer's opinion. To test this notion, Friedman and Goodman used the student interviewing task and compared an equitably paid group (hourly payment) with an overpaid group created by manipulating perceived qualifications. Overall, there was no difference between the two groups in quantity of work. However, when the sample was divided into those who originally felt qualified for the job and those who did not, the usual effect for overpayment under hourly rate conditions was found for the group who originally felt qualified. That is, those who originally felt qualified but were told they were not produced more. Thus if the experimental task is fairly simple and most subjects originally feel qualified, the increased production may be due to this mode of dissonance reduction.

Pritchard also reviews evidence from three correlational field studies (Clark, 1958; Homans, 1953; Patchen, 1961) that yield data appropriate for equity theory. The general procedure was to find naturally occurring samples which provided a comparison of equitable and nonequitable groups. However, while the results are in line with the theory, none of the studies used management samples, and the "dependent" variable in each case was job satisfaction or "feelings of inequity." Behavioral measures were not obtained.

In sum, the results of overpayment are perhaps not quite as clear as the original series of experiments by Adams and his associates seemed to indicate. In motivational terms, creating overpayment through manipulation of perceived inputs may have considerably different effects from those due to manipulation of outcomes. Also, the multitude of other ways in which inequity can arise and the numerous alternative methods for reducing inequity have not been explored. The available research addresses itself to only a very small subset of the total complex of critical questions.

A component of equity theory which has received some attention is the nature of the comparison process between the person and the Other. I. R. Andrews and Henry (1964) attempted to get at this question directly by asking a sample of managers from five firms to indicate who they used as a comparison or reference group. Their data indicate that a large portion of the subjects were most concerned with comparison groups outside the company. This trend was stronger for individuals at higher educational levels. In fact, satisfaction with pay was predicted better by an individual's relative pay standing within the entire sample than by his standing within his own company. Also, for higher level managers, pay comparisons with subordinates are more salient than comparisons with peers or superiors. For all levels, small differentials between the respondent and his subordinates were associated with greater dissatisfaction than large differentials between the respondent and his superior.

Approaching the question from a different angle, Lawler (1965) found that managers tend to overestimate the pay of managers at lower levels and also to overestimate the pay of individuals at the same level. Thus, because of the secrecy involved in management compensation, perceived inequities may be created where none actually exist. Equity theory would postulate that one way for the manager to reduce the inequity would be to reduce his effort. Unfortunately, there are no data available to suggest whether or not the secret nature of management compensation has a deleterious effect on performance.

The Effect of Incentives Other than Money on Behavior

In the context of managerial and administrative jobs, what other incentives are available besides money? Keeping the level of pay constant, we might speculate about the effects of such things as promotions, more interesting or challenging job assignments, feedback, more interesting coworkers, improved working conditions, and the like. For example, how does the *prospect* of a promotion affect job behavior? How does *obtaining* a promotion affect behavior? Does either the incentive or the reinforcement value of a more interesting task affect behavior? What is the *relative* effect of these outcomes when they function first as incentives and then as rewards?

There is a complete lack of data with regard to the behavioral effects of these outcomes, and we have no studies to cite.

Perceived Contingencies between Task Performance and Outcomes (Expectancy II)

Stimulus-response theory, expectancy theory, the instrumentality model, and common sense all stress the importance of the linkage between reward and the behavior being rewarded. That is, in order for an outcome to have a motivational effect, it must be directly contingent on the behavior. For example, if pay raises are handed out at random or as a function of seniority, then we should not expect pay to act as an incentive or reward for increasing effort. This consideration is in addition to that of whether or not the outcome (e.g., money) has positive valence for an individual at a particular time.

Aside from asking what actual behavior-outcome linkages exist in an organization, we can also ask how these contingencies are *perceived* by managers. It is the individual's perceptions that are of direct concern in the theoretical formulations we have discussed.

Lawler (1966b) surveyed managers from seven organizations, and the data strongly suggest that a very large percentage do not believe that pay raises and promotions are contingent on performance. Additional research by Lawler (1964) and Lawler and Porter (1967) examined how a global performance rating is related to a manager's perceived relationship between effort and such outcomes as pay and promotion. In both studies, managers who were rated high tended to see a higher relationship between behavior and outcomes. The same kind of result was found in a nonmanagement sample by Georgopolous, Mahoney, and Jones (1957).

Keep in mind that these studies are entirely correlational in nature. High performance may lead to a high perceived relationship between outcomes and performance rather than the perceived relationship leading to greater effort. More likely, low performance or low rewards might lead to an individual's rejection of the notion that outcomes are related to task performance.

The Nature of the Task as a Factor in Motivation

It seems obvious that the nature of the tasks making up the work role has a strong influence on an individual's motivation, as it operates through his expectancies of goal achievement. It is equally obvious that it is very difficult to define and operationalize what is meant by the "nature of the task." However, previous literature suggests at least three task factors that might be important:

1 *The kinds of skills required to perform the task.* Again, the important datum is the perception of the individual regarding how his skills match the task requirements.
2 *The general level of skill required to perform the task.* This is the same thing as goal difficulty or task difficulty. The question concerns how perceived goal difficulty influences behavior.
3 *The possible incentive value of successful goal accomplishment.* That is, the incentive value of good performance which is independent of its association with other rewards such as money, promotion, or recognition. Is good performance rewarding in and of itself?

In expectancy theory terms, the first two factors have relevance for the individual's expectancies for successful task accomplishment, and the third factor concerns the valence component. The only aspect of tasks to receive much research attention in a motivational context is the factor of level of difficulty. For example, few investigators have worried about the *motivational* implications of the "fit" between task requirements and the patterns of skills possessed by individuals.

The task goal as a mediator between incentives and behavior. In a series of related laboratory experiments, Locke and his associates (Locke, 1967; Locke & Bryan, 1966; Locke, Bryan, & Kendall, 1968) have attempted to demonstrate that the act of goal setting is the fundamental process by which an incentive exerts an effect on behavior. That is, it is a mediating process. Again, these data were not gathered from management samples, but they bear on questions which we feel have important implications for managerial behavior.

Subjects in almost all the experiments were male and female undergraduates, and the tasks which were used consisted of such things as simple addition, unscrambling the letters in scrambled words, building miniature windmills from Tinker Toys, and suggesting additional uses for common objects such as cardboard boxes. The tasks were such that 20 or more trials could be included in one experimental session. Subjects were usually given a series of practice trials to familiarize them with the task and provide the experimenters with a certain amount of normative behavior.

The general paradigm was as follows: After the experimental treatment (i.e., the incentive condition) was introduced, the subject was asked to state his intentions or goals for the next series of trials. Goal setting could thus be used either as a dependent variable, to assess the effects of different incentive conditions, or as an independent variable which might influence future performance. In this manner the way in which goal setting mediated the influence of incentives on behavior could be assessed. In some experiments the effects of specific goals set by the experiment were compared with those of instructions to "do your best." In one study the goals set by the subjects were measured retrospectively after the experiment had been completed.

The two incentives or rewards which have been studied to date are knowledge of results and incentive pay. As pointed out by Vroom (1964), knowledge of results can influence performance through its effect on either motivation or learning. In the case of learning, performance could be enhanced through identification of errors or the nature of the correct response. In the Locke studies learning effects were controlled by using simple tasks for which the correct methods are well known and by providing feedback only for blocks of trials and not for individual responses.

The following conclusions seem permissible from the data gathered in these experiments.

First, with such tasks the effects of knowledge of results are concomitant with differential goals used by the subjects. With goals held constant, knowledge of results did not produce differences in performance. This result was demonstrated in one a priori and one retrospective study. However, the question of whether feedback itself produces differences in performance goals has not been tested directly.

Second, relative to monetary incentives, two different types of goals were used and two kinds of performance measures. In two studies subjects were asked to state the *quantity* of work they were shooting for. The subsequent measure of performance was the actual quantity produced. In three other studies subjects were asked to state their *intention* regarding the difficulty level of the task they preferred. The dependent variable was then the actual difficulty of the tasks they chose (e.g., length of words to be unscrambled).

In the first two studies incentive payment had an almost but not quite statistically significant effect on the magnitude of the performance goals that were set and an even smaller effect on actual performance. However, the magnitude of the goal was significantly related to the level of actual performance.

In the other three studies incentive payment which was contingent on the number of tasks accomplished produced significant differences in both the intended difficulty and the actual difficulty of the tasks the subject selected. The direction of the changes was toward simpler tasks under the incentive condition. (The reward was for quantity, not quality.) However, with intentions held constant there were no significant efforts attributable to differences in incentive payment.

The effects of the piece rate were drastic if the subject had originally been given a set to be "achievement-oriented" and had not previously operated under an incentive condition. The analogy to the organization should be heeded. If managers are rewarded according to the goals they accomplish, then the organization must make certain that the goals represent desired behavior. In this example rewarding quantity had a very depressive effect on the difficulty of the tasks the subject chose to tackle.

In sum, the above studies suggest that incentives do not operate on behavior in some automatic, mechanical fashion, as traditional *S-R* theory might have us believe. There are conscious processes involved which tend to explain how the valence of an outcome acts on behavior.

The influence of task or goal difficulty.   We might expect perceptions of task difficulty to play a major role in organizational research on motivation because they are so directly analogous to the expected probability of success, or expectancy I, and because they have been a major part of cognitive theories for some time. Unfortunately, this seems not to be the case. In one of the few organizational studies available, data gathered in the AT&T organization suggest that if newly hired college graduates do not perceive their first job as challenging and in line with their abilities, this will lead to a higher turnover rate and perhaps to lower performance and effort (Berlew & Hall, 1966). This latter finding is discussed at some length in the next chapter.

Again we must turn to laboratory research for possible suggestions as to how task difficulty might influence behavior. We have already noted that managers as a group tend to score higher on *n* Ach than nonmanagers. Atkinson and his associates (summarized in Atkinson & Feather, 1966) have shown that subjects high on *n* Ach and low on fear of failure tend to prefer tasks of intermediate difficulty. The tasks most often used were games such as shuffleboard, ring tossing, or basketball shooting, where the difficulty of the task could be varied by varying the subjects' distance from the target. That is, other things being equal, the individual's motivation is greatest where the uncertainty of success is greatest, and this occurs where expectancy is equal to 0.50. There is some evidence (Atkinson, Bastian, Earl, & Litwin, 1960; Atkinson & Litwin, 1960) to suggest that the above may also be true for risk-taking or gambling behavior, where the individual's ability is not at issue. That is, people high in achievement motivation and low in fear of failure tend to prefer intermediate gambles (i.e., coin or die tossing), and people high in fear of failure tend to prefer either very low risk or very high risk. This finding is supported by Litwin and Ciarlo (1961), who asked supervisors and managers to make decisions in a business game where little information was available on which to base the decisions.

Also, evidence from a study by Litwin (1966) indicates that individuals high in n Ach will state higher expectancies of success for laboratory tasks when little objective information is available concerning the skills required for the tasks. This finding suggests that there may be measurable individual differences in type I expectancies under various conditions. If our hybrid model is any reflection of the true state of affairs, then an assessment of such individual differences is extremely important for understanding individual motivation in organizations.

The reader should keep in mind that the above results obtained within the context of the theory of achievement motivation deal primarily with choice behavior as a dependent variable and not effort or performance. Some additional studies by Locke, using the same sort of tasks described previously, have considered the influence of difficult versus easy goals on the amount of work performed (Locke, 1968). In one study, for example (Locke, 1966b), individuals who were equated on the practice trials were randomly assigned goals of varying difficulty for the task which involved listing additional uses for a common object. The results showed that the individuals assigned hard goals uniformly produced more over trials, even though they seldom reached the goal on any one trial (av. = 0.07) and their subjective probability estimate of reaching the goal was quite low (av. = 0.13). These results were essentially replicated in another study which utilized an addition task (Locke & Bryan, 1966). The same thing also tended to appear in Locke's (1966a) analysis of performance (nonmanagerial) in a training session. Those who, in retrospect, said they set high goals performed better than those who set low goals. In summary, Locke asserts that specific goals lead to higher performance than the directive to "do your best" and that specific difficult goals are better than specific easy goals.

Although Locke views his data as being in conflict with results from the Atkinson group, it is interesting to note that when subjects are given a choice of goals and are told to do as well as possible, they tend to set moderate goals (e.g., Locke, 1966b). Thus it is not inconsistent to say that people *prefer* tasks of intermediate difficulty but that a way to increase effort expediture is to increase goal difficulty.

However, if more difficult goals are used to increase performance, the individual must accept the new goal as a legitimate objective toward which to strive. While it may be easy for an experimenter to obtain such a commitment from college sophomores working on a laboratory task, it may not be quite so easy in an organizational setting. Organizations have historically used a number of methods to enhance commitment to higher task goals. The use of incentives is certainly one method. Punishment or reproof is another. "Participative methods" stemming from the human relations movement are yet another. Participative methods will be discussed in some detail in Chapter 17; however, their essential ingredient is that specific goals are set by group consensus, and therefore commitment is enhanced in some fashion. It follows from Locke's argument that these methods of obtaining commitment to higher goals will be effective only to the extent that the goals are specific and in some sense quantifiable by the individual.

We were able to find one study from an organizational setting which considered the influence of varying levels of task difficulty on managerial behavior. Stedry and Kay (1966) investigated the effects of differences in goal difficulty on supervisory performance in a manufacturing operation. The productivity of the supervisor's work group was taken as a measure of his performance. Two indexes were used, the ratio of actual direct labor time to the standard time. for a standard week's output (quantity) and the cost of repairing or replacing items found to be defective (quality). Two levels of difficulty were created by requiring supervisors to achieve either the 50th percentile or the 75th percentile of their weekly performance records over the previous twenty-six weeks. Supervisors were randomly assigned to one of four groups: (1) high difficulty for both criteria, (2) high difficulty for quantity and median difficulty for quality, (3) median difficulty for quantity and high difficulty for quality, and (4) median difficulty for both criteria. The difficulty levels were imposed by the supervisor's superior, and performance was then measured for a thirteen-week period. Soon after the new goals were implemented, the supervisors were also asked whether they perceived the new standards to be normal, challenging, or impossible. The most pronounced differences were found on the quality criterion. Judging the high difficulty standard as challenging led to a 28 percent *decrease* in defective items, while perceiving it as impossible led to a 35 percent *increase* in faulty units. The results were in the same direction but less pronounced for the quantity criterion. Being assigned two difficult standards led to an increase in perceptions of impossibility.

If we take the challenging versus the impossible judgment as an indication of the degree to which the supervisor accepted the new goal (level of difficulty), then both Locke's recommendation that specific hard goals increase performance and the difficulties involved in implementing it are supported. The Stedry and Kay data also make sense relative to the theory of need achievement. A "challenging" goal may be construed as neither an extremely easy nor an extremely difficult task situation.

Goal setting as task definition. In management circles the topics of goal setting (McGregor, 1960) and management by objectives have been popular for some years. At least for those sharing McGregor's point of view, the motivational implications are a major aspect of the goal-setting approach. That is, mutual goal setting between superior and subordinate is expected to elicit more commitment and effort on the part of the subordinate.

So far only one study has been done to test these notions in an organizational setting. H. H. Meyer, Kay, and French (1965) compared a traditional superior-oriented performance review with a mutual goal-setting approach in which there were more frequent discussions of performance, no summary ratings were made, salary review was *not* discussed, and the emphasis was on mutual problem solving, including both short- and long-term planning. The study had many shortcomings, as one might expect in a field experiment using relatively small samples, but a three-month follow-up seemed to indicate that the crucial influence on performance was not the mutual nature of the goal setting, but whether specific future performance goals had been set at all.

This finding is directly in line with Locke's point of view and is supported by some of the previously discussed laboratory experiments he conducted. Across several replications, the goal of "do your best" was compared with specific goals set by the experimenter. The specific goals were always set higher than the level reached during the practice trials, and they always produced greater performance than instructions to "do your best"; however, the differences between solving addition problems and the behavior of a General Electric manager must be considered.

With these kinds of data in mind we would like to argue that one could explain the effects of goal setting in cognitive as well as motivational terms. That is, the results point to the importance of the "definition" of the task to be performed. Setting specific goals should have the effect of making clear to the individual what it is he is supposed to do. This would be especially true in the organizational setting where specifying the nature of the problem is a good part of the manager's job. Certainly a lengthy goal-setting session between superior and subordinate would result in considerable discussion concerning what problems are important and what strategies might be fruitfully pursued to solve them. Thus goal setting, as opposed to a stark directive to do one's best, may have a lot to do with transforming a great deal of wheel spinning into efficient work, not because the individual would be more "motivated," but because he would have a much clearer idea of where to direct his effort. Given two individuals with an equal desire to expend effort, the individual with the greater specific knowledge concerning the nature of the organization's goals and their priorities should perform at a higher level.

Viewed from this angle, setting goals and "motivating" people are two different activities. There is first the problem of setting optimal goals (a cognitive activity) and then the problems of ensuring commitment to those goals (a motivational activity).

Managerial Motivation and Job Satisfaction

A good deal of research produced under the label of work motivation has used job satisfaction as a dependent variable rather than job behavior. By job satisfaction we mean the positive or negative aspect of an individual's attitude or feeling toward his job or some specific feature of his job. Job satisfaction is thus an internal attitudinal state and is usually assessed by means of a self-report questionnaire.

The distinction between general job satisfaction and specific job satisfactions tied to particular referents is an important one. A number of investigators have tried to break down the notion of general job satisfaction into relatively independent components (e.g., Ash, 1954; P. C. Smith, 1967; Weiss, Dawis, England, & Lofquist, 1967). The most common research strategy has been a factor analytic approach using data gathered from heterogeneous questionnaires designed to sample a wide range of specific attitudinal content. The objective is to group items into clusters or factors that are internally consistent (the items within a cluster intercorrelate highly) and maximally independent (low correlations between clusters). In order for the specific factors to have any scientific or practical importance, they must then show meaningful *differential* relationships with other variables. The internal consistency and independence of the factors supposedly result because the items in each factor reflect a common attitudinal referent in the job situation. Although the "structure" of job satisfaction thus conceptualized varies somewhat across studies, the similarities are more apparent than the differences. The referents which commonly appear are such things as pay, working conditions, supervisory practices, company policy, coworkers, opportunities for advancement, security, and the like.

Perhaps the one striking feature of the factors that have reappeared across studies is that they seem to reflect satisfaction with incentives or rewards in the job environment, or what we have been calling "first level outcomes." For this reason, it seems most meaningful to think of job satisfaction as a relative indicator of the presence or absence of certain outcomes. Several things must be kept in mind. First, high or low job satisfaction need not vary directly with the degree to which an individual's important needs are satisfied. For example, an individual may be very satisfied with his coworker relationships, but the needs for which that outcome is salient may not be very important in his motive structure. Nevertheless, a particular individual's needs certainly must play a part in determining his feelings about specific reinforcers in his job. This would explain the small but consistent relationship that job dissatisfaction has shown with voluntary turnover in nonmanagement samples. The reward level is not meeting the individual's needs, so he leaves. [1]

Second, job satisfaction need have no direct link with effort or performance. Job satisfaction reflects feelings about first level outcomes, or rewards, but rewards need not be contingent on behavior, at least performance-related behavior. Thus if rewards are not related to performance, job satisfaction will not be related to performance. We think this is reason enough for the preponderance of zero relationships that have been found in most studies that have attempted to correlate job satisfaction and productivity (Brayfield & Crockett, 1955; Herzberg et al., 1957; Vroom, 1964). We should add, however, that previous research on this relationship has dealt with nonmanagerial subjects. If rewards are more contingent on performance for managerial jobs, we might expect significant correlations.

Job satisfaction in management samples. There has been a fair amount of recent research dealing with correlates of managerial job satisfaction, but for two reasons we shall not discuss it in any detail. First, the job satisfaction variable is actually tangential to the topic of motivation, and second, extremely thorough and well-written summaries are available in Vroom (1964, 1965). We would like only to summarize Vroom's major conclusions:

1 In organizations, managers typically report higher general job satisfaction than nonmanagers. In fact, taking the labor force as a whole, the only group to show consistently higher satisfaction is that made up of members of the professions (Gurin, Veroff, & Feld, 1960). Higher level managers also tend to report more satisfaction than lower level managers (L. W. Porter, 1961, 1962; Rosen, 1961). Porter's measure is somewhat unique in that he took the difference between respondent judgments of the degree to which an outcome was actually present and the degree to which the individual felt it should be present. Porter's studies also indicate that line managers are slightly more satisfied than staff managers, especially on outcomes reflecting self-actualization.
2 A cross-cultural study using the Porter method (Haire et al., 1966) suggests that there are differential patterns of satisfaction on various dimensions across countries. The pattern seems more dependent on geography and culture than on the degree of industrialization of the country. Managers from the United States are *not* uniformly more satisfied than managers from other countries.
3 There is also some evidence to suggest that a manager's overall satisfaction is related to his perceived influence with his superior (Vroom, 1959, 1960).
4 The amount of money a manager receives is positively related to his general satisfaction and his satisfaction with pay (see, for example, I. R. Andrews & Henry 1964;

[1] See Vroom (1964) for a much more complete discussion of this point.

Mullen, 1954; L. W. Porter, 1964; P. C. Smith & Kendall, 1962). This is also true when management level is held constant (Lawler & Porter, 1963). However, with pay held constant, job satisfaction is negatively related to management level (Lawler & Porter, 1963). This suggests that equity considerations are important, and data from Patchen (1961) and Jaques (1961) tend to show that inequity is associated with dissatisfaction. The Andrews and Henry study further demonstrated that satisfaction with pay is more highly associated with differences relative to the industry norm than with differences between the individual's pay and that of other managers with the same firm.

In sum, most of the research on managerial satisfaction has been done on a very few dimensions. We know relatively little about how satisfaction with peer relationships, promotional opportunities, and the like correlate with other variables. Vroom (1965) also notes that little research has been done to try to relate personality and other measures of individual differences to job satisfaction. It would be interesting to find out how much of the variability in job satisfaction is due to differences in people rather than differences in rewards and to what extent there are interactive effects between the two.

Herzberg's two-factor hypothesis. Because it has generated so much discussion and research activity, the work of the Herzberg group probably deserves special mention. Recall that Herzberg and his associates (Herzberg, 1966; Herzberg et al., 1959) have rejected the notion of either a general job satisfaction factor or specific factors that represent continuous variables going from positive to negative satisfaction. Instead they postulate two continua, satisfaction and dissatisfaction, which are independent and which are influenced by different reinforcers or outcomes—the motivation and hygiene factors that were discussed previously.

Since the two-factor theory has been argued with a good deal of eloquence and also presents a manifestly simple hypothesis to test, it has stimulated a great deal of research. The available studies have been reviewed at various stages by R. J. Burke (1966); Dunnette, Campbell, and Hakel (1967); Lindsay, Marks, and Gorlow (1967); Herzberg (1966); House and Wigdor (1967); and Whitsett and Winslow (1967). The House and Wigdor paper includes the longest reference list, and the authors cite 30 empirical studies which have been directly concerned with the two-factor theory.

Since these authors review the available studies in some detail, we shall not attempt to duplicate their efforts here. However, we should note that they do not draw the same conclusions from reading the same literature. Unfortunately, whether or not the data lend support to the theory seems to depend to a large extent on the type of methodology which is used. There are also questions concerning whether or not some investigators have based their research on legitimate predictions from the theory (Whitsett & Winslow, 1967).

What can be concluded from the past research? If the empirical studies are examined in total, the negative evidence would appear to have an edge because it has been generated from a wider variety of approaches. Conversely, Whitsett and Winslow (1967) point out what they consider to be fundamental flaws in the negative evidence. Their major reason for disregarding most of the negative evidence is that it was generated from one or more misinterpretations of the two-factor theory. Thus if both motivators and hygiene factors are shown to correlate positively with overall job satisfaction, this is of no consequence as a test of the theory because the theory implies nothing about overall job satisfaction.

The most meaningful conclusion that we can draw is that the two-factor theory has now served its purpose and should be altered or respectfully laid aside. Theories are never true or false, but exhibit only varying degrees of usefulness. The Herzberg theory has stimulated a great deal of argument and considerable research activity. On these grounds it has been useful. However, on the basis of the data that it has generated, it also seems to be an oversimplification. Repeated factor analytic studies of job attitudes have failed to demonstrate the existence of two independent factors corresponding to motivators and hygienes. There are multiple job satisfaction factors, and their degree of dependence or independence has not been firmly tied down. In addition, Herzberg's own data, together with those of others, demonstrate that both motivator and hygiene items appear as elements in satisfying events and that both appear as elements in dissatisfying events. On the question of asymmetry, the factors Herzberg labels "motivators" are associated with job satisfaction to a greater extent than hygienes. However, the results with regard to job dissatisfaction remain equivocal. Finally, the fundamental postulate concerning the independence of job satisfaction and job dissatisfaction has never really been tested, by either Herzberg's supporters or his critics. In sum, we are now ready for a more complex and interactive view of the antecedents of job attitudes, and that is where future effort should be directed. As a final point, we would like to reiterate that in the empirical sense the Herzberg "theory" has only been concerned with job satisfaction and dissatisfaction and not with job behavior.

SUMMARY

By generalizing from rather diverse sources and ignoring the fact that much of the above research is not based on managerial samples, we can list the following as research questions that *have* been investigated relative to managerial motivation:

1 As expressed via self-report questionnaires and projective tests, a considerable amount of attention has been given to which needs and motives (second level outcomes) are most salient for managerial samples. Managers tend to value esteem,

382 Managerial Behavior, Performance, and Effectiveness

autonomy, and achievement rather than security or social relationships. The pattern of differences in expressed needs seems to be the same for different management levels as for managers versus nonmanagers and good versus poor managers.

2 A small amount of information is available concerning the expressed preferences of managers for various types of pay plans (first level outcomes). In general, managers tend to prefer their compensation in straight salary rather than in various types of fringe benefits. However, this generalization is based on rather limited information, and there may be a substantial discontinuity in preferences as salary increases. At the lower salary levels there might be a greater preference for fringe benefits and other rewards instrumental for satisfying the need for security, while at higher levels money could take on greater instrumentality for status and achievement needs. Salary level has not been controlled in previous research.

3 An even smaller fund of knowledge concerns the degree to which rewards are *in fact* contingent on behavior in organizations. Correlational data from Haire et al. (1967) suggest that they are not. In our own survey of 33 firms we found very little evidence that money was actually being used as an incentive linked to performance.

4 Some research attention has been given to the perceived contingencies between behavior and rewards (expectancy II) that managers have. The picture is not encouraging. Even if it is there, the link is seldom perceived. If basic experimental psychology has demonstrated anything, it is that contingent rewards have more predictable effects than noncontingent rewards. Much more needs to be learned about how individual perceptions of type II expectancies develop and what influences them.

5 Laboratory experiments using students as subjects have considered the effects of overpayment and underpayment as compared with those of equitable payment. Different effects are observed for hourly versus incentive payment and for manipulation of inputs (perceived qualifications) versus manipulation of outputs (pay level). In general, underpayment results in decreased output, and overpayment in increased output, except under the incentive payment condition, where changes in output would produce even more inequity. With overpayment via incentives the usual result has been an increase in quality rather than quantity. The above results have been less clear-cut when outputs have been manipulated rather than inputs. Predictions from equity theory are made very difficult by the complexity of the variables making up the input-output package and the multitude of ways in which inequity can be resolved. However, the theory presents a clear warning to organizations that they must learn a great deal more about the nature of the input-output comparisons and the way they develop and change.

6 A much larger body of laboratory experimentation has focused on goal setting and goal (task) difficulty (expectancy I) as mediators of rewards and determinants of effort expenditure and choice behavior. Several studies (Locke, 1968) have suggested that rewards or incentives (first level outcomes) have behavioral effects only to the extent that specific goals are set for the task. An even larger group of laboratory studies have demonstrated that, other things being equal, specific goals increase output to a greater extent than general directions to "do your best" and that specific difficult goals increase output to a greater extent than moderately difficult goals. General support for the laboratory results has been found in two field studies. In sum, the effects of goal setting are difficult to deny. Important questions still remain concerning how goals should be set and how commitment to

the goal should be ensured. While these questions may not be critical in the laboratory setting, they present severe problems for the organization. Also, it is not entirely clear whether the effects of goal setting should be given a motivational or a cognitive interpretation. Perhaps goal setting works because it helps define the task for the individual (a cognitive activity) rather than stimulate greater effort (a motivational process).

7 Considerable recent research effort has been expended toward studying the correlates of managerial job satisfaction, and a fair amount of knowledge has accumulated as to how job satisfaction varies with management level, salary, tenure, functional specialty, and the like. We would like to say again that studies which utilize job satisfaction as a dependent variable have only a tangential relationship to the topic of motivation, as we have outlined it, and will not be discussed further.

The above results, although helpful for understanding managerial behavior, cover only a small portion of the total range of questions suggested by our previous discussion of motivation theory. There are virtually no available data concerning many relevant questions. Some of the more important are discussed below:

- What kinds of preferences do managers have for first level outcomes (rewards) other than money? We have no empirical knowledge of how managers would trade off various external rewards such as salary increases, promotions, special forms of recognition, or different job duties. Perhaps more serious is our lack of knowledge concerning the trade-offs between external and internal rewards.
- The nature of the task governing a manager's behavior is central to understanding his motivation; however, the nature of the management job remains an undifferentiated mass. We still view management performance as a very global variable.
- Several interesting questions revolve around the relative contribution of expectancy I, expectancy II, and valence to the "motivation" of individuals. That is, which one has the most influence in a given situation?
- The development of type I and type II expectancies presents a research problem of considerable difficulty but great importance. Several studies have already shown the behavioral importance of these variables. It remains to be discovered how they come about and how they are influenced by various factors in the organization.
- Given the pervasive effects of goal setting, the question still remains of how to ensure an individual's commitment to the goal in optimal fashion.
- At a more basic research level we could ask how first level outcomes attain a particular valence. That is, for what needs are certain outcomes instrumental, and what valence do individuals assign to particular needs?

In discussing unanswered research questions, we must also keep in mind that few generalizations can be made which will be true for all people in all situations. Individual and situational differences must be taken into account early in the research enterprise, or little that is meaningful for organizations will result.

In sum, even though the study of managerial motivation in organizations presents horrendous problems, we feel there is more reason for optimism that pessimism. There is a sufficient body of theory (or quasi theory) to suggest meaningful research questions, and enough empirical research yielding meaningful results has already been done to hold out a great deal of promise for the future acquisition of knowledge.

Chapter 16: Environmental Variation and Managerial Effectiveness

Unfortunately, this chapter will be relatively data-free. We shall discuss a class of variables for which everyone suggests the need for research is great—but actual empirical activity is sparse. Consequently, most of the following material will be oriented around taxonomic problems and suggestions for what *should* be known.

So far we have discussed three classes of variables in terms of their relationships to managerial effectiveness: (1) predictors, or individual differences developed before the manager was selected for his position; (2) experimental treatments, in the form of training and development programs; and (3) organizational rewards, or motivators. However, the model of managerial behavior discussed in Chapter 2 suggests the importance of a fourth class of variables that we have labeled "situational determinants" or "environmental determinants." Since so little empirical data are available, it is proper to ask why these kinds of variables are felt to be so crucial in the prediction and explanation of management performance. There are perhaps three reasons. First, the other three classes of variables have never been able to account for much more than half the variability in measures of managerial effectiveness. In the majority of instances it has been much less than that (see Chapter 8). Much of what remains unexplained *must* be a function of differences in environmental or situational characteristics. Second, the sketchy empirical evidence that does exist suggests significant environmental effects. Third, there simply seems to be a consensus that the situation "makes a difference." It could not be any other way.

SOME PROBLEMS OF DEFINITION

It is difficult to specify what is meant by a "situational variable." Being realistic about the matter, defining such a characteristic as any variable which has relevance for management performance but which has not yet been discussed in this volume would probably be more descriptive than any other specification. Beyond this, perhaps a few additional points can be made.

The class of determinants we have in mind includes such things as the structural properties of organizations (e.g., organization size or number of levels of supervision), the psychological "climate" (e.g., pressure for production, perceived reward system, individual autonomy), industry characteristics (e.g., growth industry, competitive, tight labor market), and the specified role characteristics of the management job (e.g., formal power, procedural rules, constraints). They are properties not of individuals but of environments. Specific individuals will perceive these properties differently; however, a significant environmental effect must remain if it is to be labeled a situational variable. In analysis of variance terms, the total variability in behavior must not be explained entirely by (1) differences between individuals and (2) error. Some variability in management performance must be attributable to differences in the environmental variable, to the interaction between the environmental characteristic and individual differences, or to both. Perhaps an analogy to the weather is appropriate. Differences in temperature, precipitation, and wind velocity are general characteristics of the environment which exert an effect on an individual's behavior (e.g., he adds antifreeze to the radiator). Significant differences attributable to weather persist, even though particular individuals interpret the same conditions differently. For example, heavy snow means more indoor activity for most people but increased outdoor activity for some, and what is a "warm" day for one person may be a "comfortable" day for another. Even if there were no "average" effects on behavior due to differences in weather, it would still be an environmental variable in our terminology, if there was an interaction effect. For example, some people may become less active and some more active as the temperature changes, but the average activity level of the population stays the same.

Given the existence of a situational effect, a number of methodological and conceptual problems arise. These include such things as the form of the relationships, the processes involved, the loci of the situational variables, and the means used to measure them.

Predictors versus moderators. It is very easy to speak of situational or environmental "determinants" of managerial performance as if the linkage of environmental differences to behavior was easily understood and the causal nature of the relationships was known or could be assumed. Obviously, at the present time it is more proper to speak of correlates than determinants, even though a few experimental studies do exist. What is perhaps not so obvious is a corresponding ambiguity in the form of the correlational relationship between a situational variable and a measure of performance.

Can an environmental variable be used as a predictor of behavior, or should a direct relationship with performance be ruled out? Would it make better sense to conceive of environmental characteristics as a "moderator" of the relationship between characteristics of individuals and their performance on the job? Another way of phrasing the question is to ask whether situational variables combine additively or interactively with the previously discussed correlates (e.g., individual differences) of performance. For example, does an autonomous environment enhance or detract from everyone's performance in similar fashion, and are differences in autonomy thereby correlated with performance, or is there an interactive relationship, with particular individual differences correlated with performance only for certain levels of autonomy? The distinction is crucial in terms of how research on situational variables should be pursued and the kinds of data that should be collected. Further, successful a priori specification of the nature and magnitudes of the relationships would add considerably to the theoretical understanding of environmental characteristics. To date, the nature of the linkage between situational variables and job behavior has not been very well conceptualized.

How the environment influences the individual. Forehand and Gilmer (1964) discuss the problem of specifying how organizational environment differences are translated to differences in behavior. They mention three mechanisms:

1 *Definition of stimuli.* Environmental characteristics such as the structure of an organization, the implicit theories held by its management, or the economic condition of the industry have considerable influence on the relevant stimuli which impinge on an individual in his work role. For example, a shrinking market may elicit managerial skills associated with holding cost down, preventing waste, and increasing market share rather than those concerned with increasing production and developing new products.

2 *Constraints upon freedom.* Certain attributes of the situation may actually prevent certain behaviors from occurring. The structure of the organization may place a

number of restraints on management communication or the degree of autonomy. Such structurally imposed constraints may be either deleterious or facilitative, relative to performance effectiveness.

3 *Reward and punishment.* Besides influencing what sorts of stimuli will be perceived and what types of responses are permitted, the environment can also specify the reinforcement contingencies for various managerial behaviors. It seems intuitively obvious that the situation should help determine the behavior-reward contingencies in an organization. For example, a manager in a very autonomous organization would make much broader decisions without consulting his superior than a comparable manager in a very nonautonomous organization. The situation is one in which a great deal of independent action is rewarded. Supposedly, a lack of independent action would be punished in some fashion.

The situation a manager is in should also affect his behavior by arousing various motives. If we consider the theory of need achievement, people have a certain "amount" of different needs (e.g., n Ach, n Aff, n Pow) which are relatively permanent characteristics. However, for these motives or needs to have a significant effect on behavior, they must be aroused. In this formulation scores on need for achievement will not predict performance unless the situation arouses this need by inducing cognitions of competition with a standard of excellence. The essential point is whether different situations elicit or arouse different needs. It would seem quite likely that this is the case. For example, the need for power might be elicited more in one organization than in another.

These effects on behavior must also be considered in relation to individual differences. People have different needs and see various outcomes as more or less desirable, and these differences must be considered. As Litwin and Stringer (1966) point out, different individuals may expect different rewards and punishments for various kinds of behavior. Climate, for example, should not act in the same way for all individuals as an arouser of needs or motives.

This type of interaction has received considerable attention relative to the academic setting. Pace and Stern (1958) have suggested that the congruence between individual student needs and particular characteristics of the academic environment (i.e., potential rewards) is the focal process for explaining student achievement and change. However, as pointed out by Pervin (1968), recent research in educational settings has further suggested that a close congruence between the reinforcement patterns of the organizations and individual needs may have negative effects on performance if the individual has a negative self-image. Obviously, the interaction is a complex one.

Organizational versus extraorganizational variables. One distinction that has not generally been made in the literature is that between variables which are properties of organizations themselves (e.g., degree of centralization) and variables which characterize the outside environment (e.g., geographic location or competitiveness of the industry). Such a distinction may be important for several reasons. If an organization wants to alter the behavior of its managers by changing the situation, these two classes of variables would require drastically different approaches. It would be helpful to know which is the most salient. The appropriate prediction models may also differ. Perhaps the properties of the extraorganizational environment operate to a much greater extent as moderators or sources of interactive effects than as main effects or determinants of performance. Lastly, the methods used for measuring these two classes or variables may be far different.

Objective versus perceptual. Finally, a distinction is necessary between perceptual and objective measures of situational characteristics. The two measurement processes of (1) asking an individual how he perceives his environment and (2) defining situational variables a priori and measuring them independently yield variables of a very different order. The central issue is whether the determiner of significant effects is the situation as it actually is or as it is perceived. In the psychological literature there is considerable evidence suggesting that actual awareness of stimuli and reinforcement patterns is not necessary for behavior change to take place. There is also evidence to show that the perceived situation has a greater effect than what is actually the case. The distinction is crucial, and we shall consider it again later in this volume.

DIMENSIONAL ANALYSES OF SITUATIONAL VARIABLES

Perhaps the most frustrating feature of an attempt to deal with situational variables in a model of management performance is the enormous complexity of the environment itself (Sells, 1963). It makes the definition and measurement of situational characteristics very difficult, and a fruitful taxonomy of environments is the key to unraveling this portion of our model. Although it is here that a certain amount of empirical work has been done, the surface has barely been scratched.

Researchers concerned with a taxonomy of situational characteristics have borrowed heavily from the methodology of differential psychology and have made considerable use of the factor analytic approach. In so doing they have tended to use the term "organizational climate" in place of "environment" or "situation."

Climate Factors

One way to get a firmer grasp on the concept of organizational climate is to consider some potential properties of climate. Forehand and Gilmer (1964) feel that climate consists of a set of characteristics that describe an organization, distinguish it from other organizations, are relatively enduring over time, and influence the behavior of the people in it. Georgopoulos (1965) speaks of a normative structure of attitudes and behavioral standards which provide a basis for interpreting the situation and act as a source of pressure for directing activity. Litwin and Stringer (1966) add the notion that these properties must be perceivable by the people in the organization and that an important aspect of climate is the "patterns of expectations and incentive values that impinge on and are created by a group of people that live and work together." H. H. Meyer (1967) expands on one aspect of the Litwin and Stringer definition by suggesting that climate arises as the result of the style of management, the organization's policies, and its general operating procedures. Gellerman (1959) feels the goals and tactics of the men whose attitudes "count" are a significant determiner of climate.

From this collection of properties, components, and determiners that various authors feel contribute to climate, we might define climate as a set of attributes specific to a particular organization that may be induced from the way that organization deals with its members and its environment. For the individual member within the organization, climate takes the form of a set of attitudes and expectancies which describe the organization in terms of both static characteristics (such as degree of autonomy) and behavior-outcome and outcome-outcome contingencies.

When organizational climate is defined in this way, it can be seen that many kinds of organizational factors are potentially relevant contributors to it. The crucial elements are the individual's perceptions of the relevant stimuli, constraints, and reinforcement contingencies that govern his job behavior. For this reason, the basic data used by a number of investigators to organize a taxonomy of "climate" factors are individual perceptions of organizational properties.

For example, Litwin and Stringer (1966) report a questionnaire developed to measure organizational members' perceptions in six different areas:

1 *Structure.* Perceptions of the extent of organizational constraints, rules, regulations and "red tape"
2 *Individual responsibility.* Feelings of autonomy, of "being one's own boss"
3 *Rewards.* Feelings related to being confident of adequate and appropriate rewards—pay, praise, special dispensations—for doing the job well
4 *Risk and risk taking.* Perceptions of the degree of challenge and risk in the work situation
5 *Warmth and support.* Feelings of general good fellowship and helpfulness prevailing in the work settings
6 *Tolerance and conflict.* Degree of confidence that the climate can tolerate differing opinions

These dimensions proved to distinguish among various organizational subunits and have been incorporated into some experimental studies to be reviewed in a later section.

A broader and somewhat more systematic study of climate dimensions is described by B. Schneider and Bartlett (1968). The research sites were a group of sales agencies making up two different insurance companies. An item pool of 299 items describing various characteristics of the agencies was administered to 143 management personnel, and the responses were factor analyzed. Among other things, the respondents were asked to indicate what managers did in the agencies, what agents did, how people were treated, and what kinds of people were in the agencies. Thus, the 143 managers were not describing their own climate (i.e., the organization above them), but what they perceived the climate of the organization below them to be. Schneider and Bartlett admit the possible biasing effect of having managers describe their own agencies.

Six factors emerged. Their labels and descriptions are given below:

1 *Managerial support.* Similar to the factor of consideration found in the Ohio State studies. It refers to managers taking an active interest in the progress of their agents, backing them up with the home office, and maintaining a spirit of friendly cooperation.
2 *Managerial structure.* Refers to the manager requiring agents to adhere to budgets, be knowledgeable regarding sales material, and produce new customers. It tends to be a "sales-or-else" factor.
3 *Concern for new employees.* Most of the items are typified by a concern for the selection orientation, and training of a new agent.
4 *Intra-agency conflict.* Refers to the presence of ingroups or outgroups within an agency and the undercutting of managerial authority by the agents.
5 *Agent independence.* These items describe agents who tend to run their own business and do not pay much attention to management.
6 *General satisfaction.* Refers to the degree to which the agency sponsors periodic social get-togethers and the agents express satisfaction with various management and agency activities.

The final form of the questionnaire contains 80 items for the six factors. At a conceptual level Schneider and Bartlett view the agency climate factors both as possible predictors of later performance and as potential moderators of the relationship between selection information and performance measures. In the predictor instance an individual would be asked to respond with his preferences for climate characteristics and/or his expectancies, and they could then be correlated with later performance.

The climate factors derived in the above two efforts are meant to generalize across the perceptions of all individuals in the organization. In contrast, the two studies described below were specifically aimed at specifying climate dimensions as perceived by managers.

Taguiri (1966) asked a small sample of managers participating in a Harvard management course to name the things that "mattered most" to them in their organizations. From their replies, he developed a standardized questionnaire which he administered to a larger sample of managers and then factor analyzed their responses. Five factors resulted:

1 Practices related to providing a sense of direction or purpose to their jobs—setting of objectives, planning, and feedback
2 Opportunities for exercising individual initiative
3 Working with a superior who is highly competitive and competent
4 Working with cooperative and pleasant people
5 Being with a profit-minded and sales-oriented company

One phase of a large study on role conflict reported by Kahn, Wolfe, Quinn, Snoek, and Rosenthal (1964) also bears on the dimensional analysis of climate. During the course of the study, 53 "focal" supervisory and management positions were selected to represent the full spectrum of the managerial hierarchy. Next, an average of seven "role senders" (usually superiors and subordinates) were chosen for each focal position on the basis of the closeness of their interaction. The role senders were then asked to respond to 36 questionnaire items indicating the degree to which they advocated compliance or noncompliance with normative or expected *role* behaviors on the part of the focal individuals. The responses were factor analyzed, and five factors seemed to emerge: (1) rules orientation, or the degree to which company-oriented rules are followed; (2) the nurturance of subordinates, or communicating and consulting with subordinates, taking an interest in them, and taking responsibility for their training morale; (3) closeness of supervision, or supervising the work pace and work methods of subordinates; (4) universalism, or the degree to which the individual should identify with the organization as a whole rather than with his particular work group; and (5) promotion-achievement orientation, or the degree to which an individual should try to take advantage of every opportunity for promotion, try to make himself look good in the eyes of his superiors, and come up with original ideas for handling work.

It is extremely difficult to draw generalizations from an integration of the results of these four studies. The individual perceptions which make up the data were obtained from vastly different orientations, or "sets." Taguiri asked managers to rate *the importance,* or valence, of various organizational characteristics in terms of their motivating properties. Kahn *et al.* asked individuals (not necessarily managers) to indicate what a particular manager *should do* relative to a specific set of role behaviors. The implication is that respondents felt such role characteristics were necessary for the effective operation of the organization. In contrast, the Schneider and Bartlett items asked managers to *describe* their work groups.

A synthesis. Even though these are very different sets relative to what was required of the respondents, a good deal of communality seemed to result, at least in the outward appearance of the factors. All the studies yielded either five or six factors, and at least four seem to be common across all the investigations. Our composite view of these recurring factors is as follows:

1 *Individual autonomy.* This is perhaps the clearest composite and includes the *individual responsibility, agent independence,* and *rules orientation* factors found by Litwin and Stringer, Schneider and Bartlett, and Kahn et al., respectively, and Taguiri's factor dealing with opportunities for exercising individual initiative. The keystone of this dimension is the freedom of the individual to be his own boss and reserve considerable decision-making power for himself. He does not have to be constantly accountable to higher management.

2 *The degree of structure imposed upon the position.* Litwin and Stringer's *structure;* Schneider and Bartlett's *managerial structure;* Taguiri's first factor dealing with direction, objectives, etc.; and Kahn et al.'s *closeness of supervision* seem similar enough to be lumped under this label. The principal element is the degree to which the objectives of, and methods for, the job are established and communicated to the individual by superiors.

3 *Reward orientation.* Another meaningful grouping includes Litwin and Stringer's *reward* factor; Schneider and Bartlett's *general satisfaction* factor, which seems to convey reward overtones; Kahn *et al.*'s *promotion-achievement orientation;* and Taguiri's being with a profit-minded and sales-oriented company. These factors do not hang together quite as well as the previous two groups and seem to vary a great deal in breadth. However, the reward element appears to be present in all.

4 *Consideration, warmth, and support.* This dimension lacks the clarity of the previous three. Managerial support from the Schneider and Bartlett study and nurturance of subordinates from Kahn et al. seem quite similar. Litwin and Stringer's *warmth* and *support* also seems to belong here since apparently this is a characteristic attributable to supervisory practices. Taguiri's mention of working with a superior who is highly competitive and competent does not fit quite so easily, but nevertheless seems to refer to the support and stimulation received from one's superior. However, the human relations referent is not as clear as in the factors derived from the other studies.

It is tempting to label a fifth group and include Litwin and Stringer's "tolerance of conflict," Schneider and Bartlett's "presence of conflict," Taguiri's "working with cooperative and pleasant people," and Kahn et al.'s "universalism." All these factors seem to represent interpersonal relationships between peers, but from somewhat different perspectives. The Schneider and Bartlett and the Taguiri factors appear to fall on opposite ends of the same continuum, a kind of "cooperativeness" dimension, while the Litwin and Stringer factor reflects more of a willingness to be honest and open about interpersonal conflict, and the Kahn et al. factor represents the effect of group identification on how interpersonal relationships are handled.

A question that might be asked at this point concerns whether the comparability that does seem to exist should be a cause for rejoicing. Probably not. The factors or clusters that result from a dimensional analysis are a function of the types of individual measures that were initially included in the study.

Even though the sets required of the respondents were different, perhaps the content of the stimuli (items) was very similar across the four studies. Also, the relatively small number of factors which were found implies that a great deal of environmental variation remains to be uncovered. The tendency for researchers to cull items from the previous literature, especially that relating to studies of job satisfaction or job attitudes, may contribute to both of the above shortcomings.

Other Climate Taxonomies (Nonmanagerial)

Two other lines of evidence bear on a taxonomy of climate, although neither deals directly with the organizational environments of managers. One of these is the factor analytic work relating to the descriptions of small groups (Findikyan & Sells, 1965; Hemphill & Westie, 1950), and the other involves the description of environmental variation in educational institutions (Astin & Holland, 1961; Halpin & Croft, 1963; Hutchins & Nooneman, 1966; Pace & Stern, 1958).

Sells and his associates are in the beginning stages of a long-range program to develop measures for a broad taxonomy of environmental variables. One research avenue is the expansion of Hemphill's description of small group environments to a description of organizational environments. Hemphill and Westie (1950) originally developed 13 factors for the description of group behavior by sifting through the small group literature for descriptive items and using expert judgment to reduce an original item pool of 350 items to a total of 150. The 150 items were then "factored" into the 13 clusters on the basis of an approximation method which did not require an intercorrelation matrix for all 150 items.

Findikyan and Sells (1965) administered the items to 967 Texas Christian University undergraduates and graduate students in 60 campus organizations and factor analyzed the complete matrix. Twenty-two meaningful factors emerged, and the next steps are to develop more measures within each of the clusters and redo the analysis on industrial and military organizations. It is interesting to note that while most of the factors identified in the climate studies were found in this study as well, a number of other dimensions with different sorts of referents also emerged. Although the theoretical or empirical utility of these dimensions remains to be demonstrated, the heuristic benefit of using a different source of initial measures is substantial.

Research aimed at describing the environments of professional schools, colleges, and universities is somewhat more plentiful. The aim of such research is to describe the situation with reference to the student, and the labels placed on the dimensions bear little resemblance to those appropriate for the study of managerial effectiveness. However, the methodologies employed and the nature of the research objectives might be of interest.

Astin and Holland (1961) and Hutchins and Nooneman (1966) have attempted to develop descriptive dimensions of universities and medical schools, respectively. Their common methodological theme is the use of measures which have no within-organization variation. Astin and Holland developed objective measures of the personal or vocational orientations of the students (e.g., percentage of students in various degree areas), while Hutchins and Nooneman used a questionnaire approach (i.e., perceptions) and averaged the responses of students at each institution to each item. The item averages constituted the basic data, which were submitted to a factor analysis using observations from a wide variety of medical schools. Thus in these and other studies of school environments, the danger that the taxonomy might represent individual rather than situational variation seems to have been better controlled than in the studies of managerial climates.

Second, there has been a certain amount of effort devoted to building up construct validity for the descriptions of school environments by predicting correlations with other variables. For example, Astin (1963) was able to show that perceptual measures of student orientations were related in the predicted manner to his objective measures, and Skager, Holland, and Braskamp (1966) demonstrated that colleges with different orientations tended to produce predicted changes in a student's ratings of himself and his life goals as he progressed from his freshman to his senior year. Astin was also able to show that his objective measures were meaningfully related to the College Characteristics Index (Pace & Stern, 1958), which is a questionnaire measure of environmental variables. Hutchins and Nooneman devoted considerable effort to examining the relationships between their environmental dimensions and the average student scores on the Medical College Admission Test, the Allport-Vernon Lindzey Study of Values, and the Edwards Personal Preference Schedule. In a sense, these latter relationships should offer some clue as to how the general characteristics of the student body influence perceptions of environmental characteristics.

Lastly, the researchers interested in school environments have tried to utilize a certain amount of psychological theory to suggest which aspects of the environment were relevant. For example, in writing items for the College Characteristics Index, Pace and Stern (1958) utilized Murray's theory of individual needs and environmental press (Murray, 1938) to suggest the types of stimuli generated by the organization that would be important for the individual. Also, the objective orientation measures used by Astin and Holland (1961) were suggested by Holland's (1959) theory of vocational choice and its predictions concerning the relationships between choice and personality.

Thus the present research on university environments seems to be characterized by attempts to (1) remove within-situation variation, (2) adopt the multimethod approach, and (3) utilize previous theory where appropriate. Analogous research on managerial environments would do well to incorporate these elements.

The above studies seem to constitute the currently available supply of *empirical* attempts to derive a taxonomy of relevant environmental or situational variables. Obviously, the individual measures which have been used represent only a very limited sample of the available population. Perceptual indexes have been employed almost exclusively, and little attention has been given to classifying structural characteristics or objective situational measures.

A priori classification.   There do exist a number of a priori attempts to classify structural or objective situational variables. We shall not attempt to mention all of these, but a few examples will give the flavor. Probably the most widely quoted categorization of structural components is the one given by L. W. Porter and Lawler (1965). They mention seven such properties:

Intraorganizational
1 Hierarchical level within the organization
2 Line versus staff
3 Span of control
4 Size of organizational subunit to which the individual belongs

Interorganizational
5 Total size of organization
6 Organizational shape (tall versus flat), i.e., the number of organizational levels per capita
7 Centralized versus decentralized organization

Studies where one or more of the above variables were related to measures of job attitudes or job behavior were reviewed, and Porter and Lawler concluded that the variable of hierarchical level led the field in variance accounted for. However, most relationships were small, and the dependent variable was almost always a measure of job satisfaction. Few studies employing a measure of performance were found.

Again on an a priori basis, Evan (1963) has attempted to conceptualize the hierarchical nature of organizations and suggest operational measures for three dimensions. These are briefly noted below, along with some examples of how they might be operationalized:

Hierarchy of skills
1 Distribution of training time for the occupations or jobs making up the organization
2 Number of discriminable training time levels

Hierarchy of rewards
1 Ratio of maximum to minimum earnings
2 Salary ratios of adjacent positions

Hierarchy of authority
1 Number of levels of authority
2 Ratio of administrative to production employees

Unfortunately, no data exist concerning the intercorrelations (i.e., degree of overlap) of these variables or their relevance for the job behavior of managers.

One of the more provocative examinations of so-called objective indicators of environmental variation is reported by Hall, Haas, and Johnson (1967). They initially used the typologies of Blau and Scott (1962) and Etzioni (1961) to classify a sample of 75 organizations. As the typological basis (coercive, utilitarian or financial reward, and normative or moral commitment), the former classifies according to "who benefits" (the participating membership, the owners, a client group, or the public at large), while the latter uses "compliance," or the means by which the lower level members are induced to cooperate. For each of these typologies the frequency distributions for various specific objective measures were examined across categories. The specific measures were grouped a priori under the following labels: (1) degree of formalization, (2) the specificity of goals, (3) the type and variability of activities, (4) interdependency between organizational units, (5) emphasis on status and power, (6) the nature of external relationships, and (7) the degree of change under way. Thirty-two individual measures were grouped under these headings (e.g., type of competition with other organizations, ratio of number of formal committees to number of paid employees, number of supportive departments). However, no correlational measures were computed, and the empirical relationships between the 32 indexes were not examined. The neglect of a multivariate technique in this study is unfortunate. What is badly needed is a dimensional analysis of a large number of such objective measures and a determination of the relationship between "objective" factors and "perceptional" factors.

Seemingly, the nature of the job itself or the "task demands" should constitute an important set of situational variables influencing a manager's performance. Woodward (1965) and Fiedler (1967) have both been concerned with differences produced by variation in task demands, although from considerably different viewpoints. In her study of 100 English manufacturing firms, Woodward categorized production systems into (1) unit production, as in firms in which goods are produced in small batches; (2) mass production, as in large-batch firms; and (3) continuous process production, as in chemical refining. This typology was related in turn to each of several structural variables such as the number of management levels, the span of control in first-line super-vision, and the ratio of administrative to other personnel. This latter variable was more highly related to the type of production process than to the size of the firm. Dubin (1965) has suggested that this sort of classification should be extensively examined in terms of its effect on the type of management behavior demanded.

Fiedler (1967) operates on a much more micro level and views the task as one determinant of whether the situation is a favorable one for different types of leaders. The tasks considered by Fiedler are really "unit-type" problems in Woodward's sense and have to do with the problems faced by a work group under the direction of a specific leader. He categorized such tasks along four a priori dimensions developed by Shaw (1963): (1) decision verifiability, or the degree to which a correct solution can be demonstrated; (2) goal clarity, or the degree to which the task requirements are clearly stated and known; (3) goal path multiplicity, or the degree to which the task can be solved by a variety of procedures; and (4) solution specificity, or the degree to which there is more than one correct solution. Empirical research using this type of categorization will be reviewed in the next section.

A number of other types of situational variables could be gleaned from the literature, but the above should be sufficient for our purposes. However, as pointed out by Forehand and Gilmer (1964), these more objective types of situational indexes share some common faults in that they are often too numer-ous and too specific to be readily interpreted: "Studies that examine in isolation specific objective properties of an organization leave unanswered the questions of how properties are related to one another and how they are related to useful constructs of organizational functioning" (p. 365). Perhaps the biggest problem involved in integrating situational variables into a program of research on man-agerial effectiveness is knowing which variables to select and how to concep-tualize them.

One rather Herculean effort to sift through a voluminous number of spe-cific variables for the salient dimensions is reported by Pugh, Hickson, Hin-ings, and Turner (1968). By means of a long, painstaking series of field inter-views, the investigators were able to obtain measures of 62 different aspects of organizational structure from 46 English firms of widely varying types. Among the 62 variables were such things as the standardization of selection and ad-vancement, functional specialization, height of work-flow hierarchy, and per-centage of non-work-flow personnel. On the basis of previous organization-al theory the 62 individual measures were grouped under five a priori head-ings: (1) specialization, (2) standardization, (3) formalization, (4) centralization, and (5) configuration.

The data from the 46 firms were then submitted to a principal compon-ents factor analysis in an attempt to determine empirically the patterns of covariation among the variables. Four factors, accounting for 70 percent of the total variance, were extracted. They were labeled as follows:

1 *Structuring of activities,* or the degree to which all types of activities in the organization are standardized, specialized, and formalized
2 *Concentration of authority,* or really the degree of centralization versus autonomy in decision making
3 *Line control of work flow,* or the degree to which the work force tends to be concentrated in line jobs and the degree to which the line exercises direct control over various functions
4 *Size of supportive elements,* or the amount of activity auxiliary to the main work flow of the organization

The first two factors bear a striking resemblance to the autonomy and structure factors obtained in the climate studies using perceptual data. The third and fourth do not correspond closely to any of the previously identified climate factors, but are directly tied to the kind of objective indexes that were used. In spite of the tremendous amount of effort that went into study and the large number of variables that were used, the rather restricted range of factors which were found suggests that considerable additional research must be done before the "organizational situation" is completely described. However, the Pugh et al. study constitutes a giant step in the proper direction.

THE LEVEL OF EXPLANATION

Aside from the taxonomic question, there is another extremely important problem relative to studying the relationship of environmental characteristics to job behavior. To speak of the influence of "perceived feelings of autonomy" on managerial behavior is very different from speaking of the influence of "span of control" or some other such structural property. The linkage between environmental characteristics and behavior is much longer in the latter case and makes the eventual investigation of cause and effect much more complex. Perceptions of climate and independent measures of organization-

Figure 16.1 An explanation chain for the influence of a situational variable on organizational behavior. (*Source:* Indik, 1965)

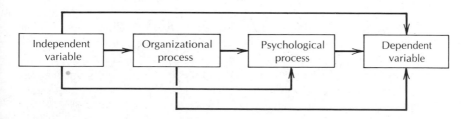

al characteristics just do not operate on the *same level of explanation*. Obviously, a systematic study of the relationships between levels must begin on several fronts if any sense is ever to come of all this.

Indik (1965) has made one effort in this direction, and a brief examination of his paradigm might be helpful. He was interested in the linkage between organization size and the degree of an individual's "participation" in the organization. Between this independent and this dependent variable, Indik postulated two types of mediating variables: (1) organizational processes resulting from the size factor and (2) psychological process. Thus there are four elements in the chain and six possible bivariate relationships that can be examined. The paradigm is diagramed in Figure 16.1.

Four different combinations of mediators were examined correlationally in three different research settings. The mediators accounting for the most variance were amount of communication and degree of task specialization, on the organizational process side, and felt attraction for other members and satisfaction with performance, on the psychological process side.

Indik's analysis makes clear that focusing prematurely on independent variables that are too distant from the behavior of interest may obscure meaningful relationships or lead to explanations for "significant" results that are misleading. In contrast, focusing only on psychological processes as antecedents prohibits being able to specify what organizational characteristics are responsible for the behavioral effects.

SOME EMPIRICAL RESULTS

As we emphasized at the beginning of this chapter, the research literature concerning the influence of the situation on managerial effectiveness is meager. Furthermore, the studies that do exist vary widely in terms of the variables and conceptual relationships that are studied. There is very little communality on which to build integrative conclusions. Nevertheless, we shall discuss, in turn, laboratory or experimental studies, correlational field studies, and studies which relate situational variables not to measures of managerial performance but to attitude and motivational variables.

Experimental Studies

Organizational climate. Both Frederiksen (1966) and Litwin and Stringer (1966) have carried out laboratory studies using "climate" dimensions as independent variables. The Frederiksen study is the most extensive and the most directly relevant for the present chapter. A total of 260 middle managers employed by the state of California worked through an In-basket Test designed to simulate the job of chief of the field service division of the Department of

Commerce. The In-basket measure has been discussed in some detail in Chapter 6. Four treatment combinations designed to create differences in climate were arranged in a 2 by 2 design. One treatment dichotomy had to do with the general prevalence of "rules and regulations." Half the subjects were informed via instructions and In-basket materials that the Department of Commerce encouraged new ideas, innovation, and creative problem solving. They were told that rules existed but that they could be broken if they got in the way. The other half were told that a very substantial set of rules and regulations had been built up over the years and had proved very valuable and that they were not to be violated except under extreme circumstances. The second treatment factor was concerned with the closeness of supervision, and the subjects were told either that the organization preferred a subordinate's work to be closely monitored or that subordinates should be allowed to work out details for themselves.

The In-basket can be scored on a large number of indexes (e.g., explains action to peers, postpones decision, involves subordinates, and takes final action). In previous research, some sixty of these initial scores were reduced to a smaller number of first-order factors, and the dependent variable in this particular study was a second-order factor labeled "productivity," or the sheer amount of work accomplished. The subjects also provided a large amount of test and biographical data which served as 21 different predictor variables. The actual dependent variable under consideration was the predictability of In-basket performance by the 21 predictors.

In general it was found that predictability was higher under the innovative climate. The details of the analysis are too numerous to give here, but Frederiksen (1966, p. 13) summarizes them with the following statement:

> It appears that the amount of administrative work in the simulated job is more predictable in a climate that encourages innovation than in one that encourages standard procedures, and that in an innovative climate (but not in a rules climate) greater productivity can be expected of people with skills and attitudes that are associated with independence of thought and action and the ability to be productive in free, unstructured situations.

Frederiksen also found that performance was more predictable for subjects who worked in a consistent climate (innovation + loose supervision or rules + close supervision) than for those who had to operate in an inconsistent environment (innovation + close supervision or rules + loose supervision).

In further analyses of the same study (Frederiksen, 1968) it was demonstrated that inconsistent climates also have a negative effect on productivity. Specifically, those subjects who were placed in a climate that encouraged innovation and was at the same time characterized by detailed supervision worked at a substantially reduced level of output. Digging still deeper in the data, Frederiksen (1968) was able to show that subjects employed different work methods under different climate conditions. For example, in the In-basket under the climate conditions permitting more freedom, administrators dealt more directly with peers, while in the restrictive climates, they tended to work through more formal channels.

In sum, the Frederiksen study yields a glimpse of the wide range of influences that climate differences can exhibit. It also demonstrates the potential power of this kind of research strategy. The conclusion is inescapable that a sophisticated research technology of organizational simulation would yield many new insights into management behavior. The research enterprise should take strong steps in that direction.

Litwin and Stringer (1966) used 45 students from the Harvard Business School and divided them into three "firms," which then had to compete in the construction and marketing of "radar equipment" manufactured from Erector Set materials. The buyer was a simulated government agency, and competition for contract awards was intense. The simulated operation, or game, required considerable organization and cooperation on the part of the 15 players. Three different climates were created: (1) an *authoritarian-structured* business, with strong emphasis on careful definition of duties, the exercise of formal authority, etc.; (2) a *democratic-friendly* business, where cooperative behavior, group loyalty, teamwork, freedom from punishment, and a loose informal structure were emphasized; and (3) an *achieving* business, where innovation was encouraged, competitive feedback was given, pride in the organization was fostered, a certain amount of risk taking was deemed desirable, and high personal goals were encouraged.

The principal means for creating the climate differences was the president of the company who was a member of the research staff and who adopted the appropriate leadership "style." The expected differences were found on a questionnaire designed to measure the six climate factors discussed earlier in this chapter. Playing of the game was continued over an eight-day period.

Significant differences in performance and satisfaction were found. The achieving business produced the most in terms of dollar volume, number of new products, and cost-saving innovations. However, the authoritarian-structured business produced finished goods with the highest quality, primarily by never deviating from the government specifications laid out in the game. After playing for seven days, the subjects in the democratic-friendly business rated themselves as being more satisfied with their jobs than subjects in the other two firms.

Several features of these two experiments have relevance for some of the more general issues with which we are trying to deal in this chapter. The dependent variable under consideration in the Litwin and Stringer study is much broader, but the source of climate differences is given a much narrower focus. That is, Litwin and Stringer consider the effects on the entire simulated organization of climate differences produced by the president of the company, while Frederiksen generates differences from much more diffuse and generalized sources, but notes their effects on only a particular organizational role. Future researchers must devote considerable attention to specifying the breadth of effect they wish to investigate if a meaningful integration of research results is to be possible. In "climate" terms, what is perceived as bad weather for one part of the organization may be good for another.

A second point illustrates a paradox that tends to arise when the experimental studies are related to the previous taxonomic efforts. Developing *dimensions* of environmental variation implies that differences among organizations along these dimensions are important. However, the treatment variables in the Litwin and Stringer study really represent modal types and not variations in a particular variable. The effects of differences in types can in no way be causally related back to the original taxonomic study. In the Frederiksen study the treatment differences do seem to reflect differences in two situational variables (rules orientation and closeness of supervision), but no indication is given as to why these treatments happened to be the ones selected or whether the two dichotomies do indeed represent two levels of the same dimension. Obviously, if experimental work is to have any scientific utility, there must be some means for relating independent variables to one another.

Third, the two studies adopted a very different view regarding the functional relationship of climate to performance. Litwin and Stringer emphasized the determinant or direct causal effects of climate differences, while Frederiksen viewed his experimental treatments as moderators of the relationship between other measures of individual differences and performance. Neither study tried to compare the relative amount of variance accounted for by main effects versus interactive effects.

Situational favorableness. Focusing on environmental variation at a much different level, Fiedler (1967) and his associates have integrated the results of their fifteen-year leadership research program around the notion of "situational favorableness." That is, the type of leadership skills required for effective work group performance is viewed as a function of certain properties of the work group situation. Fiedler has been concerned with three such properties:

1 *Affective leader-group relation.* This refers to the interpersonal relationship between the leader and the key members of his group. In the early studies this variable was measured sociometrically, but currently is being assessed by means of the *leader's* responses to 10 to 20 semantic differential scales used to rate the con-

cept of "group atmosphere." The end points of each scale are defined by a pair of bipolar adjectives, and the group's atmosphere is rated according to where it falls on the continuum. For example:

CONTINUUM

Group atmosphere

Distant ____ : ____ : ____ : ____ : ____ : ____ : ____ : ____ : Close
         1   2   3   4   5   6   7   8

Some other scales: bad-good, pleasant-unpleasant, cold-warm, quarrelsome-harmonious, worthless-valuable, and gloomy-cheerful. The basic theory of the semantic differential approach to giving meaning to concepts is formulated by Osgood (1952).

2 *Task structure.* This concerns the relative clarity or ambiguity of the task facing the work group or the programmed-unprogrammed nature of the task as it is assigned from above. This characteristic is assessed by means of four a priori rating scales which were originally developed by Shaw (1963) and which were discussed earlier in this chapter.

3 *Leader position power.* This really refers to the amount of rewards or sanctions which are at the leader's disposal and which are granted to the position by the organization. Position power is measured by an 18-item checklist filled out by an independent judge.

Measurements of these three variables are dichotomized, permitting a particular group leadership situation to be classified into one of eight possible categories. On an a priori basis, the eight categories have been arranged on a continuum defined as "favorableness," or the degree to which the leader's job of influencing his group will be easy or difficult. The category representing good leader-member relations, high task structure, and high position power is designated as the most favorable leadership situation, while a situation of poor leader-member relations, low task structure, and low position power is regarded as being the most unfavorable. While the two extremes of this continuum make intuitive sense, the intermediate steps provide a certain amount of conceptual difficulty, which Fiedler acknowledges. The complete ordering is shown below.

	I	II	III	IV	V	VI	VII	VIII
Leader-member relations	Good	Good	Good	Good	Poor	Poor	Poor	Poor
Task structure	High	High	Low	Low	High	High	Low	Low
Position power	High	Low	High	Low	High	Low	High	Low

The favorableness dimension is treated as a moderator or interactive variable which influences the relationship between characteristics of the leader and the productivity of his work group. For our purpose the productivity of the work group must be taken as a measure of management performance. However, for the reasons we have discussed in previous chapters, this may not always be a desirable criterion variable. The individual difference measure which has received the most attention from the Fiedler group is the psychological distance the leader perceives between himself and his least preferred coworker (LPC). A leader high on this variable tends to see even a poor coworker in a relatively favorable way, while a low scorer views his least preferred coworker in a very rejecting manner. The LPC is assessed by means of the same semantic differential rating scales used to assess overall leader-member relations or group atmosphere, the only difference being in the concept that is rated (group atmosphere versus least preferred coworker). The LPC is probably most analogous to the strength of a supervisor's human relations approach or "consideration" for subordinates.

Fiedler imposed his "contingency" model on data gathered from over eight hundred interacting groups operating in a wide variety of institutional situations, and he concluded that it seemed to make sense of otherwise contradictory data. That is, the correlation between LPC and group productivity (usually measured by the quality of solutions produced for a specific problem or task) was negative when the situation was either very favorable or very unfavorable for the leader but positive for situations that were only moderately difficult. This generalization was derived on an ad hoc basis from the previously collected data. Our immediate concern is with the validation of the contingency hypothesis in new experimental settings.

To date, two major validation attempts have been carried out in experimental settings. The first (Fiedler, 1966) used petty officers and recruits in the Belgian navy as subjects. Half of 96 three-man groups were led by officers, and half by recruits. In addition, half the personnel were Dutch-speaking and half were French-speaking. Thus leader position power was represented by the officer-recruit dichotomy, leader-member relations were measured by post session questionnaires, and an additional structural element was introduced by composing heterogeneous (unfavorable) versus homogeneous (favorable) groups relative to linguistic background (Dutch versus French). Variations in task structure were achieved by having the groups either work on a transportation problem involving the shortest route through several ports or compose a recruiting letter urging young men to join the Belgian navy. When all four structural characteristics were used to construct a scale of favorableness, the results of the study departed substantially from the theoretical predictions. When the correlations between LPC and group productivity were analyzed separately for the structured versus the unstructured tasks, the results tended to resemble the theoretical predictions more closely. The clearest support for the contingency model came from the two extreme categories on the favorableness continuum.

The second study was conducted by Shaw and Blum (1966) and used 18 five-man groups of United States college students as subjects. An attempt was made to hold all situational characteristics constant except for task structure, which was manipulated by having each group work on three different tasks hypothesized to vary widely in structure. These were (1) a discussion problem requiring the group to list the five most important traits a person needs for success in our culture, (2) a discussion problem requiring the group to describe which of five possible courses of action would be best for a young politician burdened by an alcoholic wife, and (3) a task requiring the group to identify five objects by asking no more than 40 questions. The rating scale measure of LPC was not used. Instead, half the group leaders were instructed to be highly directive and autocratic, while the other half were told to be nondirective and permissive. The results were generally in line with predictions from the contingency model.

Fiedler has also investigated environmental stress as a situational characteristic contributing to the favorableness of the leadership situation. In one study 19 three-person groups made up of ministers and lay leaders at a church organization leadership conference worked on composing statements of their churches' beliefs for two different audiences. Stress was introduced by calling the first statement a warm-up and giving plenty of time, while emphasizing that the second statement was a real test of leadership and allowing only twenty minutes for its completion. All participants evaluated all the solutions except their own. The results of the study suggested that a stressful situation may weaken the relationship between leader LPC scores and group productivity; however, the N was small and the experimental manipulation somewhat dubious (Fiedler, 1967, p. 206). A number of subjects perceived the first task as more stressful. Thus we again encounter the crucial distinction between objective and perceptual situational variables.

A second study (Meuwese & Fiedler, 1965) used 54 three-man groups of ROTC students as subjects and again employed group tasks centered around composing letters or position papers. Internal stress was induced by having the subjects appear in uniform and appointing the lowest ranking cadet as leader. External stress was induced by requiring uniforms and having three high ranking regular Army officers in the room as observers. In the low stress condition, civilian dress was allowed, and there were no observers. Within each experimental condition there were nine groups with low LPC leaders and nine with high LPC leaders. For one of the problems there was an interaction between LPC and stress, with low LPC leaders performing best in the low stress condition and high LPC leaders performing best in the internal stress condition. There were no differences for the external stress condition, nor were there any significant interactions for the second problem. However, when the leader-member relations measure is combined with stress to define a "favorableness" dimension, the characteristic curve appears relating the correlation of LPC and group productivity to situation favorableness.

In sum, the relation of differences in environmental stress to leader effectiveness has not been clearly demonstrated. In the ROTC study there was no overall difference in performance among the experimental conditions. That is, even though the correlations between LPC and productivity were different, the average productivity per group was not affected by the stress manipulation.

Obviously, the contingency model has not yet been sewn into a neat theoretical package, as Fiedler has pointed out (1967, p. 261). The most troublesome aspect is still the prior specification of which situations are favorable and which are not. There was some indication of a certain amount of ad hoc reweighting of the situational elements in the Belgian navy study and in the ROTC study (Fiedler & Meuwese, 1965). The general question of how much each of the situational elements contributes to the favorableness of a leadership situation also remains empirically unexplored. However, in spite of such faults, the contingency hypothesis is a provocative and extremely important contribution. It points the way others could fruitfully follow.

Correlational and Field Studies

We would now like to consider empirical studies that were conducted in naturally occurring organizational contexts. Obviously, the direction of causality is difficult to infer in such studies, but the variables tend to be "richer" in content, and fruitful hypothesis can be suggested for later experimentation.

Job challenge. Berlew and Hall (1966) performed further analyses on data gathered in the AT&T Management Progress Study reported in Chapter 9. Several performance measures were obtained for 62 individuals originally hired as managers by two companies of the Bell System in 1956 and 1957. These included the 1962 salary adjusted for starting salary, a global appraisal at the end of either the fourth or the fifth year, a composite of these two, the average of the yearly effectiveness ratings over the four- or five-year period (depending on which of the two companies the individual entered), and indexes of "contribution" and "overcontribution." These latter two criteria are related to a measure of how much the company expected of the individual on his first managerial assignment. Company expectations were rated by both superiors and subjects on 18 categories (communication skills, technical competence, etc.), and the ratings were summed. The contribution score was obtained by rating the individual's actual performance on the same 18 categories, and overcontribution was simply the comparison of expectations and actual performance. The crucial findings from the study were the significant correlations between company expectations for the first year (i.e., initial job challenge) and measures of later performance. These relationships could not be accounted for by initial differences in ability since none of the variables in the Management Progress Study designed to measure various aptitudes and skills correlated with the expectation measure. Differences in expectations seemed to be a function of the job itself.

In an earlier study using the same data, Berlew and Hall (1964) demonstrated that an individual will tend to change his performance (either up or down) to bring himself in line with company expectations. The company will also change its expectations to achieve an equilibrium with an individual's performance. The significance of both these effects was demonstrated via a partial correlation technique. To the extent that they are valid, the results suggest a dynamic aspect of situational effects that must be reckoned with. The situation may change as a function of the type of people that enter it.

Although the subjects were not managers, two other studies bear on the effects of job challenge. Peres (1966) did a follow-up study of 475 engineers hired by General Electric during the mid-1950s and attempted to determine what individual and organizational factors contributed to "salary success." At the time of hire, each subject had completed a lengthy battery of tests and biographical questionnaires from which a prediction could be made concerning future performance "potential." At the time of the Peres study, the subjects were asked to describe certain characteristics pertaining to their first full-time job assignment. The results suggested an interaction between the nature of the first job and success potential. High potential individuals achieved higher salary success if their first job was seen as difficult, challenging, and not easily handled by falling back on their college training, while the low potential subjects attained high salary success if they could successfully cope with their first assignment by direct use of their college training.

Pelz and Andrews (1967) studied 1,300 research and development engineers and scientists in five industrial laboratories, five government laboratories, and seven departments in a large university. In addition to objective measures such as reports, published papers, and patents, scientific contribution was judged by a panel of colleagues. The most successful individuals seemed to be those who occupied a position of "creative tension" between otherwise conflicting aims, such as specialized activity in a particular area versus opportunity to participate in a number of activities, or colleagues who shared similar interests but differed in technical style and strategy. Also, the most creative individuals were not those who spent all their time on research but those who had to deal with other organizational problems and tasks as well.

Obviously, the correlational nature of the above studies leaves considerable room for competing explanations. However, they provide useful hypotheses to follow up with more controlled investigation.

Field tests of the contingency model (situational favorableness). Hunt (1967) has reported a major test of the contingency model in a field setting.

Work groups in several different organizational contexts were studied. These included 18 "pure" research and "service" research groups in the chemical research division of a large corporation, 11 groups of shop craftsmen in the same company, 21 meat departments and 24 grocery departments in a super-market chain, and 15 management teams (general foreman and first level fore-men) in a farm implement manufacturing firm. Group productivity in the vari-ous settings was assessed by management ratings or group output (sales or goods produced) per unit time, where such a measure could be obtained. The rela-tive degree of task structure for the various groups was assessed via a Thurstone scaling procedure using both in-company and external judges. The other vari-ables in the model were measured in the usual way. Groups were also divided into interacting versus coacting units. Interacting units are analogous to lab-oratory groups which must interact face-to-face to yield a group product. A coacting group is a collective in which individual efforts are summed and interpersonal interaction is not fundamental for accomplishing the task. In general, the results supported the contingency model for both types of groups. However, the situational effects seemed to be accounted for almost entirely by the variation in leader-member relations, suggesting that either a less com-plex model might be needed or additional situational characteristics should be considered.

Other field studies using the contingency framework have explored ad-ditional situational variables, one of which is management level. Nealy and Blood (1968) studied VA hospital wards supervised by 21 head nurses who in turn were responsible to eight unit supervisors. In general, head nurse LPC scores tended to have negative correlations with various measures of ward effective-ness (ratings of physical care of patients, information about patients, etc.), while unit supervisor LPC was positively related. However, the Ns were quite small, and only 3 of 10 correlations were significant at $p = .05$. None of the negative correlations reached statistical significance. Other data reported by Fiedler suggest that if the task is very highly structured (e.g., that of a general foreman in an open-hearth steel plant), the correlation of higher management LPC with work group productivity may be negative. In sum, any conclusions about the influence of organizational level on the LPC times productivity cor-relation must be highly tentative. One additional finding that seems more con-clusive is that mean LPC scores appear not to vary across organizational levels. What this implies for the construct validity of the LPC measure is difficult to say.

Organizational climate. In an interesting study which deserves to serve as a prototype for many others, J. D. W. Andrews (1967) examined the effect of the congruence of organizational and individual values on managerial per-formance and advancement. Two Mexican firms that provided a clear-cut con-trast in value orientations were used as criterion organizations. One firm was judged to be highly achievement-oriented, progressive, expansion-minded, and economically successful, while the second firm was assessed as being much more conservative, less achievement-oriented, more oriented toward power relations, and less successful. All top level managers in the two firms were measured on n Ach and n Pow via the Thematic Apperception Test (TAT) and success was indexed by the number of promotions and salary increases received by an individual during the previous four years. There were no significant differences on the TAT scores between managers from the two firms, but in an analysis of variance framework, there was a significant interaction between motivational needs and type of firm. That is, advancement was greater for those individuals who had motivational needs congruent with the values of the organization. As is always the case in a field study, competing explanations are possible; however, the investigation of these kinds of interactions deserves to be pursued with vigor.

Similar research from college and university settings is reviewed by Pervin (1968). He cites data from Funkenstein (1962), Stern (1962), and his own research (Pervin, 1967) showing that a lack of congruence between measured personality characteristics, or self perceptions, and environmental characteristics predicts dropouts in a number of institutions. Since voluntary turnover is such an important outcome in the managerial population, this kind of research deserves considerable emulation in the organizational setting.

Some related field studies. In retrospect, a study by Ghiselli and Lodahl (1958) utilizes measures which seem quite closely allied with the situational favorableness dimension emphasized by Fiedler. Subjects were 18 five-man work groups in a single manufacturing plant and included one foreman and four production workers. Ghiselli's Self Description Inventory which has five empirically derived scales, was administered to all the subjects. For the scale originally constructed to discriminate between superior and poor supervisors, the foreman's score was subtracted from the highest group member score to yield a kind of "competition" index. A second index was called "self-sufficiency" and was derived from the degree of skewness in the group distribution on the Decision Making Approach (DMA) scale. This scale was originally constructed by selecting items to differentiate between different levels of management. Groups which had one high scorer and several low scorers (exclusive of the foreman) were labeled "self-sufficient" since, as measured by the DMA scale, there were already a superior and several subordinates. These two group indexes were correlated with ratings of overall foreman effectiveness, and the coefficients were —.50 and —.57 respectively. A composite of the two group indexes (simple sum) correlated — .77 with effectiveness ratings. The implication is very strong that the degree of supervisory ability already existing among the group members may have a strong influence on how easily the appointed supervisor is able to use his own talents.

We would also like to mention a study by Yanouyas (1964) which is related to the situational variables discussed by Woodward (1965) but which does not deal directly with measures of performance. The Critical Incidents Method was used to study the differences in job behavior of foremen who supervised a job-lot type of production process and foremen who dealt with a continuous flow process. The results were sketchy, but tended to show that foremen dealing with a continuous flow process spent less time training and developing subordinates but more time interacting with other foremen. Job-lot foremen spent more time enforcing safety standards, arbitrating job inequities, and performing work themselves. In meeting production schedules, the continuous flow foremen were primarily "labor pushers," while the job-lot supervisors utilized changes in scheduling and processes to meet their goals. It would not be unreasonable to expect different kinds of people to be differentially successful in these two types of supervisory jobs.

Attitudes, Motivation, and Situational Characteristics

Although the primary focus of the present volume is on performance effectiveness, a number of studies have investigated the relationship of environmental variables to other manifestations of managerial and supervisory behavior. We would like to consider briefly those which seem to have the most potential relevance for future studies of effectiveness.

Parker (1963) examined the interrelationships between situational, performance, and attitudinal measures obtained from 80 warehouse installations of a wholesale pharmaceutical company. Situational variables included the prevailing wage rate, union status, percentage of male employees, community size, and work group size, while productivity was measured by the number of items processed per man-hour, order-filling errors, and pricing errors. In addition, supervisors completed the Leadership Opinion Questionnaire (LOQ). Warehouse size was correlated low positive with the initiating structure of the supervisor (.22) and low negative ($-.25$) with work group productivity, while employment security (composite of unionization and wage rate) was negatively related to supervisory structure, order-filling errors, and attitudes toward supervision. However, these relationships were also very low. The LOQ was not related to work group productivity.

The Parker study was stimulated by an earlier investigation (Katzell, Barrett, & Parker, 1961) which tended to show that the degree of "urbanization" of the warehouse environment was related to employee attitudes and work group productivity. Contrary to expectations, the relationship of urbanization to supervisory behavior failed to materialize to any degree in the Parker study.

Analogous to the experimental studies of the effects of stress on group performance is the previously mentioned field study of role conflict by Kahn et al. (1964). In addition to the intensive study of the 53 focal managers, a national survey of 725 employed individuals over the age of eighteen was carried out via a personal interview. In both studies, the investigators were interested in the effects of role conflict produced by incompatible expectations focused on the individual. The theory of role dynamics from which the data collection efforts were developed is carefully elaborated. Individuals were characterized as being in high or low conflict roles (positions), and the conflict dichotomy was related to a number of other measures. Even though no measures of performance effectiveness were used, the pervasive and far-reaching effects of role conflict were reflected in several other variables. In general, high role conflict was associated with lower job satisfaction, less communication with other members of the organization, less confidence in the organization, a heightened sense of futility, and increased feelings of tension. The way in which these relationships are modified by various personality and structural variables was also investigated, but the data are much too broad and complex to be summarized here. Suffice it to say that the concept of organizational role and the situational forces that bear upon it promises to be a fruitful avenue for research on environmental effects.

Lastly, Tausky and Dubin (1965) studied the relationship between the nature of the first job assignment, in terms of organizational level, and the way an individual tended to anchor his managerial career aspirations. That is, does a manager evaluate his progress by assessing how far he has progressed toward the top (upward anchorage) or how far he has progressed past a certain base point (downward anchorage)? A special scale was constructed to measure this type of orientation and was administered to 337 middle managers in five business firms. The results tended to show that the higher the level at which an individual enters an organization, the more he tends to anchor his expectations in terms of the top position. Unfortunately, the effects of differential selection were not well controlled. In spite of such alternative explanations, however, the warning seems clear that as fewer and fewer managers "come up through the ranks," the incidence of frustrated expectations may become considerably greater. What this portends for the future effectiveness of the middle managers in an organization is a matter for additional research.

SUMMARY

In this chapter we have attempted to identify some of the conceptual difficulties inherent in investigating situational effects, review research dealing with taxonomic efforts, and review the empirical evidence on situational effects. On a conceptual level there is a polyglot of variables that can be subsumed under the rubric the "situation." We grouped these under the following four headings: (1) structural properties, (2) environmental characteristics,

(3) organizational climate, and (4) formal role characteristics. The relationship of a situational variable to managerial performance may be conceptualized as an experimental main effect, a predictor (in the correlational sense), a moderator, or some combination of these. Research studies have tended to focus on only one of the three at any one time. There are also serious problems regarding the "level of explanation" associated with the relationship between a situational variable and managerial performance. If the independent variable is a structural property such as organization size, the connecting chain is certainly much longer than in the case of a climate variable which is assessed by means of the individual's *perceptions* of what the organization is like.

Most of the taxonomic research has centered around dimensions of organizational climate. Even though there have been relatively few studies and they varied widely in their approach, four factors appear common to them. These we have labeled (1) autonomy, (2) structure, (3) general reward level, and (4) warmth and support. Further research should build on these efforts and attempt to determine the nature of the factor structure in different settings and how it interacts with individual differences. Unfortunately, no such beginning taxonomic work exists with regard to other types of situational variables.

At the empirical level things have not progressed very far, but perhaps a few inferences can be made. The simulation studies by Frederiksen (1966, 1968) and Litwin and Stringer (1966) strongly suggest a number of beneficial effects for organizations which maintain a consistent climate. They further suggest that if individual differences are not taken into account, there is little reason to expect *mean* differences in performance under different climate conditions. One thing these studies do not do is suggest how the influence of climate differs for different tasks. Studies of climate should take a cue from a laboratory experiment by Roby, Nicol, and Farrell (1963) which showed that a decentralized structure was best if the task required cooperative effort but that a centralized structure was best if individuals (students in this case) worked independently toward a common goal.

The work of the Fiedler group on situational favorableness is certainly the most fruitful program of research we have discussed in this chapter. The most potent variable making up the favorableness of the leadership situation seems to be the degree of task structure, and an organization would be on relatively firm ground if it tried to assign unstructured tasks to groups with low LPC leaders and structured tasks to groups with high LPC leaders. Unfortunately, there is still some ambiguity in the definition of task structure. Also, the LPC variable has not been explicated very well, and there are few converging lines of evidence to give it conceptual meaning.

Perhaps one of the most important findings to emerge from the empirical research is the importance of the initial job assigned to an individual. His expectations and aspirations regarding his career in an organization seem to be very much a function of the skill requirements and difficulty level of his first few jobs. It should be the aim of every organization to "stretch" its personnel by offering them appropriate challenges. If it does not, a self-defeating circle could be created, for the analyses by Berlew and Hall (1964) suggest that over time an individual's expectations for himself tend to approximate those the organization has for him.

In sum, the "situation" has been shown to encompass an exceedingly complex set of variables, especially when their dynamic and interactive properties are considered. Again, not much research has been forthcoming, but there is considerable promise for the future.

Chapter 17   Managerial Style: Research Results and a Social-Psychological View

So far in this volume we have dealt with the psychology of managerial effectiveness from a descriptive point of view. That is, we have asked questions concerning what individual differences are associated with effectiveness, what training and development experiences contribute to managerial performance, how managers might be motivated to alter their behavior, and what dimensions of the objective and perceived situation are salient. We have taken what we hope is an exhaustive look at the research literature in the context of trying to identify the antecedents of effective and ineffective performance. That has been our principal objective. Our approach has been psychological and has focused on the individual manager rather than the organization.

There is, of course, a voluminous literature prescribing how managers should manage, if they want to be effective. This prescriptive literature is derived from a variety of disciplines, not just industrial and organizational psychology. Although it is not our intent in this book to treat this literature in any detail, one recurrent theme *is* psychological in nature and has generated a certain amount of empirical research. "Human relations" is probably the most generic term for this theme.

THE HUMAN RELATIONS APPROACH

The human relations movement had its most recognizable beginnings in the work of Kurt Lewin and his associates and in the Western Electric studies, as characterized by Elton Mayo. Although it has been revised substantially, this theme and its variations are currently best represented in the work of Douglas McGregor (1960), Chris Argyris (1957, 1964a), and Rensis Likert (1961, 1967). These three writers are prescriptive in that they attempt to spell out the managerial and supervisory styles and practices which will result in a viable organization and in increased satisfaction and performance on the part of subordinates.

Many of the prescriptions have an organizational rather than an individual focus. That is, the behavior of the individual manager is not always the unit of analysis. Rather, attributes of the entire organization constitute the independent or predictor variables, and organizational outcomes (profits, turnover, etc.) are the dependent variables. Since the mainstream of the present volume is the behavior of the individual manager, we shall not attempt to deal with this large prescriptive literature on effective *organizations*. Again, because our approach is both individual and psychological, we shall restrict ourselves to a discussion of three characteristics of managerial behavior that tend to account for most of the research activity.

These three variables travel under various names, the most easily recognized of which are probably (1) consideration, (2) initiating structure, and (3) participation, or subordinate influence in decision making. They have already been discussed in various other parts of this book, but are briefly recapitulated below:

1 *Consideration.* Consideration, or employee-centered behavior, refers to the degree to which the supervisor or manager is warm, sympathetic, and friendly with his subordinates, is considerate of their needs, and is willing to explain his actions to them.

2 *Initiating structure.* Perhaps more commonly referred to as "production-centeredness" or "concern for production," this variable represents the sheer attention a manager gives to things such as scheduling work assignments, defining work goals, establishing procedures, and evaluating quantity and quality. However, as noted by House and Filley (1968), some instruments used to measure initiating structure include items that represent behavior which is authoritarian and arbitrary. This latter aspect of initiating structure gives it a very negativistic connotation which it perhaps does not deserve.

3 *Participation.* Whereas consideration behavior is essentially one-way, from the superior to the subordinate, and is expressive or interpersonal in nature, the central theme of participation is subordinate influence in decision making. That is, subordinates are allowed to participate in making decisions that affect them. They share power or influence with their superiors. It is unclear from the literature whether initiating structure and participation should actually be considered two ends of the same continuum or not. Empirically they have been treated as separate dimensions.

Given these variables, we can ask how they are related to managerial or supervisory effectiveness. The research surrounding this question has used two types of dependent variables and two principal methodologies. The dependent variables have usually been subordinate attitudes (job satisfaction) or summary indexes of work group effectiveness (e.g., productivity, costs, grievances, turnover). The methodology employed in the majority of studies has been correlational in nature and consists of identifying work groups whose managers are high and low on one of the three style variables and then noting the mean differences between these groups on the dependent variable. In a smaller number of experimental field studies, management practices have actually been changed for the purpose of measuring the effect on attitudes or work group performance.

MANAGERIAL STYLE AND SUBORDINATE ATTITUDES

Since the main concern of this volume is with managerial behavior and performance, we shall not dwell at length on the relationship between managerial style and subordinate attitudes. Much of this literature is reviewed by House and Filley (1968), Vroom (1964), and Likert (1961). Most of the available data concern the relationship of supervisory consideration to subordinate job satisfaction, and the results seem clear. Consideration is positively related to subordinate satisfaction. However, Vroom (1964) mentions a number of qualifications and elaborations that must be appended to such a statement.

The studies supporting this conclusion allow no inferences concerning causality. An argument could be made that satisfied subordinates elicit managerial behavior which is high on consideration, and vice versa. The same argument should be kept in mind when examining correlations between managerial style variables and productivity. Lowin and Craig (1968) have demonstrated in a simulated business office setting that changes in subordinate output can indeed produce changes in the initiating structure and consideration behavior of supervisors. There is also the problem of measuring consideration. Most studies have relied on self-descriptions. Another means for assessing managerial consideration is through subordinate descriptions of management behavior such as that provided by the Ohio State Leader Behavior Description Questionnaire (LBDQ) (Stogdill & Coons, 1957). As we have noted previously, there does not seem to be a particularly high relationship between self-descriptions and subordinate descriptions on this variable. We actually do not know whether subordinates' job satisfaction is related to *their own* perceptions of supervisors' behaviors. If there were no such relationship, it would be grounds for believing that subordinate satisfaction produces changes in a manager's self-perceptions, rather than consideration producing increased job satisfaction. In sum, the fact that a relationship exists between consideration and job satisfaction seems well established. However, several very interesting questions remain concerning the nature of the relationship and the direction of causality.

Results concerning the relationships of subordinate satisfaction to initiating structure and/or influence in decision making are not as clear-cut. Initiating structure, as measured by the Ohio State Leadership Opinion Questionnaire (LOQ), has not shown consistent relationships (Korman, 1966). On the basis of evidence from correlational studies, we can say that subordinate job satisfaction tends to have a positive relationship to degree of participation or influence in decision making (Vroom, 1964). However, when data from experimental studies are considered, the results tend to be mixed. In sum, we can make few generalizations, but perhaps we would rather not anyway. As Vroom points out, and as we are so fond of preaching, it is not reasonable to expect that the majority of employees in most situations will react in similar fashion to particular managerial styles. We shall discuss these interactive effects in more detail later on.

MANAGERIAL STYLE AND PRODUCTIVITY

Consideration. As with job satisfaction, research results consistently show a positive relationship between supervisory consideration and "productivity." Vroom (1964) cites eleven studies, among which eight showed a positive relationship, two showed a negative relationship, and one showed a zero relationship. The majority of studies used work group output or turnover as a measure of productivity, while the remainder employed ratings of the supervisor or leader. Even though most of the relationships were positive, the correlations were smaller than those for the relationship of consideration to subordinate job satisfaction. Also, none of the studies were experimental in nature, and it would make just as much sense to say that high producing groups elicit supervisory consideration as vice versa.

Initiating structure. Results with this variable are dependent at least in part on the way in which it is measured. If by initiating structure is meant devoting attention to advance planning, making specific work assignments, and specifying well-defined procedures, then there is considerable evidence to suggest that a supervisor high on this variable is given high performance ratings by his boss and tends to have a high producing unit (House & Filley, 1968). However, initiating structure as used by the Ohio State group includes such things as planning work, emphasizing deadlines, ruling with an iron hand, and refusing to explain actions. When this more authoritarian factor is included, the data become very unclear. Reviewing evidence obtained with the LOQ, Korman (1966) was able to document few consistent or even statistically significant relationships. Relationships with the LBDQ are no more clear-cut. For example, Fleishman, Harris, and Burtt (1955) found a positive correlation between initiating structure and proficiency ratings for production foremen but a negative relationship for nonproduction foremen. Halpin (1957) and Halpin and Winer (1957) found correlations of .25 and .28 between structure and rated proficiency in two studies of bomber crew effectiveness. These latter findings suggest an interactive effect between the type of job being supervised and the relationship of initiating structure to productivity, which is not an unreasonable conclusion.

Influence in decision making (participation). In contrast to that on consideration and initiating structure, research concerning the relationship of participation and productivity is largely experimental and largely indicative of a positive relationship[The antecedent experiment is, of course, the classic Lewin, Lippitt, and White (1939) study, which used eleven-year-old boys as subjects and which compared the effects of autocratic, democratic, and laissez faire leadership on group productivity. In terms of the number of tasks accomplished, the autocratic and democratic groups were very similar; however, productivity in the autocratic groups dropped off as soon as the leader left the room. The democratic groups did not require such close "managerial control."

The studies most widely quoted in support of the beneficial effects of participation are those dealing with the supervision of hourly employees on a production line. In a very well-known study, Coch and French (1948) used participative methods to introduce new production techniques to female pajama makers in the Harwood manufacturing plant. Four groups were involved: (1) a control group, which was simply given the new techniques and ordered to comply; (2) an experimental group, which elected two members to confer with management and help work out the details of the change; and (3) two other experimental groups, which participated in making decisions regarding the change. There were large differences in post change productivity in favor of the two full-participation groups. Productivity in the control group stayed below pre change levels, and 17 percent of the group quit during the first month after the change. The "representation" group was closer to the full-participation groups than to the control group.]

Bavelas (reported in French, 1950) did another experiment in the same plant and held a series of meetings with groups of sewing machine operators to set future production goals. Comprehensive feedback was provided to let the operators know how they were doing. Each experimental group was matched with a control group, and while productivity in the control groups remained relatively constant, there was a mean increase of 18 percent for the experimental groups.

Similar results were obtained with group goal setting in studies by Lawrence and Smith (1955) and Strauss (reported in W. F. Whyte, 1955). In the Strauss study female operatives on the painting line of a toy factory took over control of the speed of the conveyor belt. The result was that the speed of the line varied a great deal throughout the day, according to the desires of the group, but productivity increased by a considerable amount. In fact, it increased too much. Other departments could not supply the paint line fast enough, finished pieces piled up faster than they could be used, and serious wage inequities were created by the resulting increase in operator earnings. Consequently, the speed of the line was put back under the control of management. However, in a short time six of the eight girls had quit, and the paint department was worse off than before. This study is a good illustration of the type of commitment required of a management that uses participative methods.

Similar results, although not so clear-cut, were obtained in a Norwegian (French, Israel, & Ås, 1960) and a Japanese (Misumi, 1959) study.

Correlational data from the Michigan studies provide rather mixed support for the participation-productivity relationship. In the Katz, Maccoby, and Morse (1950) study of work groups in an insurance company, supervisors of low producing groups described themselves as supervising more closely, checking up more frequently, and giving more detailed instructions. However, this finding failed to be replicated in a study of maintenance work groups on a railroad (Katz, Maccoby, Gurin, & Floor, 1951).

One difficulty illustrated by these two studies is the fuzziness in the distinction between initiating structure and participation. If initiating structure is simply the opposite of participation, then the Katz, et al. (1950) study lends some support to the participation-productivity relationship. If not, there is no legitimate reason for discussing the two studies in this section. Unfortunately, there have been no research attempts to relate these two variables to each other.

The positive results obtained in the experimental studies just described have several distinctive features. Subjects were mostly semiskilled females on a production line, and the participative methods which were used almost always included group goal setting. That is, the jobs had clearly defined outcomes for which it was possible to set unambiguous goals. Locke's research on goal setting (cited in Chapter 15) has already suggested the powerful motivating properties of self-set goals. Also, the experiments were not terribly well controlled in terms of having a large number of subjects, random assignment of subjects to experimental conditions, and freedom from confounding influences. In the Bavelas study, for example, the experimental groups were given considerable feedback, while the control groups were not. Thus feedback-no feedback was confounded with goal setting-no goal setting, and the results of the study could have been due to either.

Two experiments which were somewhat better controlled are a field study by Morse and Reimer (1956) and a laboratory study by Campion (1968). In the

Morse and Reimer study, work groups in an insurance company were placed under a directive, highly structured type of supervision (hierarchical program) or under democratic, participative leadership (autonomy program). Considerable effort was expended toward instructing the supervisors of the two types of groups in the two leadership styles. Questionnaire follow-ups showed that the subjects did perceive the differences in the two styles. Employee satisfaction increased under the autonomy program but decreased under the hierarchical program. Production increased under both programs, but there was slightly greater increase for the hierarchical program. However, the primary criterion was a cost index, and the lower costs under the hierarchical program seem to have been achieved through a reduction in the work force. Likert (1961) points out that the superiority of the hierarchical program may not have been maintained if the experiment had lasted longer. The results seem inconclusive.

In his Ph.D. dissertation, Campion (1968) replicated many features of the Morse and Reimer study in a laboratory setting. Groups of students were asked to play a business game consisting of buying individual letters and marketing completed words according to certain rules. There were three students in a group plus a supervisor, who was a confederate of the experimenter. Groups were randomly assigned to either a democratic-participative or a directive-high structure supervisor for the first run of the game. On a second run the type of supervision was reversed. There were no significant differences in productivity for the two types of supervision. Since subject perceptions of supervisory style did not correspond exactly to what the experimenter had intended, groups were divided according to perceived influence; however, there were still no significant differences in productivity.

The difference in results between the Morse and Reimer (1956) and Campion (1968) studies and the field studies cited earlier points up the obvious fact that the effects of a particular managerial style depend on many things, such as the kinds of people being supervised and the tasks being performed. Studies by Vroom (1959, 1960) provide correlational evidence for the interaction of management style and employee characteristics. In general, it was shown that employees in a package delivery firm who were low on authoritarianism and high on need for independence tended to produce more under democratic leaders, while the reverse tended to be true for employees who scored high on authoritarianism and low on need for independence. That is, such employees tended to produce more under directive supervision. A similar interaction was found for the correlation of participation and job satisfaction. Again, the above study was correlational in that influence in decision making was measured by the self-report of the subject.

In the Campion (1968) study this same interactive effect was investigated experimentally. That is, the subjects were divided into two blocks, high authoritarianism and low need for independence and low authoritarianism and high

need for independence, and then randomized across the experimental conditions. ~~As in the Vroom study, authoritarianism was measured with the F-scale~~
~~(Adorno et al., 1950), and need for independence with a questionnaire.~~

Again, using game performance as a dependent variable, there was no
significant interaction between the individual difference variable and experimental treatment. However, when the groups were divided by *perceived* influence in decision making, results similar to Vroom's were found. That is, subjects who were low on authoritarianism and high on need for independence
performed better under participative supervision and subjects who were high on
authoritarianism and low on need for independence performed better under
nonparticipative supervision. A similar interaction was found using work satisfaction as a dependent variable.

In view of the far-reaching implications prescribed for these variables by
many writers (~~e.g., Likert, 1967~~), it is surprising that the body of empirical research is so small and that practically no attention has been devoted to interactive effects. Surely the same prescriptions cannot be made for all subordinates, all managers, all tasks, and all situations.

THE HUMAN RELATIONS APPROACH REEXAMINED

Given this brief look at the research literature concerning the effects of
management style, we would now like to view the problem from a somewhat
different perspective. Specifically, we would like to adopt a social-psychological
point of view with regard to the prescriptions concerning initiating structure
and shared decision making (participation).

Management and the initiation of structure: the unilateral fiction. An
implicit assumption in discussions of this factor seems to be that the "initiating" behavior of managers is unidirectional. That is, managers are viewed as
persons who initiate actions for others and whose interactions end once these
directives are issued. Organization charts often depict positions with arrows
pointing from higher to lower positions. A manager is often described (see Chapter 2) as one who controls, directs, gives instructions, structures tasks, etc., all
of which suggests that a manager plans, while others implement. However,
this orientation seems to ignore some crucial properties of interaction, especially "exchange" behavior (Homans, 1958).

The basic factor that is missing from these unilateral views is that persons
who interact undoubtedly behave as if relationships were reciprocal rather
than unilateral. When a request is executed, a favor is asked, or a reward is
given, it is reasonable to expect that some form of repayment will be made.
Actions can be viewed as investments which are intended to produce returns,
and the quality of interaction is affected strongly by the speed of the return,

the likelihood of return, and the magnitude of the repayment. The argument here is that descriptions of managerial initiation have unidirectional overtones, and this has diverted attention from the basic fact that expectancies concerning exchange affect the relationship between a manager and a subordinate.

A situation with no exchange is one in which a manager gives a directive and the subordinate executes it, after which a totally new interchange might occur (stimulus [S_1] $\rightarrow$ response [R_1]). This seems to be an implicit but prominent model of managerial action. However, many managers do engage in interactions which *look* like exchange. They give an order, the subordinate responds to the directive by suggesting revisions, and then the manager takes additional action. This sequence of events approximates exchange more closely, with one important exception. When the manager responds to the suggested revisions, he may often reaffirm his original remarks or at least their substantive content. Put in different terms, we have here an instance of persuasion imposed upon an exchange relationship. The main property of this quasi exchange is that hesitancy on the part of the subordinate may produce intensified efforts by the manager to be persuasive about the original directive, but the subordinate's response is viewed as nothing more than a clue that more forceful statements are needed. If this sequence of events were represented in symbolic form, it would be stated as $S_1 \rightarrow R_1 \rightarrow S_1$. The second stimulus presented by the manager is essentially independent of, and unresponsive to, the subordinate's response. A close approximation to exchange would occur when persuasion is replaced by bargaining ($S_1 \rightarrow R_1 \rightarrow S_1 \rightarrow R_1$. . .). In this sequence of events, the manager gives an order, the subordinate responds in ways which suggest that some portions of the order are unacceptable, the manager actually modifies the demands of the directive, there is a further evaluation by the subordinate, etc. The manager's modified directive *is* contingent upon the response of the subordinate, there is more explicit bargaining in the sense that the subordinate indicates the limits within which the order is acceptable (e.g., Barnard, 1938), and both parties then negotiate the width of these limits. It should be made clear that exchange processes may not be confined to simple verbal confrontations in the manager's office. The order may be given, after which the subordinate tries to execute the request and then bargains with the task setter. Furthermore, it is important to note that events relevant to an exchange might cumulate. For example, the subordinate may execute an assignment and expect that in return the manager will comply with some request, provide some commodity such as a wage increase or approval of a promotion, or allow him greater latitude to accept, reject, or modify future assignments. Our reason for pointing out these additional instances of exchange is that it is easy to confuse exchange processes with occasions of verbal feedback. The exchange processes which are relevant in the present context extend considerably beyond such interactions. They include the more basic possibilities that during interaction investments are made, and there is the expectation that in subsequent interactions the other party will take account of earlier investments and will adjust his response so that a balanced and reciprocal exchange of rewards is executed.

Sayles (1965) argues, for example, that the effective manager is one who surveys the organization, finds units which can be helpful at different stages in his own work flow, and then tries to ensure the availability of these service units by negotiating an exchange with them. In Sayles's view the manager essentially structures his relationships with service units in such a way that in return for some rewards or consideration from his unit, the service group will provide service on demands. This method of handling relationships with service groups assumes that exchange is a basic preference of persons and that if this preference is acknowledged openly, subsequent interaction will unfold with more regularity. It is important to note the particular type of group involved in this example, namely, service groups. By definition, service groups are units for which other groups initiate action. Little discretion is left to the service unit to initiate its own projects or to exercise control over inputs. Part of Sayles's argument seems to be that even though a service unit may legitimately be treated in a unilateral fashion, there are sufficient tensions which arise in such unilateral relationships so that service functions may be performed inefficiently. The manager who approaches a service unit as a unit with which to establish reciprocal rather than unilateral relationships might frequently be in a better position to obtain continuing inputs from the unit. The manager who is sensitive to reciprocal properties of relationships, handles them openly, and remains attentive to obligations and rewards that are associated with relationships is perhaps better able to stabilize relationships and to reduce dissatisfaction.

Given the basic assertion that exchange processes are imposed on managerial initiation and that definitions of managerial assignments frequently involve actions which unbalance an exchange, it is important to look more closely at some subtle properties of exchange relationships. These properties have been singled out because of their relevance for managerial action and because they suggest areas in which investigations of managerial effectiveness should be conducted. These ideas derive from several existing theories of exchange (e.g., Adams, 1965; Barnard, 1938; Blau, 1964; Homans, 1958; E. E. Jones, 1963).

There probably are vast differences in the promptness with which persons repay a favor. The parties in any exchange may have quite different ideas about how frequently it is necessary to "balance" the relationship. A manager, for example, is more accustomed to delayed rewards. His job imposes longer time perspectives, and he envisions progress in terms of more remote outcomes; thus he probably repays the investments of subordinates at a relatively slow rate. However, subordinates who maintain more limited time perspectives may expect more frequent payment. Thus a manager may conclude that a yearly wage increase or promotion is sufficient to repay the contributions made by the workers. He balances his relationships on an annual basis. The worker, however, may find such a delay too lengthy and conclude that the manager is a person who "hoards" rewards, is reluctant to repay, and is in general unresponsive to subordinates. When these impressions begin to crystallize, the worker should reduce his inputs, invest more effort in relationships where payment is more immediate (e.g., relationships with the work group), and become less satisfied with the manager. Notice that the amount of repayment is not the crucial issue here—a conclusion which managers might be tempted to make— but rather the structure of repayment. Furthermore, if the worker reduces his input when he is not repaid, the manager may respond by increasing the pressure on him to work harder. This could increase the worker's dissatisfaction since he loses even more control over his work situation, and this in turn may lead to even further reductions of productivity. The worker might conclude that not only were his contributions not repaid, but they were punished, a conclusion which should seriously undermine a superior-subordinate relationship.

Exchange has additional complexities because actions which are received obligate the recipient. If the manager receives some extra output from a subordinate which enables him to look like an effective manager, the manager should feel gratitude toward the subordinate. But there may also be some lingering unease because the subordinate has also imposed an obligation on the manager to repay the favor in the future. When a relationship is clouded by obligations, there may be an increase in tension since the manager must remain attentive to his obligations and therefore has less freedom. Furthermore, the manager's activities might be interrupted at unexpected times when the worker legitimately requests the manager to fulfill his obligation. When an obligation is imposed, there probably are no precise specifications concerning when or how repayment should occur. Control of the repayment lies in the hands of the person who *imposed* the obligation, not the person who is obligated. Under these conditions, a group of workers who are responsive to norms of reciprocity and who, *perform acts which benefit the manager* may ironically promote some dissatisfaction in the manager because they restrict the freedom with which he can structure his subsequent activities. Once obligations have been imposed on the manager, there are limits on the ways in which he can structure and assign tasks and on the number of additional demands that he can initiate with subordinates. Once a set of obligations has been imposed, subsequent interaction should unfold in a more efficient manner if new demands are made *after* rather than before earlier obligations have been satisfied. If we repeat an earlier point that managers tend to delay repayment longer than is consistent with the time perspectives of subordinates, then it seems clear that there could be considerable lingering tension in highly efficient units. The tension arises because subordinates produce beyond expected levels. This production obligates the manager to repay. The manager may not feel the need or be able to repay immediately; consequently, subordinate inputs are not reciprocated, and satisfaction and productivity decrease.

There are several possible implications of this analysis. The problem of one-sided obligations should become less serious when the manager can increase the frequency of repayment. It follows that he may need something besides delayed rewards, such as promotions, to fulfill short-run obligations. One way of providing immediate repayment is to give subordinates increased discretion over their assignments. The manager may give the subordinate more freedom to design his assignment, to enlarge his job, or to report outcomes when he wishes in a form that he prefers. Attractive as this form of reward may appear, it might have some limitations, especially with interdependent tasks. If a small number of workers are given more job discretion in repayment for benefits given to the manager, then job enlargement may impinge on other tasks and make coordination more difficult. The obligation problem might also be lessened in an organization where reminders of remote rewards are made frequently so that the workers know the obligations have not been neglected, that some repayment will be forthcoming, and that the magnitude of the repayment will match their investments.

A related and perhaps even more basic issue concerns the question of how a person signals that he expects or does not expect repayment when some input is provided and how the recipient detects such signals when there are pressures to obscure the input. Presumably detection of signals becomes less of a problem when a person's responsibilities are made explicit. When responsibilities are clarified, it should be more apparent which items are included in, and excluded from, an exchange. However, explicitness may be detrimental because "extra" inputs do not occur and performance drifts toward established job definitions (Katz & Kahn, 1966). Managers might gain some clarity in relationships if there were more explicit discussion of inputs which the subordinate feels have not been repaid and if the manager also discussed and clarified his impressions of ways in which he has handled his obligations. Among other things, we are arguing that the content of performance appraisals might profitably be expanded. Instead of focusing solely on inputs which are rewarded by money, the manager might benefit if he talked about additional sources of repayment and summarized his views about the state of the exchange relationship—whether the relationship is balanced or not—to see whether these views coincide with those of the subordinate. In this way the manager might discover inputs which the subordinate feels should be reciprocated but which have not been recognized.

In a sense we are arguing that the manager should consider more carefully a style of behavior which some would argue he should avoid at all costs, namely, bargaining. However, exchange seems to overlay managerial practice whether it is recognized or not, and unilateral persuasion tends to obstruct exchange relationships. Undoubtedly, managers may shun bargaining on the assumption that when a subordinate realizes that he has some bargaining power, he will use it in a malevolent manner. Here is one place where laboratory studies may have hindered rather than aided theories about managerial effectiveness. For a considerable time, several bargaining studies conducted in the laboratory seemed to show that when subjects negotiate, they compete rather than cooperate. However, recent studies suggest that these conclusions were premature and that they may have been produced by an artifact in the laboratory. Most laboratory bargaining studies have involved very small financial payoffs to the participants. When payoffs were small, it was typical to observe that players were competitive rather than cooperative. However, when payoffs were made much more substantial (e.g., Kelley, 1965; Radlow, 1965), it was found that competition declined sharply. The explanation of this somewhat unexpected outcome was that exercises with low payoffs were boring and noninvolving for the participants, and to make the game more interesting, subjects became competitive. However, when the stakes were higher, interest increased and competition was unnecessary.

The relevance of these findings for the present discussion is that the nature of bargaining is probably considerably more influenceable than has been realized. There is a growing body of literature which suggests that task variables, amount of monetary reward, impressions of the other participants, openness of the bargain, etc., can lead persons to be more or less competitive in bargaining relationships. Because bargaining relationships can cause sizable problems if their existence is not acknowledged, it would seem important in the study of managerial effectiveness to investigate the question of under what conditions it is possible to establish nonmanipulative bargaining.

It would be unreasonable to conclude from this analysis that persuasion should be abandoned. In any specific situation the manager has only a finite set of repayments which he can use to sustain an exchange, and it is probably essential for him to persuade the worker that these payments are attractive. But if the persuasion activity is done within the framework of exchange rather than apart from it, then persuasion should have a greater probability of being effective since it is directed at the existing structure of the relationship and is sensitive to its properties (e.g., will balance or imbalance occur?).

There is a final property of an exchange which relates closely to the preceding topic, and that is the question of the kind and amount of repayment. Here there are even fewer choices. The problem can be illustrated if we look at the instance in which a manager gives an order and the subordinate executes it. When the worker completes his assignments, he is given some compensation, which may or may not be sufficient to conclude the exchange. But notice that there has been a transfer of commodities. The worker has exchanged compliance for money. Our interest is in the question of whether such a transformation of commodities is sufficient to conclude the exchange or whether there may exist additional pressures to reciprocate the commodities in *kind*. From this perspective we might hypothesize that while the exchange of compliance for money may execute some terms of the bargain, there is lingering pressure to exchange compliance for compliance. Thus the most satisfactory relationship would be one in which the person who has been controlled then gets the opportunity to control the other person. The reason we expect that there might be some pressures to reciprocate in kind is that a sizable problem in an exchange is that persons typically overpay or underpay their obligations. When an inequitable repayment occurs, the interaction cannot conclude since there are additional items that must be reciprocated. Thus an exchange in which different commodities are exchanged may be difficult to conclude and may produce a chain of unwanted obligations.

In general, an exchange can be precarious unless there is some explicit recognition and acceptance of the rules for transformation. In the context of repayment, it is well to cite the findings of Goranson and Berkowitz (1966) concerning the conditions under which persons will reciprocate a favor which they have received. They found that a person who is helped will be more apt to reciprocate the help if the original help was initiated at the helper's own choosing than if he was forced to help. This finding, if it were to replicate, has considerable importance for the present discussion. It suggests that volition or choice is a crucial factor which determines whether an exchange will be balanced. If a subordinate receives help and interprets this help as something that the manager was forced to provide, he should feel less pressure to reciprocate it. However, if the manager views the situation differently, this reluctance of the subordinate to repay may be interpreted as ingratitude, in which case the manager might either try harder to solicit a repayment or else reward the subordinate less in the future. Notice that what could mediate the unreciprocated help is the impression that the manager did not offer help of his own volition. It would seem imporant to determine the extent to which the perception of choice affects exchange of commodities other than help.

Management and participation: the problem of indiscriminant sharing. It seems reasonable to state that a considerable portion of a manager's effectiveness is dependent on the inventory of rewards he has to dispense. Probably no manager has as large a stock of rewards as he would like, and typically he may feel quite constrained to a limited amount. However, there is one significant source of reward over which the manager usually does maintain considerable control, namely, shared decision making, or "participation."

Other writers have questioned the indiscriminate use of participation as a management technique. Schein (1965) implies that unqualified use of participation violates the simple truth that men are complex and a variety of interaction strategies is appropriate. Tannenbaum and Weschler and Massarik (1961) specify a number of points one should consider before choosing a leadership "pattern." We have already cited evidence from Vroom and others to show that participation may be a very inappropriate technique for certain types of people in certain types of job situations. We are certainly in agreement with these arguments. Our aim in this chapter is to expand upon them and formulate some additional speculations as to what might result if the concept of consideration were indiscriminately applied.

Presumably when a subordinate participates in the making of "central" decisions within his own unit, several features of this situation are rewarding. The subordinate may have contributed ideas and exerted influence over the final decision (some of his ideas are actually incorporated in the solution); participation adds to the variety of his job; he receives recognition and the chance to be more visible to his superiors; he learns more about the intricacies of the firm and is better informed when he performs his own assignment; and needs for autonomy and independence are satisfied to a greater extent than they may be on the job. These several rewards are often difficult to obtain in regular assignments; thus it would seem that the manager who uses shared decision making frequently will enhance satisfaction and bind his subordinates more closely to their jobs and their associates.

But extensive participation may also produce other effects that might cancel out, or otherwise interact with, the rewarding aspects of participation. Notice that so far nothing has been said about the content of participative meetings, what is accomplished, what the final solution looks like, the extent to which it reflects the optimal usage of resources, etc. Participation which enhances the magnitude of rewards for individuals may also be participation which is wasteful in problem solving. For example, the manager may regard participation solely as a device to increase rewards and not anticipate any useful inputs for problem solving. If he maintains this point of view, what might happen is that either participants will influence peripheral issues within the department or else their suggestions will be ignored and a solution imposed on them.

Problem solving may be influenced in other ways. Members may become narcissistically absorbed in need satisfaction (e.g., Fouriezos, Hutt, & Guetzkow, 1950) and respond to the problem solely in terms of what would satisfy them most. Subordinates may regard participation as unwarranted interference with their other activities, in which case participation reduces rather than enhances satisfaction. This latter possibility is especially likely because managers and subordinates often perceive organizational events in distinctly different ways. The manager processes information from a larger portion of the organization and employs more extended time perspectives (e.g., Goodman, 1965). As a consequence, subtle developments within the organization often assume considerable importance for the manager and prod him toward immediate action. The problem is that subordinates may view these developments as trivial and question why a group has been convened to discuss them. Thus the manager who legitimately wants to be considerate may erroneously induce participation involving problems which are crucial to him but which seem insignificant to the subordinate. Under these conditions, the supposed benefits of participation are likely not to occur. An additional consequence of participation when discrepant views exist concerning the importance of the issue is that the discussion may be utilized for other purposes. A person who has to spend time discussing an insignificant issue may be reluctant to admit that his time is being wasted. As a consequence, he may use the meeting as a forum to conduct other, more important business (e.g., to establish an alliance with another associate). If this occurs, the manager receives little help with his original problem and may discover that new problems have emerged.

An intricate but potentially crucial set of questions about participation concerns the existence of group boundaries. When a manager calls several persons together to discuss an issue, he may presume that a distinct group has been formed, while the participants may view the situation differently. The problem for the participants is that they participate in numerous meetings, and if it is unclear on what basis they have been included in a specific gathering, they do not know what they are expected to contribute. Their roles are unclear. Several consequences may occur. Katz and Kahn (1966) suggest that when the person finds himself in a setting where boundaries are unclear, he will engage in some form of behavior which is a "compromise" of the several roles in which he typically finds himself. A problem with this sort of compromise behavior is that the person might be less likely to provide any unique informational inputs for the problem which is being discussed and also less likely to become involved. Actions which represent a composite response to several different demands may also tend to be less assertive and more cautious and to involve more task-irrelevant inputs.

Frequent meetings involving partially overlapping membership in collectivities with inexplicit boundaries may have additional negative effects on problem solving. Weick (1966b) has argued that as a person's group ties multiply, there is a greater likelihood that conflicting demands for action will be generated by these several groups. If these conflicts are coupled with inexact boundaries, participants find themselves in situations of high ambiguity. Existing laboratory research in one management setting (e.g., Sherif & Harvey, 1952) suggests that as ambiguity increases, personality variables rather than task requirements exert more control over actions. This has distinct implications for group problem solving. If ambiguity generates a greater incidence of idiosyncratic activities and sentiments, there may be less chance that the group will reach agreement or even develop shared definitions concerning what the relevant problem is. Furthermore, if individual personalities and dispositions are prominent and several participants obtain some need satisfaction by acting in ways which ignore the assigned task, they might be reluctant to forgo these satisfactions and resume problem solving. If the manager tries to influence participants to return to the assigned task, he may find that persons are less rather than more satisfied as a consequence of his efforts to share decision making.

Even though managers may be experienced in handling conflicts such as the ones just mentioned, the crucial point is that the origin of the conflicts lies *outside* the control of the group leader. While the leader may be able to generate temporary conflict resolution and produce some problem solving, the assertion of individual dispositions is apt to occur again because the basic sources of this problem are left untouched. A possible reason why such a problem occurs in the first place is that the diversity of group ties, coupled with obscure boundaries and ambiguity, may leave the participants without any clear prescriptions for action. As a result, idiosyncratic guidelines could be the only remaining sources of clarity. The leader has relatively little control over these origins. He does not control all group meetings in which his subordinates participate since other executives may use their time. Furthermore, since the manager probably does not convene the same set of persons each time a new problem occurs, less explicit boundaries surround each group and occasions exist for shared norms to emerge and for shared interests to be identified. If participants are unclear about which interests are relevant to a given problem, it should be even more difficult to find areas of agreement. Even if it were possible to find areas of common interest, most settings in which participation occurs are too short-lived for these commonalities to be discovered.

In sum, the issue of boundaries suggests a number of problems which may reduce the efficacy of participation and which deserve considerable research attention. This is especially crucial in view of the fact that some of our speculations come in conflict with other suggestions derived from the small group literature. For example, some literature exists (e.g., L. R. Hoffman, 1959) suggesting that group heterogeneity facilitates problem solving. However, a manager who convenes heterogeneous groups to help make decisions may incur some of the problems discussed above.

So far it has been argued that even though participation may permit managers to increase the rewards given to subordinates, organizational properties may decrease the value of these rewards. There may be other problems with participation, one of the most significant being a possible increase in pluralistic ignorance.

The essence of this discussion is that participation tends to obscure rather than highlight individual resources, preferences, and evaluations. Individual members who disagree with emergent shared definitions may often assume that they are the only dissenters, when in reality other members might share their disagreement. In the interest of facilitating discussion and in the belief that a consensus is forming, members with divergent views may tend to assent or at least withhold dissent. Since it is difficult to distinguish between a spurious consensus and a genuine one, perhaps it would not be surprising to find that members are reluctant to express divergent views. It is important to note precisely the argument being made here. We are *not* reasserting the common folklore that organizational pressures coupled with mobility tend to produce conforming subordinates who are "yes-men." Instead, it is argued that within organizations certain basic premises seem to be held by most members. These premises might include such items as "compromise is necessary," "differences are a fact of life," "group problem solving is wasteful unless there is some consensus," etc. If these premises are shared, it would not be surprising if members tended to withhold divergent details when they sensed that a consensus was forming. Participants have some needs to confine meetings to finite periods of time, to shorten rather than prolong their duration, and to justify the value of their participation; hence they very well may feel pressures to enhance areas of agreement. Thus we might expect that members would be eager to find areas of consensus; they might interpret slight indications of consensus as promising areas for convergence and tend to overestimate the amount of consensus that actually exists. This overestimation could occur for several reasons: wishful thinking; uncertainty about the basis on which the group was formed, coupled with the assumption that others are more informed about the agenda; unfamiliarity with the other participants and their willingness to disagree openly; heightened influenceability due to the ambiguous setting (Festinger, 1954); lesser commitment to their own views because of inadequate opportunities to review and revise them; and susceptibility to a talkative person in the sense that they assume he is vocalizing a majority point of view. Thus participation may produce a setting in which members regard consensus as elusive; they are eager to find areas of agreement so that the meeting can be hastened, and they are influenceable because the setting is ambiguous. A spurious consensus should be especially contagious when the emerging consensus follows authority lines, that is, when members lower in the hierarchy sense that those who are above them are in agreement when in actuality they may not be.

An interesting example of some of the above phenomena taken from a nonmanagement laboratory study is reported by March and Feigenbaum (1960). Male discussion groups which were required to agree on the ranking of the beauty of several women shown in photographs did not arrive at a consensus which reflected the individual preferences obtained before the meeting. The individual ratings made before the meeting showed that each participant strongly favored one photograph in which the most attractive girl was in a provocative pose. Presumably what happened during the meetings is that these strong initial preferences were suppressed because each person was concerned that his associates might criticize his choice since it involved a potentially illegitimate criterion (namely, sexual arousal). Consequently, the final group rating was made on the basis of more straightforward, less threatening standards of beauty (wholesomeness, pretty smile, neatness, etc.). The relevant point for our discussion is that the final group rating did not reflect the actual preferences of any member. However, each person apparently acceded to the majority in the belief that he was the only one who had been excited by the provocative photograph.

An additional point that must be considered is that groups seem to produce a diffusion of responsibility (e.g., Wallach, Kogan, & Bem, 1964). Recently there has been considerable interest in studies which seem to show that when persons make decisions in groups, they advocate the adoption of more risky alternatives than when they make solitary judgments. It is presumed that this "risky" shift occurs because responsibility for the outcome of the decision is diffused among all members; no one person will feel wholly responsible if the risky action should fail. The implications of the risky shift are considerable. When members participate in decision making, organizations may become committed to courses of action which place their future in more jeopardy than is intended. Group decisions can outrun organizational capabilities for response. Again, however, it should be emphasized that the risky shift phenomenon is based on laboratory experiments using nonmanagement samples and simplified decisions.

Notice that the risky shift again involves an instance of pluralistic ignorance. Caution, which the members feel privately, may not be communicated in a group setting, and there emerges the impression that other participants are more daring. Once again we have a group situation in which participation may lead to leveling rather than sharpening of the differences among members.

A qualification of the risky shift effect has emerged recently in the work of Rabow, Fowler, Bradford, Hofeller, and Shibuya (1966). They found that when the adoption of a riskier position would also violate a social norm (e.g., a businessman running for Congress versus further neglecting his family), members of groups did *not* shift toward riskier positions. Furthermore, the risky shift did not occur when the group was making recommendations for someone to whom they were personally committed (e.g., a father or brother). In the original studies of risk, most of the items involved recommendations which were impersonal and did not violate social norms. Perhaps the dangers of a diffusion of responsibility may be overestimated, and yet since it might be true that within organizations there is considerable impersonalization, acquaintanceships are on a superficial basis and there is some distance between persons at the various levels.

It could be argued that organizations parallel more closely the situations investigated by Wallach, et al. than they do the personal commitment conditions of Rabow et al. Furthermore, the relevance of social norms to particular decisions may be less clear in organizations. Considering these factors, it appears that the risky shift and its attendant pluralistic ignorance may be a fruitful research area to explore in connection with the use of participation in organizations.

Recently, Ziller (1964) has proposed the outlines of a theory of individuation, which permits us to explicate in sharper detail some of the problems that a manager might anticipate when he indiscriminately shares decision making. Formally, Ziller defines individuation as "a person's subjective mapping of the social world, in which self is differentiated to a greater or lesser degree from other social objects in the field . . . the greater the number of bits of information required to locate the person, the greater the degree of deindividuation" (p. 345). It is presumed that persons have strong needs to formulate clear-cut, consistent self-definitions. According to Ziller, a person can learn something about his own uniqueness if he works alone and tests his skills, but he also needs comparative information to establish distinctive qualities. For example, it may be difficult for a group member to separate his own distinctive contributions from those of other members since the final product is a composite of contributions and the person is able to obtain few data concerning his individual worth and competence. The conditions Ziller proposes as necessary for individuation to occur within a group setting are "(a) group membership must change, and (b) information concerning the group's performance must be presented to the group members" (p. 343). These two conditions are important because they may permit the individual to infer over time what his capabilities are. Assuming that the same task is performed when members are shuffled, the individual can see how the quality and quantity of group output change as a function of different persons working with him. He can begin to disentangle his own contribution from the contributions of other persons if he is the only factor across these several situations.

While these hypothesized requirements for individuation in groups are interesting, the most relevant point for us is the apparent complexity of the process, which may result in a low probability of its being implemented within an organization. When problems are solved in groups, personnel may not change as often as is required by this model, there may seldom be a complete reshuffling of members, and, finally, feedback is often more ambiguous than would be required by the model. In short, the person who tries to gain a more explicit view of his unique capabilities may be thwarted in this effort when much of his life is spent in groups.

There are times, however, when groups and deindividuation could be important. When a person fails, he probably prefers to be somewhat anonymous, and groups may often serve this purpose. Group-centered activity also satisfies needs for affiliation, prominence, and approval, which are more difficult to satisfy in individual-centered activities. Thus persons may have strong preferences for settings in which there is individuation, but also some preferences for voluntary deindividuation. It is for this reason that Ziller proposes that his theory is a cyclical theory. Preferences for individuation and deindividuation alternate over time. Initially, a person may seek group interaction to blunt the impact of a personal failure. Group participation affords an opportunity for self-reorganization. However, as group interaction continues, as the pain of failure becomes less intense, and as group pressures make it difficult to identify areas of uniqueness, persons should be eager to leave the group or to modify it in such a way that individuated behavior can emerge.

As a final step in the description of individuation theory, it might be useful to mention several variables which could retard individuation. The reason for citing these variables identified by Ziller is that several of them seem to be prominent in organizations. Among the variables are:

1 Homogeneity of composition and external appearance
2 Use of categorical labels rather than individual names (e.g., the use of the label "waiter" in a restaurant)
3 High rate of personnel turnover, an outcome which communicates that the position rather than the person is important
4 Random assignment to jobs, as opposed to assignment on the basis of test scores
5 Interchangeability of positions
6 Minimization of personal relationships outside the organization
7 Large groups
8 Minimization of privacy
9 Denial of property ownership
10 Rigid adherence to formal rules
11 Similarity between subgroups
12 Limited choice of alternatives in a decision-making situation
13 Limited criteria of success
14 An impoverished environment which lacks novel stimuli
15 Group as opposed to personal evaluations
16 Lack of personal records
17 Group as opposed to individual products
18 Similarity of tools and equipment

If one or more of these variables were to characterize a group, it would be more difficult to locate a specific person. For example, if we tried to locate a specific waiter in a restaurant, we would require more information to find him if all the waiters were wearing the same uniforms than if they were not, if there were no personal records, if the restaurant was large rather than small, if waiters formed subgroups on the basis of the territory they worked rather than on the basis of seniority or age, if waiters serviced different tables for each meal, etc. In this example, several properties of the restaurant render individual waiters somewhat invisible; they all share an uncommon number of features with one another, and it requires considerable information before we can locate a specific person. The individuation notion essentially argues that when an outsider has difficulty pinpointing a given individual, the chances are good that the individual himself also has difficulty differentiating himself from others and discovering his uniqueness. As a consequence, he should both be dissatisfied and exhibit intensified efforts to become a distinctive individual, even if this means that he must resort to deviant behavior.

In relating the concept of individuation directly to the participation technique, we suggest that participation tends to equalize power, potential solutions are given equal weight, each person has an equal opportunity to make inputs, and, in general, extensive participation tends to make an already homogeneous group even more deindividuated. Thus it is conceivable that extensive participation can hinder rather than enhance individual growth. Obviously, there are ways in which participation can be managed to reduce this outcome. But if organizations contain relatively few settings for individuated activity and if decision making and problem solving are defined as activities which should be performed by groups rather than individuals, then managers may make it even more difficult for workers to gain self-definition. Lest it be argued that a manager can dispense with concern about the individuation of his workers, there is at least some evidence showing that there are fairly high positive correlations between individuation and morale and individuation and productivity (Ziller, 1964).

Ziller suggests that Fiedler's (1964) research on the relationship between psychological distance of leaders and productivity can be interpreted within an individuation framework. Fiedler observed that leaders who saw their "worst" and "best" coworkers as quite similar tended to have less productive groups than distant leaders who saw their best and worst coworkers as quite dissimilar. Ziller interprets this finding as evidence that the psychologically distant leader produced a more individuated work group, more distinctions were made among the workers, and the workers perceived that they were being treated more as individuals than as members of a single category, namely, subordinates. Differential treatment by the leader coupled with rewarding of accomplishments may have led to greater identity, which in turn led to higher productivity. The effective manager, therefore, is a person who uses several categories to distinguish among his subordinates. As a result, greater differentiation exists within the group, members are treated as more distinct individuals, and this treatment tends to counteract the general pressures toward deindividuation which occur in organizations.

There are several measures which might be used to assess a manager's tendency to individuate. In addition to Fiedler's "similarity of opposites" test, there are several measures which tap cognitive styles, especially the tendency to use refined or gross categories. Relevant measures of categorization behavior include the object sorting task (Gardner, 1953, p. 219), "The behavior grouping test" (Marrs, 1955), and the Pettigrew Category Width Scale (Pettigrew, 1958). Ziller argues that an even simpler measure of a manager's tendency to individuate would be his memory of pertinent biographical information about the individual members of his group.

People interested in selection frequently make extensive use of biographical information. The implication of Ziller's analysis is that these same items might be used to measure a manager's information about *other* persons. It is conceivable that biographical information used in this way might contribute a great deal more to effectiveness than such information applied only to a description of the manager himself. A final set of measures which may tap a leader's tendency to individuate are those proposed by Mehrabian (1966). He assumes that distance is indicated when a person refers to another person in terms which are "nonimmediate" (e.g., he refers to some state that existed in the past or will exist in the future or refers to only part of the object). Although Mehrabian regards this measure as a correlate of negative attitudes (i.e., people feel more negative toward those objects which are more remote), it is possible that these measures might also relate to individuation.

If we assume that people tend to prefer both types of settings but at different times, an additional implication of individuation theory for managerial practice becomes apparent relative to the individuation-deindividuation cycle. The suggestion that derives from this analysis is that the effective manager might be a person who coordinates his shared decision making with changes in individuation preference. The idea is that the manager holds meetings to a minimum when persons are satiated with deindividuated settings, but he convenes meetings when subordinates presumably are satiated with individuated settings. It may appear impossible to find subordinates with similar cycles or to detect when satiation occurs. However, these problems may not be insurmountable. For example, it should be possible for a leader to accelerate and control the speed of satiation. Through a series of planned interventions, the manager may be able to make preferences more homogeneous.

To be more specific, the preceding line of reasoning suggests that the effective manager might hold fewer meetings of considerably longer duration. The rationale for this suggestion is that by reducing the number of meetings, all persons are placed in individuated settings for longer periods of time. Eventually these settings become unsatisfactory because needs for affiliation intensify. There should be a greater receptivity to meetings when they actually are held. If the meetings are quite lengthy and varied, it is conceivable that most of the advantages of a deindividuated setting can be realized "at one sitting," and the members are then eager to return to settings which are more individualized. In this example, the manager both acknowledges the existence of individuation cycles and acts in ways which serve to stabilize these cycles.

The discussion of individuation and participation will conclude with three additional points concerning interchangeable membership, social facilitation, and relative differences in size.

One of the more intricate participation problems involves changes in personnel. Ziller's argument is that if group membership changes frequently, this could enhance individuation because the member or members who stay can infer more about their unique contributions to an aggregate product. Opposed to this advantage is the possibility that changing membership also suggests that participants are interchangeable, that positions rather than people are important. If these impressions emerge, deindividuation rather than individuation should be the outcome. The fact that changes in personnel may hinder individuation is important to consider because it is common for a manager to assume that problem solving is improved when heterogeneous resources are used. We are suggesting that while this may be true, frequent personnel changes also tend to define persons as interchangeable. Even though a heterogeneous population might improve short-run problem solving if individuals cannot gain information about their uniqueness, long-range problem solving may be hindered.

The value of participation may depend also on the response tendencies which participants have before they go into a group discussion. Recent laboratory research by Zajonc and Sales (1966) suggests that when persons perform simple tasks in the presence of other persons, motivational levels may increase. In turn, dominant responses (those which are high in the response hierarchy) are more likely to be emitted, and subordinate responses are less likely to be emitted. An implication of this finding is that the outcomes of shared decision making will depend on which responses are dominant when the group convenes. Take the case of a worker who has to participate in a deindividuated setting at a time when individual-centered activity is more important to him. We might anticipate that the most dominant responses for this person would be responses which ignore other persons and do not require their presence. Assuming such a response tendency, if this person is placed in a group setting, we would expect to find that he would not act like a responsible member, would not be especially supportive, and in general would disrupt group functioning. These outcomes might result because the responses which have been intensified are those which can be satisfied in some setting other than the group. In fact, the threat of deindividuation may make participation even more adverse than it normally is for the person in this example. If several persons try to recast the deindividuated group setting into an individuated setting, it seems likely that group problem solving would deteriorate. Performance would increase if those who were trying to remake the group actually could leave in order to work in a setting which they found more compatible. Given the possible existence of individuation cycles, it seems reasonable that if persons had available the alternative of leaving the group temporarily, the level of group productivity might be increased considerably.

As a final point concerning deindividuation, it is interesting to speculate on issues involving relative size of units. Relative to entire organizations, decision-making groups are quite small. In this sense small decision groups are more individuated than organizations. Thus it is possible that members of organizations regard organizations as deindividuated settings and discussion groups as individuated settings. If we adopt this point of view, we might conclude that members would prefer more rather than fewer meetings. Furthermore, the content of these meetings might involve more efforts aimed at group differentiation. Obviously, it is important not to lose sight of the organizational point of view when talking about small group phenomena. If discussion groups are important mainly because they are relatively individuated settings in which individuals can become more differentiated in terms of their relationship to the organization, then this is an important component of organizational effectiveness. But if participants must also make important decisions at the same time that individuation occurs, then the quality of decisions may suffer. Thus participation may serve a useful function and serve it well, but only if the manager does not impose additional burdens on the participants and if he does not take actions which obscure individual contributions. However, an individuated group need not be a group without an assigned task. There may be tasks which place a premium on differences, permit differentiation among members, and make fewer demands for interdependence and sharing. The argument here is that it is these kinds of problems which should be assigned to groups in which individuation occurs.

In some ways the present argument may seem to contradict an earlier emphasis. Earlier we argued that discussion groups may be most visible as deindividuated settings which impede self-definition. Here we are suggesting that discussion groups may also be visible as individuated settings where self-clarity can emerge. These two views are not necessarily contradictory. To the extent that the group task imposes demands for consensus, areas of similarity are emphasized, minimal differentiations emerge, and a composite product results in which individuals cannot identify their unique contribution; then the setting will be deindividuated and will heighten problems of identity. However, when differences are demanded, sanctioned, and instrumental to task performance, individuation is more likely. Thus an individuated group might be less productive than a deindividuated group on some tasks (those tasks which require consensus and high interdependence), but on other tasks (e.g., disjunctive tasks, discussed by Thibaut and Kelley, 1959) both problem solving and individuation could proceed simultaneously and in ways that are mutually facilitating. Obviously, the premium is on careful selection of the agenda items—not an easy task.

Selective participation. Several questions have arisen in this chapter concerning the value of participation. It almost goes without saying that participation is closely tied to managerial effectiveness; however, participation has been commonly viewed as a means by which the manager can increase the productivity of his department and heighten satisfaction at the same time. Despite the zeal with which this practice has been adopted, there seem to be numerous problems associated with participation, and we have tried to detail some conditions under which participation might restrict both productivity and satisfaction. Obviously, this is not the complete story, and we hasten to add that the preceding analysis does not suggest that the effective manager is one who abandons participation, but rather that a more realistic appraisal of participation is needed. Participation is like any other organizational practice: it accomplishes some ends and thwarts others. We have to find out which and when.

The preceding line of analysis involves considerable speculation, a property for which no apologies are necessary. It has been stressed throughout this chapter that investigations of managerial effectiveness have been channeled into an uncommonly narrow range of problems for an uncommonly long time. In order to make substantial gains in understanding the determinants of effectiveness, it will be necessary to make extensive reexaminations of prevailing practices and ideas. Some directions for reexamination have been mentioned in this chapter. Should most of these ideas prove to be wrong or unworkable, there is still the distinct possibility that pursuit of them may suggest additional areas in which the yield will be more substantial.

SUMMARY

In this chapter we approached some well-known research topics from a social-psychological point of view. The focus was on leadership behavior and, more specifically, on the concepts of initiating structure, consideration, and influence in decision making (i.e., participation). Initiating structure was discussed as a two-way exchange between superior and subordinate rather than as a unilateral action on the part of the manager. Persuasion and bargaining were also examined as variants of a manager's initiation of structure. Under the general heading of "participation," several subproblems were discussed, namely, the effects of ambiguous group boundaries, an organizational value system which seems to value reaching a consensus quickly (independently of so-called conformity behavior), the tendency for group decisions to be "riskier" than individual decisions, and the manager's problems in maintaining subordinate individuality under conditions of group participation. These topics were discussed in terms of some hypothesized effects on satisfaction and productivity. This latter portion of the chapter was juxtaposed against the first part, which briefly reviewed the empirical research literature surrounding the relationships of these management style variables to work group productivity and employee satisfaction.

Much the same sort of approach is adopted by Lowin (1968) in his excellent review of the literature on the effects of participative decision making. It is another example of how a different point of view can illuminate a number of important hypotheses that must be tested before research can yield generalizations that have broad utility. He conceptualizes the effects of participation in terms of the feedback it provides to the parties (i.e., a learning model) and the particular needs it satisfies or does not satisfy under various conditions (i.e., a motivational model). His analysis clearly suggests that research on the effects of participation must have a strong longitudinal component, and on this factor almost all previous research does not measure up. A recent book by Marrow, Bowers, and Seashore (1967) recounts over twenty years of experience that the Harwood Manufacturing Company has had with participative decision making, but it is largely a case study with few controls, and it is difficult with any degree of certainty to attribute the positive results to what we have been calling "shared decision making." No research studies have systematically investigated the effects of participation over time, either in the laboratory or in the field—all of which again points up the need for more appropriate experimentation, including perhaps a more sophisticated approach to organizational simulation.

Chapter 18   **Research Suggestions in Management**
Selection, Promotion, and Appraisal:
A Social-Psychological Point of View

In this chapter we would like to take a more divergent view of some of the topics that have been subsumed under the label "psychology of managerial effectiveness." Not all such topics are discussed. Our intent is to convey the flavor of some research problems that might suggest themselves from this point of view and not to lay out specific proposals. The discussion is organized around two general topics, the utility of various management personnel practices and some relatively unexplored attributes of managers that might account for significant variability in performance.

SOME CURRENT PRACTICES REEXAMINED

From the material in Chapter 2 a number of management personnel practices emerged as being fairly extensively practiced by most firms. We shall discuss three: (1) promotion from within, (2) coaching as management development, and (3) managerial effectiveness defined as "getting results." The
442

following material is frankly speculative, but we hope it will generate some new research views and fresh approaches.

Promotion from within. Almost all management positions are filled by promoting from within. There are several obvious advantages to such a practice. Promotion is potentially one of the most potent incentives the organization has to offer, although, as was discussed in Chapter 15, very little research literature surrounds the topic. It also simplifies the task of searching for promotable managers, and much more information is available on intrafirm personnel. Considerable advantages also accrue because the promoted individuals are already familiar with the firm. Training time can be shortened, and payoff is more immediate.

A number of possible disadvantages of promotion from within can also be mentioned. For example, selecting managers from outside the organization may be viewed as injecting "new blood" into the organization, thereby avoiding the stagnation resulting from "inbreeding." However, it is not our intent in this chapter to discuss research problems posed by the above. Rather, we would like to focus on questions flowing from the more social-psychological properties of the situation. Investigating promotion as an incentive or asking whether injecting new blood results in the generation of better ideas is still within the realm of individual differences and has already been discussed in a research context.

The first problem is suggested by Merton's (1957) concept of "anticipatory socialization." The essence of this idea is that persons with upward aspirations identify with the group to which they aspire and not the one to which they belong. In organizations, this can take the form of subordinates' acting like and taking on the values of persons above them and would be functional because it aids their passage into the new group *if* they are promoted. Training time is lessened, and the persons who are responsible for selection gain some idea of how the subordinate will act if he is promoted. But the group in which the aspirant actually holds membership might suffer when this pattern of behavior is adopted. The aspirant might make less of an investment in his work group because he views his performance of tasks as instrumental to promotion and derives little satisfaction from the task performance itself. The emotional tone within the group might become more tense and hostile when members perceive that the aspirant "rejects" their way of life in favor of another one, and anger could result if the person actually gets the promotion. What might happen is that the person who invested the least in the group and made the most peripheral contributions is the one who receives the most substantial reward. Serious questions concerning the value of the group and the job might arise among the nonpromoted workers when promotion occurs under these conditions.

A work group in which the anticipatory socialization pattern might be especially disruptive is one in which there is a *high task interdependence*. Within such a group, it takes only one member performing his assignment in an inefficient manner to disrupt the performance of other persons for whom the outputs of the inefficient worker are the inputs for assignments. This has the interesting implication that the position of the aspirant in the work flow should affect the degree to which his aspirations disrupt group solidarity. If the aspirant is responsible for early steps in the performance of the task, his inadequate performance should have greater impact on group productivity than if he performs later stages of the task. An aspirant who performs the last step in a work flow cannot directly influence the work of anyone else, although his shoddy "final touches" may produce resentment if the inferior quality of the product is blamed on the group rather than the aspirant. The potential disruption caused by a pattern of anticipatory socialization could thus vary with the person's placement in the work flow.

Another potential research area revolves around one of the recurrent findings in the social-psychological literature (e.g., Lott & Lott, 1965), which says that as the frequency of interaction increases, liking also increases, and that persons tend to interact with those who are similar. Suppose that over time members of a work group interact frequently, mutual liking increases, and there is the perception of increased similarity. Suppose now that one member of this group is singled out for promotion. If similarity has been enhanced, there should be considerable puzzlement concerning why this particular person was promoted. After all, most members of the group are not that different. Puzzlement may give way to resentment toward the system, and feelings about the person who was promoted might also change. Since the promotion signifies that one member is different from the others, liking may decrease because there are fewer shared interests, and subordinates might become less responsive to the "new" manager. Thus the manager who may have been picked because of his ability to get along with people may find that this ability apparently vanishes when points of similarity decrease. One might argue that these behaviors on the part of the work group represent efforts to reestablish balanced relationships between liking and assumed similarity. From such a perspective, we would expect either that the workers would minimize the differences between themselves and the manager in an effort to retain their original sentiments or that they would magnify the dissimilarities so that it would be easier to change their sentiments. The question seems quite amenable to a research attack.

Internal promotion may have other effects on those who are not promoted. For one thing, those not promoted may feel under pressure to explain and justify why they were passed over. Many potential reasons are available, some of which might prove dysfunctional for the organization. An individual could derogate the firm as being insensitive to the skills of its employees, derogate the value of higher positions, increase his valuation of nonwork activities such as family life (e.g., Festinger, 1964b), enhance the value of the present work group, leave the organization, become indifferent, or convince himself that the best man actually was promoted and then strive harder to emulate his actions and to be responsive to his directives. Only in the case of the last resolution is there a clear implication that the company will benefit from the policy of promotion. With each of the other resolutions, there is an increased likelihood that members will diversify their interest or see their present situation as less attractive than they originally thought. It would seem useful to investigate for what kinds of people and under what conditions these various reactions might be utilized by the nonpromoted individuals.

There is perhaps an even more subtle way in which the actions of the nonpromoted could change. If, within a work group, persons tend to interact in a nondifferentiated manner, similarities rather than differences become salient. If a group is basically nondifferentiated, promotion may have the effect of imposing additional differentiation because a hierarchy of skills becomes more explicit. If this were to occur, members might start to act more like people who hold specific positions. This would be most apparent in those members who, on the basis of differentiation, perceive themselves to be of low status. What is being suggested here is that as differences become crystallized when a promotion is made, performance will tend to become more aligned with these differences in status. And since most persons who are not promoted may interpret this as an indication of lower status—an indication that they are not as good as they thought they were—they will feel increased pressures to act in a consonant manner. Remote as this possibility may seem, it has been demonstrated in several tightly designed studies (e.g., Burnstein & Zajonc, 1965). For example, a person's reaction time shifts markedly in response to promotion or demotion. If a person is demoted, his reaction time lengthens significantly from its basal level, and if he is promoted, it becomes more rapid. While reaction time may seem to have little relevance for organizational behavior, it is a variable which might be expected to show fewer effects of status changes than actual managerial behavior. Thus, if a significant effect is found with such a variable, it would be wise to explore the hypothesis further in an organizational setting. This is one of the aims of experimental research that we pointed to in Chapter 14.

While these studies suggest that the person whose status is raised (he is promoted) works harder so that his output is aligned with the higher status, it is a very real question whether this improvement offsets the decrement which may occur among those who do not receive the status increment. If performance becomes aligned with social position, the manager may act in a more competent manner when his position is elevated, but the remaining workers may become less competent as a result of their lower status, which is now visible. If indeed this occurs, perhaps these effects will be fleeting and remain only until the group can ignore the manager as a legitimate person against whom they will compare their actions. Performance might then drift back to its normal level. But notice that this avenue of improvement occurs only if the group is less attentive to the manager, a resolution that may interfere with subsequent acceptance of his directives.

An additional consequence of promotion from within that might be postulated is that supervisors actually may undermine the productivity of a group by reinforcing the actions of workers who appear to be "management caliber." This might occur when certain employees are identified as having management potential and are then given special coaching by their supervisor. Coaching may create problems because the worker is reinforced for his managerial actions, and these may be incompatible with the requirements of his present job. Within the work group, his job is to work interdependently to produce an output. If the candidate imports quasi managerial behaviors into his assignment and if these alterations are reinforced by supervisors, it is possible that performance will decline because incompatible task behaviors are elicited.

Other research problems could be suggested. A policy of promotion from within means that the person's career decisions are made in terms of the company rather than in terms of the field he represents. This means that crucial portions of professional training may be omitted if they are of little immediate use in the company. The employee who adopts this pattern of life may be able to make fewer and fewer distinctive contributions to his associates. Normally this might not be much of a problem because the manager replaces one set of skills with another. However, at a time when specialization is essential to the adequate performance of complex tasks and to innovation, the loss of technical expertise through intraorganizational career development could have serious consequences.

Promotion from within might also produce a kind of anticipatory spiral effect. We have discussed the possibility of the individual who shuns his work group, identifies with the next level, and then is promoted. Once the new level is achieved, there is no reason to expect that anticipations cease. There are new levels to which the worker may aspire. As a consequence, minimal investments could pervade all levels of the organization since the performance of tasks at one's own level is slighted in favor of attentiveness toward tasks at other levels. Notice also that we have assumed for the sake of argument that the aspirant perceives accurately those actions which are characteristic of the next higher level. However, there is undoubtedly some ambiguity about which behaviors are the most crucial and the most appropriate for the next level. Consequently, errors of judgment might occur. Not only might the aspirant shirk his duties at his present level, but the anticipatory behavior which he adopts may also be inappropriate. Under these conditions the firm could be affected in two ways. First, it would be difficult to know whether "inappropriate" behaviors were due to incompetence or misinformation, and second, the productivity and morale of each work group might decrease.

Considered together, the preceding points suggest some ways in which promotion from within may prove detrimental to the organization. It would be useful to find out whether these speculations are of any consequence and whether there are alternatives which might preserve some of the advantages associated with this policy and reduce some of its possible disadvantages. It is here that experimental methodology becomes crucial. Notice that if most organizations promote from within, it will be exceedingly difficult to find organizations which employ the opposite policy. And even if such organizations are found, they will be sufficiently unique so that it would be hazardous to regard them as comparable along all dimensions except promotion policy. In the absence of natural organizations that promote from outside, the obvious solution is to create an organization which does follow this policy.

Coaching as a management development technique. Regardless of whether a firm has extensive or limited formalized training programs, it is common to find that these programs are supplemented by considerable informal training. More specifically, a superior will often single out a small number of subordinates who appear to be potential candidates for managerial positions and then "coach" them on portions of his job which he regards as important. There are certain advantages to this practice. Specialized training personnel and materials are unnecessary, and the subordinate is not absent from his regular job for long periods of time. Costly managerial time, however, *is* expended, and the addition of the coaching task may be made without any explicit recognition of this additional task when rewards are dispensed. It follows that this "informal redefinition" of the manager's job as including training with no increase in reward for this assignment may create inequity, a hidden cost. Coaching also has the advantage that instruction can be tailored more explicitly both to the company and to the subordinate. The manager is familiar with the subordinate and the company and thus is potentially better able to present more of the "unique" premises which may not appear in more general training programs. Coaching also has the advantage that it reduces the training time of the subordinate once he is promoted. If he has been coached, presumably he is already familiar with many contingencies in his new assignment.

The coaching relationship seems to be based on a rather unique structure of rewards. For example, the primary reward used to control learning consists of approval and disapproval from the coach. There is the additional reward of promotion if the subordinate learns the managerial task adequately, but this particular reward is sufficiently remote so that it cannot be used as the sole means of reinforcing the several learnings which the subordinate must master. There are also the rewards of intrinsic job interest and increased competence at a new task. Potent as these rewards might be, it is difficult for them to function in the coaching relationship because the subordinate may seldom actually be allowed to practice being a manager. A manager who coaches a subordinate cannot be too conspicuous in his training activities lest he be criticized by other subordinates for showing favoritism. The manager who resorts to coaching may find it difficult to single out a subordinate for special instruction and still maintain the impression among the remaining subordinates that they are receiving equal treatment. A more contingent and immediate reward is needed, and approval tends to be the commodity most available to the supervisor. Assuming that approval mediates much of the learning which occurs in the coaching relationship, several potential research issues become apparent. First, the attractiveness of the manager to the subordinate may be a crucial determinant of whether approval will serve as a potent reinforcement. If the subordinate has some misgivings about the supervisor, this makes it easier for the subordinate to derogate the supervisor when the latter tries to induce changes which the subordinate finds unpalatable. When discrepencies occur between a practice advocated by the "coach" and a practice which the subordinate prefers, the latter can either adopt the new practice or derogate the coach and argue that it is not necessary to make the change since the manager is misinformed, untrustworthy, biased, etc. (e.g., Aronson, Turner, & Carlsmith, 1963). A fallible manager who utilizes approval as his primary reinforcement is vulnerable to derogation. Also, when central beliefs held by the subordinate are attacked, it is probably more likely that derogation rather than attitude change will occur. As a result, the subordinate may wind up with a piecemeal conception of how an effective manager thinks and acts. Thus the subordinate would change his beliefs in areas which are of peripheral importance to him and which may also be of little consequence in accomplishing managerial tasks. The likelihood of piecemeal learning should decrease as it becomes more difficult for the subordinate to derogate the coach. From this standpoint, at least, the more competent the manager, the more effective he will be as a coach. It is difficult to find fault with competence.

A well-recognized problem with the coaching technique arises because the incumbent manager is in the dual position of coach and judge. He is visible as a person who can help the subordinate and to whom the subordinate is supposed to display most of his inadequacies so that they can be remedied before he is promoted. But if too many inadequacies are revealed, the manager in his role as judge may view the subordinate as a less suitable candidate for promotion and refuse to recommend him. When these dual functions of coaching and judgment are embedded in a single person, there are decided effects on learning and performance (e.g., Blau, 1954). The potentially most important effect is that subordinates may be more prone to conceal their performance. The judgmental rather than the coaching role may take precedence for most individuals, with the result that subordinate errors or misunderstandings of managerial tasks are not revealed. Thus the manager may feel that his protégé has learned the necessary skills, only to find that when the protégé actually becomes a manager, there are significant gaps in his technique, gaps that could have been detected and remedied earlier if the subordinate had been more open about his performance. Related to this point is a study by Maier, Hoffman, and Read (1963), in which it was found that superiors who had previously held their subordinates' position were occasionally less adequate in communicating with these subordinates than managers who had not held the position of their subordinates. It was found that subordinates were less willing to share information because they were concerned about the effect of disclosure on their chances for promotion and that superiors who had previously held the job of their subordinates developed blind spots about, as well as insights into, how the tasks should be performed.

One final point concerning the unique reward structure in coaching should be noted. When a subordinate practices some form of managerial behavior, the manager can reward either the content or the style of the performance. J. Wallace (1966) has recently shown that the choice of which aspect to reward can have decided effects on belief changes, especially when the subordinate has performed some action about which he has misgivings. Suppose, for example, that a manager coaches the protégé on ways to gain approval for a proposal given to top management. Suppose also that the proposal is one that can be justified financially regardless of the psychic costs to workers but that the protégé actually does not believe the financial considerations are paramount. If the manager has the protégé "practice" presenting a proposal (e.g., has him role play a typical presentation to a review board), the degree to which the protégé will actually come to believe that financial rather than psychic considerations are crucial may depend on how the manager rewards the performance. Wallace's work suggests that if the manager responds to the protégé by saying that the *content* of the proposal was good, there will be less attitude change than if he rewards the style of performance. The explanation of this outcome is that it is more uncomfortable for a person to realize that his action violates some basic behavioral disposition than it is to find that he can produce credible content on an issue. When a person is told that his performance was excellent, he is faced with the discomforting fact that even though he is supposedly a sincere person, he is very effective when he behaves in an insincere manner. This discomfort should be greater than the discomfort associated with the realization that he can generate plausible content that is opposed to his beliefs and can be convincing when he does so.

In the preceding discussion of performance versus content reward, we began to shift from issues involving reward to issues involving the content of coaching. We wish now to deal specifically with additional content issues in a coaching relationship. Since coaching involves a considerable amount of instruction without opportunities for practice, there is always the danger that the protégé will learn the symbols which attach to desirable organizational practice, but will not learn the corresponding techniques. In a situation where there is little chance for practice, it is possible that the learner will alter his "statements" about organizational life so that they begin to sound like those which managers make but that the learning will proceed no further. Because organizational life is heavily loaded with jargon, because much of the coach's instruction is probably phrased in this jargon, and because it is difficult to distinguish between the learning of symbols and the learning of content, this appears to be a problem that could reduce the extent to which material learned during coaching is carried over into actual managerial practice. Furthermore, since the coach is most familiar with symbols, since he wants to reduce the time which training takes away from other assignments, and since he is probably also looking for some indication that he is as effective at training as at managing, he may tend to single out symbolic changes for attention, reward them, and gauge progress according to them.

If a manager serves as a behavior model when he is in a coaching relationship, it is likely that he will also function as a model for the protégé when he is not coaching. Incidental portions of his style may be adopted by the protégé as well as those which are explicitly communicated as a result of greater attentiveness. One interesting incidental learning which may be adopted by the protégé concerns patterns of self-reward (Mischel & Liebert, 1966). When a manager approaches his noncoaching tasks, he imposes more or less stringent standards of accomplishment on himself before he is satisfied. The interesting question for coaching arises when the standards which the manager imposes on his own performance differ from the standards which he imposes on the learner. Mischel and Liebert's investigation is at best suggestive since it involves adult models for children, but the findings are sufficiently provocative to deserve follow-up with other populations. They found that when a model was stringent regarding the rewarding of his own performance but lenient toward subordinates, subordinates were less stringent when they rewarded themselves than when they observed a model who exhibited the opposite kind of behavior. The most effective situation for imposing stringent standards was one in which the model was stringent in both his own performance and his training standards. It is also important to take note of a subtle distinction in this analysis. While many coaches try to ensure success in subordinates by being lenient in the standards they impose, the subject may be learning additional things besides skills in task performance. He is learning something about the stringency of standards which he should impose on his assignments before feeling rewarded. Thus, while a coach may be able to ensure success by using lenient standards, he may also unwittingly instill lower standards for self-reward, even if his own actions exemplify the usage of stringent criteria. The simple fact that he displays stringent standards may not be sufficient to offset his lesser demands on the protégé. The result should be coupled with that obtained by Zander, Medow, and Efron (1964), who found that when observers' estimation of the level at which a group of persons would perform a group task fell *below* the expectations of the group itself, group members were less favorable toward the observers than when the standards were higher. However, they were not totally unresponsive to the lower estimates of the observers. When the group actually attained the goal which they had estimated, they were *less* willing to raise their goals on subsequent trials when the original observer expectations were too low than when they were too high. When the observers' expectations were excessive, the group raised its aspiration level when it succeeded, but it did *not* lower it when the estimated level was not achieved. These results argue that learning may benefit more when standards err in the stringent direction than in the lenient direction. It is proposed here that coaches who are unfamiliar with some of the dynamics of learning and who maintain the commonsense view that small accomplishments should be rewarded may unwittingly produce managers who are less competent than they might otherwise have been.

The fact that a coaching relationship is also informal raises additional issues. It will be recalled that the manager who tries to coach and single out the protégé for special attention must contend with the fact that other subordinates who are not favored may respond negatively to this special treatment. Thus there are pressures on the coach to be relatively discreet about the coaching relationship. This makes it rather difficult for the protégé to know when the manager is coaching and when he is not. Since clear distinctions between training and nontraining are not possible, it is probably more difficult for the protégé to know what it is that he is supposed to learn, and it is more difficult for the coach to control the learning process. The chances that the protégé will learn undesirable managerial behaviors or none at all are heightened under these conditions. Furthermore, it probably is necessary for the subordinate to remain hyperattentive to the coach so that he can detect when coaching is occurring. With this hyperattentiveness is apt to go greater adoption of practices which the coach did not intend to teach.

The equating of effectiveness with "getting results." We have already discussed this topic in terms of the problems it poses for the prediction of managerial success with measures of individual differences. We would like to consider it again from a somewhat different perspective in hopes of adding further to a fruitful research agenda.

Almost without fail, the organizations in our sample and in samples obtained by other researchers report that the effective manager is one who gets results. Whether this is a simplification made for the benefit of investigators or a basic premise within organizations, the statement is made sufficiently often so that it must be taken seriously. The criterion of results presumably facilitates personnel decisions because it specifies a rather simple rule which can be applied to numerous decisions concerning salary increase, promotion, transfer, training suitability, etc. The criterion is also apparently compatible with a basic goal of organizations, namely, to remain viable. If success is equated with viability, then a successful manager is one who facilitates the survival of the organization and who is therefore valuable. However, obsessive usage of results as a criterion for effectiveness runs the risk of impeding rather than promoting effective managerial practice. It is the purpose of the following discussion to elaborate some of the questions that must be answered if the effects of focusing on results are to be more fully understood.

When a manager is held accountable for outcomes, he is probably held less accountable for the means by which these outcomes are attained. The concept of managerial discretion (Jaques, 1956), for example, preserves the point that managers have considerable latitude in the means they use to secure outcomes. If outcomes are the salient basis on which a manager will be judged, then many of his actions will be guided with an eye toward results, but this may also mean that he directs considerably less attention to the state of the system which generates the outcomes. This selective focusing may promote some deterioration of the work-flow system. When a manager tries to meet a quota, he will probably assign tasks, make demands, and monitor in such a way that the results actually are obtained, but the problem is that the next time the group tries to meet a quota, it may have been left in a state of disarray. Excessive shortcuts could have been sanctioned, and there may have been established a set of sufficiently negative precedents and expectations so that the group will be unable to function effectively. A manager whose attention is directed toward outcomes rather than process may find himself able to do too little too late with regard to the work processes once results are obtained. It is argued that when results are the overriding basis on which a manager will be judged, he pays less attention to process and more attention to incipient outcomes while his unit is performing the task. He may prematurely request indications of work group progress and make immediate realignments of personnel and tasks when these cues are discouraging, and in making these adjustments in terms of outcomes rather than process, the manager may hasten the deterioration of the system. Even when the manager is successful in getting outcomes, if he is not mindful of the precedents that are established, he may find that his unit is less adaptable when it is given a new assignment which requires a different pattern of interaction. This is one of the explanations of the Morse and Reimer (1956) experiment, which showed that directive, authoritarian leadership can produce greater profitability, at least over the short run.

Notice that if a manager is successful, top management may respond by giving him additional responsibilities or new assignments. If the manager has ignored the processes by which the first successful outcome was achieved and fails to see what has happened to his department, it is possible that the group will falter at the new assignment. All these processes seem amenable to experimentation by means of simulated organizations or experimental field studies that abstract or preserve the relevant variables.

Another possible avenue through which a system may deteriorate involves progress reports. A manager who is sensitive to the state of outcomes and who checks frequently in order to gauge progress might decrease progress by his frequent interventions. Individuals in the work group are required to drop what they are doing, summarize their progress, and then resume their work once the report is written. These interruptions of work not only retard progress but may actually disrupt a highly interdependent, closely timed work flow and get it out of phase. This disruption of timing is especially likely if the manager monitors only selected portions of the work flow, such as the final stages. It has also been found (e.g., Pepinsky & Weick, 1961) that frequent monitoring can heighten the frequency with which workers feign or simulate productivity. In many cases it is actually possible to make it appear as if the task is being accomplished when, in fact, it is not. To the extent that frequent monitoring produces maintenance of a facade and drives actual and reported outcomes further apart, the manager has a less realistic view of the state of the system, and his recommendations will be inappropriate because they are made in terms of a stage of task accomplishment which does not exist; once this pattern becomes established, it should be more difficult to break. Obviously, there are checks built into most work systems to guard against this spiraling of ingenuous action. But if the manager is not sensitive to these indications, if he looks for incipient outcomes rather than the state of work flows, intended and actual performance may drift apart and "crash" programs will have to be instituted to salvage the product.

An organization in which managers are gauged by results is usually explicit about some of the standards against which success is judged. When standards become explicit, several consequences might be expected. For one thing, performance could tend to drift toward established standards, especially if they are resistant to change (e.g., Katz & Kahn, 1966). If standards are set high, performance might move in the direction of these higher standards (Locke, 1966b). However, if the standards are set too high and never achieved and if this is apparent to several workers, the standards become meaningless, and performance tends to be controlled by other factors (e.g., Katz, 1964). The more common situation is probably one in which standards are below what workers are capable of accomplishing, and when these lower standards become explicit, performance tends to stabilize around them (e.g., Locke, 1966b).

If a standard is made explicit, it becomes clearer when a manager has been successful, but it also becomes clearer when he has failed. While a pattern of success may be just what a firm wants to detect, what is often not realized is that the effects of failure may reduce the subsequent effectiveness of managers. Failures or ambiguous successes probably occur for most managers at some times during their careers, and a system which makes these failures distinct may retard managerial effectiveness. To see some of these potential dysfunctions when unambiguous failure occurs, it is useful to review several laboratory studies. For example, it has been found that when persons are successful, they tend to attribute the success to themselves, i.e., to some trait which they possess or efforts which they have expended. However, when failure occurs, it tends to be attributed to external sources such as the task, other people, fate, etc. (e.g., Strickland, 1958). Notice that when failure is attributed to external origins, these sources may not be under the direct control of the manager. If the causes of failure are relatively nonmodifiable, there should be less clear indications of ways in which the manager could reduce subsequent failure. Perhaps the argument can be summed up by saying that failure promotes defensiveness rather than objectivity. When failure occurs, solutions are less apparent, the search for explanations of failure is more circumspect, and adaptability may diminish.

Two final points concerning the relationships between standards and performance deserve mention. So far it has been argued that when failure occurs, a sequence of events may be triggered which could prove detrimental to the organization. However, even when success occurs, this does not necessarily imply that success will breed success. If one links together the fact that complex inputs must be coordinated for the manager to "get results," the fact that the manager who is results-oriented may be tempted to tamper frequently with the work system, and the fact that feedback concerning results typically consists of a global measure which obscures individual contributions, then there arises the very real problem of how the manager comes up with an economical explanation for his success. The manager who wants to repeat his success may have a difficult time discovering what actions he took that produced the success. If feedback is obscure, success probably gives no more information about how one should act in the future than failure does.

As a final comment concerning standards and performance, it seems relevant to pursue a suggestion which was implicit in the discussion of failure. When standards are set, it is usually clear whether these are temporary or permanent. Some standards might be only estimates which can be revised as environmental contingencies change or as new information is secured. Other standards, however, are probably less subject to revision. This difference in permanence becomes crucial when performance is out of line with standards. When such a discrepancy occurs, it is possible either for the standards to change and become accommodated to whatever level of performance is being maintained or for the performance to change toward the stable standards. The argument here is that the component which is less resistant to change will drift toward the more resistant component. Thus it becomes especially important in assessing managerial effectiveness to determine the resistance of standards. If standards can be changed, we would expect that persons would tend to perform tasks in ways to which they are accustomed and would revise the standards accordingly. If standards can be changed, dispositional factors such as need achievement should exert a greater control over performance since standards can be adjusted to support whatever action the worker takes. However, when standards are intractable, we would expect performance to drift toward standards, in which case individual differences would becomes *less* accurate as predictors of performance.

When a manager's success is gauged by the degree to which he gets results, there may be frequent problems occasioned by the fact that standards are numerous, different levels within the organization use different criteria to gauge success, and results, when they do occur, are difficult to explain. In the face of these several ambiguities, we would expect to find that managers spend considerable time searching for a subset of standards which are compatible with organizational criteria and which *also* provide evidence of progress. This search for standards could unfold in several ways, any one of which might have a decided effect on managerial performance. For example, suppose that a manager has in the past utilized his own salary level as a standard of success. Suppose now that when he tries to gauge his success by comparing his own salary with that of his peers, he is thwarted because the organization maintains strict secrecy concerning salary (Lawler, 1966b). What happens to his search for standards? The manager may try even harder to employ standards which he has used in the past. In the present case, he will try even harder to discover what other persons in the organization are being paid. As an alternative to an intensified search for familiar criteria, the manager may diversify his search and try to find other indicators that correlate with results (e.g., length of coffee breaks taken by subordinates), try to determine which criteria are weighted most highly within the organization, etc. When a search for criteria diversifies, there is a greater chance that managers will adopt "spurious" criteria and pursue goals which are irrelevant and perhaps even detrimental to task accomplishment.

Implicit in the preceding analysis has been the more general point that if criteria are unclear or are activated sporadically by unfamiliar auditors, the manager functions in a state of considerable ambiguity. From what is known about responses to ambiguity, we would anticipate that when a manager is judged on results but does not know which results are relevant, his own personal preferences and needs will gain a greater hold over the process of goal setting. As Sherif and Harvey (1952) have suggested, when situational anchors are not available as a result of ambiguity, the person resorts to internal or ego standards, which are more diverse. This means that when a system is ambiguous in its assessment of results, managers may tend to introduce their own diverse, personal criteria to gauge success. This is actually the only remaining source of standards which can produce some clarity. When idiosyncratic standards are introduced, individual work groups may be judged by very different standards and different managers might prefer different indexes, and to the extent that progress in one unit is judged differently from that in a neighboring, interdependent unit, it should become more difficult to coordinate the units. If the units are judged by different standards, they will most likely strive to achieve different ends, and this should reduce the number of shared goals. If idiosyncratic goals supplant shared goals, problems of coordination are increased, and additional strain is placed on the manager. This strain, in turn, may pressure the manager to intensify his pursuit of individual standards of success, thereby driving even further apart the interdependent units. Again we should mention that within organizations there are several checks which can arrest this spiraling of idiosyncratic goals. The point is that an organization in which managers are pressured to get results and in which potentially incompatible results are valued is highly vulnerable to problems occasioned by increased usage of idiosyncratic rather than shared standards. As standards for discrete work units become more dissimilar, problems of coordination should increase. This spiraling could be truncated in an organization which uses criteria other than results to assess managers and in which the results for which the manager is held accountable are made explicit, are not incompatible, and do not involve a diverse set of outcomes.

One final point should be noted concerning the effect on managers of the "results" criterion. This issue concerns *means ambiguity*. Throughout this book we have argued that both situational and individual difference variables are crucial in the determination of managerial effectiveness and that as conditions change, these two sets of determinants assume greater or lesser importance. The present discussion allows us an excellent opportunity to illustrate this point. It has been argued here that the situation of the manager is one in which he is responsible for outcomes but in which the means to accomplish these ends are not specified. There is more ambiguity and fluidity regarding means activities. Borrowing from the earlier proposition that under conditions of ambiguity, individual differences assume more importance as an anchorage for actions, it would appear that individual difference variables would be effective predictors of *means* activity within organizations but that they might be less effective as predictors of the "results" type of outcome. Means are more under the control of individual dispositions; consequently, measures of these dispositions should afford predictions of work process. In order to link process with outcome, additional propositions are needed; hence there may be a less than direct fit between individual difference predictors and outcomes. Several processes can lead to the same outcome; processes vary in the amount of pressure which they impose on workers to take shortcuts. Most important, different styles of managerial control have different consequences for the state of the system when it approaches future assignments. If this frame of reference is employed, it is possible to pinpoint more accurately where information derived from testing and selection can be expected to have the most impact. Since work flows are apt to be highly influenced by individual differences, this argues that process as well as outcome items should be built into selection batteries. The link between individual differences and process should be made more explicit. If such emphasis were to gain a greater foothold in investigations of managerial effectiveness, it might be possible to employ individual difference measures in a more precise manner, and it might also be possible to articulate more clearly the fit between situational and personal variables.

A REFLECTION ON SOME INDIVIDUAL DIFFERENCES

We would now like to consider some implications for using particular measures of individual differences in assessing management potential or predicting performance. Again the discussion is speculative in nature, and we are not attempting to cover all the topics that could be included. Our aim is merely to see whether some new and possibly interesting research questions can be generated.

Implicit theories of work. Managers clearly make assumptions about what motivates their subordinates. These assumptions, or "implicit theories," influence their interactions with subordinates, and yet implicit theories are seldom assessed when managers are selected. It is possible to exemplify two different implicit theories of work behavior if we abstract some of the ideas advanced by Barnard (1938) and since modified by others (e.g., Cyert & March, 1963; March & Simon, 1958; Thompson, 1961) and ideas propounded by Zaleznik and Moment (1964) and others who make similar assumptions (e.g., Argyris, 1964a; Bennis, 1966; McGregor, 1960). While the following discussion is simplified, it does suggest areas in which theories about work may diverge.

The assumptions derived from Barnard are built on a cognitive model of man, a model in which man is essentially rational and deliberate and in which conscious (as opposed to unconscious) determinants of behavior are crucial.

Although man is rational, there are distinct limitations on his ability to perceive, to forecast, and to process large amounts of information. These limitations are perhaps best described in the phrase "limited rationality," which has been used by March and Simon (1958). Furthermore, man is regarded as a person who sets satisfactory rather than optimal goals. His goals can be attained; they are set at moderate levels, and their attainment is the occasion for satisfaction.

It is interesting to note the research strategy associated with the above orientation since it actually seems to incorporate the assumptions. A prominent technology which is used is that of computer simulation (e.g., K. J. Cohen & Cyert, 1965). These simulations consist of several simple, binary choices which eventually result in a definite outcome but which, at the time of their execution, are exceedingly localized. In most experimental tasks associated with this approach, simple judgments are required (e.g., the organizational estimation exercise used by Cyert, March, and Starbuck, 1961). These tasks as well as the explanations of the results tend to bypass emotions. Persons are acknowledged to have feelings, but feelings are assumed to be of incidental importance. It is problem solving that counts. There appears to be the assumption that if jobs are simplified sufficiently, it is difficult for feelings to affect performance even if they are salient. Group processes are given scant attention, although this has been more true of recent work than it was of the original Barnard formulation. Group processes seem to be ignored because it is felt that most events occurring within the organization can be explained in terms of the behavior of individuals.

Given this capsule view of some cognitive assumptions about persons and the environment in which they work, it is interesting to examine how these assumptions might affect managerial practice. The manager who views persons in the ways mentioned above would tend to simplify tasks for his subordinates so that their assignments would not exceed their capabilities. He would assume that the routine activities will supersede planning; consequently, either he will do most of the planning or else plans will be abandoned. In the case of abandonment of plans, the manager remains inactive until some event occurs which requires a response. The manager who adopts the assumptions mentioned above might try to influence his subordinates by altering their ideas about work settings. Thus his influence attempts will probably tend to be intentional, conscious, reasoned, and logical. Also, influence may consist of attempts to change motivational patterns rather than to satisfy them. When this type of manager has an assignment which he must delegate, he should tend to delegate portions which are judged to be compatible with the limits of rationality. The manager retains for himself the task of coordinating the components of task performance. Finally, this approach is concerned with the stability and adaptiveness of organizations, and it is argued that the manager is the principal means by which this adaptation occurs. This is opposed to the view described below, which argues that workers rather than the manager are the principal mechanisms for adaptation.

A contrasting set of assumptions about persons and the conditions of effective work is presented by Zaleznik and Moment (1964). Their argument is that affective rather than cognitive processes are crucial in understanding organizational conduct. Strong emotions are presumably associated with many actions in organizations. These feelings are often aroused because of similarities between work settings and family settings (e.g., the manager assumes the role of the father), and emotions hinder productivity unless they are identified, clarified, and accepted. Furthermore, it is assumed that persons have "unlimited" rationality. They are eager to demonstrate competence and to be challenged. If workers appear to have limited rationality, this may reflect more their resignation to the minimal demands that are placed on them within the organization than the fact that limited rationality is a stable characteristic. In contrast to the use of computer simulation and relatively simple experimental tasks to study behavior, persons who adopt the approach exemplified by Zaleznik and Moment use extensive case studies of actual organizations, seldom manipulate variables, and try to develop post hoc theories that explain the events which occur in organizations.

It is important to note that investigators who are associated with this approach tend to observe organizations at times of crisis rather than at times of stability because of their strong interest in training and organizational change. During times of crisis sentiments are intense, factions are polarized, mechanisms for adaptation are strained, and the organization in general is in a fluid state. Thus it should not be surprising if the concepts associated with this approach prove to be less useful for understanding organizations when they are untroubled. Much of the routine work of organizations seems to be ignored in these formulations. As a result, it often seems that the organization viewed by Zaleznik and Moment is a more volatile institution than the organization viewed by Barnard. Also, since investigators concerned with affect tend to view organizations during times of stress, it may often happen that the persons who are most capable of easing an organization through these periods are those who possess considerable patience, resilience, and interpersonal competence. It is important to take account of this background because it argues that the approach adopted by Zaleznik and Moment may be less applicable to an understanding of the effective manager when an organization is in a relatively quiescent period, just as the Barnard model may be insufficient to explain what an effective manager does during a crisis.

In contrast with the Barnard approach, affective theories argue that workers are unaware of many of the emotional blocks concerning work and that attempts by the manager to influence subordinates by rational persuasion are ineffectual. Unless the hidden problems are clarified, managerial efforts directed toward control will be wasted. This approach emphasizes that the manager must create conditions under which persons will express their lingering discontent openly. While this may consume considerable time, it is argued that the eventual payoff will be higher than if a series of stopgap, conscious attempts at persuasion is used.

Work is viewed as essentially cooperative and as a source of considerable tension. Interdependence of tasks is emphasized, and coordination tends to be delegated rather than centralized. Jobs would not be fragmented as much by the manager who adopts this approach, or if they must be fragmented, attempts would be made either to give a worker the largest fragment possible or to increase social satisfactions. The manager who adopts this approach is more concerned with motive satisfaction than with motive change. He tries to create conditions under which competence can be demonstrated. Planning may be delegated to subordinates, or at least their active participation is enlisted. Presumably plans formulated within a group are more likely to be implemented.

Given these two points of view regarding work behavior, it is clear that managers can make sense out of organizational events in quite different ways. However, one can legitimately ask, "So what?" Since managerial effectiveness presumably is judged in terms of whether the manager gets results, it really makes no difference how he conceptualizes his situation as long as his unit remains productive and viable. But notice how these differing assumptions *could* influence whether the manager will get results. Suppose that the manager adopts the viewpoint that persons have limited rationality. He will assign minimal tasks to his subordinates, and if this is a valid representation, his unit will be productive. However, the unit might also be productive if he had totally misjudged the capabilities of his workers. In other words, productivity could occur either because people have limited capabilities *or* because they have extensive capabilities and are resigned to minimal tasks. But notice what might happen when the unit is under stress. As demands proliferate, the manager who assumes limited rationality will probably try to decompose tasks even further so that the workers can handle them. The manager with the affective orientation, however, would probably delegate even larger portions of the task to his subordinates when stress occurs. Now, if workers actually have limited abilities to conceptualize their assignments, then the manager with the cognitive orientation will have a more efficient unit in the face of increased demands than the manager with the affective orientation. But if the reverse holds true—i.e., if workers can cope with complexity—then the manager with the cognitive orientation who decomposes the task even more extensively will jeopardize rather than enhance the likelihood that his unit will survive. The argument here is that either set of assumptions may be sufficient to sustain effective relationships during routine activities, but when demands become less predictable and a unit is confronted with an unfamiliar task, then assumptions may have a sizable effect on the manager's effectiveness.

We hope that this analysis suggests some additional variables that might be considered when the task is to predict managerial performance. Notice that it also puts a heavy emphasis on the interaction of individual characteristics and situational variables.

The manager as hero. Among the prominent assumptions evidenced in current practice is the view that the manager is a hero, a central figure of strength, courage, and ability. Despite the fact that there is a growing literature concerning the situational view of leadership (e.g., Fiedler, 1967), industry has evidenced a considerable lag in the acceptance of this view. The impression that a manager is a special type of person has been strongly perpetuated by the use of trait measurements as the basis for promotion. Persons with distinctive traits are selected to be managers, and their effectiveness is then attributed to these personal properties. Such attribution neglects the possibility that the situations which confront the manager may have sizable influences on his success.

It is somewhat ironic that the emphasis on human relations training has also served to maintain the view of the manager as a hero. The prescriptions for managerial action which derive from human relations training imply that the manager is a person who is sensitive to the unique problems of his subordinates, able to identify their basic concerns or to create conditions in which the workers themselves can make these analyses, and capable of treating workers differently depending on the analysis which is made. A good example of the way in which a human relations emphasis translates into a heroic strategy is found in Schein's (1965, p. 61) description of the manager who assumes that man is complex:

> The frame of reference and value system which will help the manager most in utilizing people effectively is that of science and systems theory. If the manager adopts these values toward man, he will test his assumptions and seek a better diagnosis, and if he does that he will act more appropriately to whatever the demands of the situation are. He may be highly directive at one time and with one employee but very nondirective at another time and with another employee. He may use purely engineering criteria in the design of some jobs, but let a worker group completely design another set of jobs. In other words he will be flexible, and will be prepared to accept a variety of interpersonal relationships, patterns of authority, and psychological contracts.

Impressive as such a manager would be, the implicit demands for analysis and retention of information and the amount of attention which must be focused on individuals to implement this approach lead one to question whether the manager who acted this way would have any time or energy to perform other managerial tasks which did not directly involve people.

Managers, whether they are capable of being heroes or not, may often act as if they were or as if their jobs required such behavior. A particularly vivid portrayal of the possible consequences when managers adopt this viewpoint is found in Selekman's (1959) article appropriately entitled "Sin bravely: The danger of perfectionism." A widespread view within many companies is that persons imitate the practices of their leaders, and this imposes constraints on the manager to act in ways which he would like to have adopted. The net result is that the manager feels considerable pressure to adopt practices that look good. Expectations regarding managerial behavior often outrun actual practice, managers undoubtedly feel pressures to act in terms of these expectations, and these pressures may be enhanced if selection procedures emphasize heroic personal traits.

There are several implications of the heroic perspective. First, there is the clear suggestion that excessive demands are made of the manager and that if he is to have any success at meeting these demands, it will be necessary for him to simplify his environment.

An additional problem is that of the formulation and perpetuation of *abortive rationales* for organizational action. If persons are dependent on a hero for decisions, the chances are good that their own justifications for actions will be poorly elaborated. We might expect this because the hero is seen as a person who has a great deal of information, who is in a position to make more informed decisions, whose prescriptions are wise, and whose decision processes are unique. Given this orientation, subordinates may leave unquestioned much of what the manager prescribes, they may permit him to formulate the rationales for action, and his interpretations may be seen as "better" than those which subordinates formulate. If fewer demands are made of the superior to elaborate his rationales, subordinates remain uninformed as to the precise content of these rationales. This pattern could have very costly consequences.

If subordinates are hesitant to formulate the reasons for their actions in the belief that they do not have as much information as the manager and that they do not possess his ability to dissect and combine this information, they may perform tasks simply because they were assigned. In the absence of adequate reasons other than authoritative prescriptions for actions, several things could occur. For one thing, the actions are vulnerable. Their rationale is unelaborated and unquestioned. If some undeniable evidence appears which suggests that the action is of questionable value, the subordinate has fewer means to cope with this threat. One way in which the subordinate may respond to threat is to become even more entrenched in his belief that the action is correct and thus become less adaptive and open to information. Or he may immediately abandon the action and do something different, very possibly with just as little justification. The latter practice should promote vacillation in task performance, a response which is no more adaptive than it is entrenching. If rationales for action are unclear, we might also expect to find that persons would be tempted to invent rationales. If the person performs a task at the request of a manager and if this request is accepted and implemented solely because of the stature of the manager, there may be lingering doubts that this is a sufficient basis for action. To increase justification, the worker may accord even greater wisdom to the manager, enhance the value of the task, or derogate alternative plans of action. Any of these resolutions would serve to make the subordinate less responsive to information which suggested that the task performance should be modified. In short, he is less adaptable. Thus the manager who produces abortive rationales, rationales which are incompletely formed, may rigidify the organization. Furthermore, he could make it more difficult for subordinates to gain experience in a vital managerial task, namely, the formulation of rationales. As a result, the capabilities of persons who are potential candidates for managerial positions may be reduced.

The pattern of consequences that we have described is obviously somewhat caricatured and would clearly be qualified by individual differences. Specifically, the orientation we have discussed here parallels most nearly that of the closed-minded person described by Rokeach (1960). A prominent component of this orientation is that persons adjust to the authority and not to the content of communications and tend to adopt statements as plausible on the basis of who made them rather than on the basis of what is said. While it is true that there would be individual differences regarding the extent to which the above pattern will be adopted, what we are arguing is that the manager who acts like a hero and the subordinates who view him in this way might tend to produce a population of workers who acted as if they were closed-minded.

Definitions of what is required to be a hero differ substantially depending on how one defines a manager. For example, a manager is often viewed as a central person, a person through whom considerable information is channeled. From this viewpoint, a hero is a man who can avoid personal biases during information processing. D. T. Campbell (1958) has presented an exceedingly thorough inventory of these potential biases. To avoid such biases, the manager would have to exhibit considerable detachment, and a manager who is a hero in this sense is unlikely to be a human relations hero. The definition of the manager as one who is charged with securing adequate resources to maintain continued participation by subordinates imposes different demands. This hero is salient not because he is especially competent at the task but rather because he is able to handle those tensions which arise from task performance. Detachment hinders the execution of this assignment, and the requirements for this hero are rather close to those which are detailed in the quotation from Schein given earlier. It is also common to define the manager as a decision maker, which carries a different heroic image. The heroic decision maker is a man who processes information quickly, gives definite prescriptions without delay, makes few errors, and responds mainly when demands are made of him. This is a difficult image to sustain because a potent tool of management is the avoidance of decisions (e.g., Barnard, 1938). Furthermore, because of the ambiguity of the outcome, the generality of the decision, or the possibility that intervening events rather than the decision itself may have influenced the outcome, it is generally difficult to know whether a specific decision was correct. These factors are all common properties of decision making within organizations, and they have been noted here because they could produce disenchantment among subordinates with the heroic decision maker. The expectations of subordinates concerning the manager who makes decisions do not accord with the demands of the managerial job (e.g., Sampson, 1963). When the manager acts in ways which are unheroic (e.g., avoids making a decision), his stature may diminish.

Additional leads from social psychology are pertinent to the concept of the manager as hero. Hollander (1958) has shown in several studies that a person is permitted to innovate and have his innovations accepted only if he has demonstrated previous compliance with the norms and procedural rules of a group. The notion is that when a person conforms, he builds up "idiosyncrasy credit," which eventually enables him to depart from accepted procedures and still have his ideas considered. This suggests that the route by which a manager becomes a hero may be a significant determinant of how his ideas are accepted when they are advanced. There are also frequent suggestions in the social-psychological literature that a hero with a shortcoming is more attractive than a hero who is apparently infallible. For example, Aronson, Willerman, and Floyd (1966) found that a person of high prestige who makes a clumsy mistake (experiences a "pratfall") is more persuasive than one who does not. However, the manager who tries to appear "human" may have other problems. Zaleznik and Moment (1964) presented the concept of "status stripping" to designate the pattern of behavior of the manager who tries to deny his position of authority and act like a friend to subordinates. The principal dysfunction of this pattern—and it is a crucial one for questions of managerial effectiveness—is that it presents a rather unattractive view to subordinates of the rewards associated with being a manager. The subordinates see a person who has been elevated to a managerial position and who then tries to deny a crucial component of his position, namely, greater authority. Thus, whatever rewards are seen as important in a promotional system are undercut when those who are promoted try to act as if they were not.

Other ideas concerning the manager as hero could be developed; however, perhaps we should summarize the arguments presented so far. It has been suggested that selection practices as well as folklore perpetuate the view that managers are special persons with unusual capabilities. The set of capabilities differ depending on how management is defined, and a hero by one definition is a villain by another. Aside from this fact, there is the important point that the demands of organizational life are sufficiently diverse and numerous to make heroic actions difficult. Perhaps the biggest danger for the hero is the "fall," and organizational life seems geared toward the production of falls. A hero with whom subordinates become disenchanted is a hero toward whom they will be less responsive and who is therefore less effective.

There are probably several ways to recast the problem of managerial effectiveness to avoid some of the troublesome issues that have been uncovered. As an example, we might mention a formulation that has been developed by Zaleznik (1964). He argues that there are three main types of managerial functions: homeostatic (maintaining operations within the organization), mediative (modifying individual actions by controlling alternatives available to the worker), and proactive (changing the environment so that it conforms to resources which are available within the organization). Zaleznik proposes that individuals differ in terms of whether they are disposed to respond to ideas, persons, or a fusion of both. He suggests that the effective manager is one whose disposition is fused compatibly with a specific managerial function. Thus the individual who is person-oriented would find the homeostatic function most compatible, the idea man would find the proactive function most compatible, and the person who fuses these two dispositions should function most effectively in the mediative assignment. The implication of this analysis is that functions should be distributed among specialists, *not* embedded in a single person who is chosen because of his apparent flexibility. The particular elegance of this point of view is that it acknowledges both individual differences and a situational view of leadership. It is valuable because it suggests that it is possible to fuse both viewpoints.

The instability of ability. In our discussion of the determinants of job behavior, mention was made of the joint effects of ability and motivational variables. The nature of their joint action was purposively left rather vague because few data exist to suggest what the form of the combination might be like. In spite of this difficulty, it seems to make sense to retain these categories for purposes of psychological measurement. However, their utility becomes somewhat more questionable when the task is the appraisal of a manager's performance by his superior or a self-assessment by the manager of his own performance. Under these conditions, we wish to argue that clear distinction among ability, motivational, and attitudinal antecedents of behavior is almost prohibitively difficult, and considerable research will be required before these categories can be used effectively. Judgments of ability and motivation are influenced by past experience, familiarity with the subordinate, the present situation, and threats to the esteem of the judge. A specific behavior can be explained in several ways by a manager (e.g., Weick, 1966b), and these ways may have only a crude correspondence to the psychological dimensions used to predict behavior.

Suppose that a superior observes that a subordinate manager fails an assignment. This failure can be attributed to chance, failure to exert effort, lack of desire to complete the assignment, task difficulty, lack of ability, temporary mood, or fatigue. Notice that some of these attributions involve ability and some involve motivation, but others imply that the environment rather than the person was responsible for the failure. Any of these attributions potentially could be applied to the same action. One way in which the superior may resolve his indecision on this point is to compare the performance of the subordinate with that of other persons. If most other persons have also failed the task, the superior might attribute the failure to task difficulty (an environmental variable), but if most other persons have performed the task successfully, the superior may conclude that the subordinate manager has low ability or else did not try. Notice that once the superior has "explained" the failure, his subsequent behavior toward the subordinate should change. If the failure is attributed to the task, then the task itself may be modified or assigned to another person. Attribution of the failure to lack of ability may lead the superior to conclude that the subordinate is less suitable for a promotion and that his assignments should be simplified. If the failure is attributed to lack of desire to complete the task, this should occasion greater effort by the superior to raise the motivational level of the subordinate. Notice that if failure is attributed to lack of desire, there is no apparent reason to change the task.

On the basis of present knowledge, it is difficult to state concretely how persons choose among these potential attributions. Heider (1958) suggests at least four rules that may be used. A superior may attribute the failure of a subordinate to (1) that factor which can most readily be avoided in the future, (2) that factor which can most readily be strengthened, (3) that factor which is the least threatening to the self-esteem of the worker or of the manager, or (4) that factor which is socially acceptable. Notice an interesting implication of these possibilities. If the superior works in an organization which has an extensive testing program and in which persons are judged in terms of relatively stable individual differences, then he might prefer to assign failures to factors that can be *avoided* in the future. Such an assignment carries with it greater implications for selection procedures. But if the superior works in a firm which prefers intensive training to extensive selection procedures, then he may be more tempted to assign the cause to that factor which can be *strengthened*. Thus two individuals viewing the same behavior might explain it quite differently, depending on the personnel policies within their firm. One form of attribution is meaningful within the personnel system, while the other may not be. The relevant point is that these attributions can be influenced not by objective assessments based on clear-cut categories but rather by situational contingencies. Furthermore, attributions are apt to be influenced by previous experiences with success and failure and also by such situational factors as complexity, clarity, similarity of subordinate to other subordinates, availability of persons for social comparison, etc.

The example used in this discussion involves only attributions which the superior directs toward his subordinates. We have bypassed the entire issue of how a manager explains his *own* failures and successes. Clearly this issue could also affect a manager's effectiveness. For example, if a manager's unit is successful in meeting its quota for the month, he may explain this success by convincing himself that he is a very able manager, that he is only an average manager but "tries harder," that fate was responsible, or that his subordinates are an effective work group. If the manager supervises a large work group and has delegated large portions of the task to his workers, this may imply that he "should" explain the success by attributing it to the group (e.g., they are able, or they are highly motivated). But such an attribution may threaten the manager's self-esteem because there is the implicit suggestion that the group might have been successful even if he had not been around. If such threats are salient, then the manager may assume more responsibility for the success of his unit, an attribution which members may view as unwarranted and which may serve to depress their productivity.

The point of this discussion is that *assessments* of ability and motivation are considerably more fluid than research in the *measurement* area might suggest. It would be a mistake to reify the distinctions used to explain test results and then argue that managers perceive the world using similar categories. It seems clear that attributions can take numerous forms, and unless ability is viewed as only one form of causal attribution, it may be difficult to explain the actions of effective managers or to account for occasions when assessments made by the manager differ from the predictions made by the psychologist.

Again, we must caution the reader that we offer the material in this chapter in a very speculative manner. Almost no data exist to support or refute the plethora of hypotheses contained in these speculations. Our contention is that a great deal of research needs to be done to determine whether such factors account for appreciable variance in management behavior and that considerably more attention must be devoted to the experimental method as a means for gathering the necessary data. Many of the speculations and hypotheses should lend themselves fairly well to experimental test. Others will require a more sophisticated development of experimental technology along the lines suggested in Chapter 14. However, such developments are well within reach and, if achieved, would provide a powerful tool for investigating managerial effectiveness under various situations and constraints. Again, we firmly believe that the factors which facilitate generalization from the experimental setting to the organization are research topics of the highest priority. Only when these factors are understood will the convergent power of the experiment and the field study be realized.

SUMMARY

In this chapter selected topics which had already been discussed in previous chapters were examined from a different point of view. In line with the arguments in Chapter 14, these topics were analyzed from the vantage point of the social psychologist with the aim of formulating some tentative research questions that would lend themselves to something other than the correlational approach. Implications concerning three current management personnel practices were discussed: (1) promotion from within, (2) coaching as a development technique, and (3) equating managerial effectiveness with "getting results." A number of variables were suggested as deserving attention if the effects of these practices on management performance are to be understood. Three individual attributes of managers were given similar treatment: (1) their implicit theories of work, (2) their role as hero, and (3) their assessment of motivation and ability in themselves and their subordinates. Finally, it was argued that an appropriate experimental technology should be developed to enable another powerful line of inquiry to be brought to bear on these issues.

Chapter 19 Conclusions, Implications, and Recommendations for Research

In this chapter we compare the dominant themes in actual management personnel practices with the dominant themes from our survey of research results. Are the most widely used personnel practices also the ones receiving the most research attention? Do organizations seem to make use of available research knowledge? From these comparisons we shall try to estimate the degree of fit between current practice and research and the model summarizing the factors affecting managerial behavior presented and discussed in Chapter 2 (Figure 2.1). Finally, we summarize specific research needs derived from what we see as inadequacies in present research approaches and gaps in our present knowledge about identifying and enhancing managerial effectiveness.

CURRENT PRACTICE AND CURRENT RESEARCH

Managerial selection. In our review of current practices for selecting and promoting managers, it was apparent that nearly all decisions are based on personal interviews or on judgments made from knowledge of a manager's past job performance. Psychological tests and standardized biographical data blanks are used, but not nearly as frequently as has often been supposed. In contrast, research on the predictors of managerial effectiveness has dealt almost exclusively with tests and biographical data. Little research has been directed toward understanding more fully what goes on in personnel interviews, and few efforts have been made to improve their usefulness for predicting managerial effectiveness. At this point we do not wish to argue whether tests or interviews are better predictors of managerial performance. By now we hope we have shown the futility of such either/or questions. Standardized tests, biographical information blanks, and interviews contribute different kinds of information and may have varying usefulness, depending on the situation. Our primary point is that we are struck by the marked disparity between what is researched and what is used in practice.

Further, no research has been done on the relationship between a man's past performance and his future managerial performance, and we have no research evidence bearing on the implicit or explicit processes used by a superior when he tries to estimate a subordinate's future effectiveness on the basis of his current performance. Thus it is again apparent that certain types of information have received the most research attention as potential predictors of managerial effectiveness, but this same information has not typically been used by organizations for making actual selection and placement decisions about managers.

Closely related to this discontinuity is the finding that nearly all managerial jobs in the organizations we studied are filled by promoting men from within the company. In contrast, the thrust of much of the research literature centers on "selection" decisions instead of upon "promotion" decisions. One consequence of this emphasis is that nearly all large-scale validity studies have used global criteria of managerial effectiveness, implying that the major intent is to assess potential for the entire organization (i.e., selecting someone from outside) rather than for specific functional areas within the organization.

In view of the large number of statistical studies done to validate predictors of managerial effectiveness, one of the most surprising conclusions from our survey of current practices is that psychological test information and biographical data, even when they have been validated through elaborate statistical studies, are combined with other information (interview and past performance data) *clinically* for purposes of personnel decisions. In practice personnel decision makers use the available information in as yet unspecified ways when a man is being considered for a job, regardless of the extent of validity information available on the various predictors they choose. No research has been done which tries to describe and systematize these implicit combinatorial rules.

Research studies have also seriously underemphasized the importance of the selection ratio in managerial selection and promotion. The selection ratio is often distinctly unfavorable when a firm is faced with filling a key managerial position. Under such conditions selection may easily be transformed into highly competitive recruitment, and the organization may need to *sell* itself to prospective managers rather than select one from among a number of applicants. Almost no research has been reported in the literature on the process of job choice or the factors influencing individual employment decisions at the managerial level. Thus we have almost no knowledge of why any particular manager may choose one job over another.

Training and development. Another apparent discontinuity exists between current practice and current research when one contrasts programs designed to *identify* managerial talent with those designed to *develop* managerial talent. Undoubtedly, industrial firms spend billions of dollars annually in formalized efforts to train and to develop managers. Yet almost all the research has been concerned with selection and identification, and very little with training and development. Although the situation may be changing, there are as yet no analogs in training research to the large-scale SONJ test validation, AT&T's Management Progress Study, or Sears's extensive research on its executive test battery. Firms spend vast amounts on a wide variety of management development programs but very little on the research needed to explicate the effects of such programs.

It is also apparent that most major companies devote most of their training time to the cognitive areas, that is, to skill and knowledge courses such as accounting, business law, personnel management, computer programming, and languages. Yet the training research that is done is concerned almost entirely with human relations training via role playing, conference methods, *T* groups, and the like. Although most organizations use many different types of training programs, little research has been done to learn what kinds of training programs may be best for accomplishing specific areas of managerial effectiveness or for realizing particular organizational goals. Our current practices survey revealed that many large organizations indulge in an almost incredible variety of training activities, but the training research literature is extremely narrow in scope and heavily concentrated in just a few areas.

Rewards and incentives. With respect to managerial motivation, firms tend *not* to have current practices generally recognized as motivationally oriented. Nearly all give some mention to the probable usefulness of pay and promotion as incentives for effective managerial behavior, but with a few notable exceptions none has consciously introduced motivational considerations into its personnel practices for managers. No one seems to worry, in any explicit fashion, about what incentives the organization has at its disposal or how these are made contingent on behavior. Even more unfortunate in view of its centrality in motivational theory is the lack of attention given to the nature of the task as a determiner of effort. Again, a very few firms have tried to structure individual jobs in such a way that they provide considerable opportunity for internal rewards, but the number is woefully small.

The general lack of attention given to motivational matters in current management personnel practices is paralleled by the relatively small amount of research literature available. Recall that we had to go considerably far afield to collect any sizable body of motivational literature in Chapter 15.

In summary, then, current practices and current research seem seriously discrepant at a number of points. Organizations spend much time and effort in training, but only a limited amount of research in rather narrow areas has been done on the effects of training. Large-scale research programs have been done on test validation, but the results tend not to be used in current practices even when supposedly optimal weighting methods have been developed for interpreting test results. Perhaps an exception to this has occurred in the AT&T organization, where the early favorable outcomes from the Management Progress Study have been translated into the operational use of assessment procedures for selecting supervisors in many of the regional companies.

Lest there be some misunderstanding, we are not arguing that there is a complete lack of correspondence between research and practice or that psychological research should follow current practice and investigate whatever fads and fashions are currently in vogue. Rather, current practice should be built on research findings wherever possible. This does not seem to be the case. It would be advantageous to know why not and to discover how the energies of the researcher could be more fruitfully applied in the future.

CURRENT PRACTICES AND RESEARCH IN THE CONTEXT OF THE MODEL OF MANAGERIAL BEHAVIOR

The principal theme of the model presented in Chapter 2 and the principal theme of this book has been the importance of interactive effects between the many determinants of managerial effectiveness, for example, between personality characteristics and organizational climate. The traditional personnel selection research emphasis on simple measures of aptitudes is seen to be clearly one-sided. However, few individuals or organizations have been concerned with measuring or trying to account for the effects of situational variables, and even fewer have sought to study possible interactions between individual differences and the environment. As another example, it seems obvious that ability itself is a function of both aptitude and skill. Skill is a product of experience, and a large part of this experience may come through formalized training. Cronbach and Gleser have emphasized that a consideration of the interaction between aptitude level and method of training is crucial. If a training program can be varied to suit the particular aptitude level of each train-ee, the net result should be much better than if identical training is given to everyone regardless of aptitude level. People with high aptitude will be held below their potential by training aimed at the average man, and people with low aptitude may not profit at all from training. We need not restrict our dis-cussion to the interactive effects of training and aptitude. It is equally appro-priate for the interaction between training and personality, interest, or motiva-tional variables. A number of other obviously important interactions could be mentioned, but most of these have been touched on in earlier chapters. In particular, the importance of the interaction of aptitude, personality, and skill factors with the situational aspects of the organizational environment cannot be overemphasized. The International Harvester studies described in Chapter 13 showed clearly how little we actually know about such interactions.

How do current practices and research results and emphases look when cast against this dominant theme? In our discussion of current practices, we concluded that organizations tend often to be selection-oriented, development-oriented, or motivation-oriented in their management personnel procedures. Seldom does a firm place substantial emphasis on more than one of these areas. Such an approach precludes giving much attention to interactive effects since the organizational emphasis is mostly on just one major class of variables. Of course, there are some organizations which are exceptions, but they were few in number (only two or three) in our survey. It may be, of course, that individ-ual managers do consider these interactive components when they make per-sonnel decisions, but in practice it is very uncommon for firms to provide formal procedures for emphasizing such interactions or taking them into account.

This lack of attention to interactive effects unfortunately carries over into the research domain. Of the literature discussed, that on training research could most reasonably be expected to incorporate studies of interactive effects. How-ever, only four studies were found which investigated the interaction between training method and measures of individual differences, and all four were limit-ed in scope. In sum, the dominant theme of the model of managerial behavior lies barren and unfulfilled.

We believe that the failure of most research studies to cope effectively with the complexities of our interactive model may be one of the major reasons for the discontinuities we found between practice and research. Quite frankly, most research has been rather simpleminded. Criteria of managerial "success" have consisted chiefly of global ratings, promotion rates, or corrected salary indexes; little attention has been given to differences in the behavioral demands of different managerial jobs, and the significance of such differences has not been related to different patterns of job effectiveness; in fact, almost no one has bothered to ask what various managers actually do in their jobs that makes them effective or ineffective. Most studies have been correlational and fixated on individual differences; few have been experimental, and thus *causal* relationships have not been discovered.

In a way many research studies have effectively stripped away managerial individuality; almost nothing has been done to bring about the *individualized* pattern of prediction and managerial development that we have argued is necessary. Decisions about managers *are*, after all, individual decisions. A specific job with unique responsibilities must be filled; a particular manager shows weaknesses in specific areas, and something must be done about *him;* a manager shows flashes of excellence now and then, but seems essentially to be unmotivated. These are just a few examples of day-to-day individualized issues that arise constantly. Too many of the research studies discussed in this volume have not provided operating managers with convincing evidence that researchers have the right answers to their questions, and they in turn have gone their own way, establishing practices on the basis of fads and fashions instead of on the basis of research knowledge. This, we believe, has occurred because of a basic lack of solid evidence showing how the complex determiners of managerial effectiveness may be unraveled to yield accurate prescriptive recommendations for a firm's managerial personnel policies and practices.

AN EXPANDED MODEL

In the hope of providing a useful research guide for studying these complex determinants, we would like to expand on our original model of managerial effectiveness discussed in Chapter 2 (Figure 2.1). This more complex picture is based on our post hoc synthesis of current research and practice and is shown in Figure 19.1. The notions of the person, the process, and the product remain, but their nature is somewhat more complex.

The individual arrives at his managerial role with a particular pattern of individual differences. His skills, aptitudes, intelligence, and personality have the usual connotations, but some of the other items in the individual difference list deserve additional comment. The motivation literature suggests at least three. First, there is an individual's expectancy, or subjective probability estimate, that he will accomplish a particular task goal; second, there is his expectancy that accomplishment of the task goal will be followed by certain rewards; and third, we must consider the strength of his preferences among the available rewards. The first type of expectancy is a very important determiner of management behavior that has so far been given scant research attention in the organizational context. How an individual perceives his abilities in relation to the nature and difficulty of the task goal (i.e., a specific job)

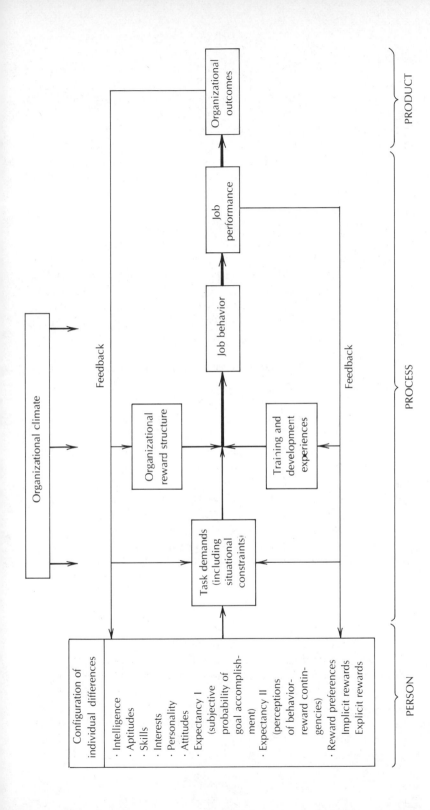

Figure 19.1 An expanded picture of the determinants of managerial effectiveness

must certainly have a pervasive influence on the tasks he selects, the goals he sets, and the effort he expends.

At this point, important questions arise as to whether people have *general* expectancies concerning the major goals of a work role or whether such expectancies are quite specific to particular tasks and must be measured in that context. It would also be nice to know how these expectancies are related to the other dimensions of individual differences (e.g., intelligence).

Although the second type of expectancy (i.e., that reward will follow behavior) has received somewhat more attention, it has still not been given its due. Lawler's (1966b) research suggests that a general disbelief in behavior-reward connections may be extensive, among middle managers at least, and that this could have a very deleterious effect on effort expenditure, choice behavior, and goal setting.

Relative to rewards or incentives we have lots of folklore but almost no data on what rewards managers actually prefer under various conditions. What little information does exist is concerned only with preferences among compensation plans. A complicating factor regarding reward preferences is the degree to which task accomplishment is itself a reward and the extent to which this reward overrides such things as compensation and promotion. That is, does the individual set *implicit* rewards for himself for reaching certain goals, and how do these interact with the *explicit* rewards provided by the organization?

Given a particular pattern of aptitudes, skills, personality characteristics, expectancies, and preferences, the individual is then faced with the task demands of his job. These are the objective (not the perceived) realities of the situation. Unfortunately, little work has been done to determine how task demands directly influence behavior and performance. The fly in the ointment, of course, is our present inability to define and measure managerial task demands. The description of managerial job behavior is still at an abysmally primitive level. The domain of management behavior remains an essentially undifferentiated mass.

To enhance the performance of managerial tasks, the organization most likely provides certain reward opportunities and training or development experiences. Again, these are the objective realities of the situation. They are experimental treatments intended to alter task behavior.

Situational variables and/or the organizational climate obviously has both a direct influence on performance and a moderating or interactive influence on the relationship of other variables to performance. We believe it makes the most sense to subsume objective situational characteristics under the label "task demands" and talk about *perceived* situational characteristics under the umbrella of "psychological climate." For example, both a shrinking market and faulty downward communication are objective situational factors that influence the task demands of the job, while an individual's perceptions of the reward structure or the degree of autonomy in his job have implications for almost every relationship contained in the picture.

Finally, at the end of all this we arrive at the output of the managerial role. It is here that we would like to distinguish between the concepts of managerial behavior, managerial performance, and organizational effectiveness.

Obviously people emit all sorts of behaviors in the context of their work role. They chat with their coworkers, schedule work for their subordinates, write reports, and discuss work problems with their peers. If we ask what constitutes job behavior in a particular role, we are asking what people actually do. That is, into what categories is job activity organized?

Two additional ingredients are necessary to turn a description of job behavior into a measure of job performance. First, the behavior category under consideration must have relevance for the organization's goals; second, differences in the skill with which these behaviors are carried out must be measured. That is, numbers must be assigned to these differences such that the scale has at least ordinal properties. Obviously, more than just one category of managerial behavior has relevance for an organization's goals, and the performance measurement must proceed along several dimensions.

Distinct from descriptions of job behavior and measures of job performance are global indexes of job effectiveness or organizational outcomes. Perhaps these can best be defined by example. Under this label we would include such things as promotion rate, salary level, turnover rates and productivity for the manager's unit, and global ratings of managerial effectiveness. Their common feature is that they are several steps removed from actual behavior. They are "results-oriented," and they typically use just one index to evaluate effectiveness. Such features make it possible for a host of other variables to influence the effectiveness index besides the performance of the manager. Obviously, attempts to predict these outcomes solely by measuring characteristics of the manager are not likely to yield much.

The final feature which makes it so difficult to predict and explain management behavior is that the picture is not static but extremely dynamic. Obviously, task demands change over time as a function of a changing environment. They also change as a result of feedback from outcomes. A manager whose unit is showing a profit simply has a different job from that of a manager whose unit is not doing well. Feedback from outcomes also must have an effect on such things as an individual's expectancies concerning task accomplishment, his expectancies concerning reward contingencies, his preferences for particular rewards, and his perceptions of climate.

The reason for two feedback loops is that there may be considerable disparity between feedback from performance and feedback from organizational outcomes. It would be interesting to speculate on the effect of an individual's knowing he has performed well but still having nothing to show for it in terms of organizational outcomes. The reverse case is perhaps even more interesting. How might an individual's perceptions and expectancies change if he originally thought his job performance was not very good but his unit turned out to look quite effective? To what does he ascribe his unit's success? How does it influence his future job behavior?

Unfortunately, research on the dynamics of managerial behavior is almost completely lacking. In fact, one of our greatest research needs is for longitudinal data gathered across an appreciable span of a manager's career. We turn now to a consideration of these and other research needs generated by our expanded model and some of the discontinuities between research and practice.

SPECIFIC RESEARCH NEEDS

Throughout this book we have been discussing the many facets of managerial effectiveness and its antecedents. We seek to identify personal characteristics suggestive of high potential for managing and to learn how latent potential for management may be made manifest. It is painfully apparent that many gaps exist in the knowledge necessary for accomplishing these two goals. We need to learn more about the critical requirements of managerial jobs, develop methods for observing and systematically recording managers' job behavior, discover the best individual and organizational predictors of effective managing, and learn which training and development methods are most likely to yield desired modifications in managers' behavior. We shall summarize here the several suggestions for needed research and the means for implementing it that we have presented in previous pages.

Job definition and task description. The Critical Incidents Method should be used to define the behavioral requirements of managerial jobs in different companies and functions and at different levels. It is necessary either to attach greater behavioral relevance to the dimensions already developed by Hemphill or, more usefully, to develop an entirely new behavioral taxonomy more exhaustive of the total domain of managerial job behavior. With such a taxonomy, steps can be taken to map thoroughly the characteristics of managerial jobs in different settings; psychometric studies can be done to determine the dynamic aspects of different managerial jobs—the extent to which each is subject to time-, person-, and situation-determined changes. As we have already said, these studies of critical managerial behaviors must look to the future as well as the past; the taxonomy of requirements must not only reflect the status quo but also describe the managerial requirements likely to be important in firms of the future.

Behavior description and performance measurement. Methods should be developed for observing and recording managerial job behavior. Discussions should be held with groups of managers in several firms, at different levels, and in several functions to build a catalog of behavioral examples or "performance specimens" to illustrate various patterns of effective and ineffective managing. Respondents should be asked to provide anecdotes describing effective and ineffective performance of managers above them, at their own level, and below them. This is necessary in order to assure that these accounts of managerial behavior will be made from the vantage point of peers and subordinates as well as from that of superiors. By using the retranslation method, knowledge gained from such discussions can form the basis for developing manager behavior checklists and job behavior evaluation forms for use in observing and recording the actual day-to-day job behavior of managers. We believe that these methods will accomplish a great deal toward overcoming errors and inadequacies that have characterized most previous efforts to observe and rate job behavior with such devices as graphic rating scales, global rankings, or forced-choice inventories. This is so because the method both incorporates an exhaustive sampling of the managerial job behavior domain and also relies on managers themselves rather than on psychologists to choose the appropriate definitions, wordings, and format. The end result should be a system for recording managerial behaviors anchored at various points by performance specimens stated in managers' own language. The system does not reflect a global or unidimensional assumption about managerial "success," but instead recognizes the possibility that different behaviors may lead to "success" and/or "failure" in any given job. With these observational measures it will be possible to learn how a manager's job behavior contributes to or deters the accomplishment of broad organizational goals. Relationships between managerial behaviors and other commonly used measures of executive and organizational success may be computed and evaluated. Thus, with such measures researchers will be able to learn how accurately different aspects of managerial behavior may be predicted and/or developed, and judgments about which behaviors to predict and/or develop can be based on empirical knowledge about relationships between specific behaviors and a myriad of other organizational outcomes, rather than seeking merely to predict these other outcomes directly, as is so commonly done now.

If these steps are taken (that is, if a taxonomy of managerial jobs is developed and if more behaviorally relevant bases are established for observing and recording what managers do), additional research in all phases of managerial effectiveness will be greatly facilitated. Methods for correcting inadequacies in much existing research and for filling gaps in current knowledge about managerial effectiveness, motivation, and training immediately become apparent. For example, we shall not need to continue to rely so heavily on global ratings and rankings, promotion rates, and salary indexes—the status quo and retrospective measures of success that have been so prevalent up to now. We shall instead be able to take account of differences in the job demands made upon managers in different functions and companies and with different levels of responsibility. Systematic study of managers' jobs should show how amenable different jobs are to change—thereby yielding knowledge about the relative importance of individual difference, organizational, and training variables in effecting required or desired behaviors. In turn, these studies will help to formulate personnel practices of selection, job placement, training and development, motivation, and organizational planning most likely to yield desired managerial job behaviors.

The focus upon studying important elements of managerial job behavior instead of upon predicting global criteria is extremely important in a number of other ways. First, it makes meaningful the measurement and prediction of relatively more short-run managerial performance factors, rather than waiting years for long-term global criteria to unfold and emerge. Experimental field studies of interactions between personal, training, and organizational variables become far more feasible; moreover, the essence of behavioral elements shown to be important in managing may readily be abstracted and studied in controlled laboratory investigations. Results from such studies can be confirmed or disconfirmed in field settings, and the outcomes will yield knowledge of far greater power for *explaining* and *understanding* managerial performance and effectiveness than any we now have.

Adopting job and behavioral taxonomies as a basis for studying managerial effectiveness also quite naturally forces greater attention on *diagnosis* as a basis for prescribing personnel practices related to managers. We have already noted the diagnostic usefulness of clinical studies in comparison with purely statistical investigations. The beauty of focusing upon behavior prediction at the managerial level is that we can take a large step toward combining the rational and analytic methods of the clinical studies with the evidence-oriented and quantitative emphases of statistical combinations. Sophisticated procedures such as synthetic validation, actuarial pattern analysis, and individualized prediction via moderator variables are available for accomplishing just such a combination, but they all demand, as a starting point, taking careful account of varying managerial job demands and behavioral requirements.

Finally, only by focusing on relevant behavioral and performance categories in managing can we hope to study meaningfully the impact of motivational variables and of training and developmental procedures on what managers actually do in their jobs.

Training and development. First, we must state quite bluntly that there is simply a great need for more research and for a wider variety of research. This may sound trite, but we are frankly surprised by the extremely limited nature of managerial training studies done thus far. Much more attention must be given to the effects of such methods as programmed instruction, on-the-job training, business games, and other simulation techniques. Many of these techniques are widely used in industry, but they have no research undergirding. To further illustrate the narrowness of the training research literature, we would again point out, as we did in Chapter 13, that the question of training content, or "what should be taught," is crucial. However, most of the training literature deals with techniques rather than content. Unfortunately, instead of studying behavioral demands of managerial jobs and relating training content to them, most research emphasis has been given to "evaluating" human relations programs. Taken together, questions related to what techniques are best for what kinds of content and how such combinations are related to managerial behavior show that the need for more and broader research has reached alarming proportions.

Second, it is important that subsequent research discard the notion that "objective" yardsticks are the best primary criteria for evaluating the effects of training. Instead, the procedures already described for developing behaviorally based measures of managerial effectiveness should be carried out, and the measures used for assessing changes in managerial behavior resulting from training. The perceived change measure used in many of the *T*-group studies is a step in this direction, but the measure is still prohibitively coarse and qualitative. Behaviorally based measures can account for far more job complexity and can be related more directly to what the manager actually does than the global "organizational" measures that have been used in so many training research studies done thus far. They can also be more easily controlled for irrelevant biases not under the control of the manager and for interactive effects which modify the relationship between training and effective job behavior.

Secondary criteria must also be improved. A fruitful approach would be to develop a wide range of realistic and complex problems or decision situations to be used to evaluate trainees' behavior before and after training and to compare experimental and control groups. These would be essentially achievement measures, but a great deal of developmental work would be necessary to ensure that they represent a wide variety of management problem and decision situations. They should cover a wide gamut—including budget control, production, public relations, staffing, and human relations problems. The taxonomy of managerial jobs and job activities developed from critical incidents analyses could well form the basis for developing these problem situations or simulated managerial tasks. This catalog of standardized situations could then be used to assess whether or not a training program is actually developing the patterns of managerial behavior claimed for it by its proponents. Training research could then use multiple criteria based on the carefully developed managerial behavior observation measures and the simulated managerial tasks. Interrelationships between the various criterion measures could then be determined. Just as in the case of selection research, training research has suffered for years from the oversimplified fixation on measuring *the* criterion at the expense of giving sufficient attention to the multiple determinants and criteria of managerial effectiveness.

Third, we must learn much more about the nature of the mediators of effective managerial performance. Until we do we can never be certain of the importance or the relevance of any particular training effort to the process of effective managing. For example, training and development of managers cannot really be conducted meaningfully until we know just how such things as "sensitivity to people," "divergent problem-solving ability," "group leadership," "knowledge of contemporary labor economics," etc., affect the patterns of a manager's job behavior. Here again, defining critical managerial behaviors across functions, companies, and levels is a significant step toward answering such questions. In gathering critical incidents, it would be well also to ask respondents to speculate on whether or not the incident might be related to the presence or absence of skills presumably taught by some of the more widely used managerial training programs. This would make it possible to develop a badly needed taxonomy of "mediators" of effective and ineffective managing and to relate this to existing training methods and their evaluation.

Fourth, a virtually untapped area, but one of fundamental importance, involves the relative effectiveness of different training methods when evaluated against common criteria. For example, is a business game a more or less effective way of developing effective decision-making behavior than case problems? What type of training program is best for influencing managers to show more "consideration" or "employee centeredness"? Criterion measures such as these have received a good deal of research attention in the literature, but no systematic efforts have been made to determine which methods are relatively more effective for producing such changes. In order to make statements of relative worth, more than one training approach must be assessed in the same study, and the effects of different criteria, different trainees, and different situational factors must be controlled or measured.

Finally, we should consider briefly the practical problems of undertaking training research in areas such as those we have outlined. It is not likely that many organizations have the resources or the desire to undertake large and complicated studies, carefully designed and tightly controlled as they must be if we are to accomplish better understanding of the process of effective managing and of methods for developing effective managers via training procedures. It is apparent that a substantial amount of training and development research must be conducted outside actual organizational settings. Problems of obtaining enough participants and of controlling irrelevant influences are too great to be handled adequately within organizations. However, doing research exclusively on college sophomores also seems undesirable. What is needed is a number of halfway houses located between the two settings. For example, business schools and university research institutes could structure their extension programs to incorporate research activities. Greater efforts could be made to recruit certain kinds of participants for such programs, and the research aim could be made such an integral part of the course structure that the student need not be bothered by the fact that he is being "researched." Also, it seems inevitable that managerial training organizations must eventually be set up exclusively for research purposes, whether in universities or elsewhere. Establishing such training research institutes has many advantages. Greater experimental control will be possible, comparisons can be made among many training methods, and multiple criteria may be utilized much more easily. One possible drawback would be the difficulty of assessing the effects of training on primary behavioral criteria of course participants after they return to their organizations; however, this difficulty would be overcome by establishing cooperative research relationships with a number of participating organizations, who would then make possible the gathering of such behavioral measures from trainees after they were back on their jobs. We feel strongly that solid training research will demand training research institutes of this type.

Motivational variables. Theories of, and research on, the role of motivation in managerial effectiveness attempt an understanding of the role of internal and external factors, and their interaction, in energizing, sustaining, and directing managerial behavior. It is clear, therefore, that the role of motivation will *not* be understood until managerial behavior is studied—observed and recorded—directly, rather than indirectly.

We should also remember that managers are people, not infrahuman experimental subjects, and a cognitive theory of motivation makes a great deal more sense than a noncognitive $S-R$ formulation. Individuals have ideas about what tasks they prefer, what rewards are valuable, and what they think will happen if they expend more effort. Many questions, highlighted by our discussion of cognitive theories and empirical research in Chapter 15, must be answered. We would like to mention again some of the major ones.

Perhaps the major consideration is learning what types of preferences managers have for both internal outcomes derived from task accomplishment and external outcomes (rewards). The roadblock to understanding managerial motivation is learning what rewards are important within these two general classes and how trade-offs are made among them.

Much more needs to be learned about perceived task difficulty (expectancy I) and perceived reward contingencies (expectancy II), in terms of both how to measure them and how they influence behavior. If a manager perceives a task as an interesting challenge appropriate for his skills and if he perceives a high correlation between task accomplishment and highly valued outcomes (rewards), we would expect him to expend a great deal of effort toward accomplishing the task.

In addition to understanding the influences of expectancy and valence, it is necessary that future research further explore the nature of the goal itself. That is, does setting specific goals influence the cognitive or motivational component of performance, and if it is the latter, how can commitment to the goal best be assured?

In this section, as is the case with other research questions, we must emphasize that the effects of expectancies, valences, and goals will not be usefully understood until some of their important interaction with individual differences is understood. It is equally important to gain an understanding of how preferences and expectancies develop and change as the result of an individual's experiences in the organization. The study of managerial motivation must become more individualized and much more developmental in character.

Situational effects. This portion of the model is somewhat like the layman's characterization of meteorology. Everyone talks about it, but no one does much about it. However, this accusation is not entirely fair, either for climatologists and meteorologists or for those studying organizational climate. Guidelines do exist, but much more needs to be done.

First, the enterprise would benefit a great deal from an incisive series of taxonomic studies. The communality across previous studies of organizational climate holds out considerable promise. The next step should be to use a number of different methods in an attempt to dimensionalize situational variables from a number of different loci (e.g., perceived climate, role characteristics, and structural characteristics). Some possible methods are questionnaires, rating scales, structured interviews, and archival records. To the extent that different methods can yield similar factors for the same loci, we have learned something about what variables to use in future research. The process of attributing meaning to situational variables must follow a course similar to that of construct validity, as described by Cronbach and Meehl (1955). That is, evidence from a number of methods and procedures must "converge" to a common explanation.

Second, the various ways in which situational differences can affect behavior must be investigated. The central question is whether a situational variable affects behavior directly, in the independent variable sense, exerts an effect only through its interaction with other independent variables and thus acts as a "moderator." Laboratory simulation would be a fruitful method for exploring this question with a number of different situational variables and a number of different tasks. The study by Frederiksen (1968) shows that this is quite feasible.

Third, the mediating variables, or process, which link situational differences to individual behavior must be mapped out. Indik's (described in Chapter 16) insightful analysis points the way for others to follow. We suspect that the number of mediating variables is not excessively large, and a great deal of understanding would result from a systematic series of laboratory studies. Promising hypotheses could then be followed up in field settings.

Finally, after significant knowledge has been acquired via the above kinds of research, we can ask a host of research questions concerning what situational and climate factors enhance or inhibit performance for different kinds of people and different kinds of jobs. The need for such research seems obvious, and it should be pursued with vigor.

Social-psychological considerations. Our approach in Chapters 17 and 18 was largely conceptual and speculative. Rather than simply reviewing specific social-psychological variables, we chose to treat the topic of managerial effectiveness from a different viewpoint—a framework derived from social psychology. *All* of Chapters 17 and 18 can be considered to consist of suggestions for areas of needed research. Here, we shall summarize only the principal themes.

First, we have argued strongly for increased use of the experimental approach in studying managerial effectiveness. This is not intended as a counterweight for an overemphasis on individual differences; instead, it is intended to "make up" for what we perceive to be an inadequate emphasis on a method of investigation complementary to correlational procedures. Experimental studies of managerial effectiveness have been confined largely to examining training effects, and few of these studies have been truly experimental. It is unfortunately true that it is just not possible to study many of the crucial dimensions of managerial behavior in a real setting. Things take too long to happen, they happen too quickly, or they happen in places not readily accessible to observation and measurement. Variables are hopelessly confounded and subject to biasing influences, and many of the measurement problems are nearly insurmountable. Moreover, degrees of freedom may be small or nonexistent (N =one organization), and randomization impossible. As a consequence, it is difficult to infer causality. By necessity then, if we seek explanation grounded in causal relationships, the salient features of the organization and of managerial behavior must be abstracted and transported to the laboratory.

We believe that heavy emphasis in the future should be given to studies which make this transportation in a fruitful manner.

Second, from our discussion of the implicit theories of work held by managers (cognitive versus affective), we conclude that considerable effort can profitably be devoted to mapping a general taxonomy of theories held by managers. Perhaps such a taxonomy will prove to be hierarchical. That is, it is possible that labels such as "cognitive" or "affective" subsume very generalized rather than specific response dispositions and that within these two broad dimensions there may be other, more specific theoretical orientations that may differentiate more finely how managers may approach specific subclasses of problems. Measuring the elements of such a behavioral taxonomy would constitute a giant step forward if we accept the assumption that a manager's implicit theory can color inferences made by him about the behavior of others in organizational settings. Managers furnish all kinds of judgmental data used by the organization to decide courses of action. To the extent that a manager's implicit theory influences his interpretation of information and the kind of information he selects, it can exert considerable influence over such things as his reactions to labor unrest, his estimates of work group capability, and his choice of different training and selection activities. For example, do superiors with a generally cognitive theory of work tend to reinforce or to punish skills learned by their subordinates in human relations training? A host of such interactions could be explored once relevant dimensions of implicit theories have been identified.

Third, our examination of recurrent themes in current organizational personnel practices suggests a number of important research topics. For example, does promotion from within actually lead to increased turnover, lower productivity, and lower job satisfaction in work units because the chosen few are aspiring to a higher level and actually receive rewards from management for a *lack of concern* with their present job? Or is the effect just the opposite, as current organizational lore would have us believe? It might be hypothesized further that the *methods* used to promote from within or hire from the outside have an effect on the productivity and satisfaction of the work group. For example, if the promotion decision is made on the basis of psychological tests and other information gathered by a central corporate staff, the managers not chosen may view the process as mystical, remote, and unfair. Conversely, such a "hidden" decision rule might provide a convenient rationalization for those left behind and thereby reduce their dissatisfaction. A number of such questions need to be asked and answered with regard to selection, promotion, and training policies followed by firms.

Fourth, an obvious implication derived from our consideration of social factors is that individual differences are certainly not the only antecedents of a particular organizational unit's performance, particularly if the performance is estimated by some global index such as profits. We have suggested that individual differences among managers may be correlated more highly with their *methods* of solving problems than with the results obtained. The actual results measure is too confounded with other moderating and contaminating influences. In contrast, correlations between dimensions of individual differences and "management style" become very important if we accept the notion that "results" are not all there is to managerial effectiveness. Here again, we can emphasize the importance of systematically observing and recording actual managerial behavior rather than merely measuring global organizational goals.

Fifth, it is clear from our discussion in Chapter 18 that a much more complex research view of participation must be adopted. A common assumption running through the training literature is that showing consideration for employees in the form of involving them in decision making is generally desirable. However, it may be genuinely undesirable, depending upon the types of interactions between people in the work group, the type of problem faced, relative uncertainty concerning the group's purpose, the role expectations of the members, and the like. If these variables are indeed important moderators of the results of participation, and the manager misreads them, he runs a considerable risk of curtailing his effectiveness.

There is also in Chapter 18 a recurring suggestion that an effective manager is one who can correctly describe his work group in terms of the psychology of its members and the social psychology of the entire group. He knows when to use the participative approach, he can correctly differentiate the unique qualities of the group members, he knows when to increase the individuality of member roles, and he correctly perceives the proper time and place for providing individuals some of the support or anonymity of the group situation. It is likely that such abilities could be used as variables with which to predict effectiveness and as dimensions along which to train. A specific case in point is the dimension of category width, which arranges people along a continuum from those who cannot differentiate stimuli into more than a few gross categories to those who can make very fine distinctions and employ numerous categories. Another example is the notion of skill in individuation. That is, are some managers more capable than others of heightening the perceived differentiation among their employees? If so, is such a skill related to management effectiveness, and under what conditions? How can it be identified and improved through training?

In general, the admonition of the social-psychological view of managerial effectiveness is that the behavior a manager emits for the purpose of being effective does not occur in a vacuum. Other people in the organization respond, and not *merely* in a compliance-defiance mode. Obligations are traded, bargaining between superior and subordinate is carried on, organizational standards remain flexible or inflexible, and so on. Such phenomena are constantly acting to alter the nature and magnitudes of relationships between relatively static variables, and these additional phenomena must be taken much more into account in future research on managerial effectiveness.

A SUGGESTED DESIGN FOR RESEARCH

We are now ready to suggest the general direction we believe future research in managerial effectiveness should take and to outline a broad approach encompassing these suggestions. So far, the research that has been done, of necessity, has been somewhat piecemeal and unintegrated. We believe it is now necessary and timely to mount a coordinated, programmatic, and additive research effort to answer many of the questions we have outlined in this chapter. First, we shall summarize the elements that should be a part of such a research effort:

1 The subjects participating in the research should come from many different firms and administrative settings; they should represent a variety of managerial functions and levels of responsibility.

2 Critical managerial behaviors in different managerial settings should be discovered and a behavioral taxonomy developed which are exhaustive of the whole domain of managerial job behavior.

3 Methods should be developed and put into practice for observing and recording managerial job behavior on a short-term, day-to-day basis. These behavioral elements, or "performance specimens," should be a major focus for prediction in both field (real-life) and laboratory settings, but they should also be studied as predictors instead of solely as criteria, and their relationships with more distant criteria such as career "success" and broad organizational outcomes should be computed and evaluated.

4 Related to the above is the necessity of studying managerial effectiveness as a human developmental process. That is, men's careers should be observed, described, and evaluated as they unfold over time. Both internal (personal) and external (organizational milieu and career interventions) factors should be examined as important variables in the developmental history of managers. Job behaviors intervening between various "way stations" in men's careers should be observed and recorded as they lead to, or are affected by, special experiences, training and development procedures, and job and organizational circumstances.

5 Measures of individual differences should encompass all the methods used in the assessment center approach as well as any additional methods which may be innovated in order to provide as behaviorally rich a system of measures as possible.

6 Methods of career intervention should be as broad as possible, including cognitive and skill training, group process and human relations training, coaching, job challenge, and organizational practices.

7 In particular, the essence of a variety of organizational practices (such as pay, promotion, job assignments, participative decision making, etc.) should be abstracted, and their effects on managerial behavior should be studied in both field and laboratory settings.

8 The predictive aspects, rather than merely concurrent aspects, of managerial behavior must be studied.

9 As has already been implied, studies should employ both experimental and correlational methodology and should be done in both industrial and laboratory settings. Findings based on correlational analyses of managerial behavior in industry should be examined for causal relationships in experimental laboratory studies; in turn, laboratory findings should be clarified, and their applicability to the actual process of managing should be determined in field settings.

10 Both statistical and clinical combinations of predictors should be tried. Sophisticated methods such as synthetic validation, actuarial pattern analysis, and individualized predictic   moderator variables should be used to enhance the accuracy of prescriptions concerning managerial personnel policies and practices.

We believe that research incorporating the above elements might profitably be undertaken by combining the resources and cooperative efforts of a number of key firms, both large and small, representing several different industry groupings. Samples of young men destined for management who are just entering upon their careers in these firms might be studied intensively during a four- or five-day "living-in" period at an assessment center. Each man would be evaluated against a series of psychological variables inferred to be behaviorally related to critical managerial job requirements discovered in the cooperating firms. During the ensuing years, these men and others in their organizations could be contacted at frequent intervals for a variety of purposes:

1 They could be reassessed in order to obtain basic developmental information about the changing patterns of aptitude, interest, personality, and behavioral characteristics during the peak productive years of managers' careers.

2 Interviews with them and with persons close to them in their organizations could be conducted in order to keep abreast of job and life experiences and their effects on patterns of job behavior and organizational movements shown by the subjects.

3 They would take part in training and development programs for purposes both of actual personal development and of conducting research studies such as those described on pages of this chapter.

4 During such training and development programs, the men might also participate as subjects in laboratory investigations designed to clarify many of the social-psychological variables discussed in earlier chapters.

As knowledge accumulated about the individual, social, and organization determinants of managerial effectiveness among these men, it would be made available to top management in the cooperating firms, who would be asked to institute managerial personnel policies and procedures derived from these research results. Because of the close liaison maintained among cooperating firms, it would be possible to evaluate the effects of those practices which are instituted.

The particular and entirely unique advantage of the approach we have just outlined is that the *same* subjects would be studied from many points of view during the crucial years of their unfolding managerial careers. This would provide the basis for unraveling the many determiners of managerial effectiveness outlined by the interactive model described in Chapter 2 and amplified in this chapter. We have already seen that the data of AT&T's Management Progress Study are beginning to yield insights about the possible interactive effects of individual difference and job challenge variables in the emergence of managerial effectiveness. The pattern of studies we have outlined here is elegantly suited for providing a rich reservoir of personal, developmental, organizational, and career information for studying just such interactive relationships. These need not be carried out in just one formalized assessment center. A series of such cooperative efforts would be best, and the format could be varied.

The payoff is apt to be extremely great, and it should not be as long in coming as it may seem at first glance. The cooperating companies, each with the support of its top executive officers, would be engaged in a significant experiment testing the feasibility of doing solid and integrated behavioral science research on a "total push" basis to solve problems arising from our current pressing need for effective organizational management. The commitment of these top men to the experiment and to the research enterprise should, in itself, assure that recommendations for personnel actions will be tried out by the cooperating firms at the earliest possible stages of the continuing research effort.

Several times in this volume we have advocated a wider and more sophisticated use of experimentation for studying management behavior, primarily for the purpose of building more useful hypotheses for testing in the organizational system. The organizational research ventures we have just described would be fertile setting for testing hypotheses generated through laboratory experimentation and simulation.

The program outlined here is an ambitious one, but its potential benefits are great. Through such an effort, much will be learned about the attributes of individuals, jobs, and organizational environments that are conducive to effective managing. It will yield knowledge allowing a more accurate identification of traits known to be associated with effective management, and it will yield training, development, and organizational planning prescriptions for maintaining and enhancing the likelihood that such traits will become manifest in the form of effective managerial behavior.

Appendix: Interview Schedule for Richardson Foundation Survey, Spring, 1966

INTERVIEW SCHEDULE

Part I

Some Identification Data

1 Type of firm

2 A very brief outline of the general corporate or organizational structure:
   a Size of company
   b Number of levels of management
   c Size of each level
   d Centralized versus decentralized

3 Position and status of the person(s) being interviewed and position of the staff group of which he is a member

4 Any special characteristics of the various management levels (e.g., lots of Ph.D.s, all have an engineering background)

Current Selection Practices

1 What sources do you use to obtain managers at each of the levels described in item 1 above?

2 Roughly, what proportion of the managers at each level come from each of these sources?

(Answer these two questions with the aid of the following matrix.)

		Presidents and board chr.	VPs, exec. asst. VPs (report to chief exec.)	Div. mgrs., plant mgrs., etc.	Mgrs. of major depts.	Second- and third-line supervisors	Other
Internal sources	Promotion from lower levels						
	Promotion from non-management jobs						
	Lateral transfer and transfer from staff jobs						
	Other						
External sources	New college graduates						
	Company recruitment from other organiza-tions						
	Executive search						
	Other						

	Promotion from lower levels	Lateral transfer	College trainees	Outside recruit-ment	Executive search	Other
Tests (what kind and what sequence)						
Interviews (number and type)						
Performance evaluation (nature of)						
Seniority or experience						
Consultant's appraisal (what kind of consul-tant)						
Application blanks (what is crucial here)						
Reference checks						
Other						
Other						

	Presidents and board chr.	VPs	Execs.	Mgrs.	Supervisors	Other
Formal courses in business methods, economics, etc. (in-plant, outside?)						
Courses in the humanities (in-plant, outside?)						
Short courses on specific topics (tax laws, speed reading, etc.)						
Short courses at a university						
Human relations training (in-plant, outside?)						
T-group and lab exercises						
Simulation (In-basket, business games, etc.)						
Sessions on communication and problem solving						
University extension (evenings, Saturdays, etc.)						
Coaching from superior (structured, unstructured?)						
Job rotation						
Other						

3 Considering each source of management talent, how does the organization decide which candidates to choose? (Use the matrix above as a guide.)

4 If executive search firms are used to secure managerial personnel, how are they used?

   a What kinds of information must the company provide to the search firm?

   b What kinds of information does the search firm provide to the company concerning job candidates?

   c What information does the company have concerning any decision rules the search firm uses to select candidates—e.g., do they use personality tests?

5 How did the organization arrive at using its present techniques to meet its manpower needs?

6 Are there any plans for developing new means of identifying and selecting potential managers; i.e., is any future research contemplated?

(Questions 5 and 6 should constitute the initial probing for any research that has been done or is being done. It can be described in detail later. If there is no research activity, then the interview can be terminated after Part I.)

Current Training and Development Techniques

1 Again, consider the levels of the management hierarchy. What sorts of training and development programs does the organization provide for the individuals at the various levels? (Use the preceding matrix as a guide.)

2 Try to get some brief notes on the following:

   a How extensively are the various techniques used at each of the levels?

   b How important does the organization feel these programs are for developing managers?

   c How long have some of the programs been in operation?

3 How is it decided whether or not to institute a program?

4 What plans does the organization have for adding, terminating, or changing programs?

5 What are the reasons for any changes contemplated in item 4 above?

   a That is, how do they evaluate these training techniques?

(Again, questions 3 to 5 can be the initial probes for research efforts. Requests for written reports and more detail can come later.)

Use of Incentives.

1 What type of incentives do you use at each of the management levels? (Use the following matrix.)

2 How did the organization decide to use the particular incentives that it does?

	Presidents and board chr.	VPs, etc. (report to chief exec.)	Div. mgrs., plant mgrs., etc.	Mgrs. of major depts.	Second- and third-line supervisors	Other
Pay raises						
Stock options						
Profit sharing or bonus						
Promotion						
Status symbols						
Creating a stimulating job						
Security						
Fringe benefits						
Providing freedom and autonomy						
Other						

3 Have any attempts been made to evaluate the relative effectiveness of these incentives?

4 Have any attempts been made to alter the organizational structure or the climate in order to enhance managerial performance?

Current Opinions Concerning Performance Criteria

1 What sorts of criteria does the organization use for judging management effectiveness?

2 Are these criteria different for different levels of management?

3 Are they formal, informal, global, specific, etc.? (This really has to be inferred from the above questions, with perhaps some additional probing.)

4 In this organization what are the prerequisites for being a good manager? (Different for different levels)

Use of Social Science Products

1 What books, articles, or other sources of information have been the most helpful?

2 Which journals are audited regularly by the personnel management and research people?

3 What research efforts reported in the literature, or at meetings, have been the most helpful in attacking specific organizational problems?

4 What "theoretical" notions from social science writers have had the most impact on personnel and management practices regarding selection and development?

5 What is your overall evaluation of the contribution organizational social science has made to selection and development problems?

6 What kinds of research would you like to see going on in universities?

   a What is your organization's biggest problem in this area that you would like to see researched?

Part II

A Detailed Look At Research Efforts

The interviewer must know what he is going to call "research," how far it must have progressed in order to be included in the review, and what sorts of related research efforts will be considered relevant—criterion development, job description, etc.

1 Some general questions to consider:
  a Why has the organization been using the selection and development procedures previously described?
  b What sorts of evidence have been or are being gathered as to the worth of these procedures?
  c Is there, or has there been, any research directed at systematically describing the manager's job and developing criteria for good and bad performance?
  d Is there any research being directed at developing new procedures for identifying and developing management talents?
2 The following are not meant to be asked as direct questions, but only to be implied or asked indirectly. The intent is to get some picture of how research gets done in an organization and its attendant problems:
  a Where did the idea for the research get started?
  b What was the original intent with regard to the goals and scope of the study?
  c How were the results intended to be used?
  d What sorts of resistances were encountered at all stages along the way?
  e To what extent were outside consultants used?
  f Did the organization perceive the research as expensive, inexpensive, or what?
  g What was the structure and nature of the group doing the research?
    (I think we are agreed that this part of the interview should have relatively little structure. However, the importance of not missing anything and getting a copy of anything written down is obvious.)

Additional "Evaluation" Information

To be answered by the interviewer after discussing the organization's research efforts with the interviewee. These points are really no part of the formal interview schedule, but something to keep in mind when the research is being described.

1 How sophisticated was the original design?
2 Was there good communication between the researchers and the rest of the organization?
3 How many interactive effects did the research try to account for?
4 Did the research try to incorporate anything we might call theory?
5 Did it recognize the multiple and possibly dynamic nature of criteria?
6 Anything at all about evaluating the utility of a decision?
7 Was the evaluation of current procedures made in terms of comparison to a priori methods?

The five management levels follow the definitions of Porter, 1964. Level 1 consists of the chief executive officer and board chairman, and level 2 includes all those who report directly to the chief executive (vice-presidents, executive assistant vice-presidents, controller, etc.). The last three categories should probably slice up the remaining management levels into thirds, tentatively labeled "executives," "managers," and "supervisors." That is, if there are nine management levels below the vice-president level, the top three would be called "executives," the middle three "managers," and the lowest three "supervisors." An alternative would be simply to number the columns of the matrix and let the interviewer use the appropriate number of columns for a particular organization. Either way the judgment problems will be a bit sticky since not everyone will provide the same kinds and amount of information about the nature of the management hierarchy.

REFERENCES

Adams, J. S. Toward an understanding of inequity. *Journal of Abnormal and Social Psychology,* 1963, **67,** 422-436.

Adams, J. S. Inequity in social exchange. In L. Berkowitz (Ed.), *Advances in experimental social psychology.* Vol. 2. New York: Academic, 1965. Pp. 267-299.

Adams, J. S., & Jacobsen, P. R. Effects of wage inequities on work quality. *Journal of Abnormal and Social Psychology,* 1964, **69,** 19-25.

Adams, J. S., & Rosenbaum, W. E. The relationship of worker productivity to cognitive dissonance about wage inequities. *Journal of Applied Psychology,* 1962, **46,** 161-164.

Adorno, T. W., et al. *The authoritarian personality.* New York: Harper, 1950.

Albrecht, P. A., Glaser, E. M., & Marks, J. Validation of a multiple-assessment procedure for managerial personnel. *Journal of Applied Psychology,* 1964, **48,** 351-360.

Albright, L. *A research study of the Vernon Psychological Laboratory Test Battery and other measures for field sales managers.* Chicago: American Oil Co., Marketing Department, 1966.

Allen, L. A. Does management development develop managers? *Personnel,* 1957, **34,** 18-25.

Alves, E., & Hardy, W. R. Evaluating supervisory training in Los Angeles County. *Journal of the American Society of Training Directors,* 1963, **17** (8), 36-40.

American Telephone and Telegraph, Personnel Research Staff. *Personnel assessment program: Follow-up study.* New York: AT&T, 1965.

Andersson, B., & Nilsson, S. Studies in the reliability and validity of the critical incident technique. *Journal of Applied Psychology,* 1964, **48,** 398-413.

Andrews, I. R. Wage inequity and job performance: An experimental study. *Journal of Applied Psychology,* 1967, **51,** 39-45.

Andrews, I. R., & Henry, M. M. Management attitudes toward pay. *Industrial Relations,* 1964, **3,** 29-39.

Andrews, J. D. W. The achievement motive and advancement in two types of organizations. *Journal of Personality and Social Psychology,* 1967, **6,** 163-169.

Andrews, K. R. Is management training effective? II. Management objectives and policy. *Harvard Business Review,* 1957, **35** (2), 63-72.

Andrews, K. R. University programs for practicing executives. In F. C. Pierson et al., *The education of American businessmen.* New York: McGraw-Hill, 1959. Pp. 577-608.

Andrews, K. R. Reaction to university development programs. *Harvard Business Review,* 1961, **39** (3), 116-134.

Andrews, K. R. *The effectiveness of university management development programs.* Boston: Harvard University Graduate School of Business Administration, 1966.

Anshen, M. Executive development: In-company vs. university programs. *Harvard Business Review,* 1954, **32,** 83-91.

Argyris, C. Some characteristics of successful executives. *Personnel Journal,* 1953, **32,** 50-55.

Argyris, C. *Personality and organization.* New York: Harper, 1957.

Argyris, C. Puzzle and perplexity in executive development. *Personnel Journal,* 1961, **39,** 463-465, 483.

Argyris, C. A brief description of laboratory education. *Training Directors Journal,* 1963, **17** (10), 4-8.

Argyris, C. *Integrating the individual and the organization.* New York: Wiley, 1964. (a)

Argyris, C. T-groups for organizational effectiveness. *Harvard Business Review,* 1964, **42** (2), 60-74. (b)

Argyris, C. Explorations in interpersonal competence. II. *Journal of Applied Behavioral Science,* 1965, **1,** 255-269.

Argyris, C. On the future of laboratory education. *Journal of Applied Behavioral Science,* 1967, **3,** 153-182.

Aronson, E., & Carlsmith, J. M. Experimentation in social psychology. In G. Lindzey & E. Aronson (Eds.), *Handbook of social psychology.* (2nd ed.) Vol. 2. Reading, Mass.: Addison-Wesley, 1968. Pp. 1-79.

Aronson, E., Turner, J. A., & Carlsmith, J. M. Communicator credibility and communication discrepancy as determinants of opinion change. *Journal of Abnormal and Social Psychology,* 1963, **67,** 31-36.

Aronson, E., Willerman, B., & Floyd, J. The effect of a pratfall on increasing interpersonal attractiveness. *Psychonomic Science,* 1966, **4,** 227-228.

Arrowood, A. J. Some effects on productivity of justified and unjustified levels of reward under public and private conditions. Unpublished doctoral dissertation, University of Minnesota, 1961.

Ash, P. The SRA Employee Inventory: A statistical analysis. *Personnel Psychology,* 1954, **7,** 337-364.

Astin, A. W. Further validation of the environmental assessment technique. *Journal of Educational Psychology,* 1963, **51,** 217-226.

Astin, A. W. Criterion-centered research. *Educational and Psychological Measurement,* 1964, **24,** 807-822.

Astin, A. W., & Holland, J. C. The environmental assessment technique: A way to measure college environments. *Journal of Educational Psychology,* 1961, **52,** 308-316.

Atkinson, J. W. Motivational determinants of risk taking behavior. *Psychological Review,* 1957, **64,** 359-372.

Atkinson, J. W. (Ed.) *Motives in fantasy, action and society.* Princeton, N.J.: Van Nostrand, 1958.

Atkinson, J. W. *An introduction to motivation.* Princeton, N.J.: Van Nostrand, 1964.

Atkinson, J. W., Bastian, J. R., Earl, R. W., & Litwin, G. H. The achievement motive, goal setting, and probability preferences. *Journal of Abnormal and Social Psychology,* 1960, **60,** 27-36.

Atkinson, J. W., & Feather, N. T. (Eds.) *A theory of achievement motivation.* New York: Wiley, 1966.

Atkinson, J. W., & Litwin, G. H. Achievement motive and test anxiety conceived as motive to approach success and motive to avoid failure. *Journal of Abnormal and Social Psychology,* 1960, **60,** 52-63.

Ayers, A. W. Effect of knowledge of results on supervisors' post-training test scores. *Personnel Psychology,* 1964, **17,** 189-192.

Bachman, C. W., & Secord, P. F. (Eds.) *Problems in social psychology.* New York: McGraw-Hill, 1966.

Bailey, J. K. The goals of supervisory training: A study of company programs. *Personnel,* 1955, **32,** 152-155.

Bailey, J. K. The essential qualities of good supervision: A case study. *Personnel,* 1956, **32,** 311-326.

Bales, R. F. *Interaction process analysis.* Cambridge, Mass.: Addison-Wesley, 1951.

Balma, M. J. The concept of synthetic validity. *Personnel Psychology,* 1959, **12,** 395-396.

Barnard, C. *The functions of the executive.* Cambridge, Mass.: Harvard University Press, 1938.

Barrett, R. S. *Performance rating.* Chicago: Science Research Associates, 1966.

Barthol, R. P., & Zeigler, M. Evaluation of a supervisory training program with How Supervise? *Journal of Applied Psychology,* 1956, **40,** 403-405.

Bass, B. M. The leaderless group discussion. *Psychological Bulletin,* 1954, **51,** 465-492.

Bass, B. M. Further evidence on the dynamic character of criteria. *Personnel Psychology,* 1962, **15,** 93-97. (a)

Bass, B. M. Mood changes during a management training laboratory. *Journal of Applied Psychology,* 1962, **46,** 361-364. (b)

Bass, B. M. Reactions to Twelve Angry Men as a measure of sensitivity training. *Journal of Applied Psychology,* 1962, **46,** 120-124. (c)

Bass, B. M. Experimenting with simulated manufacturing organizations. In S. B. Sells (Ed.), *Stimulus determinants of behavior.* New York: Ronald Press, 1963. Pp. 117-196.

Bass, B. M. The anarchist movement and the T-group. *Journal of Applied Behavioral Science,* 1967, **3,** 211-226. (a)

Bass, B. M. Social behavior and the orientation inventory: A review. *Psychological Bulletin,* 1967, **68,** 260-292. (b)

Bass, B. M., & Vaughan, J. A. *Training in industry: The management of learning.* Belmont, Calif.: Wadsworth, 1966.

Baumgartel, H., & Goldstein, J. W. Need and value shifts in college training groups. *Journal of Applied Behavioral Science,* 1967, **3,** 87-101.

Becker, G. M., & McClintock, C. G. Value: Behavioral decision theory. In P. R. Farnsworth (Ed.), *Annual review of psychology.* Vol. 18. Palo Alto, Calif.: Annual Reviews, 1967. Pp. 239-286.

Beer, M., & Kleisath, S. W. The effects of the managerial grid lab on organizational and leadership dimensions. In S. S. Zalkind (Chm.), Research on the impact of using different laboratory methods for interpersonal and organizational change. Symposium presented at the American Psychological Association, Washington, D.C., September 1967.

Bellows, R. M., & Estep, M. F. *Employment psychology: The interview.* New York: Rinehart, 1954.

Bellows, R., Gilson, T. Q., & Odiorne, G. S. *Executive skills: Their dynamics and development.* Englewood Cliffs, N.J.: Prentice-Hall, 1962.

Bennett, W. E. The lecture as a management training technique. *Personnel,* 1956, **32,** 497-507.

Bennis, W. G. *Changing organizations.* New York: McGraw-Hill, 1966.

Bennis, W., Burke, R., Cutter, H., Harrington, H., & Hoffman, J. A note on some problems of measurement and prediction in a training group. *Group Psychotherapy,* 1957, **10,** 328-341.

Bennis, W. G., & Shepard, H. A. A theory of group development. *Human Relations,* 1956, **9,** 415-437.

Bentz, V. J. Research toward the development of a multiple assessment program for executive personnel. Paper presented at the annual meeting of the American Psychological Association, Los Angeles, September 1963.

Bentz, V. J. The Sears experience in the investigation, description, and prediction of executive behavior. In F. R. Wickert & D. E. McFarland (Eds.), *Measuring executive effectiveness.* New York: Appleton-Century-Crofts, 1967.

Berlew, D. E. Early challenge, performance, and success. Paper presented at the 36th annual meeting of the Eastern Psychological Association, Atlantic City, April 1965.

Berlew, D. E., and Hall, D. T. Some determinants of early managerial success. Working paper No. 81-64, Alfred P. Sloan School of Management. Cambridge, Mass.: Massachusetts Institute of Technology, 1964.

Berlew, D. E., and Hall, D. T. The socialization of managers: Effects of expectations on performance. *Administrative Science Quarterly,* 1966, **11,** 207-224.

Blake, R. R., & Mouton, J. S. The instrumental training laboratory. In I. R. Weschler & E. H. Schein (Eds.), *Issues in human relations training.* NTL Selected Readings Series, 1962, No. 5.

Blake, R. R., & Mouton, J. S. *The managerial grid.* Houston: Gulf, 1964.

Blake, R. R., & Mouton, J. S. Some effects of managerial grid seminar training on union and management attitudes toward supervision. *Journal of Applied Behavioral Science,* 1966, **2,** 387-400. (a)

Blake, R. R., & Mouton, J. S. Using line instructors for organization development. *Training Development Journal,* 1966, **20,** 28-35. (b)

Blake, R. R., Mouton, J. S., Barnes, J. S., & Greiner, L. E. Breakthrough in organization development. *Harvard Business Review,* 1964, **42,** 133-155.

Blake, R. R., Mouton, J. S., & Blansfield, M. G. How executive team training can help you. *Journal of the American Society of Training Directors,* 1962, **16** (1), 3-11.

Blansfield, M. G. Consider "value analysis" to get the most out of role playing. *Personnel,* 1955, **34,** 251-254.

Blau, P. M. Patterns of interaction among a group of officials in a government agency. *Human Relations,* 1954, **7,** 337-348.

Blau, P. M. *Exchange and power in social life.* New York: Wiley, 1964.

Blau, P. M., & Scott, W. R. *Formal organizations.* San Francisco: Chandler, 1962.

Blocker, C. E. Evaluation of a human relations training course. *Journal of the American Society of Training Directors,* 1955, **9** (3), 7-8, 46.

Bobele, H. K., Maher, C. R., & Ferl, R. A. Motion pictures in management development. *Training Directors Journal,* 1964, **18** (9), 34-38.

Boguslaw, R., & Porter, E. H. Team functions and training. In R. M. Gagne (Ed.), *Psychological principles and systems development.* New York: Holt, 1962.

Boudreaux, E., & Megginson, L. C. A new concept in university sponsored executive development programs. *Training Directors Journal,* 1964, **18** (11), 31-41.

Bowman, G. What helps or harms promotability? *Harvard Business Review,* 1964, **42,** 6-26, 184-196.

Boyd, H. A. The buzz technique in training. *Personnel,* 1952, **31,** 49-50.

Boyd, J. B., & Ellis, J. D. *Findings of research into senior management seminars.* Toronto: The Hydro-Electric Power Commission of Ontario, 1962.

Bradford, L. P., Gibb, J. R., & Benne, K. D. *T-group theory and laboratory method.* New York: Wiley, 1964.

Bray, D. W. Approaches to management development research. Paper presented at the 70th annual meeting of the American Psychological Association, New York, September 1962.

Bray, D. W. The management progress study. *American Psychologist,* 1964, **19,** 419-420.

Bray, D. W. The management progress study. Paper presented at the 74th annual meeting of the American Psychological Association, New York, September 1966.

Bray, D. W., & Grant, D. L. The assessment center in the measurement of potential for business management. *Psychological Monographs,* 1966, **80** (17, Whole No. 625).

Bray, D. W., Grant, D. L., Berlew, D. E., Rychlak, J. F., & Katkovsky, W. The young business manager: A symposium based on the management progress study. Paper presented at the 36th annual meeting of the Eastern Psychological Association, Atlantic City, April 1965.

Brayfield, A. H., & Crockett, W. H. Employee attitudes and performance. *Psychological Bulletin,* 1955, **52,** 396-428.

Brenner, M. H. Management selection test validation. Lockheed California Company, Industrial Relations Research Department, 1963. (a)

Brenner, M. H. Personal history validation study. Industrial Relations Research Report, Lockheed California Company, Management Personnel Department, 1963. (b)

Brenner, M. H., & Lockwood, H. C. Salary as a predictor of salary: A 20-year study. *Journal of Applied Psychology,* 1965, **49,** 295-298.

Bridgeman, D. S. Company management development programs. In F. C. Pierson et al., *The education of American businessmen.* New York: McGraw-Hill, 1959. Pp. 536-576.

Briggs, L. J. *A procedure for the design of multi-media instruction.* Palo Alto, Calif.: American Institutes for Research, 1966.

Brodie, W. M., Owens, W. A., and Britt, M. F. *Annotated bibliography on biographical data.* Greensboro, N.C.: Smith Richardson Foundation, 1968.

Brooks, E. What successful executives do. *Personnel,* 1955, **32,** 210-225.

Brown, D. D. Some vital new dimensions for training. *Training Development Journal,* 1966, **20,** 21-27.

Brown, D. S. The lecture. *Journal of the American Society of Training Directors,* 1960, **14** (12), 17-22.

Brown, G. E., Jr., & Larson, H. F. Current trends in appraisal and development. *Personnel,* 1958, **34,** 51-58.

Brown, J. S. Problems presented by the concept of acquired drives. In *Current theory and research in motivation: A symposium*. Lincoln, Nebr.: University of Nebraska Press, 1953.

Brown, J. S. *The motivation of behavior*. New York: McGraw-Hill, 1961.

Brown, W. *Exploration in management*. London: Heinemann, 1960

Buchanan, P. C. Evaluating the results of supervisory training. *Personnel*, 1957, **33**, 362-370.

Buchanan, P. C. Evaluating the effectiveness of laboratory training in industry. *Explorations in Human Relations Training and Research*. No. 1. Washington, D.C.: National Training Laboratories-National Education Association, 1965.

Buchanan, P. C., & Brunstetter, P. H. A research approach to management improvement. *Journal of the American Society of Training Directors*, 1959, **13** (2), 18-27.

Buchanan, P. C., & Ferguson, C. K. Changing supervisory practices through training: A case study. *Personnel*, 1953, **30**, 218-230.

Buckner, D. N. The predictability of ratings as a function of interrater agreement. *Journal of Applied Psychology*, 1959, **43**, 60-64.

Bunker, D. R. Individual applications of laboratory training. *Journal of Applied Behavioral Science*, 1965, **1**, 131-147.

Burke, H. L., & Bennis, W. G. Changes in perception of self and others during human relations training. *Human Relations*, 1961, **14**, 165-182.

Burke, R. J. Are Herzberg's motivators and hygienes unidimensional? *Journal of Applied Psychology*, 1966, **50**, 317-321.

Burns, T. Management in action. *Operational Research Quarterly*, 1957, **8**, 45-60.

Burnstein, E., & Zajonc, R. B. Individual task performance in a changing social structure. *Sociometry*, 1965, **28**, 16-29.

Campbell, D. P. Research frontier: The Center for Interest Measurement Research. *Journal of Counseling Psychology*, 1964, **11**, 395-399.

Campbell, D. P. *Manual for the Strong Vocational Interest Blank*. Stanford, Calif.: Stanford University Press, 1966.

Campbell, D. T. Factors relevant to the validity of experiments in social settings. *Psychological Bulletin*, 1957, **54**, 297-312.

Campbell, D. T. Systematic error on the part of human links in communication systems. *Information and Control*, 1958, **1**, 334-369.

Campbell, D. T., & Fiske, D. W. Convergent and discriminant validation by the multitrait-multimethod matrix. *Psychological Bulletin*, 1959, **56**, 81-105.

Campbell, D. T., & Stanley, J. C. *Experimental and quasi-experimental designs for research*. Chicago: Rand McNally, 1963.

Campbell, J. P., & Dunnette, M. D. Effectiveness of T-group experiences in managerial training and development. *Psychological Bulletin*, 1968, **70**, 73-104.

Campbell, J. T. Assessments of higher level personnel. I. Background and scope of the research. *Personnel Psychology*, 1962, **15**, 57-62.

Campbell, J. T., Otis, J. L., Liske, R. E., & Prien, E. P. Assessments of higher level personnel. II. Validity of the overall assessment process. *Personnel Psychology*, 1962, **15**, 63-74.

Campion, J. E., Jr. Effects of managerial style on subordinates' attitudes and performance in a simulated organization setting. Unpublished doctoral dissertation, University of Minnesota, 1968.

Carlson, S. *Executive behavior: A study of the work load and the working methods of managing directors*. Stockholm: Stromberg, 1951.

Carron, T. J. Human relations training and attitude change: A vector analysis. *Personnel*, 1964, **17** (4), 403-424.

Carter, R. R., Jr. A human relations training program. *Journal of Applied Psychology*, 1951, **35**, 38-47.

Chowdhry, K. Management development programs: Moratorium for executives. *Human Organization*, 1964, **23**, 254-259.

Clark, J. V. A preliminary investigation of some unconscious assumptions affecting labor efficiency in eight supermarkets. Unpublished doctoral dissertation, Harvard University, 1958.

Coates, C. H., & Pellegrin, R. J. Executives and supervisors: Contrasting self-conceptions and conceptions of each other. *American Social Review,* 1957, **22,** 217-220.

Coch, L., & French, J. R. P., Jr. Overcoming resistance to change. *Human Relations,* 1948, **1,** 512-532.

Cofer, C. N. Motivating effects of money: Theoretical approaches. Paper presented at the McKinsey Foundation Conference on Managerial Compensation, Tarrytown, N.Y., March 1967.

Cofer, C. N., & Appley, M. H. *Motivation: Theory and research.* New York: Wiley, 1964.

Cohen, A. R. *Attitude change and social influence.* New York: Basic Books, 1964.

Cohen, K. J., & Cyert, R. M. Simulation of organizational behavior. In J. G. March (Ed.), *Handbook of organizations.* Chicago: Rand McNally, 1965. Pp. 305-334.

Cohen, K. J., et al. The Carnegie Tech management game. *Journal of Business,* 1960, **33,** 303-321.

Comrey, A. L., High, W. S., & Wilson, R. C. Factors influencing organizational effectiveness. VII. A survey of aircraft supervisors. *Personnel Psychology,* 1955, **8,** 245-257.

Crawford, M. P. Concepts of training. In R. M. Gagne (Ed.), *Psychological principles in systems development.* New York: Holt, 1962.

Creager, J. A., & Harding, F. D., Jr. A hierarchical factor analysis of foreman behavior. *Journal of Applied Psychology,* 1958, **42,** 197-203.

Croft, C. J., Kibbee, J., & Nanus, B. *Management games.* New York: Reinhold, 1961.

Cronbach, L. J. The two disciplines of psychology. *American Psychologist,* 1957, **12,** 671-684.

Cronbach, L. J. *Essentials of psychological testing.* (2nd ed.) New York: Harper, 1960.

Cronbach, L. J., & Gleser, G. C. *Psychological tests and personnel decisions.* (2nd ed.) Urbana, Ill.: University of Illinois Press, 1965.

Cronbach, L. J. & Meehl, P. E. Construct validity in psychological tests. *Psychological Bulletin,* 1955, **52,** 281-302.

Crow, R. Group training in higher management development. *Personnel,* 1953, **29,** 458-460.

Crowder, N. A. Automatic tutoring by intrinsic programming. In A. A. Lumdsdaine & P. Glaser (Eds.), *Teaching machines and programmed learning: A source book.* Washington: National Education Association, 1960.

Cuomo, S. Validity information exchange, no. 8-16. *Personnel Psychology,* 1955, **8,** 268.

Cyert, R. M., & March, J. G. *A behavioral theory of the firm.* Englewood Cliffs, N.J.: Prentice-Hall, 1963.

Cyert, R. M., March, J. G., & Starbuck, W. H. Two experiments on bias and conflict in organizational estimation. *Management Science,* 1961, **7,** 254-264.

Davis, N. M. Attitudes to work among building operatives. *Occupational Psychology,* 1948, **22,** 56-62.

Deep, S. D., Bass, B. M., & Vaughan, J. A. Some effects on business gaming of previous quasi T-group affiliations. *Journal of Applied Psychology,* 1967, **51,** 426-433.

Dicken, C. F., & Black, J. D. Predictive validity of psychometric evaluations of supervisors. *Journal of Applied Psychology,* 1965, **49,** 34-47.

Dill, W. R. Desegregation or integration? Comments about contemporary research on organizations. In W. H. Cooper, H. J. Leavitt, & M. W. Shelly, II (Eds.), *New perspectives in organization research.* New York: Wiley, 1964. Pp. 39-52.

DiVesta, F. J. Instructor-centered and student-centered approaches in teaching a human relations course. *Journal of Applied Psychology,* 1954, **38,** 329-335.

Doll, R. E., & Longo, A. A. Improving the predictive effectiveness of peer ratings. *Personnel Psychology,* 1962, **15,** 215-220.

Doob, L. W. The behavior of attitudes. *Psychological Review,* 1947, **54,** 135-156.

Drucker, P. F. *The practice of management.* New York: Harper, 1954.

Dubin, R. Decision-making by management in industrial relations. *American Journal of Sociology*, 1949, **54**, 292-297. (Reprinted in R. K. Merton, A. Gray, B. Hockey, & H. D. Selvin (Eds.), *Reader in bureaucracy*. New York: Free Press, 1952. Pp. 233-240.)

Dubin, R. Business behavior *behaviorally* viewed. In G. B. Strother (Ed.), *Social science approaches to business behavior*. Homewood, Ill.: Dorsey-Irwin, 1962.

Dubin, R. Supervision and productivity: Empirical findings and theoretical considerations. In R. Dubin (Ed.), *Leadership and productivity*. San Francisco: Chandler, 1965.

Dubin, R., & Spray, S. L. Executive behavior and interaction. *Industrial Relations*, 1964, **3**, 99-108.

Dunnette, M. D. Personnel management. In P. R. Farnsworth (Ed.), *Annual review of psychology*. Palo Alto, Calif.: Annual Reviews, 1962.

Dunnette, M. D. A modified model for test validation and selection research. *Journal of Applied Psychology*, 1963, **47**, 317-323.

Dunnette, M. D. *Personnel selection and placement*. Belmont, Calif.: Wadsworth, 1966.

Dunnette, M. D., & Bass, B. M. Behavioral scientists and personnel management. *Industrial Relations*, 1963, **2**, (3), 115-130.

Dunnette, M. D., Campbell, J. P., & Hakel, M. D. Factors contributing to job satisfaction and job dissatisfaction in six occupational groups. *Organizational Behavior and Human Performance*, 1967, **2**, 143-174.

Dunnette, M. D., Campbell, J. P., & Helervik, L. W. *Job behavior scales for Penney Co. department managers*. Minneapolis: Personnel Decisions, 1968.

Dunnette, M. D., & Hakel, M. D., Jr. Interpersonal perception and behavior prediction in the employment interview. Mimeographed proposal submitted to the Division of Social Sciences of the National Science Foundation, 1965.

Dunnette, M. D., & Kirchner, W. K. Validation of psychological tests in industry. *Personnel Administration*, 1958, **21**, 20-27.

Dunnette, M. D., Perry, D. K., & Mahoney, T. A. Criteria of executive effectiveness. AFPTRC-TN-56-73. San Antonio: Lackland Air Force Base, Air Force Personnel and Training Research Center, 1956.

Edwards, A. *Manual: Edwards Personal Preference Schedule*. New York: Psychological Corporation, 1959.

Edwards, W. The theory of decision making. *Psychological Bulletin*, 1954, **51**, 380-417.

Eisenberg, W. J. Qualities essential for supervisors. *Personnel Journal*, 1948, **27**, 251-257.

England, G. W. Organizational goals and expected behavior of American managers. Minneapolis: University of Minnesota, Industrial Relations Center. Mimeographed report, 1966.

England, G. W. Personal value systems of American managers. *Academy of Management Journal*, 1967, **10**, 53-68.

Enke, S. On the economic management of large organizations: A laboratory study. *Journal of Business*, 1958, **31**, 280-292.

Etzioni, A. *A comparative analysis of complex organizations*. Glencoe, Ill.: Free Press, 1961.

Evan, W. M. Indices of the hierarchical structure of industrial organizations. *Management Science*, 1963, **9**, 468-477.

Eysenck, H. J. *The structure of human personality*. New York: Wiley, 1953.

Ferguson, L. F. Better management of managers' careers. *Harvard Business Review*, 1966, **44**, 139-152.

Festinger, L. A theory of social comparison processes. *Human Relations*, 1954, **7**, 117-140.

Festinger, L. *A theory of cognitive dissonance*. Evanston, Ill.: Row, Peterson, 1957.

Festinger, L. Behavioral support for opinion change. *Public Opinion Quarterly*, 1964, **28**, 404-405. (a)

Festinger, L. *A technical study of some changes in attitudes and values following promotion in General Electric*. Crotonville, N.Y.: Behavioral Research Service, 1964. (b)

Fiedler, F. E. A contingency model of leadership effectiveness. In L. Berkowitz (Ed.), *Advances in experimental social psychology.* Vol. 1. New York: Academic Press, 1964.

Fiedler, F. E. Engineer the job to fit the manager. *Harvard Business Review,* 1965, **43**, 115-122.

Fiedler, F. E. The effect of leadership and cultural heterogeneity on group performance: A test of the contingency model. *Journal of Experimental Social Psychology,* 1966, **2**, 237-264.

Fiedler, F. E. *A theory of leadership effectiveness.* New York: McGraw-Hill, 1967.

Fiedler, F. E. & Meuwese, W. A. T. The leader's contribution to task performance in cohesive and uncohesive groups. *Journal of Abnormal and Social Psychology,* 1963, **67**, 83-87.

Fiedler, F. E., & Nealey, S. M. *Second-level management: A review and analysis.* Washington: United States Civil Service Commission, Office of Career Development, 1966.

Fields, H. An analysis of the use of the group oral interview. *Personnel,* 1951, **27**, 480-486.

File, Q. Q., & Remmers, H. H. *How Supervise? Manual, 1948 revision.* New York: Psychological Corporation, 1948.

Findikyan, N., & Sells, S. B. The similarity of campus organizations assessed through a hierarchical grouping procedure. Technical Report No. 6, 1965, Nonr 3436(00), Office of Naval Research.

Fishbein, M. A. Attitude and the prediction of behavior. In M. A. Fishbein (Ed.), *Readings in attitude theory and measurement.* New York: Wiley, 1967.

Fitzgerald, T. A. Compensation and pensions of executives. National Industrial Conference Board Studies in Personnel Policy, No. 111, 1950.

Flanagan, J. C. Defining the requirements of the executive's job. *Personnel,* 1951, **28**, 28-35.

Flanagan, J. C. The critical incident technique. *Psychological Bulletin,* 1954, **51**, 327-358.

Flanagan, J. C., & Krug, R. E. Testing in management selection: State of the art. *Personnel Administration,* 1964, March-April, 3-5.

Fleishman, E. A. The description of supervisory behavior. *Journal of Applied Psychology,* 1953, **37**, 1-6. (a)

Fleishman, E. A. Leadership climate, human relations training, and supervisory behavior. *Personnel Psychology,* 1953, **6**, 205-222. (b)

Fleishman, E. A., & Fruchter, B. Factor structure and predictability of successive stages of learning Morse Code. *Journal of Applied Psychology,* 1960, **44**, 97-101.

Fleishman, E. A., Harris, F. F., & Burtt, H. E. *Leadership and supervision in industry.* Columbus, Ohio: Ohio State University, Personnel Research Board, 1955.

Fleishman, E. A., & Peters, D. A. Interpersonal values, leadership attitudes, and managerial "success." *Personnel Psychology,* 1962, **15**, 127-143.

Forehand, G. A., & Gilmer, B. v. H. Environmental variation in studies of organizational behavior. *Psychological Bulletin,* 1964, **62**, 361-382.

Forehand, G. A., & Guetzkow, H. Superiors' and co-workers' descriptions of the judgment and decision-making activities of government executives. *Management Science,* 1962, **8**, 359-370.

Form, W. H., & Form, A. L. Unanticipated results of a foreman training program. *Personnel,* 1953, **32**, 207-212.

Fortune survey. *Fortune,* 1947, **35**, 10.

Fouriezos, N. T., Hutt, M. L., & Guetzkow, H. The measurement of self-oriented needs in the discussion situation and their relationship to satisfaction with group outcome. *Journal of Abnormal and Social Psychology,* 1950, **45**, 682-690.

Fox, H. Top executive compensation. New York: National Industrial Conference Board, Studies in Personnel Policy, No. 193, 1964.

Frederiksen, N. Factors in In-basket performance. *Psychological Monographs,* 1962, **76** (22, Whole No. 541).

Frederiksen, N. Some effects of organizational climates on administrative performance. Research Memorandum RM-66-21, Educational Testing Service, 1966.

Frederiksen, N. Administrative performance in relation to organizational climate. Paper presented at a symposium on "Measuring managerial effectiveness," American Psychological Association, San Francisco, September 1968.

Frederiksen, N., Saunders, D. R., & Wand, B. The in-basket test. *Psychological Monographs,* 1957, **71** (9, Whole No. 438).

Freeman, G. L., & Taylor, E. K. *How to pick leaders.* New York: Funk & Wagnalls, 1950.

French, J. R. P., Jr. Field experiments: Changing group productivity. In J. G. Miller (Ed.), *Experiments in social process: A symposium on social psychology.* New York: McGraw-Hill, 1950.

French, J. R. P., Jr., Israel, J., & As, D. An experiment on participation in a Norwegian factory. *Human Relations,* 1960, **13**, 3-19.

Friedman, A., & Goodman, P. Wage inequity, self-qualifications, and productivity. *Organizational Behavior and Human Performance,* 1967, **2**, 406-417.

Fryer, D. H., Feinberg, M. R., & Zalkind, S. S. *Developing people in industry.* New York: Harper, 1956.

Funkenstein, D. H. Failure to graduate from medical school. *Journal of Medical Education,* 1962, **37**, 585-603.

Gage, N. L., & Exline, R. V. Social perception and effectiveness in discussion groups. *Human Relations,* 1953, **6**, 381-396.

Gagne, R. M. Military training and principles of learning. *American Psychologist,* 1962, **17**, 83-91.

Gagne, R. M., & Brown, L. T. Some factors in the programming of conceptual learning. *Journal of Experimental Psychology,* 1961, **62**, 313-321.

Ganuli, H. C. An inquiry into incentives for workers in an engineering factory. *Indian Journal of Social Work,* 1954, **15**, 30-40.

Gardner, R. W. Cognitive styles in categorizing behavior. *Journal of Personnel,* 1953, **22**, 214-233.

Gassner, S., Gold, J., & Snadowsky, A. M. Changes in the phenomenal field as a result of human relations training. *Journal of Psychology,* 1964, **58**, 33-41.

Gaudet, F. J., & Carli, A. R. Why executives fail. *Personnel Psychology,* 1957, **10**, 7-22.

Gellerman, S. W. The company personality. *Management Review,* 1959, **48**, 69-76.

Georgopoulos, B. S. Normative structure variables and organizational behavior. *Human Relations,* 1965, **18**, 115-170.

Georgopolous, B. S., Mahoney, G. M., & Jones, N. W. A path-goal approach to productivity. *Journal of Applied Psychology,* 1957, **41**, 345-353.

Ghiselli, E. E. Correlates of initiative. *Personnel Psychology,* 1956, **9**, 311-320.

Ghiselli, E. E. Managerial talent. *American Psychologist,* 1963, **8**, 631-642.

Ghiselli, E. E. The effects on career pay of policies with respect to increases in pay. In R. Andrews (Ed.), *Managerial Compensation.* Ann Arbor, Mich.: Foundation for Research in Human Behavior, 1965. Pp. 21-34.

Ghiselli, E. E. The validity of a personnel interview. *Personnel Psychology,* 1966, **19**, 389-395. (a)

Ghiselli, E. E. *The validity of occupational aptitude tests.* New York: Wiley, 1966. (b)

Ghiselli, E. E. Some motivational factors in the success of managers. *Personnel Psychology,* 1968, **21**, 431-440.

Ghiselli, E. E., & Brown, C. W. *Personnel and industrial psychology.* New York: McGraw-Hill, 1955.

Ghiselli, E. E., & Haire, M. The validation of selection tests in the light of the dynamic character of criteria. *Personnel Psychology,* 1960, **13**, 225-231.

Ghiselli, E. E., & Lodahl, T. M. Evaluation of foremen's performance in relation to the internal character of their work groups. *Personnel Psychology,* 1958, **11**, 179-187.

Gibson, G. W. A new dimension for "in-basket" training. *Personnel,* 1961, **38**, 76-79.

Gilmer, B. v. H. The third crisis in industrial training. *Journal of the American Society of Training Directors,* 1963, **17**, 4-11.

Gilmer, B. v. H. *Industrial psychology.* (2nd ed.) New York: McGraw-Hill, 1966.

Glaser, R., Schwarz, P. A., & Flanagan, J. C. The contribution of interview and situational performance procedures to the selection of supervisory personnel. *Journal of Applied Psychology,* 1958, **42,** 69-73.

Gleser, G. Projective methodologies. *Annual Review of Psychology,* 1963, **14,** 391-422.

Glickman, A. S., & Vallance, T. R. Curriculum assessment with critical incidents. *Journal of Applied Psychology,* 1958, **42,** 329-335.

Goodacre, D. M., III. Experimental evaluation of training. *Journal of Personnel Administration and Industrial Relations,* 1955, **2,** 143-149.

Goodacre, D. M. Stimulating improved man management. *Personnel,* 1963, **16,** 133-143.

Goode, C. E. *Personnel research frontiers.* Chicago: Public Personnel Association, 1958.

Goodman, P. S. An empirical examination of Elliott Jaques' concept of time span. Unpublished manuscript, University of Chicago, 1965.

Goodstein, L. D., & Schrader, W. J. An empirically derived managerial key for the California Psychological Inventory. *Journal of Applied Psychology,* 1963, **47,** 42-45.

Goranson, R., & Berkowitz, L. Reciprocity and responsibility reactions to prior help. *Journal of Personality and Social Psychology,* 1966, **3,** 227-232.

Gordon, L. V., & Medland, F. F. The cross-group stability of peer ratings of leadership potential. *Personnel Psychology,* 1965, **18,** 173-177.

Graen, G. B. Work motivation: The behavioral effects of job content and job context factors in an employment situation. Unpublished doctoral dissertation, University of Minnesota, 1967.

Grant, D. L. A factor analysis of managers' ratings. *Journal of Applied Psychology,* 1955, **39,** 283-286.

Grant, D. L., Katkovsky, W., & Bray, D. W. Contributions of projective techniques to assessment of management potential. *Journal of Applied Psychology,* 1967, **51,** 226-232.

Gruenfeld, L. W. Management development effect on changes in values. *Training and Development Journal,* 1966, **20** (6), 18-26. (a)

Gruenfeld, L. W. Personality needs and expected benefit from a management development program. *Occupational Psychology,* 1966, **40,** 75-81. (b)

Guetzkow, H., & Bowes, A. E. The development of organizations in a laboratory. *Management Science,* 1957, **3,** 380-402.

Guetzkow, H., Forehand, G., & James, B. J. An evaluation of educational influence on administrative judgment. *Administrative Science Quarterly,* 1962, **6,** 483-500.

Guion, R. M. *Personnel testing.* New York: McGraw-Hill, 1965. (a)

Guion, R. M. Synthetic validity in a small company: A demonstration. *Personnel Psychology,* 1965, **18,** 49-65. (b)

Guion, R. M., & Gottier, R. F. Validity of personality measures in personnel selection. *Personnel Psychology,* 1965, **18,** 135-164.

Gurin, G., Veroff, J., & Feld, S. *Americans view their mental health.* New York: Basic Books, 1960.

Habbe, S. College graduates assess their company training. National Industrial Conference Board Studies in Personnel Policy, No. 188, 1963.

Haire, M. Some problems of industrial training. *Journal of Social Issues,* 1948, **4,** 41-47.

Haire, M. Psychological problems relevant to business and industry. *Psychological Bulletin,* 1959, **56,** 169-194.

Haire, M. *Psychology of management.* (2nd ed.) New York: McGraw-Hill, 1964.

Haire, M. The incentive character of pay. In R. Andrews (Ed.), *Managerial compensation.* Ann Arbor, Mich.: Foundation for Research in Human Behavior, 1965. Pp. 13-17.

Haire, M., Ghiselli, E. E., & Gordon, M. E. A psychological study of pay. *Journal of Applied Psychology Monograph,* 1967, **51** (4, Whole No. 636).

Haire, M., Ghiselli, E. E., & Porter, L. W. *Managerial thinking: An international study.* New York: Wiley, 1966.

Hall, R. H., Haas, J. E., & Johnson, N. J. An examination of the Blau-Scott and Etzioni typologies. *Administrative Science Quarterly,* 1967, **12,** 118-139.

Halpin, A. W. The leader behavior and effectiveness of aircraft commanders. In R. M. Stogdill & A. E. Coons (Eds.), *Leader behavior: Its description and measurement.* Columbus, Ohio: Ohio State University, Bureau of Business Research, Research Monograph No. 88, 1957.

Halpin, A. W., & Croft, D. B. *The organizational climate of schools.* Chicago: University of Chicago Press, 1963.

Halpin, A. W., & Winer, B. J. A factorial study of the leader behavior descriptions. In R. M. Stogdill & A. E. Coons (Eds.), *Leader behavior: Its description and measurement.* Columbus, Ohio: Ohio State University, Bureau of Business Research, Research Monograph No. 88, 1957.

Handyside, J. D. The effectiveness of supervisory training: A survey of recent experimental studies. *Personnel Management,* 1956, **38**, 96-107.

Harber, R. N. (Ed.) *Current research in motivation.* New York: Holt, 1966.

Harlow, H. F. Comments on Professor Brown's paper. In *Current theory and research in motivation.* Lincoln, Nebr.: University of Nebraska Press, 1953.

Harrell, T. W. Managers' performance and personality. Cincinnati: South-Western, 1961.

Harrell, T. W. *Follow-up of management potential battery.* Stanford, Calif.: Stanford University, Graduate School of Business, 1967.

Harris, E. F. Measuring industrial leadership and its implications for training supervisors. *Dissertation Abstracts,* 1958, **18**, 1513-1516.

Harris, E. F., & Fleishman, E. A. Human relations training and the stability of leadership patterns. *Journal of Applied Psychology,* 1955, **39**, 20-25.

Harrison, R. Impact of the laboratory on perceptions of others by the experimental group. In C. Argyris, *Interpersonal competence and organizational effectiveness.* Homewood, Ill.: Dorsey-Irwin, 1962. Pp. 261-271.

Harrison, R. Cognitive change and participation in a sensitivity training laboratory. *Journal of Consulting Psychology,* 1966, **30,** 517-520.

Harrison, R., & Lubin, B. Personal style, group composition, and learning. *Journal of Applied Behavioral Science,* 1965, **1,** 286-301.

Harrower, M. Group techniques for the Rorschach test. In L. Abt & L. Bellak (Eds.), *Projective psychology,* New York: Grove Press, 1959.

Harvey, O. J., Hunt, D. E., & Schroder, H. M. *Conceptual systems and personality organization.* New York: Wiley, 1961.

Hayes, J. J. Results of training supervisors in democratic concepts of leadership. *Journal of the American Society of Training Directors,* 1956, **10** (1), 24-27.

Hazeltine, B. P., & Berra, R. L. Supervisory development: The research approach. *Personnel,* 1953, **30,** 60-67.

Hedlund, D. E. A review of the MMPI in industry. *Psychological Reports,* 1965, **17,** 874-889.

Heider, F. *The psychology of interpersonal relations.* New York: Wiley, 1958.

Helson, H. Adaptation level theory. In S. Koch (Ed.), *Psychology: A study of a science.* Vol. 1. New York: McGraw-Hill, 1959.

Hemphill, J. K. Job descriptions for executives. *Harvard Business Review,* 1959, **37,** 55-67.

Hemphill, J. K. Dimensions of executive positions. Ohio Studies in Personnel, *Research Monographs,* Ohio State University, Bureau of Business Research, 1960, No. 98.

Hemphill, J. K., & Westie, C. N. The measurement of group dimensions. *Journal of Psychology,* 1950, **29,** 325-342.

Henry, W. E. Executive personality and job success. *American Management Association Personnel Service,* 1948, No. 120, 3-13.

Herzberg, F. *Work and the nature of man.* Cleveland: World Publishing, 1966.

Herzberg, F., Mausner, B., Peterson, R. O., & Capwell, D. F. *Job attitudes: A review of research and opinion.* Pittsburgh: Psychological Service of Pittsburgh, 1957.

Herzberg, F., Mausner, B., & Snyderman, B. *The motivation to work.* (2nd ed.) New York: Wiley, 1959.

Hickson, D. J. Motives of work of people who restrict their output. *Occupational Psychology,* 1961, **35,** 110-121.

Hilgard, E. R. What support from the psychology of learning? *NEA Journal,* November, 1961, **50,** 20-21.

Hillman, H. A. Measuring management training: A case study. *Journal of the American Society of Training Directors,* 1962, **16** (3), 27-31.

Hinrichs, J. R. *High talent personnel: Managing a critical resource.* New York: American Management Association, 1966.

Hoffman, F. O. The all-purpose manager: Does he exist? *Personnel,* 1963, **40,** 8-16.

Hoffman, L. R. Homogeneity of member personality and its effect on group problem solving. *Journal of Abnormal and Social Psychology,* 1959, **58,** 27-32.

Hogue, J. P., Otis, J. L., & Prien, E. P. Assessments of higher level personnel. VI. Validity of predictions based on projective tests. *Personnel Psychology,* 1962, **15,** 335-344.

Holland, J. L. A theory of vocational choice. *Journal of Counseling Psychology,* 1959, **6,** 35-45.

Holland, J. L. & Richards, J. M., Jr. Academic and nonacademic accomplishment: Correlated or uncorrelated? *Journal of Educational Psychology,* 1965, **56,** 165-174.

Hollander, E. P. Buddy ratings: Military research and industrial implications. *Personnel Psychology,* 1954, **7,** 385-393.

Hollander, E. P. The friendship factor in peer nominations. *Personnel Psychology,* 1956, **9,** 425-447.

Hollander, E. P. The reliability of peer nominations under various conditions of administration. *Journal of Applied Psychology,* 1957, **41,** 85-90.

Hollander, E. P. Conformity, status, and idiosyncrasy credit. *Psychological Review,* 1958, **65,** 117-127.

Hollander, E. P. Validity of peer nominations in predicting a distinct performance criterion. *Journal of Applied Psychology,* 1965, **49,** 434-438.

Holt, R. R. Clinical and statistical prediction: A reformulation and some new data. *Journal of Abnormal and Social Psychology,* 1958, **56,** 1-12.

Homans, G. C. Status among clerical workers. *Human Organizations,* 1953, **12,** 5-10.

Homans, G. C. Social behavior as exchange. *American Journal of Sociology,* 1958, **63,** 597-606.

Hook, R. C., Jr. Executive development: A different approach. *Training Directors Journal,* 1963, **17** (11), 29-31..

Horne, J. H., & Lupton, T. The work activities of "middle" managers. *Journal of Management Studies,* 1965, **1,** 14-33.

House, R. J. T-group education and leadership effectiveness: A review of the empirical literature and a critical evaluation. *Personnel Psychology,* 1967, **20,** 1-32.

House, R. J. Stress as a moderator of the relationship between organizational variables and satisfaction with pay and advancement. Invited address given at the University of Minnesota, July 1968.

House, R. J., & Filley, A. C. Leadership style, hierarchical influence, and the satisfaction of subordinate role expectations: A test of six leadership hypotheses and an analysis of Likert's influence proposition. Paper presented at the American Psychological Association, San Francisco, September 1968.

House, R. J., & Tosi, H. An experimental evaluation of a management training program. *Journal of the Academy of Management,* 1963, **6,** 303-315.

House, R. J., & Wigdor, L. A. Herzberg's dual factor theory of job satisfaction and motivation. *Personnel Psychology,* 1967, **20,** 369-390.

Howe, R. V. Price tags for executives. *Harvard Business Review,* 1956, **34,** (3), 94-100.

Hull, C. L. *Principles of behavior.* New York: Appleton-Century-Crofts, 1943.

Hull, T. F., & Powell, R. F. Evaluating a supervisory training program. *Journal of the American Society of Training Directors,* 1959, **13,** (11), 27-29.

Huneryager, S. G. Re-education for executives. *Personnel Administration,* 1961, **24** (1), 5-9.

Hunt, J. G. Fiedler's leadership contingency model: An empirical test in three organizations. *Organizational Behavior and Human Performance,* 1967, **2,** 290-308.

Husband, R. W. What do college grades predict? *Fortune,* 1957, **55** (6), 157-158.

Huse, E. F. Assessments of higher level personnel. IV. The validity of assessment techniques based on systematically varied information. *Personnel Psychology,* 1962, **15,** 195-205.

Hutchins, E. B. Construct validity of an environmental assessment technique for medical schools. Technical Report No. L661, 1966, Association of American Medical Colleges, Division of Education.

Hutchins, E. B. & Nonneman, B. A. Construct validity for an environmental assessment technique for medical schools. Evanston, Ill.: Division of Education, Association of American Medical Colleges, Technical Report L661, 1966.

Huttner, L., Levy, S., Rosen, E., & Stopol, M. Further light on the executive personality. *Personnel,* 1959, **36,** 42-50.

Indik, B. P. Organization size and member participation: Some empirical tests of alternative explanations. *Human Relations,* 1965, **18,** 339-350.

Ingenohl, I. Blueprint for a successful management development policy. *Personnel,* 1962, **41,** 491-494.

Jaques, E. *The measurement of responsibility.* Cambridge, Mass.: Harvard University Press, 1956.

Jaques, E. *Equitable payment.* New York: Wiley, 1961.

Jaques, E., Rice, A. K., & Hill, J. M. The social and psychological impact of a change in method of wage payment. *Human Relations,* 1951, **4,** 315-340.

Jennings, E. E. Advantages of forced leadership training. *Personnel,* 1953, **32,** 7-9. (a)

Jennings, E. E. Attitude training versus technique training. *Personnel,* 1953, **31,** 402-404. (b)

Jennings, E. E. The dynamics of forced leadership training. *Journal of Personnel Administration and Industrial Relations,* 1954, **1,** 110-118.

Jennings, E. E. Today's group training problems. *Personnel,* 1956, **35,** 94-97.

Jennings, E. E. Two schools of thought about executive development. *Personnel Journal,* 1959, **37,** 370-372.

Johansson, C. Stability of the Strong Vocational Interest Blank. Unpublished manuscript, University of Minnesota, 1966.

Johnson, J. C., & Dunnette, M. D. Validity and test retest stability of the Nash managerial effectiveness scale on the revised form of the Strong Vocational Interest Blank. *Personnel Psychology,* 1968, **21,** 283-293.

Jones, E. E. *Ingratiation.* New York: Appleton-Century-Crofts, 1963.

Jones, L. V., & Jeffrey, T. E. A quantitative analysis of expressed preferences for compensation plans. *Journal of Applied Psychology,* 1964, **49,** 201-210.

Jurgensen, C. E. Report to participants on adjective word sort. Minneapolis, Minneapolis Gas Company. Unpublished report, 1966.

Kahn, R. L., Wolfe, D. M., Quinn, R. P., Snoek, J. D., & Rosenthal, R. A. *Organizational stress: Studies in role conflict and ambiguity.* New York: Wiley, 1964.

Kaplan, A. *The conduct of inquiry.* San Francisco: Chandler, 1964.

Katz, D. The motivational oasis of organizational behavior. *Behavioral Science,* 1964, **9,** 131-146

Katz, D., & Kahn, R. L. *The social psychology of organizations.* New York: Wiley, 1966.

Katz, D., Maccoby, N., Gurin, G., & Floor, L. G. *Productivity, supervision, and morale among railroad workers.* Ann Arbor, Mich.: University of Michigan, Survey Research Center, Institute for Social Research, 1951.

Katz, D., Maccoby, N., & Morse, N. C. *Productivity, supervision, and morale in an office situation.* Ann Arbor, Mich.: University of Michigan, Institute for Social Research, 1950.

Katzell, R. A. Testing a training program in human relations. *Personnel,* 1948, **1,** 319-330.

Katzell, R. A., Barrett, R. S., & Parker, T. C. Job satisfaction, job performance, and situational characteristics. *Journal of Applied Psychology,* 1961, **45,** 65-72.

Kay, B. R. Key factors in effective foreman behavior. *Personnel,* 1959, **36,** 25-31.

Kay, E., & Meyer, H. H. The development of a job activity questionnaire for production foremen. *Personnel Psychology,* 1962, **15,** 411-418.

Keating, E., Paterson, D. G., & Stone, C. H. Validity of work histories obtained by interview. *Journal of Applied Psychology,* 1950, **34,** 1-5.

Kelley, H. H. Experimental studies of threats in interpersonal negotiations. *Journal of Conflict Resolutions,* 1965., **9,** 79-105.

Kelly, J. The study of executive behavior by activity sampling. *Human Relations,* 1964, **17,** 277-287.

Keltner, J. W. The task-model as a training instrument. *Training Directors Journal,* 1965, **19** (9), 18-21.

Kepner, C. H., & Tregoe, B. B. Developing decision makers. *Harvard Business Review,* 1960, **38,** 115-124.

Kepner, C. H., & Tregoe, B. B. *The rational manager: A systematic approach to problem solving and decision making.* New York: McGraw-Hill, 1965.

Kernan, J. P. Laboratory human relations training: Its effect on the "personality" of supervisory engineers. *Dissertation Abstracts,* 1964, **25,** 665-666.

Kiesler, C. A., & Corbin, L. H. Commitment, attraction, and conformity. *Journal of Personality and Social Psychology,* 1965, **2,** 890-895.

Kight, S. S., & Smith, E. E. Effects of feedback on insight and problem-solving efficiency in training groups. *Journal of Applied Psychology,* 1959, **43,** 209-211.

Kinslinger, H. J. Application of projective techniques in personnel psychology since 1940. *Psychological Bulletin,* 1966, **66,** 134-150.

Kirchner, W. K., & Reisberg, D. J. Differences between better and less effective supervisors in appraisal of subordinates. *Personnel Psychology,* 1962, **15,** 295-302.

Kirkpatrick, D. L. Techniques for evaluating training programs. I. *Journal of the American Society of Training Directors,* 1959, **13,** 3-9. (a)

Kirkpatrick, D. L. Techniques for evaluating training programs. II. *Journal of the American Society of Training Directors,* 1959, **13,** 21-26. (b)

Kirkpatrick, D. L. Techniques for evaluating training programs. III. *Journal of the American Society of Training Directors,* 1960, **14,** 13-18. (a)

Kirkpatrick, D. L. Techniques for evaluating training programs. IV. *Journal of the American Society of Training Directors,* 1960, **14,** 28-32. (b)

Kirkpatrick, J. J. Background history factors that lead to executive success. Research paper delivered at the annual convention of the American Psychological Association, Chicago, September 1960.

Kirkpatrick, J. J. How to select a Chamber of Commerce executive. *Journal of American Chamber of Commerce Executives,* 1961, **10** (1), 2-6.

Kirkpatrick, J. J. Five-year follow-up study of the American Chamber of Commerce standard application for employment form. Prepared for American Chamber of Commerce executives, Washington, April 1966.

Klaw, S. Two weeks in a T-group. *Fortune,* 1961, **64,** 114-117.

Kleinmuntz, B. MMPI decision rules for the identification of college maladjustment: A digital computer approach. *Psychological Monographs,* 1963, **77** (14, Whole No. 577). (a)

Kleinmuntz, B. Personality test interpretation by digital computer. *Science,* 1963, **139,** 416-418. (b)

Kleinmuntz , B. Profile analysis revisited: A heuristic approach. *Journal of Counseling Psychology,* 1963, **10,** 315-321. (c)

Kleinmuntz, B. Computer simulation of diagnostic judgments. Paper presented at the Midwestern Psychological Association, St. Louis, May 1964.

Koontz, H., & O'Donnell, C. *Principles of management.* New York: McGraw-Hill, 1955.

Koontz, H., & O'Donnell, C. *Principles of management.* (2nd ed.) New York: McGraw-Hill, 1959.

Korb, L. D. How to measure the results of supervisory training. *Personnel,* 1956, **32,** 378-391.

Korman, A. K. Consideration, initiating structure and organizational criteria: A review. *Personnel Psychology,* 1966, **19,** 349-363.

Korman, A. K. The prediction of managerial performance: A review. *Personnel Psychology,* 1968, **21,** 295-322.

Krech, D., Crutchfield, R. S., & Ballachey, E. L. *Individual in society: A textbook of social psychology.* New York: McGraw-Hill, 1962.

Krist, P. C., & Prange, C. J. Training supervisors by mail: The Railway Express program. *Personnel,* 1957, **34,** 32-37.

Kuder, G. F. *Revised manual for the Kuder Preference Record.* Chicago: Science Research Associates, 1946.

Kuriloff, A. H., & Atkins, S. T-group for a work team. *Journal of Applied Behavioral Science,* 1966, **2,** 63-94.

Kurtz, A. A research test of the Rorschach test. *Personnel Psychology,* 1948, **1,** 41-51.

Larke, A. G. Workers' attitudes on incentives. *Dun's Review and Modern Industry,* 1953, December, 61-63.

Laurent, H. Summary report of the early identification of management potential research project in Standard Oil Company (New Jersey) and affiliated companies. SONJ, Social Science Research Division, 1961.

Laurent, H. The validation of aids for the identification of management potential. SONJ, 1962.

Laurent, H. EIMP applied to the International Petroleum Co. Technical Report, 1966.

Lawler, E. E., III. Managers' job performance and their attitudes toward their pay. Unpublished doctoral dissertation, University of California, 1964.

Lawler, E. E., III. Managers' perceptions of their subordinates' pay and of their superiors' pay. *Personnel Psychology,* 1965, **18,** 413-422.

Lawler, E. E., III. Ability as a moderator of the relationships between job attitudes and job performance. *Personnel Psychology,* 1966, **19,** 153-164. (a)

Lawler, E. E., III. Managers' attitudes toward how their pay is and should be determined. *Journal of Applied Psychology,* 1966, **50,** 273-279. (b)

Lawler, E. E., III. Management performance as seen from above, below, and within. *Journal of Applied Psychology,* 1967, **51,** 247-253. (a)

Lawler, E. E. III. Secrecy about management compensation: Are there hidden costs? *Organizational Behavior and Human Performance,* 1967, **2,** 182-189. (b)

Lawler, E. E., III. Equity theory as a predictor of productivity and work quality. *Psychological Bulletin,* 1969. In press.

Lawler, E. E., III, Koplin, C. A., Young, T. F., & Fadem, J. A. Inequity reduction over time in an induced overpayment situation. *Organizational Behavior and Human Performance,* 1968, **3,** 253-268.

Lawler, E. E., III, & O'Gara, P. W. Effects of inequity produced by underpayment on work output, work quality, and attitudes toward the work. *Journal of Applied Psychology,* 1967, **51,** 403-410.

Lawler, E. E., III, & Porter, L. W. Perceptions regarding management compensation. *Industrial Relations,* 1963, **3,** 41-49.

Lawler, E. E., III, & Porter, L. W. Antecedent attitudes of effective managerial performance. *Organizational Behavior and Human Performance,* 1967, **2,** 122-142.

Lawrence, L. C., & Smith, P. C. Group decision and employee participation. *Journal of Applied Psychology,* 1955, **39,** 334-337.

Lawshe, C. H., Bolda, R. A., & Brune, R. L. Studies in management training evaluation. I. Scaling responses to human relations training cases. *Journal of Applied Psychology,* 1958, **42,** 396-398.

Lawshe, C. H., Bolda, R. A., & Brune, R. L. Studies in management training evaluation. II. The effects of exposure to role playing. *Journal of Applied Psychology,* 1959, **43,** 287-292.

Leavitt, H. J., & Bass, B. M. Organizational psychology. In P. R. Farnsworth (Ed.), *Annual review of psychology.* Vol. 15. Palo Alto, Calif.: Annual Reviews, 1964.

Levine, J., & Butler, J. Lecture vs. group decision in changing behavior. *Journal of Applied Psychology,* 1952, **36,** 29-33.

Levy, S. Supervisory effectiveness and criterion relationships. Paper presented at the 68th annual meeting of the American Psychological Association, Chicago, May 1960.

Lewin, K. The conceptual representation and the measurement of psychological forces. Durham, N. C.: Duke University Press, 1938.

Lewin, K. Frontiers in group dynamics: Concept, method, and reality in social science. *Human Relations,* 1947, **1,** 5-13.

Lewin, K. *Resolving social conflicts.* New York: Harper, 1948.

Lewin, K., Lippitt, R., & White, R. K. Patterns of aggressive behavior in experimentally created social climates. *Journal of Social Psychology,* 1939, **10,** 271-299.

Likert, R. *New patterns of management.* New York: McGraw-Hill, 1961.

Likert, R. *The human organization: Its management and value.* New York: McGraw-Hill, 1967.

Lindbom, T. R. Supervisory training and employee attitudes. *Journal of Industrial Training,* 1953, **7** (6), 17-20.

Lindbom, T. R., & Osterberg, W. Evaluating the results of supervisory training. *Personnel,* 1954, **31,** 224-228.

Lindsay, C. A., Marks, E., & Gorlow, L. The Herzberg theory: A critique and reformulation. *Journal of Applied Psychology,* 1967, **51,** 330-336.

Lindzey, G. Seer versus sign. *Journal of Experimental Research in Personality,* 1965, **1,** 17-26.

Litterer, J. A. How 47 companies measure their executives. *Personnel Journal,* 1957, **36,** 97-100.

Litwin, G. H. Achievement motivation, expectancy of success, and risk-taking behavior. In J. W. Atkinson & N. T. Feather (Eds.), *A theory of achievement motivation.* New York: Wiley, 1966.

Litwin, G. H., & Ciarlo, J. A. *Achievement motivation and risk taking in a business setting.* General Electric, Behavioral Research Service, 1961.

Litwin, G. H., & Stringer, R. The influence of organizational climate on human motivation. Paper presented at a conference on organizational climate, Foundation for Research on Human Behavior, Ann Arbor, Mich., March 1966.

Locke, E. A. The interaction of ability and motivation in performance. *Perceptual and Motor Skills,* 1965, **21,** 719-725.

Locke, E. A. A closer look at level of aspiration as a training procedure: A reanalysis of Fryer's data. *Journal of Applied Psychology,* 1966, **50,** 417-420. (a)

Locke, E. A. The relationship of intentions to level of performance. *Journal of Applied Psychology,* 1966, **50,** 60-66. (b)

Locke, E. A. Relationship of task success to task liking: a replication. *Psychological Reports,* 1966, **18,** 552-554. (c)

Locke, E. A. The motivational effect of knowledge of results: Knowledge or goal setting? *Journal of Applied Psychology,* 1967, **51,** 324-329.

Locke, E. A. Toward a theory of task motivation and incentives. *Organizational Behavior and Human Performance,* 1968, **3,** 157-189.

Locke, E. A., & Bryan, J. F. Cognitive aspects of psychomotor performance: The effect of performance goals on level of performance. *Journal of Applied Psychology,* 1966, **50,** 286-291.

Locke, E. A., Bryan, J. F., & Kendall, L. M. Goals and intentions as mediators of the effects of monetary incentives on behavior. *Journal of Applied Psychology,* 1968, **52,** 104-109.

Lohman, K., Zenger, J. H., & Weschler, I. R. Some perceptual changes during sensitivity training. *Journal of Educational Research,* 1959, **53,** 28-31.

Lopez, F. M., Jr. Evaluating executive decision making: The In-basket technique. American Management Association Research Study No. 75, 1966.

Lott, A., & Lott, B. Group cohesiveness as interpersonal attraction: A review of relationships with antecedent and consequent variables. *Psychological Bulletin,* 1965, **64,** 259-309.

Lowin, A., & Craig, J. R. The influence of level of performance on managerial style: An experimental object lesson in the ambiguity of correlational data. *Organizational Behavior and Human Performance,* 1968, **3,** 440-458.

Lundberg, C. C. Attitude change and management training: A critical commentary. *Personnel Administration,* 1962, **25** (3), 35-42.

Lykken, D. T. A method of actuarial pattern analysis. *Psychological Bulletin,* 1956, **53,** 102-107.

Lykken, D. T., & Rose, R. Psychological prediction from actuarial tables. *Journal of Clinical Psychology,* 1963, **19,** 139-151.

Lysaught, J. P. *Programmed learning: Evolving principles and industrial applications.* Ann Arbor, Mich.: Foundation for Research on Human Behavior, 1961.

Mace, C. A. Incentives: Some experimental studies. Industrial Health Research Board Report No. 72. London: H. M. Stationery Office, 1935.

MacKinney, A. C. Progressive levels in the evaluation of training programs. *Personnel,* 1957, **34,** 72-77.

MacKinney, A. C., & Wolins, L. Validity information exchange, No. 13-01. *Personnel Psychology,* 1960, **13,** 443-447.

Mahler, W. R. Evaluation of management development programs. *Personnel,* 1953, **30,** 116-122.

Mahler, W. R., & Monroe, W. H. How Industry determines the need for and effectiveness of training. Personnel Research Section Report No. 929, 1952, Department of the Army.

Mahoney, T. Compensation preferences of managers. *Industrial Relations,* 1964, **3,** 135-144.

Mahoney, T. A. Criteria of organizational effectiveness. Mimeographed report, University of Minnesota, Industrial Relations Center, 1966.

Mahoney, T. A. Criteria of organizational effectiveness. Paper presented at the 10th annual Academy of Management Conference, Midwest Division, April 1967.

Mahoney, T. A., Jerdee, T. H., & Carroll, S. J. *Development of managerial performance: A research approach.* Cincinnati: South-Western, 1963.

Mahoney, T. A., Jerdee, T. H., & Korman, A. An experimental evaluation of management development. *Personnel,* 1960, **13,** 81-98.

Mahoney, T. A., Jerdee, T. H., & Nash, A. N. Predicting managerial effectiveness. *Personnel Psychology,* 1960, **13,** 147-163.

Mahoney, T. A., Sorenson, W. W., Jerdee, T. H., and Nash, A. N. Identification and prediction of managerial effectiveness. *Personnel Administration,* 1963, **26,** 12-22.

Maier, N. R. F. An experimental test of the effect of training on discussion leadership. *Human Relations,* 1953, **6,** 161-173.

Maier, N. R. F. *Psychology in industry.* (2nd ed.) Boston: Houghton Mifflin, 1955.

Maier, N. R. F. *Problem-solving discussions and conferences: Leadership methods and skills.* New York: McGraw-Hill, 1963.

Maier, N., Hoffman, L., & Read, W. Superior-subordinate communication: The relative effectiveness of managers who held their subordinates' positions. *Personnel Psychology,* 1963, **16,** 1-11.

Maier, N. R. F., Solem, A., & Maier, A. *Supervisory and executive development.* New York: Wiley, 1957.

Mandell, M. M. Supervisory characteristics and ratings. *Personnel,* 1956, **32,** 435-440.

March, J. G., & Feigenbaum, E. Latent motives, group discussion, and the "quality" of group decisions in a non-objective decision problem. *Sociometry,* 1960, **23,** 50-56.

March, J. G., & Simon, H. A. *Organizations.* New York: Wiley, 1958.

Marriott, R. *Incentive payment systems: A review of research and opinion.* London: Staples Press, 1957.

Marrow, A. J., Bowers, D. G., & Seashore, S. E. *Management by participation: Creating a climate for personal and organizational development.* New York: Harper & Row, 1967.

Marrs, C. L. Categorizing behavior as elicited by a variety of stimuli. Unpublished master's thesis, University of Kansas, 1955.

Martin, H. O. The assessment of training. *Personnel Management,* 1957, **39,** 88-93.

Martin, M. W., Jr. The use of random alarm devices in studying scientists' reading behavior. *Transactions of the Professional Group of Engineering Management (IRE),* 1962 EM-9, No. 2.

Martin, N. H. Differential decisions in the management of an industrial plant. *Journal of Business,* 1956, **29,** 249-260.

Maslow, A. H. *Motivation and personality.* New York: Harper, 1954.

Mayfield, E. C. The selection interview: A re-evaluation of published research. *Personnel Psychology,* 1964, **17,** 239-260.

Mayfield, E. C., & Carlson, R. E. Selection interview decisions: First results from a long-term research project. *Personnel Psychology,* 1966, **19,** 41-53.

Mayo, G. D., & DuBois, P. H. Measurement of gain in leadership training. *Educational and Psychological Measurement,* 1963, **23,** 23-31.

McClelland, D. C. *Personality.* New York: Dryden Press, 1951.

McClelland, D. C. *The achieving society.* Princeton, N. J.: Van Nostrand, 1961.

McClelland, D. C. Business drive and national achievement. *Harvard Business Review,* 1962, **40,** 99-112.

McClelland, D. C. Why men and nations seek success. *Nation's Business,* 1963, **51,** 32-33.

McClelland, D. Achievement motivation can be developed. *Harvard Business Review,* 1965, **43,** 6-24, 178.

McClelland D. C., Atkinson, J. W., Clark, R. A., & Lowell, E. L. *The achievement motive.* New York: Appleton-Century-Crofts, 1953.

McConkey, D. D. Measuring managers by results. *Personnel Journal,* 1962, **41,** 540-546.

McCormack, C. *Multiple management.* New York: Harper, 1938.

McGehee, W., & Gardner, J. E. Supervisory training and attitude change. *Personnel Psychology,* 1955, **8,** 449-460.

McGehee, W., & Thayer, P. W. *Training in business and industry.* New York: Wiley, 1961.

McGregor, D. An uneasy look at performance appraisal. *Harvard Business Review,* 1957, **35** (3), 89-94.

McGregor, D. *The human side of enterprise.* New York: McGraw-Hill, 1960.

McNaughton, J. B. Work sampling at executive level. *Advanced Management,* 1956, **21,** 12-13.

McNemar, Q. Lost: Our intelligence. Why? *American Psychologist,* 1964, **19,** 871-882.

Meadow, A., & Parnes, S. J. Effects of "brainstorming" instructions on creative problem solving by trained and untrained members. *Journal of Educational Psychology,* 1959, **50,** 171-176.

Meehl, P. E. *Clinical versus statistical prediction.* Minneapolis: University of Minnesota Press, 1954.

Megginson, L. C. Management selection, development, and motivation in the United States. *Management International,* 1963, **2,** 97-106.

Mehrabian, A. Attitudes in relation to the forms of communicator-object relationship in spoken communications. *Journal of Personality,* 1966, **34,** 80-94.

Melloan, G. Young men move into executive suite faster at many companies. *The Wall Street Journal,* Aug. 26, 1966.

Merrihue, W. V., & Katzell, R. A. ERI: Yardstick of employee relations. *Harvard Business Review,* 1955, **33,** 91-99.

Merton, R. K. *Social theory and social structure.* New York: Free Press, 1957.

Meuwese, W., & Fiedler, F. E. Leadership and group creativity under varying conditions of stress. University of Illinois, Department of Psychology, Group Effectiveness Research Laboratory, 1965.

Meyer, H. D. A four year study of management promotions in the Jewel Tea Co. as related to three measures of achievement motivation. Ditto Report, Jewel Tea Co., 1963.

Meyer, H. D. Promotion probability control in using promotion as a criterion for assessment test validation. I. Assessing the probability of promotion or nonpromotion in the Jewel Tea Co. over a 5 to 6 year period. Mimeographed report, Jewel Tea Co., 1965. (a)

Meyer, H. D. Promotion probability control in using promotion as a criterion for assessment test validation in the Jewel Tea Co. II. The test validations, with promotion probability controlled. Mimeographed report, Jewel Tea Co., 1965. (b)

Meyer, H. H. Differences in organizational climate in outstanding and average sales offices: A summary report. General Electric, Behavioral Research Service and Public Relations Personnel Service, 1967.

Meyer, H. H., Kay, E.., & French, J. R. P., Jr. Split roles in performance appraisal. *Harvard Business Review,* 1965, **43** (1), 123-129.

Meyer, H. H., Walker, W. B., & Litwin, G. H. Motive patterns and risk preferences associated with entrepreneurship. *Journal of Abnormal and Social Psychology,* 1961, **63,** 570-574.

Miles, M. B. Changes during and following laboratory training: A clinical-experimental study. *Journal of Applied Behavioral Science,* 1965, **1,** 215-242.

Miner, J. B. The effect of a course in psychology on the attitudes of research and development supervisors. *Journal of Applied Psychology,* 1960, **44,** 224-232.

Miner, J. B. Management development and attitude change. *Personnel Administration,* 1961, **24**(3), 21-26.

Miner, J. B. *The management of ineffective performance.* New York: McGraw-Hill, 1963.

Miner, J. B. *Studies in management education.* New York: Springer, 1965.

Miner, J. B. Relationships between management appraisal ratings and promotions. Mimeographed paper, personal communication, 1966.

Miner, J. B. The early identification of managerial talent. *Personnel and Guidance Journal,* 1968, **46,** 586-591. (a)

Miner, J. B. The managerial motivation of school administrators. *University Council for Educational Administration Quarterly,* 1968, Winter, 55-71. (b)

Miner, J. B. & Culver, J. E. Some aspects of the executive personality. *Journal of Applied Psychology,* 1955, **39,** 348-353.

Mischel, W., & Liebert, R. M. Effects of discrepancies between observed and imposed reward criteria on their acquisition and transmission. *Journal of Personality and Social Psychology,* 1966, **3,** 45-53.

Misumi, J. Experimental studies on "group dynamics" in Japan. *Psychologia,* 1959, **2,** 229-235.

Moffie, D. J., Calhoon, R., & O'Brien, J. K. Evaluation of a management development program. *Personnel,* 1964, **17,** 431-440.

Moon, C. G., & Hariton, T. Evaluating an appraisal and feedback training program. *Personnel,* 1958, **35,** 36-41.

Morse, N. C., & Reimer, E. The experimental change of a major organizational variable. *Journal of Abnormal and Social Psychology,* 1956, **52,** 120-129.

Morse, N. C., & Weiss, R. S. The function and meaning of work and the job. *American Sociological Review,* 1955, **20,** 191-198.

Morton, R. B., & Bass, B. M. The organizational training laboratory. *Journal of the American Society of Training Directors,* 1964, **18** (10), 2-15.

Mosel, J. N. Why training programs fail to carry-over. *Personnel,* 1957, **34,** 56-64.

Mosel, J. N. How to feed back performance results to trainees. *Journal of the American Society of Training Directors,* 1958, **12** (2), 37-46.

Mosel, J. N. Evaluating the supervisors training program. *Engineering and Industrial Psychology,* 1959, **1,** 18-23.

Mosel, J. L., & Cozan, L. W. The accuracy of application blank work histories. *Journal of Applied Psychology,* 1952, **36,** 365-369.

Mosel, J. N., & Tsacnaris, H. J. Evaluating the supervisor training program. *Journal of Personnel Administration and Industrial Relations,* 1954, **1,** 99-104.

Mullen, J. H. The supervisor assesses his job in management: Highlights of a nationwide survey. *Personnel,* 1954, **31,** 94-108.

Murray, H. A. *Explorations in personality.* New York: Oxford University Press, 1938.

Murray, H. A. *Thematic Apperception Test pictures and manual.* Cambridge, Mass.: Harvard University Press, 1943. 20 pp.

Murray, H. A., MacKinnon, D. W., Miller, J. G., Fiske, D. W., & Hanfmann, E. *Assessment of men.* New York: Rinehart, 1948.

Myers, I. B. *Manual for the Myers-Briggs type indicator.* Princeton, N.J.: Educational Testing Service, 1962.

Nash, A. N. Development and evaluation of a Strong Vocational Blank key for differentiating between potentially effective and less effective business managers. Unpublished doctoral dissertation, University of Minnesota, 1963.

Nash, A. N. Vocational interests of effective managers: A review of the literature. *Personnel Psychology,* 1965, **18,** 21-37.

Nash, A. N. Development of an SVIB key for selecting managers. *Journal of Applied Psychology,* 1966, **50,** 250-254.

National Industrial Conference Board. Selecting company executives. National Industrial Conference Board Studies in Personnel Policy, No. 161, 1957.

National Industrial Conference Board. Personnel practices in factory and office: Manufacturing. National Industrial Conference Board Studies in Personnel Policy, No. 194, 1964.

National Industrial Conference Board. Office personnel practices: Nonmanufacturing. New York: National Industrial Conference Board Studies in Personnel Policy, No. 197, 1965.

Nealy, S. Pay and benefit preferences. *Industrial Relations,* 1963, **1,** 17-28.

Nealy, S. M., & Blood, M. R. Leadership performance of nursing supervisors at two organizational levels. *Journal of Applied Psychology,* 1968, **52,** 414-421.

Newcomer, M. *The big business executive.* New York: Columbia University Press, 1955.

Niven, J. R. Personal communication, 1966.

Oaklander, H., & Fleishman, E. A. Patterns of leadership related to organizational stress in hospital settings. *Administrative Science Quarterly,* 1964, **8,** 520-532.

Odiorne, G. S. The trouble with sensitivity training. *Training Directors Journal,* 1963, **17** (10), 9-20.

Odiorne, G. S. The need for an economic approach to training. *Journal of the American Society of Training Directors,* 1964, **18** (3), 3-12.

Odiorne, G. S. A systems approach to training. *Training Directors Journal,* 1965, **19** (1), 3-11.

Odiorne, G. S., & Hann, A. S. *Effective college recruiting.* Ann Arbor, Mich.: University of Michigan, Bureau of Industrial Relations, 1961.

The Office of Strategic Services Assessment Staff. *Assessment of men.* New York: Rinehart, 1948.

Ohmann, O. A. The leader and the led. *Personnel,* 1958, **35,** 8-15.

O'Neill, H. E., & Kubany, A. J. Observation methodology and supervisory behavior. *Personnel Psychology,* 1959, **12,** 85-96.

Opsahl, R. L., & Dunnette, M. D. The role of financial compensation in industrial motivation. *Psychological Bulletin,* 1966, **66,** 94-118.

Osgood, C. E. The nature and measurement of meaning. *Psychological Bulletin,* 1952, **49,** 251-262.

Oshry, B. I., & Harrison, R. Transfer from here-and-now—to there-and-then: Changes in organizational problem diagnosis stemming from T-group training. *Journal of Applied Behavioral Science,* 1966, **2,** 185-198.

Otis, J. L., Campbell, J. T., & Prien, E. P. Assessment of higher level personnel. VII. The nature of assessments. *Personnel Psychology,* 1962, **15,** 441-446.

Owens, W. A., & Henry, E. R. *Biographical data in industrial psychology: A review and evaluation.* Greensboro, N.C.: Richardson Foundation, 1966.

Pace, C. R., & Stern, G. G. An approach to the measurement of psychological characteristics of college environments. *Journal of Educational Psychology,* 1958, **49,** 269-277.

Pamplin, J. N. Executive selection in private enterprise and the federal government: An analysis and comparison. Unpublished master's thesis, University of Maryland, 1959.

Papaloizos, A. Personality and success of training in human relations. *Personnel,* 1962, **15,** 423-428.

Parker, T. C. Relationships among measures of supervisory behavior, group behavior and situational characteristics. *Personnel Psychology,* 1963, **16,** 319-334.

Patchen, M. *The choice of wage comparisons.* Englewood Cliffs, N.J.: Prentice-Hall, 1961.

Patton, A. Current practices in executive compensation. *Harvard Business Review,* 1951, **29** (1), 56-64.

Patton, A. Industry patterns of executive compensation. *Harvard Business Review,* 1955, **33** (5), 121-132.

Patton, A. Annual report on executive compensation. *Harvard Business Review,* 1956, **34** (6), 124-135.

Patton, A. Annual report on executive compensation. *Harvard Business Review,* 1958, **36** (5), 129-140.

Patton, A. How to appraise executive performance. *Harvard Business Review,* 1960, **38** (1), 63-70.

Patton, A. Executive compensation in 1960. *Harvard Business Review,* 1961, **39** (5), 152-157.

Patton, A. Executive compensation here and abroad. *Harvard Business Review,* 1962, **40** (5), 144-152.

Patton, A. Upturn in executive compensation. *Harvard Business Review,* 1963, **41** (5), 133-137.

Patton, A. Deterioration in top executive pay. *Harvard Business Review,* 1965, **43** (6), 106-118.

Peak, H. Attitude and motivation. In M. R. Jones (Ed.), *Nebraska symposium on motivation.* Lincoln, Nebr.: University of Nebraska Press, 1955. Pp. 149-188.

Pellegrin, R. J., & Coates, C. H. Executives and supervisors: Contrasting definitions of career success. *Administrative Science Quarterly,* 1957, **1,** 506-517.

Pelz, D. C., & Andrews, F. M. *Scientists in organizations.* New York: Wiley, 1966.

Pepinsky, H. B., Siegel, L., & Van Alta, E. L. The criterion in counseling: A group participation scale. *Journal of Abnormal and Social Psychology,* 1952, **47,** 415-419.

Pepinsky, H. B., & Weick, K. E. The simulation of productivity in organizations. *Personnel Administration,* 1961, **24** (6), 18-24.

Peres, S. H. Performance dimensions of supervisory positions. *Personnel Psychology,* 1962, **15,** 405-410.

Peres, S. H. Factors which influence careers at General Electric. General Electric, Behavioral Research Service, 1966.

Pervin, L. A. A twenty-college study of student + college interaction using TAPE (transactional analysis of personality and environment): Rationale reliability, and validity. *Journal of Educational Psychology,* 1967, **58,** 290-302.

Pervin, L. A. Performance and satisfaction as a function of individual-environmental fit. *Psychological Bulletin,* 1968, **69,** 56-68.

Peterson, D. A., & Wallace, S. R. Validation and revision of a test in use. *Journal of Applied Psychology,* 1966, **50,** 13-17.

Pettigrew, T. F. The measurement and correlates of category width as a cognitive variable. *Journal of Personality,* 1958, **26,** 532-544.

Pfiffner, J. M. The effective supervisor: An organization research study. *Personnel,* 1955, **31,** 530-540.

Pfiffner, J. M., & Sherwood, F. P. *Administrative organization.* Englewood Cliffs, N.J.: Prentice-Hall, 1960.

Pierson, F. C., et al. *The education of American businessmen.* New York: McGraw-Hill, 1959.

Pigors, P., & Pigors, F. *The incident process: Case studies in management development.* Washington: Bureau of National Affairs, 1955.

Piotrowski, Z. A., & Rock, M. R. *The perceptanalytic executive scale.* New York: Grune & Stratton, 1963.

Ponder, Q. D. Supervisory practices of effective and ineffective foremen. Unpublished doctoral dissertation, Columbia University, 1958.

Porter, E. H. *Manpower development: The systems training concept.* New York: Harper & Row, 1964.

Porter, L. W. A study of perceived need satisfactions in bottom and middle management jobs. *Journal of Applied Psychology,* 1961, **45,** 1-10.

Porter, L. W. Job attitudes in management. I. Perceived deficiencies in need fulfillment as a function of job level. *Journal of Applied Psychology,* 1962, **46,** 375-384.

Porter, L. W. Job attitudes in management. II. Perceived importance of needs as a function of job level. *Journal of Applied Psychology,* 1963, **47,** 141-148.

Porter, L. W. *Organizational patterns of managerial job attitudes.* New York: American Foundation for Management Research, 1964.

Porter, L. W., & Ghiselli, E. E. The self-perceptions of top and middle management personnel. *Personnel Psychology,* 1957, **10,** 397-406.

Porter, L. W., & Lawler, E. E. Properties of organization structure in relation to job attitudes and job behavior. *Psychological Bulletin,* 1965, **64,** 23-51.

Porter, L. W., & Lawler, E. E. *Managerial attitudes and performance.* Homewood, Ill.: Dorsey-Irwin, 1968.

Porter, L. W., & Mitchell, V. F. Comparative study of need satisfactions in military and business hierarchies. *Journal of Applied Psychology,* 1967, **51,** 139-144.

Potter, C. J., & Strachan, G. D. Project training groups: A "demand" technique for middle managers. *Training Directors Journal,* 1965, **19** (9), 34-41.

Prather, R. L. Introduction to management by teaching machine. *Personnel Administration,* 1964, **27** (3), 26-31.

Pressey, S. L. Teaching machine (and learning theory) crisis. *Journal of Applied Psychology,* 1963, **47,** 1-6.

Prien, E. P. Assessments of higher level personnel. V. An analysis of interviewers' predictions of job performance. *Personnel Psychology,* 1962, **15,** 319-334.

Prien, E. P. Development of a supervisor position description questionnaire. *Journal of Applied Psychology,* 1963, **47,** 10-14.

Prien, E. P., & Liske, R. E. Assessments of higher level personnel. III. Rating criteria: A comparative analysis of supervisor ratings and incumbent self ratings of job performance. *Personnel Psychology,* 1962, **15,** 187-194.

Pritchard, R. D. Equity theory: A review and critique. *Organizational Behavior and Human Performance,* 1969, **4,** 176-211.

Pugh, D. S., Hickson, D. J., Hinings, C. R., & Turner, C. Dimensions of organization structure. *Administrative Science Quarterly,* 1968, **13,** 65-105.

Rabow, J., Fowler, F. J., Bradford, D. L., Hofeller, M. A., & Shibuya, Y. The role of social norms and leadership in risk taking. *Sociometry,* 1966, **29,** 16-28.

Radlow, R. An experimental study of "cooperation" in the Prisoner's Dilemma game. *Journal of Conflict Resolutions,* 1965, **9,** 221-227.

Raia, A. P. A study of the educational value of management games. *Journal of Business,* 1966, **39,** 339-352.

Rambo, W. W. The construction and analysis of a leadership behavior rating form. *Journal of Applied Psychology,* 1958, **42,** 409-415.

Ramfolk, C. W. *Top management selection.* Stockholm: Swedish Council for Personnel Administration, 1957.

Randall, L. K. Evaluation: A training dilemma. *Journal of the American Society of Training Directors,* 1960, **14** (5), 29-35.

Randle, C. W. How to identify promotable executives. *Harvard Business Review,* 1956, **34** (3), 122-134.

Rapoport, A. A logical task as a research tool in organization theory. In M. Haire (Ed.), *Modern organization theory.* New York: Wiley, 1959.

Reed, J. H. Two weeks of managed conflict at Bethel. *Training Development Journal,* 1966, **20,** 6-16.

Roach, D. E. Factor analysis of rated supervisory behavior. *Personnel Psychology,* 1956, **9,** 487-498.

Roadman, H. E. An industrial use of peer ratings. *Journal of Applied Psychology,* 1964, **48,** 211-214.

Robbins, J. E., & King, D. D. Validity information exchange. *Personnel Psychology,* 1961, **14,** 217-219.

Roberts, D. R. *Executive compensation,* New York: Free Press, 1959.

Roby, T. B., Nicol, E, H., & Farrell, F. M. Group problem solving under two types of executive structure. *Journal of Abnormal and Social Psychology,* 1963, **67,** 550-556.

Rokeach, M. *The open and closed mind.* New York: Basic Books, 1960.

Rokeach, M. *Beliefs, attitudes, and values.* San Francisco: Jossey-Bass, 1968.

Roney, J. G. *Report on first conference on occupational obsolescence.* Menlo Park, Calif.: Stanford Research Institute, 1966.

Rorschach, H. *Psychdiagnostics.* (Tr. by P. Lemkau & B. Kronenburg.) Berne: Verlag Hans and Huber, 1942.

Rosen, E. H. The executive personality. *Personnel,* 1959, **36,** 8-20.

Rosen, H. Desirable attributes of work: Four levels of management describe their job environments. *Journal of Applied Psychology,* 1961, **45,** 156-168.

Rosen, H., & Weaver, C. G. Motivation in management: A study of four management levels. *Journal of Applied Psychology,* 1960, **44,** 386-392.

Rosenthal, R. The effect of the experimenter on the results of psychological research. In B. H. Maher (Ed.), *Experimental personality research.* Vol. 1. New York: Academic Press, 1964. Pp. 79-114.

Rotter, J. B. The role of the psychological situation in determining the direction of human behavior. In M. R. Jones (Ed.), *Nebraska symposium on motivation.* Lincoln, Nebr.: University of Nebraska Press, 1955.

Rupe, J. C. Some psychological dimensions of business and industrial executives. Purdue University, Division of Education Ref., Studies in Higher Education, No. 73, 65-95, n.d.

Rychlak, J. F., & Bray, D. W. A life-theme method for scoring of interviews in the longitudinal study of young business managers. *Psychological Reports, 1967* (Monogr. Suppl. 1-V21).

Sampson, E. E. Status congruence and cognitive consistency. *Sociometry,* 1963, **26,** 146-162.

Sawyer, J. Measurement *and* prediction, clinical *and* statistical. *Psychological Bulletin,* 1966, **66,** 178-200.

Sayles, L. R. *Managerial behavior: Administration in complex organizations.* New York: McGraw-Hill, 1964.

Schein, E. H. Forces which undermine management development. *California Management Review,* 1963, **5,** 23-34.

Schein, E. H. How to break in the college graduate. *Harvard Business Review,* 1964, **42,** 68-76.

Schein, E. H. *Organizational Psychology.* New York: Prentice-Hall, 1965.

Schein, E. H., & Bennis, W. G. *Personal and organizational change through group methods: The laboratory approach.* New York: Wiley, 1965.

Schneider, B., & Bartlett, C. J. Individual differences and organizational climate. I. The research plan and questionnaire development. *Personnel Psychology,* 1968, **21,** 323-334.

Schneider, D. E., & Bayroff, A. G. The relationship between rater characteristics and validity of ratings. *Journal of Applied Psychology,* 1953, **37,** 278-280.

Schutz, W. C. *FIRO: A three dimensional theory of interpersonal behavior.* New York: Rinehart, 1958.

Schutz, W. C., & Allen, V. L. The effects of a T-group laboratory on interpersonal behavior. *Journal of Applied Behavioral Science,* 1966, **2,** 265-286.

Schwarz, F. C., Stilwell, W. P., & Scanlan, B. K. Effects of management development on manager behavior and subordinate perception. I. *Training and Development Journal,* 1968, **22** (4), 38-50. (a)

Schwarz, F. C., Stilwell, W. P., & Scanlan, B. K. Effects of management development on manager behavior and subordinate perception. II. *Training and Development Journal*, 1968, **22** (5), 24-30. (b)

Scientific American. *The big business executive/1964*. New York: Author, 1965.

Scott, W. D., Clothier, R. C., Mathewson, S. B., & Spriegel, W. R. *Personnel management*. New York: McGraw-Hill, 1948.

Scott, W. D., Clothier, R. C., & Spriegel, W. R. *Personnel management*. New York: McGraw-Hill, 1954.

Scott, W. D., Clothier, R. C., & Spriegel, W. R. *Personnel management*. (6th ed.) New York: McGraw-Hill, 1961.

Seashore, S. E., & Yuchtman, E. Factorial analysis of organizational performance. *Administrative Science Quarterly*, 1967, **12**, 377-395.

Selekman, B. M. Sin bravely: The danger of perfectionism. *Harvard Business Review*, 1959, **37** (1), 105-118.

Sells, S. B. (Ed.) *Stimulus determinants of behavior*. New York: Ronald Press, 1963.

Selover, R. B. Identifying college graduates with high potential for advancement. Unpublished mimeographed report, Prudential Insurance Co. of America, 1962.

Serbein, O. N. *Educational activities of business*. Washington: American Council on Education, 1961.

Shaw, M. E. Scaling group tasks: A method for dimensional analysis. Mimeographed report, University of Florida, Department of Psychology, 1963.

Shaw, M. E. & Blum, J. M. Effects of leadership style upon group performance as a function of task structure. *Journal of Personality and Social Psychology*, 1966, **3**, 238-242.

Shaw, M. E., & Wright, J. M. *Scales for the measurement of attitudes*. New York: McGraw-Hill, 1967.

Shepard, H. A. Explorations in observant participation. In L. P. Bradford, J. R. Gibb, & K. D. Benne, *T-group theory and laboratory method*. New York: Wiley, 1964.

Sherif, M., & Harvey, O. J. A study in ego functioning: Elimination of stable anchorages in individual and group situations. *Sociometry*, 1952, **15**, 272-305.

Showrl, M., Taylor, R., & Hood, P. Automation of a portion of NCO leadership preparation training. HUMRRO Technical Report No. 66-21, 1966, AP-646771.

Simon, H. A. *The new science of management decision*. New York: Harper, 1960.

Sines, J. O. Actuarial methods as appropriate strategy for the validation of diagnostic tests. *Psychological Review*, 1964, **71**, 517-523.

Sines, J. O. Actuarial methods in personality assessment. In B. Maher (Ed.), *Progress in experimental personality research*. New York: Academic Press, 1966.

Skager, R., Holland, J. L., & Braskamp, L. A. Changes in self ratings and life goals among students at colleges with different characteristics. Research Report No. 14, American College Testing Program, Iowa City, 1966.

Skinner, B. F. The science of learning and the art of teaching. *Harvard Educational Review*, 1954, **24**, 99-113.

Smith, P. B. Attitude changes associated with training in human relations. *Bristish Journal of Social and Clinical Psychology*, 1964, **3**, 104-113.

Smith, P. C. The development of a method of measuring job satisfaction: The Cornell studies. In E. A. Fleishman (Ed.), *Studies in personnel and industrial psychology*. (Rev. ed.) Homewood, Ill.: Dorsey, 1967.

Smith, P. C., & Kendall, L. M. Cornell studies of job satisfaction. VI. Implications for the future. Unpublished manuscript, Cornell University, 1963. (a)

Smith, P. C., & Kendall, L. M. Cornell studies of job satisfaction. VI: Implications for the future. Unpublished manuscript, Cornell University, 1963. (b)

Smith, P. C., & Kendall, L. M. Retranslation of expectations: An approach to the construction of unambiguous anchors for rating scales. *Journal of Applied Psychology*, 1963, **47**, 149-155. (c)

Soik, N. An evaluation of a human relations training program. *Journal of the American Society of Training Directors*, 1950, **12** (3), 34-49.

Solomon, R. L. An extension of control group design. *Psychological Bulletin,* 1949, **46,** 137-150.
Sparks, C. P. Personnel development series: Humble Oil & Refining Co. Unpublished mimeographed report, Humble Co., 1966.
Speroff, B. J. Rotational role playing used to develop managers. *Personnel,* 1954, **33,** 49-50.
Speroff, B. J. The substitution method in role playing grievance handling. *Personnel,* 1959, **38,** 9-12.
Spriegel, W. R. Company practices in appraisal of managerial performance. *Personnel,* 1962, **39,** 77-83.
Standard Oil Company (New Jersey), Early identification of management potential: Social Science Research Division, Employee Relations Department, 1961.
Stedry, A. C., & Kay, E. The effects of goal difficulty on performance. General Electric, Behavioral Research Service, 1966.
Steele, F. I. Personality and the laboratory style. *Journal of Applied Behavioral Science,* 1968, **4,** 25-46.
Stern, G. G. Environments for learning. In N. Stanford (Ed.), *The American college.* New York: Wiley, 1962.
Sterner, F. M. Determining training needs: A method. *Journal of the American Society of Training Directors,* September 1965, 10-16.
Stewart, R. *Managers and their jobs.* London: Macmillan, 1967.
Stogdill, R. M. Personal factors associated with leadership: A survey of the literature. *Journal of Psychology,* 1948, **25,** 35-71.
Stogdill, R. M., & Coons, A. E. Leader behavior: Its description and measurement. Ohio State University, Bureau of Business Research, Business Research Monograph No. 88, 1957.
Stogdill, R. M., Goode, O. S., & Day, D. R. The leader behavior of corporation presidents. *Personnel Psychology,* 1963, **16,** 127-132. (a)
Stogdill, R. M., Goode, O. S., & Day, D. R. The leader behavior of United States senators. *Journal of Psychology,* 1963, **56,** 3-8. (b)
Stogdill, R. M., Goode, O. S., & Day, D. R. The leader behavior of presidents of labor unions. *Personnel Psychology,* 1964, **17,** 49-57.
Stogdill, R. M., Shartle, C. L., & Associates. Patterns of administrative performance. Ohio State University, Bureau of Business Research, Business Research Monograph No. 81, 1956.
Stolz, R. K. Executive development: New perspective. *Harvard Business Review,* 1966, **44,** 133-143.
Stone, J. *Structured objective Rorschach test.* Los Angeles: California Test Bureau, 1958.
Strickland, L. H. Surveillance and trust. *Journal of Personality,* 1958, **26,** 200-215.
Strong, E. K., Jr. *Vocational interests of men and women.* Stanford, Calif.: Stanford University Press, 1943.
Strother, G. B. Problems in the development of a social science of organization. In H. J. Leavitt (Ed.), *The social science of organizations.* Englewood Cliffs, N.J.: Prentice-Hall, 1963. Pp. 3-37.
Stroud, P. V. Evaluating a human relations training program. *Personnel,* 1959, **36** (6), 52-60.
Stryker, P. On the meaning of executive qualities. *Fortune,* 1958, **57,** 116-119.
Stryker, P. *The character of the executive: Eleven studies in managerial qualities.* New York: Harper, 1961.
Stryker, P. The pirates of management. In W. M. Fox (Ed.), *Readings in personnel management.* (Rev. ed.) New York: Holt, 1963, Pp. 38-43.
Suojanen, W. W. *The dynamics of management.* New York: Holt, 1966.
Suttell, B. J. Evaluating potential officer effectiveness in a training situation. *Journal of Applied Psychology,* 1955, **39,** 338-342.
Sykes, A. J. M. The effect of a supervisory training course on supervisors' perceptions and expectations of the role of management. Human Relations, 1962, **15,** 227-244.

Taft, R. Multiple methods of personality assessment. *Psychological Bulletin,* 1959, **56,** 333-352.

Taguiri, R. (Ed.) *Research needs in executive selection: A symposium.* Boston: Harvard University, 1961.

Taguiri, R. Comments on organizational climate. Paper presented at a conference on organizational climate, Foundation for Research on Human Behavior, Ann Arbor, Mich.:, March 1966.

Tannenbaum, R., & Bugental, J. F. T. Dyads, clans, and tribes: A new design for sensitivity training. *Human Relations Training News,* Spring 1963, 1-3.

Tannenbaum, R., Weschler, I. R., & Massarik, F. *Leadership and organization: A behavioral science approach.* New York: McGraw-Hill, 1961.

Tausky, C., & Dubin, R. Career anchorage: Managerial mobility motivations. *American Sociological Review,* 1965, **30,** 725-734.

Taylor, E., & Nevis, E. The use of projective techniques in management selection. In M. Dooher & E. Marting (Eds.), *Selection of management personnel.* Vol. 1. New York: American Management Association, 1957.

Taylor, F. C. Effects of laboratory training upon persons and their work groups. In S. S. Zalkind (Chm.), Research on the impact of using different laboratory methods for interpersonal and organizational change. Symposium presented at the American Psychological Association, Washington, D.C., September 1967.

Tenopyr, M. L. Summary of various studies on tests employed in manufacturing supervisory selection program. Mimeographed report, North American Aviation, 1960.

Tenopyr, M. L. A comparison of mental ability test scores and salaries of engineering managers. Mimeographed report, North American Aviation, 1961. (a)

Tenopyr, M. L. The relationship between scores on supervisory knowledge tests and criteria of job success. Mimeographed report, North American Aviation, 1961. (b)

Tenopyr, M. L. The validity of the Adaptability Test and the Thurstone Test of Mental Alertness in predicting the degree of success of engineering managers. Mimeographed report, North American Aviation, 1961. (c)

Tenopyr, M. L. The relationship between biographical and test variables and success as a manager in computers and data systems manufacturing. Mimeographed report, North American Aviation, 1962.

Tenopyr, M. L. Nonlinear combinations of leadership opinion questionnaire variables in predicting supervisory potential. Mimeographed report, North American Aviation, 1963.

Tenopyr, M. L. The comparative validity of selected leadership scales relative to success in production management. Mimeographed report, North American Aviation, 1965.

Tenopyr, M. L., & Ruch, W. W. The comparative validity of selected leadership scales relative to success in production management. Paper presented at the 73rd annual meeting of the American Psychological Association, Chicago, September 1965.

Thibaut, J. W., & Kelley, H. H. *The social psychology of groups.* New York: Wiley, 1959.

This, L. E., & Lippitt, G. L. Learning theories and training. I. *Training and Development Journal,* 1966, **20,** 2-12.

Thompson, V. A. *Modern organization.* New York: Knopf, 1961.

Thorndike, E. L. *Animal intelligence.* New York: Macmillan, 1911.

Tiffin, J., & McCormick, E. J. *Industrial psychology.* Englewood Cliffs, N.J.: Prentice-Hall, 1965.

Timbers, E. Motivating managerial self development. *Training Directors Journal,* 1965, **19** (7), 22-26.

Tolman, E. C. *Purposive behavior in animals and men.* New York: Century. (By permission of the University of California Press, 1932)

Tuckman, B. W. Developmental sequences in small groups. *Psychological Bulletin,* 1965, **63,** 384-399.

Tumin, M. Business as a social system. *Behavioral Science,* 1964, **9,** 120-130.

Turner, W. W. Dimensions of foreman performance: A factor analysis of criterion measures. *Journal of Applied Psychology,* 1960, **44,** 216-223.

Ulrich, L., & Trumbo, D. The selection interview since 1949. *Psychological Bulletin,* 1965, **63,** 100-116.

Underwood, W. J. Evaluation of laboratory method training. *Training Directors Journal,* 1965, **19** (5), 34-40.

Valiquet, M. I. Individual change in a management development program. *Journal of Applied Behavioral Science,* 1968, **4,** 313-326.

Veroff, J., Atkinson, J. W., Feld, S. C., & Gurin, G. The use of thematic apperception to assess motivation in a nationwide interview study. *Psychology Monograph,* 1960, **74** (12, Whole No. 499).

Vielhuber, D. P., & Gottheil, E. First impressions and subsequent ratings of performance. *Psychological Reports,* 1965, **17,** 916.

Viteles, M. S. *Motivation and morale in industry.* New York: Norton, 1953.

Vroom, V. H. Some personality determinants of the effects of participation. *Journal of Abnormal and Social Psychology,* 1959, **59,** 322-327.

Vroom, V. H. *Some personality determinants of the effects of participation.* Englewood Cliffs, N.J.: Prentice-Hall, 1960.

Vroom, V. H. *Work and motivation.* New York: Wiley, 1964.

Vroom, V. H. *Motivation in management.* New York: American Foundation for Management Research, 1965.

Vroom, V. H. Organizational choice: A study of pre and post decision processes. *Organizational Behavior and Human Performance,* 1966, **1,** 212-226.

Wagner, E. E. Predicting success for young executives from objective test scores and personal data. *Personnel Psychology,* 1960, **13,** 181-186.

Wagner, R. The employment interview: A critical summary. *Personnel Psychology,* 1949, **2,** 17-46.

Wald, R. M., & Doty, R. A. The top executive: A first hand profile. *Harvard Business Review,* 1954, **32,** 45-54.

Wall, R. G. Untangling the snarls in a job rotation program. *Personnel,* 1963, **42,** 59-65.

Wallace, J. Role reward and dissonance reduction. *Journal of Personality and Social Psychology,* 1966, **3,** 305-312.

Wallace, S. R. Criteria for what? *American Psychologist,* 1965, **20,** 411-417.

Wallach, M. A., Kogan, N., & Bem, D. J. Diffusion of responsibility and level of risk taking in groups. *Journal of Abnormal and Social Psychology,* 1964, **68,** 263-274.

Ward, L. B. Putting executives to the test. *Harvard Business Review,* 1960, **38,** 6-7, 10, 15, 164-180.

Warner, W. L., & Abegglen, J. *Big business leaders in America.* New York: Harper, 1955.

Watson, G. Work satisfaction. In G. W. Hartmann & T. Newcomb (Eds.), *Industrial conflict.* New York: Cordon, 1939.

Webb, E. J., Campbell, D. T., Schwartz, R. D., & Sechrest, L. *Unobtrusive measures: Nonreactive research in the social sciences.* Chicago: Rand McNally, 1966.

Webster, E. C. (Ed.) *Decision making in the employment interview.* Montreal: Eagle, 1964.

Weick, K. E. The concept of equity in the perception of pay. Paper presented at the Midwestern Psychological Association, Chicago, April 1965. (a)

Weick, K. E. Laboratory experimentation with organizations. In J. G. March (Ed.), *Handbook of organizations.* Chicago: Rand McNally, 1965. Pp. 194-260. (b)

Weick, K. E. The concept of equity in the perception of pay. *Administrative Science Quarterly,* 1966, **11,** 414-439. (a)

Weick, K. E. Trans-level experimentation. Paper presented at a conference entitled "People, groups, and organizations: An effective integration," Rutgers University, October 1966. (b)

Weick, K. E. Organizations in the laboratory. In V. H. Vroom (Ed.), *Methods of organizational research.* Pittsburgh: University of Pittsburgh Press. 1967, Pp. 1-56.

Weick, K. E. Systematic observational methods. In G. Lindzey & E. Aronson (Eds.), *Handbook of social psychology.* (Rev. ed.) Reading, Mass.: Addison-Wesley, 1968, Pp. 357-451.

Weick, K. E., & Nesset, B. Preferences among forms of equity. *Organizational Behavior and Human Performance,* 1968, **3,** 353-365.

Weiss, D. J., Dawis, R. V., England, G. W., & Lofquist, L. H. Minnesota Studies in Vocational Rehabilitation. XXII. Manual for the Minnesota Importance Questionnaire. University of Minnesota, Industrial Relations Center, Bulletin 45, 1967.

Weitz, J. Selecting supervisors with peer ratings. *Personnel Psychology,* 1958, **11,** 25-36.

Wherry, R. J. Hierarchical factor solutions without rotation. *Psychometrika,* 1959, **24,** 45-51.

Wherry, R. J., & Fryer, D. H. Buddy ratings: Popularity contest or leadership criterion? *Personnel Psychology,* 1949, **2,** 147-159.

Whisler, T. F., & Harper, S. F. (Eds.) *Performance appraisal: Research and practice.* New York: Holt, 1962.

Whitlock, G. H. Application of the psychophysical law to performance evaluation. *Journal of Applied Psychology,* 1963, **47,** 15-23.

Whitlock, G. H. Performance evaluation through psychophysics. Mimeographed manuscript, University of Tennessee, 1966.

Whitsett, D. A., & Winslow, E. K. An analysis of studies critical of the motivation-hygiene theory. *Personnel Psychology,* 1967, **20,** 391-416.

Whyte, W. F. Economic incentives and human relations. *Harvard Business Review,* 1952, **30,** 73-80.

Whyte, W. F. *Money and motivation: An analysis of incentives in industry.* New York: Harper, 1955.

Whyte, W. H., Jr. *The organization man.* Garden City, N.Y.: Doubleday (Anchor Books edition), 1956.

Wickstrom, W. S. Developing managerial competence: Changing concepts—emerging practices. National Industrial Conference Board Studies in Personnel Policy, No. 189, 1964.

Wilkins, L. T. Incentives and the young worker. *Occupational Psychology,* 1949, **23,** 235-247.

Wilkins, L. T. Incentives and the young male worker in England. *International Journal of Opinion and Attitude Research,* 1950, **4,** 541-562.

Williams, F. J., & Harrell, T. W. Predicting success in business. *Journal of Applied Psychology,* 1964, **48,** 164-167.

Williams, R. E. A description of some executive abilities by means of the critical incident technique. Unpublished doctoral dissertation, Columbia University, 1956.

Wilson, A. T. M. Personal communication, 1964.

Wilson, J. E., Mullen, D. P., & Morton, R. B. Sensitivity training for individual growth-team training or organizational development? *Training and Development Journal,* 1968, **22** (1), 47-53.

Woodward, J. *Industrial organization: Theory and practice.* London: Oxford University Press, 1965.

Worthy, J. C. Factors influencing employee morale. *Harvard Business Review,* 1950, **28,** 61-73.

Yanouzas, J. N. A comparative study of work organization and supervisory behavior. *Human Organizations,* 1964, **23,** 245-253.

Yoder, D. *Personnel management and industrial relations.* (5th ed.) Englewood Cliffs, N.J.: Prentice-Hall, 1962.

Zajonc, R. B. The requirements and design of a standard group task. *Journal of Experimental Social Psychology,* 1965, **1,** 71-78.

Zajonc, R., & Sales, S. Social facilitation of dominant and subordinate responses. *Journal of Experimental Social Psychology,* 1966, **2,** 160-168.

Zaleznik, A. Managerial behavior and interpersonal competence. *Behavioral Science,* 1964, **9,** 156-166.

Zaleznik, A., & Moment, D. *The dynamics of interpersonal behavior.* New York: Wiley, 1964.

Zand, D. E., Steele, F. I., & Zalkind, S. S. The impact of an organizational development program on perceptions of interpersonal, group, and organizational functioning. In S. S. Zalkind (Chm.), Research on the impact of using different laboratory methods for interpersonal and organizational change. Symposium presented at the American Psychological Association, Washington, D.C., September 1967.

Zander, A., Medow, H., & Elfron, R. Observers' expectations as determinants of group aspirations. In A. Zander, *Group aspirations and group coping behavior.* Ann Arbor, Mich.: University of Michigan Press, 1964.

Zelditch, M., & Hopkins, T. K. Laboratory experiments with organizations. In A. Etzioni (Ed.), *Complex organizations.* New York: Holt, 1961.

Zelko, H. P. Conference leadership training: A plan for practice projects. *Personnel,* 1952, **29** (1), 37-42.

Ziller, R. C. Individuation and socialization: A theory of assimilation in large organizations. *Human Relations,* 1964, **17**, 341-360.

Zigler, E. Metatheoretical issues in developmental psychology. In M. Marx (Ed.), *Theories in contemporary psychology.* New York: Macmillan, 1963. Pp. 341-369.

NAME INDEX

Williams, F. J., 180, 183
Williams, R. E., 80
Wilson, A. T. M., 247
Wilson, J. E., 317
Wilson, R. C., 111
Winer, B. J., 419
Winslow, E. K., 380, 381
Wolfe, D. M., 392
Wolins, L., 111
Woodward, J., 397, 398, 411
Worthy, J. C., 364
Wright, J. M., 264

Yanouyas, J. N., 411
Yoder, D., 24, 63, 236

Young, T. F., 369
Yuchtman, E., 102-105

Zajonc, R. B., 331, 438, 445
Zaleznik, A., 457, 458, 464, 465
Zalkind, S. S., 254, 297
Zand, D. E., 297
Zander, A., 451
Zeigler, M., 303
Zelditch, M., 338
Zelko, H. P., 236
Zenger, J. H., 311
Zigler, E., 332
Ziller, R. C., 434-438

SUBJECT INDEX